Planning and Design of Library Buildings

Butterworth Architecture Library of Planning and Design

Planning and design of library buildings

Third edition

Godfrey Thompson

Butterworth Architecture

Butterworth Architecture
An imprint of Butterworth–Heinemann Ltd
Halley Court, Jordan Hill, Oxford OX2 8EJ

 PART OF REED INTERNATIONAL P.L.C.

OXFORD LONDON GUILDFORD BOSTON
MUNICH NEW DELHI SINGAPORE SYDNEY
TOKYO TORONTO WELLINGTON

First published 1973 by The Architectural Press Ltd
Second edition 1977
Third edition 1989 published by Butterworth Architecture
Reprinted 1991

British Library Cataloguing in Publication Data

Thompson, Godfrey, *1921–*
    Planning and design of library buildings.–
    3rd ed. Architectural press library of
    planning and design.
    1. Libraries. Buildings. Planning and
    architectural design
    I. Title
    727'.8

ISBN 0-7506-1514-1

Library of Congress Cataloging-in-Publication Data

Thompson, Godfrey, 1921–
    Planning and design of library buildings/
    Godfrey Thompson.–3rd ed.
        226 p.   29, 7cm.
        Bibliography: p.
        Includes index.
        ISBN 0-7506-1514-1
        1: Library architecture.   2. Library buildings.
    3. Library planning.   I. Title.
    Z679.T53 1989
    727'.8–dc19   88-39168

Composition by Genesis Typesetting, Laser Quay, Rochester, Kent
Printed and bound by Hartnolls Ltd, Bodmin, Cornwall

Preface to the third edition

'This book is meant for beginners: not only for students but also for those, however skilled and experienced in their own professions, who are approaching for the first time the fascinating and important task of creating a new library. Its theme is that few architects in such a situation know much about libraries, and far fewer librarians know anything about architectural planning.'

The paragraph above began the preface to the first edition of this book; it was written in 1972, but it is equally true today. Considerable experience in many parts of the world has confirmed my view that a high proportion of those who are given the responsibility of creating a library are new to the task. The architect will have designed buildings before but is unlikely to have created a library; the librarian will be used to managing libraries but will seldom have been concerned with planning a new building.

In some of the sections which follow, guidance is given on operations, methods and procedures which will be glaringly obvious to experienced librarians. Other sections will deal with matters which are just as familiar to architects. Nevertheless one professional does not usually know much about the other's specialities. Throughout the book the intention has been to refer to basics which have been developed, perhaps by trial and error, over many decades. This is not to inhibit originality but to ensure that whoever proposes fundamental changes is quite clear why the basic methods were adopted and how they developed.

Although the subject is both planning and design, the latter element is considered only as it affects and is affected by the library's operational procedures. Discussions about the inter-relation between function and form have been avoided, as has reference to that element of form which is purely aesthetic and is, to a large extent, the exclusive concern of the architect. The choice of photographs has been dictated entirely by the need to illustrate planning points; if an architect wishes to obtain inspiration from photographs of beautiful libraries he or she will know where to find them.

Changes since the last edition particularly reflect the growth of electronic technology. What was on the horizon fifteen years ago is with us now, and its effects are fundamental. New techniques, new machines, are announced almost daily; the speed with which they change our world is startling. What will come tomorrow we can only guess, but it must be an educated guess. The belief is strongly expressed here that library planners, while allowing for present technology, are taking insufficient account of the changes which must inevitable come in the next three decades. It is for these decades that we are building libraries: flexibility and plenty of power points are no longer good enough.

An important feature is the consistent recording of progress through a known series of actions, so that both professionals can be sure of what is to happen at any stage and that nothing which makes a successful library is omitted. Architects are more familiar than librarians with these actions, and with the systematic recording of them, but it is most important that the two professionals are in step. The procedures recorded here may not be the same as those used in all countries but they have been tested by time and can be followed with confidence.

Because of the emphasis on common factors this book is not divided into a series of special sections, one for each category of library. Although the elements peculiar to national, academic, public, welfare and special libraries are indicated, it is regarded as fundamental that access to books and other media, the supply of information, assistance to readers by qualified librarians, are common to all libraries, as are the principles of service to users. It is by identifying these principles and applying them to each peculiar situation that one can decide on sizes, quantities and layouts, rather than by applying instant formulae, often taken out of context.

This book began in the first place as I became aware of my ignorance on becoming concerned for the first time with building a completely new library. I still see today two of the first library buildings with which I was concerned, and I know that they would have been very much better if I had had the expertise to talk to the architects on equal terms.

The best-known book in this field is Keyes D. Metcalf's *Planning Academic and Research Library Buildings*. The second edition, produced in 1986 by Metcalf's distinguished successors, is vast, encyclopedic and authoritative. The reason that there is room for another book is that Metcalf's is confined to the planning of large academic libraries in the American context and that it is written for the experienced, for experts. In serving in many countries I have had the privilege of working alongside professionals, chiefly architects and librarians, who were not expert at the task of planning libraries and who needed an introductory, general, but inclusive guide to all the multifarious factors. Some of the librarians had been informed at very short notice that they were to be responsible for the task of making a new library – university, college, public, medical, special – often not the type of library in which they had worked. They wanted a book for beginners; many of them told me that this was the book they needed.

Most of the descriptions of planning procedures and the (limited) references to the requirements of official regulations, such as safety rules or energy restrictions, are based on British practice. In some countries such regulations hardly exist, but the pattern of actions recorded here will commend itself to all who take their profession seriously. Of course it is helpful if the librarian knows something of the rules of his/her own country (the architect will be intimately acquainted with them), but it is hoped that the procedures described in this book are sufficiently logical to help anyone who is called upon to work in a foreign country.

The professionals referred to here are of both sexes but as there is no convenient pronoun in English I can only ask the forgiveness of female architects and librarians who may use this book for the frequent reference to each professional as 'he'. Attempts to reword all sentences have proved fruitless; the use of 'he or she' many thousands of times would be unreasonable.

I am most grateful to colleagues for help freely given. Outside my own country these include Professor Dr Günter Gatterman of Düsseldorf University, West Germany; E. F. Goodfellow, architect, and David Hickson, library consultant, of Perth, Western Australia; Gunnar Birkerts, architect, of Michigan; John T. Parkhill, ex-Metro Toronto Library, Canada; Ernest Siegel of Contra Costa County Library,

California; Horst Ernestus, Wuppertal Public Libraries, West Germany, and many others throughout the world. In my own country I must thank Lynn Brindley, Pro-Vice-Chancellor, Aston University, and her colleagues; Verina Horsnell, then Bibliographical Information Officer of the Library Association; Harry Faulkner-Brown, architect; P. A. Hoare, Nottingham University Librarian; James Thompson, then Reading University Librarian; Bernard Naylor, South-ampton University Librarian; Brian Baumfield, Birmingham City Librarian; Dean Harrison, Kent County Librarian, as well as those many old friends who have allowed me to bother them with visits and questions about their libraries. I thank them too for the responses in the form of the many illustrations offered for which I was unable to find room.

I am again grateful to Peter J. Bassnett of Scarborough Public Library, Ontario, for allowing me to quote from an unpublished thesis; to the American Library Association for permission to use some most valuable drawings by the late F. J. McCarthy from *Planning Library Buildings for Service*, and to the RIBA for permission to quote from its *Handbook of Architectural Practice and Management*.

I must also thank those librarians, architects and suppliers who have allowed me to draw upon their work: their names usually appear in the text; my apologies for any which may have been omitted.

My thanks to my wife, as always

Godfrey Thompson
1989

Photo Credits

Derek Balmer   7:7
Richard Bryant   6:27
John Donat   10:4, 11:1, 15:10
H. H. M. Hartog   5:4
Balthazar Korab Ltd   7:4, 7:5, 7:8
Sam Lambert   11:3
F. R. Logan Ltd   5:3
John Maltby Ltd   6:23
Paul Robinson Studios   18:9, 18:10
Thorp Modelmakers   1:4
Bill Toomey   7:6, 14:10, 14:15, 15:12

Contents

1 Libraries

An architect is unlikely to design a satisfactory library building without a clear understanding of its function and procedures. Information from the librarian will guide him in detail, but there is a danger that the librarian will assume the architect to be familiar with the type of library which is to be built. Different types of library have different spatial and environmental emphases, and it is only too easy for an architect to assume that his experience in designing one type of library can be used, with only small adjustments, in designing another. The following paragraphs are meant for architects; they give a very general outline of the purposes of the main categories of library, but it must be emphasized that there can be enormous variations within each category. 'Fundamentally a library is not a building but a service organization.'[1]

The main classes of libraries are identified below. The classification is by institutional framework; the category 'research library', for example, is not used, because many types of library serve research as part of their function.

National libraries

At the head of the formal or informal system of libraries of every country will be its national library. In the longer-established nations it will have developed from, and still be based on, an old library, often still an old library building. This applies to the British Library, the Library of Congress, the Bibliothèque Nationale and a number of others. In newer countries which have had the opportunity to start from scratch, a wider concept may have been adopted, so that the leadership of the service may be under such an entity as the National Documentation, Information and Library System of Jamaica.

Not only the buildings but also the library institutions of the older countries may have become outdated. An example of this is the British Library which, in its present form, was only created in 1973. The de facto national library up till then had been the British Museum Library, which was the heart of the legal deposit system, but the new entity was formed by incorporating other major libraries which were 'national' in that they were supported by central government funds and aimed to serve the community as a whole. The British Museum Library had been the country's greatest reference (i.e. non-lending) library, but it was partnered from the 1950s by a Lending Library of Science and Technology which was national (indeed world-wide) in its scope. These elements were incorporated into the new British Library; the Lending Library extended its scope to include all subjects and became the Lending Division of the new entity, while other divisions were created to deal with Research, Administration, Planning and Bibliographical Control for the nation. The great increase both in quantity and in type of information materials, together with the incorporation of fourteen other major special reference libraries in London, necessitated a larger and more flexible reference centre for what had become the British Library, Reference Division. The size of the endeavour, which can be judged from the sketch of the first phases, made it too large and obtrusive an element for the Bloomsbury site of the British Museum, and so it is being built on old railway premises close to St Pancras. The site area is 3.8 hectares (9½

acres), and the lowest of the four basements is 24 metres (78 ft) below the ground, and this in a heavily built-up part of the capital city. The total gross area will probably be around 200 000 m^2 (215 million sq ft), and there will be 283 linear kilometres (175 linear miles) of closed stack shelving; the amount of open shelving will depend on the approval to be given to later phases.

Another national library which does not use that designation is the Royal Library of the Netherlands. It has recently been rebuilt in the centre of The Hague, close to the main railway station in a complex which includes the National Archives, and near a large shopping centre.

These, and other very large library projects, inevitably bring into question the commitment of enormous amounts of money (by library standards) for building ever larger on the old principles, against a world of miniaturization, information held in computer databases and the possibility of a paperless society.

Newer countries, particularly third-world ones, while benefiting from western experience, have been able to take their decisions without the pressure of existing collections of many millions of printed books which have necessarily to be housed. Even so almost all countries have opted for large and often monumental buildings which are to house and process legal deposit collections, although they may also have planned to base information systems on the newer technologies. Some of them have incorporated services which have not, in the past, been considered part of a national library's remit. Thus Bosnia-Herzegovina's planned National Library will have the National Archives within the same building, but housed back-to-back with the library stock and services. Others, such as Trinidad and Tobago, plan to incorporate these into a single integrated service but not necessarily in the same building. Another variation arises from the presence of old and prestigious university libraries which had, over centuries, assumed the role of national library. In a number of countries these have become the National and University Library; examples are to be found in Iceland and in the Republics of Yugoslavia. Some countries, particularly in southern Europe, have a number of 'National Libraries', for that designation is given to the chief libraries of once independent states which now form part of a national unit.

In compiling his book on national libraries, Abdulaziz Mohamed Al-Nahari[2] sent a questionnaire to directors of national libraries world-wide, asking them to indicate what functions they regarded as important to national libraries and to rate these functions in order of priority. Not surprisingly the directors questioned gave first place to the acquisition and storage of the literature produced in their own countries; but other functions widely cited include collecting literature about their country and by writers of their nationality. Also reported were duties which show that a national library is widely regarded as the leader in all aspects of librarianship in the country. These include housing the nation's library school and, even more often, central bibliographical control, particularly to relieve other libraries of the chore of creating their own catalogue records. A very common element is a workshop of conservation, not only for the national library's own holdings but as a facility, both operating and teaching, to

1:1. Sketch of new building for British Library, Reference Division, in course of construction at St. Pancras, London (Architect Colin St John Wilson)

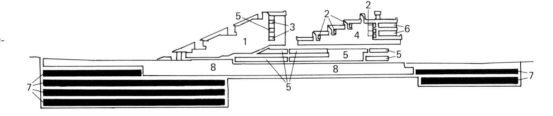

1:2. Section of future British Library building, showing extent of basements

Key to sections
1. Public
2. Exhibition
3. Reader circulation
4. Reading
5. Staff
6. Enquiry and service
7. Stacks
8. Plant

1:3. Royal Library, The Hague. Note strikingly consistent cladding and absence of sharp angles (Architects OD 205 Delft)

provide the rare and valuable skills of book conservation for the whole country. Of the functions reported in this questionnaire the ones which will make the greatest call on space will be the legal deposit element, by which everything published in the country is acquired and housed to eternity. The corollary to this is usually the production of the printed national bibliography.

The proportion of the space within the library which is dedicated to readers will depend upon the proximity of other libraries able to reduce the burden of dealing with all reader needs. If, in a developing country, the national library is the only major library in the area, it will have to adapt its services to handle the requirements of readers of all kinds. The proposed National Library of Nigeria at Abuja is such a major enterprise and therefore needs a very large building.

In earlier editions of this book it was suggested that because the building, or rebuilding, of a national library was such a vast undertaking, it was unlikely to occur very often, and so architects would not want to waste time studying the problems against the remote possibility of being involved. Since I wrote that, a number of new national libraries have been planned: some, like that of the Republic of China, are enormous; others are on the horizon; I have myself been involved in eight such projects. Because the building of a new national library will be a matter of great importance, involving central government funding on a large scale, and because its design will certainly be under considerable public scrutiny (at least in democracies), it is likely to be a matter for an architectural competition or at least for open discussion.

An important design feature of a new national library is likely to be monumentality. Although modern concepts of libraries emphasize faithfulness to function and inbuilt flexibility, other and often stronger influences may be brought to bear upon such a large visual symbol of a nation's life. A building to be created for a site of great importance, to sit beside other national institutions (parliament or palace), will almost inevitably mean that the architect's brief is to produce something which is visually acceptable and a matter of national pride, rather than a building which 'only' serves to house its intended function. In such circumstances the task of the architect is indeed a difficult one, and the temptation to please the higher 'client' rather than the mere librarian, so much more compelling. Another influence which can be brought to bear is the desire to perpetuate an element of national history or artistic inheritance: there is a strong temptation for this to become the dominant feature of the design.

State libraries

These are as different as the political and social organizations of the countries which create them. Very generally it can be said that they are the central libraries of states which form part of countries with federal constitutions such as the German Federal Republic, the United States of America and the Commonwealth of Australia. Sometimes they have the duty of providing central support (either in funding or in organization) for the state's public library system (as in the USA and Australia, in different degrees). Others are large libraries for research and scholarship (as in the GFR). Again dignity will be a large element of the design, but most of the recent examples show due concern for the importance of the function of the library. One of these, although it could be also described as a city library, is the Staatsbibliothek Berlin, the library of the Prussian Cultural Foundation. It is an impressive and very modern building, designed by Hans Scharoun and

completed in 1978, with 19 400 m² (200 000 sq ft) floor area, planned to hold four million volumes, with a further four million stored in an extension depository. Unlike most such libraries it has a lending function and is closely associated with – indeed the building contains – certain cultural institutions. In Hamburg the Staats- und Universitätsbibliothek (State and University Library) has been planned to serve more than thirty thousand students. The Alexander Library Building, Perth, the State Library of Western Australia, which acts also as a public library and as the centre for all the public libraries of the state, has a floor area of 31 000 m² (333 000 sq ft). It is a good example of a building which, far from wishing to dominate the scene, has been designed so that it will not dwarf its immediate surroundings. The artist's sketch and the photograph here show how, despite its size, it presents a modest image, responsive to human scale.

University libraries

This form of library is to be found in every country in the world, and in general its functions are similar everywhere. In studying their planning and design, we here use the term to include (British) polytechnics and sometimes very large independent colleges, but not the older universities (Oxford and Cambridge, for example, which are groupings of colleges and faculty buildings, sometimes dispersed in alien surroundings). The central libraries of some older universities are so huge and important as to be truly national in scope (Oxford and Harvard, for example). A number of the colleges and schools within such federations are themselves so large that their libraries are like those of smaller universities.

National practice in planning universities varies very widely. Fully established British universities average between 4000 and 6000 students (other than the collegiate ones, which average 10 000; London 75 000), while West German universities range from 6000 to 10 000 (with a few larger ones). On the other hand those in the United States average between 10 000 and 30 000. These numbers obviously affect both the scale of the library and the contribution it has to make. A new university, given space in which to build, usually takes the form of a campus where the library occupies a key site, easily accessible from the main thoroughfare and with all-weather approaches. The library may be associated with, or contain, a bookshop, and as it is intended to accommodate readers for long periods at a time, it will need auxiliary provision in the way of washrooms, restaurants and perhaps meeting rooms. It may have to remain open far into the night, and at least part of it may be open through twenty-four hours. Car parking can usually be ignored, as it is the responsibility of the campus planners.

Collegiate (federated) universities such as Oxford will have both a major central library, acting both as back-up and central book archive, and separate libraries in the constituent colleges, as well as a great number of small libraries in special institutions. Other universities may have permanent departmental libraries, physically separate from the central library building, or a series of faculty libraries, each with large stocks; sometimes both. The University of Tokyo is reported[3] to have had as many as 312 different libraries. Unless very considerable extra funds are made available for all these elements, they will lead inevitably to the weakening of the main collection; they also mean considerable duplication of both stocks and services; and they can lead to the staffing of branch libraries by small numbers of rather isolated librarians. One of the traditional arguments against centralization was that

1:4. Proposed National Library of Nigeria at Abuja (Architects Odeleye Associates). Model by Thorp Modelmakers

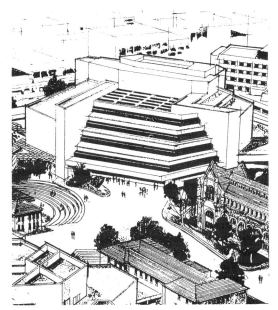

1:5. Artist's impression of Alexander Library Building, State Library of Western Australia at Perth (Architects Cameron, Chisholm and Nicol)

the central collections were difficult of access for busy academics, but the trend of the new technology will be for better communications throughout the campus. The first step towards this is probably the computer-produced microfiche catalogue of the whole collection at every service point, but a computer link is already becoming common. Nevertheless, where the weight of history does not have to be allowed for, centralization of university libraries is the more common solution and certainly the more popular with university librarians. The loosening of the barriers between disciplines and the growth of multi-disciplinary courses encourage this, and most small new university libraries are centralized. On the other hand the new university library of Düsseldorf has a central and eleven decentralized library buildings (some of them connected to the central library by an underground book delivery system). It is common for some departmental libraries, particularly those in law and medicine, to have a full life of their own, with both book consultation and borrowing facilities open to the whole university body. A number of academic libraries, especially in the United States, are associated with large medical complexes, and

1:6. Alexander Library Building, showing how it has been stepped back to prevent it dwarfing buildings nearby. The photograph shows how a large building can relate to human scales

the medical libraries can themselves be of considerable size and complexity. For comment on the sub-library, the departmental library and the institute Library, see the Parry Report.[4]

The main function of the university library is to store bibliographical and audio-visual materials and to make them available swiftly to students, faculty and research workers. A few decades ago some university librarians would have seen their main role as service to scholarship and research, but today it is generally accepted that the university library is an active participant in the teaching and learning programme at all levels and that the largest single body of users will be undergraduates. All universities have the duty of providing the tools – book, periodical, or computer terminal – necessary not only for subject interests but also for education and development of the whole university body as human beings. The library service will be a force to assist learning, teaching and research and will offer hospitality, in varying degrees, to outsiders – visiting scholars, local industry and, to a limited extent, the general public. Some universities, notably those in West Germany, have a tradition of being freely open to the public; in Cologne the university library is combined with the public library. Others pay lip-service to the facility but do not encourage it. If only because it is important to give first-year students guidance to the library's services, lecture space may have to be allocated within the library itself.

Almost all the holdings will be open for readers to search, but rare and valuable books, together with fragile materials which require special environmental conditions as well as careful handling, may be locked away and available only on application to the staff. Paradoxically books in short supply and heavy demand by undergraduates may be kept off the open shelves and issued only for short periods and under stringent conditions. Where bookshelves are not open for readers to search, the cases can be placed closer together, thus saving space. This is known as 'closed stack'. Where the great bulk of the book stock will be open to readers, seating will be needed near each section of the shelving. To provide this is so space-consuming that the rows of shelving have to be arranged as closely together as is convenient to the reader, an arrangement known as 'open stack'. A large proportion of the books can be borrowed for use outside the library, and so a control area for book issue and return will be a prominent feature. University libraries will tend to have a higher proportion of books *per reader* on issue at any one time than most other types of library; some impose no limit on the number that may be borrowed by faculty members.

Periodicals will be an important part of the storage and service problem: 5000 titles is not an unreasonable estimate. The evidence of SCONUL (Standing Conference of National and University Libraries) in the Parry Report[5] recommended 4000 titles (plus extra copies) for an established university with 3000 students. Experience today, even in the age of the so-called paperless society, shows that the proportion of library expenditure devoted to the purchase of periodicals, as compared to books, is still rising: research by Peter Mann (*Bookseller* 2 September 1988 p. 901) showed that in British academic libraries in 1982–83 book purchase amounted to 51.6% against 48.4% for periodicals. Comparable figures in 1986–87 were: books 41.5%, periodicals 58.5%.

Universities which offer services to industrial research will need to hold large numbers of reports and pamphlets. Other areas have their special needs; maps, for example, take up more space than classical texts. As the stock of the library will run into hundreds of thousands of volumes (Metcalf[6] talks about 'average libraries', albeit in the context of large American academic libraries, with stock of 2.5 million books) the library must either be spread over a vast area or have several floors; subject division of stock will be inevitable and will dictate separate shelving and furniture requirements for different areas.

The use of the building will vary very considerably at different times of the day or of the term. Entrances will have to handle large numbers at a time, yet provide security controls. Close to the entrance the area for issue and return of books will generate noise and movement that will have to be insulated both acoustically and visually from the main parts of the building, where quiet study will prevail. Loan periods may be complicated: some items may be issued for whole terms while books in heavy demand may be loaned for as little as three hours, with very strict control on return times. The movement of readers (largely young and uninhibited) to their target areas will have to be shielded in order to minimize disturbance. In some Islamic countries a major factor which has to be ascertained and taken into account in the planning of university libraries is the degree of segregation of the sexes which is required within, and at the approaches to, the building; this can be a predominant design element.

A main service area, easily accessible from all parts, will hold the common bibliographical tools. Even if the catalogues are dispersed in a system of computerizing, the large numbers of such books will take up considerable space and will be heavily used by readers and library staff. Communications in this region, as well as between it and the book shelving and supply areas, will have to be highly organized. Although for the foreseeable future the main materials to be housed will be printed books, other forms already exist in great quantities, and some will proliferate swiftly. Microforms (roll microfilm, micro-opaque, Microcard, microprint, microfiche and types of aperture card), tape (magnetic and video) and disc (audio, CD and video) all call for space and for room for inevitable expansion. Fortunately they are small in bulk and fairly simple to store; making them easily accessible to users, however, presents a more serious planning problem. Chapter 2 is one librarian's attempt to come to terms with these questions, and to offer possible solutions of a problem which will dominate library planning in the next few decades.

To provide space to seat a given number of people with adequate room to read and write is one matter: it is quite another to provide a growing – possibly an equal – number, working as individuals, not in classes, with the opportunity to use audio-visual materials and computer terminals. As part of the learning process readers may need to use sophisticated apparatus to create their own media; research workers in some arts will certainly need to do so. The parallel is with the space and equipment requirements of the university's laboratories – a frightening prospect for planners.

In all parts of the world universities have expanded in recent years, and, given prosperity, the trend seems likely to continue. In the 1960s around a thousand new academic libraries were built in the United States, although in the 1970s the figure was nearer five hundred. Certainly the number has fallen, but even in the 1980s, years of comparative economic depression, there are reported to be some sixteen new university libraries constructed per year, and that does not include extensions to existing buildings. Between 1976 and 1986, 157 new 'academic' libraries were reported there, as well as 99 additions or restorations.[7]

In the newer nations the university is not only necessary

for tertiary education but is in itself a symbol of national pride. The range of its activities will differ widely according to the pressures and priorities of the particular country. In the early days emphasis is likely to be on the most essential services – training doctors, administrators and the teachers who are to train the next generation – but a greater sophistication soon arises. In older countries such as India there is great emphasis on all aspects of high-level education and research, but along with these is a seemingly insatiable demand for first-degree courses in all fields, which often leads to a concentration on a degree-awarding syllabus. Whatever role the community calls upon the university to play will directly affect its library.

Paradoxically the continued expansion in the richer countries is bringing its own problems. Although in Britain only the largest modern university library (Edinburgh) is of 30 000 m² (300 000 sq ft), there are several in the United States which are over 50 000 m² (500 000 sq ft), and the Robarts Library of Toronto University is more than a million square feet (96 000 m²) on sixteen floors and has a capacity of five million volumes. Some will feel that collections of this size are self-defeating in the difficulty of locating and delivering books to readers. This problem of continuous, endless, expansion was specifically set, by the (British) University Grants Committee, to a committee under Professor Richard Atkinson. That body reported:

'We felt bound . . . to question the concept of providing for the whole of a library's existing stock and anticipated accessions, since it rests on the assumption of indefinite accumulation, possibly at a high rate of growth, which would lead in a comparatively short timespan to financial and reorganisational problems of such magnitude as to pose a threat to the university library system, even if substantial funds were available to sustain it.'

The committee's recommendations, since put into force, were for (in very general terms) a 'self-renewing' library of about 300 000 books with provision for improved co-operation between universities and with the British Library. The recommendations of the Atkinson Committee[8] will be considered in more detail in Chapter 19, 'Standards'; some views upon the growth problem in a world of information technology follow in Chapter 2.

In large libraries the enormous runs of bound periodicals eat up a high proportion of shelf storage space, and so a policy decision by the librarian to use microforms for the storage and retrieval of periodicals can have an important influence upon the stack requirements and thus on space planning. In terms of numbers the greatest use of the library is by undergraduates, who, while needing access to large holdings of books and periodicals, make intensive demands upon a comparatively limited range of materials. There are advantages in providing for students a smaller library devoted largely to their immediate textbook needs and with a suitably cheerful environment; on the other hand there is the real importance of encouraging in students the habit of browsing in a large collection. The Parry Report[9] discusses undergraduate collections, browsing rooms and libraries in halls of residence, all of which can affect the planning of the main library. There are very few under-graduate libraries in Britain (although Glasgow had one as early as 1939, and there are a number of undergraduate collections); but such libraries have the helpful effect of freeing the main library from undergraduate pressure and have been the fashion in some American universities for decades now. Even there, however, doubt has been expressed about their value; unless they have very large stocks they may tend to become holdings of 'set books', encouraging the undergraduate to limit reading to essen-

tial texts, a trend which is against the basic principles of university education. An extreme example of this is the fashion for quite large libraries, entirely for undergradu-ates, with a comparatively small book stock but plenty of space, and with an atmosphere which encourages their use as a social meeting-place, especially for new students. Any form of separate provision for undergraduates will tend to free space in the main library for post-graduate and research workers who need carrels and other secluded, or specially equipped, seating facilities. It can also enable the main library to spend more time on its important creative activities – literature searches, the compilation of biblio-graphies for research, the production of current awareness bulletins and other direct contributions to the life of the university.

In order to do all this the university library must be a processing plant and to a lesser extent a factory. New books must be selected, the requirements of the depart-ments coordinated and assessed, the books ordered and accepted on arrival in quantity, to be sorted, passed along organized lines and through a processing sequence before they can take their place on the shelves. Some volumes will need to be treated in a repair shop or bindery, either outside the library or as part of the flow-line itself. Business affairs and general accounting work generated by the library will have their spatial and service needs, and the usual arrangements will have to be made for the staff, including food, recreation and toilets.

A complication for many universities is that they own special subject collections of books which may have begun as the private property of a devoted professor or donor but have grown and become a source of pride. As such they get priority and sometimes expand until they are a matter of national importance. The long-term financial effects of such collecting could create their own problems; the collections are too important to be neglected but no extra funds are available. This was one of the special concerns of the Atkinson Committee.

Some new universities have begun with a few faculties and the intention of adding more as the opportunity occurs; in these circumstances space for expansion of the library will be essential, as will a high degree of flexibility. It has to be remembered that space is needed not only for subject collections which are to be added but for the additional staff to operate them. Communications have to be planned so that the new elements can be incorporated, and this includes possible future extensions to the building. In the same way new materials and communication methods, including those not yet invented, have to be allowed for. Obvious examples are the coming of microforms, tele-vision, video and computer-based information retrieval systems.

Fortunately, most entirely new universities have space in which to plan; because they are often built in open country, their buildings can be designed for expansion more easily than can those within cities. The upgrading of existing colleges within cities and their physical expansion present a much more difficult planning problem and offer a task challenging enough to stimulate any architect. A very interesting, and not uncommon, practice is to associate a library school with the university library. This has obvious advantages in enabling the student librarians to use the university library as a workshop, but it is a factor which the architect has to allow for in his design.

College libraries

Colleges vary enormously in size and function but many consist of a single large building of which the library occupies a floor or a wing. A college which has its own campus is best thought of as a small university. In general what has been said about university libraries applies on a smaller scale to college libraries, but because colleges generally include fewer residential students than universities, there may be more emphasis on the issuing of books for use outside the building. The staff's bibliographical activities will include providing reading lists and bulletins to exploit the library's resources, both in association with the curriculum and for general cultural ends. Some colleges make use of recreational literature to encourage reading among students who are not basically book-orientated. This means that there will be attractive browsing areas with paperback books, displays and other features more usually associated with the public library. Any special features the college may use in its educational programme (film theatres, for example) will have repercussions on the library's activities and services.

All colleges will have an active programme of teaching directly associated with the use of the library: such a programme will be particularly extensive in colleges of education and will call for a large space allowance, possibly in adjoining lecture rooms. The requirements include facilities for efficient handling of large numbers of readers, easy access to books, quiet study conditions and encouragement of private reading. Because their subject range is limited (when compared with universities) and the emphasis is more directly on teaching, colleges may be particularly advanced in their use of non-book resource media. Because these media are in so many ways extensions of the book form, the librarian will be in charge of the entire work of the college in this field; he will therefore require both space to store these materials and workshops and laboratories where the forms may be prepared, processed and presented. Video tape is an example; to the college librarian it will be not only a form of recorded information but also a way of using many of the library's special resources in live teaching sessions.

In many modern colleges (as in many schools) the library has changed its identity and is no longer merely a place where books are housed. The students' increasing involvement in its activities, and their participation in its work, make it a workshop for their creative self-education and an environment in which they can express themselves by using its materials and techniques. If the classroom is now where they are stimulated to use their minds, the library is a place where the resources can be found to follow up this approach, and where they can create something unique to themselves; this act of creation is a fundamental part of the aim of education today.

In some circumstances, particularly where suitable sites are scarce, it is possible for the public library and the college library to share space and staff (and, to some extent, stock). Arrangements will have to be planned so that college and public readers are able to use the service at the same time without disturbing each other; that means some form of physical division. This can work effectively, but it needs clearly thought-out principles and firmly applied rules. It can be used to save space, but the full financial commitment of each side must continue to be made; it should not be a way of saving on book purchase.

Because colleges operate as independent entities, book intake and processing areas similar to those of university libraries will be needed. The basic difference between the institutions is that college library stocks will be neither so vast in number nor so comprehensive in range as those of universities and they will more directly echo the subject emphases and limitations of the college.

School libraries

At one extreme will be the primary school library, which may be a few books housed centrally in an informal atmosphere and supplemented by collections in classrooms; at the other extreme – rather like a college library in miniature – will be the library in a senior school with a large pre-university group.

It is commonly said that the library is the heart of the school: this truism certainly has meaning if we apply it to the central position which it should occupy in the school's internal layout. The illustration from the American School in London shows how the library holds a position which is both central and easily accessible from all parts of the school. It is vital to prevent it being used as a passageway to and from other areas.

Because a school must be designed as a single entity, the architect will have limited freedom to express originality in designing the library. Encouragement of use must be the keynote, the comparatively small stock of books presenting few storage problems. In other ways also the traditional school library is easy to plan; much less space will be needed for preparing books for the shelves, particularly if, as is commonly the case, the school is associated with a central supply organization. A rest room and other facilities for the library staff will be found in the provision made for the teaching staff. Because librarians and teachers will be in close contact with individual readers, control and security arrangements can be less stringent. On the other hand, no institution is changing so fast as schools. Where classrooms have disappeared and individual learning takes place in flexible areas within open-plan rooms, the library will act as the centre in which all the resources of modern education are housed and from which they are supplied (and indeed created) for the whole school. It will be the place to which children and staff come to choose and to read books as well as the storehouse and working centre for all the school's library resources: in fact the term

1:7. Library of the American School in London

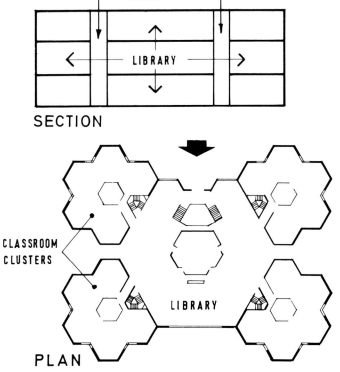

COMMUNICATION
CORES

LIBRARY

SECTION

CLASSROOM
CLUSTERS

LIBRARY

PLAN

'school library resource centre' has in many countries replaced 'school library' as its designation.

Here are housed film reels, strips and loops, audio and video discs and tapes which can not only be used on the appropriate machines by children within the centre but can also be piped by sophisticated switching installations to both individuals and groups at the discretion of the teachers. It is also the duty of the resource centre to produce teaching and learning media for specific needs by drawing upon its own holdings and borrowing from other centres. Students themselves can create such media within the centre.

In some schools the resource centre has the task of serving as the link with all outside sources of information and so contains the terminals communicating with databases in the educational complex or elsewhere. It is within the library that the pupils become familiar with, and competent in the use of, computers. The direct teaching in this field may be carried out by specialists, but the network will be based on the library/resource centre where all the information is grouped. This arrangement may require the architect to create a cluster of specialized service units of which book collections are only a small part.

As these alterations transform the traditional function of the school library, so they have repercussions in every aspect of its design. If the trend in school design is towards clusters of study areas of which audio-visual projectors and picture transmitters are the focal point, rooms can become wedge-shaped, perhaps with sloping ceilings. The library resource centre, offering the same facilities, may also change shape so as to offer good viewing and listening positions. Lighting will need to be far more flexible when there are functions other than book-reading to be accommodated; the different lighting levels needed for various audio-visual conditions must be obtainable at the touch of a switch. Acoustic problems will be quite different from those of the past, and electrical outlets will need to be more numerous; conduits for remote control apparatus will be a normal provision.

The architect who has to plan a new school library will not necessarily find that the project is to create such a sophisticated entity. The education authority or the head teacher may have gone only a short distance along this road, but at the very least the switch of emphasis from teaching to learning will mean the need both for more space and for the more flexible use of the space, while the hospitality to advanced technological ideas and equipment will alter the conventional image.

Whether or not audio-visual materials are held in any quantity, the usual storage, study and browsing areas will be needed, as well as locations where students can study individually. Where space is available, these can be in the form of carrels; in other libraries they may be merely quiet areas within the perimeter of shelving. More and more schools feel the necessity for group viewing and listening rooms as well as seminar rooms, and because of the importance of having information materials to hand, they are being associated with the library. As the barriers within the schools come down, the library occupies a focal position, its information pervading all learning activities at all times. To an architect this can be an exciting challenge; it is also a very difficult one.

Public libraries

This extract from the UNESCO *Public Library Manifesto* states the purpose of the public library in convincing terms:

'The public library is a practical demonstration of democracy's faith in universal education as a continuing and lifelong process, in the appreciation of the achievement of humanity in knowledge and culture. It is the principal means whereby the record of man's thoughts and ideals, and the expression of his creative imagination, are made freely available to all.'

Public libraries are to be found in all parts of the world but in their present form they are a product of western nineteenth-century philanthropic ideals. Their original aim was to give to the newly literate masses a little of the opportunity for wide reading which the rich already possessed. British librarians believe that their public library system is as good as any in the world, but excellent examples are to be found in Scandinavia, West Germany and many parts of the United States. Very many public libraries are to be found in countries of the socialist bloc, but for political reasons there is a basic difference in the provision of any title which the reader may request.

In the third world the position varies widely, largely for economic reasons; when the basic essential of living are in short supply, libraries will not often be given a high priority. Most countries which were once in the British Empire possessed basic public library services, and in many they have developed admirably.

This book deals with library buildings, permanent structures which are a feature of a community and its area. There are many alternative methods not studied here which are used when it is not appropriate to build a permanent structure. The best-known examples are trailer or caravan libraries which can be towed to a site and left there for a short period before being collected and taken to the next site. Other types are container libraries which are delivered and collected by a lorry, or where shelving and counters are mounted on rollers and then rolled onto the floor of a local school or community centre for a brief period of service. Much more widely used are mobile libraries which simply draw up at a predetermined, and pre-advertised, site, usually on a weekly schedule, open for business and then move on to the next port of call. These are not necessarily substitutes; the small or isolated pockets of population they serve would never warrant a full-time building and they save readers having to make difficult journeys to the nearest permanent library.

Despite the prevalence of these substitutes, and despite financial restrictions, it is true that if an architect is given the task of producing a library building anywhere in the world, the odds are very heavily on its being for a public library. In Britain about 700 public library buildings were opened between 1973 and 1983,[10] and although many were conversions and extensions this is still an impressive achievement. In the United States there are reported to be about 100 new libraries and 150 adapted, usually small, ones each year: at the moment there are said to be 586 in progress.[11] In these circumstances it is perhaps surprising that specific reporting of a new public library building is much less common than for an academic library. The main reason is that public libraries are usually small; large ones are rarer, but when they do arrive they can be striking. Among the most famous of recent European examples are the Mitchell Library, Glasgow (extension only), 35 000 m^2 (375 000 sq ft), Rotterdam 24 000 m^2 (260 000 sq ft) and Birmingham 21 000 m^2 (220 000 sq ft). There are numerous city centre libraries of from one to seven thousand square metres (ten to seventy thousand square feet). The majority of public library buildings, however, are not the large and striking pieces of architecture which make the reputation of an architect. Nevertheless the challenge of producing a good, attractive, small public library is a very real one; in some ways the problems to be solved are more difficult than those of a large academic library where the features are common to many buildings already created and discussed. An academic library is made to carry out fairly clearly defined tasks; in every country the needs of faculty, researchers and students are basically similar. The public library is quite different, because (with the exception of large libraries with a centre-of-network function) each has a separate, different and largely indefinable community to serve. Some are in areas where there is a homogeneity about the neighbourhood – small country towns, commuter suburbs or industrial estates – but most serve a mix of all types and consequently of all needs. In answering this need, the architect is going to be more involved in area planning matters than with other types of library. The building he designs has above all to attract people to use it. Siting, position in relation to traffic patterns and the habits of local residents, are of the highest importance. In assessing and handling these questions he will use some of the techniques of retail store planning: the same will be true of much of the detail design.

Public libraries, though a common institution, have developed in different ways in different countries. In Scandinavia there arose (or, certainly, developed) the concept of the culture house, a centre for all the cultural activities of a town, usually a medium-sized one where theatres, concert halls and galleries would not be financially viable. Such buildings need to be particularly flexible, as they will have to accommodate exhibitions, music and theatrical performances as well as libraries for all ages, and will probably include restaurants. This all-inclusive cultural complex may be appropriate in a medium-sized town or in a suburb but is unlikely to be necessary in a city large enough to have its own theatres, concert halls and galleries; it would be too expensive for a small town. In the USSR and other East European countries there are vast numbers of trade union libraries, which are a kind of public library not common in the West.

The public library is usually funded by the government of the country, directly or indirectly. In some countries it will be under a ministry of libraries or of education or of information. Whichever is in control will affect the emphasis of the service. At the worst the library can become the place where government handouts and political leaflets are publicized. In other countries there will be a degree of delegation to local government control. In Britain the service is, in practice, completely part of the local government service but the Ministry of Arts and Libraries has a (seldom used) supervisory role and the government does, in the long term, hold the purse strings. Whatever the overall power, there is a fundamental difference between the services to large cities, medium-sized towns and the countryside. In Britain the public library service operates under 166 authorities, divided into two different types. On the one hand there are the Metropolitan Districts (that is, the great conurbations) and the Metropolitan London Boroughs, which resemble them in their concentrations of population. On the other hand are the counties, which serve the medium-sized towns, small towns and villages in the country. In practice, the situation is not quite so tidy because there will be isolated knots of people to be served within city boundaries, and usually quite large towns in county areas. Sophisticated information and study requirements, even access to databases, can be needed by those who live far from permanent library buildings, and it is the duty of the public library to serve them all. In some countries, small towns may retain their independence but arrange to supply the more sophisticated services to their readers by voluntary association with other libraries in a grouping for which they make a financial contribution. However they are organized, a salient feature of all public

library services is the degree to which they have developed inter-library cooperation, particularly for the loan of books; this grew naturally from the difficulty of meeting specialist demands from their readers within the limits of comparatively small book stocks. In Britain, more than half a million books each year are borrowed in this way from other libraries. This development has been assisted (and in some measure replaced) by the services of the British Library Lending Division at Boston Spa, from whose vast stocks 150 000 are loaned in addition to the more than two million supplied in photocopy form.

Central libraries for towns and cities

These are extremely complex organizations: they may have to be:

1. Administrative and distribution headquarters for a system with as many as a hundred branch libraries, serving a large population with an infinite variety of needs, and issuing as many as 10 million volumes per year, with the purchase, intake and processing of up to 100 000 books per year.
2. The book-lending, consultation and study point for the town centre, in addition to being the referral place for the more advanced bibliographical enquiries of the entire area.
3. A collection of research libraries, housed together and used by a clientele basically similar to that of a university but with an even wider intellectual spectrum and including the information needs of local industry and commerce.

Because of these very different functions, the central library will need to be more sectionalized in its operations than any other type. In carrying out the duties listed above there will be division by function (reference, lending, information, recreation, children's) or by subject (e.g. art, science, commerce, music). There are a number of different ways of arranging this division: one is to have a general library near the circulation control counter in the centre, with subject libraries radiating off it. Another, the so-called 'service in depth', has the reference and lending books shelved together in a single sequence; the most popular books (recreational reading) are placed at the front, less popular subjects further back and the least used of all at the rear. This principle is best followed in an open area, with perhaps a change of floor level but with a visual link. It has the advantage that readers of serious subjects automatically get the quietest part of the library. Whichever method is to be used will be explained by the librarian in the brief. Common to them all will be the problems of control, security and economy of staffing.

The range of materials to be housed will be similar to that of a university library, but there will be large stocks of fiction and children's books which are not retained as consistently as are books in university libraries; this is because it is more common for public libraries to discard books when they are worn or superseded. On the other hand there will be holdings of manuscripts (and often local archives) as well as rare books for which special conditions of atmosphere and security have to be provided.

In some cases large collections have to be housed in closed stack (that is, not open to readers to visit), which will be economical of space but often heavy in floor loading. The greatest part of the book stock will be laid out to attract readers on 'open access'. This uses more space but is essential to the purpose of a public library. However shelved, stock must be organized so that it can be easily and economically traced and brought to the reader who asks for it. Conditions of use of the material will again be similar to those of a university library except that pressure of demand will be greater at peak times of the day (i.e. outside normal working hours) and more evenly spread throughout the year.

Technological advances in communication methods will affect the central library at least as much as they will any other kind. The city central library was a pioneer in the provision of media other than books. Audio and video discs and tapes, both music and spoken, are provided for use on the premises and also for borrowing; photographs, prints and original works of art are displayed and in some cases lent for appreciation in the home. In Britain, cooperation with other social services and involvement in networks to help many community needs is bringing a new extension to the already wide scope of public library work. These innovations involve public libraries of all kinds but the greatest pressure (and response) comes from the central library in the heart of a large conurbation.

Requests for expansion of space will usually be given less automatic official support than those of college and university libraries. This is not because the growth of demand is less but because there are (or appear to be) alternatives or palliatives for the problems of the over-crowded city central library. The decentralization of some of the services is usually possible and is cheaper than an extension to the building. This reluctance to allow expansion is often unfair because the increase of university student numbers and the coming of such ventures as the Open University have added greatly to the pressure on the large city library. It is evident also that users will turn to the central library for the new information retrieval services now available to the public, from viewdata to full databases.

Central libraries for counties

These have some of the concentrated lending, reference and information supply features of city central libraries; their extent depends on the size of the town in which the library is situated. In addition to these the county library will have, much more than the city library, the task of serving as headquarters for the library services of a large region. This may include other towns as well as villages and isolated communities. The greatest emphasis therefore will again be on acquisition, storage, processing, distribution and communications; the latter element will include not only answering enquiries and sending books, other materials and information swiftly to individuals in all parts of the county but also running a service by van or mobile library to isolated areas. Library services to assist or supplement those in schools are a common feature; this may involve a permanent but changing collection of books suitable for children in a room which teachers can visit regularly. In the same way the service to welfare homes, hospitals and house-bound readers, together with the transport and other requirements, will have to serve a much greater area than the city. The central building will include garages for transport vans and mobile libraries as well as easily accessible short-term collections for delivery throughout the county.

Branch libraries

In both town and country these exist to serve their immediate catchment areas, but in large or widely spread systems there may be district or regional libraries which in addition act as headquarters for smaller, often part-time, libraries in surrounding areas. Branch libraries generally offer a service of books (and often of pictures, records, tapes, discs and so on) for loan to people of all kinds and all ages; they also provide minor reference and study facilities for both adults and children. Branches which are open full-time will house between 6000 and 50 000 books, the vast majority on open access, that is spread on shelves from which readers will help themselves. A smaller number of books will be kept in a quiet study area as a reference library, while others will necessarily be held in operational reserve. Where a full-time branch library cannot be justified because of the smallness of the immediate population, a part-time service may be given, but the book stock should not in any case be less than 5000.

The primary design and siting requirements are that the building shall be very easily accessible for the general public and that they shall be attracted to use it. At peak times large numbers will do so, perhaps several hundred in an hour. Again control and security arrangements are important features of the planning, as is economy of staffing. Workrooms will be needed for staff, but the basic processing work on new books will have already been carried out centrally for the whole system. Of the two types of service which the branch library has to give – lending and reference – the former must have much the greater emphasis. Newspapers and periodicals will be read at tables within the open area. In the past there was usually a children's room in larger branches but now it is common for it to be merged with the general open area; children will certainly be catered for, often in large numbers, but the tendency is for barriers to be broken and a single integrated library designed, with areas for choosing books, for quiet study, for quick reference and for children's facilities, all separated only notionally by furniture and layout within a single open-plan room. In branch libraries, attention to children's reading needs is most important, because children will normally tend to use the local branch library rather than travel to the large library in the town. All librarians recognize the importance of inducing young people to make the transition from reading as a child to reading as an adult. For this reason young adults' sections may be found; experiments in this direction have been made for many years now, but most librarians are as yet unconvinced that such sections are a desirable feature. On the other hand the age at which children are considered old enough to be catered for in the main adult library has been steadily falling, at least in Britain. At one time it was fourteen, but now it is more likely to be twelve or even eleven, the ages at which the transition to secondary education is made.

The social contribution the library has to make in its own particular situation and to its own particular community may drastically influence both siting and design. In a small town the library can be the heart of the community and, given flexible planning, the building can serve as exhibition centre, lecture hall, meeting-place and small theatre. It can also support and provide accommodation for a multitude of community clubs and activities. Anyone particularly interested in these matters should see *Designing a Medium-sized Public Library*,[12] which not only surveys the problems but proceeds to design a suitable library on an actual small town site.

At the other end of the scale the library may be incorporated with a public building having a different purpose, such as a town hall. This was common in the past, but if a library cannot stand alone today it is likely to be found in a shopping complex (which is ideal for catching the attention and serving the needs of those who are doing their shopping) or a community project such as an arts or education complex. A recent British example is the Abraham Moss Centre in Manchester, which occupies 3.4 hectares (8½ acres); it houses schools, an adult education centre, swimming baths, restaurants and a wide range of social services, and has as its heart a public library designed to serve users of all these multifarious activities. The social planning of an area – the creation of hypermarkets, for example – can change the library's emphasis and even its opening hours. Car parking space is less of a problem in such cases, as a complex is likely to have its own parking space.

Other types of libraries

The library types which follow are given less attention, not because they are unimportant but because they are less likely to have their own buildings. Almost all form part of the building of a parent institution.

Hospital and welfare libraries

Library services for those in hospital and welfare homes are essential both for the sick and for the staff. At the very least they can be justified because they provide for those who are unable to visit other libraries, but, as the large and growing literature on the subject shows, they are now recognized as an important sector of the professional library scene. The recreational library services vary in size from the small rooms in welfare homes where the elderly residents may read or borrow books, to those in large hospitals which resemble a small public library. Teaching and university hospitals and medical schools will have their own professional libraries. In general hospitals there is often a library complex with services to staff and patients in separate but adjacent areas. This is generally the most economical and effective method of giving satisfactory service to both sides.

Hospital libraries are seldom separate buildings, except in large mental hospitals situated in open country. Usually the main planning question to be solved is the siting of the library within the hospital, particularly its relation to other hospital services. The library for both patients and staff must be as central as possible for service to the wards and also near lifts and toilets. However, a multi-disciplinary library for doctors, nurses, administrators and other professionals supplementary to medicine has to be related to the facilities for post-graduate and nursing education. In designing a patients' library the architect will be especially concerned with the access needs of the physically handicapped.

The importance of libraries for hospital patients is being increasingly recognized, as the value of reading as a practical therapy to alleviate worry and boredom is accepted. The literature of bibliotherapy is constantly growing, and a number of interesting books are listed in the Bibliography, p. 218.

The official British guide *Library Service in Hospitals*[13] says:

'An efficient trolley service visiting each ward at sufficiently frequent intervals to enable the service to be used properly is required for patients who cannot leave the ward. Patients who can do so should be encouraged to visit the library and make their own selection from the shelves. . . . The library service might also include the maintenance of a stock of gramophone records and the provision of sets of plays for play reading.'

To this should now be added audio and video tapes and discs. A professional librarian in charge of such a service may also need adjoining space where rehabilitation

activities such as poetry and play reading by small groups, can be organized.

Quoting *Library Service in Hospitals* again:

'The purpose of the staff library is to serve the needs of the hospital medical, dental, nursing and other professional medical staff; and to provide a service for general practitioners, local authority doctors and other professional people who work in the National Health Service outside the hospital and who make use of the hospital's postgraduate training facilities.'

Developments in the field have been rapid within the last few years: the latest revision of the Library Association's *Hospital Libraries*[14] deals separately with the library and information needs of medical and other professional staff, including those in regional libraries, post-graduate medical centre libraries and those for nurses in training. After decades of comparative indifference, official support is at last being given to these important services. There is real scope therefore for architects to design units which, while providing separate staff and patients' libraries of different degrees of complexity according to the nature of the hospital, can associate them together to make full use both of stock and of library staff time. If such a library complex can also serve the local general medical practitioners (and such schemes are already in action), the integrated service becomes of value to a wide range of people.

For all the information needed on this subject the essential book is *Hospital Libraries and Work with the Disabled in the Community*,[15] edited by Mona Going.

Prison libraries

These libraries are doing a great deal towards the successful rehabilitation of those who are confined within prison walls. No other community consists of active people with so much time on their hands; in no community is there greater need for the opportunity to read a wide and inviting selection of books. The architect may think it unlikely that he will be asked to design such a library; so much the worse for us all, because a prison library – planned to attract and to look like a public library 'outside' – could have a civilizing influence in a world where the primitive too often rises to the surface. Pioneering work is being done; public libraries assist with book stocks and staff advice. Problems exist, of course, and it would be absurd not to acknowledge them, but a well-designed library can make its own small contribution towards solving these problems. The Summer 1977 issue of *Library Trends* was devoted to library services in correctional facilities.

Special libraries

The term is used to denote libraries which are *not* university, college, school, hospital or public libraries. Despite this negative description special libraries have some important positive attributes in common. Their collections are usually limited in subject range but can have very great depth of coverage of their particular specialities. They are perhaps the most positive and active of all libraries in that they are the least inclined to sit and wait for their clientele to approach them. They not only acquire source material but also produce it by scanning and abstracting from a wide range of sources to meet the exact, and predicted, needs of their users. They are certain to rely more heavily than other types of library on technical equipment – photocopiers, microforms and in particular the new information technology. They serve as information centres for their parent institutions, and because of their dynamic approach the planning of their layouts is less easily predictable.

Because of the great growth of electronic technology and the realization that an efficient supply of information is vital to success, special libraries have grown more than any other type of library in the last two decades. With the changing patterns of business and industry this growth is likely to continue. They may have to handle other functions, including catering for the educational and recreational needs of the members of their organization, but undoubtedly an efficient and up-to-the-minute information service is the very essence of special library work.

Among the chief divisions of the genre special library are:

1. *Government bodies* Here the service will be to the government itself, to the legislature or to a special section of government; those serving sections of the civil service will become very specialized indeed and may also be the main library giving a service to the general public on that particular subject. The latter element is usually subordinated to the official one and may be inhibited by the need for official secrecy. Governmental libraries, cooperating and perhaps training together, comprise an impressive section of the library and information profession.
2. *Major industrial headquarters* These libraries can be very large indeed and in some cases will have been planned to organize a network of information services to vast complexes spread over the entire country; they may have central and branch libraries each with its own specialized or merely regional service.
3. *Learned institutions and research associations* Obviously the service to members is the main interest but again such a source of specialist knowledge will recognize its obligations to scholarship by cooperating with other libraries. The range of specialities here is very wide indeed, from pure art to applied science and technology.
4. *Professional associations, societies, and trade unions* The collecting of information in its own field for the use of its own members must take priority, but the library will cooperate with other libraries and may also do some public relations work for the parent body.

5. *Commercial and industrial firms* There is an enormous size range here, from the library of a large manufacturing organization to that of a small firm of lawyers, architects or stockbrokers. Here, as in most special libraries, the use of computers to create databases, or to give access to other sources, will be of primary importance. In this field, special libraries will always be the leaders. If the firm is large enough to have its own training scheme, the library may take part, not only by supplying the literature but by preparing its own bibliographical guidance to the trainees. A regular feature will always be the preparation and circulation of current awareness reports to various levels of research and management.

There are other categories of libraries which are 'special' in that they are devoted to a particular field of scholarship and which are not necessarily a part of any academic organization. To refer to them as 'research libraries' is a piece of cross-classification, because many different types of libraries are planned to facilitate research. Examples are the library and archive entities devoted to the presidency of certain United States Presidents, or built around the papers donated (and often endowed) by the estates of statesmen, and collections of material about a race or religion which have become worthy of organizing into an important research source.

To lay down guide lines for planning libraries of such a wide variety is impossible without knowing their specific purpose and function. To generalize, special libraries tend to be small, but there are exceptions. Some, in large complexes of scientific establishments, may themselves have sub-libraries, comparable to departmental libraries in universities. Siting problems are generally similar to those of school libraries; a central position easily accessible from all parts of the institution is desirable, preferably near the main (ground floor) entrance but not usable as a thoroughfare. This is the usual stipulation, but in a recent article an American architect[16] claims that use of the library rises dramatically when it is planned deliberately to be used as a passageway. One would appreciate the views of particular librarians on this claim.

2 Libraries of the future

This chapter is intended for those who have not followed the changes which electronic technology has brought into libraries during the last thirty years. Normally well-informed librarians will find that what is written here has nothing to offer them.

When planning a library building we are hoping to provide the framework for a service which will be in operation in two or three years' time and which will continue to serve for 'the future' – at least twenty-five years, probably much longer. We plan so that the service will be as effective and appropriate at the end of that time as on the day of opening. To do this we have to be confident in our ability to visualize the users and their needs in (say) thirty years from now. This is a daunting task. In whatever form information may be stored in the future, it will continue to be the business of the library to obtain, house and process it for readers. To plan for this without knowing what form it may take is a seemingly impossible task and adds force to the well-known dictum that 'long-term planning is impossible'. Although more new techniques and materials become available to us every year, the planning team in every project will in practice tacitly accept a freeze date, planning according to what is available at that time and not according to what might one day become available. As an attempt at flexibility, however, certain steps can be taken towards accommodating future changes which can be dimly discerned, accepting that such steps will always weaken, or make more expensive, the plans for the known present. A common allowance is based on the belief that there will be a decrease in material storage and a relative increase in the space required by each seated reader. For example, microforms take up only a fraction of the space needed to house a similar amount of text in book form, but each user will need access to a reading machine. The relevance to computer storage and use is even more dramatic.

Those who attempt to predict the future of the library fall into two camps. The traditionalists say that books, attended by professional organization and skills, have more than just information to offer. 'Information', they say, is the fashionable concept of the moment; in some fields – medicine, chemistry, technology, for example – it is at the heart of things, but for human beings in general it makes a very small contribution compared with knowledge, wisdom, enrichment of the soul and of the quality of life. To this thoughtful comment the traditionalists tend to add less acceptable ones which are in reality based on continuity of practice, the ubiquity of the printed form with its many conveniences, and above all the resistance to change of those who maintain the riches of the older institutions. The more forward-looking thinkers, on the other hand, point to the potential which the new technology has for making information of all kinds available to users more swiftly and cheaply (in terms of human time and effort). Lest this be thought visionary, they can point to the acceptance, against enormous inertia, of the technological changes which have already entered our lives. As I am neither computer specialist nor seer, I can only contribute by tracing briefly the changes that have taken place in libraries in the last few decades and leave it to the professionals concerned with each planning project to decide for themselves where they believe the future lies. A

complication to even this cautious approach is that changes are taking place at such a speed that anything written today is bound to be out of date by the time this book is printed.

How it began

From the middle of the fifteenth century printed books joined manuscripts as communicators of ideas. For the next three and a half centuries the only major change was the increasing relegation of the manuscript form to a subsidiary, usually an archival role. Libraries steadily increased in size with the great growth of printed book production, but no change of practice took place until the late nineteenth century, when lending books for use off the premises became common; the material loaned was no different. Gradually other forms crept in – film, gramophone records, radio – but it was only after the Second World War that these became serious partners to books and the library service began to change with the opportunities they offered. At no time were they thought of as replacements for books rather than supplements to them.

The first really revolutionary arrival was miniaturization in the form of the microfilm. Although it was a century old as a technique, it was adapted and heralded, particularly by Freemont Rider,[1] from 1936 onwards as the way to solve the overcrowding problems caused by continual growth of book stocks. The microfilm never did replace the book, but after its general acceptance in libraries by the 1950s, by which time automatic cameras were in general use, it provided space-saving advantages, particularly in the storage of long, logical sequences such as runs of journals and newspapers. It was also of great value from the 1960s in replacing crumbling old volumes and as a short-run publishing device, making out-of-print books available to libraries without large back stocks; in particular it helped libraries in the developing countries to obtain those standard works without which it was difficult to operate. In general, however, the impact of microfilm was less than had been expected; but this was not because the technique itself was at fault. Forms convenient for special purposes arrived – microfiche, Microcard, microprint etc. Ultrafiche carried miniaturization still further and put the complete Bible onto a single 35 mm square film; the whole of *Books in English* was published in ultrafiche in 1972. The service weakness of all microforms was that there was no truly hand-held way of reading the text (although a lap-reader to read a thousand pages was produced). A major drawback, the slowness of production and the cost of converting print to this form (except in publishing conditions), was removed when the computer gave it both a new dimension and a new direction. Today it is used more than ever; for example the eighteenth-century *STC* (*Short Title Catalogue*), which in 400 000 bibliographical records represents two million copies held in over a thousand libraries world-wide, is available on microform (and also through a computer). Microform records produced by the computer are widely used as the catalogues of many libraries.

Because first the microform and then the computer were so far-reaching in their potential effects, it should not be forgotten that other technical devices were making their presence felt in libraries. The simple photocopying machine, once a mere office convenience, has become one of the most important elements of the service. Its use to produce a substitute for the original printed text, not only of journal and newspaper articles but also (often illegally) for whole textbooks in those libraries which are unable to buy multiple copies of most-needed works, has made it of prime importance. Many colleges and universities provide rows of photocopying machines, usually coin-operated and sometimes with a cavalier attitude to the rights of copyright holders. This is a small matter (except for the authors and publishers) compared with the question of payment for access to the computer's potential sources world-wide. Someone has to pay: is it to be the library or the individual enquirer? Fortunately this is not a problem which need concern the building planners.

Other machines were brought in to relieve the tedium and cost of the record-keeping necessary in increasingly busy libraries. The tape typewriter was certainly a step in the right direction. Others (like the Vannevar Bush Rapid Selector of 1939, which selected extracts from microfilm on request and displayed them before the reader) certainly worked, but the automation of information did not develop in that direction. Advances in general office technique were adopted and adapted: telex and fax are examples of machines which were of limited application at first but where technological improvements eventually made them of great value. The automation of circulation records was attempted by photocharging methods, by punched-card systems and sometimes by a combination of the two. Small wonder that when the potential of the computer began to be apparent, librarians should welcome it above all as a way of replacing repetitive and boring library tasks; to suggest at this early stage that it might be an alternative to the traditional ways of supplying information would have been out of the question.

The computer was, for our purposes, a product of military research in the Second World War, and it entered library operations in the 1950s. The possibility of putting information in a minute form into a database and retrieving it at will led to the development of the computerized catalogue where bibliographical information (catalogue entries) could be recorded so that both staff and readers could obtain access to it. A further step was the centralizing of such records so that colleagues (or customers) could draw on ready-prepared entries in a database, eliminating the wasteful and tedious practice whereby many staff in many different libraries catalogued the same books at the same time.

The computer-produced records were at first far from attractive; large rolls of paper with entries in a very undistinguished type face were bound into clumsy volumes, but they were comprehensive, could be supplied in a number of copies and could be replaced at regular intervals, thus ensuring that they were up-to-date. Above all they relieved staff from unnecessary repetitive tasks; no new additions had to be made to the old card catalogue, but for the moment computer product and card catalogue existed side by side.

The next step, putting the whole of the library catalogue into the computer and making it available on-line, was slower in arriving, but when commercial firms offered retrospective conversion by contract, it meant the beginning of the end for the vast rows of card catalogue cabinets which had for so long dominated reader service planning. Access to the catalogue could now be obtained from any number of points in the building through small-screen terminals, VDUs (visual display units). An on-line catalogue

for reader use was first introduced in 1967 by the Medical Research Library, State University of New York, and in the same year OCLC, the first major regional centre, was founded; it began with batch mode cataloguing but went on-line in 1971. By 1985 it was serving nearly 3000 libraries, and it now has a bibliographical database containing over 16 million records, 2 million of them in non-book form, in more than 300 languages. This is an individual organization, but Americans are already looking ahead in referring to a 'national database' which would comprise a number of such organizations combined – OCLC, RLIN, WLN and LC.

Through the 1960s and 70s new developments followed each other at great speed. An integrated system (including acquisitions, serial control and cataloguing) began to be set up by the University of Chicago in 1966, and the New England Library and Information Network started a cataloguing system in the same year. Circulation control systems were introduced (at Southampton University and several United States ones) in 1969. Computer typesetting was used to produce the INSPEC journals by 1969 and the British National Bibliography from 1971. In 1972 UNESCO published ISDS (International Serials Data System) for periodical control, but by then such events had become so commonplace that a full history would show many developments in many different fields, sometimes overlapping, sometimes being abandoned; there are far too many to list here, even in outline.

More recent technological advances include the laser-read compact disc, produced for the home market but which proved to have great potential for information storage; by the late 1980s runs of journals were made available from existing database producers on these small inert discs, the library profession's own LISA (Library and Information Science Abstracts) being one of the first. Video discs, with a vast capacity, began to be used for the storage and retrieval, through a local computer, of visual images in colour as well as text.

Today a great number of libraries of all kinds have one, or both, of the two main library computer services which are available from many different sources. The first is the housekeeping function – circulation control, access to the library's own catalogue, stock control etc. – usually on a stand-alone basis; the second is access to bibliographical and other databases through cooperative, network, or host. The two functions – housekeeping and database access – are at the moment usually on separate systems, but it cannot be doubted that they will be completely integrated in the near future. As commercial firms woke to the importance of the library market, more and more databases were produced and firms offered turnkey systems at competitively lower costs. Today the library professional press bristles with advertisements for bigger, better, cheaper systems.

In earlier days the most common way for a library to obtain access to a computer's services was to join others in a queue to be allowed time from its parent institution's mainframe computer. Such machines, very large and expensive, requiring special air-conditioning and secure housing, would be held by a university's computer centre or a local authority's headquarters. The library, among others, would be allowed to use the mainframe for an allotted number of hours per week; its transactions would be submitted to the computer, and returned, in batches. The next step was for the library to have its own minicomputer, which gave freedom for real-time use and could be connected to a mainframe with its vastly greater capacity. The coming of the cooperatives gave access to mainframes dedicated to library processes. The library's own minicomputer, hardly bulkier than a home freezer, could handle the immediate transactions such as circulation records, while the more elaborate needs, such as the creation of the catalogue from bibliographical records, might still be accomplished by batch use of the parent mainframe. Some libraries acquired bibliographical records at regular intervals on magnetic tape from organizations such as the British Library, and those records were then matched against the library stock, given minor amendments to conform with local precedent, and added to the catalogue. At first, only numbers (such as the International Standard Book Number, ISBN) could be searched, but before long access could be by author, title or subject. There were many variations in this progress, including some false starts, and others which depended on the availability of computer services and funds. Today, whether or not the library is a member of a cooperative or network, it is likely to have reasonable computing power in-house; the move is towards remote access to databases but local control of the manipulation of the records. On-line public access catalogues are gradually becoming the norm, and there are a variety of computer-based turnkey systems available with integration of two or more technical processes. Access will be by micro (or personal) computer, and the library will be able to have one or a hundred, according to how many its system can accept and its funds support. The siting of the mini is not difficult, although it must be insulated from changes in temperature and humidity, and often electrically and audially shielded. For the rest, it is only a matter of providing a supply of 'clean' electricity (that is, free of fluctuations and of induction from other users) and the installation of wires, through ducting, to where the terminals are to be placed: the librarian will require the right to change these at will. Some terminals will be devoted to staff use; others, with more limited access ability, will be placed strategically for the use of readers. To operate the terminal and bring the information to the screen, there will be controls varying from light-pens (hand-held or built into the counter top) for circulation control, to the usual QWERTY keyboard and screen-touch devices. Some of the terminals will have printers attached, so that whatever appears can be printed, but these will usually be confined to sections which are under direct staff control.

In addition to the usual advantages to a library of access to a database, bibliographical or not, the developments have produced other contributions. Access is increasingly available to material which is being recorded for the first time because of the advantages which the computer offers. For example a British Library survey at Loughborough University of Technology showed that very little 'grey material' (a category comprising published documents which are usually local or of non-book format) is entered into the national bibliographical records. Steps are now being taken to bring it into the British Library database.

These activities in the library field have taken place against a background of general acceptance of new electronic technology in the home. Television became a familiar part of the home from the late 1940s and was followed by colour TV and in the 1970s by home video in colour. Viewdata began in 1973 and together with the Teletext systems made the visual supply of factual information on a screen, as well as interaction via the home television set, commonplace. Other, less immediately relevant, advances entered normal life; it became routine to access bank records and to obtain cash this way, and even the ubiquitous telephone was affected. The increased capacity of wires, with the introduction of fibre optic cabling, made less impact on the public than using a telephone handset without wires. Cable and satellite television are still spreading, with what long-term effect we do not know. All these steps depended on two elements: their market potential and the presence in the home of certain requirements for the particular mechanical or electrical advance; without these – electricity, the television set, the telephone – and without the expectation of a reasonable level of prosperity and leisure time, the developments would never have taken place. A sequence of random inventions from research laboratories will lie dormant until such time as the right conditions for acceptance of the new product are perceived.

The growth of computers in schools was affected by the belief among parents that familiarity with the machine would give their child an educational advantage; and this belief (right or wrong) also boosted the sale of computer games. These people, the parents and the children, are the users of libraries and so they are not disturbed at the changes which electronics had brought there. In their local public libraries they now consult terminals to see what is happening in the neighbourhood, to look at up-dated lists of job vacancies, and to find out about their rights as citizens from government, welfare and social service files. In some places they can order from the local bookseller, via the library computer, books they have seen on the library shelves; in others, disabled people in their homes can get in touch with the library computer to order groceries for delivery from a local store. These services vary widely according to the policy of the local authority, but they are becoming more and more accepted. A much higher level of sophistication produced the BBC Domesday Project, which is now used in schools and local history libraries. It is a self-contained unit with a small dedicated computer searching two video discs which contain 250 000 pages of text and 24 000 maps, together with pictures in colour, statistical tables and many other features, in an interactive, user-friendly mode, easily understood in a few moments by a normal citizen. (The fact that this librarian, raised in the traditional manner, should use such terms without wincing shows how far we have all travelled.)

The position today

The libraries which make most use of advanced computer-based information sources are those in the fields of science and technology. The earliest of the databases in those fields, now have enormous holdings. DIALOGUE, an early leader, now contains several hundred different computer subject files. Medical research has always been to the fore in the use of computers to provide the data with which it works, and MEDLINE is used world-wide; there are many other databases serving specialist aspects of medical science such as pharmaceuticals and drugs. Educationalists have used ERIC for many years now, and lawyers can access databases such as LEXIS for full text case law on-line. The number of databases is now very high; certainly there are over 3000. The number of 'hosts', organizations through which these databases can be accessed, is over 1000 and continually growing. The BLAISE service is thecentre of British Library activities, and by the use of BLAISE RECORDS, machine-readable records from one of the largest MARC databases can be accessed on-line or supplied in tape form. The British Library's ADONIS document delivery service has begun to supply (at first) several hundred bio-medical journals on CD/ROM (Compact disc, read only memory) and deliver them to major document centres world-wide. A further step, the APOLLO Project, is to make the delivery direct by facsimile through satellites, the result being printable by compatible computer anywhere in the world.

Naturally all these schemes depend on finance and facilities being made available by government or semi-government bodies. It will no doubt be many years before these steps are used in ordinary libraries, but by late 1989 the reasonably forward-looking library (in the West) will be using high-speed electronic mailing, fax and other modern office machines. Its computer equipment will not be that with which it began to automate: most such machinery is now 'written off' after about seven years, and some libraries are already on their third round of computing systems. This has great implications when overall comparative costs are being considered, and it may have to be noted for its possible effect upon interior planning and space allow-ances.

In such a library the new technology will be used for the following purposes:

1. *To order books and journals*, check them off on receipt and handle accounts. Once a new title has been entered for ordering, the record will be accessible through a terminal, not only by the staff but also by the reader in different parts of the library or in its branches. The reader is thus able to see not only what items are in stock but also what is on order.
2. *Catalogue books* or other items, either in-house or by retrieving the text of the catalogue entry from the network or cooperative which the library chooses to utilize. Contact can be by dedicated line or by the use of the telephone system. The library's own cataloguers will be able to add to or amend the centrally produced entry so that it accords with local bibliographical procedures. Once the record is entered it becomes accessible to both readers and staff.
3. *Circulation* records based on minimal identification entries for both books and readers, drawing information from the bibliographical records already in the cata-logue if desired. From these, the system controls the record of issue and return of books, locates books by showing at which branch or library they are housed and whether they are at that moment on issue or on the shelves. The system handles reservations, trapping the books when they are returned, automatically prepares notices relating to circulation and gives the librarian all the information drawn from issue and stock records that he will need. This information helps the librarian to control his book selection and its expenditure in a way that earlier systems could not do. Readers may use terminals to see what books they have on loan or on reserve.
4. *Information* is made available on-line to enquirers, firstly from locally produced sources such as community and local history material. From a terminal, readers can consult a guide to the library, or they can access on-line, from any branch library, reference material, such as bibliographies and encyclopedias, which the central library may hold in full text on, say, compact disc. There may also be discs holding runs of journals which are similarly accessible. The next step is access to any of the 3000-plus databases throughout the world, via hosts who offer these services. Each particular library's attitude to charging for open-ended searches will vary greatly according to its policy and funding, but few will give readers absolute carte-blanche.

This, in the broadest and most general terms, is the picture of the library today among forward-looking, but not especially advanced, systems. It does not apply all over

the world, because of the obvious limitations of finance, technological awareness or even the presence of a stable electricity supply in some developing countries, but it is the path they are likely to follow. They will also be able to advance without the expensive early experiments and avoid the dead-ends. They may also manage to sidestep that concentration on methods of processing information which has so dominated the West and be able to move directly to serving their readers from the ready-processed material at hand.

Language still influences the speed of the adoption of the new technology; because of early Anglo-American work on the creation of machine-readable databases from the holdings of the British Library and the Library of Congress, English-language records are well-established world-wide, but much work has yet to be done to create the basis of large cooperative bibliographical ventures in some other languages. This is not to suggest that English is inherently better but that it, and even more the Roman alphabet, now have decades of development for the purpose behind them.

Immediate prospects

Any library must reflect the changes of need in the community it is built to serve, and it is obvious that all communities' general cultural and informational expecta-tions have changed greatly. The second generation brought up with television, and the first with video, in the home is approaching maturity. Children to whom com-puters are commonplace are now in universities and beyond. In childhood they used them as toys; in their schooling the child-computer link was already challenging the predominance of the teacher talking to them. They probably played chess against a computer, and when they reached the age of higher education they found it perfectly natural to take their problems to a terminal and to interrogate whatever sources were made available to them. In the academic library it is already very much less important to place terminals where staff can show new entrants how to use them; the machines can now be dispersed so that each reader can use one near where the books or journals he needs are shelved. The speed of this advance will vary; it will be most developed in the special academic libraries, particularly those in the fields of medicine, law and technology. Public libraries will tend to be behind, because although they serve the technological-ly advanced younger readers, they must also be at the service of the pre-computer generations. Computer systems will certainly be in general use, but the procedures will be adapted to cater for those to whom the techniques are less immediately familiar.

This is not merely a revolution in methods and procedures. To have information on-line entirely changes the importance of location. If a reader sitting at a work-station can interrogate databases in distant places, there is less need to travel; if the home library's short-loan collection (the books most in demand for courses) can be accessed and studied on-line work can be done from a terminal in a bedroom. It will be possible to off-load (build up his own files on disc) and submit essays on disc. Integration of different courses, perhaps from different universities, can be easily effected, and an inter-disciplinary approach can become normal. When these opportunities are considered against a background of increased amounts of leisure throughout the community, it encourages the belief that there will be a great growth in informal and in continuing education – a real social revolution. The parallel with 'home working' is obvious;

actual attendance of any student (of any age) at a college (to say nothing of attendance at its library) becomes a matter of little moment, perhaps only for the social interaction. How much greater the effect upon the researcher whose specialist journals are increasingly being replaced by electronic (paperless) publishing, who will communicate with his peers by computer conferencing, and will 'publish' into a database after his text has been refereed by distant colleagues.

Before accepting this as a picture of the inevitable future, we are bound to ask who is going to pay for it. The scholarly journal is a case in point: a scholar, or the library, has always had to pay for a great deal of information he did not need in order to get the little he did need. A computerized, profiled service can reduce the supply to what is of importance to the individual reader. This may mean the decline, even the demise, of the scholarly journal at a time when, by all the evidence, the amount, and proportion, of academic library budgets allotted to journal subscriptions is greater than ever before. Since the seventeenth century the production of scientific literature has doubled every ten or twenty years, but the scientists of today cannot read more than their predecessors could. If we accept the easy way out and decide that only journals in specialist research subjects will cease to be printed, we have to ask who is to create the text to be entered into the databases and who is to pay. More than that: we have to ask who will store the totality of that information so that it can be retrieved later; it is hardly likely that the publisher will do this in the long term.

One possible answer to these questions is the proposal for a Knowledge Warehouse (KW). Publishers would supply to KW a copy of the tape or disc containing their text. KW would store it, index it and add it to the general index it is building up. Researchers would use this index and ask for extracts from the text; whole subjects could be gathered onto a CD/ROM, and this would be of great value to serious workers in any field, a version of their own special subject library. Experimental work is now going on in Britain,[2] but difficulties of copyright, terms and so on have yet to be overcome. As with so many new projects, the position may be quite different by the time this book is printed.

A journal on compact disc (CD/ROM) is cheap because it is produced for a mass market; to make a specific compact disc for one's own library is much more expensive. It is therefore most important to consider market factors when trying to visualize the way ahead. This applies to the arguments of the traditionalists: if browsing (and serendipity) are indeed important features of libraries, and if we accept that screens are not acceptable for browsing, we have to ask who, when the book stock is no longer the chief source of information, will pay the costs of supporting the book stock purely for browsers. Certainly electronic advances have been accepted most easily into fields such as medicine, science and technology where the meaning of the information is more critical than the way it is expressed. Literary and historical source materials are 'only' texts, but how soon what appears on the screen will be accepted by scholars as a complete substitute for the original is an open question. The smallest effect is likely to be upon voluntary reading, whose effects range from the broadening and deepening of cultural experience to relaxation and recreation.

To what extent CD/ROM, by providing in a portable form extracts from what is already on a database, will reduce the need for access to the on-line base is an unknown factor. It appears to be cheaper for a heavy user of information bases to obtain the whole of the contents of a particular file on disc and be able to access it without extra cost, but this is understood by the hosts also and they are not likely to sell cheaply and so risk losing the income from their present on-line customers. It must not be forgotten that a CD/ROM cannot be updated, so its great advantage will remain with finite information. Vendors do of course offer to bring the disc information up-to-date by selling on a replacement basis. Discs are an ideal format for bibliographies, and they are now on the market offering up to five million MARC records, book reviews and other bibliographical requirements, cumulated every three months.

Also on the market are the new Write-once (programmable) versions of compact discs; and the imminent arrival of the erasable optical disc will change the picture entirely. CD/ROM has so far been a publishing device, but the new versions can be created in-house, opening a completely new world. Its disadvantage is that it is expensive and it may be superseded (but not for publishing purposes) by Digital Paper, which ICI have now produced.[3] This is said to have the same basic recording features as other optical storage media, but its enormous capacity and flexibility, together with its low cost, could make it an alternative to read-only discs and a major alternative to microforms where it is not only cost-competitive (for example, for archival purposes) but offers much easier access.

In the short term there are a number of developments on or very near the horizon. The optical disc, already offering 400 000 pages of text on a single 300 mm (12 in) platter, may soon be cheap enough as a publishing medium for a library to use it for the housing of vast runs of information. A number of writers, including Roy J. Adams,[4] believe that we are on the brink of yet another advance 'with the promise of fully integrated search and document delivery services yet to be fulfilled'. Optical character recognition devices, already available, will become cheaper, as will machines capable of reading directly from bound books and converting the data for storage and processing through networks. A printer which will enable a reader to print out swiftly and cheaply what he has raised on his screen, the machine being based on a laser print head, capable of operating in facsimile, digital printer and photocopier mode, will soon be with us; the 'electrobook', which will enable readers to carry around, add to electronically and read from a required text, cannot be far away. The obvious question to be asked is what is the position of the library in this electronic future? Is it to change into the place where all computer-based information is stored and accessed, or will it be completely bypassed, remaining only as the holder of printed material while databases become available direct from the home?

Small changes in organization to meet the new progress have already been made: libraries have been combined with computer centres, and even with educational media production units, but these do not appear to have been a success. It is already technically possible for the text of the whole of the world's library holdings to be entered into databases. The technology and the capacity exist, but there can be a wide gap between technical possibilities and drastic changes to existing practices: adopting ambitious advances can be a difficult undertaking. The story of the 'Scholar's Workstation' project[5] at Brown University is of interest for those who see the immediate future for universities as a 'highly computerized wired campus'. It illustrates the difficulties which ambitious and forward-looking schemes carried out by enthusiasts may meet from uneven technical advance, enormous and usually underestimated costs, and the need to carry the whole university community with them at all levels and at all times.

There is already a growing gap between those who are expert and enthusiastic about the new technology, about how it can revolutionize learning, and those who are expert on specific sections of the information itself. It is vital that this gap should be bridged and that the library shall not become simply a supply organization for information which has been placed in a machine-readable store, its curators unable to comment or give guidance on the value of the information itself. A chasm lies ahead; there is a great and fundamental difference between converting a library's catalogue for on-line use and putting the text of the library stock into a computer. A catalogue, in whatever form, is only a guide to, and a way of tracing, the contents; and in the long run it is only the text that the user wants. That the whole text can in the future be made available on-line is no longer in doubt; what is still unsolved is whether the end product will be acceptable as a substitute for the original documents and whether the high costs can be justified.

As we look back at the changes brought about by electronic technology during the last thirty years, it is hard to avoid the conclusion that advances over the next thirty years are likely to be at least as dramatic. The breakthrough has already been made, the computer and its products are already a part of everyday life; the voices saying that the book can never be rivalled are becoming faint. In order to get a picture of the library of thirty years ahead it is no use seeking a consensus among present-day librarians; we must turn to those who are doing the research into the future of communications. We will find it difficult to credit some of their predictions; but then we did not believe Licklider[6] twenty years ago when he predicted that the library could be replaced by direct information supply to the user. He has discussed the problem again[7] at a point halfway between the date of his original book and the arrival of the twenty-first century, and we would be rash not to consider his views.

'Expert systems', largely formed from research in the field of medicine, have problem-solving abilities and it may be that soon these will be a kind of consultant on highly specialized topics. Feigenbaum,[8] working in the field of artificial intelligence, predicts that we are moving from data-processing to knowledge processing; that the next generations of computers will communicate with their users in speech rather than by keyboard and screen; that 'natural language' use is possible in the not too distant future, with possibilities far ahead of the stilted and restricted vocabularies in use today. The introduction of metaphor comprehension and the ability of the computer to use common-sense reasoning lead us towards a world where computers will speak to other computers in order to solve our problems. Few of us are competent to follow far in these discussions, but we have learned better than to dismiss them.

The planning of libraries for an unknown future

To the library planner the timetable is all-important. He or she knows that drastic changes will come, but also knows that the rate of change will depend less on the ability of thinkers than on the funding which will be approved.

Given sufficient thought and backing it became possible to put a man on the moon, but the financial effort could not be sustained at the same intensity. While the hardware, the storage and retrieval devices for use in libraries, will become smaller and cheaper, the increasing complexity and the cost of manpower are combining to make the software far more expensive; the resulting trend will certainly be towards off-the-shelf rather than tailor-made software solutions.

Despite the enormous changes which the new technology has brought there are some, highly esteemed, who still say that the changes in the immediate future will not be fundamental; some claim that the impact of the computer in libraries has been 'disappointing'. In 1967 a conference which included senior librarians, architects and computer specialists from the United States and Canada[9] concluded:

'In sum, it is the consensus of those who participated in the conference that for the next twenty years the book will remain an irreplaceable medium of information. The bulk of library negotiations will continue to be with books – although the science and technology sections will shrink. Remote retrieval of full texts in large amounts over long distances will not be generally feasible, and the continued use of a central library building will still be necessary.'

'The next twenty years' from 1967 brings us to 1987, and most readers will support that judgement. With much more vision, the same conference recorded the following view:

'If it is a fact that in the future the bulk of knowledge will be stored on magnetic tapes or greatly reduced microforms and fed into computers; that information transactions will be negotiated through terminals located at home, in the dormitory, the classroom, the office, or in service stations remote from where information is stored; and that information will be transmitted to users over long distances, then it is imprudent, if not illogical, to plan costly structures to house non-existent books and their readers.'

Taking that statement seriously, and disregarding all the 'ifs', it is a cause for concern that nothing has been done in those twenty years which gives us the belief that library planners do look ahead.

The first important question is how much an allowance for change in the future should alter the allocation of space for book storage as against reader seating. The most authoritative of sources, the 1986 second edition of Metcalf,[10] continues to say of university libraries: 'Doubling the collection size in sixteen or seventeen years has been true in the United States for at least two centuries . . . after maturity, growth slackens to doubling in twenty-five to forty years'. Later: 'In most cases this type of technology [micro-reproduction and video disc] will serve to supplement rather than replace the book as we know it. While growth rates will be affected, collections will continue to grow for the indefinite future.' Again, later: 'So it seems certain that university libraries as well as college libraries will grow at least for the immediate future in their requirements for book collections and campus space'. From such an authoritative source these are disturbing statements; to be fair, they should be read in context in Chapter 1 of the second edition of Metcalf[10].

It is over fifty years since Freemont Rider[11] reminded us that if libraries continue to grow at the rate shown above, then there is a predictable time when the whole land mass will be covered with libraries. He was speaking of the United States, but the principle applies, if in a lesser degree, elsewhere; ubiquitous and blinkered book collecting and storage on such a scale seems to bring into question the whole rationale of academic library provision. If these libraries exist to make the *text* of information sources available (and surely this must be the primary purpose), then it appears to follow that the best, the quickest and the most economical methods of doing this should be used. If such methods are able to supplement these texts with other contributions (commentary, illustrations, variants, background facts etc.), brought in front of the reader in the same medium and at the same time, then to insist that books should continue to be piled up in such vast numbers with ever-increasing difficulty of access, seems both short-sighted and extravagant. For every library to continue to obtain and store to eternity, individually and idiosyncratically, goes against all library thinking of the last half-century. National, and in large countries regional, libraries must of course continue to acquire and hold materials comprehensively as an archive or as a back-up, but the key words for the future must be cooperation and acceptance of technological advance. The world's resources are too limited for each to go his own way forever. Perhaps it would be too hopeful to suggest that resources saved by cooperation and the use of the new technology could help to develop libraries in countries where provision is urgently needed. All influential library thinking, from Rider in 1936 to the Atkinson Report[12] in 1976, has led to the same conclusion: the world cannot afford indefinite expansion of the housing of books on all subjects, in all libraries; certainly not out of public funds.

For the library planner there are two certain comforts. First the continuing build-up of such vast quantities of books can only take place in a few rich countries; there is much work to be done elsewhere, particularly in bringing the rest of the world's libraries up to a decent standard. Second, to plan for a future with impending drastic but unpredictable changes hanging over it is both exciting and challenging. Our expertise is needed in both these fields.

3 Begin at the beginning

Even a librarian has to admit that the finished product, the new library, will show the influence of its architect far more than of its librarian, and that the architect is the real creator. Although Le Corbusier said that architecture only exists where there is poetic emotion, design is not a matter of self-expression but is a solution to a particular problem. The architect will always be trying to create the perfect machine, and so it is of the greatest importance fully to understand the exact function which the library is being created to perform. Similarly no librarian can be content with a machine that works perfectly if it does so in an unattractive or unsuitable atmosphere. It is equally important therefore that the librarian should understand the aesthetic objectives.

Given two competent professionals, the result should be a library which fulfils both requirements and, even more important, is satisfactory, both aesthetically and practically, to its users. This is not always the case; a look at libraries shows that in many of them there has been a gap, a lack of understanding and cooperation. Over and over again the student of library architecture sees an attractive building which just does not work as a library, or an efficiently working library which creates the wrong mood for those who use it.

The division of duties between architect and librarian seems to be rational: the librarian tells the architect by means of a brief (the American term is 'program') what the proposed library has to accommodate and what functions have to be housed. The architect has to create a building which will meet these requirements and will also be acceptable (even commendable) architecturally. This division seems clear, but is it really reasonable? An architect is trained to assess needs and analyse problems in many human service situations; could he not write the brief himself? This is done in some fields (and is claimed by a small number of architects to be part of their ambit), but for the creation of a library it would be most inadvisable. Neither the architect nor the chief executive of the parent institution can define the exact needs without having had considerable working experience of libraries. The librarian, however experienced, will be able to do so only after consultation with senior colleagues, with maintenance staff and perhaps with readers. To leave an architect without an adequate brief is not to liberate his genius but to limit his potential. An architect is a specialist in designing to meet client requirements, not in either guessing or dictating what those requirements should be. Collaboration at all stages, not least in developing the brief, is the only way to utilize the entirely different skills of the two professionals.

Each profession has its own peculiar language, and this can be a source of misunderstanding. Librarians are aware of the common usage of such words as 'planning' and 'design', but in the architect's world their meaning is at once wider and yet more specific. 'Planning' begins with the assessment of the library's total potential contribution to the community, the establishing of priorities and relationship with other social, cultural and educational services, securing a viable fiscal base, the siting, and then the organizing of the internal spaces. The term is also met in the wider sphere of regional and town planning, the latter particularly in the case of public libraries, and campus planning in the academic field. Later each function of the library will have to be planned, that is organized, both for its own effectiveness and for its relationship with the other operational activities.

'Design' has artistic implications: as applied to library buildings it consists of devising a satisfactory environment in which the already planned series of operations can take place. Design cannot begin until overall area planning has been completed and will therefore start later in time. On the other hand planning will not cease at the early stage but will have to continue after consideration of the inevitable restraints which the proposed design will have to circumvent. The definitions, however, are far from exact: the architect will refer to stages of his work as 'outline planning', 'detail planning' and so on, but these uses of the term refer to the organization of his own concepts so that he may arrive at the design he has visualized.

Normally planning will begin the process, but real planning, by both librarian and architect, will continue throughout the various stages of the design.

A major hazard is that the librarian may not be absolutely clear in his own mind when he puts a particular stipulation in the brief. This is a very important point: if he himself is not quite sure exactly what is the functional end to be achieved, he cannot expect the architect to provide the perfect framework. Take for example the requirement for a room for occasional extra-library activities. The librarian may have in mind lectures, recitals and so on, but he may not have worked out the exact range of activities the room is to house or defined clearly in his own mind the term 'occasional'. Would the occasions be daily, monthly or yearly? If the exact functions and their frequency are not made specific, the space itself is bound to be ill-conceived and areas associated with it will be over- or under-provided. Very often the result is a room which is too lavish for a simple series of talks, having rudimentary stage fittings, lighting and projection apparatus, but not sufficiently equipped to be used for even the simplest stage presentation in costume. Many librarians have such rooms and find them an embarrassment.

The librarian has to write the brief; approaching this task can give the unique opportunity to take a long, hard look at present processes and procedures to see whether they are adequately serving the real purpose of the library. It is the best chance to use operational research methods which simulate activities and experiment with models to find the best possible procedures to use in the new library. At its extreme this means that a team of experts will have to be employed; this may be justified on the grounds that such an opportunity will save money in the long run and is never likely to recur. Systems analysis can be of great value in presenting an accurate picture of the structure and of the processes which it employs. If time and money permit, a full systems evaluation can follow with a survey of how effectively the system now analysed is serving its purpose. The systems techniques are of course a much larger enterprise than operations research; both are more used, and more fashionable, now that computers play such a large part in library systems.

First actions

The creation of a new library, for many of those involved and for many institutions, will be literally the event of a lifetime. It calls for the expenditure of a great deal of money – usually public money. It is obvious that the initial cost will be high, less obvious that this cost is small compared with the running costs throughout the life of the building. The capital cost of the project is central to all early discussions. In part this is for political reasons: some form of higher authority has to be approached to give the money or the permission. Less consideration will be given to the running costs, although they will in time involve much more expenditure. Some of this could be saved by using more expensive materials and methods in the first place. Every librarian knows that funds for maintenance and staffing are very hard to obtain, and that 'impressive' exteriors, cheap materials and designs which necessitate high staffing levels will mean buildings that are expensive to run. This knowledge and his consequent apprehension make the librarian's views essential in all discussions. The programme of actions and sequence of events which are traced in this book are the recommended, and fortunately the normal, ones, but there are many cases where less than perfect procedures have been followed.

It is horrifying that binding decisions about a proposed library have often been taken before appropriate professional advice has been obtained. Many a library has been built before a librarian was appointed; the scale and position of a library in a new college or school has often been fixed by spatial and positional allocations within the building long before thought has been given to the library's role, and before a librarian has been allowed to speak for its needs. This has happened also where an authority accepts an architect's (or developer's) proposals, supported by sophisticated presentations, for a large cultural complex including a library. The library space may have been allocated, the activities breezily shown by words, diagrams, perhaps models, without a library brief being used. At such an early stage, it will be said, there is no need for details to be considered, but it is often true that if the scheme shown by model and small-scale sketches is approved it will later be found impossible to change spatial and service allocations to produce a viable library. In one glaring recent example of my experience the library was placed on an upper floor of a complex, with generous lifts for the public but no lift or hoist at all for the reception and dispatch of materials. The key figure here is the architect: he should have consulted the librarian (or at least a librarian) from the beginning. Similarly there are occasions where a developer provides the shell of a library building in unofficial exchange for planning permission, leaving the interior to be fitted out by the authority. This can be disastrous, because the architect of the shell will not have had the cooperation of the librarian who is to operate the future library, and also because two different architects will have been involved, perhaps with a time-lag between their contributions. There are cases in newly developed countries where furniture salesmen have persuaded the authorities to let them design the interior of a library (on a turnkey basis) without benefit of either brief or independent architectural advice. Binding decisions have been taken by authorities on the suitability of a certain site without consulting the architect, who may later find it unacceptable on planning or design grounds. If a librarian is concerned in the original decision in such a case, he should point out the need for an architect's opinion.

Outside factors often override the early decisions; social, political, educational and financial considerations – in many cases the very factors which lead to the creation of a new library – will inevitably take precedence. A new branch of the public library in a previously unserved area will be prompted in the first place by the presence of a community of citizens who are aware of the cultural and educational advantages to be gained by having a library in the area, but it is only when these needs are formalized and expressed through the machinery of a local council that they approach reality. Decisions by a commissioning authority will evaluate comparative importance and will assign to the proposals a place among others in a list of priorities.

In large organizations this means putting it into a rolling programme of capital projects, and in order to do this, the first rough estimate of costs will have to be made. This will be done by the finance officer, who, with the assistance of the official architect or surveyor, will use published (and updated) figures of building costs for projects of a similar size and kind. To these will be added the costs of loan charges and other overheads, and so a certain figure will stand in the programme associated with the proposed library. Because of this it often happens that the 'guesstimate' assumes the role of a financial limit, which may cause difficulty when firm and detailed costings, based on a full study of the situation, are produced at a later stage. In a similar way the proposal may acquire site associations or social emphases from its early processing and before professional officers have reached the stage of reporting in full. This is not the ideal method of conception, but we are not living in an ideal world. There is no shortage of professional expertise available to an authority: what may be lacking is the decision at a very early stage to assemble a body of experts and to encourage them to work as a team, their proposals being submitted to the authority at each progressive stage. For a team to work effectively, each member must appreciate the peculiar skills of the others and there must be a crystal-clear understanding as to the respective spheres of action and powers of decision. Lack of this understanding has been the greatest single cause of failure in the past.

The moment when the idea of a new library first begins to take shape is not always easy to identify. Some projects are statutory: a new secondary school *must* have a library. Sometimes the need for a library is so obvious as to make the provision automatic: a new university certainly *will* have a main library, and it *may* have secondary ones (although even this obvious dictum can be challenged by the Inter-University Library, near Lyons, France, established to serve a number of universities in the region). Nevertheless, there will be many occasions when inclusion of a library among the facilities of a new project will not immediately occur to the planners: for example, it has taken decades of persuasion by librarians to make hospital authorities take seriously the idea of a hospital library. Similarly many commercial firms have yet to perceive the advantages of having an efficient library information service.

The project normally first acquires a form when it is drafted by a librarian: his proposals will be studied and possibly drastically amended by his governing body – be it library committee, university council, local council, board of governors or board of directors; theirs is the decision and theirs the control at all stages. It is therefore in the librarian's mind as he first drafts proposals for a new library that we can recognize the moment of conception, but from this very first moment he will need specialist information and specialist advice. He or she will in fact be making a preliminary feasibility study and will begin by drawing upon his own experience and that of others who have had to solve similar problems. Looking at the simplest example, providing a branch library for a new housing estate, he can turn to published information on similar projects; for Britain the most obvious example is the Library Association's *New Library Buildings* series,[1] which periodically covers new libraries in Britain, giving details of area served, size and cost, as well as simple floor plans and photographs. In the United States the December issue of the *Library Journal* summarizes new buildings and extensions, both public and academic. Similarly librarians of medical centres, hospitals, schools, colleges and universities can turn to their colleagues or to relevant detailed reviews of similar projects in either library or architectural professional journals.

The librarian will soon find that he is faced with hundreds of questions for which his experience, and that of his own profession, can produce no solution; for these he will need to consult legal, financial and other officers to help him to forecast whether it will be possible to create a suitable library under the powers of the institution and within its financial abilities. Because the project will usually be associated with some particular site, the librarian will already have made informal enquiries as to the availability and conditions of use of that site. This may have involved planning officers or surveyors who will make general comments on his ideas, but they will not be concerned with the specific requirements of this particular project, only with its possible place in the area. When the librarian considers he has sufficient relevant information he will report to his authority, summarizing both the need and the recommended functional solution, explaining the advantages he believes the new library will bring. In the case of a commercial firm he will emphasize the economic benefits the library would contribute to the efficient operation of the undertaking. Where such basic arguments are superfluous, for example in the building of a new university, he may give his views upon appropriate organization – either central library facilities with close links to specialist schools, or a network of libraries within the campus. He will make no references to matters of design or structure, nor will he attempt more than the vaguest indication of possible costs.

At this early stage, dealing only with a known need but with little idea of building size or problems of construction, to obtain even the vaguest cost estimate is difficult. In large authorities the committee is likely to instruct a quantity surveyor (or whatever building cost expert it employs) to produce an estimate which will take its place in the authority's rolling capital programme. The quantity surveyor will look up standard building costs per square (or cubic) metre or foot for buildings of a similar nature. Using the librarian's rough estimate of size (probably based on reports of similar projects), he will multiply to produce the first cost estimate. The authority may also require a preliminary estimate of annual running costs, which will take its place in the total predicted annual cost figure.

Even if the authority does look favourably on the proposal it is unlikely at this point to do more than give approval in principle. The librarian may have to satisfy it on points which are in doubt and perhaps prepare a second report, before the authority agrees to appoint an architect for the scheme. This is not always done in the same way. The authority may employ its own architect to make a feasibility study, with a preliminary estimated budget, and, if this is acceptable, appoint an outside architect to design a library within the financial and other limits recommended. This may be done in order to save professional fees and in the belief that the authority thus retains greater control over the project: an odd but prevalent notion. Other ways are to appoint an architect to prepare a feasibility study and then

re-appoint him to carry on with the scheme if the proposal appears to be satisfactory, or to appoint an architect to design a library, produce all documents necessary for the building contractor and then leave the scene, the authority itself, through its own architect, inviting tenders and supervising the building process.

In some countries there is an official architect for each region, in government employ, who will take on all the projects within his area of responsibility. In the normal way an architect will be appointed with a written contract, in Britain either on the model approved by the Royal Institute of British Architects or on the authority's own pattern; if in private practice he will be remunerated according to the published scale of professional fees, which is generally a percentage of the final total cost of the project. If the contract is a lengthy one he will have the right to interim payments (as will the consultants); these matters will be detailed in the contract documents. Whatever the method of appointment chosen, the architect will be tied to the authority by contract, and one of the obligations will be to report at specified intervals upon progress and upon financial implications.

The way in which an architect is chosen will differ widely, not only in different countries but in different circumstances in the same country. Unless the choice is already dictated by a decision to use the same architect for the whole of a campus or a complex, it is most usual for the authority to survey past work done by architects who have been recommended to it. Who draws up the original short-list? Possibly the authority's own architect will have a part to play; the RIBA (or its equivalent in other countries) may provide a list of suitable firms. Whatever method is used, it will be found that the principle is to use a firm of architects which has already done good work on a similar project. This seems hard on newcomers, but presumably they have to build up a name by concentrating on small jobs.

Another much publicized method is to hold an architectural competition. Here designs are invited from architects, or a selected number of them, and the creator of the design which is finally chosen is awarded a prize, or the job, or both. Sometimes the prize-winning entry is widely publicized to obtain public reaction; if this is unfavourable the whole project may be re-thought but commonly the prize-winner gets the job. In the case of a prestige building a competition is quite a common way to choose both a design and an architect: the RIBA Directory contains regulations for such competitions. However, even if the new library is to be a prestige building the method is still dangerous. The brief for the competition will have to be drawn up in great detail by the librarian working in a vacuum, or alternatively with an architect who will not be responsible for the design. There can be no satisfactory contact with the competing architects, including the ultimately successful one. Such a system is often the perfect example of how not to use the best available talent to create a solution; but the highly praised new university library of Düsseldorf was designed after a competition which had thirty-five entrants. The entries to a competition show what very different ideas are possible: an example of the ingenuity of a number of architects given the same problem is to be found in the entries for the new Nationalbibliothek in Frankfurt-am-Main (West Germany).[2]

In Britain the costs of the entire project will usually be met from one financial source, the authority's central funds. Large private donations are almost unknown in the public sector (although they do occur, if rarely, in universities), mainly because of a tax structure inhospitable to potential donors. This may deprive the librarian of 'pump-priming' advantages but at least the architect is spared the task,

3:1. University of Düsseldorf, West Germany. View of library building from south-east (Architects Volkamer, Wetzel and Beckmann)

common in some American academic libraries, of isolating, in cost and design, a section of the building so that it can be financially debited (and publicly credited) to a particular donor.

The total cost estimate will have to be broken into its major elements, not only so that the authority can assess the relative proportions of expenditure proposed but also because official cost targets and funds are often based on separate main divisions – site cost, building cost, services, furniture and so on. This is also helpful when making comparisons with other projects, because it is obviously unfair to compare schemes when costs can vary enormously with factors such as a free site or communal main services. In the case of a large project, approval, if only in principle, may have to be obtained from the ultimate financial overlord: in Britain, this will be a government ministry for a public authority, and the University Grants Committee for a university. No project can begin in earnest until it has received approval at a high 'political' level. Whatever body is responsible for the decision and the concomitant expenditure is referred to in this book as 'the authority', be it council, senate, board or other body. All major stages of the programme will have to receive approval from this authority, but in practice it is certain to delegate its day-to-day powers to a committee. The committee, which has power delegated to it to make all but the most formal and legally binding decisions, may be a standing committee of a council, board or firm, or it can be a body specially appointed for this purpose and meeting only to review progress on the library project. Such a body will be referred to here as 'the planning committee'. If the librarian wishes to confer with his senior library subordinates he may set up a group to meet regularly and call it a committee, but that is his own affair. In this book the library professional contribution is covered by the term 'the librarian'. Similarly any representative of the architectural firm who is authorized to take action is here called 'the architect'.

When the architect has been appointed, although required to report on the proposed design and its financial implications and to await approval at every stage, he or she has in fact become responsible for the end product, the completed building. This responsibility cannot be borne by one person alone; the project must be the result of team-work, with the architect as leader of the team and its spokesman.

The design team

In a large project the team will include experts from many different fields. Even with a large team, only a few will be actively engaged at any one time. Some will be brought in for consultation at very infrequent intervals; others may make their total contribution once and for all at a very early stage. The following cast-list of a design team is based on the requirements of a very large and complicated library. In most library projects the number involved will be very much smaller, but special knowledge will always be needed; many specialists are in fact members of the firm which we are for convenience calling 'the architect'.

Architect

Leader of the team. He or she will have had specialist education at a school of architecture; in Britain a full-time student cannot quality in less than seven years, of which four to five are spent in school. If successful he is then entitled to become a corporate member of the RIBA and to be registered as an architect under the Architect's Registration Acts 1931–1938. Under these acts it is an offence for any person who is not registered to carry on any business under any name, style or title containing the word architect.

An architect is not a builder; he is above all an artist, but in order that he may apply his designs and control the whole operation of erecting a building, he has to learn to understand fully the work of a great number of specialists who will be called into action. Although he may employ, or cause to be employed, experts in structural engineering, soil mechanics, electrical, ventilating and heating (among others), he will still himself be familiar with the work they perform. He will have a good knowledge of scientific management and will order his complicated procedures in a systematic way: his own technical field is well documented and his office will include an effective specialist information service. He is an organizer and an entrepreneur, familiar with property values, commercial development possibilities and ways of financing building operations of all kinds. He must be able to work with, to persuade and be accepted by, the planning authorities on whose permission so much depends.

The RIBA[3] distinguishes two functions of the architect: '(1) The management function – to ensure that the project as a whole is well run, and to coordinate the process of design. (2) The architect's function – to contribute particular architectural skills.

The complexities of his world are vast: he is responsible for the safety of the structure under all conditions, and for ensuring that it complies with all regulations and by-laws. He has an obligation to see that his client is given the best possible value for money but also that contractors and sub-contractors are treated fairly. He is employed by the client but has to act as a judge in matters affecting both those who provide the money and those who receive it for work done. The legal implications of his work are considerable, not only in respect of his own direct responsibilities but also because of the maze of official permissions and rules which he, on behalf of his client, neglects to follow at his peril. In the vastly complicated world which he rules he is at great financial risk for every possible error and omission.

In Britain about one-half of architects work in private practice; about two-fifths work in public offices (for central or local government); others are employed by industrial and commercial firms. They are not all engaged in designing new buildings: many of them specialize in other sections of their complicated world, but we use the term here to refer to the senior members of a firm who have the major responsibility in respect of a new building project. When the project has reached a certain stage, the day-to-day work may be delegated to a 'job architect', a less senior but nonetheless well-qualified person, and it is with him that the librarian will have most close contact. Although the architect will work on both the artistic and technical aspects, there can be no separation in his mind between purely aesthetic and practical considerations: one has to be made to serve the other.

Because the result will depend so much on the architect's own judgement he will wish at an early stage to make his own assessment of the problem facing him, and this is what he has been trained to do. His design will attempt to meet the client's vision of function but not the client's vision of a new building. He will design to satisfy not only the needs of which the client is aware but also those which he does not know that a successful design can satisfy. The architect is not, therefore, simply carrying out his client's orders; it may be claimed that as an artist and a servant of the community he has a primary duty to the library's users and to the people at large. This may seem exaggerated but it has an element of truth; the RIBA *Handbook*[3] is worth reading on this point. For further information on the relationship between architect and client, see *Working with Your Architect*.[4]

Librarian

He or she will not necessarily be the chief librarian; but may be the professional member of the library staff appointed to act on the chief's behalf in this particular operation. If responsible for all new building in the library system he will in time develop an expertise which can be of great value to his employer in future projects. In the past, particularly in small libraries, the chief librarian had to fit this task into an already busy working life, and little opportunity therefore arose for him to develop a working relationship with the architect. The librarian will be a senior member of the profession, and in Britain will be one of more than 14 000 chartered librarians. Library school education will have included both theoretical study and periods of working practice in different types of library. Today the principles and practices of information handling are basic to courses. The title 'Chartered Librarian' carries the designation 'Associate' or 'Fellow of the Library Association' (ALA or FLA). The fellowship is now awarded only as a higher qualification to experienced librarians who produce a thesis or similar acceptable contribution to advanced study.

Because the profession is highly organized (through the Library Association, its branches, groups and sections, as well as through other specialist bodies), the librarian will almost certainly have spent a great deal of time visiting new libraries and studying new methods and developments. He will have this advantage over the architect and may be able to suggest machinery and equipment which the architect may not have met. Because the library profession is information-based, he will be better-read in the practices and developments in his own field than most professionals.

He will act for the client, representing his authority in day-to-day decisions, always in close contact with the scheme and keeping clearly before him the functional aims of the proposals. Because he represents the client, many architects do not accept that the librarian should be considered as a member of the design team, arguing that on the one hand he does not have a technical background or training and on the other that as the servant of the authority he would be in a difficult position when the team's proposals were put up for ratification. I believe this is a fallacious view and one which leads to the gaps which so often develop between the two sides. The librarian is an expert in his own field, which is vital to the project, and he has special knowledge of the peculiarities of his own library: knowledge which the architect would find difficult to obtain in the time available. If the librarian is party to the discussions, other than the purely technical, he can make a most valuable contribution, if only in the negative way of seeing functional flaws in the proposals at an early stage and so preventing waste of time. He will not attend the majority of the daily working meetings, but then neither will other specialist members of the team. His great value is to be on hand to clear up possible inconsistencies in the brief and to talk over alternative ideas.

Library consultant

The use of an experienced librarian as library building consultant is rare in Britain, although more than twenty years ago the Parry Report[5] recommended it for university projects. It is perhaps a comment on British architects that they do not appear to feel the need for specialist information from outside their own ranks. In some countries it is so common as to be an accepted part of large schemes. The consultant's great value is that he brings direct experience of library planning which may be missing in the team. He will be able to compare the proposals with similar jobs on which he has worked and may identify future flaws at an early stage. Because he has some knowledge of the architect's world he will have a better grasp of what the architect needs to know. Being a librarian he will be able to understand easily what the local librarian wishes to have and he will be skilled in brief writing. Not the least of his merits is that he will be able to devote to the task that attention to detail which the local librarian could not give because of his other duties. This is a very important point; one of the common reasons for unsatisfactory library buildings is that the librarian simply did not have the time to give to the innumerable problems which arise. Being an interpreter for the librarian and adding from his own knowledge are valuable assets, but the consultant does not cut the librarian out of the picture. One of my own problems in developing countries was that they wanted me, as their 'expert', to get on with it, not talk about it. The first difficulty, as always, was to find out what the client, whether or not represented by a librarian, really wanted. A library consultant should not be expected or allowed to produce a ready-made brief; he is helper and adviser. His fees will add slightly to the overall cost but they can save many times this amount by unique expertise.

The other professionals who are members of the design team may all be employed in the firm of architects; in Britain it is more common for them to be independent specialists, and the following descriptions are based on that situation.

Quantity surveyor

A key figure, employed ideally (and commonly) on the recommendation of the architect at an early stage. His link with the architect will be close and should be formed in mutual knowledge and confidence. His main task is to estimate, from the architect's drawings at every stage, the probable cost of the work and to assist him in evaluating the various alternatives open at any time in different constructional systems, details and materials, and even alternative types of contractual arrangements with the builders. His value will be apparent from the beginning in assisting with the first rough estimates of cost and will continue throughout every subsequent operation. He assesses the value of building work in progress and recommends the amount of interim payments on account. In carrying out his responsibilities he will work closely with all the other specialists concerned in the building operation to ensure an accurate valuation, both of proposals and of work already carried out. In Britain it is common for his appointment to be by contract to the client, to whom he reports, and not to the architect, although he will work closely with the latter. He will have little direct contact with the librarian, because he is primarily there to give financial expertise to the architect and to the authority.

Specialist consultants

There can be almost as many of these as there are problems to be solved. Soil surveys, structural design, heating, acoustics, electricity, ventilating, mechanical equipment, security, interior design – all these require expert attention. The architect may have the expertise within his firm, or he may recommend to the client what specialists should be appointed. His advice in this matter is valuable because these consultants will form with him the design team. If at all possible his preferences for

appointment should be followed; this is important because he will then have around him people in whom he has confidence. The number appointed will depend on the complexity of the project and whether such experts are already available on his, or the authority's, staff.

Clerk of works

The architect will generally advise the client authority as to whether or not the job merits the appointment of an official to supervise the building work on its behalf; the decision will depend largely upon the size and complexity of the scheme. 'Clerk of works' is a long-established term of which British practitioners are proud; in other countries the post is known by such titles as building inspector or site supervisor. When building begins he assumes great importance because he is constantly on the site, supervising the work on the client's behalf to see that the architect's intentions, as expressed in the plans, drawings and specifications which form part of the building contract, are followed in every detail. The architect carries responsibility for general, but not constant, supervision, and it is this constant element which the clerk of works particularly supplies. Thus, although he is employed by the client to see that it is getting what it pays for, his work is also an extension of the architect's supervisory function. The clerk of works is in fact the counterpart of the builder's foreman and will work closely with him, as well as checking on his work, to ensure the smooth progress of the job as well as the efficient and accurate construction of the building. He takes no part in design and becomes necessary only when building contracts have been allocated. For a full definition of the clerk of works' responsibilities, see the RIBA *Handbook*.[6]

Despite what may appear to be a proliferation of experts forming a large and unwieldy team it must be made clear that for the great part of the time it is the architect who alone, or with one or two colleagues, works to produce the proposals. He himself will consult specialists, receive and incorporate their ideas, or the constraints which they have to report, into his slowly forming concepts. He will call the librarian and other members of the team to join him when he has questions to ask or proposals to discuss. The team exists but it is not in session continuously, or indeed often.

The librarian will not be the authority's only representative involved in the project. There are a number of other persons – perhaps we should call them office-holders – who are certainly not part of the design team but who have a part to play at intervals throughout the scheme. They include the following.

Chairperson

A responsible member of the board who will act on its behalf between formal meetings. In an educational establishment this may be the principal, or his representative. He is unlikely to take part in regular teamwork but it is important that he be kept informed, that discussions take place and informal agreement be reached, before proposals are brought to the board. In particular he will be consulted, or kept informed, on all policy matters which do not necessarily need the authority's formal decision. To the inexperienced it is surprising how many policy decisions arise, particularly in a complex building project with some amenities and access routes common to more than one entity.

The authority's planning officer or surveyor

Will take the wider overall view of the area and make recommendations to the authority on space priorities in accordance with the needs of the community as a whole. His contribution may be completed at an early stage, but in some cases he will be involved whenever proposed changes affect the pre-conceived use of the site. If he is also the local authority's Planning Officer he will certainly be concerned throughout the project. If not, he will be able to assist when applications have to be made to the local authority.

The authority's finance officer

Will be called upon to comment upon the estimates and all financial proposals and will need to be kept fully in the picture so that he can arrange for payments to be made, even at quite early points in the programme. For example, trial bore holes may be required before a decision can be reached about the suitability of the site; throughout the programme he will be paying instalments of fees to the various consultants.

The authority's own architect

If such a post exists and if he is not also the architect to the scheme, he may be given specific duties at an early stage, such as advising on the possibility of a scheme or helping to write the brief. He may also be used as a watchdog to see that the project is proceeding satisfactorily, but this is a potential source of professional conflict and should not be necessary.

The authority's clerk or legal officer

Will be concerned throughout, both with the presentation of reports to the authority and in drawing up contracts; he will also be involved in approaches to outside powers (ministries particularly) for requisite consent.

Other officers of a local government authority

Several of these will have to comment on, and recommend for acceptance, various aspects of the proposals. They can include police, health, roads, fire and other officers but sometimes, and always in the case of non local government libraries, some or all of them may be 'outside powers'. If they are officers of the library authority they can be represented directly on the controlling committee, where contact will obviously be more direct and efficient.

Future users of the library

Users may be represented at some committee or discussion group by a readers' and/or staff delegate. In universities and colleges this is a not uncommon arrangement because both staff and users are organized and identifiable. This applies to a lesser extent in some types of hospital, but in public libraries only the staff are likely to be involved. This is because the council members are themselves elected to represent the views of the citizens – the potential users – and it is often held that direct reader-representation means that self-appointed pressure groups will exert undue influence.

Channels of communication

From the outset it is vital that everyone concerned shall be absolutely clear as to the powers, responsibilities, progress procedure and methods of communication which shall apply. Similarly nothing can be more chaotic than for an architect to be instructed by one person or committee and then be responsible for the results of his work to a different body. In all projects there must be a single line of communication from the authority to the architect; it would be ideal if this could always be the librarian or library consultant. In practice the building committee or board will usually require the architect to report direct to it and attend meetings held to discuss the report. This leaves the librarian as a kind of professional consultant at a time when he is the officer most concerned with the resulting library. When there is a library consultant the position is easier, as he can join the specialists, leaving the librarian to sit with the board as its permanent official.

The relationship with specialists must also be clearly defined. Although they work with the architect it is common for them to report direct to the committee. If the authority already has its own consultant on a certain aspect, such as security, then it must be made clear whether the architect has access to him or whether this consultant is to report direct to the authority. In the latter case the librarian should act for the authority so that the architect is still dealing with a single representative of his client.

Four full reports are usually called for from the architect: the feasibility report after a survey of the possibility of carrying out the required project; the outline planning report after an outline plan has been completed; a scheme report with sketch designs; and a final report when working drawings are produced. In each report a cost estimate will be given so that the authority can see whether the project is on target and still acceptable financially. In small projects there may be fewer reports: in very large ones there may be regular reports and additional ones on special aspects of the scheme which are particularly important. When the architect wishes to tell, first the librarian and then, after discussions, the board, what he proposes and to seek their approval he will communicate not only in words but in plans, drawings, sketches and perhaps models. He will have to bear in mind that while these media are the common currency of his own world, they are not as familiar to the librarian. The latter will be accustomed, and eventually happy, to study floor plans at 1:100 (or ⅛ in: 1 foot) but will find elevations and sections much more difficult to grasp. Detail from one-tenth up to full scale he will find very difficult indeed (especially joinery sections) and the spatial relationships between plan and section the most complex of all. On the other hand he may be seduced by the charm of 'artists' impressions' and isometric drawings, while failing to grasp the essential points the architect is trying to show. Architectural models and videos he will love, but these are always expensive. More comments about plans and particularly the story which the different scale versions try to tell are given on p. 101. This is not to suggest that the librarian is a dilettante, happy to play with the toys of another's world. The point is that it cannot be assumed that, because the librarian has been supplied with some plans, he understands and accepts everything. Teamwork means understanding, and it will be important for the architect to spend time in patiently explaining the significance of the plan's features in order to be sure that they are fully understood. As any experienced librarian knows, working with an architect has drawbacks which arise from the latter's responsibilities.

Because he has a critical job to do and has always to balance one need against another, with constant heart-searching, and because he is often a persuasive speaker, the architect may find it easier to mould the librarian to his own ideas than to produce yet another compromise solution. This can be unfortunate; I have known examples where it was disastrous. Only a patient understanding of the librarian's point of view and continual cooperation can give a satisfactory result.

From their many meetings, architect and librarian will learn to understand each other's aims and intentions. On a particular subject which is under discussion, such as heating, acoustics, security, the specialist in that field will be present and will take a leading part, the architect having often to act as interpreter. At even the most informal of these meetings certain agreements will be reached; it is absolutely essential that minutes be kept of these agreements. They should be drawn up by the architect and circulated for confirmation. This may seem bureaucratic, but in fact it is a sensible precaution; where the backgrounds of the participants differ so widely, each member may leave the meeting with a different view of what has been agreed. These minutes will form appendices to the brief and are the architect's authority for spending time and money in developing certain lines of action.

3:2. Design programme

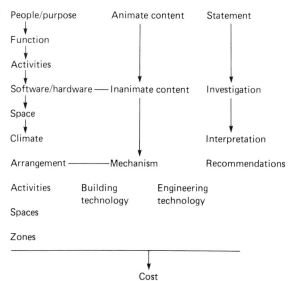

The programme of action

To the architect the creation of a new library is just another job; he will set about it on a programme of operations familiar to him through his training and experience. To the librarian the experience will probably be new, and it will be a great help to him to know exactly what the architect is doing at any one time and what he will turn to next. This will reassure him during the inevitably long periods in which he receives no communication from the architect. This programme (and the time schedule of operations which the architect will draw up and which will be referred to later) will keep him informed. This design programme has been expressed as shown in Figure 3:2.[7]

Table 3.1 Summary of programme of action
Inception of project
Setting up the design team
Primary brief:
statement of aims
contents to be accommodated
activities and users
life of building, flexibility and expansion requirements
special physical requirements and conditions within the building
site location and limitations
security
communications
cost limits and controls
consents
time schedule (from client's viewpoint)
Feasibility study:
use of site: site investigation
space relationships
structural implications of space relationships and physical requirements
cost feasibility
feasibility report
Secondary brief:
pattern of operations
verification of amplification of information
contract policy: client nominees; proprietary libraries (where applicable)
maintenance policy
Outline planning:
planning principles redefined
division into major areas: reader circulation
Scheme design:
planning the structure:
flexibility
structural grid: columns
floor loadings
service equipment: stairways
internal environment
column sizes
construction
services
Detail design:
layouts and critical sizes
book accommodation
reader service areas
staff areas
non-assignable areas
furniture and fittings
floors
circulation
lighting
enclosing elements and finishes
Security and protection
Physical conditions
Cost studies
Final report
Production information:
drawings, schedules and specifications
bills of quantity
tender action
project planning
operation on site
completion

An agreed programme will not obviate the need for continual discussion. It will be found that the same matters arise at several different stages of the programme for different reasons. The programme not only lays down a progression through a sequence of actions known to all who are to be in any way concerned in it; it is a chain in

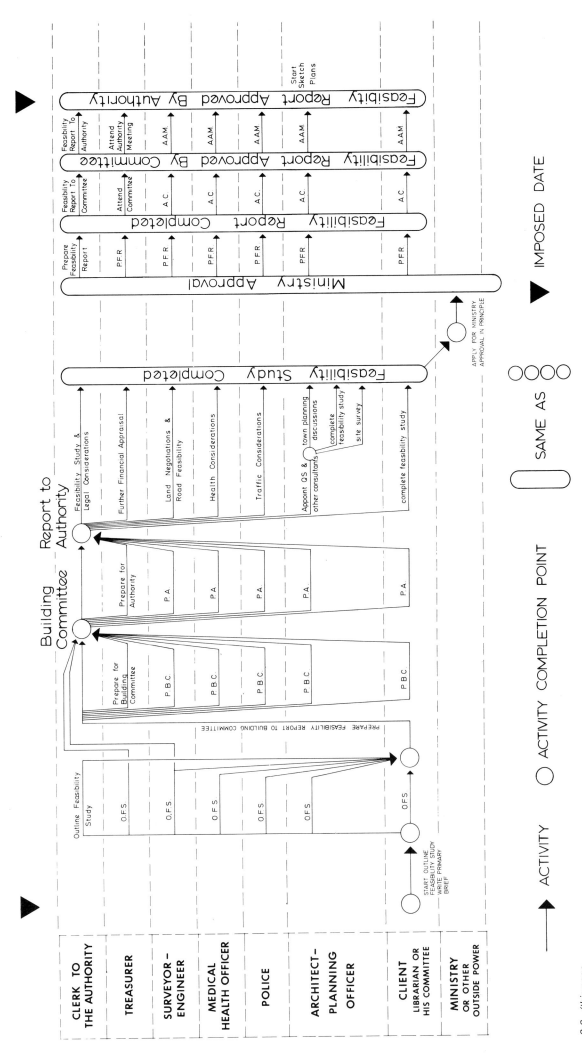

3:3. (this page and opposite) British local authority procedural network

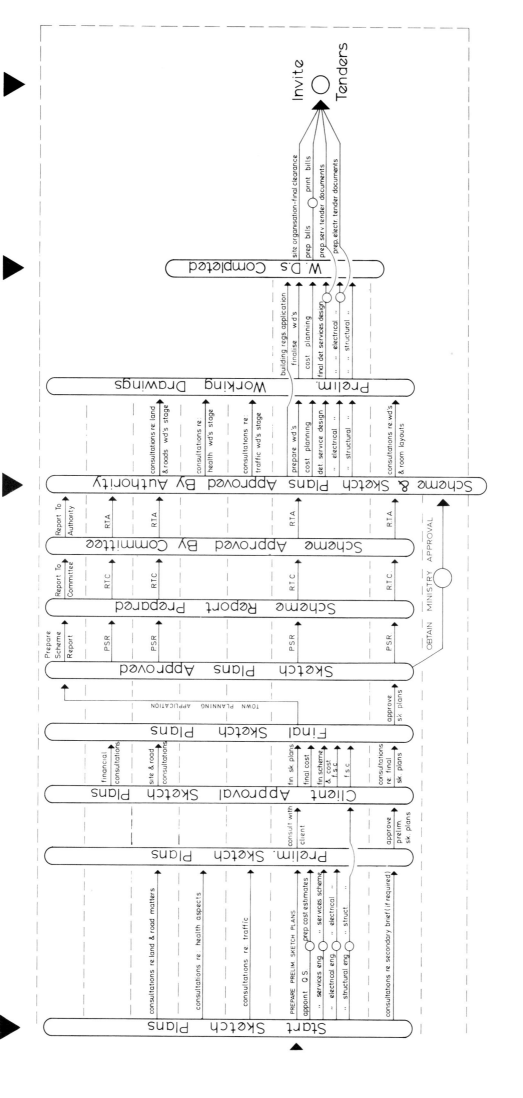

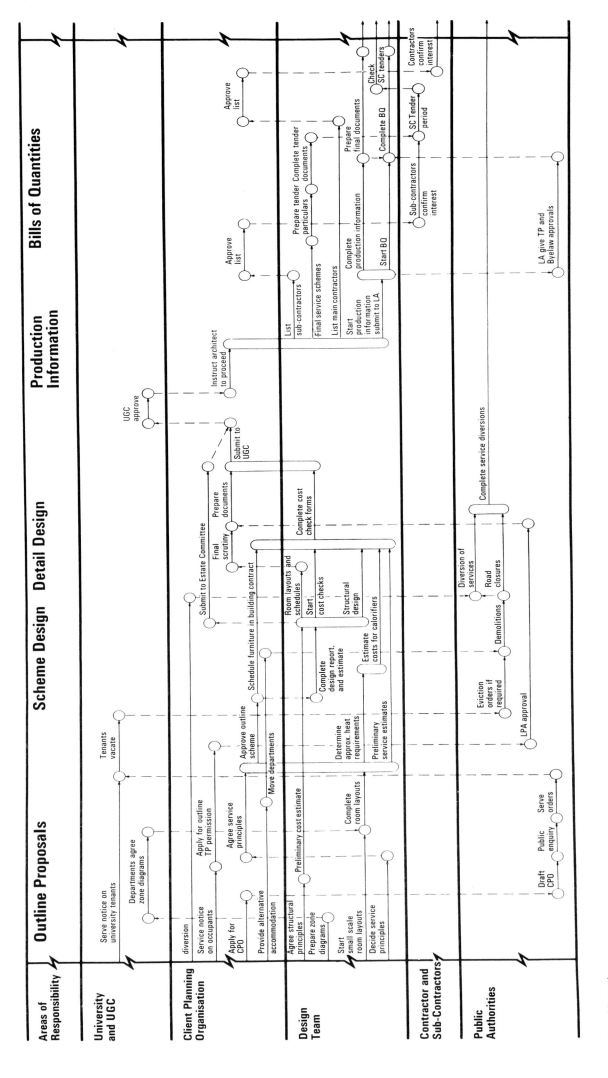

3:4. Network analysis for a university

which all links are interdependent, and in which one single omission can cause a complete breakdown. Approval for each step in the planning must be obtained, either from the authority itself or from an outside body, and without such approval all future actions will be impeded and the entire programme can come to a costly standstill.

In parallel with the list of actions which are being carried out by the design team is a sequence of actions by all the powers and officers who will be concerned in the project; this can add up to a formidable list. To lay down a full and exact record of all actions which must be taken can be a daunting prospect; where such a building project is a regular occurrence – in the case of large university or local authority, for example – it is common for a network analysis of the operations to be undertaken (see pp. 28–29).

Although the architect will be free to set his own programme, in Britain it will usually be based on the RIBA's 'Plan of work for design team operators'. This plan, and the *Handbook of Architectural Practice and Management* of which it forms a part, deals with the systematic planning of the design process in much greater detail than the librarian will ever need, but from it he can see the main sequence of activities. From this point on, the arrangement of this book is based on a typical programme from an *Architects' Journal* briefing guide; in order to make the librarian familiar with a likely sequence of events, a summary of the programme is set out in Table 3:1.

Those concerned with creating a very small library, one within a building, or with converting existing buildings to make a library, may find this an over-elaborate proposition, but even in the most modest scheme the principles still apply, although it will be found in practice that some sections will require little or no attention. The great advantage of an agreed programme of this kind is that it reduces the likelihood of mistakes arising from the librarian's failure to communicate vital information, having assumed that the architect already knew about it. The oft-quoted example of the primary school provided with washbasins in every classroom (as requested in the brief) but not with a supply of water at these points (as it had not been requested in the brief) may be untrue, but it draws attention to a real danger. If the librarian stipulates one need in great detail the architect is entitled to assume that his other needs have been similarly included.

Network analysis

In large projects the architect will be responsible for an enormously complicated operation and he may make use of the techniques of network analysis to control activities of great complexity whose interdependence in both time and action is such that a sequence of steps must be meticulously followed in order to avoid disastrously expensive delays.

In Figures 3:3 and 3:4 two examples are given of networks applicable to building operations in which a librarian may become concerned. The university example (reproduced by kind permission of the RIBA) shows the great complexity in university building work. It is not particularly designed to apply to university *libraries* but shows clearly the large number of officers, committees and other powers who will inevitably be involved in the project.

The example in Figure 3:3 shows in more detail a programme network for a public library building; note that the architect concerned is the authority's own architect and planning officer, and is therefore more closely involved in the committee procedure than would be the case if a consultant architect had been employed. Also more events concern officers within the authority than is the case in the

university example; this is because, in this particular instance, the authority was itself a planning authority, and therefore some consents were obtainable through officers of the authority (e.g. the planning officer, medical officer of health). The analysis is in two stages: the first concerns the actions leading up to the acceptance of the feasibility report, and the second that applying to the production of the sketch plan and working drawings. In practice the architect will use a third network to control activities at the stage of tender and construction on the site, but these will be of little real concern to the librarian.

Despite their apparent complexity these networks are basically simple, showing the progress of activities (indicated by arrows) in an exact sequence as they lead up to certain events (indicated by circles). These events are key points beyond which no progress is possible without some form of authorization; where such events involve a number of officers or committees simultaneously the circles become ovals to show who is involved. Many of these events will have predetermined dates (e.g. meetings of the authority council).

Architects are familiar with network methods which are part of the technique of critical path analysis. The analysis is also useful to the librarian (as well as to others involved) because it ensures that no one can be in doubt about the next step in the programme and who is to take it. If the librarian is to play his full part and keep abreast of progress, he should at least know something of the methods used. A network such as this need not be created anew for a library project, because the responsible officers of the authority may have already prepared and used a similar scheme for other building projects. All that will be necessary will be for minor amendments to be made where procedures are deemed unnecessary, for the identity of the client to be established and for the relevant officers or committee to be identified. Such a network will have time implications, and progress will obviously depend on the degree of completion of one activity before the next can take place. From this basis will be produced the timetable of operations that will form part of a periodic report from the architect to the authority.

In a smaller project the same principles will apply; many parts of the programme can be omitted, but only after the section has been read, understood, and the appropriate actions taken.

Standards

One of the librarian's most obvious tasks is to tell the architect, by means of the brief, how big the library is to be. He should do this not in square or cubic metres or feet, a judgement alien to his training and experience, but in numbers of readers to be expected (and at what times), numbers of books to be housed, equipment to be installed and reader services to be provided. He will also say how long he expects the building to last and how much room for expansion and allowance for change is required.

The information falls into two categories: persons (both readers and staff) to be accommodated, and material to be housed. More complicated is the information he has to convey about the functional relationship between them, a factor which strongly affects the design. These matters are for the librarian's decision alone, given the concurrence of his authority. Where his task is to transfer unchanging operations from an old library to a new one he will already have the practical local experience to visualize the new service in quantitative terms, although one should never forget that a new library will always attract more readers and need more staff. Similarly it is easy enough for a public librarian who has to create a new branch library basically similar to those he already runs, to find what numbers of readers and books have to be accommodated. It is simple for a school librarian to know how many scholars he has to seat but not so simple to discover what book stock provision should be made. It may be very difficult indeed for a librarian who has to create a completely new library of any kind, and perhaps most difficult of all for a college or university librarian when the library is to form part of a new venture, whose boundaries, both physical and intellectual, have yet to be clearly defined. In such cases, very clear thinking is needed.

The librarian will get his greatest help from a study of similar projects carried out by others. Reading, visits, correspondence with colleagues, all these will help him to produce an estimate of the quantities concerned – books, readers and services. Unfortunately, the figures he obtains in this way are not likely to impress his authority when he seeks its concurrence. He would find it helpful to be able to quote official standards relevant to his own case; published guide-lines describing official or cooperatively agreed levels of size, staffing, equipment and, above all, finance, which have been appropriate for producing a library to an acceptable standard.

Such guide-lines seldom exist; the most helpful figures are derived from the experience of other librarians. 'Official' statements normally turn out to relate to financial limits, the main yardstick with which officialdom is concerned. As Havard-Williams has said, 'Whether you have one seat for every three students or every ten will depend on whether the financial authorities are convinced that it is an essential service to provide seating on the scale 1:3 or 1:10.'[8] The figures which can be obtained from fairly official bodies are consistent neither in level nor in approach. In a college library the authorization may be in terms of percentage of seats and number of books per student; in a public library it may be volumes per head of population; in a hospital library, expenditure (or number of books) per patient. It is not that there are no published standards, but that they are diffuse, inconsistent and irrational. Those which exist have emanated from many countries and have not been codified into a single document.

At international level the work of the Standards Committee of the International Federation of Library Associations and Institutions has produced, and continues to produce, valuable work, but because of the immense variation in the development, attitudes and authorities in different countries, standards must inevitably be less than precise in their application to particular libraries. Even IFLA's *Guidelines for Public Libraries*[9] says in its introduction:

'It is the task of library authorities and their chief librarians to assess needs, determine priorities, and quantify the resources required to meet the needs of their communities. Recommendations as to desirable levels of provision, based on past experience in quite different circumstances, are bound to be unreliable and misleading. We have therefore made no recommendations regarding areas of buildings, numbers of staff, or the quantities of books and other materials which libraries of different kinds should provide. We have discussed these questions in general terms. . . .'

The major authoritative and official standards for libraries of all kinds, together with implications to be drawn from governmental statements, are given in Chapter 19 of this book, with quotations from *Standards for Library Service* by F. N. Withers.[10] This book, a most valuable research project which was written under the auspices of the International Federation of Library Associations for UNESCO, covers public, school, university, college, special and national libraries. Its value is limited only by the fact that it is becoming dated and by the great difficulty of making comparisons among such diversity. These standards and the recommendations of the appropriate professional bodies which are given together in Chapter 19 may serve as a rough guide and possibly as a source which may help to impress and persuade an authority, but they are not quoted in detail because it is essential that they be read in context. Librarians will (should) already be familiar with them; architects may find them of value because they can help in the task of relating requirements expressed in numbers of persons and books to appropriate allocations of space.

4 Primary brief

Throughout the programme of creation, the library's functional requirements must be kept constantly in mind. Book accommodation, reader seating, materials, access, reader service, security and so on, each raises questions which cannot be resolved once for all but must be reconsidered in each succeeding context, decisions at one stage affecting possibilities at the next. The first step will be when the librarian, familiar with the needs of the future library, assembles his thoughts, perhaps even before the architect has been appointed. Next comes the stage of expressing the library's needs in a brief, and then the architect, after studying the brief and knowing some of the constraints, makes his first tentative space allocations and arrangements. Discussion with specialists will follow, and all the implications will be studied with great care in the preparation of the feasibility report. When this is approved the architect will begin to plan in outline and then in detail, and at each stage he will want to ask the librarian to amplify or perhaps to amend the recorded requirements. Right through the programme the same library functional needs will continue to be under review from the points of view in turn of site, traffic routes, approaches, structure, heating, lighting, ventilation, safety, security, interior design – and always costs. For these reasons the same series of functional topics will recur in this book, chapter after chapter, just as they do in the creation of a library.

The library situation

When designing a library the architect is forwarding a service whose rationale is not easy to assess. There is no easily defined 'purpose of a public library'; the contribution a library has to make to the community reflects something special in the nature of that community and in the particular direction of development which the library, among other instruments, exists to further. It cannot be assumed that the public library is just a collection of books made conveniently available; its role is much more sophisticated, more dependent upon and involved in certain trends in the community's unconscious aims – 'self-improvement in an atmosphere of freedom'. In an institution the purpose of the library cannot be understood without knowing both the purpose of the institution and the essential contribution, recorded or implied, which the library has to make in it. It cannot be assumed that a college or university library is similar in needs to one in which the architect may previously have been concerned: the speed and degree of technological change will have effects which are peculiar to a certain situation.

It is small wonder then that the library profession has acquired an approach for which professional training gives only a broad basis and in which much depends on experience and on the vision of the individual. If an architect has to be taken on his own terms because he is an artist, then a librarian has a similar claim because of the essentially pragmatic nature of his craft.

Starting work

It is now the librarian's task to start the programme by telling the architect what the client, that is, the authority, wishes to create. This is done by means of the brief, which is basically a statement of purpose, with requirements in terms of accommodation, function and standards. The brief should provide the basic information required by the architect so that he can begin work towards a design solution.

Although it is possible to have a verbal brief, common sense dictates that it should be written in order to serve as a source of reference. It is no exaggeration to say that this is the most important part of the whole scheme; however magnificent an architect's creation may appear to be, it must fail utterly unless it meets the need for which it was designed; however skilful the architect may be in solving a problem, the solution is useless if he has not grasped the problem's true nature and extent.

While the primary brief is primarily a statement to the architect of a problem, with all its implications in the fields of space and organization, it has a secondary value in that writing it forces the librarian to clarify his mind and to examine the organization and methods of his present – and so of his proposed – library. The first requirement, then, is that the librarian should be quite sure in his own mind exactly how the new library is to operate, both generally and in detail. Vagueness at this point will inevitably result in an unsatisfactory end product. He will already have prepared for his authority a statement of the aims and purpose of a new library, in general exhortatory terms. What he has to write now must be more constructive, detailed and professional. To equip himself to do this he must read, visit, compare and, above all, think hard. Even if he is lucky enough to be able to employ a library consultant or professional brief writer, he must still know exactly what he wants; the consultant can handle the operations within the programme, but the librarian in charge of the project carries the full responsibility. He produces the brief and if possible has it endorsed by the client authority. This is valuable for several reasons, not least because the architect is entitled to have a document which will be his mandate to spend valuable time in working in a certain direction. At its most elaborate the brief can be divided into three elements:

1. A statement of the purpose the library is to serve and the place it is to occupy within the social, educational or commercial framework: the library's relationship to the other institutions, departments or sections of its environment.
2. A detailed record of the library's exact requirements as an operational unit, including quantities of books and other materials to be accommodated, the readers to be served, their needs and the times when they will be presented; staff to be housed; and the physical relationship between these different elements, together with an indication of how each will change with the passage of time during the expected life of the building.
3. A record of the limitations imposed by the authority: the chosen site, any known height or access restrictions, together with the financial and other controls which have been determined.

In a small and uncomplicated project these three elements may be combined in one simple statement. In any large scheme it is better for them to be elaborated systematically, if only because team consultation can then take place on each section, as questions arise in the mind of the architect moving towards his solution. In this book the statement of general aims is included in the brief, although in the event it is often produced as a separate document. What has so far been called 'the brief' is in fact the first stage, the primary brief. The secondary brief is created when the architect has completed his feasibility study and realizes that there is more that he needs to know. Some librarians have produced one single, comprehensive brief – or have appeared to do so. In fact they are certain to add to it when the architect indicates in which fields he needs more information. I myself have found it much better not to list minor requirements – furniture, movable equipment, minor communications machinery, signs and so on – until the architect has shown the proposed room layouts after his decisions on spatial relationships. Such factors as windows, heating and cooling arrangements also have too great an effect on operations to be anticipated. On the other hand some matters of this kind have to be in the primary brief because they will affect the structural decisions or the overall spatial relationships; major book transport machinery and special mechanical equipment which is very heavy or will need a water supply must be included in the primary brief, although the full details can wait until later in the programme.

Although the brief will be chiefly in words there will also be diagrams – for example of area relationships, access priorities, material and reader progress routes. It is most important that the librarian should express these essentially spatial factors in a merely notional manner and not restrict the architect by prejudging the way in which he will solve the problems. Areas should be shown very roughly and without any attempt to formulate their shape, otherwise the architect would be justified in considering the diagrams as an exact indication of required area shapes and sizes. Where a particular requirement concerns matters affecting the whole building, for example communication networks, they are better tabulated, so that the whole question can be studied separately.

When the librarian has sent the completed primary brief to the architect he should, as far as is humanly possible, stick to it. Inevitably changes will be made, but they should arise from changed circumstances, not from changed ideas. The time for the librarian to think hard is before writing the brief, not afterwards. Any necessary changes must be notified in writing to the architect as soon as possible: all changes cost time and money, but the later in the scheme they occur, the more expensive they become. At a certain point, usually before detail design begins, the architect is entitled to impose a freeze date, a point beyond which no changes to the brief should be made; changes after that date may be inevitable but they will be very expensive indeed.

In the brief it will be necessary to call for flexibility – a factor that often bedevils the solution proposed in response to the statement of the problem. Few libraries are now created except as part of larger organizations, and on the change and development of those organizations library design is utterly dependent. But flexibility is an expensive luxury and it should never be used as a substitute for forethought.

Statement of aims

Perhaps the most difficult part of the brief to write, this statement has to express clearly and concisely the part the library is intended to play in the life of the community or of the parent organization. The terms of the statement need to be quite different from those the librarian used when he presented to his authority a case for creating a new library; no polemics are called for, no generalizations on cultural, social or economic advantages to the community, but a definition of objectives, both immediate and long-term. In order to do this it may be necessary to explain the programme and objectives of the parent institution itself.

This is particularly important in the case of a school, where the library's contribution depends directly upon the educational methods to be used. In the traditional pattern the school library was a place where books were kept and where children went to read them at certain hours; today in increasing numbers of schools the library is a dynamic centre which exploits media of many different kinds and which is continually in action, with contacts in both directions from each element of teaching and learning. The relationship with the school's computer-based activities has to be made clear; what is the extent of the library's involvement in familiarizing the pupils with these? Unless the architect knows all this, he can hardly design a framework suitable for the proposed activity.

it is equally important for the statement to show what the library has not to do. A library in a hospital may be planned to serve the recreational needs of the patients, or of a certain section of the patients, the medical staff, the technical staff, the professional and recreational needs of the nurses. The combinations of these variables are infinite and the architect must know exactly which applies in a particular case. It is sometimes suggested that this can be found out by the architect while he walks around the old library asking questions; this may be so, but it is essential that what he finds out should have the approval of the official who has been given the responsibility of deciding. To pick up staff ideas and assess them is the duty of the librarian and not the architect.

From the statement, the architect will see a picture of the library as a service and from this he can visualize the environmental conditions he must create to meet the aims. The details of the library's activities – users, contents and methods – will be discussed later: there is no reason for this first summarizing statement to record the planned programme of operations, only the end which the new service is being created to achieve.

Contents to be accommodated

Because shelving space is so valuable, and because library stocks are still expanding in line with the information explosion, it is every librarian's duty to consider possible economies in the storage of books.

The period when the librarian is really thinking hard about a future library is the ideal time for him to be looking at the book stock as a very expensive user of space. This great mass of books is going to be uprooted and transferred to a new home, and it is the unique opportunity to grasp the nettle and to have the stock organized in the best possible way. The ideas he considers will make him wince: they go against all his experience and they mean extra work, but it is now or never. Here are some:

Weeding the stock
This is a very unpopular suggestion which will raise the hackles of most librarians; it implies that their stock contains dead wood, and they may see it as a criticism. Choosing which books to relegate or discard is a wearying and worrying job; no one enjoys it, but it is at the heart of the professional role of a true librarian. It is his duty to ensure that every volume in stock justifies the high cost to the community of storing it.

Separate storage of less-used books

All libraries place the most-used books in priority positions; this principle can be extended, after a survey of stock use, to the creation of shelving sequences based on frequency of use, the least-used books being housed most economically, the most-used closest to the service point. The new university library at Lund, Sweden,[1] has its open stack shelf space equally divided between three subject areas: the ground floor holds the publications of the most recent ten years, the first floor the previous ten years, and the rest is in the basement. Presumably this means a continuous and, one would suspect, expensive programme of stock assessment by date.

Surveys of the use of materials in large libraries (Fussler and Simon[2]) seem to lead in a general way to the conclusion that books which have not been used for several years are not particularly likely to be used for several more years.[3] It should be possible to make a systematic survey of the library's stock, identifying books which fall within this category, and removing them to a place where storage is cheaper. The literature on the subject is worth studying carefully to balance pros and cons. Books which have been established as likely to be the least used can be stored in various ways to save library space.[4]

Off-centre storage

Housing books in warehouses away from expensive sites saves a great deal of space, but at a high cost in delay in retrieval and consequent reader frustration. Access to this separate storage will be slower and more expensive, and there is always the book or section of books which suddenly comes into active demand because of a shift in public interest or in the curriculum; nevertheless considerable saving could result. Because the number of books to be stored in remote locations will increase and in time become massive (unless weeded regularly), this seems to be a case where the identification of locations, updated constantly, plus a good delivery system might be acceptable, although it will always be unpopular with those who have to wait for their books.

Cooperative storage

Schemes whereby libraries cooperate for the common storage of books in little demand are already in operation, with some success. Which of these is available will depend on the size of the country. In Britain the facility is highly developed through the service of the British Library, Lending Division. This national institution is situated in open country but has well-organized communications with the whole of Britain. It holds vast stocks of books from which it lends, or photocopies, to help libraries of all kinds. Unwanted books may be offered to the BLLD; if it accepts them, the local librarian can send them with a clear conscience, knowing that a request for a loan will be met at very short notice. If BLLD does not want them it is because it has sufficient copies to be able to meet demand, and again the librarian is assured that getting rid of his copy is not a dramatic and final action. It all depends on estimated frequency of use.

Storage in basements and stack towers

Numerous examples of this solution have appeared, and the architect will know the relative advantages and disadvantages, in both design and overall cost. See Chapter 6.

Sizing

Because the height of the shelf must be determined by the height of the tallest book on that shelf, the more single-size sequences there are, the more economically the stock can be shelved. The necessary disadvantage of single-size sequences is that the reader has to look in several sequences to find the book he needs; even if the different locations are recorded on the catalogue entry, confusion will still be caused. This disadvantage naturally applies less to little-used books in closed stacks, so the possible space savings in closed stacks by storing according to size must be considered.

J. Grady Cox[5] approaches this problem from a mathematician's angle. He quotes earlier claims of space gains in storage by size, ranging from 25 per cent (Rider) to 250 per cent (Midwest Inter-Library Center), but his own conclusions are less easy to summarize without extensive quotation. He sees two possible methods of using sizing. 'Within shelf' has several given shelf heights running throughout the stacks, each in its own shelf location sequence; in order to locate a book in this arrangement it is necessary to know first the size sequence and second the location symbol. 'Within stack', on the other hand, uses only one shelf height in one group of stack units; in this case it is necessary to find the group of stacks holding the size of books and then trace the location symbol within those stacks. Cox shows that the 'within stack' system gives slightly better space saving. He also shows that between three and five is the best number of size sequences in most situations.

Further space savings can be made when the top shelf of a shelving unit is open, that is, has no enclosing canopy; theoretically there is no limit (other than the ceiling) to the height of books on it. However, as only one extra row of books can be installed, unless further fitments are added, the full gain is achieved only when tall books are stored on the top shelf – not a practice which many librarians will relish.

Against all these space gains – and they can be considerable – must be off-set the cost of selection, transfer, alteration to records and other initial costs. These will be very small indeed in the long run compared with space savings over many years, but the cost in staff time of continual access to these books may be high. The librarian must be very sure that the possibility of frequent retrieval has been well assessed and can be discounted.

Conditions of access

In addition to listing the quantities of material, the librarian must also show:

1. Access conditions under which material is to be housed.
2. Size sequences in which books are to be shelved and the quantities in each sequence.
3. Allowance to be made for future expansion.
4. The librarian's preference as to shelving.

Each of these factors is of great importance and must be considered carefully before being committed to paper; but it should be remembered that the architect is at this stage concerned only with general space allowances; there will be no need to go into such minor matters as the number of reference books in the children's library.

Different shelving conditions

The variations are:

1. Books which are to be freely available to readers in fairly spacious browsing conditions (open access).

Table 4.1 Materials to be housed: number of books

	Under 250 mm (10 in) tall		Over 350 mm (10 in) tall		Laid flat	
	At opening	In x years	At opening	In x years	At opening	In x years
Open-access areas 1 Bibliographical 2 General reference 3 Special reference (commercial, technical, etc.) 4 Adult lending 5 Children's lending 6 Local history 7 Music 8 Arts 9 Others *Closed-access areas* 10 Local stacks for 3 to 9 above 11 General stack 12 Compact shelving stack 13 Special collections 14 Extension services stack*						

Number of books per metre or foot run of shelf in each of sections 1 to 14 above . . . .
Top and Bottom heights of shelving preferred in sections 1 to 14 above . . . .
Distance between stack centres preferred in sections 10 to 14 above . . . .

* These cover 'supply stocks', housed to be sent to branch, school or welfare libraries.

Table 4.2 Materials to be housed – other than books*

	Location†	Open access		Closed access		Method of storage
		At opening	In x years	At opening	In x years	

Periodicals:
   Current only
   Current plus x back issues
   Back issues
 Newspapers:
   Current only
   Current plus x back issues
   Back issues
 Sheet maps
 Photographs
 Prints
 Broadsides
 Cuttings
   (no of boxes)
 Slides
 Pamphlets
 Sheet music
 Audio discs
 Audio tapes
 Video tapes
 Video discs
 Microfilms reels
 Microfiche
 Microcards
 Film reels
 Film strips
 Pictures
 Other materials
 Catalogue cards						

* Any non-book form that has been bound up to form a volume, or is to be kept in boxes and stored in book shelving, will be recorded under books.
† Show in which of the sections 1 to 14 in table 1 material is to housed.
‡ Audio discs may be laid flat, stored on edge in pigeon holes or in open trays; audio and Video tapes may be displayed or stored in boxes or drawers; microfilm may be in boxes on shelves, in vertical files and so on. See Chapter 14 for alternative methods.

2. Books to be housed more economically in formal rows of shelving but still available directly to readers (open stack).
3. Books to be housed as closely (and therefore economically) as possible because only staff will have access to them (closed stack).

Ways of computing space allocation for each of these categories (including compact storage methods) are suggested in Chapters 13 and 14. Normally public, hospital, school and some college libraries will use open access with a small proportion of closed stack; large public libraries will use open access but with a larger proportion of closed stack. Most university and some college libraries will be very largely open stack with a small proportion of open access (chiefly reference and biblio-graphical tools) and with a varying, but usually small, proportion of closed stack (e.g. rare books and special collections). It should be pointed out that whether or not the library is to lend books for readers to use off the premises (which will involve space-consuming issue-and-return machinery) does not necessarily depend on the variations given above. Open access and open stack can be for reading only on the premises; the shelving economy usual to closed stack can be stipulated in home loan conditions. The picture has to be made absolutely clear.

Size sequences

It is seldom possible to have just one sequence of books, but in most libraries more than 90% of books are less than 280 mm (11 in) tall, and these can all be shelved in one sequence. In popular libraries a very high proportion of books are less than 250 mm (10 in) tall, and such libraries can house the great bulk of their open-shelf stock on bookcases with shelves at 280 mm (11 in) centres; encyclopedias and quick reference books can be at 330 mm (13 in) centres, and other books in a single oversize sequence at 500 mm (20 in). There will be very few books larger than this in open access libraries, and these will usually be laid flat. At this stage it will be enough to compile a rough estimate of books for each operational section, subdivided into those under and over 250 mm (10 in) tall (popular libraries; 280 mm (11 in) tall in other libraries) and those few which need to be laid flat: a sampling of the stock will easily give such a figure. Depths of books need not be considered here – in general tall books are also deeper – but thickness is important. The thickness of the average book in each of the operational sections should be given by quoting the number of such books per running metre or foot, because without this information numbers bear little relation to space requirements. Some music scores are very thin, most directories are thick; so much is obvious, but further variations in any particular situation will be unknown to the architect. The matter is too important for him to walk around making guesses. The whole question is considered in greater detail in Chapter 13.

Expansion allowance

The demand for more and larger libraries continues unabated in many parts of the world, although there have been signs of a slowing down in some western countries. Even here the check may be only temporary; as we have seen, the library of the future may continue to grow despite miniaturization and the database. Growth of demand, official policy on education, a steady increase in the number of books published each year (or the increased opportunity to obtain books from abroad) may make this an inevitable process and continue the call for more space for books and readers. Planning a new library takes several years: the stock to be accommodated on opening day will be larger than it was when planning began. To spend a great deal of money on a library that will be inadequate in a few years is so patently absurd that it is absolutely essential for the librarian to estimate the size of the library at a given future date and to relate all his space requirement to that date. Havard-Williams[6] points out that a university library growing at the rate of 5% a year, and starting with a stock of 600 000 volumes, will have to house 2 032 000 after twenty-five years. This indicates the seriousness of the problem. Where plans for expansion in the immediate future are restricted the task is even more difficult: is the librarian to accept that an imposed 'no growth' is to last for all time, or should he not plan for an expanding future, even though he may only be allowed to build a first, and more modest phase? Public and other more popular libraries will grow less dramatically because they discard more books, but every librarian must think hard, choose a date at the very least ten years ahead, and plan to have sufficient space to house books and serve readers at that date. Ten years is suggested, not because a new library building will be expendable in that time but because predicting for the conventional thirty years ahead is today beyond the powers of most people. These figures alone are not enough to enable the architect to make effective plans: even if enormous expansion is expected after a few years, no one would would wish to open a new library that is three-quarters empty. The architect will plan for expansion, both in general and in detail, at the same time producing a library of acceptable form on the day of opening. It is therefore necessary for two sets of figures to be provided when expansion is expected: those applic-able on the day the library opens, and those which will apply at a chosen date some years ahead. It is difficult indeed to provide such figures, but they must be provided, and only the librarian can do it.

Shelving

The space allowances which the architect will make to house the materials listed will depend on the height to which books are to be shelved, the distance apart of the stacks and a number of other factors. On these matters the librarian should indicate his *preferences*; he cannot be more specific because structural and design considera-tions may prevent the architect from being able to accept these preferences as positive instructions. In practice the matter will be settled later in discussions within the design team.

The great bulk of the material to be housed will be in the form of the hardbacked book; a separate record must be made of each of the other forms and their quantities. In many libraries there will be a surprisingly large number of other forms. Methods and space requirements for their housing are discussed in Chapter 14. The operational divisions in Tables 4:1 and 4:2 are those of a large public library building with conventional references, lending and children's services, but the principle can easily be applied to any type of library. Something along these lines will serve as a useful guide when completed as conscientious-ly as possible and handed to the architect.

Activities and users

The architect will have a general idea, both from the statement of aims and from his own experience, of the likely activities within the building, but this is not good enough; he needs to know in some detail how the librarian (representing the authority) visualizes them in operation. It is important that this information be given in a systematic pattern; if a particular activity is omitted the architect is entitled to assume that it is not to be included.

The total activities in the library can be separated into two sections:

1. User activities, their quantity, frequency and timing, and staff activities in serving users.
2. Technical services – staff activities in providing the framework for user service.

The information should be given to the architect in two ways: the first will list all major activities in the library, with an estimate of the numbers of persons (both staff and readers) involved, and the hours when these activities will take place. The second, in the form of a series of diagrams, will show the practical relationships between these activities and the priorities in terms of nearness and separation, which the librarian would wish to give to them.

These priorities will apply to both the relative proximity of activity areas, and the access routes between the areas.

List of activities and users

The list should show both *what* is to happen and *when*. Hours of opening must be given, together with an estimate of the varying amount of reader use of each section of the library during those hours. Many points will be difficult to predict, but it is up to the librarian to attempt it. However, inaccurate estimates turn out to be, they will certainly be more realistic than those which anyone else could make. Some terms may need explanation: 'reference library' may seem self-explanatory, but what will the readers be doing there? Browsing, consulting books or studying for long spells? Standing as well as sitting? If the answer is 'all of these', then it would be useful to attempt to estimate the proportions of users engaged in each activity and at what times the proportion can be expected to change.

The extent of use of computer services must be spelled out. Is there to be a Central Processing Unit (CPU) within the building? If so, it will need specially insulated conditions and room for the specialist staff. Are terminals to be placed on tables, so that plenty of plug points is the only special requirement, or are there to be full work-stations in some areas? The size and layout of such fitments is not in consideration at this stage, but space needs have to be estimated. A few years ago it was very common to have a 'computer terminal room' to house the equipment, but now most large machinery is housed elsewhere; nevertheless there may still be a need for a separate room, now to be used either for familiarizing new students with that particular library's computer procedures, or as a practice room fitted with a number of terminals.

The changes which are occurring, and will go on occurring, in the methods of serving users, have to be visualized by the librarian, and it is his responsibility to estimate how these will affect both the operation and also the equipment which the new library will need. Some developments which are at an early stage may well be common practice by the time the new building is opened; in predicting the future in this way the librarian is on his own. He must allow, not for what is going to happen, but for what is likely to happen, and lay down instructions in the brief on this matter where he is both specialist and bearer of full responsibility.

User services
Hours of opening
Peak hours of the day
Peak days of the week (also of the year, particularly in educational institutions)
Numbers of readers present (where applicable these figures should be provided separately for each major section of the library):
    at peak hours on a peak day
    at normal times
Length of time readers will stay (where applicable these figures should be provided separately for each major section of the library):
    at peak hours on a peak day
    at normal times
Number of reader seats to be provided (at date of opening and at a given future date) in the areas listed below; where applicable give separate figures for open seating areas and closed carrels (open carrels and semi-carrels can be thought of as furniture in open seating areas); indicate where microform reading machines and computer terminals will be required:
    bibliographical
    general reference
    adult lending
    children's library (give age range)
    young adults' library
    short-loan collection
    periodicals
    newspapers
    music
    special reference (commercial, technical etc.)
    local history
    arts
    archives
    other departments
    typing rooms
    other areas (exhibitions etc.)
    outside the building or in courtyards
Associated activities – number of seats in:
    story hour rooms
    creative activity rooms for children
    language learning areas ⎫
    meeting rooms (give   ⎪
  hours of opening)   ⎪
    lecture and film shows   ⎬ Indicate general nature
  (give hours of opening)   ⎪   of equipment
    music recitals (give hours⎪
  of opening)   ⎪
    exhibitions (give size and⎪
  basic purpose)   ⎭
Facilities for individual readers (as distinct from audiences) showing location and numbers:
    document copying (staff or reader operated?)
    television
    computer terminals
    video-tape reproduction
    microform viewing
    sales points
    external book return slots
    leaflet or pamphlet racks
    poster display (signs for guidance are considered elsewhere)
Public refreshment services:
    hours of opening
    number of seats
    type of service and staffing
    type of refreshment
    water dispensers

Storage of readers' belongings (with location):
    number of coat hooks
    number of lockers
    briefcase or handbag accommodation at tables
    attendant-operated bag and cloak deposit stations
Public lavatories (with preferred location):
    numbers to be catered for – men and women
    type of towel system
    incinerators
Public telephone(s) (with location)
First-aid room for public use
Other provisions – book shop, vending machines etc.

Staff activities in serving users
Direct reader service: number of staff on duty at the
    following points at normal and peak times in each of the
    sections listed under 'Number of reader seats' above:
        security points
        book issue and return   } giving the association
    counters   between these two
        readers' enquiry desks
        other
External activities for which the library is to be the
    headquarters; number of persons to be catered for in:
        branch library supply and service area
        school library supply and service area
        welfare libraries supply and service area (handi-
        capped readers, prisons, housebound readers etc.)
        privileged readers (for example, a room for teachers
    to select books from a display range. These areas will be
    fairly small in many libraries but large and important in
    others, particularly in county library headquarters)

Mobile libraries and vans: number and size of vehicles to
be housed and their servicing requirements (petrol, oil, air
etc.)

Technical services
Staff working accommodation, each with number of staff to
be allowed for at peak times, with type of staff involved
(clerical, porters, attendants, etc.):
        administrative offices, clerical, typing, machine
    operating
        executive offices (indicate each post)
        secretarial offices
        accessioning area
        cataloguing area, both cataloguers and typists (in
    some special libraries such intensive activities as
    scanning and abstracting are, for convenience, included
    here)
        processing areas
        receipt and dispatch area
        post room
        telex centre
        xerox room

                             The complexities of
                             these departments
    photographic laboratory   necessitate separate
    bindery or repair room   statements of their
    printing department   equipment and opera-
    conservation department   tion before the architect
                             can estimate space
                             needs: see Chapter 16
        poster artist's studio
        workrooms (indicate location)

Staff rest accommodation, with numbers; if there is to be a
physical division (such as for men/women or staff/porters),
then separate numbers must be given:

    lounge   } With general indication of range of
    tea room   } equipment needed
    kitchen   }
    staff lavatories (with numbers, men and women, for
    all locations)
    lockers, number and location; to be sited in or near
    rest rooms or lavatories? (Will staff go direct to rest
    areas on arrival to remove outdoor clothing, or
    should a locker area be provided near the staff
    entrance?)
    staff first-aid room

Other areas (in square metres or feet) with location if more
than one:
    stationery store
    furniture store
    cleaning materials stores (with water and sinks?)
    other stores (stacking chairs, display screens etc.)
    strongrooms (with indication of degree of security)

Other facilities
parking:
    number of cars   } At peak times; controlled
    number of motor cycles   } or uncontrolled; covered
    number of bicycles   } or uncovered; staff only or
                             } both public and staff
pram park: number, inside building or under canopy
outside
points where dogs may be tethered outside building
access for disabled persons (other than the statutory
provision)

Sizes of areas and their relationship

An alternative, or perhaps additional, way of showing the
amount of space needed for the various sections of the
library is to draw up a scale diagram. The example given
here is one the librarian of the University of York included in
his brief: it is of particular interest in that it can be
compared with the result – the plans of the four-storey
building showing the archtiect's design solution. From
these it is clear that the spaces shown within a perimeter
had no exact positional significance, although certain
relationships were implied by their proximity in the
diagram. It also shows the confidence which obviously
existed between librarian and architect and which must
have resulted from a number of amicable meetings.
Without such understanding a diagram such as this would
risk misinterpretation.

Relationships between areas

Up to this point the brief has been a specific and detailed
statement of requirements. There follow sections of more
general comment on matters relating to the operating and
environmental conditions of the future service. These are
for the librarian to decide; it is certainly possible, and not
uncommon, for such matters to be left for the architect to
raise when he finds that he needs the information, but the
principle followed here is that it is better for them to be
dealt with in the primary brief. After having read the brief
the architect will be in a position to ask more specific
questions. Moreover, it is safer for all possible points to be
covered in a systematic document that will make
absolutely certain that they do come to the team for
consideration.
    One of the earliest decisions the architect will be called
upon to make concerns the relationships in space between
the various operational areas and the priority of access

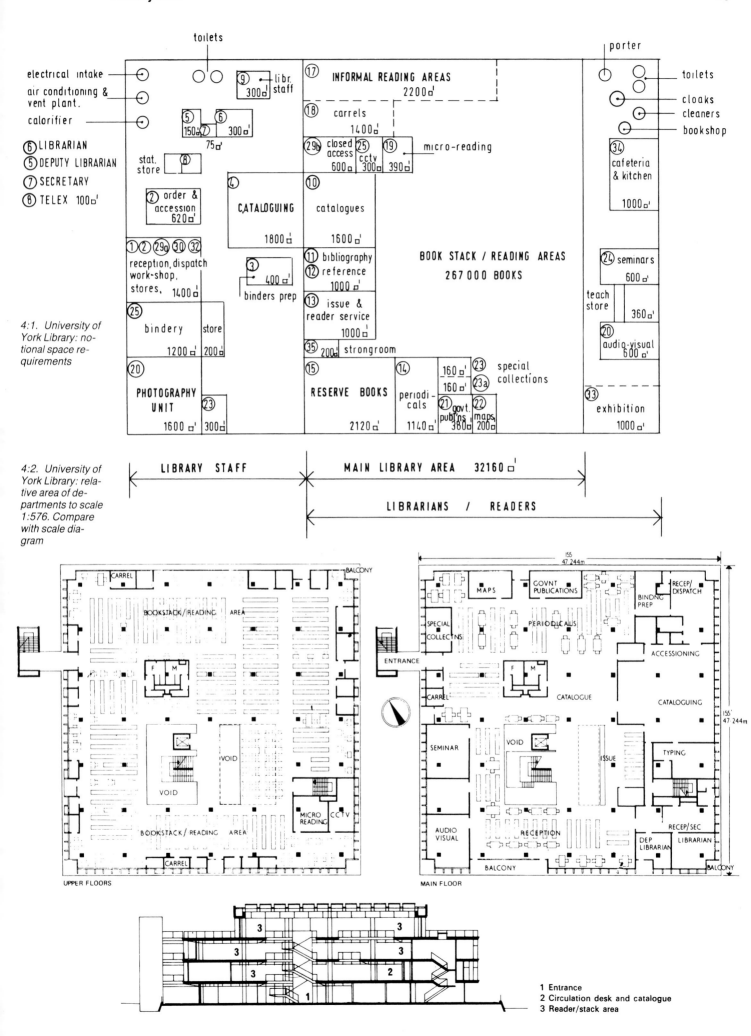

4:1. University of York Library: notional space requirements

4:2. University of York Library: relative area of departments to scale 1:576. Compare with scale diagram

toilets

electrical intake

air conditioning & vent plant.

calorifier

⑥ LIBRARIAN
⑤ DEPUTY LIBRARIAN
⑦ SECRETARY
⑧ TELEX 100 □'

stat. store

⑨ libr. staff 300 □'

⑤ ⑥ ⑦ 150□' 300 □' 75 □'

⑧

② order & accession 620 □'

① ② ㉙ ㉚ ㉜ reception, dispatch work-shop, stores, 1400 □'

④ CATALOGUING 1800 □'

③ 400 □' binders prep

㉕ bindery 1200 □' store 200□'

⑳ PHOTOGRAPHY UNIT 1600 □' ㉓ 300□'

⑰ INFORMAL READING AREAS 2200 □'

⑱ carrels 1400 □'

㉙b closed access 600 □' ㉕ cctv 300□ ⑲ 390 □' micro-reading

⑩ catalogues 1600 □'

⑪ bibliography
⑫ reference 1000 □'

⑬ issue & reader service 1000 □'

㉟ 200□' strongroom

⑮ RESERVE BOOKS 2120 □'

⑭ periodi-cals 1140 □'

160 □'
160 □'

㉓ ㉓a special collections

㉑ govt. publns 360□ ㉒ maps 200□

BOOK STACK / READING AREAS 267000 BOOKS

porter

toilets
cloaks
cleaners
bookshop

㉞ cafeteria & kitchen 1000 □'

㉔ seminars 600 □'

teach store 360 □'

⑳ audio-visual 600 □'

㉝ exhibition 1000 □'

LIBRARY STAFF | MAIN LIBRARY AREA 32160 □'

LIBRARIANS / READERS

UPPER FLOORS

MAIN FLOOR

1 Entrance
2 Circulation desk and catalogue
3 Reader/stack area

routes between them. A good example is the photocopier: a piece of free-standing equipment, it would normally be listed in the secondary brief among other minor items, but the recent expansion (almost explosion) of its use in academic institutions has made it a major service to readers. The librarian must now show how many photocopiers there will be and where they are to be housed: it will usually be within supervisory distance of a staff service point.

The obvious need is for the librarian to show by means of a diagram which sections should be closest together, which fairly close, and so on. A little experience will show that this can be an exceedingly difficult task; any such diagram must invariably carry inferences as to the positioning of the areas, and this is a matter which the architect must approach with a completely open mind in order to develop a design. Precommitment by the librarian, even if inadvertently, can have a surprisingly hampering effect on the architect: the information needed can be best given by means of a table as shown in Figure 4:3. This table shows the relative proximity between the main sections of a medium-sized public library, in which one loan control is to be centrally placed and so outside any single department, and where the children's department has its own cloakrooms.

The architect needs to know not only which sections are to be close together but also which should specifically be placed far apart: for example noisy working areas (bindery, typing rooms etc.) must be kept away from quiet public study areas. He also needs to know where the relative placing of sections is immaterial to the librarian – this is all positive information. Figure 4:4 shows departmental relationships in a large library (now built) where a second phase, a future extension, had from the first conception to be specifically allowed for. A far more advanced example of such an analysis is to be found in the *Site Selection Study* of the Metropolitan Toronto Library Board.[7] This used an interaction matrix to chart the degree of interdependence of each component of a future central library with all other components. Ninety-nine basic components were identified, giving 4901 separate interactions to be considered. This exercise concerned the planning of the central library services of a metropolitan area, not merely those of a single building, but it is nevertheless well worth studying.

Relationship between sections in a multi-storey building

When the library is obviously going to consist of more than one floor the librarian must say not only which areas need to be close together, but also which need to be on the same level, listing them again in order of priority. Attention will first be directed to the main (usually ground) floor, because it is obviously sensible that areas most used by

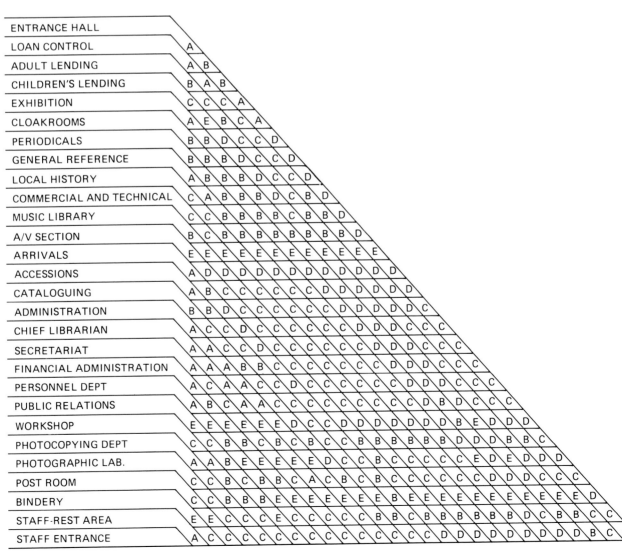

4:3. Proximity relationship between departments. A = as close as possible; B = close; C = immaterial; D = separated; E = as far away as possible

	ENTRANCE HALL	LOAN CONTROL	ADULT LENDING	CHILDREN'S LENDING	EXHIBITION	CLOAKROOMS	PERIODICALS	GENERAL REFERENCE	LOCAL HISTORY	COMMERCIAL AND TECHNICAL	MUSIC LIBRARY	A/V SECTION	ARRIVALS	ACCESSIONS	CATALOGUING	ADMINISTRATION	CHIEF LIBRARIAN	SECRETARIAT	FINANCIAL ADMINISTRATION	PERSONNEL DEPT	PUBLIC RELATIONS	WORKSHOP	PHOTOCOPYING DEPT	PHOTOGRAPHIC LAB.	POST ROOM	BINDERY	STAFF-REST AREA
LOAN CONTROL	A																										
ADULT LENDING	A	B																									
CHILDREN'S LENDING	B	A	B																								
EXHIBITION	C	C	C	A																							
CLOAKROOMS	A	E	B	C	A																						
PERIODICALS	B	B	D	C	C	D																					
GENERAL REFERENCE	B	B	B	D	C	C	D																				
LOCAL HISTORY	A	B	B	B	D	C	C	D																			
COMMERCIAL AND TECHNICAL	C	A	B	B	B	D	C	B	D																		
MUSIC LIBRARY	C	C	B	B	B	B	C	B	B	D																	
A/V SECTION	B	C	B	B	B	B	B	B	B	B	D																
ARRIVALS	E	E	E	E	E	E	E	E	E	E	E	E															
ACCESSIONS	A	D	D	D	D	D	D	D	D	D	D	D	D														
CATALOGUING	A	B	C	C	C	C	C	C	D	D	D	D	D	D													
ADMINISTRATION	B	B	D	C	C	C	C	C	C	D	D	D	D	D	C												
CHIEF LIBRARIAN	A	C	C	D	C	C	C	C	C	C	D	D	D	C	C	C											
SECRETARIAT	A	A	C	C	D	C	C	C	C	C	C	D	D	D	C	C	C										
FINANCIAL ADMINISTRATION	A	A	A	B	B	C	C	C	C	C	C	C	D	D	D	C	C	C									
PERSONNEL DEPT	A	C	A	A	C	D	C	C	C	C	C	C	C	D	D	D	C	C	C								
PUBLIC RELATIONS	A	B	C	A	A	C	C	C	C	C	C	C	C	C	D	B	D	C	C	C							
WORKSHOP	E	E	E	E	E	E	D	C	C	D	D	D	D	D	D	D	B	E	D	D							
PHOTOCOPYING DEPT	C	C	B	B	C	B	C	B	C	B	B	B	B	B	D	D	D	B	B	C							
PHOTOGRAPHIC LAB.	A	A	B	E	E	E	E	E	D	C	C	B	C	C	C	C	C	E	D	E	D	D	D				
POST ROOM	C	C	B	C	B	B	B	C	A	C	B	C	B	C	C	C	C	C	C	D	D	D	C	C			
BINDERY	C	C	B	B	B	E	E	E	E	E	E	B	E	E	E	E	E	E	E	E	E	D					
STAFF-REST AREA	E	E	C	C	C	E	C	C	C	C	C	B	B	C	B	B	B	B	B	D	C	B	B	C	C		
STAFF ENTRANCE	A	C	C	C	C	C	C	C	C	C	C	C	C	C	C	C	D	D	D	D	D	D	D	D	B	C	C

4:4. Departmental relationship diagram for a large library; planning for minimal essential services, with indication of those for the second phase to follow soon afterwards

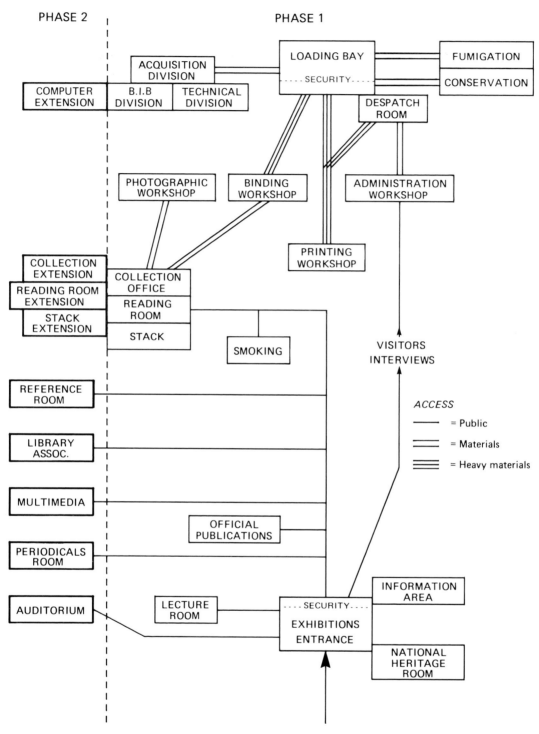

4:5. Progress of readers through a very small branch library

4:6. Progress of readers through a medium-sized public library

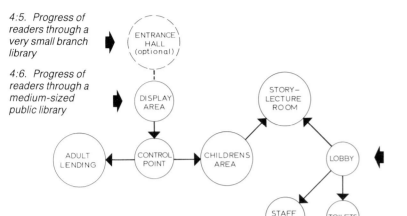

4:7. Progress of readers through a small research library

4:8. Progress of materials through a library

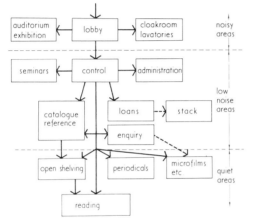

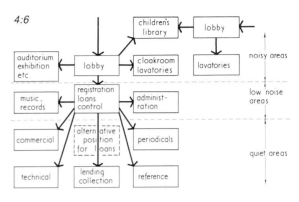

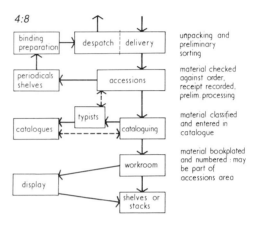

4:9. Traffic at different times of day

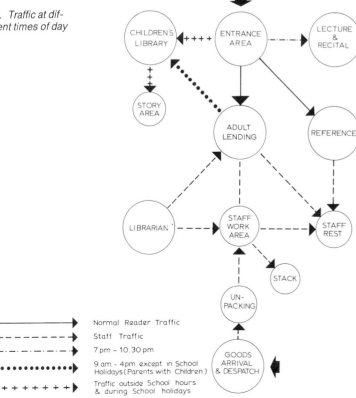

readers should be nearest to the entrance. It should not be forgotten that readers (particularly serious students) are not at all reluctant to use upper, and therefore quieter, floors if lifts or stairs are adequate.

Among the factors to be considered in this example of a central public library are the following (under each heading the numbers indicate priority):

Same floor as main entrance
1. Exhibition area
2. Loan control
3. Adult lending library
4. Children's library
5. Cloakrooms
6. Periodicals room
   etc.

Same floor as goods entrance
1. Unpacking area (must be the same level)
2. Accessions area (same level, unless a goods hoist or two-level ramp is to be provided)
3. Bindery (same level, unless a goods hoist or two-level ramp is to be provided)

Same floor as adult lending library
1. Department workroom
2. Department stack
3. Children's library
   etc.

Same floor as general reference library
1. Local history library
2. Technical library
3. Departmental workroom
4. Closed stack (if not on the same level, a book hoist will be needed)

It is not necessary to spell out that public access between departments not on the same level will be by both lift and stairs. Access for staff may be by stairs alone where distances are small, staff movement is not very frequent and no loads are carried.

Access routes

Area relationships are closely concerned with access routes: to operate efficiently the library must be planned so that there is minimum interference with the main routes through the building for both readers and materials. These routes are best indicated by simple diagrams showing notional areas linked by arrows. Priorities can be shown by changes of colour or markings of the arrows. The areas should not be shaped, nor should the diagram attempt to show their relative sizes.

In small libraries the relationship and reader routes can be illustrated very simply: in less simple cases it will be necessary to show how and when they will vary at different times of the day.

An example is given in Figure 4:10 of a diagram which concerns the technical processes to be carried out in a university library: again it was produced by the librarian of the University of York and given to his architect as part of the brief. Although he has shown the main progress taking place and indicated where sections form separate natural divisions, the librarian has been careful not to scale or shape his diagram in a way that might limit the architect in his response. The design solution can be seen in the plans on p. 40. At this stage the information given concerns only the placing of operational sections and the access routes between them. Traffic patterns within each area, and the layout of furniture and equipment which will depend on these patterns, will arise at a later stage. Similarly the diagrams and lists will show only the progress of people and materials through the building. Telephone and other methods of communication which have no direct bearing on the space allocation will be shown in a separate communications chart in the secondary brief (see Chapter 8). The transport of small amounts of material (single books, photocopies etc.) is a matter of document conveyance and is also dealt with in Chapter 8, but major transport machinery can have an effect on structural decisions and will be included further on in the primary brief (Chapter 5). Although the question of floor surfaces is

not to be considered here, the librarian should indicate where special surfaces will be needed; he does not have to stipulate the material to be used (see Chapter 17), but any unusual weight to be carried or special wearing qualities needed must be reported. The architect may need to take this into account when planning a particularly type of floor construction.

Producing the 'Activities and users' part of the brief will inevitably require a great deal of time and thought, but without this information the architect is likely to produce proposals that are quite unacceptable to the librarian, and much expensive time will have been wasted.

Life of building

Expansion

When drawing up his requirements, in terms of both materials and use, the librarian will have in mind a date, which he has agreed with the architect, up to which these requirements will be valid. In most types of library, evidence suggests that some expansion will be called for in the foreseeable future. Outside factors of great importance such as the effect of continuing growth in both publishing and education will inevitably mean an increase in reader demand; to be balanced against these is the growing replacement of books by other forms of communicating information. During the last thirty years the production of material which any serious library must stock has grown enormously. The newer forms such as audio and video tapes, discs and cassettes now arrive in great numbers, but if we consider only book production we can see what an effect this growth must have. Taking book publication in Britain, we find that the total number of titles published[8] in 1947 was 13 046; in 1957, 20 719; in 1967, 29 619; in 1977, 36 322; and in 1987, 59 837. And this is the position in what is beginning to be known as the 'paperless society'. Whether these figures will continue to increase is an open question, but it must be remembered that these are trade figures and do not include the vast numbers of government publications (40 000 new patent publications are issued each year) or the mass of 'grey materials', much of which libraries must stock. The growing awareness of, and demand for, books published abroad adds to this already impressive expansion of material to be acquired and housed.

In the field of formal education numerous official

4:10. University of York: librarian's progress diagram for technical service

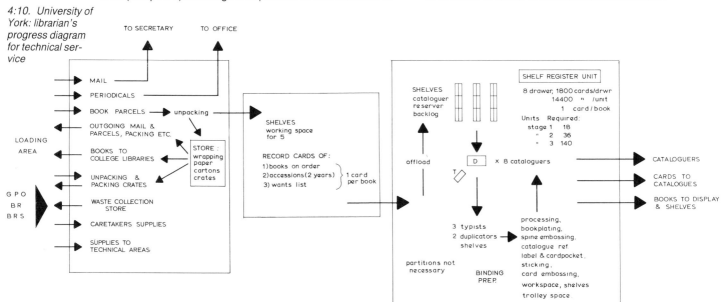

statements show that the apparently endless increases in student numbers may be affected, in some countries, by a decline in the birth rate. In Britain the number of full-time students receiving higher education, which had been steadily increasing since the Second World War, will be between 33 and 70 thousand less in 1996 than it was in 1985. As we have seen when considering the effects of the new technology, it may be that there will be a great increase in the numbers of part-time students of all ages. The fluctuations in both book production and numbers of people receiving some form of education are felt most dramatically in some of the developing countries. Here the salient factors will be government decisions on the funds to be made available for book publication or import and on rises in the level of education. It is to be remembered that in these countries increased demand will result not only from future expansion in education but from the cumulative effect of the present and much improved levels.

Although predictions of expansion are thoroughly familiar to this generation of librarians and must be faced, it is of vital importance that they should not be taken too literally. They are growth factors and must be assessed while bearing in mind other developments which might work in the opposite way. Even if we know that publication and reader demand will continue to increase for the next twenty years, this does not necessarily mean that a new wing must be added to a library to cater for the pressure on space. As we have seen in Chapter 2, it may well be that factors such as computer databases, cooperative provision of storage and miniaturization (as well as technological innovations as yet unknown) will produce such a drastic

reform in space use that no overall increase will be called for. It may be that the need in the future will be, not for more space, but for a greater opportunity for flexibility in the use of that space.

But, because a new library will have to last for a great number of years, it will at the very least be helpful if space can be allowed for expansion: the drastic alternative is planned obsolescence. If there is room on the site where a new wing may be built in the future, this must be a feature of the brief. If no such space exists but long-term expansion is nevertheless expected, the architect may be asked to plan to add floors to the building at a later date. He can deal with either contingency only if he knows about it from this very early moment, but even so he may not be free to plan for a stipulated future expansion on the site if other requirements in the brief tie his hands. For example, a librarian who insists on maximum daylight provision forces the architect to install a great amount of glass in the walls, making lateral expansion expensive; in these conditions expansion could perhaps take place upwards but would be better by extension at an angle to the initial building. It is obvious that this must be allowed for at an early stage. Future expansion upwards is a highly questionable idea; the disruption of the existing services is only one of the prices to be paid. At the least it calls for different foundations and a heavier structure which will add greatly to the initial cost.

When expansion within a given period is a known requirement (and a great number of university libraries in periods of 'temporary' economic difficulty are being planned in self-contained phases) the architect can allow

4:12. Nottingham University Library: Level 2 as originally planned. It was described thus in the official brochure: 'The main floor. The public enter at this level, and it is here that most of the general business of the library is transacted, where the main administrative departments are located, and where facilities for refreshments and relaxation are provided. The main stairs are close to the entrance, and visitors are provided with a clear unobstructed progress to the issue counter and enquiry desk. On approaching the issue counter, the reference and general bibliography collections are to the left, and the library's catalogues to the right. The short loan collection, a special service for students, is located near the issue counter. The coffee bar and smoking area is to the right as you enter the building. Beyond the issue counter the open-plan library administrative area, which includes the cataloguing and acquisitions departments, leads into the staff rest and refreshment area. The public exit to the building, on this floor, incorporates an anti-theft device to prevent book losses.'

4:13. Nottingham University Library: Level 2 as altered after thirteen years' working experience

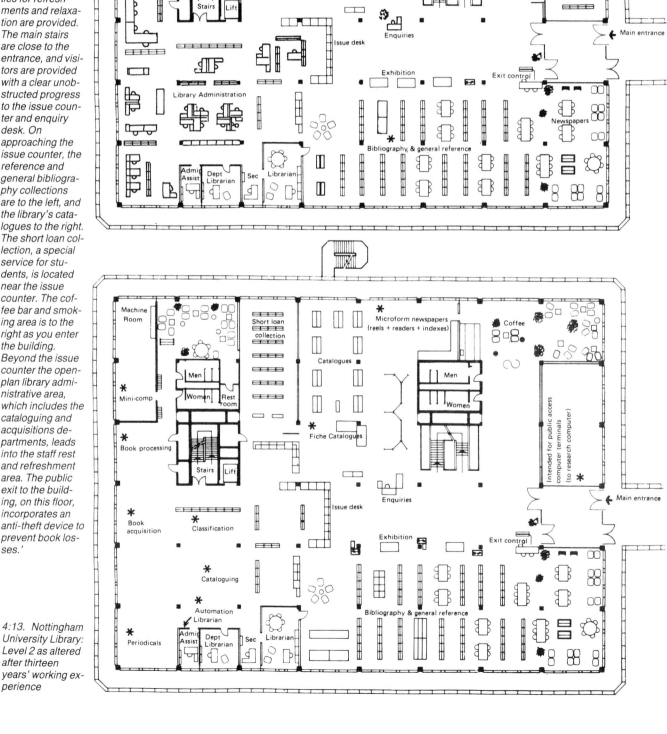

for this by using partitions for perimeter walls and removing them later to fit an extension onto the library. Many examples of this have been seen: demountable walls can be of wood or of brick. In the library of Nottingham University, (4.11) the architects stated 'By using precast panels of a light colour with brown glass windows future extensions to the building can be added with a reasonable assurance of being able to match the existing panels. The units are designed so that they can be removed from the facade and reused in the extended building.'[9] Similar arrangements were intended in Bristol University library, but could not be fulfilled. 'It had been originally intended that stage 1 of the library would be followed by stages 2 and 3 . . . and the west wall had been designed as a temporary structure . . . the economic situation made the provision . . . for further stages unlikely in the near future and the same type of concrete panel was used on this wall as on the others, though the method of fixing would make it possible to remove and reuse the panels when the time came to extend the building.'[10]

Expansion downwards may seem to be a desperate measure, but several recent library projects have included this element, chiefly for underground expansion of storage, although the Radcliffe Science Library, Oxford, has built reading rooms below ground, and there is a growing number of underground libraries, the Sedgewick Library, University of British Columbia at Vancouver, and the Stellenbosch University Library, South Africa, being well-known examples. At the State University of New York at Buffalo the subject libraries within the stack are under each appropriate faculty building, the general collection being under the open area between. The separate faculty in each building will thus have access to its own section of stack. Such developments may become increasingly necessary under the twin pressures of shortage of space and need for quick access to collections continually increasing in size. Where land prices are very high, such as in the centre of great cities, branch libraries have been successfully placed in the basements of office blocks (such as Shoe Lane in the City of London), but this is a matter of siting not of expansion.

Flexibility

Because so many of the famous public buildings of the last century were designed to impress and were known more for their classic monumentalism than for their functional efficiency, many librarians will express themselves strongly in their opposition to this type of building. Modern methods of construction – notably the use of columns to carry the structural load, the walls being merely curtains hung from a framework – have given the architect freedom to design so that there need be no irremovable internal divisions, the only limit to absolute flexibility being the service cores, staircases, lifts etc., which are usually grouped together.

The term 'flexibility' is commonly applied to this facility, but perhaps 'adaptability' is more appropriate. The concept can be extended as far as the complete open-plan library, where almost every free-standing item of furniture and equipment can be moved to give service in any other part of the building. Some librarians have jumped with relief to the idea that such flexibility is the solution to all space problems, but it is important to stress, what every architect knows well, that for such open-plan layout a price must be paid. If absolute flexibility on each floor is required, then the architect will be limited in his choice of design solutions. For example, it is difficult to feature sections of roof lighting or to emphasize control areas by

altering ceiling heights without either limiting flexibility or making expensive arrangements so that these features can be moved to other parts of the floor if required. Absolute flexibility means that lighting, heating and floor loading must be planned everywhere according to the highest special requirements of the most intense individual demand; this is possible but it is expensive. Air-conditioning will cost more because controls have to be installed to provide the variations which full partitioning would normally give. Moreover it is wasteful of space, because the flow patterns of circulation that separate the islands of activity use up more space than a lesser number of corridors. From the librarian's operational angle it makes for disturbance to readers from traffic to and fro as well as a lack of privacy (perhaps acceptable in private offices) and causes extra trouble in keeping the inevitable work mess away from public view. The main disadvantage is that it produces a monotonous interior, because the floors, the ceilings, and even the partitions give a large and identical vista in whichever direction the reader may look. Some variation can be achieved, but it still makes it more difficult for the interior designer to produce interest and sparkle, to create a distinctive internal environment.

The librarian should state clearly in the brief exactly how much flexibility is required (for example, he is hardly likely to want the right to be able to move the main entrance up to a higher floor), leaving the architect to worry about the extra cost. He should, however, satisfy himself, by a study of some examples of yesterday, whether expensive and design-inhibiting flexibility has been used enough to justify its costs.

The British library most famous for full flexibility, using the open-plan methods made famous in German office buildings as 'Bürolandschaft', is that of the University of Nottingham. This library serves the faculties of arts, education and social sciences of the university together with the sub-department of manuscripts and the photo-graphic and printing units. It is of four stories, but the slight slope of the site allows the main entrance to be on Level 2, with a number of functions, plus a service entrance, on Level 1. It was opened in 1973; the two layout plans of the main entrance level, with differences indicated, show how much change has been made between 1973 and 1986. It will be seen that the short-loan collection has been moved from near the front door to a position close to the main circulation counter; reasons include economy of staffing and reduction in cable-runs for the on-line issue system. On Level 1 there has been a good deal of movement round an expanding printing and photographic unit. The micro-forms room has also been changed to a store, with microforms being dispersed to subject areas. A new bay for microfilm newspapers has been created on Level 2 north of the east core. One change which does not show up in these plans is on Level 4, where the seating area east of the core (right-hand side of the plan) has been turned over to shelving. Some of the reader places have been absorbed elsewhere – including other libraries in the system – but there is a slight overall reduction; this is not likely to be a problem in view of lower student numbers than originally projected.[11] It may be objected that a number of these changes could have taken place under a less flexible plan, but many will envy the librarian the opportunity to respond to change in such a confident manner.

These opportunities seldom exist in small or medium-sized public libraries. In each case the librarian must make up his mind what to ask for in the way of flexibility within certain zones, and the architect will work out how he is able to respond.

5 Primary brief (continued)

Specifications and special physical conditions

It is not the librarian's duty to attempt to instruct the architect in matters concerning the structure, materials or appearance of the future building, but it will be necessary to communicate to him any client requirements that will limit his freedom in this field. The building may have to form part of a campus, a cultural centre, or a shopping precinct where conformity with certain design principles is considered essential.

Similarly the architect can be relied upon to produce atmospheric conditions for the interior of the building which conform to best modern practice, because there are authoritative manuals at his disposal, but they will not deal specifically with libraries. He must be made aware of peculiar library requirements and also of any special conditions which may apply in this project. If rare and fragile material is to be housed, the architect will make special arrangements for light, heat and humidity control for the appropriate sections of the building. For example, if fumigation is used in the conservation of old material, then special ventilation arrangements will be needed.

The question of whether to ask for full air-conditioning is a difficult one. Although air-conditioning is undoubtedly the best method at present available for providing clean air of the correct temperature and humidity, it has drawbacks: its machinery and trunking use space and limit flexibility. Above all it is expensive; the cost of a good installation can be very high. It needs a completely reliable electricity supply, or the result, particularly in a humid climate, can be much more damaging than natural ventilation. Konya,[1] dealing with the especially difficult problem of smaller buildings in tropical climates, states categorically that well-designed buildings can give comfortable conditions without the use of expensive, energy-consuming mechanical equipment. This is only possible if, from the very beginning, the influence of climate on the overall concept, the layout, the orientation, shape and character of the structure is taken into account. On the other hand, Metcalf[2] writes that 'many would say that wihin a few years a non-air-conditioned academic library will be a thing of the past'. This was published in the United States in 1986 and presumably is meant to apply only to that country. In some instances it may be that having full air-conditioning is as much a matter of prestige as an essential service. The Parry Report[3] stated that full air-conditioning was 'essential' for British university libraries, but the University Grants Committee has not yet given unqualified approval to this recommendation in financial terms. Even if the library cannot afford full air-conditioning initially, the architect can be asked to allow ducting and space so that plant can be provided when funds become available. This will not be easy.

If old or fragile materials are to be displayed, or if paintings, prints or photographs are to be featured in an exhibition or art gallery area, the architect will need to plan suitable housing conditions. The librarian should not go too far into practical details such as lighting levels unless he is qualified in this specialist field (it will be a great advantage if he can make himself competent enough to discuss such matters with the architect). The recommendations of the Illuminating Engineering Society[4] on the lighting of libraries are the basic source and are simple to quote. The architect will know about the expectations of those who are to use the library, but he needs to be told what types of materials are likely to be exposed and for what periods they are to remain on display. The architect will also be aware of legislation requiring special conditions to be provided for the disabled (in Britain, the Chronically Sick and Disabled Persons Act 1970) and will take these requirements into account in terms of access to all sections of the library by disabled people. He will see that ramps or lifts are provided so that handicapped people are not debarred by stairs, but he needs to know what special allowance should be made in this particular library situation so that disabled persons, particularly those in wheelchairs, can have access to catalogue cabinets, book shelving and other facilities. The (British) law, if strictly interpreted, decrees that wheelchair users should have equal opportunities, which means that no stack should be higher than could be reached from a wheelchair; but this would be very difficult to arrange in a busy library (see Chapter 13). Special design for this purpose will often affect provision for the general reader, and the matter is for the librarian (and perhaps the authority) to decide. Hospital and welfare librarians will deal with such problems constantly but in too many libraries this question is not taken seriously enough.

Under 'Activities and users' (Chapter 4) information has already been given about rest and eating facilities, but if, for example, smoking is to be allowed in all, or any part, of the library the fact must be stated in this part of the brief. Although it may seem obvious, it would be as well to tell the architect which areas are to be particularly designed to allow quiet, undisturbed study and which areas can have an atmosphere of businesslike bustle. When in doubt it is better to include information which might appear obvious rather than risk a misunderstanding.

The site

Libraries which form part of a larger organization in a building complex will seldom have much say in the choice of site. In a university the master plan will probably have fixed the library site. In a school or hospital the library site will usually be a section of a building rather than a piece of land on which to build. Even here a conflict of interests is certain to arise. The library will need to be central, easily accessible for all major activities of the institution, close to a main entrance though never usable as a thoroughfare (but see p. 12). These will also be the requirements of most other special interests within the organization, and the library is unlikely to get absolute priority. If the ideal, centrally situated position is denied to the library, there is consolation in the fact that such a position would almost certainly prevent lateral expansion. The public library, on the other hand, must take the question of site selection very seriously, because so much of its success in attracting readers will depend upon its position. There may be little choice: the site may have been earmarked for years even though the money or permission to build could not be obtained. If there is a choice the librarian will discover what the architect already knows well, that he will have to deal with many agencies before he is able to persuade the authority to accept what he has chosen. In most cases there will be officers to be consulted, committees to be persuaded and some opposition to be overcome before a suitable site can be secured, but first the librarian must be clear in his own mind what features of a particular site are important to him.

In the case of a public library that is not to be a part of any cultural or educational complex, he will want a site which is central and easily accessible from main traffic routes by those it is designed to serve. Some interesting studies[5] have been made of the criteria needed when choosing sites for public libraries in new towns. The conditions of these surveys are ideal for a clear study of principles because the areas are unencumbered by existing buildings. The studies have been particularly directed to the importance of the siting relationship between the public library and other crucial elements of community life – houses, shops, industry, civic centres and so on. The methods used in assessing the various social factors will be new to most librarians, particularly the use of mathematical models and cluster analysis.

A very fine example of site selection by highly systematic procedures is to be found in the *Site Selection Study* of the Metropolitan Toronto Library Board.[6] Here the team considered ten sites as potential locations for a new central library and after questioning all the experts available, both planners and librarians, distilled the requirements into fifty-eight evaluative criteria (excluding site cost). Each criterion was given a number relative to its assessed importance, tabulated and totalled, in order to 'prove' which site was the most suitable. At the head of the table of 'first-level criteria' were 'metro-wide access', 'development potential of the site' and 'availability'; in the second-level criteria, and awarded a higher relative score, were such factors as 'positive contact with major pedestrian ways', 'positive contact with public open spaces' and so on. Few situations will ever call for such an elaborate approach; critics have suggested that the wrong questions were asked, but the undoubted success of the Metro Reference Library gives a riposte, and the methods used are worthy of study. Another interesting study[7] was carried out for the new building of the University of Groeningen, Holland, where the financial effects of different suggested sites were scrutinized.

Working without the benefit of such expert help but with his own experience as guide, the public librarian will usually recommend a position where a great many people come for other essential routine needs – shopping, public transport, other cultural and recreational centres and so on. The most suitable association has always been found to be with shopping, but local authority representatives usually tend to favour a site near the town hall on the grounds of civic dignity. All public librarians will oppose the suggestion, always made by town planners, that the library should be placed in a quiet backwater and so ease the pressure of demand for 'main street' sites. A key position in a busy street may be expensive but, like any other businessman, the librarian knows that out of public sight is out of public mind, and an underused public service is potentially a waste of money. A good comparison is between the central libraries of Manchester and Sheffield, the only two large central libraries built in England during the early 1930s; Manchester has a central library on a magnificent site and, partly because of its grandiose architecture, is known to every citizen and serves as a symbol of the city; Sheffield's functionally better-planned library is in a central backwater and attracts fewer new readers. A strong argument for the quiet area in the past was the problem of noise, but this is much less important today because it can largely be controlled by the architect.

In practice it is only possible to build when a site becomes available. Compulsory purchase powers are seldom used to make space for libraries in Britain. The question is usually one of balancing the pros and cons of building on a not-quite-perfect site against those of losing the chance to build while waiting for the perfect site.

Because the public library will serve its community far into the future it is important to take into account the position, so far as it can be estimated, in thirty or forty years' time. Despite the steadily increasing use of city centre libraries, account must be taken of the tendency for urban centres to become depopulated. If the centre of a large city is likely to be cleared of residents in the future it may be that its library should be planned to serve the day-time business community only; library services for residents would then be based in residential community areas, or even in large shopping complexes outside the city. On the other hand there is some evidence that residents are showing a tendency to return to the 'deserted' down-town areas. Perhaps the siting priorities of the future should be concerned with vehicle rather than pedestrian access; this might mean that the ideal site will be one close to main motor roads and with large parking provision. Far-fetched as this may seem at this moment, it is probably more realistic than to use very expensive space within a city for car parking space for library users. The high proportion of the 'library' space devoted to parking in large libraries today throws into relief a problem that will grow larger every year.

A parallel problem concerns the administrative head-quarters of a large public library system. Traditionally housed in a central library in the heart of a city, it is becoming ever more expensive to maintain and less convenient for delivery and dispatch of books. A separate headquarters outside the central area of the city with better vehicular access and a much lower rent might offset the disadvantages of separation of the public service from the central administration, particularly as communication systems have become so much more efficient.

The explosion of the traditional central library into a series of smaller buildings, each housed among the people it is intended to serve, may be the way of the future. Business libraries and day-time lending libraries in city centres, arts and music libraries near cultural and educational precincts, technical libraries close to industrial complexes – these suggestions, anathema to the librarian who regards each member of the community as a potential user of each section of the service, may have to come unless future funds are provided on a more generous scale than at present. Where any choice is open to him, the librarian should strongly resist the suggestion that the library should share premises with any other activity. A combination of social services within a single building has immense appeal to planners, but such schemes are seldom successful as sites for libraries. Any experienced public librarian knows that a shopping centre is a more effective (and cost-effective) site than a social or educa-tional precinct. Whatever the social reactions, problems are inevitable on the structural side; different services have their own individual spatial and operational needs which can seldom be catered for efficiently in the same building. A library works best when it is planned as a library, not as a part of a multi-purpose building: if a new library can be financed only by becoming part of a commercial block, or with shops below or offices above, then the librarian will have little choice, but even if he is given the priority ground-floor position (and in some countries this seldom happens) he will find that the structural module has to be chosen to suit an alien purpose and that large pillars and ducts will be needed to carry services to other floors.

It is obviously of the greatest importance that, if a choice of site is possible, the architect as well as the librarian should be closely involved in the decision.

Security

This is more a problem for the librarian than for the architect. It is not the layout or the design of machinery which are difficult, but the policy as to the extent to which security of the book stock is to be maintained at the expense of freedom of access by readers.

Ideally, in an educated society, there should be little need for barriers and checks; in practice, this is not so. The reasons which lead to loss of and damage to books and other materials should be discussed by the design team in order that they can be fully aware of the difficulties and of the acceptable risks. The problem is a very real one in universities, colleges and large public libraries, all of which will hold stocks of rare books; 'rare' in this context can refer to those which are in excessive demand and scarce as well as to those of a high monetary value. Where most of the stock consists of books in fairly even demand and the titles are easily replaceable, as in most public lending and school libraries, it may be easier to 'trust the people'; the resulting losses, though costing money to replace, will not be as damaging to the library as when intrinsically valuable items, or books in great demand, are lost. Whether the authority is prepared, like a supermarket management, to accept a certain level of losses as an operating cost is another matter; the authority may feel that its duty to the public calls for a high level of security, even though the cost be higher than that of possible losses. There follows the question of what the authority is prepared to do when theft or attempted theft is detected; educational and other 'closed' institutions may be able to use their own sanctions, but a public library has little alternative but to prosecute, at a cost that will almost always be uneconomic in the particular case but which, by the resultant publicity, may deter other potential thieves. An outline of the problem is given here: possible solutions are considered in Chapter 12.

Theft of books

Book thieves are motivated by:
Cash value Except in rare book libraries this reason is less common than might be expected. Because most library books are 'mutilated' (in the sense that they are marked with ownership stamps and labels) they are not generally saleable. The great exception is the rare and valuable book, but these books will usually be kept under lock and key and issued under strict conditions upon proof of identity. Highly professional thefts do take place, but this is not the common denominator.
Ad hoc need Students are the main culprits here. They 'must' have the book for their studies; the conditions of study in the library do not appeal to them or they want to continue studying after hours (perhaps because they have left it so close to examination time). The books they need may be unobtainable in the circumstances they have created, so they steal them. This is anti-social and hinders their colleagues who do obey the rules.
Absent-mindedness Many books are taken by honest people who find them in their possession when they get home and are too embarrassed, or too lazy, to return them.

Mutilation of books

This is another form of theft; it is caused by:
The collector One of the great menaces to libraries of all kinds. Fundamentally decent people often become unbalanced when under the spell of a devouring hobby. Every reference librarian knows how much care has to be exercised when issuing volumes with illustrations of old trains, trams, ships and so on, even in well-supervised reading rooms. Hobby fanatics will use razor blades held in their palms or thin knives slid from up their sleeves to cut out desired sections; their ingenuity is worthy of a better cause. A similar menace is the student who needs an article or an illustration for his work. A free, or at least subsidized, photocopy service can be of help. One of the worst examples in my experience came in dealing with graduate students in art colleges, who need illustrations for their theses; because colour pictures in major art works are often printed on both sides of a page, two copies of the same work were mutilated so that the student could stick the illustrations into his own work.
The prints thief The vogue for framed engravings, particularly maps, has produced a type of thief who specializes in cutting engravings (or lithographs) out of historical books, especially those concerned with topography or costume, in order to sell them to unscrupulous dealers. Such thieves often work in teams, one acting as a decoy.

This may seem a sweeping condemnation of the community, but, as every librarian knows, book thieves and mutilators form a very tiny proportion of readers. The problem is how to deal with them without disturbing general freedom to use the library. Methods of doing so are considered in Chapter 12. At this stage the architect will need answers to the following questions:
Is a physical barrier or control to be placed at the exit from the building, or from any room, and is it to be manned?
Is a detection device to be installed, and if so has the librarian decided on a particular product?
Is a bag and coat deposit station to be installed, and if so is its use to be compulsory? If it is, then an estimate will need to be made of the highest number of coats and bags which will need to be housed at any one time. This point needs to be taken seriously; a busy library which proposes to use such a method for the first time will find that an alarming amount of space is needed for storage. Is the station to be manned, or is there to be locking self-service equipment?

Safety

By training and experience the architect is competent to design a building which is safe for people to use; indeed the law lays upon him very stringent duties in this respect. The effect of the legislation for disabled people has already been mentioned, and he or she will pay close attention to the need to prevent fire, flood and other hazards and to arrange for the handling of any subsequent panic. Because of the peculiar properties of library materials, chiefly books, defence against hazards will be different from those of other buildings, but there are a number of techniques and proprietary equipment with which he must make himself acquainted. These are dealt with in some detail in Chapter 12 and they are only referred to here because of their possible effect on matters which are the concern and the responsibility of the librarian. The latter will know of special material (rare books, for example) to which special attention has to be given; he may also have had both experience and strong feelings about the use of

5:1. Transparent-sided lifts in Metro Reference Library, Toronto (Architect Raymond Moriyama)

5:2 and 5:3. Escalators in Birmingham Central Library (Architects John Madin Design Group)

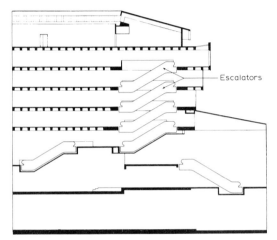

Escalators

5:4. Escalators in Rotterdam Central Library (Architects Bakema and Weeber). See also 5:5 over

5:5. Escalators in Rotterdam Central Library

Key
1. Entrance
2. Newspaper-room
3. Shop
4. Reception
5. Circulation centre
6. Exhibition hall
7. Direction and admin.
8. Theatre
9. Information dept.
10. Literature, history
11. Art, music, film, video
12. Science, technology
13. Social sciences
14. Ventilation trunking
15. Escalators

sprinklers, fire alarms, anti-flood measures and so on. If so, it is at this point that he should make his views known in the brief. Normally any proposals from the architect about defence against hazards, including fire exits, will be discussed in detail with the librarian at a later stage. Although fire exits are statutory requirements, they can strongly affect the operation of the library, and after discussions it may be possible for the architect to make provision which does not clash with the librarian's functional requirements.

Movement of people

Horizontal circulation of people is a normal factor to be taken into account in the design of the overall layout. The quantities will be known from 'Activities and users' (Chapter 4), the directions from the circulation and traffic diagrams. Traffic flow is subject to mathematical calculations; sources are available to provide formulae, standard space allowances for people moving through buildings, doorway and corridor widths and so on. Unless a moving floor track is to be installed (unlikely in libraries), there will be little to affect structural planning.

Vertical conveyance on the other hand can have great significance. A lift (elevator) in a tall building can be a major structural matter, so the requirement (and the building regulations) will be studied at an early stage. Although the various pieces of equipment which move people vertically within a building are well known, and comparisons in cost, speed of operation, numbers conveyable, reliability and so on can easily be made, their visual effect can be a matter of major importance. Although lifts are usually tucked away discreetly in corners as part of service cores, they can also be used as major features of the internal decor. The transparent-sided lifts in the Metro Toronto Library and Alexander Library Building in Perth, Western Australia, are not original, in that they have been a feature of opulent department stores and hotels for years, but they bring a new dimension to the users' idea of a library, and children love them. They are becoming widely used in other large atrium-type libraries.

Similarly, escalators can convey users up to the various service floors quietly and efficiently, like those in the Birmingham Central Library (although here the visitor does not get an overall view of the library), or they can be an ostentatious feature of the interior design, as in the Rotterdam Central Library. This uses up a great deal of space and distracts some readers, but it also attracts many others and makes the building famous: this is not a negligible factor in a public library. These are very important matters for the architect to take into account, and the brief should give him all the relevant facts as well as conveying the feelings of the librarian. It is for the architect to make the decisions (or rather the detailed proposals).

The position and style of a staircase seems a minor matter in comparison, but it can have an effect not only on access but on security. The librarian will take this latter point seriously, and he will also be concerned that a proposed open staircase does not cause the visual and aural distraction to readers which has been a feature of some modern libraries. There is undoubtedly a temptation which some architects cannot resist to make a feature of a large central staircase, and this is a form of the monumentalism which librarians try to avoid. The question is considered again in Chapter 6; Figure 6:27 (the Free University of Berlin Library) should be studied with care.

Materials circulation

Because 'materials' in a library consist largely of books, and because the librarian will be very experienced in handling books, his special knowledge will be invaluable. 'Books are different', and they cannot be treated merely as objects of a certain size and weight; whatever methods are used to move them must allow for variations in handling according to the value and the fragility of different volumes.

Books in a library present three entirely different handling problems:

1. Distribution after arrival, through the preparation processes and then on to open or closed shelves.
2. Replacement on shelves after readers have borrowed and returned them.
3. Retrieval of books from closed stack and their return after use.

Distribution of books after arrival
The progress of books through the processing section has received too little attention. The number to be handled hourly may be small but over months and years multiple handling can represent a very expensive use of staff time. In many libraries, day after day, staff manhandle parcels from delivery, up steps, onto book trolleys (which were designed for quite a different purpose), along corridors and into passenger lifts, crossing public access routes and wasting an incredible amount of time. A little thought at the planning stage can make a great deal of difference.

Loading and unloading
The main feature of a loading bay should be a ramp or platform so that transfer to and from a van can be made without a change of level. If materials are to be received at two separate levels, say a bindery on the ground floor and accessions department on the floor above, a mechanical two-level ramp can provide a good solution. The delivery route to the unpacking point should have been given its degree of priority in the 'Activities and users' section of the brief, so that the architect will have made the route direct, unimpeded and clear of other routes.

Horizontal conveying
In many libraries members of the staff have to carry parcels of books, the greatest concession to automation being the book trolley. Where large numbers of books are involved and there are changes of level in their progress from section to section, thought should be given (by the architect, at the request of the librarian) to providing more labour-saving methods, possibly including horizontal conveyors automatically picking up books from vertical ones. Few libraries are likely to need these or tracked trolley systems or powered rollers, but some may. On the other hand, gravity roller tracking, possibly telescopic and removable, would be a boon in many existing libraries' processing departments. A good example of planning book movement on a large scale was shown in the British Library, Lending Division, at Boston Spa. This building was from the beginning planned to handle individual requests in great numbers and at high speed; a continuous belt carries trays which hold books hooked to an overhead conveyor with sophisticated control features. However, experience with even such a well-planned system has shown that it can have psychological disadvantages. The arrangement whereby a single person stationed at each section of the immense stack collects books from his own area as he receives a request and feeds them onto the conveyor can certainly be economical of movement but

5:6. Telelift showing book container pivoting so that vertical motion, both up and down, is practicable

5:7. Telelift conveyor in action

5:8. Book transfer by sliding down smooth metal surface: the screw

5:9. The discharge point (Inter-University Library, Lyons)

leads to boredom and potential loss of efficiency. The limitations of the human machine should not be ignored in this planning.

In less advanced systems some form of closed container will have to be employed. Containers may also be needed where automatic book hoists are used. These can incorporate automatic signal devices which, when pre-set at the dispatching point, cause them to stop and move out horizontally at the appropriate floor. Other containers can latch onto moving tracks and move, not only horizontally but also vertically; a most ingenious balancing device enables them to swing so that books are not tipped out.

Simple containers will be needed to assemble books in bulk for transport to different parts of the building or to branch libraries. Too little attention has been paid to the design of these containers; factors to be considered are:

1. Size relative to the channels or positions in to which the containers will have to fit, particularly if they are to be stacked when not in use.
2. Weight and size should be related to the reasonable lifting capability of those who have to handle them.
3. Material – both its durability and its effect upon books. Wicker boxes have often been used because they are light and cheap, but after heavy use they tend to splinter and damage the books. Plastic and fibreboard are the best materials today, but if containers made of these are to be regularly loaded onto vans they may have to be bound with metal or framed in wood.
4. Handles and method of labelling to show contents and/or destination; small points, perhaps, but such matters should be thought out at the beginning, not after the need has been discovered.

Vertical conveying
Alternatives for this purpose include:

1. Trolley into passenger lift: obviously inconvenient in staff time and in interference with other services. The walls of the lift cage will have to be protected, at least at the level where they might be bumped by a trolley, with a lining material, usually a belt of metal which cannot be easily damaged.
2. Special trolley lift: better; a signal system will be needed to tell staff to take the trolley out at the appropriate floor.
3. Book hoist: this will of course take smaller numbers but it should be large enough – 635 × 455 mm (24 × 18 in) – to take bound newspapers. Again, light or sound signals (or both) will be needed to indicate arrival. Firm discipline for immediate clearance of hoists will be needed or chaos will result.

Improvements on the old book hoist are available, including semi-automatic loading and unloading and automatic selection of floor for delivery. One type uses a platform, counter-balanced by a spring so that it remains still when holding an empty container; when a loaded container is placed on the platform it swings towards the centre of the elevator and the container is picked from the loading platform automatically by pegs on the elevator chain. When the chosen floor is reached the container is automatically discharged.

The best-known system in Europe is the Telelift. In this a carrier engages in a track which travels from stack to service point and back again on the endless belt system, electronically controlled. The striking feature is that the belt, complete with carrier, can climb up and down walls, the books in the carrier being suspended in an inner container which pivots with gravity. It is certainly an experience to see for the first time a line of carriers climbing walls in their journey. The system is also used

through underground tunnels to transfer books from one building to another and back again. This is used to send books between some branches and the central library of Düsseldorf University. At another extreme is the system used in the technical university at Delft, and seen here in a more striking form in the Inter-University Library at Lyons, which takes the form of a giant screw of polished steel, down which the books slide slowly from the balcony of a stack to the ground-floor reception point. No energy is needed for this system, but the books cannot be sent back in the same manner.

Requirements such as these must be thought out by the librarian at a very early stage and incorporated in the primary brief. Almost all these installations will have spatial as well as structural implications; some book hoists can be free-standing, but even these will have to be associated with other core elements, and the architect must know what is needed in this field before he proceeds to the feasibility study.

Books are not the only items which have to be moved about a library but most of the others – documents, microforms, discs and so on – are much less bulky and present fewer problems. The item causing most frequent movement is probably the photocopy. Photocopies can be placed in containers in book delivery systems or can be handled by special conveyors which have their own routes; see p. 56 below.

Retrieval from stack

Closed stack is certainly the book storage method most economical of space, but to obtain quickly every book that every reader requires becomes an expensive operation and one calling for special study. Ways of organizing the stack so that readers can be placed as close as possible to the books which they are, statistically, most likely to call for, is considered in Chapter 6. We discuss here ways of getting the book into the reader's hands. In the simplest case the reader will enter the call number of the required book on a slip and hand it to a member of the staff who will check it for accuracy and fetch the book. In a large library this process will not be feasible, because the stack is likely to extend over several floors. Such a stack can be divided notionally into sectors, each with its own staff. Because of the long opening hours of libraries, a large number of staff will be needed for this operation, so any method which can reduce that number deserves careful consideration. Some of the methods of communication considered here (e.g. telephone and fax) will not interest the architect at this stage because they need only wire connections, but others which use heavy machinery, particularly hoists and automatic retrieval systems, will be important to him because of their effect on the structure, or at least on the planning of floors and ceilings. The operation itself can be broken down into the following parts:

Receiving and checking the call slip prepared by the reader. Because readers can so easily misunderstand the location information it is never advisable to allow slips to be dispatched unchecked to the stack. A preliminary glance by the librarian on duty may save much fruitless searching.
Transmission of the call-slip information to the appropriate stack sector. This will usually start from the enquiry desk, but in a large system with enquiry points throughout the library it will be necessary to have a distribution centre for routing the slips, or the information on them, to the appropriate sector of the stack (see alternative methods below).
Searching for and delivering the book to the reader This usually involves some method of moving the book vertically

(see above). The machinery used can be designed for the purpose to take a very few books or the general book hoist can be shared with other functions such as book distribution to departments. The use of passenger lifts for this purpose is most uneconomic and should be for emergencies only. In practice, delivery will be to the staffed point within the reading area; careful planning can ensure that staff do not have to go to the delivery point to fetch books. From here the staff or attendants may take books to the reader, the number of his seat being found on the call slip. Alternatively an illuminated panel near the staff desk may indicate to the reader that his turn has come and the book is ready for collection. It is fair to say that I have seen this, and much more complicated notification systems, in many libraries, but most have been abandoned.

Returning the book to the stack. From reader to staffed desk, to stack centre, to stack sector and so to the shelf place; the reverse of the actions above but always more difficult because returned books must go to their specific place on the shelves, or chaos will come.

Retrieval communications
Methods of sending call-slip information to the stack include:

Facsimile transmission This system copies the call slip and reproduces it in stack. It is necessary only to insert the slip in the machine; no other staff time is needed. It has the advantage of leaving the original of the call slip at the enquiry desk, so no duplicate has to be produced there. To the cost of the transmitter and receiver (or a more expensive transmitter-receiver which permits two-way communication) is added only a pair of wires and a negligible use of electricity. The drawback is that the scanning system involves a slightly delay while it is operating, and the next slip cannot be inserted until the previous one has been completed.

Pneumatic tube This is much the most common method and has been in use for many years. Modern systems use plastic conveyors with outside measurements only 60 mm (2⅜ in) in diameter, running in plastic tubes, with comparatively small power plants. The old problem of noise has been largely overcome, but the system can never be absolutely silent. The setting of a control on the carrier can, by the tripping of levers, direct it to the appropriate sector of the stack. This system is better when it is installed in a new building where plans can be made in good time to accommodate the network of tubes.

Gravity tubes This is the cheapest and the quietest system, the slip needing no enclosing carrier (like mail drops in hotels), but it is possible only where there is a vertical direct fall.

Document carrier There are several varieties: document lift, drag-band or travelling double-belt. All have their advantages and disadvantages. Much depends on the angles round which the flexible belts have to travel and the space available for the width of the belt. They are very fast and may be seen in airports, transporting documents from office to counter and return.

It is advisable for the librarian to study manufacturers' trade catalogues in this field, because the operation vitally affects the running of the library and the sequence of actions is more familiar to him than to the architect.

It is possible to dispense with the call slip, although experience has shown the value of written, staff-checked book requests. Methods which can be used include:
Telephone Cheap to install but expensive in staff time

(because it takes two people to pass a message). There is always a risk of mishearing.

Telex (teletype) This calls for more expensive equipment, particularly if there are many reader service points. It takes only one staff member to send the information because the recorded message can wait at the receiving end until staff are ready to deal with it. Again a copy can be retained at the sending end to provide a duplicate.

Visual display unit Very quick and efficient, and the variations possible are enormous. The requests which are keyed in will await their turn on the receiving VDU; a number of keyboards can connect with a central VDU. It is possible to allow readers to key in their own requests, but the risk of error is high; if stack staff have to query requests, time will be lost.

Automated book retrieval

Any method which could reduce staff involvement in the time-wasting and laborious business of fetching books from stack would be a boon. Several methods of varying complexity, have been devised. Brawne[8] describes the Bibliofoon system which was installed some years ago in the Technological Institute at Delft, Holland.

Here the reader dials the call number of the required book on one of several phones situated in the public areas near the catalogues. The call is monitored electronically to see that the book is not already on issue; if it is not, a switching system causes direction lights to appear in the stacks guiding the attendant to the appropriate tier. The call number of the book appears on a digit indicator tube close to the appropriate stack: the attendant removes the book and dispatches it by a system of spiral chutes and conveyor belts to the issue point. He also presses a button which causes the call number of the book to be automatically recorded at the issue point. If the book is not on the shelf the attendant presses a different button which records the number of the wanted book at the loan centre, so informing the staff that the book cannot be found. The loan centre therefore knows about the transaction, whether it is completed or not.

This scheme has certain sophisticated advantages over earlier methods and it could presumably be developed further by the use of computers and by a mechanical book return system, but it still requires the time of an attendant to find and dispatch the book and, more important, both his time and his judgement to reshelve it.

A great step forward was made by the Randtriever produced by Sperry-Rand Inc. Essentially this is a method of storing file boxes in stacks where they can be packed closely (and therefore economically of space) because they are to be retrieved entirely by machine and no space for human access is required (other than a minimum for maintenance engineers): in fact, stacks can be as high as 7264 mm (23 ft 10 in). The file boxes can be designed to carry books, say three or four to a box. When this installation is included in the plans for a new library, therefore, the maximum height can be used by putting the equipment in a complete deep basement, thus eliminating the need for floors to house conventional stacks. This itself produces a saving in structural costs. It is in use for shelving and retrieving files; several such library installations were built, both in the United States and the Netherlands, but it does not seem to be available today. Nevertheless it is based on sound, and revolutionary, principles, and it is worth studying. More information is given in earlier editions of this book.

A less dramatic method, developed by the materials handling industry and using similar principles, has the title

AS/RS and is described by John Kountz.[9] Again books and other items are stored in bins, being identified, retrieved and eventually returned to their place by computer. Space savings are again very great, but the advantage of this system over the Randtriever is that comparatively small units can be built to order and so it need have much less dominance over the planning of the building. Such methods are similar to storing and retrieval methods for office files in quantity, of which several examples are on the market.

Cost in use

This term denotes the complicated exercise by which the architect will establish the factors in shape, structure, materials and so on that will produce the most economic new building. The complication arises from the need to arrive at a balance of initial and running costs, and this involves attempting to correlate two sets of cost figures which have entirely different bases. Initial costs are predictable; running costs depend on many uncontrollable and unpredictable factors. Obviously the total initial cost of the building will be small compared with the running costs throughout its life (though much will depend on the life-expectancy allowed in the calculations). It is therefore important that the librarian should understand the principles underlying the architect's decisions and that he should bear cost-in-use considerations in mind when drawing up the brief. An interesting series of articles in the *Architects' Journal*[10] on cost-in-use studies for the design of new schools is a helpful introduction to the subject.

Although every feature of the design affects this issue, there are three fields in particular which should be considered by the librarian at this point and on which his comments and recommendations may help the architect when he is considering his first sketches. They are:

1. The requirements for environmental conditions (heating, lighting, ventilating etc.).
2. The employment of maintenance staff.
3. The employment of library staff.

Environmental conditions

Because of the technicalities involved this must eventually be a matter for the decision of the architect on the advice of the appropriate specialist consultants. Nevertheless they are planning, as far as is practicable, to meet the requirements of the librarian, and if he asks for too critical a range of temperatures and humidity levels, highly sophisticated equipment will be necessary. Not only will this be much more expensive initially, but its running costs may include labour charges for maintenance engineers. If such costs would be unacceptable, then the architect cannot meet the librarian's stipulated figures, or if he does it will mean finding money from other areas; this may seem obvious but it is worth taking seriously. A librarian who asks for perfection in certain fields when he is well aware that the future running budget will be limited is simply creating a situation where economies will eventually be made in the one truly flexible item in his budget – the book fund.

Maintenance

When the architect has completed the building and left the scene, maintaining the building will be the librarian's responsibility. For this reason he will be well advised to state clearly to what extent the architect is to be restricted in his choice of materials and methods in order to plan for economy of maintenance. Because the need for constant maintenance in certain parts of the building (such as the entrance hall) can cause chaos in the service and add enormously to costs, the librarian is within his rights in doing this, but he must remember that any stipulation of maintenance-free materials and equipment is likely to add heavily to the initial cost. He must sum up the factors applicable in his own case. For example, doubling the number of fluorescent tubes in each fitting and having switches to turn on the second tube when the first fails is particularly efficient, but it is expensive initially; alternatives such as this can be found in almost every part of the building and its fittings. If for financial reasons it is decided that maintenance staff will be available for a strictly limited number of hours a week, the architect should be informed. If cleaning can take place only in the late evening or early morning (common in schools and busy public lending libraries), or if all major maintenance tasks can be carried out only in college vacation time, then these limitations must be made clear, as they may affect the choice of materials – particularly flooring. Electrical fitments which require skilled attention may be inappropriate in a small branch library with only one general-duties janitor. For instance, the fashionable cluster of lamps hung high over an entrance hall requires at least two workers with long ladders whenever a single bulb fails – a major drawback if the branch library is several miles from central servicing departments. Similarly windows which can only be reached by using special equipment, or a floor which needs sanding and resealing at regular intervals, can be a permanent embarrassment.

Staffing

A major factor in the cost of running a library service is the number of points which must be manned at all times. With long opening hours and allowing for shift working, sickness and holidays, at least two staff will have to be allocated on the establishment for each point. To provide more points than the librarian really needs for his service requirements is a major financial hazard, so a good understanding between librarian and architect on this matter is vital.

Economy of staffing is a particularly important question in small libraries where the number on public duty at off-peak times must be minimal. Placing a children's library where it can be visually supervised from the lending counter at quiet periods, rather than putting it on a different level or in a separate room, can make a great different to staffing needs. The design and layout of control counters is critical; if only one person is available at off-peak times, then an island counter is essential (see Chapter 15). Similarly, separate entrances to a building or to a single section will present control problems and if the librarian asks for such an arrangement he must realize that it will mean either extra staff or some loss of control.

One cause of conflict can be the librarian's insistence on visual supervision of every part of the library where readers are allowed. This will probably clash with the architect's design ideas; in the past bookcases were often sited so that they radiated from a single control desk, allowing a view of every part of the library. Other alternatives are now possible provided that the problem is clearly stated at an early stage.

End of brief

The brief may seem to have developed into a formidable document, particularly in a large undertaking. The architect will supplement it by asking questions and by himself exploring factors which will affect his decisions. He may survey the community to be served, the characteristics of the locale and the potential readership to satisfy himself as to the true, if unwritten, needs of the people. Architects are trained to make this kind of preassessment, and in many projects it is an essential exercise. Such an assessment should first have been made by the librarian (or library consultant), who will have specialized knowledge of both the service and the community, but this does not mean that the architect will not wish to make his own survey. He should, however, be provided with a full record of the librarian's views and these views should be given careful consideration.

From this point onwards the architect, as leader of the team, will ask, examine and propose. The librarian's task will be to study the architect's proposals, be quite sure that he understands all their implications, and comment on them. Having written the brief, the librarian must be prepared to stand by it: he may agree to changes suggested by the architect, circumstances may alter, but should not change his mind about his own requirements unless it is absolutely inevitable. All change costs money, and the later the change, the more expensive it becomes. This emphasizes yet again how important it is for the librarian to know exactly what he wants before he writes the brief.

Cost limits and controls

The authority may have stipulated a firm cost limit for the project. This is a perfectly reasonable requirement (although impractical unless it allows for inflation). it is a factor which the architect will take very much into account in his feasibility study. The cost limit could have been based on cost per book, per reader, per square metre or foot of floor space, or a proportion of the cost of a project of which it is a part (e.g. a new college). In practice it will constitute a sum of money; even when permission from higher authority (e.g. government) is given on a cost per square metre or foot basis, there will in practice be a predetermined sum of money which may not be exceeded.

Before a cost limit is stipulated it should be clearly understood that, if the quantity requirements of the brief are firm, the architect may have to use lower standards of quality (in materials, finishes, etc.) in order to meet it; this will be clearly shown in his feasibility report, where responsibility for acceptance is firmly placed upon the authority. If possible the accepted target figure should be one that arises out of the feasibility study, or an amendment to that figure, not one that was arbitrarily chosen before studies were even begun.

In setting an initial cost limit the authority should consider very carefully what its impact will be on the cost-effectiveness of the space provided. The more effective the use of space, the greater the purely financial cost, because of the additional seating, shelving and furniture which can be accommodated. In general the larger the library, the smaller the proportion of non-assignable areas (i.e. architectural features such as walls, columns, vesti-bules, stairways, etc.) required, so that an increase in size may produce functional economies. A fairer cost criterion might be the cost per reader, or per book housed, but it is difficult to see how such a true cost-effectiveness can be computed for a library. Designing down to a price can mean that extra library staff will be needed for service and security, and this will have to be paid for in the long run. This underlines the importance of including in the brief all possible information about operating conditions.

In order for the cost limit to have any real meaning, it must relate to a particular moment in time. In periods of

inflation the architect cannot be responsible for increases beyond, for example, the time of tendering, unless a given allowance for inflationary price rises is to be included. If all tenders exceed the limit and reductions are necessary, the librarian will have to decide what to give up: if this is not done, cuts will have to be made in the standard of items which can still be controlled – floor coverings and finishes – and this can mean a poorer appearance, reduced comfort and possibly higher costs of maintenance and renewal. A cost ceiling based on the cost of a similar library elsewhere should not be hastily applied without very careful study of possible hidden differences. Construction may be more expensive on one site than another (such as a crowded situation in a metropolitan area or where a token service has to be continued from part of the site while construction is in progress).

When the architect knows the proposed cost limit, he will begin, with the quantity surveyor, to assess the proportion which can be notionally allocated to the various building elements. Throughout the progress of the project he will maintain, and where necessary amend, his apportionment so that no one element is allowed to cost disproportionally more at the expense of others. When, at a later stage, he receives the recommendations of the various specialist consultants he will compare the cost implications of each with his original, theoretical, allowance and so retain continuous cost control of the operation.

Consents

The consents from outside powers which have to be obtained at various stages of the programme are many and varied, and it is right that this should be so. The community has to be protected against the results of irresponsible building, but the restraints which are used to provide this protection mean extra work and extra time in any building project. In the comments which follow here (and later in the book) British practice may at times be referred to specifically, but every country will have its own system of controls and the underlying principles remain the same. In some, all powers may be held by a single central authority; in Britain the powers are divided between central government and each of two levels of local government (just as in other countries the powers can be federal, state, city or county). Planning approval is needed because of the possible effect of the proposed building upon its neighbours and on the environment. The Building Regula-tions are generally concerned with the interior of the building to see that methods and materials of construction follow the recommended practices in the interests of safety in all its aspects. These powers are derived from laws and their application is delegated, but they can be exceedingly complex and their operation is at times decided by what is in effect case law. For planning approval the position has been made a little easier for the architect in many circumstances by a system whereby consent can be 'deemed to have been given'. This means that in certain predetermined situations, and especially in small projects, power to approve is delegated to planning officers and the case does not have to be argued through a committee, thus simplifying formal approaches. Another advantage is the extension of General Development Orders which can allow automatic consent in a fairly typical situation. Some of the limitations apply to all buildings (e.g. the local authority's planning approval), while others apply only to certain kinds of buildings (e.g. building and fire regulations for public buildings).

Some of the chief (British) controls and their authority are:

1. Planning (both outline and detail) and utilization (purpose of building), appearance, height etc. – local authority and central government.
2. Traffic matters – local authority and police.
3. Conformity with local building by-laws – local authority.
4. Drainage, sanitation and matters concerning the handling of food – local authority, usually through its health department.
5. Fire safety – local fire authority.
6. Working conditions – factory inspectorate (for both offices and 'factories', which can include library binderies).

For a fuller list, see the RIBA *Handbook*.[11]

Undoubtedly, the most important of the powers belong to the local authority in its capacity as local planning authority. This body will have to be consulted from the earliest moment in order to obtain outline planning approval, and the final scheme, in every detail, will have to be submitted to the same body (and in some degree to the central government) for final approval. What the librarian seldom appreciates is that this is not just a matter of submitting drawings and receiving them back stamped 'approved' or 'disapproved'. While the architect is conceiving possible solutions to the problems raised by the brief, he will have to turn, time and again, to the planning officers to see whether what he has in mind would be acceptable to them. Planning powers cannot be neatly defined in published regulations; they are developed locally by the council on the recommendations of its officers and sometimes other bodies: for example it is usual for planning authorities to accept the views of the fire prevention officers. New proposals are tested against agreed planning ideas which are continually being developed. The reply to a request for approval is seldom a simple yes or no; the planning officers are working towards a concept of a satisfactorily planned area as their council has decreed; they may make concessions towards an architect's ideas in one direction if he will meet their wishes in another (usually a more important one). The result is an almost continuous dialogue in which the personal qualities of the architect are of real importance. If he is peremptory and unyielding in his approach, he is less likely to be met with a reasonable answer than if he is flexible and willing to compromise. Because planners are interpreting the law, and because new laws are promulgated, it is not uncommon in large-scale (and therefore slow) building projects for alterations to the plans to become necessary even at a late stage and long after permission had been granted. This can cause considerable (and expensive) alterations: the architect will see what softening of the blow he can obtain by discussion with planning officers but in many cases it is literally a case of 'back to the drawing board'. Less dramatic but nonetheless very important for the librarian to note is that consent must be obtained from some authority for almost every major change he causes the architect to make. This means more time, more delay, more expense.

In addition to compliance with statutory powers, the architect is responsible for seeing that his proposals do not affect the rights of others. He will need to use legal expertise in his search for any possible restrictions upon the use of the land which may form part of the site, as well as for any effect which the proposed building may have upon the access routes, rights of way, rights of natural light of adjoining properties. He may have to consult the company which is to give the insurance cover to the building; to neglect this can mean either alterations or increased premiums later.

The librarian will state in the brief if any consents have already been obtained, for example planning approval in principle for the use of the site for library purposes. The architect will certainly double-check, but a record of previous discussions with the planning authority is very important.

Timetable

When the initial proposals for a new library were approved in principle, the authority had in mind a general idea of a date of completion, and this date may have been communicated to the architect. It may be that after preliminary studies he will find this date unrealistic and he will say so in his feasibility report. If the authority accepts the report it will also accept the timetable which the architect then proposes. This will show approximate dates for submission of the various reports and drawings which mark the salient points in the operation; it will be kept up to date (and inevitably amended) by such devices as bar charts, but it should be distinguished from the schedule which the architect will keep in a far more elaborate form to assist him in controlling the work. This is a sequence of the related and interdependent activities for which a logical and pre-planned order is of the first importance.

Study of brief

The architect will by now have received a great deal of information but before he can make use of it he will have to use a number of conversion factors. To take the easiest example, he will have been asked to provide seating accommodation for a certain maximum number of readers. Before he can work out space allocations he must know not only how much space an average reader takes up when seated at a table but also the space allowance within the building to be allowed for each reader – a very different matter because of the need for movement of readers, access to tables and immediate circulation space. To this he will add the space for general access routes, for readers to consult books on shelves and many other factors.

No architect is likely to start to measure books and readers to see what space they occupy: he will expect to use established standards for each element. Unfortunately the experts disagree on almost every aspect of library estimation, not out of cussedness but because conditions and materials in libraries vary so enormously. When a basis for estimation is quoted in this book the rationale of the measurement is indicated, so that the architect can decide whether or not it applies to his particular situation. If ready-made guides are accepted without question, the variations in space which could be assumed are simply enormous.

At this early stage the architect will wish to make a very rough assessment of the space requirements of the various areas; he cannot afford to go in to detail yet, but he would like to have a general idea of the total square or cubic metres or feet involved. This is where the library consultant can show his real value, but in his absence the architect will be glad of the roughest general guide to the space requirements of a given number of books and readers. He may do this by resorting to various formulae such as the cubook (p. 143) or the VSC (p. 202). Unfortunately these and other ready-made guides have often been used out of context, without consideration for the great variations between libraries of different types.

In theory the architect will take the quantitative requirements of the brief (number of readers, of staff, books etc.)

and multiply by known space allowances for each person and book, to produce a total for the various service areas; then he will allow an amount for the support services needed and add a proportion (which he is qualified to decide) for architectural and circulation space. This is the theory; in practice each architect will have his own ways of tackling the problem, and his 'guesstimate' will be affected, especially in the case of academic buildings, by the guidelines or limits laid down by higher authority. These are usually based on space allowances per head of student and staff in each particular category. In public libraries it used to be common to use a 'space per number of population' yardstick, often quoted in the United States as 0.55 square foot ($0.05\,m^2$) per capita, but this is seldom used today, and the only internationally accepted recommendations are those recorded below in Chapter 19.

To supply height, depth and space conversion factors which can be applied to libraries of all kinds is an impossible task, but sometimes an architect may like to have figures to give him even the roughest idea of what space is likely to be needed. The tables below, based chiefly on findings recorded throughout this book, are given reluctantly and without a specific authority quoted for individual figures. The findings can be dangerously wrong if used without careful attention to the conditions stipulated. They may be useful when there is a great hurry, but they are no substitute for using the basic figures given in appropriate sections of this book and adapting them to the circumstances of a particular case.

Shelving space allowances

Open access (particularly in popular libraries)

Number of books per 900 mm (3 ft) shelf ¾ full: 24
⁴⁄₅ full: 26

These figures can be used to calculate the number of books per tier by multiplying by the number of shelves, usually between 3 and 6. Allow for 5% of the books being oversized and housed at 3 shelves per tier.

Overall height of wall shelving (see Table 13.1):
   adult, 6 shelves 2 m (6 ft 6 in)
   children, 4 shelves 1.5 m (5 ft)
Height of island bookcases:
   adult, 3 shelves 1.35 m (4 ft 6 in)
   children, 3 shelves 1.35 m (4 ft 6 in)
Depth of single-sided tier:
   230 mm (9 in)   Depth of shelf 200 mm (8 in):
Depth of double-sided tier: see p. 137
   450 mm (18 in)
Distance between free-standing bookcases: 2 m to 3 m (6 ft to 10 ft): see pp. 140–141

Space allowance for single copies of periodicals on
   face-forward display: $0.093\,m^2$ (1 sq ft) each copy
1000 shelved books take up: $16\,m^2$ (172 sq ft)
Overall capacity in rooms with 3 m (10 ft) ceilings:
   65 books/m^2 (6 books/sq ft)
   22 books/m^3 (0.6 book/cu ft)
The overall capacity figures apply only to the rooms which contain open access materials. The overall figure for the whole building will vary enormously according to the design but will be much lower, say from 30 to 50 books/m^2 (3 to 5 books/sq ft). For the cubic equivalent, divide by the ceiling height in the appropriate measure (metres or feet).
Weight of 900 mm (3 ft) shelf ¾ full of 'normal' books: 12 to
   16 kg (27 to 35 lb)
Weight of 900 mm (3 ft) shelf ¾ full of directories,
   bibliographies or bound volumes of journals: 22 to 25 kg
   (50 to 55 lb)
For shelves four-fifths full a simple arithmetic calculation is needed. There will seldom be more than three or four such shelves per tier in open-access conditions.

Open stack (particularly in academic libraries)
Tiers 2.3 m (7 ft 6 in) high under 3 m (10 ft) ceilings in optimum grid and gangway conditions:
   6 shelves at 345 mm (13½ in) centres:
      120 books/m^2 (11 books/sq ft)
      40 books/m^3 (1.1 book/cu ft)
   7 shelves at 300 mm (11½ in) centres:
      140 books/m^2 (14 books/sq ft)
      47 books/m^3 (1.4 book/cu ft)
1000 shelved books take up $5.57\,m^2$ (60 sq ft)
For the effect of variations in grid sizes and gangways, see pp. 144–148.
Bound periodicals, per single-sided tier 900 mm (3 ft), ¾ full, 5 shelves: 75 volumes
Reports and pamphlets in lateral filing cabinet, single-sided, 900 mm (3 ft) wide, 1.8 m (6 ft) high: 750 to 1450

Closed stack
Tiers 2.3 m (7 ft 6 in) high under 2.5 m (8 ft) ceiling in optimum grid and gangway conditions:
   6 shelves at 345 mm (13½ in) centres, ¾ full:
      160 books/m^2 (15 books/sq ft)
      64 books/m^3 (1.9 book/cu ft)
   7 shelves at 300 mm (11½ in) centres, ¾ full:
      200 books/m^2 (19 books/sq ft)
      80 books/m^3 (2.5 books/cu ft)
Compact book storage, 7 shelves:
   330 to 650 books/m^2 (30 to 60 books/sq ft)
   133 to 260 books/m^3 (3.7 to 7.5 books/cu ft)
The manufacturer will be able to produce the exact figures in this case.

6 Feasibility study

The approach to the study

As we have seen, a kind of feasibility study may have taken place even before the formal appointment of the architect: the university surveyor or city architect may have been required to see whether a library would be possible or economically feasible on a suggested site. Now the appointed architect will begin the design process by preparing a firm proposal to the authority, complete with notional costing; if this is approved, more detailed work can proceed.

The design process involves the reconciliation of two opposing classes of information: clients' requirements as expressed in the brief (i.e. what the need is) and the constraints acting upon a possible solution (i.e. the factors which will tend to prevent the fulfilment of these needs). The first step in designing a building enclosure therefore is to identify and record both requirements and constraints as far as they are known, together with the general background information which forms the context of the design problem. Because so many elements of a library are common to all buildings, and others are common to all public buildings, the architect will be dealing with matters which are thoroughly familiar to him and quite outside the librarian's province. For the rest of the programme, as followed in this book, matters which concern the architect only – form, structure, mechanical services, layouts, exterior cladding and so on – will be discussed solely as they impinge upon the librarian's direct concerns. Other features still within the architect's jurisdiction, such as lighting, floor covering, shelving, furniture and so on, will be considered in more detail because the librarian will have something to contribute from his professional training and experience. He will know, and need to know, less about them than an architect does, but will look at them from a different viewpoint and background. Familiarity with various alternatives and their particular strengths and weakness in a library context will enable him to see the functional problems against a range of possible solutions. For example, it is not his concern to stipulate categorically the flooring material to be used, but he should record the required contribution, physical, acoustic and psychological, which the flooring will have to fulfil. When he sees what flooring materials are proposed, he will comment on them from his own experience and from his studies of other libraries, and a dialogue will begin because in such a case both sides have something to contribute.

Having studied the brief, the architect has the client's requirements before him; he will himself have considered the more obvious of the constraints upon his freedom. Now he has to approach the problem of design, and his first action is probably to assess the ability of the allotted site to house the quantities indicated in the brief. These, which were expressed in terms of numbers of people and numbers of books and other materials, have to be translated to space requirements; this is to be done while holding firmly in mind the purpose of the library and the activities to be carried out in the various sections.

The architect will eventually fix upon a requirement in terms of floor space, and he must look at the site to see how much freedom is given to him. If, within the ground space and the building height allowed, he finds that there is plenty of room, he can pass on to the process of design unrestricted. If, on the other hand, he finds that space will be tight, he is going to have to design a compact, economical building and omit all thought of space-consuming extras, as for example overhanging upper floors or architectural spaces within the perimeter of the site.

He will also analyse the needs of the future users, and these will influence his thoughts about such matters as floor-to-ceiling height, numbers of floors, partition spacing, services and so on. The brief will have itemized users by number, but also by characteristics relevant to the situation (age, sex, rank – which confers privileged spaces in some academic libraries), as well as those factors which might affect their use of the building (e.g. physical disability, social background – as in centres for the disadvantaged – and so on). The nature of the expected occupancy, long-term or short-term, continuous or intermittent, active or sedentary, purposeful or casual – or the proportions of all these within the proposed library – have to be studied.

The architect will then assess the most important constraints and be in a position to begin the process of design. It is difficult to dissect this process and fit it into a programme of activities because it is composed of both rational and intuitive elements. The whole question of the design process is constantly being studied in research organizations, not only the mental processes by which creative ideas evolve but also methods by which these can be stimulated and systematized. These studies are important both in producing more effective creativity in a designer and in encouraging group decisions as well as participation in an area where the initial impulse arises from an irrational, and therefore highly selective, judgement.

In the *Handbook of Architectural Practice and Management*[1] an attempt is made to outline the process of design by dividing it into a series of phases: 1, Assimilation; 2, General study: Part I, Investigation of the nature of the problem; Part II, Investigation of possible solutions or means of solution; 3, Development; 4, Communication. Another way of looking at the same programme is shown in Figure 6:1, from the *AJ Handbook of Building Enclosures*[2]; it is the basis for the Design Guides published by Butterworth Architecture.

It is made clear in the RIBA *Handbook* that 'in practice the mental activity [of the designer] tends to make short flashes from one phase to another according to results achieved and the ideas that are stimulated by the work'. It is obvious that, while there will always be feedback of ideas from later to earlier phases, the more effectively the earlier stages have been thought out, the less delay will arise from later rethinking.

These matters are fundamental to the professional architect's world and are mentioned here only to show how complex and personal must be this stage of the operations. To the librarian the position is that the architect, having received a full statement of the client's requirements and knowing the site, has to consider how to accommodate these requirements in an acceptable way while bearing in mind certain constraints.

At its simplest, then, the architect, knowing the required functions, contents and physical conditions, has to associate them on a known site, place them in a spatial

6:1. Design process

COLLECTION OF DATA

DATA REQUIRED

design requirements
- building type, purpose, occupancy
- flexibility of internal spaces
- security, protection
- users' preferences
- environmental requirements

design constraints
- client's economic policies
- client's building economic policies
- cleaning, maintenance policy
- design life, durability
- availability of resources
- construction programme
- dimensional basis
- insurance, fire brigade, legislation

design context
- site, climate
- programme
- structural context

performance requirements for building fabric
- structural, fire resistance, security
- design life, durability
- cost limits
- environmental performance

DESIGN OF EXTERNAL ENVELOPE

TAKE BASIC DECISIONS
POSITIONS, SHAPES AND SIZES OF OPENINGS
walls and roofs
- consider access and egress
- consider view
- consider daylight and sunlight
- consider ventilation
- consider noise
- consider heat
- review decisions

CHARACTERISTICS OF OPENINGS
walls and roofs
- consider heat, air and sound control
- consider light, view and privacy

CHARACTERISTICS OF SOLID FABRIC
- review earlier structural decisions
- decide solid wall fabric
- decide solid roof fabric
- decide solid lowest floor fabric
- review decisions

TAKE DETAILED DECISIONS
solid fabric
- decide details of wall fabric
- decide details of roof fabric
- decide details of lowest floor fabric

openings
- decide details of wall openings
- decide details of roof openings

junctions
- decide joint sizes
- decide joint shapes
- decide joint materials

TAKE FINAL DECISIONS
whole envelope
- finalise drainage
- finalise cleaning and maintenance
- finalise appearance
- finalise cost plan
- review decisions

DESIGN OF INTERNAL DIVISION

RELATE DESIGN DECISIONS TO PERFORMANCE REQTS.
partitions/floors/ceilings
- adjacent elements
- structural requirements
- support/fixing facilities
- radio-active screening
- dirt resistance
- thermal performance
- sound control
- light and view
- ventilation
- fire resistance/security
- accommodation of services
- durability, maintenance, appearance
- dimensional considerations
- cost plan check

relationship which will enable the known functions to be performed, and choose a suitable 'envelope' in which to enclose them. In practice this is a process of trial and error: during the design process the architect will have visualized many different solutions and sketched many 'envelopes', testing each against the known needs and restraints. The relationship of operational sections, movements – human and material – provision of mains services, consideration of external elements, natural light, noise, access routes – all these factors will be used in shaping and refining his early vision. Some of the factors affecting his aesthetic conception are given below; there can be no rigid order in which these matters are considered and he will continually hold them in mind and balance them against other factors which must be largely subjective. At this stage he is concerned to see whether the project is feasible; later, in his outline planning, and then again in scheme design, he will be concerned with the same subjects but for different reasons and in different degrees of detail. It is never possible to say dogmatically that heating problems, for example, are considered at a certain stage, reader circulation at another stage. The architect will work with his technical experts in collecting information, trying out ideas, measuring, costing and comparing alternative ways of providing a feasible solution.

In all this work there will be the limitation of constraints. They will be multifarious: in Britain many will be official and statutory – overall town planning regulations (limits on height, colour, and style of cladding), fire and safety rules, sanitary considerations and the ubiquitous Building Regulations. In some countries they will be less stern and restrictive. To these can be added the constraints laid down by the client – required life of the building, degree of flexibility and so on – and the limitations imposed by the building industry of the country – controlling dimensions which make possible the use of prefabricated elements (doors, windows etc.) and the limits of building methods available (affected by access to the site). But everywhere the most limiting constraint will be the authority's cost target. Almost every design decision the architect makes will be dominated by this; almost every architect 'could have done better' if he had not been hampered by cost limits.

Site feasibility

The selection by the authority of the site for the future library has already been mentioned. In too many cases this has been settled long before the architect comes upon the scene, but in some cases he may already have been involved, particularly when the library is to be within a university campus. The choice of site is absolutely crucial for the project. In his study of the Sedgewick (underground) Library in British Columbia, Mason[3] quotes the architect Richard Henriquez of Todd and Henriquez as saying 'I learned that form does not follow function; form follows site.'

It might happen that the architect is forced to report after investigation that the chosen site is not feasible for the successful accommodation of the proposed materials and functions. He may make alternative suggestions, either a change of site or (more frequently, in view of the possible firm pre-commitment to the site) a variation in the proposals in the brief. Where a separate building is to be erected, the points which follow below must be given close attention: where the site is within an existing complex or part of a building designed basically for other purposes, many of the points are inapplicable.

From the requirements of the brief and his knowledge of the site, the architect will already have arrived at general ideas as to height and shape of the building. He must now consider:

1. *The relationship with existing buildings* in the immediate neighbourhood, with regard to both the general environment and possible limitations on his freedom to plan.
2. *The adequacy* of the site for future extensions to the building, if this has been a requirement of the brief, and the relationship of the library to other buildings which may later share the site. In particular, immediate external circulation routes will need careful study and discussion with those who will be responsible for other buildings.
3. *External traffic patterns* in the neighbourhood as decreed in the overall traffic plans; whether they allow, or restrict, road access to the building in a way considered suitable.
4. *Noise factor* If noise from the immediate surrounding area is inevitable (traffic, student movement and so on), provision for protection must be made in the structure, layout, surfaces and external environment.
5. *Immediate surroundings* – whether space is available for gardens or other areas to insulate the library from its neighbourhood or to improve its appearance.
6. *Car parking* – a fast-growing, space-consuming requirement which may have been indicated in the brief. Cooperation with other occupiers of the complex may be possible or there may be opportunities underneath the building. The planning authority or the police will be concerned in consultations on this subject.
7. *Pedestrian access routes:* the possible need for weather protection for readers approaching the building.
8. *Access for servicing* may be a major problem and may have to be kept quite separate from the public approach.

Other equally important considerations in the viability of the site require the expert advice of the specialist consultants (especially engineers) who form part of the design team and who must now be approached. Points include:

1. *The geological basis of the site* A soil engineer may be needed to advise as to its suitability for bearing a multi-storey structure. A layer of rock immediately below the surface may mean that the excavation of basements would be too expensive; water hazards may be similarly restricting, or there may be mining subsidence problems.
2. *The adequacy of mains services* – water, gas and electricity supply, drainage and sewer access. Plumbing and drainage experts may be needed and almost certainly consultants on the heating, cooling, ventilating or air-conditioning system envisaged; at this stage only general principles and major drawbacks need to be considered.
3. *The suitability of the site* for incorporating the trunking and machinery for mains services. This will include study of the access routes, both those needed for the construction of the building and maintenance and renewal of the services themselves and those for vehicles used by service engineers. If the brief required provision for possible expansion to be made horizontally, then preliminary planning will be complicated by the need to place access routes and physical services where they can be used in the expanded building of the final concept. Unless it is absolutely essential, possible expansion should be confined to a single direction only.

When these and other aspects have been considered and assessed, the architect is in a position to study the question of the orientation of the building, to make the best use of both site and design. He must study the impact the future building will have on the passer-by, on those who will see it from local vantagepoints and the way it will declare itself on the skyline.

He will be concerned with the effect of natural light at various times of the day and the way that wind and rain will affect the building from different directions. This will mean a study of prevailing winds and climate, because siting and orientation can have a strong effect on thermal efficiency. He will also need to make basic decisions, in consultation with the local planning authority, about the main access route and the approaches to other possible entrances to the building.

The form of the building

The most immediately obvious result of the design concept will be the external shape (form*) of the building. The architect will wish to create a shape which not only encloses the functions satisfactorily but also makes a certain impact upon the user and the passer-by, interacting with its surroundings in an agreeable way. He will also have the not unnatural wish to achieve some degree of originality. In this lies temptation; he will do well to visit some 'striking and original' library buildings and note the price which users and librarians have had to pay for this originality in terms of inconvenience, extra staffing and large heating, ventilating and maintenance bills. A few architects, mainly eminent practitioners with a 'style of their own', have been notorious in the library profession. Keyes Metcalf, whose experience of library planning is never likely to be equalled, 'had the distinct impression that there had been an unfortunate tendency in recent years (reversing the trend of the first decade after the Second World War) on the part of some of the more capable and better-known [American] architects to attempt to attract attention by glamorous and exciting buildings which subordinate function to other features'[4].

The question of the librarian's legitimate interest in the appearance of the building cannot be swept away by such clichés as 'To the client the function; to the architect the form.' The end product has to fulfil an overall function in serving, attracting, and making comfortable, future readers, and the architect is bound to design to meet the requirements of the brief in these respects. For an architect to claim that he himself can decide these matters by a number of visits to other libraries is absurd; a librarian's lifetime experience, together with his unique view of the future service which his library has to give, is indispensable. As civilized people, librarians should be concerned that the future library is as aesthetically acceptable as possible; if it becomes famous for its beauty they will be the last to complain. On the other hand those librarians who still complain about 'architectural monumentalism' (by which they mean classical monumentalism) are out-of-date. Contemporary architects have reacted against this style far more than have librarians, and there is little danger of it today. Indeed the fashion throughout this century has been moving more and more towards simple, uncluttered buildings. The modular planning made possible by new building methods led a reaction against fixed-function

buildings (including libraries), but by the 1960s flat, soulless glass boxes were out of favour and we are seeing a return to a reinterpretation of traditional forms but designed around the functions which they are to house.

It is obvious that the architect's concepts will be influenced (or even determined) by his professional education and experience. His studies will have included a detailed analysis of all the styles of the past and he will have examined the seminal buildings. However, the greatest single influence upon him will be the immediate environment: unless specifically authorized (as, for instance, Rogers was at the Beaubourg), he is not likely to create anything startlingly at variance with the architecture of the particular place and time. A site, especially a restrictive site, will limit him; when he has to design for a wedge-shaped site between roads he is tied to a tight, balanced building and is unlikely to be able to produce originality. Original forms *are* produced, and, within limits, the librarian should provide encouragement. It may be that the present-day equivalent of monumentalism is the love of artistic gimmickry, such as fountain courts and gardens, open stairways to mezzanine floors, and glass walls. Quite distinct from this movement, although perhaps attributable to the same pressures, is a reaction in architecture against the harshness (raw concrete) and the grandiose character which have been evident in recent decades. There are signs of a return to cosiness, to a feeling for the greater importance of ornament, to human scale. This is the business of the architect and not the librarian, but the latter will inevitably feel its impact. Because his mission is to encourage and attract people to his library and to serve them in surroundings designed to help rather than impress by magnificence, he may welcome it.

In some cases the brief may have made clear exactly what form of building is to be provided and even the way it is to relate to its environment. An extreme example was the new library for Glasgow University, where the architect was told that 'an essential consideration in design was that while the new library should dominate the university development on the north side of University Avenue, it should nevertheless be compatible with the Gilbert Scott building which is the most significant of the university's existing buildings.'[5] It should be remembered too that despite all the talk about the unsuitability for library work of a classically monumental building, the client has the right to demand such a structure from the architect; in that case it will probably choose the architect specifically for his expertise in this sort of work.

The design of the building enclosure and its divisions will normally be approached after the basic position and orientation of the building on the site have been tentatively decided and after decisions have been taken on general building form and structural type – load-bearing walls, pitched roof etc. The question of the relationship between major elements to be housed, particularly large closed stack areas and the readers, will also be influential. In the relationship lists and diagrams the librarian may have asked for a pattern of association between activity areas which will be virtually impossible except in a spherical building; this the architect is unlikely to provide, but he might be tempted towards a circular one. There are precedents – not only the well-known ones of the British Library Reading Room, the Library of Congress, Manchester Central Library and the Brotherton Library of the University of Leeds, but also a number of small lending libraries. At least one of these should be visited and its problems studied before such a risk is taken. Similar parallels of great value can be found with other 'original' shapes – there is little which is really new. The square

*To an architect the term 'form' connotes a number of factors including space, size and mass which have to be organized in an ordered way; for a librarian the term will usually mean the visible external shape which is only one element of it.

6:2. Glasgow University Library (right) (Architect William Whitfield)

6:3 and below. Crescent-shaped library: Chandlers Ford, Hampshire County (County Architect)

6:4. University of Qatar at Doha (Architect Kamal El Kafrawi)

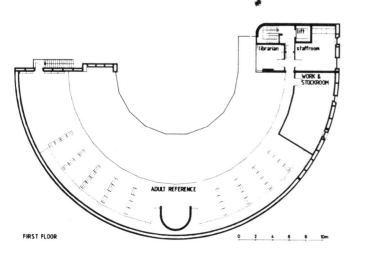

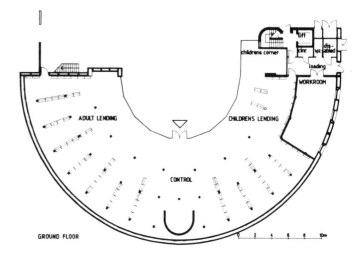

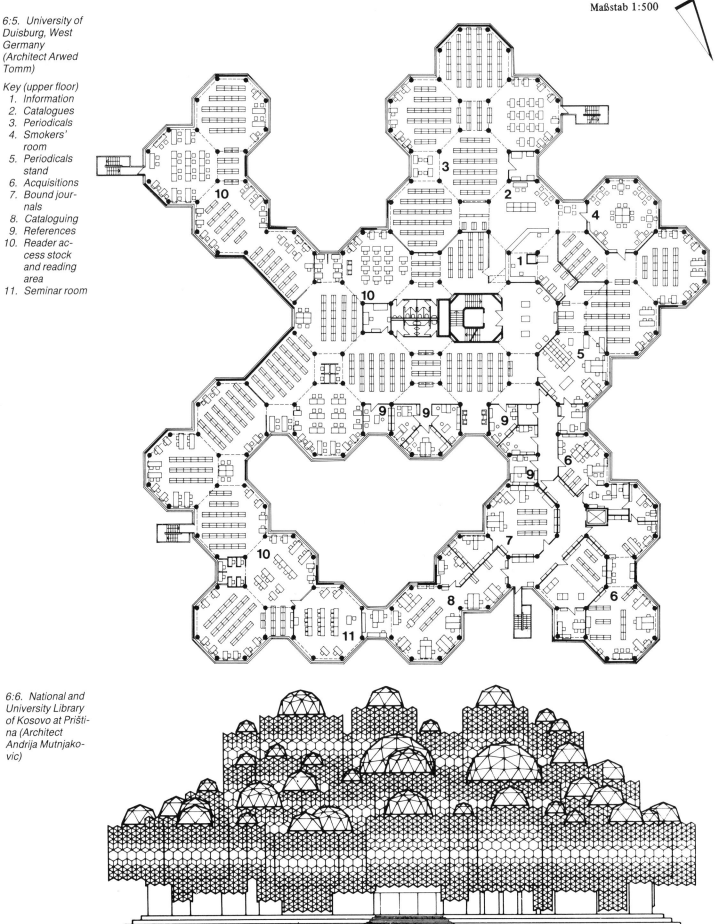

Maßstab 1:500

6:5. University of
Duisburg, West
Germany
(Architect Arwed
Tomm)

Key (upper floor)
1. Information
2. Catalogues
3. Periodicals
4. Smokers'
   room
5. Periodicals
   stand
6. Acquisitions
7. Bound jour-
   nals
8. Cataloguing
9. References
10. Reader ac-
    cess stock
    and reading
    area
11. Seminar room

6:6. National and
University Library
of Kosovo at Pristi-
na (Architect
Andrija Mutnjako-
vic)

6:7. National Autonomous University of Mexico (UNAM) Library (Architect Juan O'Gorman)

6:8. San Juan Capistrano Public Library, California (Architect Michael Graves)

6:9. English village library: Burnham, Buckinghamshire (County Architect)

shape has many advantages, particularly minimum distance between extremities, maximum opportunity for re-arrangement and, above all, an external wall-to-floor ratio which produces economies both in building costs and heat losses through external walls. Walls, particularly those containing windows, are expensive, so a square shape is comparatively cheap, although the proportion of cheapness falls as upper floors are added. The proportionate gain in construction costs against other shapes, even rectangles, and the fact that the larger the single-floor square the cheaper, are well brought out in the *AJ Handbook of Building Enclosure*[6] in a way which even librarians can understand. On the other hand it is fair to say that a rectangle may have advantages by reason of possible use of beams and a one-way structural slab system. Obviously there will come a point where lighting, heating and ventilating costs have to be considered: it used to be said that no part of a library floor should be more than 13 m (40 ft) from a window for natural light, so that would limit the building to 26 m (80 ft) deep. In the same way when natural ventilation is to be used the building will have to be narrow. Another limit will be the maximum distance which the fire regulations will allow between any reader and the fire exits. From the functional point of view in an academic library the deep square is attractive because bookstacks can be housed in blocks in the centre with readers placed on the perimeter where there can be natural light. Nevertheless the point will come when horizontal movement becomes so excessive as to be counter-productive, but in general it is true that the most economical building in both construction and energy costs is one of a square shape and on not more than three floors. Faulkner-Brown[7] has shown that heat loss is proportional to the amount of permanent walling (assuming that the insulating qualities of the walls are fixed factors) and that such walls vary between 10% and 20% of the total construction costs.

In a high proportion of cases, however, particularly in public libraries, the architect will not have the freedom to choose the basic ground plan. The requirements of the brief may tie him to finding a solution of a problem involving vital relationships with other buildings within a complex. Such a position arose when the board of the University of Ulster decided that it required a library on the 'spine' principle in order that the various subject collections should be sited in proximity to the appropriate teaching and study areas. Again, a board decision of the Robarts Library of the University of Toronto required the architect to provide 950 lockable carrels, each to have an outside-facing window. This, and other reasons, 'generated the triangle, the geometrical form that provides the greatest perimeter area for any given square footage'. It is only fair to add that Mason,[8] who quotes this from his excellent critique of the library, describes the triangle, as a library shape, as 'a common cliché which did very poorly for school libraries in the 1960s'.

More commonly the site itself may dominate the ground plan in circumstances where a square would be wasteful of space. In other cases the architect may feel that in the particular environment a square would be both inappropriate and dull – and it is he who is making the decision. Circular, triangular, crescent-shaped (Figure 6:3), octagonal (Central Library, Houston, Texas); I myself have been asked to work on plans for a star-shaped library building, but fortunately the design was rethought. Sometimes it is incumbent upon the architect to design a building whose exterior is to be a reflection of national or even religious feeling. The library of the University of Qatar at Doha (indeed the whole university) consists of a series of interlocking octagons (the octagon is of course of great significance in Islamic art). Ventilation is provided by a sophisticated system but it is housed within the traditional wind-towers of the Gulf. (The University Library of Duisburg, West Germany, also uses a basic ground plan of interlocking octagons, but they do not dominate the external appearance.)

The National and University Library of Kosovo at Priština is another example of a building which uses forms derived from the region's past, in this case Byzantine and Turkish. One of the most common characteristics is a square building bearing a dome, and this has become a symbol of the spirit of Kosovo. A similar feeling affected the library of the National Autonomous University of Mexico, although it did not determine the ground plan. Instead the walls were almost entirely covered by the mosaics of architect-artist Juan O'Gorman, which celebrate the history of Mexico.

Less dramatic, but equally reflective of the spirit of the community, are the illustrations of the public libraries of San Juan Capistrano, California, and Burnham, Buckinghamshire. One represents a Hispano-American, the other an English village, feeling.

In the West the square ground plan is chosen usually for mundane reasons, economy and efficiency of operation and maintenance being major factors; but there may be disadvantages. In very many cases a square shape on plan seems to mean, automatically, a flat roof. Although this may be reasonable, and is of recent years by far the most common roof, it has one disadvantage which many libraries know to their cost: it can leak. Indeed there is a strong body of opinion in the building trade which holds that there is no such thing as a leak-proof flat roof. This may be challenged in the unusual case of the University of Leicester (see p. 111), which has twin lakes on the roof,

partly to help with thermal control, partly to produce a reserve of water for the mechanical services, but also because a roof which can never dry out can be made watertight. Apart from this unusual idea, however, the *Architects' Journal* reported that 'over one third of the flat roofs of 323 Crown buildings surveyed three years ago leaked and over half were considered unsatisfactory.'[9] This comment could well be brought to the attention of the architect.

In some very small libraries there will be little real choice as to shape. If it is to be an independent building using minimum ground area and open plan, then maximum use must be made of natural lighting, and this usually means a single-storey building with window walls and/or roof lights. There must be adequate space for the circulation of the numbers of users (estimated by means of a survey), a central main entrance, a control counter combining maximum opportunity for supervision with economy of staffing, and nominally separated areas for adult reading, children's reading and 'other activities' as defined in the brief. It is still worth consulting Wheeler and Githens' *The American Public Library Building*,[10] although it is almost fifty years old, because it records just about every possible combination of room positionings which can be dreamed up for a small public library: many of them date back to the Carnegie recommendations of 1911 but are still viable.

Examples of plans here show a minimal public library plan; apart from the possible use of a basement for storage and staff toilets there is little real difference between these

6:10. Library of 180 m² to 270 m² (2000 to 3000 sq ft)

6:11. Library of 460 m² to 930 m² (5000 to 10 000 sq ft)

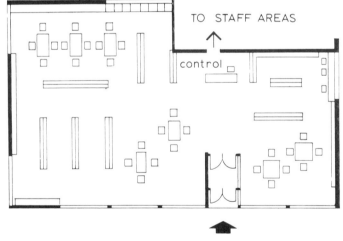

6:12. Small special library

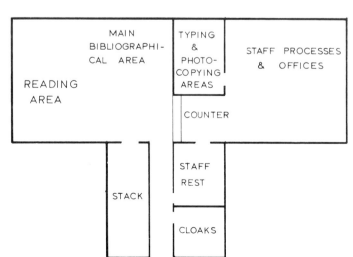

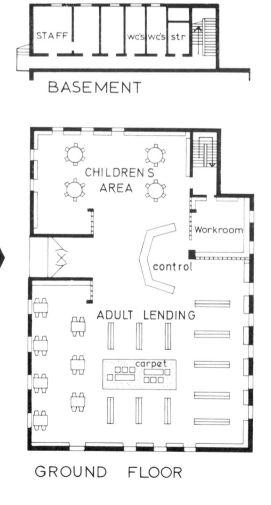

plans. The difference in the resulting buildings will depend on the flair of the architect and the arrangement and style of furniture.

The appropriate space allowance by population is laid down in IFLA Standards (see Chapter 19), but when considering a floor area of more than say 1000 m^2 (10 000 sq ft) to serve a population much above 10 000, complications arise, chiefly because the demarcation between reader service areas must become more clearly defined. Much depends also on the social requirements of the region: a very detailed study of this subject was carried out for the British Office of Arts and Libraries using the actual needs of a town with its complications of siting and environmental compatibility.[11]

A small library which must occupy a part of the building of the institution it serves, particularly a school, hospital or special library, seldom has freedom to choose the perfect shape. The area will often be the wing of a building, and because the heart of these libraries will be a staffed information and service point, and the two main elements a reading area and a staff area, L and T shapes are commonly used, the entrance and the reader service point being at the junction of the laterals. An obvious layout is shown in Figure 6:12.

Structure

With the clients' requirements, the general constraints, a feeling for form and some idea of his preferred solutions to internal space considerations in mind, the architect will now turn to a fundamental matter which is no concern whatever of the librarian: that is, the structure. As in all aspects, the element of cost (both cost of construction and cost of running the building) will dominate the architect's thoughts. The brief will have informed him of the required life of the building, and he will know how the desired flexibility will affect his thoughts on the load-bearing structure. Even in his preliminary sketching he will have ideas about the basic structural elements and the methods of construction to be used. He will be very conscious that different methods can cause perhaps the greatest of all variations in the overall cost of the building, and if for this reason only he will give them very careful thought. If the building must be multi-storey and without internal load-bearing walls (in the interests of flexibility), then he will be very much concerned with the size of the structural grid and the columns. The latter, especially if they are intended not only to support a building several stories high but also to carry ducts, may have to be wide; the result could be a forest of columns almost as inhibitive of change as the internals walls they superseded.

A decision has to be made as to the size of the square or rectangle which is to be the base for planning structural support. First the designer determines the minimum sizes of essential basic spaces within the building (e.g. floor-to-ceiling heights, door head heights etc.). He will then select heating and ventilating controlling dimensions (working sizes, not basic sizes). By dimensional coordina- tion, which relates dimensions to the size of building components and assemblies, a rectangular and three- dimensional grid of basic modules will be established. The architect can then choose the one most suitable for his purpose. The controlling dimensions for spacing structural elements on plan on axial lines (which is what concerns us here) are usually, in Britain, in multiples of 300 mm* (with

100 mm as second choice). If columns are established in multiples of 300 mm (from 900 mm up), then the grid will be continuous throughout the floor and can be easily used in plans. Of course grids cannot be considered on plan alone, and vertical controlling dimensions, on the same principles, will also be determined. There is a difference between the planning and the structural grid, but this is a matter which the architect understands completely and of which the librarian needs to know only the basic facts. Suffice it to say that a three-dimensional framework has been notionally created which will accept standardized components with 300 mm as the basic module. These are basic, not working, sizes, and consequently make no allowance for joints and tolerances, which have to be specified separately.

Despite this emphasis on the use of prefabricated elements, the bulk of the work will take place on site, and the architect will use his design skills to minimize on-site construction costs. The design will largely decide cost levels because of its decisions on the provision of expensive elements (windows, for example). Such vari- ables, which can be of great cost importance in a small building, will matter much less in a large one, where specially manufactured items become both comparatively and actually cheaper since they are used in large numbers.

In most modern library buildings there is a framework on the exterior, and columns within, the building being without load-bearing walls. (Although exterior curtain walls have been described as 'non-load-bearing', they are in fact loaded horizontally by wind force and vertically by their own dead weight. The point is that they do not carry the structure; it carries their weight.) Under this method internal walls can be merely divisions, whether made of brick walling or fabric partition: they will be changeable according to the requirements of the brief. The specifica- tion here of frequency of possible change (every month or every ten years) will guide the architect in the choice of partitioning material. Where a number of fixed-function reader service areas are planned, zones of flexibility can be established within those areas.

The choice of the structural grid can be a complex matter: for example, in a multi-storey structure, alien factors such as offices over, or a car park under, the library may mean a number of different, but related, grids within the building. In most circumstances, however, the grid should be based upon the needs of the clients: in this case, the librarian and the readers. The grid chosen, and in particular the column spacing, will have a strong influence on the efficient use of the library space by its effect on the siting of shelving, reader seating and furniture, and above all in determining the amount of book stacking that can be installed. The Causewayside Building of the National Library of Scotland uses a grid of 900 × 900 mm, chosen deliberately because of the book shelving length, and this size is used throughout the building, even on the cladding (see p. 143). The columns exist, of course, to support the weight above, and their configuration will reflect this in one of a number of ways. In the case of the Causewayside Building, 'the floor slab is in the form of a coffered slab on a 900 mm module with solid sections immediately over the columns. The reinforced concrete columns are a uniform size throughout the building to suit the layout of the bookstack area and they have a capital to match the floor slab coffers.'[12] The relationship between the number of

---

*Although equivalence in sizes between metric and imperial systems in this book are, in accordance with normal practice, rounded up (because they refer not to the components

themselves but to the spaces required to house them), this does not apply to modules where metric and imperial sizes must be used separately.

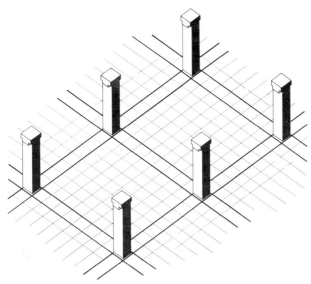

6:13. Uniform-sized columns with capitals arranged to match floor slab coffers. (Causewayside Building, National Library of Scotland, Edinburgh; architects Andrew Merrylees Associates)

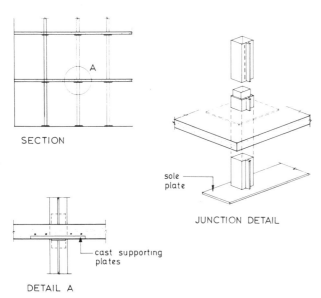

6:14. Metal uprights supporting a reinforced concrete floor

SECTION

A

sole plate

JUNCTION DETAIL

cast supporting plates

DETAIL A

6:15. Self-supporting double-height stacks, complete with their own lighting (Schulz GMBH Speyer, GFR)

books which can be efficiently housed and the structural grid is dealt with in Chapter 13, but it is not the only point of importance; if the grid allows for tables with seating between columns for six readers instead of eight and leaves unusable space in other areas, then the loss to the library as a working unit can be considerable. The grid should also allow for offices of reasonable sizes to be planned by fitting demountable partitions without column interference.

The Danish State Library Inspectorate's committee has published a detailed survey of module planning[13] and has made very definite recommendations. The committee first considered using functional modules based on various shelf lengths and found that no generally accepted shelf length would produce a structural module that would be acceptable for efficient shelving arrangements, both in linear run and in width of stack placing. They then took what they considered the optimum bookshelf centre-to-centre distance for a small public library (3 m), and argued that only this size of functional module can be efficiently used to obtain a suitable structural grid size; indeed they go further and suggest that 'at every stage of the work of planning, the library's functional module should be used directly as the layout or planning module of P = 3 m.'

The arguments are well worth considering but two points should be noted: First, the standards are meant to apply only to small public libraries (library premises in areas with populations between 5000 and 25 000) in Denmark. In larger buildings it is reasonable to take into account much larger structural grids which will offer greater flexibility. Second, the possibility of using different shelf lengths within a single library is given full weight. Possibly this factor could be discounted in larger libraries because of other difficulties which may arise when it becomes necessary to move shelves around to accommodate changes in book stock positioning.

In large libraries the positioning of the stacks (especially closed-access stacks, which will be packed more closely) is vital. Books in bulk are heavier than readers, and if a large part of the book stack is to be kept in closely packed conditions, then it is important at the planning stage to establish where it is to be placed. This problem was handled in the past by separating book storage areas from reader areas. Historical examples are given by Thompson[14] and Brawne,[15] and this is briefly discussed on pp. 79–80. To obtain a fair measure of flexibility in such conditions, the most usual arrangement in academic libraries today is for the book stack to form the core of the building, leaving thte perimeter for reading areas, making the best use of window light.

Other alternatives are still used, particularly in closed-access situations. The stack tower, which has economic advantages (and requires less aisle space), had a vogue, but it is often expensive in retrieval and impracticable where reader access may be desirable at some future date. The Robarts Library of the University of Toronto has book stacks on Floors 9–13 of its fourteen floors, with compact book storage underground. This is not likely to become common practice. Some libraries of an earlier period contained multi-storey stacks, one book stack supporting others, not as part of the structure of the building, with integral stairways and catwalks. After a period of neglect, such systems are once again offered commercially. The uprights of the stack shelving system can be used to support a reinforced concrete floor, usually with the assistance of a capping plate. There are complications in such a proposal, conduits, for example, needing to be set into the concrete. These systems produce savings on the basic structure, but it is important to check that they comply with the building regulations.

Instead of having a whole floor of reinforced concrete supported in this way, gangways only may be supported, the bookshelves being bracketed from the pillars which run through the floors. Where two or three floors only of book stacking are concerned this can be a viable, and indeed a very attractive, proposition. Proprietary shelving manufacturers offer such multi-tier systems in steel and they are very well suited for making use of areas of very high ceiling, for example in converting a warehouse to library use. Being basically a shelving system and non-structural, it offers great flexibility.

The architect also needs to know the basic lengths and widths of stacks and, in very general terms, how they are to be accommodated in the various reader service conditions. This he should find in the brief: standard shelving is traditionally made in 900 mm (3 ft) units, and if mass-produced shelving of this size is to be used in a large stack area the grid should be chosen so that shelving can run in either direction, with 5.4 m (18 ft) as the probable minimum acceptable length between columns, and 8.1 m (27 ft) the maximum. This is very general: in practice it is the between-column distances in both directions which are the deciding factors as far as stacks are concerned, although the architect has many other factors to take into account. Similarly, if we take 1350 mm (4 ft 6 in) as a common size for the distance between stack centres in open stack conditions, a square size divisible by both 900 mm (3 ft) and 1350 mm (4 ft 6 in) will theoretically enable the direction of runs of stacks to be altered by 90° if required.

Because the sizes we have been considering are nominal ones, the answers in practice are not so easy. A 900 mm (3 ft) shelf will not really fit in a 900 mm (3 ft) bay because of the way the elements are measured; similarly, because a standard 900 mm (3 ft) stack bay is measured from centre to centre of units, six such units will not normally fit into an exact 5.4 m (18 ft) length. In the same way, because the planning grid square, to the architect, may run from centre to centre of the columns, the resultant space is not the same as that between faces; the thickness of the columns will be a decisive factor. It is vital that the actual, not the nominal, sizes of all elements are known. This is not to say that the convenient size of shelving bays or reading alcoves must dominate structural planning. If circumstances require, the architect must study the possibility of using shelving equipment of special dimensions to meet a particular situation. He must certainly discuss such a proposal with the librarian: by contrast the librarian's stipulation of a certain type of shelving might be a major consideration in the architect's decision about the structural grid.

Columns

The choice of columns for a library without load-bearing walls can be a crucial factor. In most aspects – material, strength, shape – the architect and his structural engineering consultants alone are concerned. In the positioning of the columns throughout the library and the size of the columns (and, perhaps even more, the size of the housings), the librarian is directly interested. Column placing is a direct result of the structural grid chosen, although the columns are not necessarily placed at each corner of the grid. The positioning of columns at intervals inappropriate for the library's economic operation – shelving, reading, staff siting – can be a disaster.

In areas planned for formal rows of book stacks (or which might be used for them at some future date), the size on plan of a pair of columns should, for efficiency of shelving, use up together not more than one shelving unit:

two 450 mm (18 in) columns within a stack run will therefore cause the loss of only one 900 mm (3 ft) shelf and not upset the run of the other stacks. If the columns must be larger than 450 mm (18 in) in one direction, it is better to have the longer side within the the stack run, even accepting the loss of two shelf tiers, than to have it protrude into the between-stack space and thus force stacks further apart, with a much greater loss of shelf space. It is possible to utilize the wasted space by making special shelves (at extra cost and loss of flexibility) or by putting in short consultation or reading shelves, but these are poor expedients. Rectangular columns will, of course, limit flexibility in that a 90° change of direction of the stack runs will not be possible without loss of shelving efficiency.

In the Düsseldorf University Library the columns on the perimeter are 600 × 600 mm (2 ft × 2 ft), but in the middle of the floor they are 1000 × 600 mm (3 ft 3 in × 2 ft 0 in). This has no effect in the open areas (although in theory it is a bar to future change), but it is a disadvantage in the stack, although the bookcases have been placed parallel with the longer side, as explained above. Serious consideration of the practical use of spaces left between columns, or outside columns, is always essential.

The between-column distance should also be suitable to accommodate settings of tables and chairs, combinations of shelving and furniture, as well as to allow for standard-width aisles. 6900 × 6900 mm (22 ft 6 in × 22 ft 6 in) or 8400 × 8400 mm (27 × 27 ft) have been cited as the optimum sizes for grid squares in large libraries (for reasons given in Chapter 13). Obviously the larger the clear space between columns, the better for the library's purpose, but there is a great deal more to the matter than this. The grid square can seldom be used absolutely consistently throughout a library building of more than one storey: some features such as entrance halls and lecture rooms may need special arrangements whereby the columns bound larger areas. If column thicknesses are to vary on different floors (for example thicker ones on the lower floors to support the structural load), the grid square available for library use will also vary slightly.

Column sizes will depend on the structural decisions, such as fire resistance and whether they are to contain service ducts. Air-circulation ducts inside columns have the advantage that air can be directed out into semi-isolated areas such as carrels. In order to carry these ducts the column housings may have to be rectangular, one section containing the ducts and the other the support. The architect may choose this system rather than house the ducts under the ceilings; as efficiency of shelving is affected by larger columns, he should put the matter to the librarian in terms he can understand. An interesting variation is found in the Birmingham (England) Central Library, where the large columns necessary to support an 11 m (36 ft) grid square, and to house ducts, have been made cruciform on plan, individual casual seating being features against some column spaces. It should not be forgotten that columns can not only carry ducting but may be valuable as outlets for power or communications wiring (just as the wiring can travel through the posts which are part of the proprietary partitioning systems).

Librarians will always prefer columns to be square (or within a square on plan) and as small as possible: 200 mm (8 in) square metal columns suit admirably, but if such columns are used, especially in public areas, they should be painted in bright colours to make them noticeable; neutral-coloured metal columns are a potential hazard, as readers often walk into them. Such small columns are seldom possible in multi-storey buildings because fire regulations (in Britain) decree that all columns which

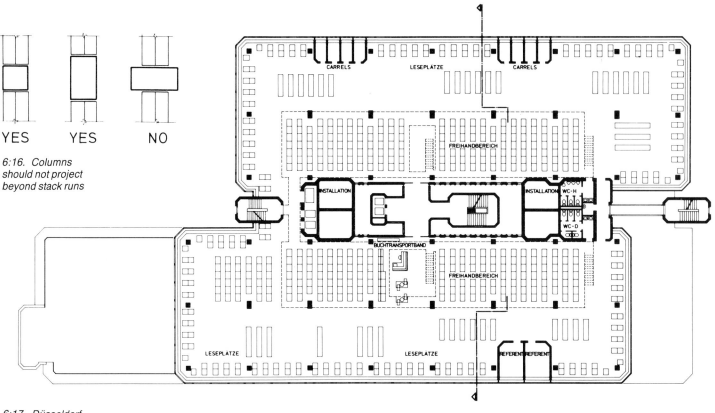

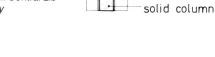

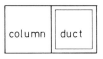

YES   YES   NO

6:16. Columns should not project beyond stack runs

6:17. Düsseldorf University Library: effect of column spacing on book stack distances

6:18. Effect on grid squares of columns of differing thickness

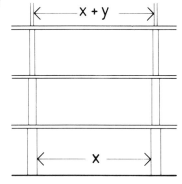

x + y

x

6:19. Cruciform columns: Birmingham Central Library

— seating
— ducting
— solid column

— seating
— solid column

6:20. Column and duct in one housing

| column | duct |

6:21. Seats around columns: Metro Reference Library, Toronto

support upper floors must have a certain number of hours' fire resistance. This is usually achieved by housing them in concrete, although there are alternatives. Circular columns leave awkward, dirt-attracting spaces on the floor around them; if they are absolutely essential (when converting an existing building, for example), it is possible, in reader service areas, to 'lose' them by fitting seats or even book shelving around them. Columns with a plastered surface need to be protected against the impact of book trolleys. The prevalent fashion for white-painted columns may be visually attractive but should be accepted only after serious attention to the maintenance costs involved; readers inevitably handle columns as they pass them, and many libraries are marred by grubby, finger-marked columns. 'Washable' is a word librarians have learned to dread.

As we have seen, it is common in areas such as entrance halls, lecture rooms and so on for some columns to be omitted to give larger open spaces. It seems to a librarian, therefore, that it would be structurally possible for similar larger spaces without columns to be provided elsewhere also – even in stack areas. Although the librarian can take no useful part in the studies and discussions in this part of the programme, his primary brief could indicate areas (or rather parts of the functional pattern) where open, columnless spaces would be of critical importance. If it is proposed to cantilever out beyond a line of columns to gain space on the upper periphery (and provide valuable shading for the floor below), the extra space, however attractive, can be wasted unless it is at least 1800 mm (6 ft) wide and so usable for tables or shelving bays.

Columns should be uniform in section throughout their heights; the splaying of column feet will impede the use of book trolleys and can be a safety hazard. Tapering columns, which seem to attract some architects, can cause loss of shelving space: bookcases cannot be fitted close to them without looking awkward. A space left between column and a bookcase or another fitting must be clearly wide enough for a reader to pass comfortably. A narrow space, aesthetically desirable in order to allow the column to stand clear, may leave readers unsure as to whether they are to pass through it; inevitably some will squeeze through and the result again will be a grubby column. A common difference of view between architect and librarian on the subject of columns is that in an open, visually important public area, the architect may see columns (if they are essential structurally) as a feature of the interior design. The librarian, on the other hand, is likely to regard them only as hindrances and a cause of wasted space. Discussion on this subject at an early stage is vital: cost enters into it and may well be the determining factor.

Floor loading

To provide adequate foundations and a sound building with strength to withstand the required loads in all parts is a matter for the professional expertise of the architect and his consultants. To them a load is a force, and the term is used to describe those outside forces that act on a building structure. There are three kinds of load:

1. *Dead loads* from the weight of the building itself.
2. *Imposed loads* (live loads) of the people, furniture and materials in the building.
3. *Dynamic loads*, usually natural forces such as winds, or even earthquakes. They are not concerned in this discussion.

Forces are measures in kilograms force per square metre, or in pounds force per square foot; loads in building involve the factor of acceleration and are measured in Newtons per square metre (N/m^2) or more usually kN/m^2; in some countries the term Pascal is used for Newtons per m^2; again in structures usually k/Pa. One lbf per square foot is the equivalent of 0.04788 kN/m^2 or k/Pa.

What concerns us most here is the peculiar nature of library loads, in particular books, which when stacked closely together are heavier than an inexperienced person realizes. 'Normal' books weigh 11.4 kg to 13.6 kg (25 lb to 30 lb) per single run of a 900 mm (3 ft) shelf three-quarters full; but certain categories (bound periodicals and directories, for example) can weight as much as 25 kg (55 lb). Taking the two extremes, then, 11.4 kg (25 lb) to 25 kg (55 lb) for a normal 900 mm (3 ft) shelf three-quarters full, we can say that in a seven-shelf double-sided stack run 5400 mm (18 ft) long with a 1000 mm (3 ft) between-stack distance in a 6900 mm (22 ft 6 in) grid square, the books would weigh between 1.2 kN/m^2 (25 lb/sq ft) and 2.6 kN/m^2 (55 lb/sq ft). This is books alone; the architect can find the weight of shelving from the manufacturers' brochures as well as any other contribution to the imposed load for which allowance has to be made. The simple calculation above can be made with different weight

estimates with the help of the diagrams on pp. 144–47.

The extremes quoted above are indeed extreme; although, as stated, a shelf of heavy books can weigh as much as 25 kg (55 lb), there are very unlikely to be seven such shelves fitted into a single stack tier. The estimates can only be very approximate; 900 mm does not really equal 3 ft; calling shelves three-quarters or four-fifths full can only be a rough (and temporary) guess. For this reason it is considered better here to give the bare ingredients of a calculation to be done with a knowledge of local conditions than to provide an 'instant formula'.

If compact shelving, usually rolling stacks, is to be installed, a high floor loading is called for not only because the machinery and closely packed books are themselves heavy but because the imposed load, upon which the floor-loading factors being considered here depends, is concentrated and not diluted by the unstocked floor area which usually tends to lower the distributed load figures. Such a load can be very much higher than normal book stack weight; firms who make the equipment will be able to supply the exact figures.

Special consideration needs to be given to the equipment of a repair shop or bookbindery: guillotines and presses can be very heavy indeed. It is possible for such spot loads to be positioned along the lines of the load-bearing beams, but this is a limitation on flexibility. It should also be remembered that allowances for imposed loads should apply throughout the expected life of the building; changes in position may occur in the future when the reasons for the original placings have been forgotten.

In theory, to obtain full flexibility in a multi-storey building one has only to know the maximum weight per square metre or foot to be carried anywhere in the building and allow for this everywhere; in practice, high loading levels have to be paid for in some way – larger columns, smaller grid squares, more expensive floors, deeper foundations. Economies may be obtained by sacrificing some flexibility in order to lower loading requirements, for example, by placing the heaviest loads – ventilating plant or rolling book stacks – in a basement.

The floor loading that may be regarded as permissible for libraries varies according to the uses of the different areas. The official British code[16] gives the figures shown in Table 6:1.

Floor loading will also vary according to the structural characteristics of the floor concerned. In Britain the University Grants Committee recognizes three characteristic floor structures[17] and provides standard equivalent uniformly distributed loads (udl) for them:

1. Structures capable of distributing a udl of 6.3 kN/m^2 (133 lb/sq ft) in the direction at right angles to the line of the book stacks, e.g. in-situ reinforced concrete. This loading is permissible if the floor-to-ceiling height does not exceed 2.75 m (9 ft).
2. When there are no spreaders for the loading, beams should be designated to carry a udl of 7 kN/m^2 (150 lb/sq ft).
3. If floor-to-ceiling height is greater than 2.75 m (9 ft), udl load is reckoned as 700 N/m^2 (15 lb/sq ft) for every extra foot height of potential book stack.

In quoting to the structural engineer the maximum load likely to be required in the building, the architect can use the published experience of many library planners. Faulkner-Brown[18] has said:

'In order to support either book stacks or reader spaces, the maximum superimposed floor loading takes on the nature of a constant. It is currently 7 kN/m^2 (150 lb/sq ft).

There is no evidence to show that the floor-loading figure of 9.5 kN/m^2 (200 lb/sq ft) quoted in *Bricks and Mortar-boards*[19] is necessary. Experiments that have taken place tend to show that 5.75 kN/m^2 (120 lb/sq ft) live loads might be enough.'

This is not to suggest that the floor loading needs to be the same throughout the building unless a very stringent requirement for full flexibility is to be met. In the Alexander Library Building in Perth, Western Australia, the floor loading is 6 k/Pa for reading rooms, 7 for offices, 12 for open-stack and 15 for compact stack.[20]

Heating and ventilating

The services aim to provide thermal comfort and atmospheric conditions acceptable to both staff and readers, as well as conditions in which books and other materials can be satisfactorily preserved (see Chapter 10 for details). The methods used in providing them affect the project in both space needs and costs, both initial and running. The heating consultant can provide costs of the alternative methods; the architect will balance cost against space elements in the various proposals. These services are expensive: every architect knows that in an effectively designed library the envelope itself should protect from the outside atmosphere and its vagaries, leaving only the minimal provision to be made by mechanical and electrical services. Nevertheless, as a rough guide, heating, lighting and ventilating represents 20–30% of the structure costs. Air-conditioning can add between 10 and 15% to these: Cohen[21] says that full air-conditioning can add 60% to the building construction costs.

Separate estimates will be produced for the running costs of the three elements (HLV), although they are inter-linked in many ways; for example, heat produced by a high-level lighting installation can sometimes be utilized in the heating system; conversely it is largely heat produced by lighting (and by humans) which cooling equipment has to handle. The costs are also affected by design factors; the lighter the structure, the greater will be the need for cooling and insulation against external heat; in a large building with heat-resistant windows, internal areas will need cooling more than perimeter ones.

Heating and ventilating services, especially in multi-storey buildings, will almost always require some heavy equipment. Even underfloor electric heating may require a special transformer. The choice and design will be matters entirely for the architect and the mechanical consultants, but the librarian is interested in the amount of space the equipment will take up and its position. Briefly the alternatives for housing heavy service equipment are:

1. *On the roof:* not very usual (except for lift housing), but it has been done and has advantages for the intake of air for ventilation and air-conditioning plant.
2. *In an outbuilding:* expensive both in site use and in heat losses in transfer to the library; on the other hand district heating may be supplied from a campus, and small loads of electricity can come from a nearby transformer without the need for internal machinery. If a larger load is needed – the figure has been quoted as low as 100 kW – a special transformer will be needed in the building or nearby. (In order to relate this figure to a librarian's experience, one large electric fire uses 3 kW.)
3. *In the basement:* the obvious place for very heavy machinery with possible savings in loading levels but occupying an area that could be utilized for compact shelving, which is also very heavy; it can have the advantage of minimizing structure-borne noise.
4. *On an intermediate floor* of a tall building: unorthodox, but is said to offer savings in trunking costs because of its central position. It is obviously unpopular with the librarian, who 'loses' a floor (although experience has shown that the lost floor is simply ignored in time); it may also be expensive in terms of sound insulation.

The first and second methods appeal most to the librarian in that they do not use any of the space he needs for library operations.

In the library of the University of Newcastle upon Tyne, heating and ventilating services are provided in four equal zones, each using a small self-contained air-conditioning

Table 6.1 Permissible floor loadings

Use to which building or structure is to be put	Intensity of distributed load			Concentrated load to be applied, unless otherwise stated, over any square with a 300 mm (1 ft) side		
	kN/m^2	kgf/m^2	lbf/ft^2	kN	kgf	lbf
Libraries: Reading rooms without book storage	2.5	255	52.2	4.5	459	1012
Rooms with book storage (e.g. public lending libraries)	4.0	408	83.5	4.5	459	1012
Stack rooms	2.4 for each metre of stack height with a minimum of 6.5	245 for each metre of stack height with a minimum of 663	15.3 for each foot of stack height with a minimum of 136	7.0*	714*	1574*
Dense mobile stacking on mobile trucks	4.8 for each metre of stack height with a minimum of 9.6	490 for each metre of stack height with a minimum of 980	30.6 for each foot of stack height with a minimum of 201	7.0	714	1574
Corridors	4.0	408	83.5	4.5	459	1012
Toilet rooms	2.0	204	41.8	—	—	—

* Fixed seating implies that the removal of the seating and the use of the space for other purposes is improbable.

unit. This keeps the length of air ducts very short, so that low-velocity fans can be used, requiring much less energy. Another arrangement, in the proposed National and University Library of Bosnia-Herzegovina at Sarajevo, has a separate air-conditioning installation for the closed stacks, which are on the top two floors, so that the air-conditioning in the reading areas can be switched off at closing time.

In a truly open-plan building, where acceptable environmental conditions have to be the same in every part, the problem of housing the service ducting can be difficult. Solutions include:

1. *A complete service floor:* this can be a space containing ducts between the concrete (structural) floor and the walking floor, which is supported from it on steel piles. This system is widely used in television studios, where it is undoubtedly necessary because of the mass of wiring and the danger of induction, but it is very expensive. Against the extra cost must be set the elimination of the need for a false ceiling. This saves not only costs but vertical space and could even allow the insertion of an extra floor in a planned tall building.
2. *Ducts within the structural beams or floor slabs* can give a considerable space saving by eliminating the false ceiling, but inspection access could prove a problem.
3. *Ducts exposed under the floor above:* fashionable recently, even to the extent of drawing attention to piping by painting it in violent colours; can save the cost of a suspended ceiling.
4. *Within a suspended ceiling:* the most common, with many variations; can fit in well with the decor and add sound insulation, but there can be problems with compartmentalization for fire defence.

In the design of all service installations in libraries, high priority must be given to sound insulation of plant and equipment. Buffer zones (corridors and storage rooms) have to be established around heavy machine rooms. Not only do the main plant, boiler, fans, refrigeration plant and pumps produce noise; ducts and pipes distributing air and water to the building transfer it, often to the most sensitive areas. Local equipment such as convector fans must also be silenced. Access for maintenance is another important matter: some equipment requires regular maintenance, and unless access points are carefully placed, considerable disturbance to readers can result. Heating and ventilating machinery positions which are not well thought out can prove very expensive in their effects on library functions and space. Walls occupied by air intakes or radiator grilles may be lost to the librarian as shelving space. A recent British prize-winning library, which shall be nameless, has heating fitments fixed at intervals on the floor of the open lending library area. No librarian would award a prize to this arrangement.

Building height

The architect's own assessment of the contents to be housed, tempered by local planning requirements, is likely to have already established the overall height of the building. By varying the structural design it is possible to get more or fewer floors into a building, depending largely on the acceptable floor-to-ceiling height of the rooms and the necessary thickness of the floors. Other factors, both structural and financial, will have to be considered. It is not a matter to be taken lightly, but if a library building can have either five floors, each with a floor-to-ceiling height of 2.75 m (9 ft) and floor thickness of 900 mm (3 ft), or six floors of floor-to-ceiling height of 2.44 m (8 ft) and floor thickness of 600 mm (2 ft), then an extra one-fifth of the total floor area of the library is gained – an extremely important matter. Of course it is not as simple as that; to build

22. Newcastle University Library: ducting arranged to serve four equal zones from four separate air-conditioning units (Architects Faulkner-Brown, Hendy, Watkinson, Stonor)

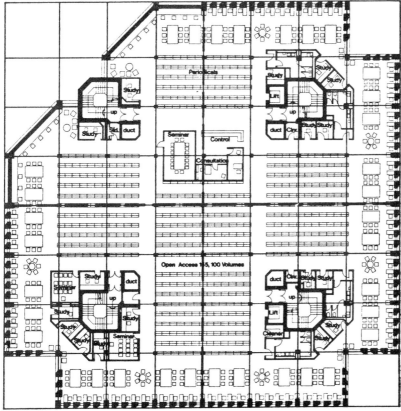

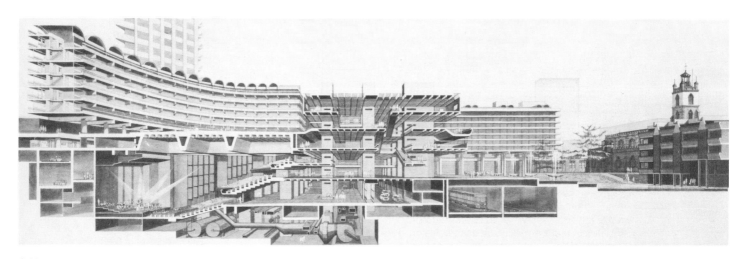

6:23. Barbican Centre; architect's drawing of one section (Architects Chamberlin, Powell and Bon)

narrower inter-floors involves structural engineering decisions. For example, loading requirements for the entire building may have to be increased, necessitating heavier foundations; in addition the costs of a complete extra floor have to be met. Conversely there may be cost compensations; in some types of structure, more and shallower floors can mean fewer brick or tile facings (but probably more windows) and the air-conditioning may be more cost-effective. Lower ceiling heights and different service duct distribution can eliminate the need for false ceilings, although visible pipes are not always liked. These matters are for the architect and his structural engineer; what very much concerns the librarian is the total area available for his operations and the floor-to-ceiling heights.

Large multi-storey complexes are a completely different world, one full of difficulties. Structure, access routes, lifts, escalators and other elements will be common to a number of basically different operations, and library requirements are often but a small matter. The service engineering needs will be enormous, and if the complex includes a theatre the complications are horrendous. The architect's drawing of a section of the Barbican Centre (Figure 6:23) illustrates some of the problems the architects faced, even in the relationship between floors.

Number of floors

Because movement of readers and operations of staff are more efficiently carried out in a horizontal than a vertical

plane, and because second and subsequent floors need complicated mechanical services, lifts and staircases, a single-storey library is usually the most economical. Not invariably, however: in a very large building on one level the horizontal distances involved must pose serious problems. In theory one needs a second floor when horizontal movement on a large ground floor becomes less efficient than vertical movement to an upper one; in practice it is when the ground-floor site gives too little space for all the activities required. Tregenza[22] says: 'the proportion of floor areas that is not directly profitable tends to increase with the height of the building (because of lifts, access stairs and escape stairs)'. And, later, 'a low building extended across the site also increases [the proportion of unprofitable space] but horizontal circulation space may be usable for other purposes (display, exhibitions, etc.).. . . . In general the cost of internal circulation . . . is lowest when the form of a large building is a low compact block.' Note that this applies to a large building. The architect will also bear in mind the requirement of expansion and may consider making the foundations sufficiently heavy to allow for a further floor or floors to be added later. This is theory: in practice there are serious objections to later expansion upward. Building operations are violent, noisy and dirty, and when carried out on top of an already operating library they are very costly indeed. It is often better to build at the outset more floors than are at first required; they can be used for other purposes until the library needs to expand. Usually such a

6:24. Loughborough University of Technology, Pilkington Library; height limited by area planning decisions. Building designed to take advantage of sloping site with main entrance at a middle floor (Architects Faulkner-Brown, Hendy, Watkinson, Stonor)

decision will have been made by the authority at an early stage, but fundamental thinking by the architect can produce such a possible solution in the feasibility study.

Because he is an expert on the optimum use of space the architect may suggest radical solutions which had not been envisaged in the first concepts; many a scheme has been rethought and a new brief prepared because the architect made proposals including ideas which were new to the client. The site itself may offer interesting opportunities: a sloping site can make possible both a variation in floors and an alternative to having a ground-floor entrance. An entrance at the middle level on such a site can be a most useful expedient, because the distance to be travelled from the entrance to any area in the library is less than in any other arrangement of floors. Although such a decision is usually forced by town or campus planning considerations, there are occasions when it has proved so effective that artificial slopes are reported to have been created especially for the purpose.

In ways such as these the architect can make a virtue of an awkward site and at the same time create an unusual design at a lower cost. When floors are planned on different levels or in differing sizes the effect throughout the building can be most striking (for example, the Humanities Library, University of California at San Diego, and, in a lesser degree, Essex University), but there is always a space loss compared with the simple cube. It is up to the architect to reconcile the balance of advantages and disadvantages before making his proposals.

Floor-to-ceiling height

In a single-storey building there are obvious psychological advantages in having a reasonably high ceiling; the added costs are not excessive. Similarly on the ground floor (or,

more accurately, the entrance floor) of a multi-storey building the architect will wish to create an inviting prospect, possibly with a vista which takes the eye deep into the building. If there is insufficient space to provide a specific entrance area to give this required effect (and functionally the entrance hall is often largely wasted space), then the architect will probably wish to achieve his aim by building a high ceiling throughout the whole entrance floor level. The librarian's priorities will be quite different; because the entrance floor is used by all readers, he will want every inch of it for library services. A fashionable compromise is for the areas beyond the entrance hall to be open but with a partial mezzanine floor around or in the rear of the room, an open staircase forming an attractive and eye-catching feature in the middle of the room. The librarian will consider such proposals with caution; to some extent a mezzanine is a fixed-function element and a bar to flexibility: unless it occupies a large part of the area (60% has been suggested as a practical figure), the space thus made available for book and reader accommodation may be poor compensation for the loss of a possible whole extra floor. Because lifts are difficult to install here, readers will be inconvenienced by having to climb stairs to use key sections of the library, and staff will have many extra journeys to fetch and carry books for them. The needs of disabled readers must also be taken into account. The first reading floor itself may suffer by having in parts a low ceiling which makes readers feel cramped.

A different approach to this common problem is shown in the Düsseldorf University Library, where the double-height entrance floor is at the front and the back is occupied by two floors of single-height administration areas. Whatever proposals the architect may have in such matters, he must take into account the requirements of the brief and in particular the librarian's view that efficiency in housing books and readers is at least as important as the psychological effect of an imposing entrance hall.

In formal study areas where on entrance the eye can travel right down the room, the ceiling needs to be of a height of at least 2500 mm (8 ft 3 in); where pressure on space is less acute, 2750 mm (9 ft) would be better, to avoid a claustrophobic effect. Metcalf[23] says: 'A room 7.6 m × 11 m (25 ft × 36 ft) which is enough for thirty-six readers is not unpleasant with a 2540 mm (8 ft 4 in) ceiling if ventilation is adequate.' If the vista through the room is broken by high bookcases or partitions, for example in a university stack reading room, where in modern practice the stack occupies the centre and tables the perimeter, a ceiling as low as 2340 mm (7 ft 8 in) can certainly be acceptable. For efficiency in such cases, a stack seven shelves high, giving an overall height of 2300 mm (7 ft 6 in) is necessary; a 2340 mm (7 ft 8 in) ceiling here may seem close but if the lighting arrangements are carefully considered it can be achieved. To have to reduce the height to six shelves because of lighting problems would,

6:25. Birmingham Central Library, showing cores at corners and potential for change of floor areas.

6:26. Building with outside staircase, leaving library area free

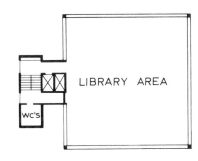

versely construction requirements for deep beams will appear to lower the ceiling height. In the Manchester Central Library a mezzanine floor was inserted into an area which had a total floor-to-ceiling height of only 4530 mm (14 ft 10½ in), the ceiling height of 2135 mm (7 ft) under the mezzanine being made tolerable by having a series of partial voids in the mezzanine floor to break up the tunnel effect.

Position of stairways

In a multi-storey building the positioning of the core of stairs, lifts and other services will be one of the architect's major considerations. If placed centrally, they may need shielding to remove audial interference with serious reading, they may block the vista through the library, making self-location difficult, and they can seriously hinder library operations. If placed off-centre, they will limit the potential for change of activities in the future. In both cases it will be necessary for dead areas to be left around the entrance to the stairs (if only for fire safety reasons) and this wastes space. In many very large university libraries (and in the Martin Luther King Library in Washington DC), there are four cores, evenly spaced, and with columnless areas between the four cores. A rather similar arrangement is to be found in a very different structure, and without the regularity (and perhaps monotony) of these large university floors, in the Birmingham Central Library, West Midlands. Here, staircases, escalators and lifts are provided in the core areas on every floor because of the very heavy traffic; lavatories are on alternate floors only. The plan (Figure 6:25) shows how the main floor areas have been left clear and flexible, even for change between stacking and seating, with security control localized on exists and entrances.

Stairs entirely outside the building leave a good open-plan area for library use and would be very desirable from the librarian's point of view. The difficulties are the single entrance, or at best a limited number of entrances, to upper floors which create crowded traffic routes and bottlenecks, possible security hazards unless lockable doors are installed on all floors; and above all fire regulations. Staircases are not a popular building feature with librarians. They can create audial and visual disturbance and they seem to lure many architects into attempting 'striking features'. Ironically, if such staircases are left open for aesthetic effect, the fire regulations may require the installation of a fire staircase outside the building in addition. Large open staircases, particularly symmetrical pairs of stairs rising imposingly from entrance halls, have proved to be a source of wasted spaced as well as trouble and expense.

6:27. Dominance of stairways (Free University of Berlin; architect Schiedhelm)

of course, be absurd. Readers in the perimeter areas, possibly sitting close to windows, will not be unhappy with such a ceiling height. Construction in reinforced concrete using honeycomb ceilings can given the feeling of greater height (and can house lighting installations), while con-

7 Towards a feasibility report

Most of the matters which are vital to design decisions at this stage have now been considered. Two have been left because although they are basic to the design their influence on the function of the library is very strong. These are the effects on space allocations of the way books will be delivered from closed stack and the question of windows.

Space implications of stack placing

Just as there are advantages in having a direct vertical association between the major services – lifts and staircases, water and sewage lines – so there can be a gain in having such a connection between service stations on each floor and the book stacks which will supply them by hoist or conveyor machinery. To site all such service points close to liftshafts would impossibly limit the flexibility of reader services, but to insist that this vertically-operating machinery should be placed in easily accessible open areas for better reader service will restrict the architect in his freedom of design. Whatever solution the architect may propose to a problem which so directly involves operational matters must be discussed with the librarian.

In large projects, which will inevitably be multi-storey, the architect has to conceive a relationship between large masses of books and large numbers of readers which will give the required degree of freedom of access. In the case of a very large closed-stack system, that is, one where readers are not allowed access to the stacks, he will wish to keep the mass of books housed closely together for space economy and he will study the various classical alternatives of relationships with reader spaces. Thompson[1] illustrates five such plans:

1. Reading room above and stacks below.
2. Central reading room surrounded by book stacks.
3. Reading room in front and book stacks behind.
4. Book stacks in the form of a tower with reading rooms in what is virtually a separate building.
5. Central book stack with surrounding reading rooms.

Imagination could suggest other alternatives but there are many working examples of these five which may be studied to determine their strengths and weaknesses. Figures 7:1 and 7:2 show two famous examples which illustrate diametrically opposite ways of dealing with this problem. Manchester Central Library placed the books in the centre, with subject departments radiating, allowing readers to choose to be near where most-desired books were stacked. There is, of course, no opportunity for expansion in this arrangement. The proposed National Library of Nigeria at Abuja gives the reader the chance to sit near his main subject interests, knowing in which stack

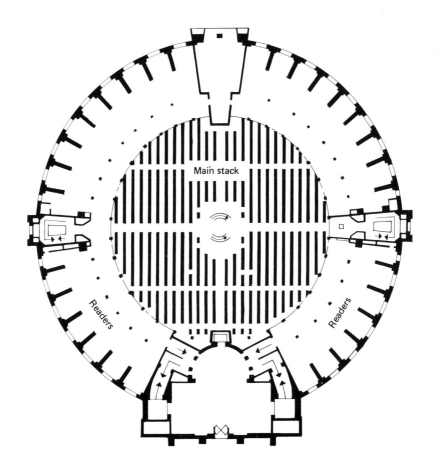

7:1. Manchester Central Library: stacks in centre, readers on perimeter

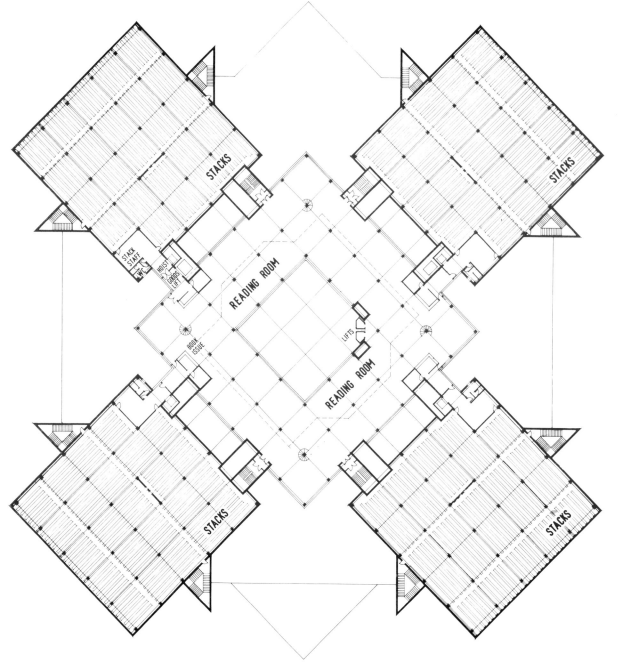

7:2. Proposed
National Library of
Nigeria at Abuja:
readers in central
block, stacks in
four independent
buildings linked
by supply bridges

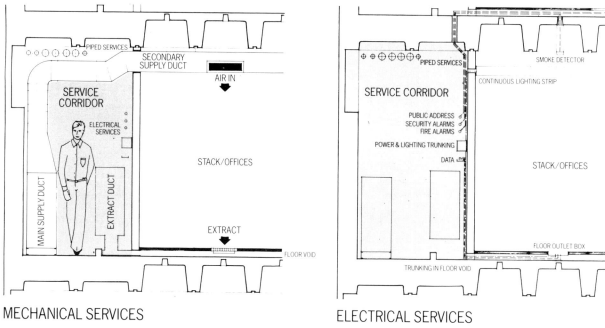

7:3. Cause-
wayside Building,
National Library of
Scotland, Edin-
burgh, showing
how the centre of
the building is left
free for books
(and readers) by
placing all ser-
vices on peri-
meter. This also
serves to insulate
the stack against
damp penetration

MECHANICAL SERVICES

ELECTRICAL SERVICES

and at what level they are to be found; the stacks are housed in four independent structures outside the main building, with links to each reading room.

Methods of storing books in quantity can affect the design at an early stage, as for example when the brief calls for compact-storage stacks as a main provision, as distinct from the normal practice of having a few rows, perhaps on a low level, as an addition to normal shelving. Loading here will be critical, and the necessary allowances must be made from the earliest stage, or never. The new Causewayside building of the National Library of Scotland was planned in many ways around the stacking. Phase 1 has a usable area of 6613 m² (71 000 sq ft) out of a gross area of 8828 m² (95 000 sq ft): 'The book storage areas are . . . the principal building element and form the large core of the plan. The flexible elements – the services and vertical means of access (stairs and lifts) – are on the perimeter, forming an outer ring which acts as a buffer for noise, heat gain and heat loss.'[2]

In an open-access or open-stack library such questions will be less dramatic in that most reading areas will also house books and the problem will be more closely bound with degrees of reader access and priority placings of particular services. Here the flexibility requested by the librarian may be achieved by having some of the internal walls removable, so that space allocations can be altered at a future date. The brief must state how 'temporary' such partition walls are to be; it would be a serious error if a flimsy demountable partition with low noise-insulating qualities were installed when changes were known not to be needed for some years. In such a case a brickwork partition could have been installed, as the cost and trouble of alteration would form an acceptable part of a future major change. The exact opposite applies when partitioning is to be demounted at weekly or monthly intervals. If even more frequent changes are needed, such as to give privacy for lectures and introductions to the library, a folding screen from column to column may be the least inconvenient method. The use of portable screens in truly open-plan manner has influences on visual and audial conditions which the librarian would be well advised to study in other libraries. The architect will also need to make a survey of the reader circulation routes that follow from his trial space allocations, with particular attention to the main entrance and exit. For reasons of security it is assumed that wherever possible there will be only one main entrance and one main exit, and that they will be located together. The obvious solution is for this to be placed in the centre of the ground-floor perimeter of the building, but in many cases the special nature of the site will prevent this. Placing them off-centre may be important to the design concept. From the brief the architect will see the priority the librarian wishes to give to certain functional areas; applying this priority rating to the spatial allocation which is already crystallizing in his mind he will arrive at a first idea of the interdependence of operational areas, which is, in many ways, the most important spatial factor in the whole concept. In doing so he will try to disregard the many matters of detail that will constantly arise.

Prefabricated libraries

Examples of these are when a 'systems building' technique is to be used. When materials and labour were scarce in Britain immediately after the Second World War cooperative ventures were developed by local education authorities who began to plan primary schools with 'kit' components. (Ironically, after the situation improved and permanent building began again it has happened that some of these prefabricated buildings were converted for use as village libraries.) From these beginnings emerged CLASP (Consortium of Local Authorities, Special Programme) and, after its initial great success, other similar bodies. At first the scheme concentrated on free-standing school buildings for which the components were virtually prefabricated, producing very considerable savings in both design work and construction on the site. There are now a number of such consortia working in wider fields of education and in local government generally, especially in housing. No longer confined to producing simple buildings but obtaining advantages by the standardization and coding of products, such schemes may attract authorities which are already using them in their education or housing interests. If a large local authority plans to build a dozen or more libraries to serve village communities there are obvious advantages in such standardization of parts, and the architect may be told to incorporate such materials and units in his work.

There is some resemblance between these schemes and the 'complete library service' offered by certain library supply firms. These are based on a series of structural units, similar to those used to produce classrooms or offices, which can be assembled to produce a surprisingly wide variety of enclosures. Terrapin International offer such buildings based on units of 1200 mm (3 ft 11¼ in) giving clear internal spans up to 9.6 m with a ceiling height of 2.355 m (7 ft 8¾ in) or 2.955 m (9 ft 8 in). Spans of multiples of the module can give areas of almost any length without internal columns, provided that they are planned in a given series of patterns. If unusual shapes are required, internal columns will be necessary for support. Non-load-bearing wall panels 1200 mm or 2400 mm wide are located between timber or steel columns. The suspended ground floors are supported on brick or concrete panels, or alternatively construction can be on a solid concrete ground slab, with thermal insulation if required. The buildings can have either flat or pitched roofs and comply with the appropriate Building Regulations.

The great advantages of such a system are not only its cheapness and speed of erection but the economy offered in the design process, so often a bottleneck in architects' offices. It can be a most useful expedient where a service has to be provided on a certain site but where financial support for a full-scale building is not available. Such package libraries, complete with the makers' furniture, fittings and accessories (and of course with all mains services connected), can be thoroughly viable library buildings.

If such a scheme is chosen it might be argued that there is no need for a separate architect. This would be highly dangerous: an architect is a professional whose services are entirely at his client's disposal to safeguard his interests. Commercial undertaking can never do this impartially: by definition they are partial, because they have something to sell. It is also a complete misconception to imagine that a client is saving architects' fees in such a case; the fees are hidden in the total costs. A repeated design will always be cheaper, if usually less effective, then one conceived for a special purpose.

Spatial analysis

Analysing the proportions of the building which are to be allotted for the various purposes is a complicated exercise. In the first place a basic volumetric analysis will distinguish between:

1. The total volume: that contained by the external

7:4. Duluth Public Library, Michigan: stilts setting perimeter of the building over a pavement (Architect Gunnar Birkerts and Associates)

7:5. Duluth Public Library, showing the columns rising through a public area

7:6. University of Hull: wall of windows sloping downwards (Architects Castle Park Dean Hook)

7:7. University of Bristol: individual windows sloping downwards (Architects Twist and Whitley)

perimeter and the height from the lowest floor surface to the outer surface of the roof.

2. The total contained volume, which is in effect the volume of air contained within the visible parts of the exterior.

3. The equivalent volume, which is calculated by multiplying the floor area by a standard floor-to-floor height of 3 m (10 ft).

The balance area (the American term is 'non-assignable space') is that portion of the total space which is not usable for the library's direct purpose. It therefore includes walls, columns, entrances, vestibules, corridors, stair wells, and other spaces used for transport and communications, unusable spaces under sloping roofs and so on. It does not include stores, workshops, kitchens, changing rooms or any areas which help the library to perform its function.

A distinction of more immediate use to the librarian is one between 'functional', 'auxiliary' and 'circulation' space. The term 'auxiliary' refers to areas which house activities concerning the building but not its operation as a library – such as heating, lighting, ventilation, as well as open spaces. In circulation space it is usual to distinguish between primary circulation space, which is the main arteries; secondary, which joins sections and groupings; and tertiary, which is within working areas. The widths of these circulation corridors will be in descending order from 2 m (6 ft) for the main ones to 750 mm (2 ft 6 in) for paths between desks. It is generally held that a library can be considered functionally inefficient if the balance area occupies more than 25% of the equivalent volume. An interesting exercise in architectural design potential is shown in the *Site Selection Study* of the Metropolitan Toronto Library Board.[3] This applies relevant criteria about

7:8. Duluth Public Library, Michigan: window sloping to bring indirect natural light into room. 'Daylight bouncing from the silver-coloured exterior metal panels beneath the sloping windows to the tilted white metal panels over windows and tables. . .'

spatial relationships and critical placing to both plan and isometric drawing, working without any design preconceptions. The conclusions drawn, especially those relating to the positioning of the stack in a large central library, are most illuminating.

Differences in basic design can have a dramatic effect upon the proportion of total volume which is available for the various purposes, from the running of the building itself, general circulation space and direct library service activities. The librarian's chief interest will be in seeing that his operative areas occupy as high a proportion of the total as possible, but this is a matter which is fundamental to the design, and he can only offer pious hopes.

The attitude to basements is a case where the views of the two professions may diverge. The librarian, with experience of ever-growing demands, will always call for the greatest possible usable space within the building, and especially valuable to him will be that which is easily accessible from the entrance floor. Basements, however, can cause both trouble and expense, because of the effect of earth pressures, the presence of water (even underground streams) and, in older cities, the existence of service pipes and drains. The new British Library building in London is being erected amid such hazards, all capable of being solved but at some extra cost.

In the building trade generally the view is that basements should be avoided except where land values are exceptionally high. The entrance floor, so vital to library service, need not be on the ground floor; for example, Loughborough University's Pilkington Library (p. 76), built on sloping ground to conform with environmental site requirements, has its entrance on the second floor, thus providing many advantages of speed of access over the traditional vertical floor relationships. Obviously the importance (and the cost) of the entrance floor will vary in proportion to the number of floors in the building, but to the librarian its great importance lies in the way it concentrates readers for essential actions before they disperse to their special needs, and in its visual impact: it sets the tone – severe or welcoming – and he will always give it a high priority.

The relationship between the height of the building and the library's usable space will be affected if the architect chooses to design the library on stilts. There was a vogue for this style some years ago: it may fit in with a particular environment (and even provide useful parking space) but it adds to the construction costs and means that every

reader must progress to a floor above the ground (with complications for the disabled). Librarians seldom like it, but the Duluth Public Library, Michigan, boat-shaped and with stepped cantilevers, inward-sloping windows and a long overhang above the street pavements has been much admired.

The points raised here are only a few of the many questions inevitably affecting a judgement which is basically an aesthetic one tempered with practical considerations. Certainly the greatest influences on the architect's judgement will be his training, professional expertise, experience and, above all, the personal factors which make this an extremely difficult subject to rationalize. Completely different solutions will occur to him, be given tentative shape and be discarded for others, although it is often true that an architect is working towards a concept that was in his mind from the beginning. Gunnar Birkerts, architect of the Duluth Public Library, 'believes that an architect's generation of form is largely intuitive, drawing on a lifetime's accumulation of remembered visual images as they mesh with the physical necessities of a given job.[4] What is certain is that no other member of the team has any part in this operation; the power of the authority in this matter was largely delegated when it chose this particular architect to design its library.

Fenestration

The size, style, placing and even the materials of windows are vital to the building in many ways, and the architect will have spent many hours trying out his first tentative ideas and working towards his final solution. The topic has been left to the last because it is one which a librarian can appreciate and on which he will have strong views, for a number of very different reasons. He will not understand the full contribution of fenestration to the final building, but he knows that the windows will have an important effect upon the internal environment as well as upon the running and maintenance costs, so he will want to know what is being proposed and, to a limited extent, why. Before going too far with his design concepts the architect will digest all factors affecting, and being affected by, the various proportions of glass in the outer walls. The very need for natural light in libraries is by no means universally agreed. Metcalf[5] says that even a large reading area completely without windows is acceptable to readers, both physically and psychologically. Thompson[6] on the other hand believes that daylight is essential. There are few libraries completely without natural light, so our direct experience is to this extent limited; but medical literature leads us to believe that there is no physical need for natural light in normal conditions. Whether there is a psychological need is another matter. Some experts hold that the eye needs a longer view as a relief from short-distance concentration, but, as librarians know, many readers choose to sit well away from windows, even directly facing walls; it seems to be largely a matter of personal opinion. It is interesting to note that an American university library is reported as requiring 'seats facing inwards from windows to avoid the distracting view.'[7] Nevertheless even if a window is not absolutely necessary it seems to be accepted that, where possible, readers should be given the chance to look outside the room. This can be achieved, without suffering the disadvantage of having continuous rows of vertical glass windows in perimeter walls (which we shall discuss later in many contexts), by a number of expedients, including narrow strip windows in an otherwise blank wall (the Lyndon Baines Johnson Library, University of Texas at Austin) and windows sloping downwards so that direct

sunlight does not penetrate into the room. Examples shown here are of Hull University, where whole window walls are arranged in this way; Bristol University, where smaller groups of downward-sloping windows are used; and Duluth Public Library, Michigan, where light without direct sunlight is obtained from windows which look down from the first floor of a library on stilts. In Leicester University (p. 165) the concrete external wall has horizontal slit windows along the line of reader seating, this side of the building being within a shell of reflecting glass. British Building Regulations,[8] stiffened by the energy crisis, limit the proportion of window to external wall to a maximum of 35% (single glazing), but the University Grants Committee lays it down that no more than 25% of the external wall may be glass. There seems to be a consensus among university librarians that if window size is to be limited, horizontal slits are better than either vertical ones or fewer rectangular windows: as always, much depends on the overall design. Certainly to provide natural light for reading purposes there is no need for the vast expanses of glass walling which have been common in recent years. This is for the architect to decide: on one hand he will feel that the

mass of a building without windows can be overpowering; on the other he will have to consider the implications of his fenestration proposals and decide whether it is reasonable to accept the many disadvantages, among which are:

1. The need for machinery to control the considerable heat gain and loss; in more than one glass-walled building, dissipation of heat costs more than heating and lighting.
2. The need to control the effect of direct sunlight on readers and books: this can be by shades or light-breaks outside the building, by special glass, double-glazing with blinds, or by slanting the heads of windows downwards; all have disadvantages in cost, cleaning, operation and maintenance.
3. The possible need for a higher level of artificial lighting in areas away from window light, in order to balance the brightness of direct sunlight and to mitigate the sense of deprivation in readers who can see a bright sky. Darkened glass in windows can help to overcome this problem, but it is not cheap and can be depressing.
4. The loss of wall shelving space and of flexibility in both seating and shelving.

In all, it can be said that walls with large areas of glass are not usually suited to libraries. In open-access conditions clerestory windows (small windows running along the higher part of reading room walls) may be an acceptable compromise; they can give the desired impression while allowing shelving to be installed on the lower part of the walls. However, with this type of window, light is directly in the eyes of the reader as he chooses books, and for this reason it is rejected by many librarians. Clerestory windows within a light well from which the light can be reflected are very acceptable but may waste much space. Narrower but full-height windows on one plane of a zig-zag are a possible compromise, but again there can be a serious problem of glare from outside at certain angles of the sun.

In single-storey buildings roof lights are still a possibility. They were very popular over a long period because they gave a source of natural light which spread evenly throughout the rooms. They became fashionable in the 1930s under the influence of the Finnish architect Alvar Aalto, much the most famous of modern library architects. He used roof lights in his library in Viipuri, Finland, designed as early as 1927; these freed the walls of the need for windows and enabled him to use several shelving and reading levels within a single space. The principles used were widely imitated from the 1930s to the 1960s, but they had the disadvantage of the great variation of light levels caused by the changes at different times of day or year.

In addition to the necessity of lighting the interior there is the great attraction which a well-lit 'shop window' of glass exerts on passers-by, and this is important for public libraries. Outstanding recent examples are to be found in Michigan City and the New Orleans Public Library; a large number of small public libraries in Britain make use of this appeal. If the architect has in mind such a design he must be clearly aware of the accompanying disadvantages – limitations on shelving space, trouble and cost caused by heat gains and losses, as well as humidity problems and glare.

Before artificial lighting became as efficient as it is today, natural light was essential in all reading areas. In a very large building this forced the architect to provide internal light-wells so that all rooms could have natural light. In small libraries of all kinds the interior court performs something of this function. Light comes in from above and serves each level, care being taken to see that it is indirect and 'washes' from light-coloured surfaces. On the ground level the open court can be used for outdoor reading where the weather permits; otherwise it can be a garden, more a design feature than a source of usable light. In countries where sunlight is reliable but not excessive, such a court serves well as a safe and attractive reading area for children.

An extreme form of the classical light-well is the atrium, familiar from luxury hotels and department stores. Here the main internal space within a large library is open, the functional areas being placed around the perimeter as a series of balconies. Well-known examples are those of the Metro Reference Library, Toronto, and the National Library of Mexico, where two separate buildings are linked by a transparent roof to form a kind of atrium.

In all buildings of this kind the open space in the centre gives an unrivalled feeling of openness, but there are a number of disadvantages. Access from section to section is complicated, noise may rise in the atrium, and there may be difficulties with fire regulations. However, librarians who attack the concept because it 'wastes cubic feet' may be guilty of muddled thinking; much depends on the space

available (i.e. the opportunity to build higher). Nevertheless atria are likely to be expensive and not only in structural costs. The attractiveness of this style can sometimes be obtained without such extremes. In a 'normal' large library building, there will be floors on top of other floors, connected only by stairs, lifts and service cores. The vista from most parts of the building will then be limited to a single floor with a fairly low ceiling. To get the gains of the atrium without using up so much space has been well achieved in the Alexander State Library Building of Perth, Western Australia. Here the balconies are much larger in comparison to the open space, and the upper floors in fact project further than the lower ones. The view from both the main entrances, and the view back from the stairs and transparent-sided lifts, give a feeling of light and space as well as helping to orientate the visitor. A much more limited version is the simple balcony or mezzanine over part of the ground floor, much used in libraries of all kinds.

If the architect has any such proposal in mind, he must first discuss it with the librarian as soon as he has made a tentative choice. Design is certainly his responsibility but in a matter which will so dramatically affect both the appearance of the library and its reader service conditions it is his undoubted duty to ensure that the librarian, as the client's specialist representative, accepts his views.

There will always be some form of natural lighting in libraries (except perhaps underground ones, and many of these have forms of laylights). Artificial light will certainly be needed; the architect will know of the IES recommendations on lighting levels for different library functions[9] and, with his lighting expert, will have studied the contribution which both natural and artificial lighting make to the appearance of the library. They will also remember that the cost variation of different lighting plans and levels can be very considerable, in installation, consumption of current and bills for cleaning and maintenance. The cleaning (and at times the maintenance) of complicated window and artificial lighting fitments is a recurrent nightmare in many libraries. In large buildings, particularly of an irregular shape, the architect may have to allow for balconies, gantries or suspended cranes when direct human access is not otherwise reasonable.

Reviewing progress

Now that the major factors affecting the structure, the exterior appearance and the major services have been dealt with, the architect may take the opportunity to review once again his tentative proposals, to check that they are likely to fulfil the needs of his client and, even more important, of the future users of the library. Harry Faulkner-Brown, a very experienced library architect, has laid down a number of desirable qualities for a library; he was thinking of university libraries, but the principles apply everywhere. These have become widely known as his 'Ten Commandments' and are repeated here, with his permission, because they can serve at this stage to remind the architect what it is that his designs are hoping to achieve. The Commandments state that a library should be:

1. Flexible, with a layout, structure and services which are easy to adapt.
2. Compact, for ease of movement of readers, staff and books.
3. Accessible, from the exterior into the building and from the entrance to all parts of the building, with an easy, comprehensive plan needing minimum supplementary directions.
4. Extendible, to permit future growth with minimum disruption.

7:10. National Library of Mexico: double building linked by translucent roof

7:11. Jordanhill College of Education Library, Glasgow: typical arrangement of partial mezzanine allowing natural light to main reading hall. Note individual shielded seating effect, economically obtained

5. Varied, in its provision of accommodation and reader services to give wide freedom of choice.
6. Organized, to impose appropriate confrontation between books and readers.
7. Comfortable, to promote efficiency of use.
8. Constant in environment, for the preservation of library materials.
9. Secure, to control user behaviour and loss of books.
10. Economic, to be built and maintained with minimum resources both in finances and staff.

Cost feasibility

Before he spends too much time developing his first sketches, the architect will need to know whether what he has in mind is possible within the overall cost allotted for the project. Even if no firm limit has been given he must still have a rough estimate of probable costs; limits of cost per square metre or square foot may be laid down (or strongly 'recommended') by outside authorities (in Britain the University Grants Committee or the Department of Education and Science). In any case he will have to present cost feasibility proposals to his client authority and so will need to see the overall financial position before he proceeds to more detailed planning.

The quantity surveyor will have been working alongside the architect, costing his various proposals. Other members of the team, such as the engineering, structural and service consultants, will prepare their own estimates of the different solutions which the architect may advance experimentally. Every proposal will have its own economic implications and every decision its cost consequences, and these must be kept under review if the budget is to be met. Even minor matters need to be assessed for their cost effect: the architect's wishes in the matter of finishes (floor and wall coverings, door furniture and so on) may not be detailed until a much later stage, but the quantity surveyor will need to have a general picture of the quality standards of such items if he is to assess their probable contribution to the final costs. For example the architect may decide

that the use of laminated glass, heavy plastic or polycarbonate sheeting is justifiable in situations where vandalism may be expected and the extra costs must be allowed for.

Cladding

The architect's decision, a common one, to opt for a building with steel or reinforced concrete framing, hung with slabs of cladding purchased 'off the peg', instead of the solid, load-bearing walls of the past, will have its own cost implications. It may be bewildering to a layman that the Auditor-General's Report (1966–1967), quoted by Derrick Oxley in the *Spectator* (4 March 1972), stated that 'industrialized building is more expensive than traditional.' Without doubt there is more to this question than the cladding itself; but it can be fairly stated, with considerable relevance to recent libraries, that glass walls are very dear, and irregular glass walls even dearer. Old-fashioned brick walls are, by comparison, very cheap, and they weather well. On-site assembly of prefabricated components favours lightweight construction, but the architect's willingness to have such components as are available from manufacturers does tend to produce monotony of form and crudity of detail. Examples are the slabs of off-white concrete in seemingly endless rows, streaked and stained by the weather. Developing countries are more likely to use in-situ rather than pre-cast concrete building methods because manual skills are available and sophisticated machinery is not. This has often produced genuine originality, not just gimmicks.

The cladding will have a great effect upon the appearance of the building and thus on its appeal to potential users; it will also be an important item in the cost, but it is entirely the architect's business, subject to planning approval, and no comment is called for from the librarian. If he does strongly object to the appearance of the building, as shown in the sketches or models submitted by the architect, he will have to make his views known to his authority when the feasibility report is being considered. In such a case the authority might ask the architect to make an alternative suggestion: happily this is a most unlikely occurrence.

The architect should allow for the effect of weathering upon the external materials. The horrible examples, daily before us in the West, of the fashion in the 1960s for massive public buildings with shuttered concrete exteriors is a warning.

Brick helps to camouflage weather marking because of the small variation in colouring from brick to brick, but efflorescence in brickwork can produce unsightly white staining. Other materials can have their problems: for example, mosaic-tile cladding has a poor record for staying fixed in wet countries. It is of the very greatest importance that the librarian should not have to find money in the future to maintain the external fabric. The fine appearance of the attractive external metal sheathing on the new Rotterdam Central Library is paid for by the high cost of annual specialist maintenance. The librarian has the right to expect his future library to look good throughout its predicted life, not just at the opening ceremony.

The report now prepared by the architect will be his own responsibility, although it will embody the professional expertise and advice of various specialists. With the appropriate sketches and a summary of costs, it will be submitted to the authority (committee, board or other body), but it would be wise for the architect to explain it first to the librarian: if cooperation and teamwork are in evidence this will certainly happen. The librarian wants to know what is proposed so that he can study the implications from the viewpoint of the one who will have the task of running the future building. If he finds some of the proposals unacceptable or if he has serious doubts, there is time for a discussion to take place, for explanations, amendments if necessary, without bringing in other bodies. As the librarian is likely to be asked at the committee meeting for his opinion of the proposals, it is well for him not to come 'cold' to a complicated set of sketches. Furthermore, a feeling of solidarity between the appointed architect and its own librarian will tend to give the authority confidence in the proposals.

The report will then be considered by the authority, who may accept or reject it, or accept it with certain stipulated modifications. These may be so drastic as to call for a further report and amended costings. If the report is accepted (or if any proposed modifications are easily acceptable to the architect) he will proceed to the next planning stage. In some circumstances it will be necessary for him to be formally appointed to carry out the rest of the work, and the specialist consultants may have to be re-appointed also. At the same time the authority should declare its contract policy: whether the building work is to be carried out by competitive tendering or by a modified form of tendering, or whether the authority intends to have any of the work carried out by its own works department.

Timetable

Included in the feasibility report was the architect's assessment of the time to be taken by each element of the project, and an overall time for its completion. He will make it clear that this is only an estimate, not a promise, because so many factors will be beyond his control. It might prevent possible confusion if a distinction is here made between a programme and a timetable: a programme consists of a record of related activities, its basis being that these

activities shall be carried out in a logical order. A timetable on the other hand is simply a list of events set out against a list of dates; it may be shown in the form of a bar chart, or series of such charts, but it relates only to time, whereas a programme has also to show how each operation depends on the previous one; it can also be used to plan for the supply of resources at each stage in order to conform to the dates in the timetable.

This timetable will be accepted by the authority, or the architect may be asked whether it can be amended in any way. Sometimes it is possible to shorten the period (the only amendment any authority is interested in), but this will be at a price. Additional cost will be caused by the allocation of extra staff and probably by overtime working by the eventual building contractor. Perhaps the most important way to save time and therefore control costs is for the authority to give the architect enough time to complete his contract drawings and bills of quantity in sufficient detail and authorize him to resist all change, for change is always very expensive. The position today on building delays has become critical. While there is always pressure by the client to complete the building in the shortest possible time, this often results in the preparation of information being rushed and inadequate. This is always bad policy because a contractor, working as he does in the competitive climate imposed by the need for tendering, can pick on any inadequacies in the information provided and claim, with justification, that he was delayed by not knowing clearly how he was expected to proceed. Under the terms of the building contract he may claim extensions of time for uncertainties which cause delay, and in such a case he is entitled to be compensated for any resulting loss.

Another result of over-hasty preparation of contract information is that the architect will tend to leave certain matters to be sorted out later by including estimated provisional items and prime cost sums in the bills of quantity. There is a perfectly legitimate reason for doing this where work has to be undertaken by specialist or nominated sub-contractors who will have special skills in technical fields. The architect may not wish such specialists to be appointed before the general contractor has been chosen, since the contractor may have worked with particular firms which he would like to use again, or may have objections to other firms proposed. The danger of leaving too many specialist jobs to be allocated is that it creates problems of organization, programming and control which may give the contractor legitimate cause for claiming extensions of contract if any of the specialists default. Such claims can be substantial and make complete nonsense of budgetary control.

Thus thorough preparation by the architect of all information before tender stage will make for a smoother run and, in the end, a cheaper contract. If he has enough time, items which in a rushed job would be the subject of later decisions can be detailed and the responsibility for them placed squarely on the general contractor. The contractor can be far more effective when dealing with firms working directly for him than with firms nominated by, and accountable to, the architect. The question of the right to charge for supervision does complicate the issue; the elimination of all nominated sub-contracts, with the whole burden of organizing the contract falling direct onto the general contractor, is the ideal, but it is seldom achieved.

The timetable, then, is associated with the cost estimate, and the architect will be prepared to give an alternative estimate for a different period if necessary.

8 Secondary brief

When the feasibility report has been accepted and the draft timetable agreed, the architect will need more detailed information before he can proceed to the next planning stage. If team consultation has been continuous throughout there should be no doubtful points in the brief to be elucidated, but there will certainly be need for amplification of detail. In addition, because the spatial relationship between the various sections has now been tentatively established, the architect is ready to consider in more detail the layout of each operational section, including the identification in general terms of the furniture and equipment. The librarian in his turn has been able to see from the sketches (or models) which form part of the feasibility report the position of the different operational areas and their inter-relationship. He is now in a position to formulate with some confidence his needs in the way of furniture and equipment of all kinds.

The architect needs to know a good deal more than this and he may draw up a questionnaire for the librarian to complete; it both pinpoints matters on which he needs further information and provides a document for the team to discuss. From experience I feel that this can distort the picture: it is better if the librarian himself prepares a full list of everything that is needed, including, in places, comments on how they are to be used. This is because the subject is the operation of the library, not just items to be purchased.

The architect already knows in general terms the contribution each operational section is to make and the degree of priority in the proximity between them. He now needs to know:

1. The pattern of operations to take place within each section.
2. The communications to be established between them.
3. Further requirements which were not detailed in the primary brief, particularly furniture and equipment.
4. The librarian's preferences in regard to all furniture and equipment.

In order to produce this information the librarian will prepare a secondary brief.

Many successful libraries have been created without the librarian being involved in such matters: many architects believe that they themselves, by observation and experi-ence, are the best judges, but it is the theme of this book that the best results are obtained by pooling the experience and expertise of all the professionals involved and by free discussion within the team. The architect is likely to disagree with some of the librarian's suggestions, but it is most important that he should have them before him.

Pattern of operations

An internal traffic diagram for each of the sections which formed the space relationship table (p. 41) will be needed. There will be three different types: administration; technical (that is, book preparation) services; and reader services.

Administration

The primary brief will have shown the position this suite should occupy. At that stage there will probably have been a discussion within the team, because the wish of the librarian that he and his immediate entourage should be within control distance of the main reader services (usually on the ground floor) may clash with other calls upon prime areas. This is a very good example of how a friendly relationship within the team can provide the best possible result. This result can be a compromise: direct supervision of the main reader services obtained by siting a senior staff member's office in a position of control, the chief librarian's suite (including reception and offices) being in close contact with the supervisor but in a rear area or on another floor. This sort of planning is the speciality of an architect.

To make a flow chart to show the operations within the administration section is simple; if an open-plan layout is proposed, the degree of audial and visual privacy required must be made clear. One well-known librarian, who was a complete devotee of the open-plan library, insisted that he alone needed absolute privacy for his office. Not an encouraging example to his staff.

Technical services

An example of the progress of a book or other item from its arrival in the library, through the various sequential processes to its destination on a shelf, should be shown in a flow diagram, with an indication of the concomitant operations which it generates. Each of the sections involved is a workshop which the architect will have to plan, and to do so he must know in some detail what operations take place, in what order, and what special conditions are involved. Once again the librarian should not attempt to place these operations in any particular position, but show their working relationships and priorities of proximity so that the architect can plan an acceptable and economical layout.

It will not be necessary to tell the architect that typists require decent working conditions or that the layout of a bindery must conform with Factory Act regulations; this is his business. The librarian's concern is to show how he wishes each section to operate and to indicate how much freedom he needs to allow for possible changes in the future. This will enable the architect to check his space allocation for each section and to design a layout. It will also guide him as to the exact needs for such elements as lighting, heating, windows, electric points, water supply and disposal.

Some sections of the technical services can be planned simply as open-plan offices (the cataloguing section, for example), but others are extremely complicated and must be shown with great care. Chief among these are the photographic workshop, the conservation section and the library bindery: a flow chart for the latter is shown in Figure 8:2, but it must be amended according to the work it is to do and the equipment and methods to be used.

Reader services

Reader services vary according to the infinite and unknowable trends of individual readers' demands, as well as a gradually changing pattern of library use. Some patterns are predictable: for example in the case of a new public branch library it may be possible to foresee the general character of use, in numbers of readers at times of

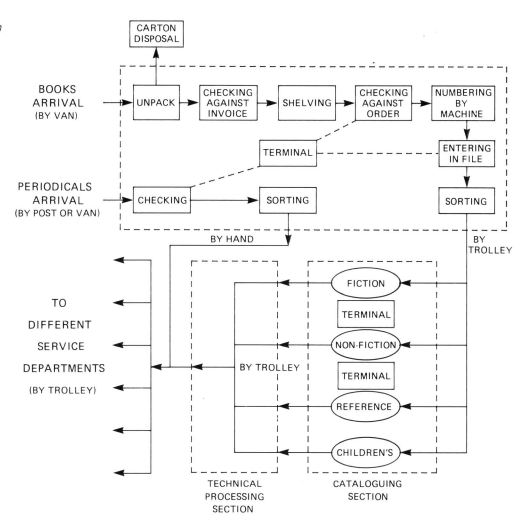

8:1. Flow diagram of materials intake through processing sections of a public library

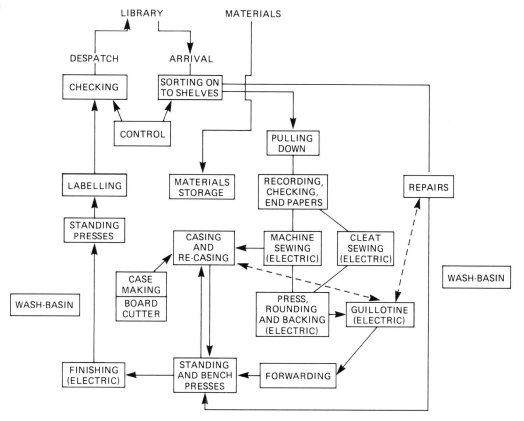

8:2. Flow diagram of a library bindery

the day and their traffic routes. In a small research or school library, use may be forecast with even more certainty. Even in a new and complex library, however, certain assumptions can be made; although there is no 'average reader' the actions of certain large groups are predictable. The casual reader, the undergraduate, the research worker, have elements in common in their use patterns, although one person may himself at times form part of another group. It is most valuable now for the librarian to observe closely and even to put himself in the position of each of these groups in turn and try to visualize what he will do when he enters the library. The picture of the service which emerges may be very different from the librarian's usual view.

Not all readers find libraries inviting places; many combine inability to understand a catalogue with a built-in reluctance to ask the staff for help. How can such a reader be induced to help himself or to allow the staff to help him? The positioning of catalogues and readers' advisers' desks alone is not the complete answer, but careful consideration of the layout can be a first step towards solving the problem. In a multi-storey library it can be helpful to the reader to have a consistent and recognizable layout pattern of tables, stacks and readers' advisers' desks on each floor. This can do more than complicated colour coding to make the reader feel confident of his location: the better-planned the library, the less need for guiding notices.

By drawing upon his experience the librarian can plan a compromise based upon reader needs, economy of staffing and estimated traffic patterns. The result, a notional placing of the operational activities and predicted readers' movements within each section, can take the form of a traffic diagram. It will be the architect's task to give this his skilled attention, to translate it into spatial terms and eventually to prepare a layout which includes the positioning of furniture and equipment.

In lending libraries the traffic pattern will be simplified, in that most readers will go first to the book-return counter and then split up into various routes, going to the book-issue counter before leaving. Sections which use physically different forms for a similar purpose, such as audio-visual departments with their wide range of media, will present more complicated problems. A flow diagram of a music, audio disc and tape department is illustrated in Figure 8:3; any analysis of reader activities which the librarian can make will enable the architect to use the experience of the librarian to help him to visualize the service. In addition to drawing such a diagram for each operational section the librarian may be able to clarify his original estimate of reader use. Now that he can see the place which each section will occupy in the building and its physical relation to other sections and access routes, he may be able to say that at a given peak hour, 200 readers will enter the section, that 100 will go direct to the study area and remain there for at least one hour, that fifty will go direct to the quick reference area and then to the study area, that twenty will go direct to the catalogue and so on. Such prognostications are very difficult to produce and may turn out to be wildly inaccurate in practice, but the librarian's experience is the only possible source for such an assessment, and without it the architect will be less well-equipped to proceed with his work.

Communications

The relationship between readers and materials was indicated in space relationship diagrams, materials flow charts and traffic route diagrams: from these the obvious channels and machinery can be planned. Special attention was drawn in the primary brief to equipment which might affect structural planning (lifts, hoists, escalators etc.) It is basic to an architect's work to plan methods of communication for both people and materials which are needed in

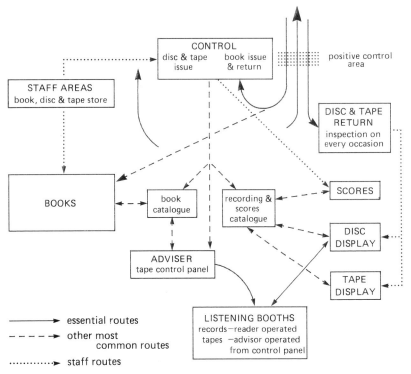

8:3. Flow diagram of a music, audio disc and tape department

different sections of any building; but forecasting the communications equipment to be used in a library is not quite so simple. One becomes aware of the possibility of a form of communication only when there is a reasonable chance that it can be given practicable form. Before closed-circuit television appeared no one ever asked for a direct visual link between widely separated departments; before fax became sufficiently sophisticated no one demanded a fast document delivery method. As in so many cases the availability of the equipment came first; it is therefore of great importance that the librarian should be aware of systems which might serve his purposes. The normal way for communication requirements to be shown is for a schedule to be prepared showing, room by room, what form of communication will be needed; but in a very small library it will be enough to prepare two simple tables, one to show 'who is to speak to whom' and one for 'what is to be sent where'.

Telephone – external

Where the library is to form part of a larger establishment which has its own central telephone exchange (switchboard), it is usually sufficient from the readers' point of view if incoming calls can be routed directly from that exchange to the required section of the library. The librarian will see that the exchange operators are adequately briefed on the range of activities of each section. If, however, the library is independent of such a group exchange, then the question to be decided is whether it is more efficient and economical to have a private exchange (which means that the reader's call will be handled twice) or whether each major department, and especially its most-called services – renewals and enquiries – should have a separate number. The disadvantages of the latter are the cost of extra lines (to be offset against the savings in not having a private exchange and operator) and the frustration caused to the reader who calls what he thinks is the correct department only to be told that he must ring another number. The availability of more sophisticated telephone equipment now gives the freedom to switch directly from department to department, phone outside the system and make internal calls on the same equipment. Nevertheless the need for a central reception phone is likely to remain in busy libraries not served from the exchange of a parent institution.

If the library is large enough to have its own exchange it should be placed out of sight and hearing of the public services. Except in the largest libraries, where more than one operator may be needed, the exchange should be near enough to a staff workroom for relief to be available at short notice. In small libraries where an exchange cannot be justified, the placing of the main incoming lines presents problems; too often they go to the circulation counter, where calls interfere seriously with public service. An estimate should be made of the frequency of calls to the various sections (book enquiries, information enquiries, book renewals and so on) and the telephone placed where the greatest number of calls can be quickly handled with the minimum interference with other services. In a branch public library the best place is often the enquiries desk; even though this may mean that a professional member of the staff must take all calls it may be better than interrupting the relatively busier 'books-in' counter. At busy times the flow of book-renewal calls can be a great problem: is such provision necessary? Would it not be better to have a longer period of loan and to ban phone renewals, which are largely motivated by a wish to avoid paying fines? The whole question of telephone enquiries

needs careful thought before any decisions are committed to paper. In most libraries a high proportion of such enquiries can be answered from a comparatively small collection of quick-reference books, and there is something to be said for the system where all information enquiries go directly to one of a group of telephones situated beside a revolving bookcase which holds a collection of quick-reference books; these telephones would be permanently manned by staff devoted entirely to the task; the number of telephones in use varying with known peak periods of demand. The annoyance of bells ringing can be avoided by substituting light signals to indicate a call to a continuously manned desk. If such a solution is too expensive the librarian may have to consider whether telephone calls should necessarily take priority over readers attending in person. The telephone can be a bully unless handled efficiently. Once again this is a matter where information databases accessed by the enquirer may soon provide a different solution.

Telephone – internal

Recent advances in telephone systems enable a wide range of internal calls to be made on the telephones for external calls. Can this arrangement supersede the usual internal communication link? Telephonic communication is not cheap; the demand for more telephones within the building (and demand always grows) can add considerably to the running costs of the library. On the other hand it is much better to have an adequate network planned beforehand than to add lines later. In some organizations it

Table 8.1 Communications list for a large college library complex

Key: A Outside line
B Internal telephone
C Close-circuit TV link
D Telex link
E Document facsimile transmission link

	A	B	C	D	E
Book return counter	1	1	–	–	–
Readers' adviser's desk	1	1	–	1	1
Periodical control desk	–	1	–	1	1
Map room	–	1	–	–	–
Special collections room	–	1	–	–	–
Stack control centre	–	1	1	1	1
Photographic section	–	1	–	1	1
Xerox section	–	1	–	1	1
Telex centre	–	1	–	1	1
Bindery	1	1	–	–	1
Closed-circuit television	1	1	1	1	–
Audio-visual room	1	1	–	1	–
Seminar room	1	1	–	1	–
Chief librarian's office	1	1	–	–	–
Deputy librarian's office	1	1	–	–	–
Administration office	1	2	–	–	1
Secretary's office	1	1	–	–	–
Cataloguing department	1	3	–	–	–
Accessions department	1	1	–	–	–
Delivery and dispatch office	1	1	–	–	–
Unpacking room	–	1	–	1	–
Staff rest-room	–	1	–	–	–
Building supervisor	1	1	–	–	–

may be necessary to trace certain members of the staff who have several working bases, and in extreme examples a pocket point-to-point radio might be justified. If so, this should be included in the brief, because it is obviously more efficient to install an aerial loop in a new structure than in a completed building. A pocket paging device might be acceptable as a much cheaper alternative.

Table 8:1 shows the communications list for a large college library. Many libraries will need a much less elaborate network. It is possible to give this information in the form of a diagram, but a list is entirely adequate and less liable to cause confusion. The list does not of course include terminals used for bibliographical purposes.

New communications technology

The coming of closed-circuit television gave libraries the opportunity to bring to a reader in a remote part of the library (or campus) a page of information, instantly, without the reader leaving his work. This was a great step forward, but it has several drawbacks, the most important being that it is wasteful of staff time (if economical of the reader's). This has been replaced by the much more efficient computer terminal but only where the required information is already on the local database or is available through a network. To type information into a central microcomputer and then switch it to an outstation, or to use telex, takes up the time of a member of the staff; fax is preferable here if the information is on single sheets, otherwise it must be photocopied first. In the case where a library has an encyclopedia or the full text of a journal on CD/ROM, a branch library with a terminal can consult it immediately, but the number of such text holdings in the immediate future must be limited. New machines can also replace the traditional methods in such fields as video for story hours and fax for book requests from enquiry desk to stack. As there are no structural implications, the architect will be concerned only with the effects upon the layout of the service areas and the provision of wires and power points. If the librarian intends to bring in computer services for the major bibliographical functions of the new library, the effect upon all sections will be so fundamental that a special and highly detailed report must be issued for approval by the authority and then passed on to the architect.

Human movement

The information about movement of people, both readers and staff, was given in the primary brief because it is vital to the layout and, where major equipment such as lifts and escalators might be needed, will have important structural influences. Now that the basic decisions have been made there are other questions which require an answer:

1. Is access to certain floors to be restricted to staff? If so, will special locks and keys be necessary?
2. Will 'staff only' lifts be needed, e.g. for use with book trolleys?
3. Are lifts to operate in a different way at peak times from other times?
4. Is special provision to be made for the disabled, even on mezzanines?
5. If continuous lifts, such as paternosters, are to be used, what provision will be made for the disabled or the elderly?

If it has been decided that escalators are to be installed it is likely that the librarian will be less familiar with their qualities than with those of lifts. Escalators can deal with very large numbers indeed, and they can be reversible,

taking readers up only during the day but bringing large numbers down quickly at closing time. Alternatively, an upward escalator only may be provided, leaving readers to use stairs for downward journeys. Switched-off escalators can of course function as stairs. Escalators can be efficient but they have some drawbacks (apart from high cost): they will need far more horizontal space than lifts and will therefore be a major factor in design (see pp. 51, 53). Because of fire regulations, safety shutters will have to be fitted, and stairways have to be installed in addition to either lifts or escalators. The relationship between these facilities affects both reader traffic routes and planning considerations. Built-in powered chairlifts for the disabled should not be forgotten. Ramps should not be disregarded; they are psychologically more acceptable than short flights of stairs as well as being essential for the disabled. They should be specifically provided for the approaches to fire exits.

Fire regulations will also decide where emergency exits are to be placed. These, although obviously essential, are the despair of librarians because they so often make nonsense of the proposed security arrangements. Fire exits and the equally difficult problems of locks and keys are discussed in Chapter 12. Both are subject to regulations but are also matters of library policy, and the librarian has to make up his own mind before asking the architect to give a technical solution.

Main entrance and exit doors deserve particularly careful study. Will a lobby be needed to prevent draughts affecting staff who are on duty at a counter just inside the entrance? This is essential unless revolving doors are installed. A heat curtain may be expensive but perhaps could be justified: it is astonishing that these devices, which have proved so effective in department stores in many northern countries, are seldom to be found in libraries: too expensive? If revolving doors are proposed, is there provision for a by-pass at peak times, and can the doors be swung aside to allow furniture and similar items to enter the building?

These are all points which the librarian must think about and then formulate into questions for the architect to answer. It is difficult to say exactly how a secondary brief should be written, because it is not only the way of providing the more detailed information which is now required but also a response to the feasibility report. Once again it is vital that the librarian understands exactly what is proposed in that report.

Furniture and fittings

The critical sizes and the layout of these items are dealt with in Chapters 13 and 14; the choices available and their relative merits in Chapter 17. To the question 'Who is to choose the furniture?', the answer is that the design, material and colour of the furniture and fittings are always a fundamental part of the interior design, for which the architect is responsible. If there is a separate Interior Design Consultant he will have a valuable contribution to make, but it must be within the visual framework created by the architect. On the other hand, the librarian will be dependent on the functional efficiency of the furniture and fittings for the successful running of the library and for seeing that the atmosphere created is suitable for the needs of the readers, so he must agree every item which is proposed. Undoubtedly the best way is for the architect and librarian to discuss the matter together, see the coloured brochures issued by the very many firms operating in this field and together visit a library in which the favoured firm's products have been in use for some

8:4. Effect caused by light washing from translucent ceiling over white surfaces: Royal Library, The Hague (Architects OD 205 Delft)

were tested, and the decision made, by the members who were to sit in them. This decision included all the chairs for the library; the librarian protested in vain. Had a good relationship existed between him and the architect this need never have happened.

In some contracts the free-standing furniture and equipment will be designated 'prime cost' items. This can mean that the architect will allow an estimated sum for them in the budget but not purchase them unless specifically authorized. In these circumstances, discussion and cooperation can take place, but its chief value to a librarian is that as the purchase of these items will have to be formally authorized this will give him the opportunity to take part in the decision-making.

For some years levels of comfort in libraries have been rising steadily, and present-day readers expect much higher standards than in the past. The architect knows this; there is no need to spell it out in the brief. Because he is responsible for the allocation of costs within the agreed total sum, the architect must decide what standard of fittings, furniture and finishes the proposals can support. He may wish, for example, to make savings within the overall total by using the furniture and equipment from a single manufacturer's range because there could be contract cost advantages. In all such cases it is essential that the librarian examine the specification for, and actual examples of, every piece of furniture or fitting it is proposed to purchase, so that he can check its suitability for its future function. If something is not suitable he must say so firmly: in good conditions he can work out a compromise with the architect. In bad ones the matter will be referred as a dispute to the authority. This is something to be avoided if at all possible.

Shelving

What material and design would the librarian prefer, and why? It is worth asking this question, and in particular the second half of it, so that the priorities can be identified. What degree of adjustability is required? Is it the same in all areas? What is to be the height, depth, number of shelves, distance from the floor, of the shelving? How many size sequences are there to be in each area? Does the librarian prefer canopied or topless shelving, and why? Is there to be fitted case lighting? These matters are considered in some detail in Chapter 13.

Other considerations

Lighting

Published lighting standards will be studied by the architect (who may also have the advice of a lighting consultant), but satisfactory lighting conditions are very largely a matter of experience and judgement. As it is impossible to ascertain the preferences of the future users, the views of an experienced librarian or, better still, a library consultant can be of great value. Lighting is dealt with in detail in Chapter 11, but anyone concerned with the design of lighting for a large university or college library should read Mason[1] for his terrifying cautionary tales on the matter which he, who has surveyed very many libraries, declares to be the greatest failure of library architects. Matters which are vital to the librarian are maintenance (particularly the problem of changing worn-out tubes and bulbs) and cleaning. These are often treated as though they were inevitable but they can be alleviated by careful choice of fittings and equipment. It is up to the librarian to make the architect aware of the high importance he attaches to this subject.

time (the firm will know which library to suggest). They should test everything (and that includes sitting on the different chairs, writing at the tables and so on) and come to an agreement about each item. The architect can then be relied upon to negotiate the best possible price for the objects. The worst possible way is for furniture salesmen to be allowed on the scene before a definite decision has been made; they are experts, in many different ways.

In one case known to me a large public library was to be part of a city hall complex and a policy decision had been made to choose a single design of reading chair for the whole complex because of the favourable price obtainable for large quantities. The majority of the chairs were for committee rooms and offices; examples were brought into the committee meeting and, as seemed reasonable, they

8:5. Good reading light, but how are the windows to be cleaned? Will it be expensive?

Walls and surfaces

A high proportion of the internal divisions of many libraries will be covered by bookshelves, either in cases or on brackets, the perimeter walls, particularly window walls, being left for readers. Above the shelving and on blank walls, the architect will plan colour and texture as a part of his design. The librarian will have two legitimate points of interest here – the acoustic qualities of the surfaces and, more important, their maintenance cost.

Wall surfaces, particularly those which can be touched by readers, will soon need cleaning. This raises two questions: the cost of cleaning and the effect regular cleaning will have on the durability of the wall covering. High-gloss paint is certainly the best from this point of view, but it is often considered institutional in appearance and it has disadvantages of high reflectance of both light and sound. These disadvantages are not insurmountable: sound absorption can be provided in other ways, by floor or ceiling, and light reflection can be controlled by careful siting of light sources.

The fashion among architects for rough, hammered and pitted concrete surfaces, if only on columns, causes particular cleaning problems: the surfaces hold dust – indeed the pitted concrete seems to product dust – and they cannot be 'wiped down'. To a librarian it might seem better not to use such surfaces within a library, but if an architect chooses to do so he must be pressed to see that they are effectively sealed and cleaning instructions recorded.

In most cases it is a counsel of perfection to say that all internal surfaces should be permanent and never require renewal. This would be an enormous advantage throughout the life of the building, and it could be done. It is not up to the librarian to say how, but he should request as strongly as possible that this be taken into account in the choice of internal surfaces.

Notices

Whether or not it is strictly within the architect's province to design all the lettering depends on circumstances. He will certainly deal with the major items, and it would be intelligent to make use of his professional expertise. Time and again one visits a recently opened library to find it disfigured by notices of a quality, fount, style and colour which clash with the internal design. In a fine new library people will expect lettering in impeccable taste. If possible, the architect should choose the lettering to be used throughout, including shelf guiding, and the librarian should always keep to that style. Similarly all notice boards, inside and outside the building, should be part of the overall design.

It is now the job of the librarian to list all the notices which will be required, their comparative size and wording, and their position inside or outside the building. He will say which need to be illuminated after dark and whether a large logo (even a neon sign) is to be provided. The choice of the lettering is not his concern.

Maintenance

A librarian must never forget that during the expected life of a building, operational costs will be very much greater than the initial ones. Of the operational costs, maintenance of the fabric will be a major element. On the whole the time and money spent on maintaining public buildings such as libraries is very much lower than in comparable commercial buildings, and consequently many libraries have a run-down appearance after a few years of service.

Governing bodies find it expedient to defer redecoration as an economy; wood surfaces and seat coverings become worn in ways that would not be acceptable to commercial firms conscious of the importance of their image. Perhaps the fault lies as much with librarians as with their masters, but whatever the reason the architect must plan to keep to a minimum the need for cleaning, replacement of worn-out items, redecorating and attention to mechanical fittings. The times and conditions under which cleaning, maintenance and redecorating can be carried out will now be notified to the architect. For example, major maintenance in a school or college may have to be confined to school holiday times and in a college to vacations, but in a public library, open fifty-two weeks each year, all maintenance may have to take place while people are using the library (the cost of nightwork being prohibitive). The architect will need to bear these facts in mind when choosing materials, finishes and methods of construction.

The architect's proposals, in the form of the feasibility report, will not contain the detail which will appear at later stages in the programme. Some items of great concern to the librarian will appear in the specifications only at a very late stage, but if he is uneasy, now is the time to raise any matter which causes him concern. He can do so in design team meetings, but it is always as well for an important matter to be presented in writing (and a copy filed).

Some of the following points therefore could be posed as queries in the secondary brief. They are all the architect's business, and he *may* have them in hand. Nevertheless, it does no harm to bring them to his attention and it may avoid at a late stage in the programme that dread response 'It is too late now.'

1. *Doors* Will the machinery of main entrance doors be sound enough for the very heavy use they will receive; if they jam or break down, how will readers enter the library while repairs are in progress?
2. *Windows* Is the control machinery (if any) easy to operate or does it require equipment and ladders? Can it be secured against interference by readers? How are the windows to be cleaned? Will the cleaning be particularly expensive?
3. *Light fittings and large windows* Will they need special scaffolding in order to clean them, or will it be built into the structure? Can they be cleaned by one person, or will a team be needed? Can fittings be changed as a routine every few months, rather than piecemeal as they break down or wear out? If they are to be changed as a whole at specified intervals, will there be adequate lighting if some bulbs or tubes fail before the time for renewal arrives?
4. *Roof glazing* (if any) How is it to be cleaned and how often? Would it not be worth fitting glass pyramids, steeply sloped so as to be as far as possible self-cleaning?
5. *Power points and water taps* Will there be enough of these within a reasonable distance of every area where a cleaner is to operate? Are there adequate and well-sited cupboards for cleaning materials, and have cloakrooms been provided for cleaning staff?
6. *Redecoration* (interior and exterior) How often should it take place? How long are the fabric or other coverings of chair seats expected to last?
7. *Floor coverings* Are worn areas to be replaced in sections, or must the whole area be renewed? If in sections, is there any guarantee that matching pieces will be obtainable in the future? How often must floors be cleaned and how often resealed? How long will the operation take?

8. *Heating and ventilating machinery* What happens if it breaks down? Is there to be a maintenance contract? If so, what will it cost? How long will the library be without services when a breakdown occurs?

9. *Lighting* Is there to be any emergency provision in case the lighting system should fail? (In a building where hundreds of people can be trapped in the dark, this needs serious consideration.) Is there to be an emergency supply for other electrical requirements?

Not all the questions listed above are strictly concerned with maintenance but they are all matters which might place the librarian in difficulties after the architect has left the scene. It would be ideal if the authority has its own buildings or maintenance officer who can take part in enough of the later discussions to have a good knowledge of how the library is being built. Otherwise the architect must record his recommendations as to the cleaning and maintenance schedules for all areas. It would be possible, at a price, for the architect to take part in the supervision of maintenance for a limited number of years after the opening; this seldom happens.

Client nominees

The architect is well acquainted with the materials and services offered by suppliers in many fields, and any comment by the librarian will usually be superfluous. There are exceptions, however, when the librarian (with his authority's approval) feels strongly that some firm's equipment or materials are so exceptionally suitable for the project that he will require its use in the library as a 'client's nominee'. The reason for this stipulation is usually the desire to achieve uniformity within an institution or a system of branches. Other cases occur with library supply firms who make furniture and shelving based on unit factory-made components. These can include a very wide range of designs, although the basic materials and size modules will be the same. The price advantages are undeniable. Some of the firms also offer advice both on design and layout of furniture and shelving as part of a package deal – 'free' if the merchandise is purchased; because of their very wide experience over many years and in many countries this advice can well be of great value. This is a difficult matter: the architect, when conceiving a design, will include a vision of the furnishings in it. To force him to use alien designs, materials, and above all colours may upset his whole conception. On the other hand, the financial advantages of mass-production of this kind are undeniable and if the brief shows that such equipment or furniture is a client nomination, then the architect can plan accordingly from his earliest designs. The expertise in such specialist firms also helps to avoid the pitfalls inherent in using firms without such wide experience. Even if no client nominees as such have been stipulated, the architect will allow in his estimates certain prime cost sums for specialist materials and services which he does not consider to be within the competence of the contractor himself to provide. These are chiefly proprietary products such as lifts. With all specialist work, hardwood flooring, for example, it is well for the contractor to be asked whether he wishes to tender for it; this he may be able to do through a specialist firm which he himself will appoint. Prices have to be watched carefully, but as a general principle the more control the contractor has over specialists the better; sub-contractors imposed by the architect can be a source of friction, whereas if the builder himself appoints a specialist he has responsibility for the performance and can apply pressure without reference to the architect. The question of the general contractor's supervisory fees needs to be discussed and findings recorded.

Further information

The architect himself may ask for the following facts in a questionnaire, but it will save time if the librarian takes steps to supply the information as part of the secondary brief:

1. What sort of vehicles make deliveries, how often and at what times? Should unloading take place under cover, or are the loads so small that this requirement is unimportant? What tables, benches, racks and so on will be required for packing and unpacking? How much packing material will need to be stored nearby?

2. What machines are to be used in each staff work area? How many typewriters, duplicators, photocopiers and other machines, particularly those which call for power supply points?

3. What are the details of the equipment mentioned in the primary brief as reader service aids, such as microform readers, and photocopiers? Will there be ancillary items; e.g. if the photocopiers are coin-operated, is a coin-changing machine needed?

4. Will cleaning be by contract, or will the library have its own cleaners? Are there strict limits upon times when cleaning may be done? What are the preferences for materials and methods (such as vacuum dusting of shelves)? Are any unusual provisions needed for storage of cleaning materials? In which areas will cleaners' sinks be wanted?

5. How much waste accumulates weekly, and how is disposal to take place? Does the local authority supply special bags for its disposal? (The architect can certainly find this out for himself, but it is the librarian's business to be sure.)

6. Where is postal delivery to be made? Entirely through a postal slot or by bag delivery? If there is to be book-return slot for use by the public, are the books to remain in a box behind the slot, and if so, how many is it to hold?

7. Has the librarian a preference for lobby, porch, canopy or 'dripping area'? Should absorbent mats be provided, or will 'barrier mats' be supplied on a contract basis? Where are cigarettes to be extinguished and discarded, and umbrellas left?

8. What sort of cycle stands will be needed? Dog rails? For how many dogs? What security must there be for a pram park?

9. What of signposting? Will a crest be used? Is the main sign to be large or small, lit or unlit, eye-catching or discreet? In how many places will there be notices to give times of opening of the various services?

10. Are there to be internal and external displays? How big will they be, and how much security will they call for? Lockable glass cases, or just noticeboards? Baize, peg-board, or pin-board?

11. Will there be shelf, tier or case guiding, or all three? What is the preferred method and material? How often are guides likely to be altered or moved? Must the guiding be protected against vandalism?

12. Where are trolleys to be parked in off-peak times? Are they to be used as relief shelving; has the 'hod' method been considered? (This is a system whereby trolleys have removable shelves which can be fitted, complete with their books, on to special tiers of shelving.)

13. Are floral displays, changed regularly under contract, desirable or financially acceptable?

Table 8.2 Equipment lists

Reader service areas
acoustic hood for telephone
audio cassette players
audio tape players
bell alarm for closing time
blinds
blotters
bookcase guiding
book return box
book supports
book trolleys
building directory
calculators
CD players
CD storage
CD/ROM equipment
change machine
circulation desks
clocks – electric
closed-circuit television
coat hanging units
communication system
cupboards
curtains
date indicators
date stamps
desks – staff
detection equipment
display cabinets
display stands
doormats (dirt-absorbing)
electric erasers
electric fans
emergency exit alarm
   systems
emergency lighting
equipment trolleys
exhibition cases
exit signs
filing cabinets
film loop projectors
film strip projectors
fire alarm (whole building)
fire extinguishers
first aid equipment
floor guides
floor polishers
floor washers
gramophone record
   cabinets
gramophone record players
kikstools
key cabinet
light boxes
light tables (for map
   consultation)
map cabinets
media storage equipment
message pads
microfiche readers
microfilm readers – 16 mm
microfilm readers – 35 mm
microfiche reader printers
microfilm reader printers
mirrors
pegboard display units
pencil sharpeners
photocopiers – coin-
   operated
pinboards
plan cabinets
plant containers

public address equipment
return book box and slot
shelf label holders
slide projector
stack end desks or shelves
staplers
storage cupboards
strip index units
tables (readers)
tables (tracing)
tape recorders
telephones
telephones for public use
television receivers
terminals
tier guiding
torches
turnstiles
umbrella stand
vending machine
video disc players
video recorders
video tape players
wall display boards
waste bins

Audio-visual area
amplifiers
audio tape splicer
audio disc player
background projector and
   supports
back projection screens
blackout curtains
cable release
CD player
film projectors
film strip projectors and
   holders
film strip viewers
film viewers
filter holder
filters
floodlights
headsets
lens hoods
light dimmers
long-focus lenses
loop projectors
loudspeakers
magnifier
microfilm camera
micro lenses
microphones
opaque projectors
overhead projectors
pentaprism viewfinders
portable screens
projector screens
radio receivers
slide copier
slide mounting equipment –
   electric and/or manual
slide projector
slide projector – magazine-
   programmed
slide viewers
slide viewing light boxes
spotlights
studio electronic flash unit
tape decks
tape copiers

tape players
tape recorders
television camera
television monitors
tripods
video disc recorder
video tape recorders
video players
waste bins

Seminar rooms
audio cassette players
blackboard – wall-mounted
blackboard – portable
blinds
chairs
clocks – electric
cupboards
curtains
dais
desks
display stands
emergency lighting
equipment trolleys
film projectors
film loop projectors
fire alarms
fire extinguishers
headphones
overhead projectors
projection screen
projector stand
projectors
shelving
tables
telephones
television receivers
video recorder
video disc player
video tape player
wall display boards
whiteboards

Technical services
adding machine
adhesive tape dispensers
blotters
book hoist
calculators
coat hooks
coat stands
collator
communication system
dictating equipment
electric eraser
electric stylus
fire extinguisher
first aid box
franking machines
hand drier
key cabinet
kikstools
lettering sets
media storage equipment
microfiche reader/printers
microfilm reader/printers
mirrors
numbering machines
offset printing machine
paper chopper
paper drilling machines
paper punches

paper stitchers
pedal bins
penstands
pencil sharpeners
photocopiers
rulers
shredding machine
sink unit
staff lockers
staple extractors
staple gun
stapling machines
stationery cupboards
stools
string dispenser
strip index units
tables
table lamps (adjustable)
tape measures
telephones
trolleys (industrial type)
typewriters – electric
typewriters – electronic
   composing
waste bins
water boiler
weighing scales
wire cutters
wrapping paper containers

Chief librarian's suite
adding machines
adhesive tape dispenser
armchairs
ashtrays
blotting pads
bookcases
calculators
cassette players
chairs – chief librarian,
   secretary, clerks, typists
clocks, electric (including
   master clock)
clothes brushes
coat hanging units
coat hooks and stands
coffee-making equipment
coffee table
collator
communication system
crockery
crockery cupboard
cupboards – steel
cupboards – wood
curtains
date indicators
date/time stamps
desks
desk extensions
dictation equipment
door signal
electric fans
electric fires
electric kettle
fax transceiver
filing cabinets
fire extinguishers
key cabinet
lettering sets
message pads
microfiche reader/printer
microfilm reader/printer

mirrors
numbering machine
paper chopper
paper knives
paper punches
pedal bins
penstands
photocopiers
pinboards
plant containers
refrigerators
safe
shelf units
shredding machine
stapling machines
stationery cupboards
stencil trays
storage bins
string dispensers
tables
table lamps, adjustable
tape measure
tea-making equipment
telephones
telex terminal (live)
towels
trolleys
tumblers
typewriters
umbrella stand
video player
wall display boards
wardrobes
word processors

Staff room and toilets
armchairs
ashtrays
bicycle racks
blinds
breadknife
chairs
coat hooks
coat stands
clothes brushes
coffee pots
coffee urn
cooker – electric or gas
crockery
crockery cupboard
curtains
cutlery
dishwasher
dusters
easy chairs
fire extinguisher
formica-topped tables
frying pan
hand dryer
incinerator
kettle
mirror
mops
pedal bins
plant tubs
plants
rack for tea towels
refrigerator
saucepans
shower
shower curtains
soap dispenser

Table 8.2 Equipment lists *(continued)*

staff lockers	toilet roll holders	coat hanger	*Building maintenance*	electric fires – portable
storage bins	towel holders	couch bed	block and tackle	first aid equipment
storage cupboards – kitchen	towels	cupboard	book hoist (unless in-built)	fumigation equipment
tables	umbrella stand	first aid box	burglar alarm	humidifiers – portable
table lamps	vacuum cleaner	pillows	carpet cleaning utensils	hygrometer and other test equipment
tea cups and saucers	washing up bowl	sanitary bucket	carpet shampooing machine	mops
tea pots	waste bins	stretcher	dehumidifiers – portable	vacuum cleaners
telephone	water boiler	table, chairs	dustbins	waste bins
tin-opener		tea-making equipment	dusters	window cleaning ladders
toaster	*First aid room*	waste bin		
	blankets	water flask		

Many of these points are considered in more detail in the chapters which follow, and such a list can never be complete; to attempt one is to stimulate the mind into turning out problems which can be studied before the plans have crystallized, and for which the best solutions may be too expensive if left until later stages. The trouble with such a list is that it is not systematic and so it is very easy to omit something of importance. By far the best way is for the librarian to visualize every area of the future library, section by section, and to make a detailed list of every single item which will be required there. It is a daunting task and, as no two libraries are exactly alike in their needs, it cannot be borrowed from another project. The lists here (Table 8.2) concern a large college: they do not indicate numbers required but will serve as an aide-mémoire. A successful series of lists has the added advantage of staking a claim for many small items which the librarian would like but has doubts of being able to get from the always depleted budget available to him at the conclusion of a major building project.

Equipment lists

An example of an equipment list arranged by areas appears, as already noted, in Table 8:2.

Visits and reading

With the help of the foregoing information from the librarian, the architect will use visits, reading, observation, user survey studies and any other relevant sources to amplify what he already knows and to throw more light on the problem. Meanwhile the specialist consultants will be carrying out studies relevant to this stage of their own work. For example the heating and ventilating engineers, now that the type of equipment which they proposed has been approved and its position allocated, will work on further details of installations and trunking. Each member will advise the architect on the design influence of the various alternatives and keep the quantity surveyor informed of all financial implications. The architect will of course bring to all meetings his own appreciation of modern development in design and materials. It is at this stage in the planning that the team will toss around and discard ideas in profusion. It is far, far better to 'waste' a little time at this stage than to complete a library only to find that a a new

method or a new material would have drastically improved the result.

Visits

Visits to new libraries may seem to many to be light relief. In fact they are an exhausting and necessary duty: wherever possible they should be carried out by the architect and the librarian together, preferably at an early stage. There is much to be said for further visits now that choices of furnishing, finishes and equipment have to be made. In most cases the responsibility lies with the architect, but experience has shown the value of joint visits. The principle that a librarian and an architect studying a library together will come up with a vision richer than either could achieve separately is behind the activities of the Architect–Librarian Working Party of the Library Association. It proved conclusively that the contrast provided by the separate angle of approach of the two professionals gives an entirely new dimension to the resulting picture. For tactical reasons it may be advantageous to take on the visit the leader of the authority's governing body; this particular occasion could be a return visit to the building which originally appeared to offer the most acceptable parallels.

Perhaps the most valuable exercise of all is to ask the librarian of a newly completed library what he would do if he were starting again with hindsight; the result can be most illuminating. It is a mistake to visit only renowned or 'successful' libraries: the reasons for the comparative failure of others can prove of great value. It may also be found that popular votes of success or failure have been too hastily expressed.

Reading

There is a great deal of published information about new libraries. Articles appear in the library professional press, but many of them are submitted by the librarians responsible for the new libraries and so are inclined to be uncritical. Each December issue of the *Library Journal* (US) is devoted to the subject but is mainly statistical.

Articles in the architectural press – in Britain chiefly the *Architects' Journal* and *Architectural Review* – are better, if fewer. Because these are written from the architect's point of view they complement those written from the librarian's angle (although some also include an assessment by a librarian).

9 The rest of the programme of action

The feasibility report, with its timetable and cost implications, has been accepted by the authority; the architect has studied the secondary brief and has turned also to other appropriate sources of information. His original planning concepts may now need reconsidering in the light of new or expanded requirements from the secondary brief and from the information gained in studies and visits. This is also the point where he has another long hard look at his draft sketches to see whether he has really made allowance for all the important factors. Is the shape truly functional? Are there as few changes of level as possible? Are all areas easily accessible, especially for the disabled? Have the elements restricting flexibility of function been reduced to an irreducible minimum?

The architect will also incorporate the results of his dialogue with the various specialist consultants. Has full account been taken of the need to suppress noise? Are all those windows necessary for lighting, or, if they are purely for aesthetic effect, is not the price to be paid for them too high? Is it not worthwhile after all to install a more sophisticated ventilation system, and if so where could the heavy plant be located? Will it not be necessary for maintenance staff to be given living accommodation on the premises to look after the service equipment, even at the extra cost and space loss so caused?

These random points are but a few of many, and with each further step in the planning and design process the opportunity for change becomes rarer and more expensive.

Auxiliary areas

In studying his drafts and proposals the architect will want to be sure that he is using the space to the best advantage and that the proportion which can be used for the library's own operations is as high as possible; with this the librarian will be in full accord. At an earlier stage the architect distinguished between operational space and balance areas (non-assignable space). He will now look again at the latter, distinguishing between the circulation space which is inherent in the design and the space occupied by auxiliary areas. He may compare the results with published figures which illustrate desirable ratios and with plans of comparable projects in order to see that he has done his sums right. He may need to sub-divide, at least notionally, the auxiliary areas in order to check the suitability of his proposed allocation.

The auxiliary areas may be divided into service and environmental areas.
Service areas Main services: heating chambers, ventilating and air-conditioning plant, electricity sub-stations, distribution and meter rooms, water tank areas, service equipment stores, cleaners' rooms and distribution ducts.
Sanitary.
Welfare: cloakrooms, rest rooms, canteens, staff rooms, bicycle stores, garages.
Environmental areas These are less easily defined because they arise from the architect's vision of the library as an attractive contribution to community life. They may include open spaces where sculpture can be displayed, areas with walls for paintings and displays generally, permanent art features (sculptures, murals etc.), gardens,

internal courts with fountains or other pleasant features. To these must be added space needed for purely architectural reasons.

The librarian will obviously be interested in seeing that as high a proportion as possible of the building is available for his operations and would be happy to be able to find 'standard' figures which he could check to see that the architect is achieving this. There is, however, a limit to the value of systematizing and comparing space ratios, even between libraries of a similar type, and here the limit has been reached. The architect decides on the environmental factors inherent in his design; he needs to bear in mind the proportions which he has notionally allowed in his planning, but beyond that he must use his own judgement. If a librarian is unhappy with the ratios in this respect, he is challenging the acceptability of the whole design; this is a serious matter and only friendly persuasion can be used.

The ratio of both auxiliary and circulation areas to the whole will tend to fall as the size of the library increases; a large library is therefore usually more functionally efficient than a small one – in this respect at any rate.

Flexibility and adaptability

Once again these important facets will be under discussion. Unless a completely open-plan library has been agreed upon, the architect is likely to find the librarian's requirements in this field particularly irksome and perhaps entirely impracticable within fixed cost limits. Flexibility will be much easier to provide in a single storey than in a multi-storey building because mechanical and sanitary services can usually be grouped together in a corner and there will be no need for lifts or stairs; if a single roof span is possible there need be no fixed structural elements to prevent a complete open-plan layout. With an even lighting plan, the same flooring materials throughout and the use of demountable partitions, there is little difficulty in arranging a thoroughly flexible layout. The open-floor, single-room plan, divided only by low bookcases, has been widely used in popular libraries of all kinds.

In university libraries, where the number of books easily accessible is higher and the intensity of use per volume may be lower, the problem has a different emphasis than in public libraries, where open-plan designs, as well as offering infinite flexibility, give unity to the space and lead readers to notice and perhaps be drawn to books on all subjects. Such a layout produces a feeling of space and of colour (because books in publishers' jackets are themselves particularly colourful). Browsing areas can be notionally limited by bookcases lower than eye-level and by changes of furniture design; more definite breaks, such as those between browsing areas and offices, can be marked by tall bookcases (which must of course be solid-backed). Bookcases like these, single-sided with panels on the reverse, are used effectively to make a division between a reading area and a main library corridor. The chief difficulty in open planning arises when attempts are made to accommodate both quiet (reference and study) and noisy (popular lending and children's sections) within the same open plan. Although this will be almost inevitable in smaller self-contained libraries, great difficulty will be found in preventing aural and visual distraction. Because all furniture is movable within open plan, the operational success or failure will be in the hands of the librarian, who will be able to arrange the furniture according to his own ideas. The distractions should not be overlooked: in the offices for which open plan was originally designed there was an internal discipline which is not to be expected when children can enter study areas. The extreme example of the large open-plan areas in the library of the Centre Pompidou in Paris, where informality and the mixing of books, audio-visual equipment and a stream of visitors produce uproar and visual chaos, is a warning. This is entirely in the librarian's hands: from the architect's side there are no real solutions, but noise problems may be partly alleviated by the generous use of noise-deadening material and by installing low-level hum to absorb peak sound frequencies. To prevent visual distraction it is sometimes possible to arrange higher bookcases as divisions and face all serious study seats away from reader movement. Use of semi-carrel fitments, or placing seats beside windows or in alcoves made of book-lined walls is no disadvantage if sufficient space can be left around each reader to prevent the feeling of being penned in.

In multi-storey buildings, however, the position is very different; the structural requirements and the need for stairs and lifts will inevitably entail fixed elements, and it is therefore much more difficult to allow for full flexibility. If the architect has played his part and designed a structure which can give as much flexibility as possible, the librarian, now he has studied the plans, can indicate exactly the zones in which he needs the opportunity to change, allowing the architect to provide the limiting and sometimes dull fully-flexible squares only where necessary. Where the need for flexibility can thus be identified, opportunity for future change can be found without resorting to full open planning.

Large central libraries will have areas, and possibly whole floors, devoted to open-access conditions but also areas or floors for closed stacks. University libraries will have large areas of open stack and various smaller areas, special collections, for example, in closed access. By placing closed stacks at typical open stack distances – 1400 mm (4 ft 6 in), the area can if desired be changed to open access without alteration. Open stacks can be closed merely by fitting barriers or hinged gates. The only cost caused by this interchangeability is that the closed stacks cannot be arranged as economically as they would be with narrower aisles. To interchange either of these stacking methods with open access, however, means that the floor loading must be based on the highest single requirement, and this may cause extra structural costs. If this is accepted, and the grid and column sizes are carefully planned at the outset, it will be possible for stacks and bookcases to be resited when required without waste of space. The effects of this flexibility on lighting and floor finishes will be considered in later chapters.

In the Birmingham Central Library the reference floors have a large central void, the closed stack forming one L shape, the other L holding the combined open-access and reading area (see plan, p. 77). This offers unique advantages: the closed-stack contents can relate to each subject area located conveniently at hand and there is good flexibility, although a partition wall would have to be removed to change the closed-stack area to public use. The method depends on having a high level of loading throughout and is assisted by the use of a large 11 m (36 ft) grid square and a consequent absence of the usual forest of columns.

At the library of the University College, Cardiff, it has been possible, by using a structural grid of 13.5 × 9 m (44 ft 6 in × 29 ft 6 in), to have only six internal columns in each floor area of 1685 m^2 (18 000 sq ft): an immense advantage in potential flexibility. The floors spanning between in situ concrete frames consist of inverted U-shaped pre-cast concrete units which, when assembled, provide ducts for the distribution of conditioned air and act as the ceiling containing the lighting fittings and acoustic baffles.

Position of operational areas

The positioning of areas for the various reader services, and the layout within each area, are matters on which the architect will spend many hours, and it is only to be expected that several drafts will be considered before a detailed proposal is put forward. Even after his insistence on the ubiquitous 'flexibility' the librarian will have very strong feelings on this vitally important point, and will know how important it is that readers are served in positions relevant to the function, not where the architect happens to have placed the facility, perhaps to make the area symmetrical. When making the initial allocation of areas for the different operational needs of a large library, the architect will inevitably find that demand for main floor (usually ground floor) space will be far in excess of what is available. With the librarian he will settle first what *must* go there – main entrance, goods loading, parking for mobile libraries – and second, those features which the librarian would *prefer* to have on the ground floor, such as circulation counters, quick reference and the most used departments. In these decisions, the needs of users are paramount; where certain services are likely to be well used by older people, and therefore probably a higher proportion of the disabled, they must be placed as near to the entrance as possible and on an easily accessible level.

The often despised basement can, with careful planning, be used for meetings, which, in community services, may take place in the daytime. Access need present little difficulty. Certainly in a public library this is more important than making the decision on grounds of the 'importance' which professionals might give to particular subjects. In the Central Library of Newcastle upon Tyne the lending library was situated on the ground floor but the central readers' advisers' desk and public catalogues were sited on the first floor. The City Librarian[1] reported that readers were reluctant to go up to the first floor for these services, so that it became necessary to create a second readers' advisory post on the ground floor. A similar layout could well have been planned in an undergraduate library without the same adverse reader reaction. Other cases occur when the ground-floor entrance to a main-street public library is only large enough for a guiding display or possibly a general enquiry point, in addition to stairs, lift or escalator. This may be the price which has to be paid for a prime site. If a central public bibliographical area, including card catalogues, is to be placed on the ground floor, then the housing of cataloguing staff can become critical; as a backroom activity it might seem reasonable to place it on an upper floor, where there is less demand for space, but this can necessitate either the creation of a staff catalogue separate from the public one, or alternatively (and usually in addition) frequent journeys by cataloguing staff to public catalogues. Both expedients can be very expensive indeed and the librarian may insist that at least some provision be made on the ground floor for cataloguing and cognate staff processes. The replacement of the card catalogue – whether by computer-output microform (COM) or on-line terminal – does at least completely solve this problem.

The chief librarian may require that his own office should be on the ground floor so that he can keep an eye on the key points. If, however, he controls a large institution, having secretarial office and visitor reception areas, he should yield priority of site to his line staff. Although new books and other materials will almost certainly arrive on the ground floor and will progress directly to accessioning and other processes, there will be cases where it is worth the extra trouble and expense of having newly arrived materials conveyed to an upper floor in order to free the most easily accessible floors for readers.

All these library service priorities have planning implications which can be decided only by discussion. Sometimes an architect may tend to mass spaces rather than base them on function, and this can lead to his thinking of the form of the building from the outside. It may also lead him to make the ground floor an architectural or display space, causing every reader to make his way upstairs or to use the lifts on every visit. Libraries on stilts are still to be found, especially where the open ground space meets environmental needs, possibly as a garden. It is an expensive provision, even if the open space becomes a much-needed car park.

Subject departments

An alternative to the traditional division of public library buildings into lending and reference sections is the creation of subject departments which combine all reader-service functions for a single subject within what is almost a separate library. Each department may be self-contained in having its own issue and return counter, but until recently it was normal for this function to be centralized and placed so as to control entrance and exit of the building. One of the great advantages of computerized book-issuing systems is that the terminals can be duplicated and placed anywhere, each having full access to, and interaction with, the library's issue-return-location-reserve (and often security activation and deactivation) centre. Because of this, the question of the security of entrance and exit can be considered in an entirely different context. The subject department principle is in effect used in most university libraries, with a central bibliographical area provided separately, but its application to public libraries is comparatively recent and is confined to those which can afford the extra space and extra staff which this system undoubtedly requires. In general, the trend to subject-departmentalized public libraries will call for larger buildings. Even when this principle is not fully adopted, most public libraries will create some subject departments, particularly where non-book materials form a significant part of the stock. Music, discs, tapes, films, prints, painting and so on need separate treatment, if only for their peculiar handling and issue problems.

Medium-sized public libraries, lacking the space or money to apply subject departmentalism overall, may use various diluted versions based on a so-called 'service in depth' with conventional large, open shelving areas, but keeping together specialized material on subjects within certain interest groupings. Another step in this direction, but a much more perfunctory one, is division of the book stock and reader service into serious (information) and popular (recreation). An area will be given over to fiction and popular non-fiction, and another to serious non-fiction associated with reference books or having the reference area adjoining.

This pattern is chiefly confined to very small public libraries where such a notional division is all that can be expected for a village community. Nevertheless this subject is treated very seriously in *Designing a Medium-sized Public Library*.[2] Such service divisions are critical in smaller buildings and should be decided in the first place by the librarian, but the implications will influence the architect in space allocation and choice of furniture as well as the internal environmental design, which will have much to contribute in such limited buildings.

Single-room libraries

Most very small libraries are on single floors, open access and open plan. They are in effect single rooms, the main layout factors being the position of the windows, entrances and mains services. These libraries give a good opportunity to practise layouts, the possible variations being small. In such simple cases the librarian's ideas as expressed in the brief and particularly in the traffic diagram can be very swiftly incorporated into sketch plans.

Most books on library planning contain floor layout plans of large buildings: because they look simple and are interesting to study they can lead the librarian to believe that the placing of free-standing furniture is a really important part of the planning process, whereas in fact it is a simple and pleasant exercise which can be repeated until a satisfactory result is obtained. The real value of such plans is to students, enabling them to appreciate the dangers of inflexibility in structural elements and to visualize traffic and use patterns in different situations. The result of such study should be reflected in more efficient briefing, not in attempts by a librarian to translate these requirements into graphic terms.

No great harm will be done if a librarian does sketch out such a layout as an example, but only for a single-room situation. Once the position gets more complicated, and space relationships, circulation, and a thousand other factors outside his experience and training have to be considered, he must bow out. The more he has studied the question, however, the more valuable will be his comments upon the architect's layout proposals, after testing his functional requirements against the architect's own rationally designed layout.

Rooms for special purposes

Small public libraries, particularly those which treat seriously their position as a community centre, may need to provide lecture, film and music recital rooms. If these activities are to take place after the book service has ended for the day, it is possible for them to utilize certain library areas for the purpose by moving the furniture and using flexible partitioning. This practice was common in Britain in the 1930s. A converse arrangement was to use the local schoolroom after classes had ceased for the day, lockable bookcases being rolled out and a counter erected so as to form a simple public library. These seem reasonable expedients when space is short and a room will be needed only when another activity has entirely ceased; but it is seldom very successful and is to be deprecated except where there is the direst shortage of space and money.

The library profession has found from bitter experience that dual-purpose rooms, and particularly dual-purpose furniture, are a menace. A possible exception is the adaptation of children's libraries for occasional use for story hours, but even here a specially designed alcove proves a great advantage with a very small loss of space. An alternative is to provide a story hour room (without 'kiddy-winky' atmosphere) which can be used for adult meetings in the evenings, but it is a poor expedient.

Most structural factors will have been largely predetermined by tentative decisions made at the feasibility stage: number of floors, positioning of heavy loads, choice of heating and ventilating machinery and so on. All implications of such decisions must be considered carefully. In the past most libraries were of the fixed-function type, consisting of a network of rooms, each designed to house some specific operation. This method should not be brushed aside, for it had many advantages: in a known situation it was economical of space, in that each operation could be neatly framed, and it allowed each room to have a character and atmosphere suitable for its purpose. Dignity was obtained by impressive entrance halls and lofty reading rooms, and intimacy was created in other rooms by bookshelves enclosing pockets of seating for readers. This is still by far the best method of planning and building in circumstances which can be confidently expected never to change. Memorial special collections are a good example.

Outline planning

During the process of producing outline plans, cooperation between members of the team will be close. The librarian will be party to many of the discussions and will have answered questions and made comments as requested. Up to this point he will certainly have seen the plans which were produced as part of the feasibility stage, but now for the first time he will be given plans to take away, to study and to discuss with his specialist departmental heads. He may wish to involve staff members at other levels and perhaps a union representative; this is a matter of tactics and is for him alone to decide.

At this stage he must be sure that he himself thoroughly understands the plans, because he will have to interpret them to his staff. The ability to read plans is not usually part of the training of a librarian, and he has therefore to learn a new technique. The first matter to be taken seriously is the scale. This will be stated on every drawing; those which the librarian will study are likely to have a drawn scale also, and this can be a great help; but he can easily use a small-scale rule. Plans which have so far been discussed in general terms may include block plans of the neighbourhood, which will often be to the scale of 1:2000, and site plans to a scale of between 1:500 and 1:200, which will enable him to visualize the building in its immediate surroundings. The drawings which he will now handle will be internal location plans with a scale from 1:200 to 1:100, and these will enable him to grasp all he needs to know of passage routes and the location of furniture. Later in the programme detail drawings will be presented to him with a scale from 1:5 to full size, but he will only study these when he is considering the details of a piece of furniture in which he is specially concerned – such as the construction of the counter.

For the present, then, and at sketch design stage, he will be concerned with plans from which he can visualize the whole library and how its operations are to take place. He will soon find floor plans easy to understand and will see on them figures which show the difference in level from floor to floor. These figures are all relative to key reference planes which, as far as libraries are concerned, means a certain (usually the main) finished floor level.

Drawings showing the vertical aspects of the plans – elevations and sections – are more difficult to visualize; it takes practice to be able to think in terms of the structure as seen from one of the directional lines marked on each floor plan, usually shown as A–A, B–B and so on. With a little tact it may be possible to get a lesson from a friendly architect; it is absolutely essential that the librarian should understand these plans, though sections in an irregularly shaped building can be very difficult.

By the time the librarian has grasped the scale and the basic layout of columns and changes of level as shown in the architect's drawings and has acquired enough confidence in his ability to estimate the scale without having to check anew every time, he can carry out that most helpful and illuminating experience, 'walking the floors', mentally measuring himself against the routes, through the doors, up the stairs. As he does so he will get to be conscious of the ceiling heights around him, the location of the windows and their height and size. When he has confidence in this, he can look at the orientation so as to know at what angle the sun will be visible through a window and at what time of day and which days of the year. As he 'stands' in the future library and looks around, he can see the routes which readers and staff will use, see where the stairs, lifts and entrances are, and try to anticipate any visual or audial distractions. It may help if he makes paper cut-outs of furniture and equipment to the scale of the floor plans, trying out the positioning of tables, bookcases, counters and other free-standing essential of the service. This will give him a clear idea of the space each item will occupy, how much has to be allowed for those who will work there or walk around the piece of furniture or equipment.

This exercise can be helpful, but it must be realized that it is only an exercise. It can lead to better-informed discussions with the team but it must not be regarded as the way to position furniture. The interior design will have been visualized with the furniture in certain positions; it is inevitable that in the future, changes will be made to the placings, but until after the official opening it is better for it to be left where the design expert put it. It is equally important that this expert is thoroughly aware of the functional needs of the library and the views of the librarian. As the architect proceeds to the next steps – the scheme design and detail drawings – the librarian, who by now has a full picture of the library, can develop his own views on such practical matters as shelving, reading conditions, ancillary user requirements, physical conditions, lighting and security. The chapters which follow deal with each of these subjects in turn.

Outline proposals

At the conclusion of the outline planning stage the architect will probably be required to submit a report embodying all his conclusions and proposals up to this point. It will be his responsibility to coordinate and apply all the proposals made by the various specialists. Their recommendations will have been notified to the quantity surveyor, who will have been analysing the cost implications of every tentative decision reached by the team, and its relation to the cost limits. The report will include outline plans and elevations, possibly isometric drawings or an artist's impression, even a video or a model (although this is more likely at the feasibility stage). Some of the proposals submitted in the feasibility report may have to be amended and resubmitted to show the most up-to-date proposals. With the plans will be a new estimate of costs, broken down into various major headings but not usually detailed. The authority will be asked to approve this report before the team goes on to the next stage, that of developing the scheme design.

The architect may have to bring to the authority's

attention certain matters requiring a specific decision; for example, after full consideration of all alternatives, the team may have decided that certain of the brief's requirements are impossible within the limits laid down, either by the statutory authorities or by the client, particularly as regards cost limits. These matters will be for the authority to decide and the scheme cannot proceed until either the architect's proposals are accepted and the limits modified, or the brief is amended so that the team can work out acceptable proposals.

Outline planning, sketch and scheme designs are not exact disciplines. In a small project the process will be a single flow with periodic and routine reports of progress but no formal submissions stage by stage. In larger and more complicated projects there will be a firm division between the various steps. These are usually the schematic design stage, the design development or preliminary drawings stage (which includes complete floor plans, elevations and sections) and the working drawings stage.

Scheme design

With the outline proposals agreed, the team now sets out to prepare a full scheme for the project, going through the same procedure once again, each member carrying out further studies of his own special subject and its implications with regard to the plan as a whole. The proposals from each specialist will then be more specific, especially in space, access and loading, the effects of which will be most important to the entire plan. The specialists will also provide more details of prices, so that the quantity surveyor can continue working towards a more realistic cost estimate.

The librarian will be concerned with many of the ideas, particularly those relating to layout, use of space and their functional implications. By this time the plans will be so far developed that every change will have an effect on space allocations already made, and it is likely that the librarian's operational intentions will be affected. A very common example is that the heating engineer finds that in a certain area he will need a wider duct than had earlier appeared to be necessary; the architect will alter his drawings accordingly. The change may make a passage-way narrower than is acceptable and the obvious remedy would be for a nearby readers' service point to be moved a few feet. The librarian realizes that this would result in a changed relationship with a book hoist that would increase the action needed to obtain every book from stack, and so add to the staff's work every working hour throughout the life of the building. He will report this to the architect, who after discussion, probably involving the heating engineer, will attempt to resolve the problem in a way acceptable to all concerned.

This example is not meant to show that the librarian's requirements are more important than those of any other officer, but that if he had not been kept informed, plans would have crystallized to a point when it would have been too late to make a change; the necessary alterations would have had expensive repercussions throughout the building. From this point in the programme, therefore, the librarian must be constantly involved and the developing plans must be sent to him for comment.

What if his voice is ignored? This may seem to be anticipating trouble, but it is trouble which is too often met. In discussing with a librarian the weaknesses in operation of his new library, one too often hears: 'I pointed out to the architect that this would make the library too hot/cold/ noisy/cramped, but he assured he that this would not be

so.' It is an undoubted failing among some architects that at such an advanced stage, when any change can have serious repercussions, they find it easier to reassure the librarian than to rethink the whole sector. What can the librarian do if he has reason to believe that one of the architect's proposals will turn out to be a failure in terms of the library's operations? If teamwork has been effective it will never happen, but the unpleasant possibility must be faced.

It must be accepted that the librarian is employed for his professional judgements just as much as is the architect. The librarian's judgement has no standing in technical matters of library building, but it is pre-eminent where the library's future running is concerned. A serious disagreement, therefore, is a matter for the librarian's professional conscience; if he feels that his requirements are not being met then he must inform his masters of this fact, having given the architect notice that he will do so. A professional librarian, responsible to his authority for the effective operation of a library, cannot sit by and see erected a building which will, in his opinion, suffer from an avoidable operational inefficiency. In such a case the authority has no alternative but to consider this as a dispute between two professionals and it must either decide arbitrarily or appoint another person, perhaps its own architect or another librarian, to give an opinion. If the architect's views are supported, then the librarian can be content that he has done his duty; if he stands silent out of awe or friendship for the architect, he is betraying his professional trust. It must be said that such an event is very unlikely to occur if the librarian has been accepted as a member of the team and not as a 'client representative' who should stand on the side-lines.

By the end of the scheme design stage the architect will have completed planning in general and made decisions on all matters except those of detail. Outline specifications will have been drawn up. Among other things outline specifications will lay down the basic building materials to be used, but facings will have been specifically proposed and agreed at feasibility stage. Any necessary approvals will once more have been obtained from the various powers. The result will be the presentation to the authority of a completed scheme with a full explanation, references to the brief as it developed during the stages of consultation, a cost plan and a timetable. Only when the authority accepts this scheme and all its implications, including costs, is the architect able to move on to the next stage.

By the time the general outline of structure and layout have been established, a number of areas will have been identified where decisions need to be made, at first in fairly general terms, and then, as the scheme progresses, in some detail, ending in a full and definitive statement of instructions to the contractor. In these subject areas the architect, or the specialist concerned, will think out and test proposals, developing them at successive stages and bringing conclusions to the team to be tested for their effect on the spheres of responsibility of the other members.

Detail design

As the scheme develops, it goes into more and more detail, and some of the drawings are produced to a larger scale; some, especially joinery, will be at a scale of 1:1, that is full-size. Although the architect will be continually reassessing his proposals he will not now have to report to the authority in such a formal manner as in the earlier part of the programme. It is likely that periodical progress reports will be called for, and certainly any variations which involve changes in cost or timetable will be spelled out; but in general it is now teamwork all the way. In particular each specialist will have to watch carefully the development of the design detail for implications which may affect his own field; this applies to the librarian also. The project then moves on to its next phase – producing the full details required for making the working drawings, schedules and specifications to be used by the building contractors when they come to construct the library.

Working drawings and specifications

Producing the mass of working drawings will take time; accompanying the drawings will be schedules and specifications, detailed statements of materials to be used, methods of construction, and required standards and tolerances. These documents will be too numerous and too complicated for the librarian to handle, but he should see the ones with which he is concerned, however technical. It is here that the full value of a library consultant is obtained: he will have the specialist knowledge and the time to study the drawings and schedules in detail and to interpret them in the light of the library's functional needs.

In the case of very large and complicated projects, detailed specifications for the whole building may not be produced, but the architect and quantity surveyor may together prepare, for incorporation into the bills of quantity, specification clauses covering the work: the working drawings themselves will have many specification notes on them. On certain aspects of the building there may be separate specifications, for example on structural reinforced concrete and on service installations. In a large project the complexity of the building makes preparation of a specification for every operation an enormously complicated task out of line with modern building practice, which tends more to elemental drawings and production information.

For small projects today, as in the past, specifications are produced, trade by trade, in great detail as to quality, workmanship and method. When read in conjunction with the drawings they should define exactly how a building is to be constructed. Specifications are the architect's responsibility, but because both quantities and prices are involved a large part in preparing them must be played by the quantity surveyor. For special work he will have had to prepare special bills in advance so that they can form the basis of prime cost sums to be allowed within the tender. Specifications must be highly detailed and precise, with reference, in Britain, to British Standards and Codes of Practice. Any looseness here may be the case of dispute later, which can be very expensive, not only for the client but also for the architect, as he can be held liable for instructions which allow of more than one interpretation. The recommendations of the various specialist consultants – heating, sound, ventilating, electrical, structural – were included in reports submitted when each stage was completed. The details of these requirements will now be embodied in a complete specification which will contain all the relevant elements.

From the specifications and the working drawings, the quantity surveyor will now draw up bills of quantity: in practice the operations being described here do not form a series. One set can be worked on before the previous operation is completed, but the order used here is the common one.

Bills of quantity

These documents are exact and very detailed statements of the quality and quantity of all materials to be used, and are accompanied by a specific pricing. This pricing is a highly skilled operation which is the basis of the quantity surveyor's profession; it involves a very full knowledge of every detail of each operation to take place during the construction, and an absolutely up-to-date knowledge of the current prices for every class of material as well as the time-cost of each operation. The figures produced in the bills will be gathered into subtotals, then into a grand total. From these total figures the architect will be able to see how his apportioned cost allocations have been followed and where his running estimates have proved incorrect. He will have many discussions with his technical team members and will revise and reconsider in order to produce the desired result.

The final figure will be critical in the architect's scheme; to it he will add the other costs involved – fees, consent costs, and so on – together with those which may already have been incurred, to arrive at a grand total which should correspond to the estimate agreed earlier by the authority. Naturally the amounts will seldom correspond exactly and the architect will consult with his team to see whether it is feasible to bring the figure down to the original estimate (it could be that the final figure is lower than the original estimate, but it seems never to be so). If he finds that the increase is unavoidable, he has no alternative but to report yet again to the authority, asking whether the increased figure is acceptable. If cuts are judged to be necessary, then much work has to be done in deciding what features have to be omitted and where lower standards can be accepted.

Although this total is referred to here as the 'final' figure, it is still in effect an estimate. It is the cost for which the architect believes it will be possible for the building to be completed. If the 'casting off' of quantities and costs has not been done with absolute accuracy or with correct judgement of current prices, then tenders received will be different from the total, and again the architect has either to recast and replan or return to the authority with a request for an amendment of the total sum available.

Tenders

It is usual at this stage to invite tenders. Tenders may be advertised openly, or selected contractors (known to have had experience in carrying out this class of work) may be invited to tender. In the case of a building to be charged to public funds the former method may seem to be the most open and honest, but it has some disadvantages. The authority has the right to know that the contractor has the necessary financial soundness for such a large undertaking may decide to appoint only a firm which has already had practical experience in the field of public building. If the authority has such preconceptions it would be wrong to encourage firms without the requisite qualifications to spend the large amount of time and money needed to submit a tender.

When the tenders are received (usually under legal stipulations of secrecy and strictly controlled delivery), they will be considered by the authority along with a report from the architect on any factor which, from his expert knowledge, he might wish to bring to their attention. This could include his own assessment of the particular contractor, a report on other buildings recently carried out by him and so on. The architect has an important task in commenting upon a particular tender, and he may not recommend acceptance of the lowest tender if, for example, he judges that the large margin between the lowest and the next tender casts doubt upon the soundness of estimating by the firm offering the lowest one. Acceptance of an abnormally low tender can land the client in serious trouble if the contractor has underpriced to such an extent that he cannot meet his financial commitments. The authority may disregard the architect's advice – the decision is their responsibility and the lowest tender might be accepted against the architect's advice. Although the principle of the acceptance of the lowest tender, after all details have been produced, is normal, there are advantages in the 'controlled cost plus' system where a tendered price is accepted earlier in the programme and amended by experience (and by agreement) as planning proceeds. The advantage of this system is that the builder can be involved in the later design stages; this can sometimes produce cost economies.

Tenders may be invited for several different parts of the project, or a single overall tender may be called for, prime cost sums being included within the global sum for special contract items such as machinery, equipment or loose furniture. Alternatively some of these, particularly loose furniture, may be excluded in order to save the contractor's percentage profit charge. Contractors for these special sections may be nominated, or the sections themselves may be subject to tender. It will be clearly indicated in the main contract what responsibilities lie upon the contractor for the work of the various sub-contractors or specialist suppliers. The main contractor will normally be required to supervise the sub-contractors as far as seeing that their work is acceptable, but not be expected to be entirely responsible for their performance.

This method of fixed price tendering is the most usual one, but in recent years of continuously rising costs it has proved difficult to apply to very large projects. A firm tendering for work which may take months or even years to complete will be unwilling to commit itself to a figure when cost increases, over which it has no control, can arise. Even if the total figure is projected ahead with percentage increases to allow for estimated rises in costs over the period of the contract, the tenderer will still be at the mercy of such uncontrollable forces as labour difficulties, shortages of materials and rapid inflation. For these he will wish to claim additional costs which cannot be estimated at the outset but he knows that the authority will be unwilling to agree to them.

To resolve this difficulty there are various alternative methods of tendering. One is to enter into a contract on a fluctuating basis. Here the current prices of materials and labour are included for all aspects of the work, and increases in the costs of these, as ascertained by the quantity surveyor, are added to the contract sum as they arise. The advantage of this method is that the contractor is not expected to gamble on possible variations in the rates that he will have to pay for materials and labour, and knows that he will be paid a fair sum to cover such increases. If the contractor has to allow for unknown future increases he will naturally price above the highest level of increase that he can anticipate in order to cover himself for the risks involved. Another danger is that he will underestimate the possible rises and, being bound by contract, have to face unpleasant surprises caused by circumstances beyond his control. This in turn can lead to genuine financial embarrassment or even bankruptcy, which is certainly not in the client's interest. The disadvantage of accepting a 'fluctuating' price is that the authority will not know its total commitment until it is too late to make savings if the cost comes out above what it is prepared to spend.

Another alternative is to deal with the tender in two stages: in stage 1 firms are invited to tender on the basis of the priced bill of quantities prepared by the quantity surveyor. From these tenders a firm is chosen and then, at stage 2, that firm is brought into consultation and cooperates with the architect in completing a firm bill of quantities from which a target price is produced, including a set percentage for management and profit. A contract is then drawn up, acceptable to both sides, which apportions between them the sum of money, either above or below the target figure, which the project will finally cost. The system is very complex and places upon the architect a greater responsibility in checking true actual costs for goods and labour than if he had only to certify that the work was carried out correctly.

This is a highly specialized business, particularly in the case of projects which may take several years to build. The work of drawing up the contract itself takes time and inevitably involves the legal departments of the authority as well as the architect and the contracting firms. From this point the team is enlarged by the addition of the representatives of the various contractors and sub-contractors. The architect will have already been busy planning the construction project, and much depends upon the efficiency of his plans.

Site work

At the appropriate time the contractor will be given access to the site under exactly stipulated conditions, and work can begin. During the whole period of construction the architect* will visit the site, usually in the person of the 'job architect', the member of his staff who has been placed in day-to-day charge of the project. He is responsible for general supervision but is not normally expected to be constantly on the site. In large jobs constant supervision will be provided by a clerk of works (inspector, supervisor), who inspects the work under the architect's instructions but is appointed by the client. His job is to ensure that the architect's intentions are fully realized and to keep records of progress, to warn the architect of difficulties and anomalies in the information and record time spent by the contractor on works measured at daywork rates.

The contractor has accepted a price for a job on certain strict conditions, and if these conditions are not met he will have the right to claim extra payment. Conversely if the contractor does not meet his exact obligations, he will cause delay and extra costs through the effect which the variation will have upon others. In all this the architect and clerk of works will be closely involved and in many cases entirely responsible.

The architect may feel, therefore, that at least he should be spared the librarian's attention but, unfortunately, this cannot be. Throughout the entire period of the construction there should be contact between members of the team. Although the librarian will not understand much of what is going on, he can prove of value in simply watching and noting if anything seems to him to be wrongly sited or sized. At the very least he must be able to approach the job architect and to ask questions. It is important that the librarian should understand that any desired alteration he might wish to have made at this stage can cost a great deal of money. Because his authority has accepted the

*This is the procedure where the architect has been retained to see the job through. Although this is normal in Britain, in some countries it is common for the architect to be dismissed at this stage and the contractor supervised by one of the authority's own officers.

architect's proposals he is committed to them; hence the great importance of his understanding them. If he now has second thoughts and wishes to make alterations, they will be extra to the scheme for which the architect has received full acceptance, and extras must be paid for, both their individual costs and those of any delays they may cause and effects they may have on the whole job. It is most important also that any changes, or even comments, which the librarian wishes to make should be communicated only to the architect. If the librarian asks the contractor to make alterations, even in such a small matter as the position of door fittings, he is likely to cause chaos, and to commit his authority to extra expenditure. This is particularly important because of the penalty clauses: these parts of a contract place financial penalties on the contractor, should he fail to complete work by a stipulated time. When the contractor accepts such a clause he does so on the condition that he shall be uninterrupted in his work as prescribed.

The application of penalty clauses is fraught with legal difficulties; the contractor will accept responsibility for the delay only where he is undeniably at fault. If he feels that the prescribed conditions have been violated he will resist them and a legal battle will take place. The legal position is not simple and it may be necessary for the authority to prove that it has been caused actual financial loss by the delay – not always easy in the case of a non-profit-making body such as a library. One of the claims which a contractor may make in defence of his own timetable is that it was disrupted by requests from the librarian. This is not as far-fetched as it sounds: if a librarian has been so ill-advised as to go direct to the contractor and ask for a small alteration, the contractor may claim that a representative of the authority has enforced changes outside the contract.

An even more petty matter can cause trouble: the librarian may wish to use part of the building which appears to be completed in order to move in some of his stock or equipment to save time at the end of the project; unless he does this with the full consent of the contractor, through the architect, the contractor can later claim that this was not in the contract and that it caused delays. Even if legal action against a contractor is successful it is an unhappy and expensive state of affairs.

Because the architect is retained by the authority he is responsible to it for all aspects of the project, but he is not entirely its employee in his dealings with the contractor. As a professional he has an ethical responsibility for the relationship between the authority and its legally contracted construction firm; he holds here something of the position of referee, and this responsibility must be fully accepted by both sides. The architect also has responsibilities to nominated sub-contractors to see fair play in their relationship with the main contractor.

While construction is in progress, seeing that work goes according to schedule will not be the architect's only preoccupation: he will also be engaged in analysing the management and progress of the job, feeding back progress reports to his technical team and constantly reconsidering the methods and timetables in the interests of greater efficiency. Few jobs proceed exactly as they have been visualized, and after each site inspection he will expect to receive comments (and probably complaints) from the various people involved – contractors, sub-contractors, engineering specialists and so on – which call for continuous adjustment to the programme. In such a complicated operation these people's interests may often conflict, and the architect will act as judge on the different claims and counter-claims. He will have the task of assessing the work as it progresses and (with the clerk of

works and the quantity surveyor) certifying for payment the sums claimed by the different contractors which become due as certain agreed portions of their task are completed. He must keep his eye on the overall programme and timetable; if delay is inevitable, he must report at the earliest opportunity so that adjustments can be made. Some delays, such as those resulting from exceptionally bad weather or strikes, are inevitable, but they are always unpopular. Trouble may arise as a result of the architect's own specifications. If for instance the stipulated plaster fails to dry in the period allowed, there may be delay before paint can be applied and this can set off a chain-reaction of delay throughout the finishing. He has to report this fact and accept financial liability on behalf of the authority. On the other hand the contractor may have laid a screed which does not meet the architect's specifications and he will require it to be taken up and relaid; this will involve delays and extra costs which he will certify as being due to breach of conditions by the contractor, recommending that the extra cost be charged him. This may seem a gloomy picture, but the complicated process of erecting a large building can seldom be expected to run exactly according to plan.

Even at the date of handover of the building by the contractor there will almost inevitably be 'outstanding items' which could not be completed on time. The librarian should receive a list of these from the architect and he should delete items from it as they are completed. When the time comes for the contractor to leave the site it is most important that the list should be checked carefully. Despite all promises, it is much more difficult to get outstanding work done by the contractor once his workmen have left the site. Outstanding items of furniture will not normally fall within the main contract, and it is the architect whom the librarian must badger to see that all items included actually arrive. Surprisingly long periods can elapse before outstanding items of all kinds are cleared up and, as in all planning actions of the librarian, it is important that systematic and up-to-date records be kept if the completed library is to match that which was planned by the architect and accepted by the librarian on behalf of his masters.

Moving in and the official opening

Generations of librarians have found that these operations, the culmination of a successful programme, cause more headaches than the planning process itself. Certainly each calls for meticulous preparation. There are a number of books about 'the move'; the best of them are based on the writer's personal experiences of such operations and are worth reading for helpful tips. This writer, whose personal experience in the field has been considerable, feels that what 'moves' have in common is comparatively unimportant. The principles are easily worked out; everything depends on the factors of a particular case and on the resources, especially in enthusiastic helpers, which are available. It is above all an exercise in leadership. At the official opening, when tributes are paid to the skills of the architect and the industry of the contractors, it is particularly gratifying if a word of praise is given to the librarian and his team for a successful move.

The years ahead

It is indeed a fortunate librarian who can run the new library without experiencing any trouble from the building. There are almost inevitable teething troubles, and the architect should have made it clear to whom complaints are to be addressed after the building is in use. It is only reasonable that the authority's own workers can be called in to deal with minor matters – sticking doors, leaking taps (faucets), for example. It is important that the library should have been supplied with a complete set of 'as-built' drawings: these, as the name implies, show in full detail the whole building exactly as it was built, which will seldom be exactly as it was planned, so that workers in the future will know how to repair and to amend. There is usually a specified period during which the contractor is required to return to attend to all complaints, a portion of his payment being retained for a time against this performance.

The architect will certainly be expected to adjudicate on any disputes with the contractor about troubles which occur during this stipulated period. This is certainly the architect's business, but he should be asked to put the librarian in the picture in order to avoid misunderstandings.

10 Physical conditions

In temperate regions it will be taken for granted that an architect is competent to create a building with a comfortable internal atmosphere because he is familiar with all the factors. Because of this, when the librarian considers conditions of comfort for readers and staff he takes it for granted that the building envelope will protect the library against outside influences and thinks little about a factor which is of very great importance in many parts of the world – the climate.

Climate

In tropical and sub-tropical zones, where the effect of the climate is felt very directly, the architect knows that it will have a strong influence on his designs. In particular his decisions as to form will depend very much upon conditions outside the building. Moreover he will have to take into account the expectations and habits of the potential users. For example in some countries rain is very persistent and it can be assumed that readers will arrive with raincoats and umbrellas which will have to be accommodated. In parts of South-East Asia, however, the rain is continuous at some seasons, so much so that people hardly bother with protective clothing, knowing that they are warm and will soon dry out once in the library. The problem here will not be raincoat storage but dispersal of condensation produced by the human body.

Because architecture is an international discipline its practitioners may be called upon to work anywhere in the world; nevertheless the export of design solutions which worked well in one country can (and often does) produce unhappy results elsewhere. In order to take the effects of the climate into consideration the architect will have to obtain data for the region, analysed month by month, to enable him to build in harmony with the local climate. Although the librarian does not have to be concerned with the problems he will have a legitimate interest in the proposed solutions; in some circumstances he himself will be more familiar with the local climate and its effects on reader habits than the architect.

Where either professional has to work in another country, he will find his life and work affected by the local climate. Many people just accept the differences without giving thought to the factors which cause, or strongly influence, them. Countries are thought of as hot, cold, wet, dry and so on, but the variations, by day or by season, have to be considered carefully so as to plan and to design appropriately.

Solar radiation is the dominating influence in all climatic phenomena, the intensity varying according to the earth's distance from the sun. As the radiation passes through the earth's atmosphere, part of this radiation is reflected back by the surface of clouds, and other parts are absorbed by atmospheric ingredients. The great differences in direct effect of the sun on ground surface are not only that of cloud as against clear sky but also according to the degree of pollution in the atmosphere. However, the intensity of the direct radiation does depend ultimately upon the solar altitude, since that determines how much atmosphere the rays have to traverse.

As the surface of the earth receives and absorbs energy its temperature increases and it too radiates energy; as the atmosphere absorbs some of this reflected energy (more in proportion than it absorbs direct radiation), its own temperature is raised and it in turn radiates heat, some of which goes back to the earth which may by now be cooling. Solar radiation varies greatly with the geographical location, the altitude and the weather. In general the greatest amount of radiation is found in two broad bands between 15° and 35° latitude, both north and south of the equator. Here there is usually a relatively thin surface layer of earth, which heats and cools quickly, so that in the deserts the surface temperature may become very high indeed, but at night the position is reversed so that heat is quickly lost to the open sky, and cold nights result. The second highest amount of radiation is in the equatorial belt between 15° north and 15° south, which has high humidity and is frequently cloudy, so that the proportion of diffused radiation and radiation reflected back from the clouds is high. These, together with the rich moist soil, produce very much less difference between day and night temperatures.

Although there are numerous 'local' climates, the major zones are:

1. Warm-wet zones (both equatorial and tropic-marine).
2. Warm-wet and hot-dry zones (both savanna and uplands, with considerable seasonal differences).
3. Hot-dry zones (arid and semi-arid desert).
4. Sub-tropical zones (Mediterranean and American humid).
5. Temperate zones where there are no extreme daily fluctuations of temperature and humidity, although in some parts there are very considerable differences between summer and winter conditions.

In any of these very different regions the architect employed will have to study the conditions carefully and design so as to take advantage of benign factors while minimizing the disadvantages. To do this must inevitably have a strong influence on the form of the building. Charles Correa, a distinguished architect with much experience of designing in India, has said 'Form follows climate.' For those who may be interested in the way in which civilizations have over the centuries developed a unique building style to handle local climate extremes, Konya[1] is both informative and interesting. He quotes the Mahoney Tables, which provide a guide to design in relation to climate, using readily available climatic data. A step-by-step procedure in the tables leads one from climatic information to specifications for optimal layout needed at the sketch design stage.

Conditions for human comfort

Because one of the prime functions of any building is to protect its users against the main hazards of the climate, it should be designed to repel, absorb or filter hostile elements. This applies in all parts of the world, but most of all in the hot climatic zones. An important factor is the maintenance of the thermal balance between the human body and its environment. The conditions under which such balance is achieved and the state of the body when it reaches equilibrium with the surroundings, depend on a combination of many factors: some are individual (activity, acclimatization, clothing), while others (air temperature, radiation, humidity and air movement) are environmental factors. The body maintains a constant internal temperature by releasing superfluous heat to the environment and there is constant exchange of heat between the body and its surroundings which may take place in four physically different ways – conduction, convection, radiation and evaporation.

These physical processes depend on the factors of air temperature, radiation, humidity and air movement already mentioned, each of which may aid or impede the dissipation of surplus heat from the body. A clothed person does not usually lose a great deal of heat by conduction, and this process is limited to the local cooling which occurs when parts of the body come into contact with cold materials; bare arms on cold table-tops, for example. The heat exchange by convection depends chiefly on the temperature differences between skin and air and on how much the air is moving. On the other hand, radiation (in these circumstances) depends almost entirely on the difference in temperature between the skin and the walls and windows which surround it.

The body gains or loses heat by these processes depending on whether the environment is colder or warmer than the body surface, so that the position in cold countries and hot countries is exactly reversed. The difficulty of designing in temperate climates is that outside daily temperatures are rarely consistently colder or hotter than the human body, whereas comfort depends on keeping the internal temperature of the body within a certain range. When the surrounding internal temperature is above 25°C (77°F) the clothed human body cannot get rid of enough heat by either convection or radiation, and the sole compensation is loss by perspiration. As the body is almost always at a higher temperature than the air in a library, the aim is to stop excessive loss of body heat, caused chiefly by convection. If air is still and its temperature is between 20° and 22°C (68° and 72°F), readers (in Britain) will usually be content. The range of temperatures given by the University Grants Committee is between 18.5°C (66°F) in winter and 21°C (70°F) in summer. In the United States a number of authorities give 21°C (70°F) for the winter and 27°C (80°F) for the summer as the highest temperatures suited for books and humans. In different countries the comfort requirements will depend on habit as well as such factors as style of clothing and familiarity with heat or cold. Much depends too on readers' personal preferences; experience has shown that many notice and dislike changes of temperature more than conditions which are either a few degrees too hot or too cold. If readers are moving about and carrying books (in lending departments, for example) the acceptable temperatures can be as low as 13°C (55°F). Here, where visits are fairly short and outdoor clothing is commonly worn, the comfort of the staff who have to work at desks for long periods can be the critical factor. All this applies in still air; the presence of considerable air movement can drastically alter comfort expectations.

When wishing to stipulate levels of temperature (or humidity) for his future library, the librarian should consult experts (or published recommendations) *of his own country*. Circumstances can differ very widely.

In this discussion of conditions within library buildings the emphasis has been on the comfort of those using them. This is because, in general terms, books and other materials will be safe in temperatures as low as humans can tolerate. The great dangers to library materials are excessive heat and humidity, very low humidity, and the effect of air pollution from nearby industrial installations.

Heating

In small libraries staff comfort may be achieved by providing local heating at enquiry counters and in work rooms; the essential here is a system that can quickly be altered to compensate for a fall in temperature without making readers in outdoor clothing feel uncomfortably warm. Complete sealing of external doors against wind and rain is important; revolving doors are good, and heat curtains which conserve the heat already inside the building can be most effective. Because books keep better at lower temperatures, the lowest acceptable level for humans is generally satisfactory for book preservation. In little-visited rare book storage rooms a much lower temperature is ideal, with consequent fuel savings.

In theory the correct relationship of air temperature and surface temperature within a library can be obtained by 25% radiant heat and 75% convection heat. For comfort of readers seated for long periods, feet should be warmer than heads, and this can be achieved by underfloor heating, either electric or by hot water coils. This method has the additional advantage of not taking up space which could be used for bookcases or tables. If this system is to be employed, the architect will have to allow for it at an early stage when he chooses the flooring system. It used to be said that staff who stand all day dislike underfloor heating because it 'draws the feet', but this objection does not seem to be heard today. Ceiling heating panels offer similar space-saving qualities, but heating above people's heads results in a feeling of stuffiness. The abomination of high-level gas radiators should never be tolerated: working long hours under these invariably produces headaches. Low wall panels are a possible compromise if wall space can be allowed, but they tend to create dust patterns on the walls. The use of heating panels in the lower part of full-length glass windows can serve the second purpose of a safety measure. Heating can be combined with ventilation by bringing in heated air at low level through walls or hollow columns and extracting it at a high level; some heating arrangements used to do the opposite but were often ineffective because the hot air tended to stay at high level. If blown hot air is employed it should be directed across exposed walls and windows to reduce their cooling effect rather than into the room, where readers may feel it as a draught. There are advantages and disadvantages in each method, and this is a matter to be discussed with the architect or, even better, with the heating expert direct. The placing of radiators and convector heaters is a matter of much concern to the librarian. Wall radiators not only prevent the wall from being used for shelving but also waste space by creating 'dead' areas alongside the radiators. Much worse are free-standing radiators and convectors, which can be both hindrances and dangers; the only possible solution here is to have the heaters built into library fittings, but even then they are not particularly efficient and are a bar to flexibility. Radiators built into the safety rails along balcony edges can be acceptable unless these areas are to be used for study tables.

The choice of heating fuels will not lie with the librarian although they can seriously affect both the operations and the running costs of the library. The normal alternatives are solid fuels, oil, gas and electricity. Faber and Kell[2] give a table showing relative fuel and labour costs, but it would be a bold person today who would predict the relative price and availability of these fuels throughout the life of the library. Solid fuels are dropping out of use in industrialized countries, but there are many regions where both the fuel and the labour are available locally. There may also be a political element in the choice of fuels, priority being given to the fuel which is home-produced. Solar heating can be a real bonus where there is enough sun; there are a number of well-known libraries using this method. It should not be ignored in the less sunny climates because the photovoltaic solar cell is going to be much more efficient than the cumbersome heat panels, and it may be that solar heating will become normal in the majority of countries in a few years.

Cooling

In temperate zones libraries are free from the problems caused by excessive natural heat which apply in the tropics, and so cooling is necessary mainly to dissipate heat produced by people in the library, by solar gain from sun-facing windows in the summer, and by very high lighting levels. It should not be forgotten that the installation of more and more electronic equipment will add to the heat load for the cooling system to handle. In situations where full air-conditioning cannot be installed, adequate mechanical ventilation can provide conditions which are generally satisfactory for readers but less definitely so for fragile books. Much depends upon the structure of the building; in an atrium where there is a large body of air which will move with heat, ventilation can be obtained by thermostatically controlled vents in the roof which open automatically. It should not be forgotten that fragile materials were adequately preserved in temperature countries for many centuries before forced ventilation or air-conditioning were invented, because the heavy structure of the buildings evened out changes in temperature from outside elements. In certain areas with low ceilings, forced ventilation may create an uncomfortable draught, and natural air cooling would be preferable; the old-fashioned punkah fan has proved to be surprisingly effective in a number of modern buildings, although it is visually and perhaps audially intrusive. Free circulation of air is essential, and here the open-plan system shows its value. In heavily shelved stack areas, particularly if the stacks are closely fitted to floor and ceiling, there is a distinct gain in having some open centres to double-sided stacks so that air can circulate more freely between rows of books.

If unprotected from the sun, buildings with large areas of glass windows suffer from enormous solar heat gain in the summer, leading to high internal temperatures. If the building has a lightweight structure the low thermal capacity of the building aggravates the problem, and large rapid temperature fluctuations can occur inside the building with little delay between a temperature change outside and a corresponding change inside. This is in striking contrast to the situation in traditional, relatively massive enclosures where the building tends to 'iron out' and delay temperature changes, so that the heat of the day is not radiated within the building until night-time, when it is less of a nuisance or even a benefit.

In some modern buildings, even in temperate climates, cooling is the largest single service cost – far higher than heating or lighting. Librarians who have not experienced this problem would be advised to read an account[3] of the alterations and adaptations needed to make one of the earliest and most famous all-glass-covered buildings in London suitable for general office use without discomfort and to see how much it cost.

Another difference between the climatic zones is the angle at which direct sunlight becomes a hazard to the readers because it strikes windows and raises the heat level. A single sheet of glass allows 80% of the solar heat to enter; moreover, because it allows short-wave solar

radiation to pass through but not the long-wave radiation emitted by objects or surfaces in the room, the heat which enters is trapped and can raise the internal temperature far above that outside. In temperate zones, balconies, the extension of the roof line to form an overhang, and other forms of providing horizontal shade should keep out the sun in the summer and admit it in the winter, but in the tropic zones even the low sun of morning and evening can be very hot: obviously orientation is all-important. Horizontal screens are most effective against a high sun and are normally used on the exposed north or south sides (according to which hemisphere is being considered). In equatorial zones, both sides must be protected because of the sun's path. The nearer the library is to the equator the more effective it is to screen the facades with a roof overhang such as those used in houses in equatorial regions. Planting trees and shrubs nearby also helps to shade walls and windows.

One of the greatest disadvantages of sunlight in tropical countries is glare. If it comes direct from the sun it is easy to plan shading, but in hot dry regions the reflection from the ground (usually of a light colour) and nearby buildings can cause great discomfort. Balconies, special attention to the design of windows and baffles immediately within, can all help; for comments on glare as a factor in reader comfort, see Chapter 11.

Vertical screens in the form of closely placed columns, fins or louvres are useful against low sun on the east and west facades. Combined vertical and horizontal screening – the egg-crate grille, for example – can be effective. Whatever type of screening is used should be placed outside the glazing, be of low thermal capacity materials to ensure quick cooling after sunset and should be designed to prevent reflection into the building. In Düsseldorf University Library the sun-blinds are made of a very strong glass-fibre mixture; one is fastened outside each window, but they are electrically driven in sectors from a staff-controlled switchboard on each floor. The librarian[4] reports that experience has shown them to be very satisfactory. The small screening devices illustrated in Figure 10:3 would not be drastic enough for really hot regions but can serve well in temperate zones.

Special heat-reflecting glass, often combined with double glazing, is another possible solution but has a high initial cost, can produce a gloomy internal atmosphere, and might be difficult to clean. The reflecting glass shell around the concrete walls of Leicester University Library stands clear of the structure, thus trapping air which serves to insulate the building, but cleaning will certainly be a major problem. (Note also the 'twin lakes' on the roof: they serve to prevent the roof from drying out – a major cause of leaks – and also act as a reserve water supply for air-conditioning.) Double glazing may be inevitable if very low outdoor temperatures are expected. If venetian blinds or curtains are proposed the librarian will again need to consider the cleaning and maintenance problems. If glass roofing is to be installed, motorized horizontal blinds may be needed, if possible controlled automatically by light-sensitive cells. A cheaper alternative is to apply a transparent film to the inside face of the windows and roof lights which by reflecting sunlight (and ultra-violet light) reduces heat transmission by 25–75%, depending upon the density of the film employed. The question of the need for windows was considered in the feasibility study, as was the orientation of the building.

Humidity

Humidity is the dampness or dryness of air, for our purpose the air inside a building. The basis of judgement is the amount of moisture held by the air being measured, as a percentage of the maximum amount of moisture which could be held by air *at that temperature*: this is called the relative humidity. It is affected by a number of factors such as the humidity and temperature of the outside air, how much that air enters the building directly, and, very important, the moisture produced by humans inside the building. One has only to think of large numbers of readers coming into a warm building from the very cold atmosphere outside, and the water vapour which they exude, to realize that the warm air, which holds more moisture than cold air, will have a high relative humidity. The problems of humidity are often disregarded in popular libraries; it seldom affects humans or modern books in common use at library temperatures, but it is of vital importance in those which contain certain classes of materials, chiefly older, fragile documents.

Low humidity dries out papers as well as skins (vellum, parchment); it is also damaging to papers made of woodpulp from the late nineteenth century. Incidentally it allows static electricity to build up in certain circumstances (particularly where carpets of man-made materials are laid) and causes minor shocks from metal fitments such as handrails. To off-set low humidity, moisture can be sprayed back into the air as it enters or is re-circulated. This is usually done in ventilation ducts, but there are drawbacks (such as rusting) unless the task is undertaken scientifically. High humidity, on the other hand, provides the conditions under which mould flourishes. To control this the air is dried as it passes through the ventilation plant; this will of course produce water – often a surprisingly large amount – and arrangements have to be made for its disposal. To obtain the desired humidity level in all parts of a library can be an expensive undertaking (especially when the conditions outside are extreme), but there are cheap ways of providing it within limited areas, such as rare-book storage rooms. Here humidifying (adding moisture) can be carried out in the ducting special to those rooms or, even more cheaply, by free-standing electric

humidifiers emitting moisture into the air. In the same way the air supplied exclusively to those rooms can be dried by passing it through de-humidifiers which include a refrigerant circuit or by the use of spot de-humidifiers which absorb moisture; here in particular it will be necessary to remove the water at intervals. In exhibition cases, trays of silica gel perform the same function.

In Britain and most temperate countries these conditions are not a real problem, although warm, moist air inside the library will produce condensation on meeting the colder glass of windows; in extreme examples this can run down and damage woodwork below. The only satisfactory answer is double glazing, which adds to the expense.

Recommended levels for relative humidity in libraries are well known, and are referred to below. In a sealed building with air-conditioning these levels have only to be stipulated and the correct conditions should appear – at a price. It is nonetheless important to watch the humidity level where fragile materials are stored and to see that doors and windows are not left open to let in very damp (or excessively dry) air from outside the building. The use of books or manuscripts for short periods in uncontrolled conditions is seldom important, but where they are exhibited for long periods humidity must be watched.

In general the recommended humidity level in libraries is between 45% and 55%, the latter being the better figure. Special stipulations may be made for unusual materials; film can crack in conditions of low humidity, and its coating can be damaged if the humidity is too high.

For most temperate climates the above figures are satisfactory but in Finland, which experiences intense cold for several months each year, the question of humidity levels has been given special attention. Finnish Standard SF 3540 (LSO 2830) stipulates the levels shown in Table 10:1. The humidity levels shown for reading rooms and stacks are much lower than would be recommended in most temperate climates, and the top figure for the storing of microforms would not be accepted in many countries.

An unusual condition occurs when materials exhibit signs of mould even though the temperature and humidity levels appear to be correct. This may be caused because materials have earlier acquired spores in a place where

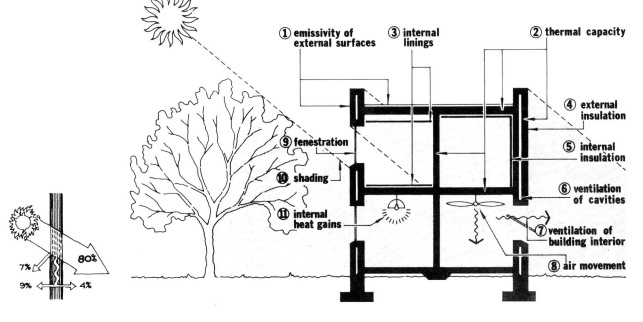

10:1. Key diagram to the factors which influence peak temperatures attained in buildings and which the designer may therefore manipulate to avoid summer overheating

10:2. Solar heat gain through a sheet of clear glass (Allan Konya)

① emissivity of external surfaces   ③ internal linings   ② thermal capacity
④ external insulation
⑨ fenestration
⑤ internal insulation
⑩ shading
⑥ ventilation of cavities
⑪ internal heat gains
⑦ ventilation of building interior
⑧ air movement

7%   80%
9%   4%

1 External building projection

6 External retractable louvres

9 Midpane retractable louvres

12 Reflective curtaining

2 External horizontal visor

7 External retractable vertical blinds

10 Special glass

13 Internal retractable louvres

3 External vertical screening

8 External retractable horizontal blinds

11 Reflective coating to glass

14 Internal retractable vertical slats

4 External vertical louvres

5 External horizontal louvres

10:3. Externally mounted solar screening devices; Midpane and anti-sun glass solar screening devices; Internally mounted solar screening devices

10:4. Twin 'lakes' on roof: Leicester University Library (Architects Castle Park Dean Hook)

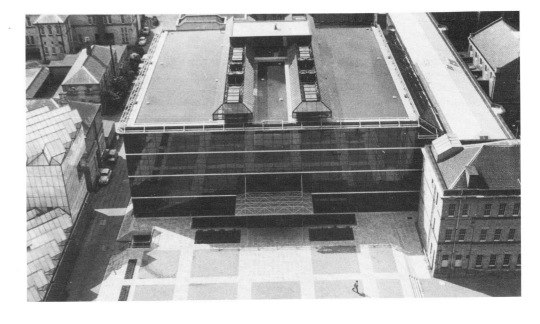

humidity was high and were then moved to a library where warmer temperatures allowed the spores to develop. The disease may not become visible unless for example the air-conditioning breaks down temporarily. The remedy is thorough cleaning and fumigation: the problem should not recur. The damage caused by the acid which accumulates in paper after storing in polluted atmospheres can be dealt with by a process of mass deacidification, but this is a very large-scale and expensive operation.[5]

Air-conditioning

The advantages of full air-conditioning should not be taken lightly. The Parry Report[6] says:

'Firstly, solid particles of dirt and liquid gaseous forms of acids suspended in the atmosphere have a seriously deleterious effect on books and manuscripts, resulting under the worst conditions in complete destruction of bindings, paper and vellum. Secondly, even in Britain, excessive changes of temperature and humidity accentuate this deterioration and can also lead to additional destruction as a result of the growth of moulds, fungi and bacteria which such conditions favour. For these reasons it is essential that for the best conditions for the preservation of books, the atmosphere should be free from dirt and acidity in gas or liquid form and that the temperature and humidity should be controlled; in fact these conditions are obtained only by the installation of full air-conditioning plant (water washers to extract liquid or gaseous acids, filters to remove solid dirt, heating plant and refrigerating plant). In areas of highly polluted air it is our view that library stocks, housed both in reading-rooms and stacks, can be preserved only in a fully air-conditioned atmosphere.'

For most libraries these arguments may seem a little strong; the very real advantages of air-conditioning have made it something of a status symbol, but it should be remembered that it is expensive (in many cases its costs are about double those of the total of other heating and cooling methods) and that it is not a package solution to all ills. It calls for a dependable electricity supply, because a breakdown will change humidity levels and can have disastrous effects on fragile materials, worse than if there had been no air-conditioning. It must also have an adequate water supply and usually needs special engineering skills in attendance. It is very common indeed for it to be noisy, and it is not always effective in providing consistently acceptable conditions, but its greatest drawback is the vast amount of space needed for its fans, ducts and machinery. In some cases the need for these seems to have been the predominant factor in the design of the building.

Air should be changed at the very least three times per hour; it depends on the area of the library and the time of year. In Britain six is the normal figure (ten in toilets), but there are eight changes per hour in some modern universities, and thirty have been reported in a recent art gallery. The air intake per cycle should be 25%, although this is often reduced to 15% for the sake of economy. The air should be drawn in at a high level, where pollution may be less, and should be mixed with the existing air before it reaches the heaters and coolers, to prevent hot air forming a layer over the cold; much depends on the cubic capacity of the building and the number of people in the areas. If smoking is allowed anywhere in the building, the air from that section should not be re-circulated without filtering. If noxious chemicals are used in a bindery, conservation areas or photographic laboratory, the air should be expelled directly to the outside. On the question of air filtration, Mason[7] is as always both expert and forthright, but this is a very specialized field where knowledge comes from long study and instant formulae are not really acceptable. It is best to tell the ventilation expert what the library's needs are and to seek his advice.

Although most libraries today are virtually sealed, it will be necessary for some windows to open, preferably key-operated, in case the air-conditioning fails or there is a power cut. If air-conditioning is to be installed only in certain parts of the building, lobbies or air traps will be needed so that the effects will not be lost by outside air being admitted.

These comments from the appraisal in the *Architects' Journal* of the air-conditioning system in the library of Leicester University (Figure 10.4) are worth noting[8]

'The building has been designed as a sealed and virtually air-tight unit with minimal window openings and this has necessitated the installation of an air-conditioning system capable of providing comfortable conditions for the occupants and keeping the books in a clean, stable environment. The conditions to be maintained are: internal temperature 21°C (70°F) ± 2°C (3°F) (when external temperature varies between 1.0°C (33°F) and 26.5°C (80°F)); internal humidity 50% RH ± 5% (when external RH varies between 100% and 44% RH). The architect and the services engineer have together designed a building which, because of the mass of concrete in the structure and the use of concrete ducts to carry conditioned air, has a high thermal capacity. This leads to a time-lag in the heating or the cooling of the structure and makes close control and quick response impossible. Continuous operation of the plant was one of the specific parameters of the mechanical design and avoided problems of thermal shift and expansion effects on the structure itself.'

For technical details of the highly complicated subject of air-conditioning the standard authority is Faber and Kell.[9]

A few years ago to propose full air-conditioning for a library would have seemed a counsel of perfection, but surveys[10] show that over 90% of new public libraries built in the United States are air-conditioned. This is obviously the trend (where money is available), and it is far more economical and efficient to install air-conditioning in a building while it is being erected than to add it later. Even so it is not a complete answer: it is not uncommon today for large libraries, especially in universities, to be planned with full air-conditioning but with heat-absorbing glass walls. This can be troublesome because the heat can cause thermal stress within the glass and require special glazing techniques. Even so, much of the heat absorbed by the glass will in time pass into the building unless double glazing is used: again more expense.

Ventilation

A small library with a continuous movement of people through its doors, situated in an area where there is little atmospheric pollution but where the electricity supply is far from reliable, has a number of reasons to look for more economical alternatives to air-conditioning. A library with which I was concerned in Costa Rica on the Continental Divide was cleverly orientated to take advantage of the prevailing fresh and clean winds. Here the air movement was beneficial, but it should be noted that this solution is not acceptable for tall buildings, because of the effect of wind pressure, or (by British Regulations at any rate) for any room occupied by more than fifty people or where there is more than one person for each 3.5 m³ (12.5 cu ft). Nevertheless there are many occasions where natural ventilation still has a part to play; I was particularly impressed at a small branch library in Porus, Jamaica, by the way the architect had taken advantage of prevailing climatic conditions to include natural vegetation to protect the building against high winds and had installed low-level

Table 10.1		
	Humidity	*Temperature*
Reading rooms and stacks	30%	20–21°C (68–70°F)
Microform archives	30–40%	15–25°C (59–76°F)
Archives	45–55%	18–20°C (63–68°F)
Magnetic tape	48–52%	18–20°C (63–68°F)

Table 10.2   Comparison of environmental conditions – heating and ventilating

	Edinburgh	Bristol	Nottingham	Newcastle
Mechanical services	Full air-conditioning	Air-conditioning in part of basement; artificial ventilation in all other areas; heating from external source (boiler)	Full air-conditioning: heating from university district heating system converted to right temperature by heat exchangers at the library, then to the heater batteries of the air-conditioning system	Full air-conditioning
Temperature	20°C (68°F)	21°C ± 1.67°C (70°F ± 3°F)		21°C ± 3°C (70°F ± 5.4°F)
Relative humidity	55%			50% average (55% maximum)
Air changes per hour	5	9		6
Filtration	To 5 micron size; air washer			
Heat gain	Projecting floors, double glazing, heat-absorbing glass on south face; fixed louvres on east and west faces	Heavy structure provides high degree of insulation; low proportion of windows to walls. Louvres on south-east (admin.) area of ground floor	Low wall-to-floor ratio; overhang on floors 1 and 2. Brown glass on windows	Building has high thermal performance construction; very small window-to-wall ratio
Additional heating	Perimeter heating under windows			Heat generated by lighting and occupants in centre can be transferred when required to perimeter
Zoning	Two zones on each side of building on each floor			Four discrete plants each serve a quarter of each level
Comment	Air-conditioning was given priority by both librarian and architect	Unable to obtain funds for full air-conditioning		Single plant room on the roof is directly connected to each of four cores. Free cooling and heat reclamation techniques used

ventilation grilles along the walls, under bookcases: both economical and efficient. Konya[11] is again helpful on the ways buildings have developed in tropical countries to take advantage of natural ventilation.

Forced ventilation, usually by fans in ducting, can build up a higher pressure inside the building than outside, causing external doors to fly open; higher pressure can be very useful in areas where the exclusion of dust is a priority, microform storage rooms, for example. If the pressure inside a building is lower than that outside, readers may find difficulty in opening the outside doors.

General atmospheric control

Whatever methods are proposed by the architect for the correct atmospheric conditions, the librarian should watch the following points:

1. *Demands on space and limits on flexibility* caused by the various installations.
2. *Possible noise* caused by air-conditioning, forced air circulation or cooling plants.
3. *The need for central thermostatic control* of heating equipment to avoid wasting staff time in attending to individual switches (the latter will be needed in rooms where special conditions are required, so it must be arranged that central controls can be overridden).
4. *The location of all controls* and thermostats where staff only may operate them.

5. *Fixing overall heating and ventilating levels* at those suitable for reader service areas and not for staff workrooms where local controls can operate and windows be opened.
6. *Special ventilation requirements* for areas where fumes may be produced (fumigation equipment is a good example).

Table 10:2 compares the heating and ventilation provision in four British university libraries.

Noise

External noise

Some libraries will inevitably be close to sources of external noise, ranging from aircraft and road traffic to the sound of typing in nearby offices and students on pathways. These the architect will deal with by designing suitable enclosing walls and windows or by planting trees and shrubs which attenuate the noise to an acceptable level. There is no need for the librarian to enter the world of the sound-reducing qualities of different walls. This may seem inconsistent with his involvement in measurements in the section on lighting (Chapter 11); the reason is that while lighting can be affected by the librarian's own actions when the library is operating (re-siting tables, switching on lights at certain times, drawing venetian blinds and so on), there is nothing he can do about external noise (except close doors and windows).

Table 10.3 Comparison of disturbance levels

	Edinburgh	Bristol	Nottingham	Newcastle
Visual disturbance	Segregation: the entrance and circulation desk area is separated from all other areas. A lift lobby within the central core is closed off from the two undergraduate reading floors by a glazed partition. Groups of readers are isolated from the core and from each other by stacks	Reader seating on reading floors is on perimeter, with stacks between these and most human movement	The entrance area is part of the large open-plan library area with the circulation counter deep inside. Considerable movement to and from entrance and circulation desk gives a severe test to the excellent acoustic conditions. The entrance level holds staff working area, general periodicals and reader refreshment facilities, all in open plan, but is little used for serious study	Reader seating on reader floors is on perimeter with stacking between these and most movement
Aural disturbance	Sound-absorbing materials: acoustic ceiling tiles are used throughout. Carpet is used throughout the two undergraduate reading floors, but in reading areas only on stack floors. Fixed double glazing	Carpet tiles (rubber on main entrance concourse). Acoustic tile ceilings; group reading areas have been surrounded by screening acoustically treated on the inside face	Carpet tile flooring; acoustic tile ceiling, with saw-tooth profile and horizontal shields at intervals; these reflect the sound down to the carpet in each section rather than further into the room	Carpet tile flooring, deep acoustic absorbing wings in ceiling
Noise criteria level*	25	35; 40 dBa		43 dBa

* The noise criteria levels from equipment are the common levels for equal sound pressure over the eight octave bands (IHVE Guide, 1965).

Internal noise

To plan and design so as to produce an environment audially acceptable to readers and staff will be part of the architect's task, but he will have to bear in mind the degree of acceptance of noise in the country where he is working. The idea, normal in the West, that the quieter the library is, the better is not necessarily accepted in some other parts of the world, where a cheerful hubbub seems to be part of the way of life. I have seen hundreds of undergraduates working in reading rooms with stone floors while the chairs were constantly being scraped backwards and forwards: the noise always made me wince, but none of the students seemed to notice anything amiss. Dead silence can make people uneasy, and when the slightest sound is heard it has a distracting effect out of all proportion to the level of the noise. An environment acceptable to readers includes a noise level that is familiar and not obtrusive to them. The question of noise must be kept in mind when planning internal traffic routes; by examining sketches, especially room elevations, the librarian can learn to trace ways in which noise might travel: this is another reason for him to be able to interpret plans and elevations confidently. High and resonant ceiling surfaces can be very difficult to handle acoustically: the hard high domes of old-fashioned reading rooms produce echoes of surprisingly long duration. The ideal reverberation time is less than half a second, but longer times, up to one second, can be accepted if necessary: aim for the lower figure. Windows can reflect sound badly; the greatest single step forward has been the installation of acoustic tile or fibre suspended ceilings, although most librarians think that a pile carpet on felt makes a greater contribution: this is because carpet tends to suppress the noise of foot traffic, which is particularly distracting. A less striking, but still important, influence is a wall of books, but it must be of significant size

compared to the open area; book alcoves suffer less reverberation than open areas.

The provision of materials which give sound absorption and sound insulation will be a major step towards a successful environment. Technically sound absorption is the prevention of sound reflection and is particularly connected with the reverberation time within a certain space. For this there will be acoustic tiles on the ceiling and carpets on the floor, but curtains and other soft-surfaced hangings will make a contribution. In fact carpets absorb high frequencies better than low ones, so that sharp irritating noises tend to be blurred although low rumbles, like muttered conversations and air-conditioning hums, may still be heard.

Sound insulation, is more complicated, being concerned with the prevention of transmission of sound from one space to another. It calls for acoustic isolation of an area by the use of materials to block ways in which sounds can come through from other rooms, using baffles in ducts, upward extension of partitions and breaking up of areas with partitions and bookcases. In open-plan libraries the very extent of the unrestricted space, together with carpets and acoustic ceilings (especially with panels of a saw-tooth profile and vertical divisions which serve to limit noise and direct it downwards rather than along the room), can be surprisingly quiet; on the other hand, there is often an uncomfortable deadness about the acoustic environment (see the illustration, p. 120).

If we presume that the architect will have planned to insulate (or isolate) those parts of the service machinery which can produce structure-borne noise, the noise inside a library consists chiefly of conversation, frictional noises (chairs scraping hard floors and the impact of heels on hard surfaces) and mechanical noises (from book hoists and typewriters). Staff discipline can eliminate a good deal of noise: librarians on duty are often less inhibited in their conversation than readers, and a resonant voice speaking into a telephone can carry a long way. Acoustic telephone hoods are seldom popular with busy staff, but their use may have to be enforced. It also helps to plan groups of similar activities together and in libraries used by large numbers of young students to provide outlets for conversation in the form of group discussion (or relaxing) rooms or other areas where talking need not be discouraged. It may also be useful to provide a level of hum, of a frequency chosen by an expert (white noise). This will not itself be noticed but will cover some of the distracting sound, particularly the higher frequencies. It is often suggested that air transmission through ducts can be utilized to provide such noise, but my experience is that it would be better to plan for silence from the ducts. Too often the noise comes unwanted; it depends on how much you trust the ventilating engineer. In entrance halls and areas where noise will not disturb readers the architect may plan for a lively level of sound.

There are no definitive standards for acoustic matters but it is often said that the maximum of internal noise level in a library should be 50 dB; but that measurement is itself a ratio and much will depend on the users and the country. Table 10:3 shows the noise level and both the aural and visual distraction in four British university libraries. Another university (York) was originally much less satisfactory in these respects. A survey[12] reports that 'Most readers are disturbed, both visually and aurally, by movement of other readers around the library, as the noise is carried from one floor to another via the light wells, and readers are constantly aware of the movement of people. Rain on the roof light causes considerable noise.' For these reasons it became necessary to add a shield above the counter to protect readers in the upper floors from the noise rising up the open well, and an inner skin was added beneath the glass roof to prevent rain noise.

For a good account of the seemingly simple, but actually very complex and difficult, problem of library noise control, see Thompson.[13]

11 Lighting

Choosing the lighting for a library is a complex matter, because lighting has to serve several entirely different purposes and is a question of balancing priorities. It must allow reading to take place in comfort and should contribute to the internal appearance of the room, and, to a lesser extent, to the external impression upon passers-by. On the negative side it must not dazzle, tire the eye, be intrusive to serious workers or raise the internal heat level. It must be quiet and economical, needing as little maintenance as possible. To meet all these criteria there will be artificial light, which, within limits, is controllable, and natural light, which is very much less controllable but 'free'. Because the human response to light is largely subjective, or at any rate conditioned, there are no absolute standards by which success can be judged, and the librarian's experience can be as sound a guide as the architect's. Even a specialist lighting consultant will be expert on the best methods rather than the most acceptable results. One has only to contrast the high level of lighting in a supermarket, designed to enhance the appearance of the goods, with the low level in some restaurants, planned to give a romantic atmosphere, to see what an important effect lighting can have on an interior.

Even in the most easily measurable aspect of lighting, the intensity, standards differ so widely that we are not justified in presuming that the librarian will present the problem and the architect provide the solution. Certainly in the matters of aesthetics and the means of providing light the architect is master, but for the satisfaction of a reader's lighting needs there is no authoritative technical solution, only numerous opinions.

The standard authority in this field is the Illuminating Engineering Society (IES), both British and American societies having the same title and initials. To add to the confusion there is little conformity between the codes and technical reports of the two bodies. The element most quoted from them is intensity of light, the most obvious of the questions to be considered but by no means the most important. In using light to contribute to the overall design the architect will employ variations not only of intensity but also of quality, colour, direction, shape (as created by the fittings) and contrast to contribute to both operational efficiency and interior design. These variations will enable him to indicate change of mood in different parts of the building and to produce interest, quietness, sparkle or whatever effect he wants to achieve. In doing so he must take care that reading conditions are not impaired and must assess what levels of glare and contrast are acceptable.

The librarian will also be concerned about the lighting's effect upon the materials in his care. All paper, vellum and parchment, as well as the words or other marks upon them, can be damaged by light, as can other sensitive materials which the library may hold. While he will be most concerned about old and valuable material, the librarian will not forget that paper of the mechanical wood period (from the late nineteenth century) is particularly vulnerable. The damage is chiefly, but not entirely, caused by ultra-violet (UV) radiation emitted by all white light sources, daylight being the most dangerous. The rate of damage will depend on the intensity of the light, in which distance from the object will be a major factor, and the length of the exposure; in general it will depend directly on the product of these two elements – the higher the intensity, the greater the damage; the longer the exposure, the greater the damage. These matters will seldom be of any consequence when materials are being studied by readers, but if they are displayed for long periods the results can be very serious.

Sensitive materials should not be exposed continuously to a level of more than 50 lux (for lighting measurements, see below). As daylight of this level would be too low to be acceptable for the environment of a public exhibition, an artificial light source must be used, because it is more easily controllable. As it would obviously be inconvenient to withdraw an exhibition every few hours, a common answer is to arrange for displays of the most sensitive materials (old manuscripts, watercolours etc.) to be covered with curtains which can easily be drawn aside by viewers. Where this cannot be done it will be necessary to control the UV radiation from both natural and some artificial light sources. The lighting of display and showcases is considered in more detail in Chapter 17. Tungsten incandescent lamps do not emit very damaging UV rays, but fluorescent light tubes do, and some quartz iodide lamps are particularly dangerous; on the other hand tungsten lamps emit much more heat. (These comments are generalizations; the architect may be aware of recent developments which invalidate them, or manufacturers may claim that they do so.) The most effective method of preventing UV damage, and the only one in the case of natural light coming through glass, is to interpose a screen of transparent UV-absorbing film between the light source and the object. This can be special glass or, less expensive, a coat of varnish or a plastic sheet; their relative efficiency, and cost, will need to be studied. Fluorescent tubes coated with an UV-absorbent film are now available – at a price. Common sense must be used; for example fluorescent lights three metres (ten feet) above an object are not likely to be a great danger, but direct sunlight is always dangerous.

Natural light

Natural light is 'natural'; people are familiar with it and like it; sometimes they feel deprived when they are without it. Its colour rendering is either better than artificial lighting or at least it is what the human eye has been accustomed to. It is theoretically free, but to provide it satisfactorily can be extremely expensive.

Single-storey buildings can use roof lights which give good general lighting throughout the area; its drawbacks will be dealt with later. Side windows are another matter, because they seriously affect both the structure and the design. Their size and positioning is a major design element and is dealt with in Chapter 7. Over the years it has been found that for small public libraries in temperate countries a very acceptable design provides full glass walls on both sides of a single-storey rectangle with heavy overhangs to prevent direct sunlight entering. Such a solution is cheap and it is liked. The disadvantages are that there is a high rate of heat transfer through the glass, especially by reflectance from hard, light-coloured surfaces outside, and high noise admittance, unless expensive glass is used.

In the case of a deep building where window light does not reach the full depth of the room, the ceiling and floor become important reflectors. In the deep square building which we have found to be economical in many ways, windows can provide adequate lighting up to 10 m (30–35 ft) if supplemented by a little artificial lighting, but only up to 6 m (20 ft) – some say 8 m (25 ft) without any: it depends on the reflectance and colour from surfaces in the room (and on personal preference). To have windows on only one wall not only reduces the penetration of light but can produce excessive contrast, which may be reduced if the inside surfaces of the walls are white.

Natural light brings with it a number of other serious disadvantages. The necessary apertures created through wall or roof impose severe restrictions upon the architect's freedom of design, as well as on the flexible and economic use of floor and wall space. Moreover protection has to be installed against the concomitant heat, cold, glare and often noise. Solar radiant heat, usually the most severe of these discomforts, can be partially deflected and its absorbance and transmittance reduced by the installation of special glass and shading fixtures on or outside the windows (see Chapter 10). In arid areas glare is caused chiefly by sunlight reflected from the surface of the ground or from light-coloured walls of other buildings. A traditional way of overcoming this is by keeping the windows on external elevations small and few in number, with larger low-level windows overlooking a shaded internal courtyard. It is also important to keep the interior walls around the window openings light in colour to reduce the apparent contrast between sky lighting and the interior.

Intensity

As we cannot control natural light intensity at source, we plan the fenestration in order to achieve our aim. We use the daylight factor, which is the ratio of illumination of a point in the interior to the unobstructed horizontal plane at ground level. The intensity of outdoor illumination under overcast sky is internationally accepted as 500 lm/ft^2 (5000 lux); therefore if we wish to achieve a minimum horizontal internal illumination of 30 lm/ft^2 (300 lux) at desired points, the daylight factor would be 6%. In practice there can be enormous variations in outdoor intensity. Although variations in the level of natural light in Britain show only thirteen times more between a summer noon and a winter afternoon,[1] American investigations show variations of forty-eight times at 46° latitude.[2] These are natural light intensity levels; obviously shade conditions within the building have also to be taken into account. In equatorial and wet-dry tropic regions the variations will be very much more drastic. Even in temperate climates, Thomson[3] says that an object in a daylit gallery may receive 100 times more light on a sunny day than on a gloomy one.

As the human eye is very sensitive to change, variations of a small fraction of this amount are unacceptable in continuous reading conditions. Also the continuous change in the angle of the light, though gradual and predictable, is often disturbing to the serious reader. Very sophisticated equipment can be installed whereby photo-electric cells detect variations in the level of natural lighting and change the artificial lighting provision to compensate. These are expensive and are chiefly to be found in art galleries, where a constant light level can be critical. For purely functional efficiency it would be much better to use only artificial, and therefore controllable, light. Library

rooms without natural light have been provided in many parts of the world and are physically acceptable, but it may be decided that natural light is desirable for psychological and aesthetic reasons. The problem will be to control the natural light, and to bear in mind its various and changing effects when planning an artificial lighting system suited to the needs of the different users of the library. It will also be necessary to use light-coloured surfaces inside the building to reflect as much daylight as possible without the glare produced by too much direct sunlight.

Artificial lighting and measurement

Standards of intensity are based upon the light-emitting power of a candle, and the intensity is expressed in candelas. The illumination, which is technically the amount of light radiating inward from an imaginary sphere around the light source, is measured in lumens, and the spread of light over the area of one square metre is measured in lumens per square metre, known as lux. In the United States the unit is the lumen per square foot (still sometimes known as the foot-candle), which (obviously) relates to the spread of light in lumens over a square foot. The numerical relationship between the two units is one of direct metric conversion of area, one lux being equal to 0.0929 foot-candles (lumens/ft^2); one lumen/ft^2 equals 10.764 lux. To plan a lighting scheme in full it would also be necessary to bring in the factor of luminance (brightness), which can be expressed either in fundamental units (candelas/ft^2 or /m^2) or in terms of the equivalent illumination related through reflectance (the foot-lambert or its metric equivalent, the apostilb). For a full explanation see Hopkinson and Collins[4]; see also the IES Code.[5]

Librarians should generally confine their observations to levels directly related to the IES recommendations.[6] If it is planned to use a light meter to determine the light level at a reading table, the correct instrument must be used (not the meter for calculating the correct exposure for photographs), and measurements must be taken on the horizontal plane at 850 mm (2 ft 9 in) above floor level or at the normal working height. It should be noted that light from any source decreases with the square of the distance

Table 11.1 Recommended lighting intensities

	Recommended illumination (lux)	Limiting glare* index
Reading rooms (newpapers and magazines)	200	19
Reading tables (lending librarires)	400	19
Reading tables (reference libraries)	600	16
Counters	600	19
Closed book stores	100 (on vertical surface)	—
Binding	600	22
Cataloguing, sorting, stock rooms	400	22

* These figures represent the maximum acceptable degree of glare for the room in which each activity is to take place. The IES *Glare index* is widely used for comparison purposes throughout industry and its levels are stipulated in lighting contracts.

from the source, and that illumination on a surface varies as the cosine of the angle at which it reaches the surface. There is also the factor of the reflectance of other surfaces, including the table-top: to know the light power of a source therefore is not in itself very helpful.

Intensity

These recommendations (Table 11.1) are of course very general and should not be applied uncritically; for example the wide variation between the lighting for reading rooms and for reading tables is based on the difference between casual reading and concentrated study, which will apply only in particular circumstances. There is also the point that human eyesight becomes less efficient with age, and this must be taken into account.

It should be noted that the levels given here refer to the 'maintained' intensity, that is the operating level when the lamps are well used and have a normal accretion of dust and dirt, not the level of a brand new lamp. The former may have only two-thirds the intensity of the latter. The steady escalation of lighting levels in libraries (in America they are usually noticeably higher than in Britain) is an intriguing phenomenon. A recent article on American public librar-ies[7] states: 'Candlepower per square foot had risen gradually until the energy crisis of the 1970s prompted the lighting engineers to substantially lower standards . . .'; and later: 'General reading rooms for instance were once thought to require 100 foot-candles; they are now said to need 50 foot-candles, or even less in some instances.' It is interesting to note here that British recommendations quoted above are for 200 to 600 lux – that is between 18.6 and 56 foot-candles.

The editors of the second edition of Metcalf[8] report that in 1970 they saw lighting in a library rest room that exceeded 180 foot-candles (1936 lux). They also quoted the 1981 edition of the (American) *IES Lighting Handbook* as suggesting 5 to 10 foot-candles (54 to 108 lux) for inactive stacks and microform reading areas; 20 to 50 foot-candles (216 to 540 lux) for active stacks, book repair and binding areas, cataloguing, circulation desk, audio-visual reading areas and map, print and picture rooms; and from 20 to 100 foot-candles (216 to 1080 lux) for reading areas, depending on the nature of the detail, age of readers and other factors. These high levels of lighting intensity mean a greater consumption of electricity and so are likely to be confined to a few rich countries. In poorer countries it is not only a matter of economizing on electricity but of planning to create conditions which are familiar and acceptable to the people. A visitor to a rich country (not necessarily in the West), seeing these glittering expanses of light, might at first be envious, but can take comfort in the fact that energy conservation needs are inevitably going to bring the levels down. Moreover, it must be repeated, there is no evidence at all to show that high levels produce better reading conditions. Mason[9], who of all library consultants is the most critical (and the most interesting) on library lighting, says: '70 foot-candles (750 lux) of good quality light for all reading and work areas. Intensities below 50 foot-candles (520 lux) drive students away'.

Medical evidence indicates that the human eye has not changed in the last few decades and that no present-day reader's eyesight would be strained by reading in the conditions familiar to our fathers, even though today such conditions would be regarded as intolerably gloomy. We tend to forget that to read black print on white paper is not difficult visually. The eye will not be damaged by bad lighting, but 'information collection' may be less efficient.

A conclusion from research that is of particular interest is that people who have the same standard of visual acuity (sharpness of vision) do not necessarily perform visually with the same ease. Further experiments[10] led to the conclusion that an increase in the intensity of light on the task material considerably improved its readability for the average person up to a level of 300 lux (approximately 28 lm/ft^2), but that the improvement after this point is much less dramatic, even though it does continue. On the other hand people with poor sight benefit more from increased levels of lighting than do people with normal sight. It is also notable that people in different countries react in different ways to lighting, perhaps because their eyes become conditioned to the levels and changes to which they have become accustomed. It is important to note that visual comfort (a crucial matter) appears to be more affected by increased luminance of the surrounding area than is the actual task of reading. An increase in the surrounding luminance to thirty times that of the reading matter certainly impairs the reading performance and increases discomfort (see 'Contrast' below).

Uncomfortable conditions of luminance of the surround-ing area are also likely to give rise to complaints of glare. Normal reading (and in serious working conditions reading includes note-taking) can take place perfectly adequately with a general lighting intensity of 150 lux (14 lm/ft^2), but few librarians today offer such a low level. Investigations by Blackwell[11] produced interesting conclusions:

'The light intensity we require depends drastically upon the task we are to perform. This conclusion supports the idea of localised lighting for areas where the *most* difficult tasks are performed. . . . The data certainly suggest that more light is needed for many tasks than is needed for well-printed books.'

Tests by the (American) Illuminating Engineering Society led them to recommend 70 foot-candles (753 lux), because the lighting needed for reading medium-hard pencil marks on white paper was used as a basis. Is this a fair assessment of study use?

Tests leading to this recommendation (quoted by Blackwell) suggest that by the same reasoning the level required for comfortable reading of 8-point printed type need be only 15 foot-candles (164 lux). In open-plan office areas in Continental Europe it is common to find 1000 lux (93 lm/ft^2) on table-tops, but this appears to be higher than in Britain, where 650–750 lux (60–70 l/ft^2) is more normal. The whole question obviously needs further scientific study before categorical statements can be justified.

A psychological factor to be taken into account is that the reader will be happy to work in a bright area within sight of other areas which are less brightly lit, but he will suffer a sense of frustration if he can see areas brighter than the one in which he is working. This must be allowed for in the layout by isolating from any brighter areas rooms where intensive study is to take place.

Reading is not the only activity which concerns the librarian: in matters of general display, the best guide is the IES report on the lighting of art galleries and museums,[12] which gives many examples of the problems and recommends solutions.

Contrast

Eye fatigue is caused mainly by glare and excessive contrast. The romatic picture of a reader in a dark room working with a pool of light on his book shows an unhealthy situation. Extensive investigation of the best lighting for comfortable working shows that the aim should be smooth graduation in brightness from the book itself to the immediate surround (the table-top) and finally to the general background. A ratio of luminance (photometric brightness) of about 3:1 between page and table-top is probably best, and more than 5:1 is bad for continuous reading. The ratio between the page and the rest of the room can certainly be five times, but how much above that is not authoritatively stated anywhere. Perhaps, again, it is largely a matter of what one has become accustomed to.

If the page of the book is white, the table-top should certainly not be white or too light, but it is also important that it should not be too dark; certainly it should not be black. The general background should be less bright than the table-top, but not excessively so.

Books are normally printed on white paper of a reflectance of 0.7 to 0.8. If the table-top has a reflectance of about 0.2 to 0.3 (Munsell values 5 to 6*) and is illuminated more or less uniformly, the recommended luminance ratio will have been achieved. To give acceptable conditions the colour and material of the table-top and the surrounding areas will have to be balanced, so lighting cannot be considered in isolation from interior decoration, which includes choice of furniture.

The luminance of the background will naturally vary enormously; there will often be bookcases close to the reader and their luminance will be less than that of the table-top, but light-coloured walls and ceilings as well as open spaces also form part of the background and will have to be taken into account. A great deal depends on the reflectance factors of the various colours and materials in the room: figures for these are readily available, and the interior designer would take them into account in his designs. Unless the walls are panelled in dark wood, and provided that some light is cast upwards to a light ceiling, the background is not likely to appear too dark.

In libraries there is usually a fair amount of light shining upwards from bookstack lighting, but where there is none, it is desirable to direct some light towards the ceiling; panels which act as reflectors behind high-level lights will direct some light back towards the ceiling to reduce contrast. This may not be necessary if the floor is of a very light colour (Munsell value 6 or more), in which case there may be adequate reflection from the general lighting. Where bookcases are close together this may not be so since they will obstruct a large proportion of reflected light. To avoid distraction it is important to avoid too much upward light; while indirect lighting gives character and charm, its use as a sole source is especially to be deprecated.

The human eye responds more directly to change than to intensity itself, and much depends on the 'adaptation level', the level to which the eye has become adapted in the previous few minutes. Because the eye's response to change is proportional to the existing light, an increase in level from 20 to 30 lux will produce the same psychological benefit as an increase from 100 to 150 lux. Brock Arms[14] says:

'One group of readers was subjected to 30 foot-candles (323 lux), another group to 50 foot-candles (538 lux) and another to 70 foot-candles (735 lux). At the end of thirty minutes of general reading tasks, the three groups were exposed to a series of progressively higher levels of illumination. Each individual in the experiment was then asked to mark the level at which he found the light most comfortable for reading. The majority of people who had

*For a definition of Munsell values, see IES *Technical Report 14.*[13]

adjusted previously to 30 foot-candles indicated a level near 30 foot-candles. The group who had adjusted to 50 foot-candles marked a level near 50 foot-candles. The group which had adjusted to 70 foot-candles marked a level near 70 foot-candles.'

Glare

Strong light shining, or being reflected, into the eyes causes glare, and this not only irritates but makes the pupil contract so that it is less efficient for its purpose. The extent of the glare depends on a number of factors: the brightness itself, both from the source and from reflection, the size and position of the source and the number of sources in view. It follows that there is more danger of glare in open areas because of the greater number of direct sources and ways of reflecting them. Blackwell[15] shows that the angle at which the light source is visible is absolutely critical and that the best results are achieved when light is obtained from as large a percentage of the ceiling area as possible. After a scientific analysis he concludes: 'Thus we can say categorically that the best lighting installations can provide the visibility criterion with less than one-fourth of the light level required with the worst lighting installation.'

There are a number of scientific ways of measuring glare, but they are based either on a study of directly comparable environments (difficult with libraries) or on the subjective reaction of a sample of users. Both methods are too involved to be discussed here.

The most obvious way to control glare might seem to be to direct all light sources downward (where it will be important for table-tops to be matt, not shiny). This method can shade readers at tables from angled emissions of light and is most commonly found with individual table lights, which will be needed for special tasks (study of prints, for example). They are liked by readers, but each would prefer to be able to adjust them to his own requirements, and this can be difficult (except in carrels) because of the effect of glare on other readers. Table lights for two readers sitting opposite each other should not be provided unless there is a light shield between them. The light emitted should extend beyond the table-top so that readers can lean back with books in their hands if they wish. Individual table lights should be chosen with the needs of left-handed people in mind. These lights do not illuminate surrounding book-cases at all, and although very effective for study conditions they are not so good for casual reading because they do not provide enough light for books held for reading at an angle to the table-top.

Large shades around incandescent lights are commonly used to control glare but there will be a great loss of lighting efficiency and limits upon interior design. Such methods attempt to prevent points of light entering the eye direct from light sources. This can be done by totally indirect lighting, that is by directing all light upwards to a light-coloured ceiling, but it is not to be recommended where continuous study is taking place. It would be ideal if reflecting surfaces could be arranged so as to surround completely the reading position, but this is seldom possible to arrange in an open area. Light directed downwards from a fluorescent source, particularly if it is unshielded, will reflect back from white paper, especially art or machine-polished paper; really glare-free conditions are obtained only when the source is diffused by an efficient filtering medium and reaches the reading surface from as many indirect points as possible. The shielding of fluorescent lights with a plastic cover does reduce glare, and a cover also has advantages in avoiding the

11:1. Bare fluorescent tubes on ceiling: not acceptable for study conditions

11:2. Fluorescent tubes in trough of light-coloured acoustic control material; this spreads the light and reduces the contrast. The vertical shields limit the spread of glare to readers some distance away but not to those reading nearby

11:3. Low level of general lighting from fittings in coffered ceiling supplemented by light from arrangement of more heavily lit bookshelving areas in alternate floors and individual lighting at two-sided tables: Birmingham Central Library

11:4. General lighting from high windows lightly curtained, bowls on ceiling as well as bookcase and single table lighting (Schulz GMBH Speyer, GFR)

11:5. Pattern of sockets in a suspended ceiling: sockets can be grouped into circuits

concentration of points of light common in single-source elements such as bulbs in fittings, but it also reduces the efficiency of the light source: the quality of the light then emitted, and the extent of the reduction of efficiency, will of course depend on the proprietary shield used, and many of the cheap ones are appalling: here expert advice is essential. Blackwell[16] says: 'The best material (multi-layer polarising panels) permits use of three times as many foot-candles without discomfort as the worst materials (perfectly diffusing panels).'

Some diffusers which use glass polarizing elements to break up the light can be most effective as well as attractive. With all this information and the new products to hand, it is surprising that we see so many libraries with the rows of fluorescent tubes which we have learned to dread. Open tubes fixed to ceilings in particular produce considerable glare and should never be accepted for reading areas. The use of light-coloured troughs above the tubes (also serving as acoustic baffles and false ceilings) is rather better, especially if vertical breaks are added at intervals to interrupt the lateral spread of light. Nevertheless it is my view (and I take heart from the fact that Mason feels the same) that in serious reading areas there is a danger that the tubes will catch the student's eye at times. Shielding tubes with open-bottomed 'egg-crate' fitments (one of the real abominations of modern lighting) directs the light downward but does not prevent points of light

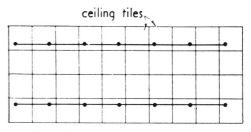

• 5 amp, 3 pin socket
— conduit

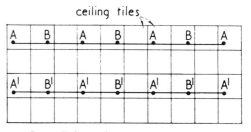

• 5 amp, 3 pin socket
— conduit

catching the unwary eye and causes great irritation. People who are studying do look away from the book at intervals – probably more often than they realize – and for this reason alone glare-producing fitments are unacceptable.

Colour

Colour of lighting affects the reader's response to the visual environment, but, within reasonable limits, it has no direct effect on the eye's efficiency (although some colours are obviously unacceptable for tasks such as reading). The appreciation of the colour of lighting does not correspond with any scientific measurement, but neither is it truly subjective, being influenced by human experience as well as the relation to other colours within view at the same time. To obtain a suitable colour rendering by using 'cold' or 'warm' fluorescent lights is therefore no answer on its own, because an area with a certain lighting colour can look warm in a very white room and cold in a yellow one. Daylight and tungsten incandescent lamps are on the whole neutral in tone, although UV filters will alter the colour, and different reflecting surfaces will have an effect.

The appearance of a library interior, and the feeling of comfort while engaged in tasks such as reading, depend on the quality of the lighting. This, as we have seen, is improved by control of glare, variation of contrast and, to some extent, the use of colour. It also depends on the quality of the fluorescent tubes: those with especially suitable colour renderings are often less efficient in converting electricity into light and therefore more expensive. Increasing the level of lighting without paying expert attention to the other factors can produce some of the worst results and also add appreciably to the cost.

Flexibility

Obtaining complete flexibility (for example in open-plan conditions) would appear to involve having the highest level of absolutely even lighting everywhere in the building, but in practice this will be limited by having different kinds of lighting in entrance halls, lobbies, corridors and other areas which are hardly likely to be converted into stack or reading areas. To have a high level everywhere would be very expensive, and for aesthetic reasons the architect will not be happy to have evenness visible in all directions. To cut down current consumption (and heat rise) and ignoring the use of heat-exchanging systems (which have their own problems), it is obvious that if general lighting can be reduced from 750 to 500 lux (70 to 47 foot-candles) there will be a significant saving, so a compromise would be an overall shadowless illumination plus the provision of numerous electric points so that spots may be added, local lighting is made possible, and fittings can be altered when a change of use is required. It should also be remembered that if an open-plan library is ever fully partitioned (the opportunity to do this is one of its advantages) there will be no light switches in the newly partitioned areas.

A very convenient means of providing lighting from above is to have a demountable ceiling with tiles approximately 600 mm (2 ft) square, of which any can be replaced by a fluorescent fitting. Several proprietary ceilings of this kind are on the market, and light fittings are available to fit the same suspension members; a further advantage is that air supply, or even full thermal and ventilation control, can be installed without ducts. For ease of alteration it is desirable to provide one 5-amp three-pin socket outlet either above each ceiling tile or one to every two, three or four tiles. The layout can therefore be altered

completely by interchanging the lighting fittings with blank tiles. All fittings should be provided with short leads and fused plugs so that they can simply be plugged into the nearest socket.

Although this method involves a comparatively large number of sockets, only a few are likely to be in use at any one time and the cost can therefore be reduced by grouping them into a few circuits each controlled by a miniature circuit-breaker combining the function of fuse and switch. Change can be achieved by plugging a fitting into either an A or B socket (11.5). Each fitting should be protected locally with a fused terminal block or a fused plug top. Such methods of recessing fluorescent lighting in the ceiling are widely used in single-storey open-plan libraries, the counter area being distinguished (and lit more intensely) by hanging incandescent lamps in striking shades. Unless such lamps are hung from the same trunking system and its replaceable tiles, there will be an immediate bar to flexibility. For a fully illuminated ceiling, moulded plastic translucent panels or continuous corrugated strip give a good spread of light, particularly if there is space in the false ceiling to put a good distance between the material and the light source. Reflectors positioned behind the light source will add to efficiency. Such translucent sheeting can be used to admit natural light also (under suitable laylights), with artificial light being both a supplement and a substitute by time-switch or light-level detector switch.

In all these systems which use fluorescent tubes on, or flush with, ceilings, the quality of lighting will depend on the efficiency of the diffuser and fittings of the proposed system, and these should be seen in action before a decision is made. The other extreme is to have a fairly low level of overall lighting with direct individual lighting to reading desks and to bookcases. From the point of view of the serious reader and searcher for books (and that, after all, is what really matters) this is a most attractive proposal, particularly if the desk lights can be fitted with individual controls to vary the intensity of each light, but it requires very expensive and elaborate planning if flexibility is to be retained. The scheme used in the Central Library at Birmingham is to relieve the low general lighting level with a change of ceiling height (by the use of voids through ceilings, staggered on alternate floors) and with floor electric points on every 1375 mm (4 ft 6 in) grid square throughout reading areas to allow for separate lighting on every study table. This achieves good flexibility at the cost of a most elaborate wiring network in the flooring; if the floors are to be carpeted it also means that holes must be made to allow the wires through, and there must be carpet plugs to fill in the holes over any points no longer in use owing to a change in layout. Sockets fitted above the floor covering should never be permitted. A reasonable compromise is to have a medium level of overall lighting with the facility to plug in a table lamp wherever higher levels are particularly required; certain tables can be specified for the purpose.

Areas devoted to microform reading and perhaps to banks of computer work-stations may need a lower level of overall lighting. No formulae will help as much as trying out the machines under various lighting levels. A generous method is to provide local fittings with dimmer switches so that readers can adjust the light to their own needs. This provision can be useful in 'wet' carrels also.

Bookcase lighting

Illumination of bookshelves is difficult to arrange satisfactorily if full adaptability is to be retained. The IES Code[17]

11:6. Lighting across stacks: greater flexibility, but level of light on book surfaces will be reduced

11:7. Lighting along stacks: books rather better lit but there will be difficulties if the stacks have ever to be moved

11:8. Vertical bookcase lighting; not common (Schulz GMBH Speyer, GFR)

11:9. Stack lighting with sensor to switch on when human presence is detected (Ex-Or Ltd)

recommends a minimum illumination level of 50 to 100 lux (4.7 to 9 lm/ft^2) on the vertical surfaces of bookcases, and it is clearly important that no light should shine into the eyes of people choosing books. In open-access or heavily used open-stack conditions, illumination can best be provided either by general room lighting (such as fluorescent tubes set into coffered ceiling panels with removable plastic shields), by direct shelf lighting or by a combination of the two.

General lighting has the advantage of giving complete flexibility in the positioning of stacks and reading areas, but unless there are many light sources readers may cast shadows on the books.

Stack lighting

This is affected by the closeness together of the stack ranges and by the need for flexibility for any future re-arrangement. For these reasons the fluorescent light fittings (preferably recessed) should run across the direction of the stacks at 900 mm (6 ft) intervals. This gives a more even light than tubes running along stacks, but if the tops of the stacks are less than 250 mm (10 in) from the light source it may be necessary, because of the shadows and possibly heat problems (even with fluorescent tubes), to return to the usual expedient of having tubes running between the stacks and in the same direction; this gives better light on the shelves but is a bar to flexibility, as there will be great problems if stacks are moved. In this case the gaps between ends of tubes should not be more than 600 mm (2 ft), because the light does not spread well along the line of tubes and would give very poor light on bookcases which may be on walls at right angles to the stacks. It is possible to have tubes running along the tops of stacks and reflecting off a white ceiling, but this will mean a greater stack ceiling gap and thus higher ceilings or lower stacks; it is also relatively inefficient in the use of current. Direct shelf lighting can be mounted on each case, with a pelmet, or for each row by stand-off fitments. The farther the stand-off the better: 450 mm (18 in) is desirable, 230 mm (9 in) barely acceptable.

By such means it is easy to light the upper shelves adequately (although shadows can be a problem) but lighting on the lower shelves falls away drastically, by the square of the distance from the light source. To increase the light falling on the lower shelves it is desirable to have a light-coloured floor, or at least a strip of floor about 300 mm (1 ft) wide in front of each bookstack with a reflectance of about 0.4 (Munsell value 7), although this does not really compensate for the falling off in illumination. An unusual form of bookcase lighting is that of tubes vertically up the sides of cases; it is illustrated here, but I have never used it and so cannot comment.

Another, very different, example of a combination of general lighting and individual case lighting occurs when a

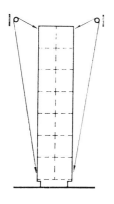
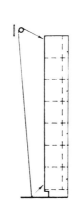
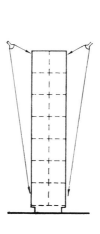
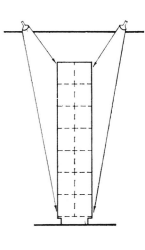

11:10. Fluorescent tubes lighting bookcases; light reflected from the floor can improve the lighting of the lower shelves

11:11. Spotlights can give brighter light and may be recessed if the ceiling is low

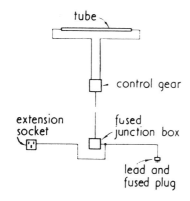
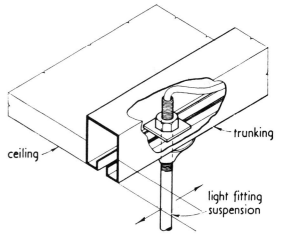

11:12. Trunking channels at right angles to the bookcases will enable light fittings to be moved to suit different shelving layouts

11:13. Wiring diagram for bookcases; control gear can usually be concealed on top of the unit

tube

control gear

extension socket

fused junction box

lead and fused plug

ceiling

trunking

light fitting suspension

11:14. Adjacent bookcases can usually be connected to each other, thus reducing the number of floor outlets required. In practice there is every opportunity to alter the position of the cases when needed

11:15. Alternative patterns for floor trunking. The fishbone layout (left) is cheaper

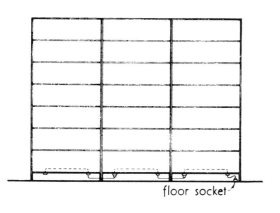

floor socket

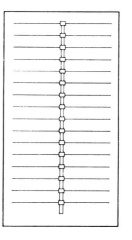
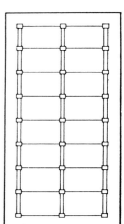

low level of illumination is provided between stacks as a safety measure, individual lights for each section of stack being switched on when required and possibly being turned off by a time-switch. The trouble with time-switches is that they tend to go off when the reader is still in the stacks, causing not only annoyance but the need to go to the stack-end to press the switch again. Some form of overall lighting left permanently on is better in these circumstances. A recent idea is the sensor switch which puts the light on whenever a reader comes into a particular aisle and switches it off when there is no one present. Although not entirely foolproof it has proved very effective and, like the time-switch, will make considerable savings in current consumption. Some manufacturers claim that these installations will pay for their fitting in three years. These systems should not be used with the old-fashioned fluorescent fittings which wear out quicker when switched on and off repeatedly. The starters and condensers of modern fluorescent lighting appear to have eliminated this drawback.

Lighting for open-access areas

In areas with high ceilings where bookshelves form alcoves against walls and where each alcove has a reading table in the centre, fittings hanging from, or mounted on, the ceiling can give enough light on the tables and in the room generally, but they seldom light the bookshelves adequately. It is difficult in these cases to provide pelmets or spotlights on the shelves themselves because they conflict aesthetically with the high ceiling and the alcoves. Lamps with large translucent shades on each table are often useful, not so much to light the tables as to cast light on the bookshelves.

Direct bookcase lighting can be arranged so that each bookcase is provided with a pelmet behind which is mounted a reflector-type fluorescent tube. The tops of the pelmets can be closed in or left partly open to throw light onto the ceiling. Some upward lighting is usually preferred, but screening may be necessary to prevent unsightly shadows. If required, the pelmet can be cut away and provided with holders for translucent frames carrying subject titles. It may be convenient to mount the fluorescent gear on top of the bookcase with small leads only running to the tubes. Light-coloured flooring with a high reflectance (not carpet) can add lightness to the bottom shelves. An expedient used in open-access libraries is to tilt the lower shelves upwards to catch the light, but this has the disadvantage of increasing the depth of shelving as well as looking untidy. Its use in close stacking would be most uneconomical of space.

An alternative method is to use incandescent spotlights carried on a frame or pelmet fixed to the top of the bookcase. Spotlights can be directed downwards and so diminish the contrast between the illumination of the upper and lower shelves; again, beware of shadows. On the other hand, the life of spotlight lamps is limited, maintenance costs are high and it is very difficult to prevent glare from some angles. Each spotlight has to be directed individually and there is always a tendency for small spotlights of neat design to work loose owing to cyclic heating and cooling as the lamps are switched on and off. Where accessible to the public, lamps are also vulnerable to interference.

Adjustable spotlights recessed into the ceiling can be used where siting of bookcases can be accurately determined in advance and the ceiling is low. Change can be obtained if the system of removable ceiling tiles referred to earlier is used.

In areas used for bulk storage of books in stacks it frequently happens that when the library is first opened the stacks are spaced quite far apart. As the stock builds up, more stacks are added and the spacing is reduced; so incandescent or fluorescent fittings which are ceiling-mounted between each pair of stacks must be movable as the stack positions are altered. One solution is to mount the lighting fittings on a simple trunking system on which they can slide. The space between the fittings is closed by a blanking piece, and as racks are added it is necessary only to shorten the blanking pieces, slide the fittings along and add the extra fittings at one end. There are several proprietary trunking systems, some for flush and some for surface mounting, which enable this to be done economically with the minimum of disturbance.

The easiest way to permit movement of bookcases is to provide each case with built-in lighting which can be moved with it. This can be achieved by bringing all wiring to a junction box at the bottom of the bookcase with a lead and socket. Each bookcase can then be connected either to a floor socket or to an adjacent bookcase.

Floor sockets can be installed in a simple grid system for complete flexibility. Each socket can serve a row of cases and therefore the grid of sockets need not be very dense: 1.2 m to 2 m (4 ft to 6 ft 6 in) centres should be enough. In any floor trunking system the junction boxes constitute the most expensive item, so it is desirable to adopt a fishbone layout which reduces the number of boxes.

In most cases absolute interchangeability will not be needed, since certain areas (walls, for example) will always be used for shelving and other areas (in front of windows, perhaps) will always be used for tables. Floor trunking and ceiling sockets need be provided only in those areas where the layout may be changed. By these means, reasonable flexibility can be obtained at comparatively small cost. Such identification of reasonable limits can achieve a great saving.

The use of high-intensity lighting units (particularly metal halide) appears to be growing. These, in small fitments, can be ceiling mounted, incorporating their own directional reflectors, to light wall shelving. They produce a great amount of light but if used in conjunction with some diffused room lighting, do not cause shadows. It is not advisable to use them for free-standing cases as the glare could be intense. Because they are so small and so powerful they are often directed towards the ceiling to produce indirect lighting.

Whatever equipment the architect chooses need not be the same in all sections. He can design so as to have top daylight to perimeter carrels, vertical wells with light washing along reflecting surfaces for some areas and local table lighting for serious study conditions. A good mix of lighting methods can contribute a great deal to the charm as well as the efficiency of the internal environment.

Cost

To step up the intensity of lighting can be expensive, not only in the cost of the extra electricity used, but in the provision of more fittings and machinery and in the consequent higher cleaning and maintenance bills. As lighting in all its ramifications can account for as much as 10% of running, cleaning and maintenance costs, this can be very serious.

The efficiency of a lighting installation can be measured and expressed in lumens per watt. Examples of typical installations are given in Hopkinson and Collins.[18]

Of the usual alternatives, fluorescent lighting has been found to be cheaper than filament bulb lighting if it is used for more than three-quarters of an hour per day (180 hours a year), but a true costing can be computed only after taking into account the costs of the initial installation, periodic cleaning and later replacement, as well as the length of life of bulbs and tubes. It is commonly said that a filament lamp costs one-fifth as much as a fluorescent tube, uses five times as much electricity and lasts one-fifth of the time. Metal halide lamps, producing very high-intensity light, are economical if only because fewer of them will be needed; but they also have acceptable efficiency and long life. The cost advantage of low-level indirect lighting combined with local (task) lighting should not be forgotten; because the lights can be switched off when not in use, a great current saving can be obtained.

In his feasibility study the architect may go so far as to make a rough estimate of lighting costs (taking into account the number of hours when lights will be in use, the cleaning and replacement schedules and the likely labour costs). These estimates should be considered carefully. Where the library forms part of a large complex (a university, college or school, for example) the authority may call for comment from its own officers, who can compare the levels and costs with those in other parts of the institution. If the costs are deemed to be too high, the architect may have to amend his proposals. In making his plans the architect may draw upon the expertise of a lighting consultant, but it is rare for this expert to report direct to the authority. Because lighting is so vital a part of the aesthetic effect the architect intends to produce, he will usually decide to reserve the final decisions to himself. At present very much the most common form of general lighting for reading areas consists of fluorescent tubes, either fitted to or free of the ceiling, or else recessed into a false ceiling, and usually (but not always) cased in diffusers. The effect is bright and economical in the use of electricity, but it is also soulless.

Table 11.2	Efficiency of lighting installations
Fluorescent tubes	*Light output (lumens)*
80 watt	3 100 to 4 850
65 watt	2 700 to 4 400
40 watt	1 700 to 2 600
Filament bulbs	*Light output (lumens)*
25 watt	200
40 watt*	390
60 watt*	665
100 watt*	1 260
200 watt	2 720
500 watt	7 700

* Coiled coil.

Maintenance

Because of high labour costs and the unpredictability of the falling-off rate of their efficiency, fluorescent tubes are now usually replaced periodically in bulk, rather than piecemeal as a single tube fails. This can result in lower lighting levels in certain areas while replacement is awaited. To overcome this by having higher lighting levels than are needed at first, so as to allow for failure, is wrong; a better method (at a higher initial cost) is to have two, or even three, tubes in a fitting; one to come into operation automatically, or be switched on manually, if another should fail. Easy access to fittings is also an item of economic importance in maintenance; ornamental clusters in high ceiling areas which require scaffolding for lights to be cleaned or replaced are a librarian's nightmare.

In open areas all light switches should be sited where they are entirely under staff control, the whole area being lit or unlit as one unit. Local control may be needed for areas near windows, where lights will be needed less often, but these again should be controlled by the staff. A system of switches operable only by key is worth considering. Individual carrels will have their own switches, but time will be saved if all these can be overridden by a master switch so that staff do not have to check that each light is out at the end of the day. A similar arrangement is economical for closed stacks: switches for each stack ensure that lights can be put on when needed, but all lights should be controllable by a central cut-off at closing time. Main aisle lighting can be exempted from this central control, so that patrol and cleaning can take place at night. In small libraries all switches should be at the counter.

The librarian's tasks

With regard to lighting, the librarian's chief tasks are to indicate in the brief the purposes of the different functional areas and say where special circumstances call for different levels of lighting. He will be ill-advised to venture too far into the technicalities of lighting levels, quality and so on, but he may wish to draw the architect's attention to an existing library which has the kind of conditions he would like to achieve. When he receives the sketch plans he should carefully study the position of the reader and the light sources, natural and artificial, and try to visualize the possible effect of glare and contrast: at first he will find this difficult to do. He must also insist on seeing a mock-up of one of the proposed light fittings in operation, both in day-time and night-time conditions, and listen for the hum of the starters and check whether fluorescent lights interfere with audio-visual equipment. If the architect thinks this is unnecessary, quote to him Mason,[19] who says that in his long career as a consultant the light fittings which have been first proposed in his projects have always ranged from the mediocre to the horrifyingly bad. The provision of suitable lighting is the architect's business, but it is the weakest point in modern library design, and the librarian has to live with the results.

As in so many fields of library planning today, technological developments offer a range of lighting innovations, some of which may change drastically the opportunities open to the architect. For the last three decades the choice has been confined to incandescent lamps or fluorescent tubes, but now smaller, more efficient alternatives are on the market. It must be assumed that the architect will be familiar with them and may utilize them in his designs.

The librarian will not know from early sketches what type of fittings will be stipulated, so it is important that he should discuss the whole matter with the architect. Among other things he has to visualize the cleaning and maintenance problems with which he will have to deal after the architect has left the scene.

Table 11:3 shows the lighting conditions in four very similar small British university libraries, with comments upon the degree of adaptability and the environmental effects.

Table 11.3   Comparison of environmental conditions – lighting

	Edinburgh	Bristol	Nottingham	Newcastle
Lighting levels	377–430 lux at table-top. Stack 129–161 lux on vertical surface	450 lux at table-top and average elsewhere	377 lux (35 lm/ft) at table-tops and bookstacks. 'As an economy measure 50% of the fluorescent tubes have been removed but in most areas 350 lux lighting levels are achieved at table-top height.'	Not less than 400 lux in all usable areas
Ceiling height	2450 mm (8 ft)	General 2700 mm (9 ft). Perimeter reading areas 2300 mm (7 ft 6 in)	2450 mm (8 ft) but with deep modular panels making troughs for the fluorescent tubes	2550 mm (8 ft 6 in)
Artificial lighting	Fixed continuous recessed fluorescent lighting strip at 1375 mm (4 ft 6 in) centres along bookstack aisles across width of building	Low-brightness prismatic panels semi-recessed into the ceiling. Tungsten over seating around perimeter including tables	Fluorescent tubes shielded by modular V-shaped ceiling panels with vertical wings which both reflect light and limit its spread	Fluorescent tubes shielded by modular ceiling panels with vertical wings
Natural lighting	Continuous full-height glazing; fixed horizontal louvres on east and west faces; south face with tinted glass shielded by projecting floor structure	Ground floor tinted windows protected by overhang; large corner windows on 1st floor; downward sloping windows on 1st and 2nd floors	Bottom two floors fully glazed with brown tinted glass and with cantilevered overhang. Upper floors vertical slit windows with glazed feature at cut-off corners	Windows protected by vertical fins beside reader seating; window size kept small to conserve energy
Adaptability	Bookstacks are restricted to the 1375 mm (4ft 6 in) module in the direction and position they are now in so as to maintain an even distribution of light. Lighting conditions are suitable for readers over the entire floor area. Bookstacks cannot be placed within 1825 mm (6 ft) of windows on south face	Stacks movable; partitions for admin areas are of concrete block but demountable. Different lighting on perimeter	Open-plan layout giving full flexibility throughout except for single core. Same lighting in most open areas of library	Reader areas entirely flexible except for four cores

12 Security and protection

In theory the degree of security required and the priority to be accorded to it were recorded in the primary brief. In practice this is not an easy matter for the librarian to tackle. He can indicate which portions of the library need special protection – strongrooms for valuable books, for example – but can hardly tell the architect to arrange that the building is to be burglar-proof, because that is a term with special implications. This chapter is designed to help understanding of the problems which may have to be faced and to suggest some possible solutions. It has to be accepted that higher degrees of security not only inhibit the architect in his design solutions and add to the cost; they also diminish, to a greater or lesser extent, the reader's freedom to enjoy the library. There are three categories of hazard: natural forces (fire, flood and 'Acts of God'); outside thieves, burglars and vandals; and, by no means the least, readers.

After considering carefully the possible dangers and the possible defences, the librarian will be in a better position to indicate to the architect what are the parameters in this particular library, so that it can be designed for crime prevention and for protection against other dangers.

Fire

All libraries – the buildings, the people inside them and the materials – must be protected against hazards. Of these, by far the greatest is fire, and the damage which often accompanies it, caused chiefly by smoke and water.

To what extent is it justifiable to incur considerable expense and inconvenience to readers where there is little danger and the materials are not difficult to replace? As part of the Library Technology Project, Gage-Babcock and Associates Inc.[1] made a survey of fires in libraries in the United States, comparing them with similar occurrences in other public buildings and studying the main causes of the fires. One of their first findings was that libraries are among the institutions in the category of lowest fire risk. Nevertheless, the researchers point out that the data make it clear that libraries in themselves are no safer from harm than other buildings.

'The idea that books do not burn easily is a dangerous half-truth. When they are tightly packed on the shelves, they do burn at slow rate. However, in a situation of multi-tier stacks with unrestricted passageways and openings in the floors permitting vertical draughts, intense fires can build up in the stacks very quickly.'[2] The attack on the 'myth of the non-burning book' was taken further in *Managing the Library Fire Risk*,[3] which quotes an experiment carried out with a solid block of books and paper under carefully controlled conditions; a temperature just short of 2500° Fahrenheit was generated.

Even if books do not burst into flames easily they, and the carpets and other materials near them, smoulder and produce smoke. In fact it is smoke which usually billows up the 'funnels' within the building. Smoke is particularly dangerous to life, not only because of asphyxiation but because of the panic it can cause. It must be clearly understood that a great danger can exist even without flames.

In every aspect of planning, great attention will be paid to fire dangers. This is one of the most constricting of factors on the freedom to design. The danger will be a major consideration in planning structure, structural materials, floor thicknesses and all interior materials. Official fire regulations determine the compartmentalization (that is, the division of areas into 'boxes') and the intervals at which these must be separated by fire-proof barriers. Because fires feed on oxygen, the control of ventilation is vital, and this can affect the size, positioning and materials of windows and require fire shutters for escalators. In designs of the atrium variety there will be special problems to be overcome because the upper 'balcony' floors are at risk from a fire below, for which there is a natural funnel; the upper floors may have to be enclosed.

Nevertheless the smoke has to be dissipated; in a recent small atrium public library in Britain,[4] 'a sophisticated sprinkler system operates throughout the building and is associated with alarm bells. If the alarm is raised, fans in the atrium roof and some of the windows on each floor level open automatically to clear the smoke'. Fire doors or the dampers in ducts may have to be fitted with fusible links so that in the event of a fire there will be an automatic cut-off.

There will also be very stringent rules about the distance which any theoretical reader may have to travel to get to a fire exit. The needs of the disabled have to be considered, because lifts are usually out of action when a fire occurs. There will be danger of fire from adjoining property, and it may be necessary to plan for fire-insulating spaces or walls. The Robarts Library of Toronto University has double exterior walls connected by a thermal break, but this is a fourteen-storey building, the largest university library in the world, and so a special case.

If a fire does start, its progress through the building must be delayed as much as possible, and this depends not only on the material on which it can feed (books, paper, furniture and so on) but also its passage through walls, doors and ceilings, as well as on the air which can reach it. A door that is quickly consumed by flames, a lift shaft or stair well which allows air to be funnelled upwards, a weak wall – all these are hazards to be guarded against in designing for fire protection. Regulations require that doors and other barriers must have a stipulated fire-resistance period. The criteria for determining this include stability, integrity (existence of openings in the barrier) and insulation (heat passing through); in general the requirement will vary from half an hour to four hours, the latter being where the library is what is deemed a separate building (including one within a complex if there is a floor between library and underground car park). It should be noted that a heavy but combustible barrier (such as thick hardwood) can often resist fire longer than a thin non-combustible one (such as thin sheet steel). The choice of furniture is also affected: some paints allow flames to spread along a surface more quickly than others. Polyurethane foam and polypropylene covering on chairs can be very fast-burning and can produce toxic fumes.

This is the world of the architect and the fire prevention officer. There are very strict rules which must be obeyed, the fire authority having to be consulted at every stage of the planning programme. In many cases the fire insurers will add special requirements. This aspect of the programme is quite outside the experience of the librarian but it is part of his job to know about fire exits, and the detection and suppression measures to be used, so that he can drill his staff to remember them clearly and make full use of them almost instinctively. It is even more important for him to play his part by ensuring careful discipline in organizing and inspecting the storage of materials so that loose papers, spare packing papers and so on are never left near possible (even remotely possible) fire hazards. It is perhaps significant that most fires begin in basements. With one important exception the greatest causes of fires are the heating and lighting systems. The exception referred to is smoking: investigations show this to be by far the greatest single cause of library fires; staff and reader discipline is the only answer.[5,6] Regular patrolling by a library employee whose duties include following a prescribed path through the building at regular intervals, day and night, checking for possible fire danger is of great value. Where this is not possible a substitute can be found in various mechanical systems, including closed-circuit television, to keep an eye on particularly vulnerable areas. At the very least the architect should arrange that identifiable danger points (e.g. smoking areas) be isolated from vulnerable materials.

Detection

Automatic fire detectors are sophisticated devices which can give early warning of a fire developing both locally, with the detector placed on the underside of the ceiling, as well as in general service areas such as ventilation ducts.

There are four types of detectors in general use:

1. Heat (detecting temperature above a certain level).
2. Heat rise (detecting a sudden rise in temperature).
3. Optical smoke (sensing when smoke obscures glass in the fitting).
4. Ionization smoke (sensing a presence of particles even before smoke is visible).

The choice depends on the estimate of the nature of the danger. When loose papers burn, the heat can quickly be high enough to trigger a heat or a rate-of-heat-rise detector, but the general library hazard is of smouldering books and carpets. Ionization detectors are best, but in areas where smoking is permitted they cannot reliably be used, and here the rate-of-heat-rise detector is best. Modern detector fittings can easily be removed from the ceiling for maintenance.

Suppression

When a fire has been detected there are two immediate requirements: to alert the fire station and to try and put the fire out. Alarms must be planned to notify the nearest fire station direct; a two-tier system (phone the library fire officer, who then phones the fire station) is unacceptable. For quick suppression of the fire there must be a system of local extinguishers in whose use the staff have been well trained. It is unfortunate that these appliances (and, even more, coils of fire hoses) take up much space and are unsightly. Many charming interior designs are ruined by the red horrors whose site is decided by the fire authorities, whatever the architect may desire.

The best answer is an automatic sprinkler system associated with the automatic detector device. Strictly localized automatic mist-sprinkler response to a fire-activated (or smoke-activated) warning would certainly soak the outsides of the books on (say) a single tier of stack. If this extinguishes a fire, the resultant drying-out operation of the affected books would be a small price to

pay to prevent a disaster. It will be even cheaper when considered against the alternative, which is the entry of firemen pouring thousands of gallons of water over the book stock.

Sprinkler devices are:

wet pipe system with pipes containing water and a head with a seal which melts under heat and sprays water around; it was this method which gave sprinklers such a bad name.

dry pipe system: there are several types but in each the water does not enter the local pipe until the detector operates.

Sprinklers have variations in their area of operation; a strictly local one can be set to spray on a very small area where the fire has been detected.

Such detection and sprinkler systems have great value in stacks, particularly closed stacks which may not be visited frequently; but in open-reader areas they are very vulnerable to the practical joker with a cigarette lighter.

The use of gas to kill fire in rare-book and archive areas can be very effective. Carbon dioxide can kill a fire in a matter of seconds in a confined area but it is space-consuming (in the storage of bulky CO_2 cylinders), expensive and can be a risk to human life in certain circumstances. Halon gases are now common and can be installed in neat fitments to kill fires immediately in special closed areas. Gases are not suitable for open public areas, and should be used sparingly because they contribute to the destruction of the ozone layer. The advice of fire prevention officers is essential, because they can discover special features of a situation which would seldom occur to the layman.

Escape

The very stringent nature of fire regulations in most countries is made necessary by the horrifying examples of what can happen if hundreds of people are trapped in a public building when a fire starts. Consequently the architect's plans will be rejected by the fire authorities unless they meet these requirements. They will not only stipulate how many fire exits must be provided, and their width and location, but there will even be detailed instructions as to the size and style of wording of fire exit notices. This is very laudable; but any exit is a chance for the opportunist thief. The librarian will want a method which allows immediate escape in case of fire but is secure on ordinary occasions. There are a number of alternatives: the most primitive are 'push-bars'. These are considered essential in theatres, which combine people in mass with a high fire-risk environment, but they spell disaster to the security of a library's book stock. Even an alarm fitted to them will only tell the librarian that he has lost more books. The break-glass system, with a key or an opening handle behind it, may be old-fashioned but has psychological advantages, especially if fitted with an alarm. Its main disadvantage is that it is attractive to vandals; it also calls for immediate and well-rehearsed action when the alarm sounds.

Electronically operated locks can be useful. Here the system secures the lock during normal times but releases it automatically when the fire alarm is activated in the building. These locks are designed to be 'fail-safe' so that if there is a breakdown of the electronic system they will automatically unlock.

Multi-storey buildings are particularly difficult, because a fire staircase can give access to supposedly secure regions. It is important that when the librarian has studied the subject he should make his attitude clear in the brief, so that the architect can investigate what is available on the market and get the fire authority's approval for a plan to meet the needs.

Flood

Water has probably damaged more libraries than fire, and the architect will be aware of the possible danger from water pipes within the building (and even water mains near basement stacks). The few inches below the lowest shelves of bookstacks will give protection for a time, but detection of a flood is seldom automatic and it may be necessary, in underground areas, for water-breaks to be formed to isolate and limit any danger. In certain circumstances it may also be expedient to build special walls to protect underground storage areas from possible external flooding, but this need will have been indicated at an early stage in the report of the geological survey. It should not be forgotten that one result of a flood, even if water remains below the lowest level of actual book stacking and does not soak the books, is the creation of a very humid atmosphere for some considerable time, even in an effectively air-conditioned building, and this can activate mould in older books and manuscripts. To have the areas heat-dried as soon as possible is a priority, even if it means temporarily removing the books from the building, because a temperature rise, except in strictly controlled areas, would also cause damage.

Flooding can cause whole sections of the book stock to become completely soaked, which can also occur when water is used to put out fires. Recent advances in conservation techniques have made this less of a nightmare than it used to be. If books can be freeze-dried immediately, the drying-out process can be controlled and the development of mould prevented. Even in his old building the librarian needs to keep in touch with any centralized body which can offer the facility to handle masses of soaked books. If not, a kindly deep-freeze store manager may be willing to help with what has proved to be a surprisingly effective method of initial treatment.

It may also be necessary to take special steps to design a building which will be as secure as possible against any other 'natural' hazards to which the region may be prone. Architects in the earthquake belt have experience of building so as to accept earth movements by means of flexible and compensating elements in the structure. Even so there have been examples in recent years of considerable damage to libraries, and it appears that in certain countries the matter needs more attention. The same is true of rather lesser convulsions such as hurricanes and tornadoes. The architect will take the record of past events in the region into account in his structural planning as well as in such matters as fenestration and escape routes.

Reader hazards

Book theft

To protect the library against this common and, alas, growing habit there are two major weapons: supervision of exits and compulsory depositing of cases and bags in a cloakroom.

Supervision of exits
The obvious protection against theft is to have some form of inspection at exit points, although such supervision will always create a bottleneck.

During the last century the attitude to inspection in public libraries has turned a complete circle. For many years all public libraries were closed-access, readers being separated from the books by a barrier; each book was identified from the catalogue and was requested from a member of the staff who went to fetch it: it was usually already out on loan. Later, indicators were installed, machines showing which books were in and which were out, but no reader was allowed to handle a book until it had been issued.

Towards the end of the nineteenth century (in Britain) came the move to 'safeguarded open access'. It is difficult now to understand the furore the proposals caused, but at the time there was bitter controversy between those for and against the new method. Open access won, at first gradually, then in a landslide, and readers were admitted to the shelves. The exit counter in this system was fitted with a locking wicket which was released by a staff member to allow the reader to leave only when the book had been checked out. For years these wickets were in widespread use, but many librarians remember that even then they were often permanently locked open, partly because they irritated honest readers and partly because the greatly increased use of the library was not matched by an increase in staff or space; so the system became unworkable. During the last forty years more and more libraries moved away from both the lockable wicket and the bottleneck counter which dominated entrance and exit routes; counters were placed further and further from the entrance to make the library's atmosphere more welcoming. It is for the authority (through the librarian) to decide how much control is to be sacrificed in order to produce an attractive and cheerful library. Certainly the architect would welcome the disappearance of the island enclosure grimly guarding entrance doors.

Sadly, book losses have become so high in libraries (as in all stores with openly displayed merchandise) that the atmosphere of freedom has reluctantly been abandoned. Safeguards have returned and consequently there are bottlenecks; books in most demand are often issued to readers only after direct request to the staff. The wheel has turned full circle.

In small libraries, control will have to be exercised from the counter and the readers' advisory desk, often the same place, within a single room; but in large libraries, particularly multi-storey academic libraries, control will be carried out at a special position dominating the entrance and exit to the building. This can be a glass-sided cubicle manned by security staff who have no other task, and who have positive control over exits, with facilities, as well as authority, for examination of readers' cases. 'Glass-sided' has been stipulated here because attendance at entrance and exit doors can be a draughty business.

Turnstiles, after a long period of discredit, are to be seen again. Modern versions appear less forbidding than the old types, but they are always unpopular because they are restrictive and imply mistrust. Because of this it is common for their operation to be a rather perfunctory and shamefaced business which leaves them open to the opportunist thief. When installing them it is necessary for the librarian to be absolutely clear as to the way they are to be used, and the staff must be put in the picture from the beginning. Fire exit regulations must be carefully watched, and it will be necessary for turnstiles to have fast and complete release mechanisms.

A comparatively recent development is the detection system which operates a locking wicket and sounds an alarm whenever an attempt at unauthorized removal is made. In these systems each reader passes out of the library (or out of a single room) through a bottleneck across which is an invisible magnetic or, more usually today, electronic field, which may cause the alarm and locking device to operate. The trigger varies in the different proprietary systems but is generally a piece of material hidden in the book. Recent systems have considerably reduced the size of the trigger and increased its effectiveness; this is an area where we can expect electronic technology to produce ever more useful and unobtrusive security.

In reference libraries where no books are issued for use outside the library the system is fairly simple: all books will activate the alarm if they are removed; similarly it can be used for 'reference only' books in other libraries. Some systems offer the advantage in these conditions that the detection posts can be as far as 3.6 m (12 ft) apart, thus avoiding a bottleneck with its unpleasant connotations. In lending libraries there are two kinds of system in common use. In the bypass method all the books are potentially alarmed: each book which is to pass the detector screen at the issue counter must be handled by a member of staff, who will pass it behind the field produced by posts across the issue counter exit. In newer versions the staff member who issues the book can place it on a moving belt built into the counter-top so that the book goes behind the screen and is collected by the reader (12.1). Even so the issue counter must be placed near the main exit. In the full-circulation system the book is desensitized at the issue counter so that it can pass the field and is resensitized when it is brought back to the return counter, after which it can take its place on the shelves. The great advantage of this is that there can be issue counters anywhere in the

library. With some computer issue systems the book is sensitized and desensitized as part of the issue process as it passes over activating machinery built into the counter top. All that is necessary at the exit is a detection screen to provide a field across the doors. There does not have to be a guardian in permanent attendance there, so long as a well-rehearsed routine is set in motion when the alarm sounds and the turnstile locks. If there is a guardian on duty there he can also handle the business of checking readers' bags.

In some methods the trigger is a diode transmitter which is no larger than other triggers but is activated only by a receiver sensitive to the same frequency. This eliminates the false alarms from metal objects in readers' pockets which were a feature of earlier magnetic systems, although false alarms can still happen when 'transmitters' operating on a similar frequency (such as switched-on calculators or even hearing aids) are carried; but this of course is a far less frequent event than mere pieces of metal. The possible effect on 'heart-pacers' has also to be considered.

The architect has only to see that electricity is supplied at the exact point required and that there is an adequate safety bypass to satisfy fire regulations. He may find it irksome to have to incorporate this alien element within his interior design, but manufacturers can supply products in different colours and coverings. Nevertheless at the moment there are undoubtedly drawbacks, including:

1. The high cost of the detection machinery and the need for special control furniture.
2. The narrowness of the field; 900 mm (3 ft) is the usual maximum.
3. The cost, especially in staff time, of inserting the triggers in many thousands of books.
4. The time consumed in operating the system (although not much in some methods).
5. The false alarms caused by objects in readers' possession, or by nearby electrical installations (more likely to occur in some systems than in others).
6. The possible need (in some systems) to reactivate the trigger, which may lose its effectiveness;
7. The challenge to the inventive student to find a way of beating the machine.

Against these disadvantages must be set these systems' undoubted success in reducing book losses. No manufacturer claims that his system is foolproof, but the moral effect is certainly good; it has been found that it is not necessary to protect all books, as the knowledge that the scheme is in operation acts as a deterrent to potential thieves.

Banning cases from book areas
Another solution is to require all cases to be deposited in a controlled section just inside the entrance hall but outside the entrance barrier. To be without a case can be a considerable inconvenience to a serious worker, but he can adapt himself to this rule.

Bags can be handed over to attendants on duty and a token receipt given, but before embarking on such a plan the librarian will do well to assess the total peak use, the very large amount of space required to house the bags, and the high cost in staff time of operating this system during the long opening hours of a modern library. The number of readers who return for re-access to their cases can be surprisingly high. An alternative is to provide lockers with removable keys and make their use compulsory; again it will be necessary to check that the large amount of space needed can be made available. For extra

12:1. By-pass system. The book is permanently sensitized so that it can pass the control bottleneck at the counter only when the staff member who issues it passes it behind the barrier

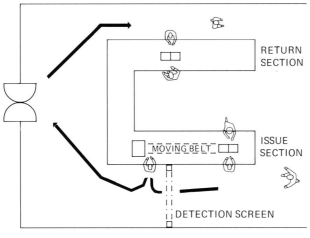

12:2. Full-circulation system. Here the book is desensitized at the issue counter so that it can pass the barrier, which can be some distance away at the exit door. When the book is returned after loan, it is resensitized before being returned to the shelves

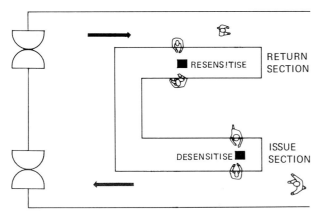

security, and to avoid having extra clothes, particularly wet coats, inside reading areas, it can be decreed that coats also are deposited. To avoid heavy staffing costs it may be possible to use a locking hanging system for clothes and cases, the reader taking the key while he is in the building and using it to release his coat or bag when he leaves, the key then remaining in the lock for the next user. A disadvantage is that an irresponsible person can remove keys: it may be necessary to issue keys from a manned service point although there is no guarantee that keys will be returned unless an elaborate signature book is used, with consequent pressure on busy staff.

Both bag and clothes lockers are common in university libraries on the European Continent, but they are seen less often in Britain, perhaps because the very large numbers in a small entrance space make lockers impracticable.

It will be necessary to display a notice disclaiming responsibility for loss of, or damage to, any items left in deposit areas. If deposit is compulsory this seems iniquitous, but there appears to be no alternative.

In some universities and colleges it is the practice to demand that all cases and bags be opened for inspection. This, though a sound solution, may cause congestion at busy periods and understandably irritates readers. A possible alternative is to check certain bags at random, say one in five, but this too can cause personal problems. The writer has a vivid recollection of many acrimonious interviews with readers who resented being chosen for such a search after other readers had passed unchallenged; it may be difficult to persuade a reader that he is not being victimized. The only reasonable solution is for the rule about random search to be very clearly advertised in the entrance hall and on membership cards.

The searching of cases is not foolproof, as books can be hidden in clothing (and in women's handbags), but it has the advantage, if a book is detected, of demolishing the excuse that the reader had not really intended to take it out of the library. It does not help in the case of the reader who conceals a book on his person: many ingenious methods have been devised, and here the detector system can prove its worth.

All such controls must be sited so that no alternative exit from the building is possible, and there should always be a turnstile or other positive check to restrain the reader until the bag inspection has taken place. When contemplating any such methods the librarian will be wise to take advice of his authority's legal expert and to see that all staff are aware of the legal position.

Windows, especially in quiet corners of the library, should be lockable; it is not unknown for a reader to open a window from the inside and hand out or drop books to an accomplice.

Mutilation of books

Many libraries have suffered from professional thieves (often operating as gangs) who cut prints from older books and sell them individually. Protection against this is possible only by adequate supervision. Even if attendants are employed specifically for this purpose it is very difficult for them to see everything, especially if one member of a gang is acting as decoy. To expect professional staff to carry out this supervision in addition to their other duties is hopeless. Nevertheless, alert staff and attendants can do a great deal. The use of convex mirrors is a good example where the psychological results of awareness are probably more effective than any actual detection they do. The architect may be able to help in specified areas by positioning a control desk so that it overlooks certain tables at which users of valuable books can be required to work. The use of strip-silvered (Venetian) glass in doors of staff areas has a deterrent value; in Manchester Central Library the grilles between closed-stack and reader areas have a similar effect, in that the reader can never be sure that he is not being watched. The use of closed-circuit television to keep readers under supervision can have great psychological value, even if it is not possible for surveillance to be continuous. A drawback of CCTV is that even with wide-angle lenses on the cameras, the field of vision is seldom sufficient for full protection, and more cameras will usually be needed than was at first envisaged. This will mean either a bank of screens, which all have to be kept under supervision, or a switching device (controlled or automatic) to a single screen: this is expensive and cannot provide continuous control. Where books particularly vulnerable to mutilation are issued for use outside the library, a system of checking before acceptance back can be used. The name of the borrower and a note on the physical condition of the book when it was issued is recorded on an enlarged version of the common book card and retained with the reader's ticket until the book is returned. The method is cumbersome but prevents the reader from claiming that the book was damaged when he borrowed it. The staff member inspecting it on its return will sign to indicate that it has been returned in good condition; as the reader's name has been recorded, the inspection can be done at off-peak time. The system is of course very time-consuming.

Designing for protection

There are many different aspects of security to be considered and they include the planning of a possible illegal entrance to the building, from fall-pipes, skylights and manholes, perimeter security as a whole, and the provision of adequate external lighting. Climb-proof paint may not seem a very important accessory, but it can be of great value where there could be access to a flat roof, especially one with some upstanding feature to provide concealment.

To protect rare and valuable items, specially planned security accommodation will have to be requested in the brief. The provision could be a strongroom that is 'fire, flood and thief resistant'; within it could be a burglar-proof safe. The degree of protection given will depend very much on the price the library is prepared to pay. When planning such an installation, the architect will bear in mind that it is not only the doors which have to be resistant to attack but also the walls and the ceiling. He will consider in particular the position of the strongroom in relation to external walls and roofs.

All matters concerning the protection of the building from possible break-in while the library is closed require the attention of a security consultant, from whom the librarian can learn about the protection devices available. Apart from solid doors and walls, and good locks on windows, much depends on whether the building is to be patrolled after closing time. If not, and if the value of the contents warrants it, a sensor which detects the presence of an intruder into a key area can be most effective in giving immediate alarm. The introduction of the silicon microprocessor to security systems has changed design thinking and improved capability to an unprecedented extent, and new systems should be investigated. Methods at present on the market include:

1. Microwave dopplers, which send microwaves at ultrasonic frequencies and detect any change in reflection from objects within the area.

2. Acoustic microphones with electronic monitoring, which detect unusual sounds while ignoring natural ones.
3. Volumetric devices, which measure the change in electrical capacitance when a person enters the room.
4. Infra-red sensors, which detect the heat given off by a person.

All these devices only sound alarms and will be ineffective without a well-planned procedure of reaction to the alarm. Police support often depends upon the reputation for reliability of the device: they suffer too much from false alarms. Much depends too on the value of the portable property. In exhibitions of particularly precious (and saleable) items, protection must be a highly professional service to meet highly professional dangers. Where particularly valuable items are kept in display cases it is more economical to have these cases individually wired to alarms. A cheaper alternative is to have windows with wiring incorporated in the panes, so that if the window is disturbed or the glass broken a circuit contact is completed and an alarm sounded. Security consultants recommend a combination of good break-proof fittings with an alarm system, but such systems are only as effective as their weakest point.

A recent need is to protect portable computer hardware. Specialist firms have produced equipment designed to create continuous links between items at single and multiple work-stations without interfering with the flexibility of use. Again the alarms thus activated are only useful if the staff know how to handle the crisis.

In addition to these, and for use in protecting the building while it is open, there is the option to have security measures openly displayed so that all but the most sophisticated criminals will be warned off. The psychology of the potential criminal has to be studied; in the same way it is vital to repair the effects of any vandalism immediately, so as not to give ideas to others.

Other dangers

As well as the losses caused by readers, by opportunist thieves and by professional burglars there are those attributable to vandals and to politically motivated extremists, even arsonists. In some areas the trend towards open libraries with inviting shop windows has had to be reversed and libraries built which are less easily damaged in riots or when a protest is made. From the design point of view this is bad news; if it is in the brief the architect can certainly give this sort of protection, so that the building looks like a fortress, but the decision is a political one and rests firmly on the shoulders of the authority which is responsible for the security of the environment. It would be foolish to suggest that this will not be needed in the future. Even in less dramatic situations there may be need to plan for emergencies, with individual communication devices for staff members who may be isolated or at risk. Panic buttons connected to manned positions or control panels and portable alarm devices may seem easy to provide, but their necessity should be indicated in the brief so that the architect can allow for them in his plans.

Locks and keys

This mundane matter is in fact of great importance. At a late stage in the planning the architect will want to know the priorities in preventing entry through doors, and who, and in what conditions, is to be allowed to hold keys. The technology of the locksmith is very advanced, and a high level of security can be obtained, at a price. The price is not only money but a carefully thought-out system of masters, sub-masters and ordinary keys so that security can be combined with speed of access for whose who need it. Among costs to be considered are those of replacing combinations in locks periodically when, as always happens, key losses and changes of staff have made the system vulnerable. Once again recent electronic advances are likely to alter the whole picture.

A good security consultant is worth his fee, if only for his ability to look at a proposed scheme and to point out how it can be circumvented. If such expert advice cannot be obtained, the librarian should at least read a book written by such a consultant.[7, 8, 9]

Safety

A hazard which is less dramatic than those which have already been considered is that which affects both readers and staff in their movements because of design faults. Architects will have this constantly in mind, and safety hazards caused by slippery floors, loose carpets and concealed steps should never occur. There is little even a vigilant librarian can do until the building is almost completed, when his knowledge of the daily routine gives him the chance to anticipate trouble. Doors are particularly dangerous; strains, exertion injuries and, above all, walking into glass commonly occur. Even the compulsory coloured lines across doors, which must be used to draw attention to the presence of glass, can be unnoticed and a horrifying accident happens. Just before the time of handing over the new building it is a good idea for staff to walk through and use all furniture and doors with possible hazards in mind; it is even better for a wheelchair user to try out the facilities to test them before it is too late.

13 Layouts and critical sizes: shelving

Once the architect has settled his ideas about the structure, the cores, the heating and ventilation machinery, ducting and the other essential physical features, he must turn to each of the operational areas and consider in more detail how he is to provide for the layout of furniture and equipment, even though much of it will be free-standing. The size of each operational space will have been decided by the brief and the budget, which means the amount of space which the authority feels that it can afford.

In a single area of the library, or in a library which is in effect a single room, the librarian may be quite capable of arranging the furniture; librarians have had experience of the exercise of cutting pieces of paper to the shape and scale size of items of furniture and equipment and arranging them on a plan to make a satisfactory layout. It will always be found that there are numerous ways of arranging the pieces and that some are more effective in their use of space than others.

A simple example concerns the placing of readers' tables and chairs. Reed[1] demonstrates that a number of single tables and chairs close to, and facing, walls or windows use less space than a similar number placed against, but with tables at right angles to, walls or windows, while if the tables and chairs are placed in open space they need even more room. This is because, as Reed suggests, there is an unusable 'halo' (he uses the figure of 450 mm (18 in)) around each working area, and the halo's shape will vary with its position within the room. It has never been suggested that the reader at a table will actually occupy the nominal 2.3 m² (25 ft²) allocated; a more normal figure is 1 m² (10 ft²), the rest being allowed to provide for a share of the aisles and necessary open spaces in the room, but not outside it. Similarly bookcases placed along walls occupy less space than those placed at right angles to walls, while the latter use much less space than island cases.

In the following sections critical sizes will be discussed for the various items of operational equipment, but in every case sizes and dimensions will vary according to the placing of the items relative to other items, to the walls and passages and to the peculiar requirements of the type of library. Types of shelving available, the materials from which they are made, and factors affecting the choice are dealt with in Chapter 17.

Book shelving

The material to be housed for both staff and readers consists largely of bound hard-backed books. Furniture has certainly to be planned to hold microforms, sheet maps and computer products, and sometimes for charter rolls, broadsides, rolled maps, prints and other inconveniently shaped material, but for the immediate future the bulk of holdings of libraries of all kinds will continue to be in book form. University and special libraries in particular may have large numbers of periodicals, but, except for recent issues, they will take the form of bound books, or boxes which can be shelved as books.

The architect will know from the brief the quantity of material to be accommodated; his object will be to house the books in a way acceptable to those who have to handle them, in an aesthetically suitable form and as economically as possible as regards both space and money. It is obvious that if he can house more in a given space he will save costs; in the case of large libraries with stocks running into hundreds of thousands, or even millions, this can be a most important factor. If seven shelves can be installed per tier instead of six, there will be a gain of one-sixth of the storage space; if aisle widths can be reduced, more ranges can be installed; but if the object is to make books available to humans, the cramming of more and more books into a given space is far from being the only consideration.

Sometimes the inconvenience caused by shelving books very closely together may be out of all proportion to the gains. A library which can afford space for a large entrance hall, a relaxing area and perhaps a car park cannot be well advised to pack books too closely together when the space gained is comparatively small. To take the economical planning of shelving so seriously as to allow it to dominate reader service, ceiling height (and so lighting), and possibly the number of floors which the building can hold should call for a very careful reappraisal of the relevant factors and their effect on the overall budget.

Book and shelf depths

There is little to be gained by the use of the traditional descriptions of book sizes – folio, quarto, octavo and so on – as they are both imprecise and difficult to determine. It has been well established that in most libraries, at least 90% of the books are less than 230 mm (9 in) deep – that is, from front to back, from spine to fore-edge. In popular libraries of all kinds this is certainly so, except for the high proportion of picture books in libraries for children; music and open-shelf bibliographies and reference books will of course be deeper. Discounting these, and those libraries which have special problems because they hold large stocks of bound newspapers, music or art books, most libraries can save space if they standardize shelving at 230 mm (9 in) deep; indeed most popular libraries can afford to standardize at 200 mm (8 in) deep. The small difference between these figures may not be important in the majority of libraries, but if double-sided cases can be limited to 400 mm (16 in) deep, more ranges may be fitted into the intensive shelving area of a large library, and this can be very valuable.

A compromise which can allow the slight cost saving of having shelves 200 mm (8 in) rather than 230 mm (9 in) deep, without loss of flexibility, is to have a backless double-sided case 460 mm (18 in) wide, but to fit 200 mm (8 in) shelves, leaving a nominal 60 mm (2 in) gap in the middle of the stack. Books up to 250 mm (10 in) deep can then usually be shelved by overlapping across the centre, because the book opposite will probably be narrower. This will reduce the number of books requiring oversize shelving, but in public areas such 'see-through' shelving is sometimes unpopular with readers.

It is necessary to consult proprietary shelving suppliers to see what is available ready-made. Shelving made to individual specifications is unnecessarily expensive, except for very large orders or in countries where there is no library furniture industry and all items have to be made locally.

It is also possible to house books deeper than 230 mm (9 in) in closed stacks by allowing them to protrude over the fronts of the cases, although this is untidy. Systems shelving units offer the opportunity to fit deeper shelves, particularly when held on brackets from wall strips; this gives some advantage in flexibility. One large manufacturer (Terrapin Reska) offers shelves 200 mm (7⅞ in), 250 mm (9¹³⁄₁₆ in), 300 mm (11¹³⁄₁₆ in) and 350 mm (13¹³⁄₁₆ in) deep, fitting any of them on to its uprights or wall strips. On the 200 mm (8 in) shelf of a double-sided case, a lip at the back of the shelf can be used when books are up to 200 mm (8 in) deep; if deeper books are to be accommodated on the same shelf, the lip can be removed so that the books can protrude over the inner edge into the gap between the shelves.

Books more than 230 mm (9 in) deep can be housed on special runs of shelving 300 mm (12 in) deep, but the great majority of such books will also be too tall for normal shelving, and so oversize shelving bays must be provided to hold them. It is usually better to have both deeper and taller shelves for this purpose, so as to accommodate the vast majority of books in only two sequences. But in stack conditions, where the extra inches can be vital to shelving economy, it may be preferable to follow Poole,[2] who says: 'As a rule of thumb it may be assumed that a normal [American college] installation will require 80 per cent 200 mm (8 in) shelves, 15 per cent 250 mm (10 in) shelves and 5 per cent 300 mm (12 in) shelves'. It is debatable, however, whether the space saving is worth the disadvantage of having three sequences instead of two; this is discussed under 'Closed stack' later. It should be remembered that to have normal books on deep shelving means that some will be pushed to the back: a great inconvenience.

Shelf length

In Britain and the United States the standard shelf length has for many years been 914 mm (3 ft). It has been held, without any scientific research to uphold the statement, that the reader's eye cannot encompass more than 3 ft in one glance. The late F. J. McCarthy produced the study shown in Figure 13:2 for the feasibility of scanning a

1219 mm (4 ft) shelf. Shelves longer than 914 mm (3 ft) are practicable now because U-section steel offers a greater rigidity than either wood or the older type of metal shelving. Longer shelves may save some space (if the intended use is planned when the module is chosen), but the gain is slight and the shelf usually has to be rather thicker than the 20 mm (¾ in) of the conventional wood shelving. What is important is that the shelf-length unit shall be consistent, or at least that there shall be as few different sizes as possible. Any librarian who has had to move books and shelves in a library where some shelves are not *quite* the same length will echo this from the heart.

It must be noted that if using recommendations in imperial sizes, the translation to metric measures must be exact (and vice versa). A 900 mm shelf is actually ⁹⁄₁₆ of an inch shorter than 3 feet; although in some cases the two may be interchangeable, it will depend on whether the manufacturer is quoting actual or nominal lengths. A misunderstanding here can have detrimental effects upon stack capacity. At the moment several manufacturers of systems offer 750 mm, 1 m and 1.5 m shelves; these can fit in with different modules but not with existing 3 ft bays, or indeed with any imperial sizes.

Shelf height

The question of the height of books is more important because it affects the distance between shelves and so decides the number of shelves which can be fitted to a tier. If equally convenient for the reader there is obviously a great gain in space if more shelves of books can be accommodated. In most libraries it is possible to house at least 90% of the books at 280 mm (11 in) centres (that is, from centre to centre of the shelves themselves). This, with 20 mm (say, ¾ in) for shelf thickness, means 260 mm (10 in) clear and, allowing 13 mm (½ in) for fingers to be inserted above the top of the book, will accommodate a 240 mm (9½ in) book comfortably and a 255 mm (10 in) one without too much trouble. Such an arrangement can have many advantages in housing the maximum number of books within convenient reach of the average reader. In closed stack (and almost equally in open stack serving a large student population), it is common for seven shelves to be

13:1. Lip and non-lip shelves

13:2. Scanning a 1219 mm (48 in) shelf

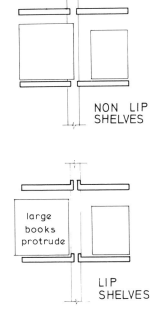

NON LIP SHELVES

large books protrude

LIP SHELVES

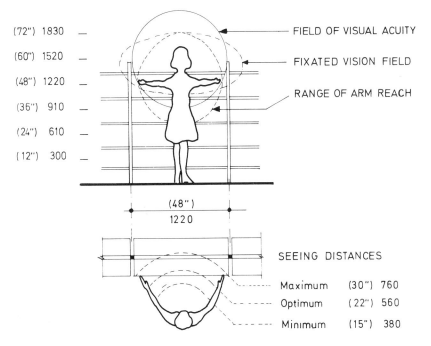

(72") 1830 —
(60") 1520 —
(48") 1220 —
(36") 910 —
(24") 610 —
(12") 300 —

FIELD OF VISUAL ACUITY
FIXATED VISION FIELD
RANGE OF ARM REACH

(48")
1220

SEEING DISTANCES

Maximum (30") 760
Optimum (22") 560
Minimum (15") 380

13:3. Dimensions of different percentiles of adult male and female wheelchair users. These dimensions relate to people who use standard wheelchairs and who have no major impairment of upper limbs (New Metric Handbook)

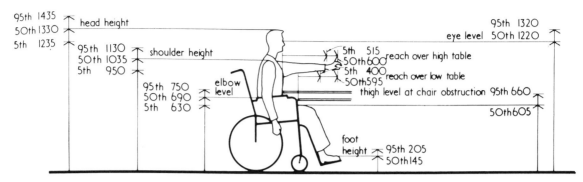

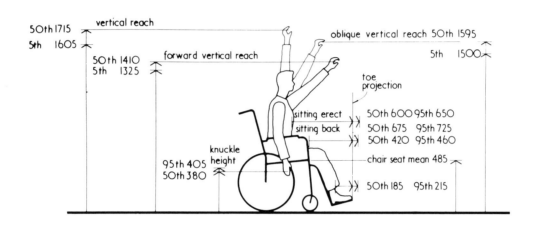

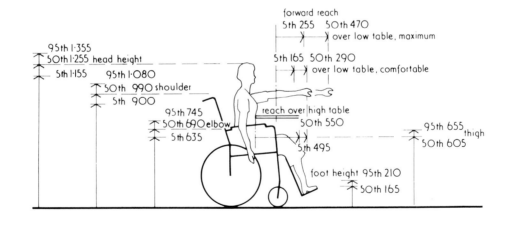

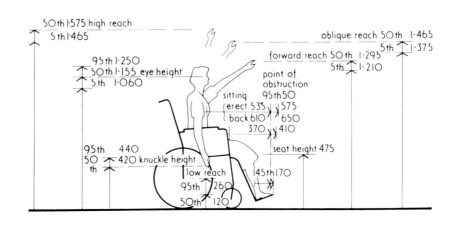

fitted. This is commonly done by having shelves at 300 mm (12 in) centres, which will hold a very high proportion of all books, and a base-plate (combined with bottom shelf) not more than 100 mm (4 in) from the floor. So under a theoretical 2.286 mm (7 ft 6 in) overall height of fascia, the top shelf will be around 1930 mm (6 ft 4 in) from the floor. This is not a comfortable height for a short person to reach; also a bottom shelf no more than 100 mm (4 in) from the floor means squatting or twisting the neck; but most British and United States universities use it, presumably without too many complaints. If 280 mm (11 in) centres had been used with a 150 mm (6 in) base-plate, the top shelf would be at 1830 mm (6 ft): an improvement in comfort at both top and bottom which will still hold more than 90% of books in most libraries.

A conventional expedient has been to allow one deeper shelf per tier (usually the bottom one), but this can never accommodate the really large books. In popular libraries it is best to set out firmly to have only two sequences: one at 280 mm (11 in) centres and a special oversize sequence which can be clearly labelled and referred to by location symbol on the catalogue entries. This does not apply to the quick reference collection; it is more economical of space to house it in a special tier at 330 mm (13 in) centres than in a run with much smaller books.

In public, hospital and welfare libraries, which can

expect to serve a number of readers in wheelchairs, it should be noted that most women can reach to 1375 mm (4 ft 6 in) and most men to 1500 mm (5 ft) from wheelchairs, so that with 300 mm (12 in) base, four shelves at 280 mm (11 in) centres, together with a fascia, most readers will be content. The same case can have three shelves at 350 mm (14 in) for oversize, and shelving of this kind will give a feeling of openness and allow an attractive vista across the room.

A decision on shelf distances is vital if fixed shelving is to be used, because it determines absolutely the size of the bookcases; but in practice it is also advisable with adjustable shelving. In open reading areas the top and bottom lines of shelving units can be important in the appearance of the room, and the height of these visual horizontal lines (and of course the distance between them) can severely limit the use of even infinitely variable shelf fittings. This should not be taken too far. I know a case where a most attractive run of low island cases was designed especially to allow a vista across the room: it would hold only two shelves of books, but an additional 75 mm (3 in) to the overall height would have allowed a third shelf to be fitted. In popular lending areas of public libraries there is today more emphasis on the comfort and ease of readers, especially the elderly and disabled, than on packing as many books as possible into a given area or

13:4. Optimum shelving conditions for adults (top), teenagers (centre) and children (bottom) (F. J. McCarthy)

Table 13.1 Shelving sizes

Bottom space	300 mm (12 in)									400 mm (15 in)								
Fascia	50 mm (2 in)			75 mm (3 in)			100 mm (4 in)			50 mm (2 in)			75 mm (3 in)			100 mm (4 in)		
Shelving space, i.e. no. of shelves at 280 mm (11 in)	4	5	6	4	5	6	4	5	6	4	5	6	4	5	6	4	5	6
Overall mm height: inches	1475 58	1750 69	2030 80	1500 59	1775 70	2050 81	1525 60	1800 71	2085 82	1550 61	1830 72	2110 83	1575 62	1850 73	2135 84	1600 63	1880 74	2160 85

even making it look neat. In such an area it is very convenient if the bottom shelf starts at 300 mm (12 in) from the floor and the top shelf at 1500 mm (5 ft) from the floor (or 1375 mm (4 ft 6 in) if it is to be acceptable to wheelchair users). With shelves at 300 mm (12 in) centres and a narrow fascia, such a case will give four shelves and can house the great majority of books. The same case with three shelves at 400 mm (16 in) will certainly hold all the oversize books such a library is likely to have.

It is common for architects inexperienced in library matters to give too much emphasis to the appearance of shelving, particularly the neatness and sense of order to be obtained when shelves can be in continuous parallel horizontal lines on a long wall; the resultant inflexibility can be a high price to pay. Nevertheless the overall height of shelving in an open-access library must be an important factor in the design. Wall shelving should never be higher than 2 m (6 ft 6 in) to the very top; this will give a 300 mm (12 in) base, six shelves and a fascia. An overall height of 1.8 m (6 ft) is usually better and gives five shelves. The height of an island case depends on its position: where a vista is called for, 1375 mm (4 ft 6 in) is a good height and 1500 mm (5 ft) is the maximum, but for cases at right angles to wall shelving the wall shelving height may have to be followed for appearance' sake.

Where at all possible, all shelves for use by the general public should be 300 mm (12 in) from the floor. For island cases, a 400 mm (15 in) space at the bottom gives a surprising improvement in appearance, because light shines from under the case, particularly when reflective flooring is used. The depth of the fascia must be considered before a decision is made; if a generous space is needed for tier guiding, then room for shelving is likely to be reduced. In closed and open stack, tier guides are less important than in open access, and more economical use can be made of every inch of the space. (For types of guiding, see p. 187.)

Rather than make an arbitrary decision as to overall height it is better to make simple calculations from a list of alternatives such as Table 13:1. In stack conditions the bottom shelf can be much closer to the floor, and consequently more shelves per case are common.

When adjustable shelving (including wall-mounted bracket shelving) is to be used, this may seem over-elaborate but it can be a useful exercise to produce a figure which can then be tested for other combinations of shelf spacing. The final choice will affect the appearance and efficiency of the library for many years. The sizes discussed in the table are for adult libraries, but as books for older children are similar in size, the important factor for children's libraries is convenient access heights, which obviously differ according to the age ranges of the children concerned. Figure 13:4 shows the best shelving heights for adults, teenagers and children.

The Danish State Library Inspectorate[3] decrees a height of 1600 mm (5 ft 4 in) in junior schools, but this seems high. In junior schools and parts of children's libraries the bottom shelf can be as little as 75 mm (3 in) from the floor, because small children like to sit on low stools or on carpeted floors. Common sense and familiarity with children's needs will dictate the answer. A practice to be deprecated is that of buying standard shelving units for a whole library and then leaving the top shelf empty, or blanked off as a display shelf, in the children's library. If a library is worth providing, it is worth planning according to the needs of its users. Recommendations on shelving for children's libraries are given in *Library Resource Provision in Schools*,[4] issued by the Library Association.

In special libraries, particularly those serving commercial and industrial firms, the layout of shelving and its association with reading needs will indeed be 'special' and individual. The total book capacity will be small (compared with university and central libraries), and the accent will be on speed of access to the material. There will seldom be any call for very long runs of books or need for large open seating areas, and it is common for individual study tables to be placed close to, and often within, the shelving runs. Because there will be comparatively little browsing or casual use, books can be housed seven shelves high, and runs of bound periodicals and reports, being in very great demand, are likely to be positioned close to the focal point. Current issues of periodicals and reports will usually have absolute priority; periodical shelves adaptable within proprietary shelving runs have much to commend them here.

The layout of such libraries will be complicated by the need to house banks of vertical files, terminals and photocopying equipment in tight operational areas convenient for instant use. The concentration upon speed and efficiency of operation in a library designed specifically to meet a known and limited need will dictate layout of shelving; because the needs of each special library *are* special, it is impossible to generalize, but a sound survey of the problem has been produced by Anthony.[5]

Shelf loading

Poole[6] says: 'All standard book shelves in the United States are presently designed to withstand loads of 40 lb/sq ft (2 kN/m^2) with no permanent deflection and with no temporary deflection in excess of ¾ in (20 mm).' In Britain this depends on the specifications of individual manufacturers, as no standards exist (performance tests for various types of shelving would be an asset to the profession). Poole also noted that 12 in (300 mm) gramophone records produce a load factor of 49.5 lb/sq ft (2.39 kN/m^2) on a 12 in (300 mm) shelf. However, the present writer's experience has shown that there are runs of books (directories and bound volumes of periodicals, for example) which weigh much more than 50 lb/sq ft (2.4 kN/m^2). If an average book weighs between 1 and 2 lb (0.5 kg and 1 kg), then a 3 ft (900 mm) shelf of such books, three-quarters full, weighs between 25 and 50 lb (11 kg and 22 kg).

Some guides discuss the weight of a square foot (or metre) of books, but this is seldom of any value, not only because 'average' books vary greatly between different types of library but also because on the shelves a 1 ft (300 mm) run of average books will take up a very irregular space; to render this as if it were a square or cube serves no useful purpose. The relative bearing qualities of wood and metal shelving are considered in Chapter 17.

Books per shelf

This subject has generated a surprising amount of heat among the experts, mainly because they seek a general solution to a problem with so many variables. Shelves may be completely filled in closed-access conditions with a completely finite stock, or in other than subject sequences (for example where large runs of little-used serials are housed), but in few other cases. Even in a normal closed stack, space must be left for additions within a classified subject sequence. To study possible situations whereby more books or less books might be accommodated by leaving more or less space empty per shelf is only of use when making space estimates for the housing of enormous collections.

In practice books will be placed on the shelves as long as shelf space conveniently remains. In open stack, where books are continually being removed from the shelves, and even more in open access, where there must be room for a great deal of casual handling, from a fifth to a quarter of the shelf should be left empty, if only to make life tolerable for staff who have to insert returned books. This space allowance has to apply right up to the end of the life expectancy of the building; the notion that a space is left on a shelf for expansion, and that when all these spaces are filled the library is ready for replacement, is based on some of the woolliest thinking in the profession.

Table 13:2 gives a generally accepted estimate for shelves *three-quarters full*; because books vary so much in thickness, all 'averages per foot' must be vague. Other inconvenient details are ignored: there can be a difference between nominal and actual shelf sizes; 3 feet does not

really equal 900 mm, and so on. For general estimating purposes, however, this table is accurate enough.

Fixed and adjustable shelving

It seems reasonable to suppose that to obtain the best use of space within each tier, adjustable shelves should be used – adjustable either infinitely, by Vernier-type fittings, or, more usually, by 25 mm (1 in) divisions. Such methods are normally used, but mainly from habit more than clear thinking. The size range to be housed is not large: shelves at 28 mm (11 in) fixed centres will accommodate well over 90% of the books, and the remainder will need special oversize shelving. Shelves can be fixed at intervals of slightly more than 230 mm (9 in) to hold the bulk of the stock, but 280 mm (11 in) centres are more convenient and hold a higher percentage.

Fixed shelving has the advantage of giving a neater and more regular appearance, and in many cases it is cheaper. If a lending library uses shelving at 280 mm (11 in) shelf centres (height), with reference shelves on 300 mm (12 in) and encyclopedias etc. at 330 mm (13 in) (or both the latter on 350 mm (14 in)), it is surprising how little adjustability will be missed.

Adjustable shelving will definitely be needed in the following circumstances:

1. Where the need for a single sequence of books to contain a large proportion of the library's stock is greater than the need to make the best possible use of space: for example, in a closed-access special library where books are added to stock in the order of receipt.
2. Where the stock contains separate long runs of large and small volumes (e.g. bound periodicals and annuals) without any certainty that their location can remain fixed.
3. For housing bound volumes of newspapers: these should be laid flat and, because of the variation of thickness in volumes over the years, much space will be wasted unless shelves are adjustable. (Paradoxically such newspaper storage cases are seldom offered with adjustable shelves.)

Adjustable shelving allows greater flexibility, and in particular the opportunity to fit an extra shelf into each bay of popular books (especially fiction) without having to commit that bay to holding fiction for ever. On the other hand many experienced librarians would be surprised if they discovered just how seldom the vaunted flexibility was in fact used in their libraries, and what it had cost. The position is altered when 'systems' shelving is used. Because these products are assembled from standard components they offer the economic advantages of mass production, and they can give flexibility at no extra cost. (See Chapter 17.)

Tilted shelves

Lower bookshelves can be tilted slightly upward so that the sloping book spines are easier to read and better lit. This is largely a matter of taste; there are proprietary bookcases of this kind on the market, but, because they take up considerably more floor space, they are seldom used except in casual open-access conditions. The County Libraries Section of the Library Association[7] states that 'a rake of 150 mm (6 ins) in the overall depth of the shelves (i.e. the bottom shelf is set forward 150 mm (6 ins), so that the whole bookcase slopes and all the shelves are slightly tilted) can be recommended as satisfactory and aesthetically pleasing; this does not cause books to slide back on

Table 13.2 Number of books per shelf		
Type of book	*Number per 300 mm (1 ft) run of shelf*	*Number per 900 mm (3 ft) run of shelf*
Children's books	10 to 12	30 to 36
Loan and fiction stocks in public libraries	8	24 to 25
Literature, history, politics and economics	7	21
Science, technology	6	18
Medicine, public documents and bound periodicals	5	15
Law	4	12
Averages	7	21

painted shelves, but polished hardwood should be finished with a matt or eggshell finish.' An extreme example of this in Grimsby Central Library has the lower shelves quite heavily tilted, the shelf depths varying from 200 mm (8 in) on the top shelf to 690 mm (27 in) on the bottom one. Some may consider the effect grotesque, and the upper shelves are certainly further away from the reader; the arrangement takes up space; of course, but it is only fair to say that Grimsby reports favourable reader reaction to the experiment. A compromise is to have only the bottom shelf tilted, and this can be done, even in stack, at a smaller loss of space. Unless the lighting is particularly bad it is difficult to follow the reasoning of those who would do this in a formal stack at the price of placing stacks further apart.

Layout of shelving

Except in popular open-access rooms where the book shelving plays an important visual part in the internal environment, the aim is to house as many books as possible in conditions convenient to both staff and readers. It is very necessary, therefore, to take account of the human engineering elements; arbitrary recommendations are no substitute for a study of the measurements relating directly to those of the human body. The drawings in Figure 13:5 show better than any table the distances, heights and depths which are convenient for readers.

These are the best conditions for reader use, but the librarian may decide that some slight inconvenience would be acceptable to readers in the interest of housing books more economically. The decision will depend on the expected clientele (stacks mainly for undergraduate use can start lower and end higher) and upon the type of shelving; for this reason the housing requirements considered in detail later are dealt with under the separate headings of closed stack, open stack and open access.

It was suggested earlier that the architect should choose a structural grid which can relate to the module most vital to his client's interest, and that this is the unit of shelving (see p. 69). Where large numbers of books have to be accommodated in stack conditions the positioning of the columns is perhaps the most important factor of all, and this will have a very close relation to the structural grid. If a grid of 11 m (36 ft) can be chosen (an expensive and much-to-be-desired luxury), the columns will be so far apart that stack shelving distances will no longer be critical; but where such a large grid would be an impossibly expensive structure, then, if a standard 900 mm (3 ft) shelf is to be used and the stack centre-to-centre distance is to be 1375 mm (4 ft 6 in), the most suitable grid size is 7 m (22 ft 6 in) square.

In the brochure of the new Causewayside Building of the National Library of Scotland[8] (Figure 13.6) it is stated that:

'Following the analysis of the typical requirements for the storage of books, bound newspapers and maps, and the access needs of staff and readers to this material, a planning module of 900 mm (3 ft) has been adopted and a structural bay size of 7.2 m × 8.1 m. This in turn relates directly to the lengths and widths of mobile stackage and mobile map cases and to the economic bay size for the structure taking into account the configuration of the site.'

Because of the greater strength of tubular steel shelving, shelves of 1375 mm (4 ft 6 in) can now be used, and these can be fitted into the same grid with a slight loss of efficiency; a larger grid, preferably 8.25 m (27 ft) square, would be an advantage. The architect and the structural engineer will have other factors to take into account, but in general the grid chosen should be a multiple of both 900 mm (3 ft) and 1375 mm (4 ft 6 in) (or of other shelf lengths which are to be used). Many of these points are well illustrated in the plans of Düsseldorf University Library on p. 72. A grid of 8.4 m (27 ft 7 in), with a module of 1.2 m (4 ft), accepted closed stack at 1.2 m (4 ft) centres, giving six stacks per grid square, while open stack at 1.4 m (4 ft 7 in) gave five stacks per grid square. Although the librarian would have preferred 1.44 m (4 ft 9 in) he was limited by official standards and thus by the grid chosen. The plans also illustrate clearly the loss of shelving space caused by having some columns 1000 mm (40 in) in one direction as against the 600 × 600 mm (2 × 2 ft) in other parts. They also show how much more disruptive to shelving it would have been if the stacks had run across the larger sides of the columns; even so flexibility is affected.

The discussion which follows is based on the holding capacity of a 'grid square'. It should not be forgotten that the between-column spaces often form a rectangle (see the Causewayside example above). The decision depends on the planned structure. The figures given here can nevertheless be used as a basis for similar computations in a simple diagram of rectangles.

The Danish State Library Inspectorate[9] recommends a 'layout module' of 3 m, using shelves 1 m long. This can be used with grids of 6 m, 9 m or 12 m; the idea is applied with ingenuity, and the simple diagrams show spacings of shelving, furniture and equipment based on the 3 m square. Within this square the Inspectorate distinguishes between three shelving conditions:

1. General open access: stack centres at 3 m, aisle width 2.56 m.
2. 'Near-stack' (open stack): stack centres at 2 m, aisle width 1.56 m.
3. 'Near stack' (closed access): stack centres 1.56 m, aisle width 1.06 m.

These figures are designed for small single-storey public libraries, where there will seldom be columns to complicate the issue. Columns waste vital shelving space, and the librarian will wish to see them as small in plan as possible; steel columns 200 mm (8 in) square have a great appeal except in public areas, where they are usually both ugly and a safety hazard – people walk into them – but the architect will have to take into consideration structural strength and many other factors (such as fire regulations requiring steel to be enclosed in concrete). In a 7 m (22 ft 6 in) grid square, columns should preferably be no wider than 450 mm (18 in), so that two columns cause the loss of no more than a single 900 mm (3 ft) tier in stack shelving. If the columns have to be as large as 760 mm (2 ft 6 in) square, then 7.3 m (24 ft) square is probably a better grid size.

Closed stack

This forms a major part of the book housing of national, large city and county libraries, and may be required in a lesser degree in libraries of all kinds. The shelving will be arranged to make the maximum use of space, and this will usually mean double-sided stacks, with single-sided stacks along walls. Because the distance, however small, by which stack width can be reduced will add to stack capacity (in theory, at any rate), between-stack distances will be as narrow as possible, the deciding factor probably being access by book trolley. The minimum between-stack distance is probably 600 mm (24 in), but this makes access difficult even for staff and, particularly where oversize

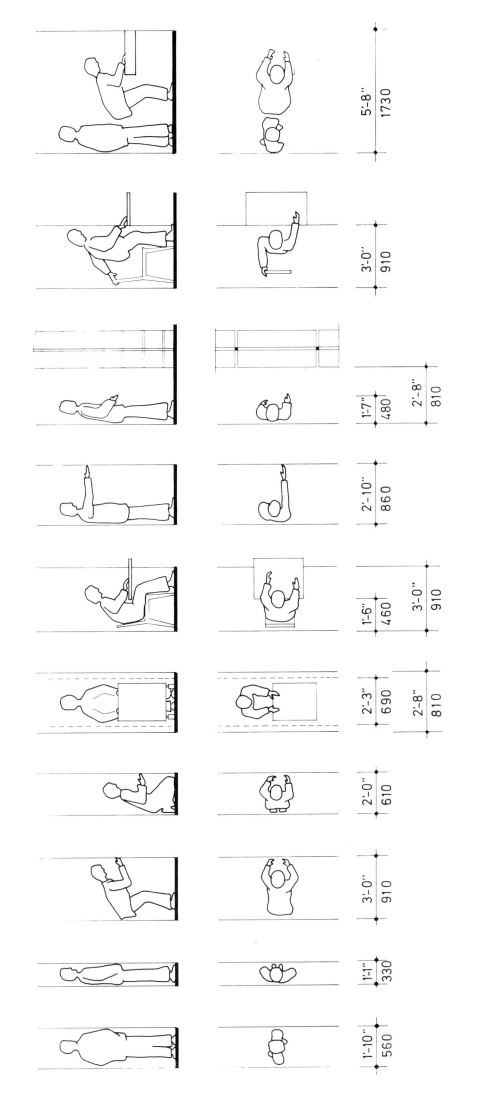

13:5. Minimum clearances for various attitudes in shelving areas

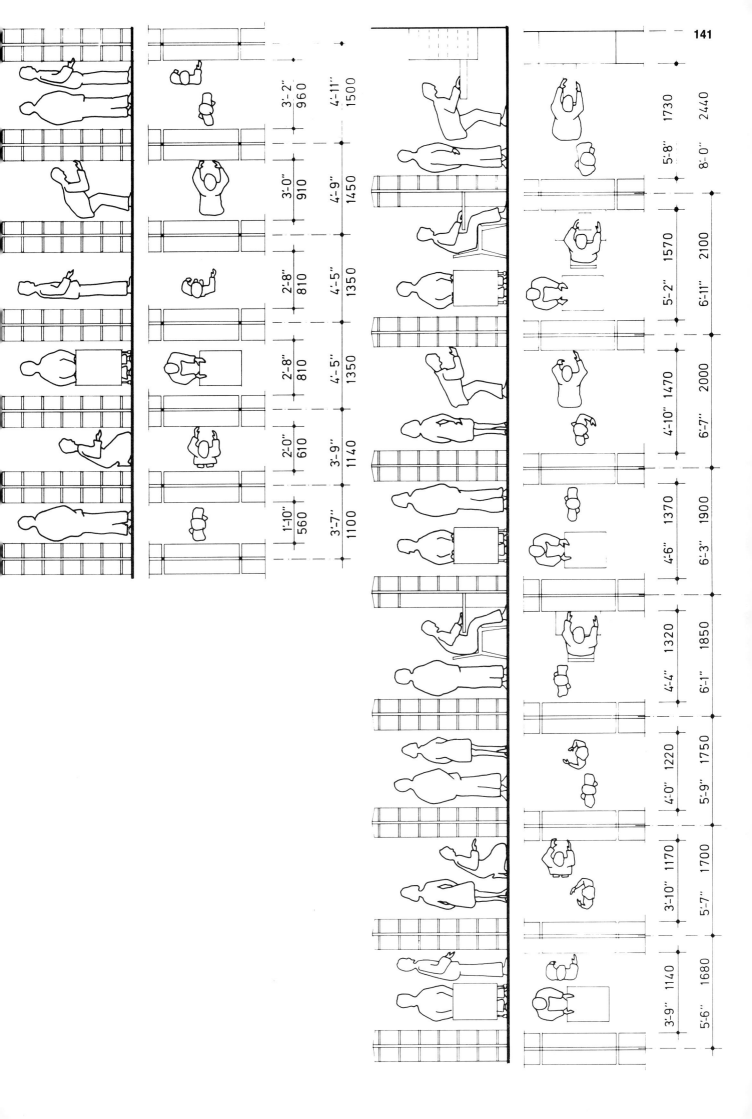

3'-2"	960	4'-11"	1500
3'-0"	910	4'-9"	1450
2'-8"	810	4'-5"	1350
2'-8"	810	4'-5"	1350
2'-0"	610	3'-9"	1140
1'-10"	560	3'-7"	1100

5'-8"	1730	8'-0"	2440
5'-2"	1570	6'-11"	2100
4'-10"	1470	6'-7"	2000
4'-6"	1370	6'-3"	1900
4'-4"	1320	6'-1"	1850
4'-0"	1220	5'-9"	1750
3'-10"	1170	5'-7"	1700
3'-9"	1140	5'-6"	1680

Table 13.3 Closed stack: alternative layouts and capacities

Grid size	Stack centres	No of double-sided stacks	Books per grid square		Books per ft²	
			One aisle per square	One aisle every other square	One aisle per square	One aisle every other square
Imperial sizes (ft in)	*(ft in)*					
18	3 7†	4	6174	6804	19	21
20	4	4	7014	7644	17½	19
24	4	5	10458	11214	18	19½
25	3 7†	6	12810	13692	20½	22
25	4 2	5	10962	11718	17½	19
25 6	3 8†	6	13104	13986	20	21½
27	3 10	6	13986	14868	19	20½

					Books per m²	
Metric sizes (m)	*(m)*					
6.5	1.1	4	6160	6860	204	226
6	1.2	4	6860	7560	191	210
7.2	1.2	5	10276	11116	198	214
7.5	1.25	5	10780	11620	192	207
7.7	1.1	6	12992	13972	219	237
8.4	1.2	6	14364	15344	204	217

†Almost: more acceptable with stacks only 405 mm (16 in) deep

books are shelved on lower portions of the stack, 685 mm (27 in) is the minimum practical figure.

The use of wider-based stacks as an aid to stability has been proposed, the narrowing of aisles at the bottom being acceptable because the shoulder is the user's critical width. This would certainly make trolley use difficult.

Shelves can be fitted close to the floor, leaving only a very small space to keep the books clear of dust; the bottom space should be filled in to facilitate cleaning. In basements it may be a useful precaution to have a higher bottom space as an emergency aid in case of flooding. The shelves may run close to the ceiling, but shelving to an overall height of more than 2.3 m (7 ft 6 in) will mean that the highest book-holding shelf is at least 1.9 m (6 ft 3 in) from the floor, and so some members of the staff will need step-stools in order to reach these books. In theory this is no great inconvenience; in practice such stools get misplaced around the stack, block trolley routes and waste time. Tiers of eight shelves are therefore seldom convenient; moreover, deliberately to install a higher ceiling solely in order to allow increased shelving height can be uneconomic if it adds to structural, heating and ventilating costs. Stack lighting, a crucial matter when shelving is to run close to the ceiling, is considered separately in Chapter 11.

Because staff only are to have access to the shelving, provision of cross-aisles is less important than it is for readers. Each cross-aisle will of course reduce the amount of shelving available, but too few aisles will waste staff time in walking around long unbroken stacks. At various times large libraries have installed horizontal conveyors within closed stacks, but it is doubtful if the savings of time and energy are worth the inevitable limiting of access to the shelves. If the conveyor can transport books beneath the floor in stack and up to the access point on other floors, as does the Telelift (see p. 54) in Düsseldorf University Library, it will not interfere with access to stack shelving, although books have still to be carried to each of the three supply points in the basement stack which deliver books to a single service point on each reading-room floor. Other systems have used horizontal conveyors on top of the stacks; if there is ceiling space to spare (and if the horizontal distances are long enough) this is possible, although the only examples in my experience have fallen into disuse. Usually walking aisles are more common; a compromise is to have one cross-aisle for every other grid square; with a 5.5 m (18 ft grid) this will reduce the potential stacking by one-twelfth. With an 8.25 m (27 ft) square the reduction will be only one-eighteenth, but there will be a 16.5 m (54 ft) run of unbroken stack to be negotiated.

Within each size of grid there is a limited number of possible combinations of shelving. Knowing the between-stack widths and the shelving requirements, the suitable one can be chosen. The plans in Figure 13:7 are based on the recommended grid size of 6.9 m (22 ft 6 in); the following points have been assumed:

1. Shelving 7 shelves high at 18 books per 900 mm (6 books per foot because the books will usually be of a more 'serious' nature, also to allow for insertions).
2. Columns not more than 500 mm (18 in) square.
3. Stacks (double-sided) 500 mm (18 in) deep.

Before making use of these figures the following important qualifications must be accepted.

The figures refer to the great bulk of book stocks which can be housed on stacks seven shelves high, and this usually means with shelves at not more than 300 mm (12 in) centres at the most.

Special spatial calculations have to be made for books too large or too deep to be shelved in this way.

If narrower stack centres are used, some main aisles must be provided at 1375 mm (4 ft 6 in) minimum for trolley access.

On the other hand it may be possible to fit more than the twenty books per linear metre (six books per linear foot) which has been allowed for here; in little-used stacks, or where additions to stock are rare or do not have to be inserted in a systematic sequence, the allowance could be twenty-three or twenty-four books per linear metre (eight books per linear foot), giving an increase of one-third

13:6. Cause-wayside Building, National Library of Scotland, Edinburgh. The 900 mm planning module of the interior is picked up in the fenestration and roof detailing, lying like a net over the building (Architect Andrew Merrylees Associates)

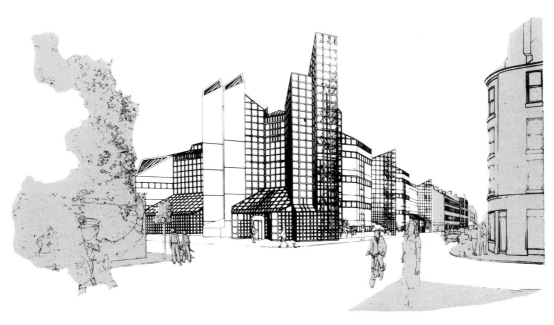

above these capacities. Stack stability is less critical here, because it is usually possible to have stack-to-stack bracing (and, better, of course, stack-to-wall bracing) from the tops of the stacks. Such an idea for a public area would be rejected as unsightly.

The questions of shelving oversized books in both closed and open stack need careful thought. If three sequences are tolerable, it is possible to allow for certain tiers to have four shelves rather than seven, and for other tiers to be devoted to very large books. Even so it will be impossible to house all large books in this way: in Guildhall Library there is one book nearly 2 m (6 ft) tall. Any book more than 500 mm (20 in) high should be housed flat; cases for such books will need more space, and it is better to place them against walls, where the slightly increased depth will hardly be noticeable.

Shelf depth allowances for large books complicate the planning of large and regular stack areas. Poole,[10] referring to shelf depths, says '. . . 80 per cent 8 in (200 mm) shelves, 15 per cent 10 in (250 mm) shelves and 5 per cent 12 in (300 mm) shelves'. The 10 in (255 mm) books might be accommodated in backless 18 in (450 mm) double-sided stacks by overlapping onto the other side, where books will, by the law of averages, be narower, leaving only 5% to be housed on 12 in (300 mm) depth shelving. It would save space to have the latter on the single-sided stacks, which will almost certainly be installed against walls somewhere in the store where an additional small increase in depth from the wall will have little effect on space planning.

On the alternative spacings used in both open and closed stack examples, certain figures of books per m^2 or ft^2 have emerged, but because these stacks do not hold oversize books, to this extent the figures must necessarily be false for overall application. For this reason these examples cannot be quickly used to deduce the total stack floor area required from a given total book stock. Perhaps the best method for doing that is the one almost sixty years old now, proposed by Henderson[11] and known as the 'cubook' formula.

This has been more often quoted than understood: 'In estimating capacity then, the unit is a *hypothetical* book. It is important to bear constantly in mind the abstract nature of the unit, and not to confuse it with the actual book. . . . A cubook is the volume of space required to shelve the average book in a typical library.' Henderson took a 'typical' reference library as one with 85% of books under 290 mm (11½ in) high, 13 per cent between 290 mm (11½ in) and 480 mm (19 in) high, and 2 per cent over 480 mm (19 in) high (shelved flat); he allowed 10% of each shelf empty for ease of book-handling and produced a formula: '100 cubooks will occupy a standard 900 mm (3 ft) section or will run 33⅓ per foot of single-faced tier.' To obtain the number of 900 mm (3 ft) tiers theoretically required to house the stock, therefore, it was necessary only to divide the total stock number by 100. By applying this formula to a stack shelving area with a 2300 mm (7 ft 6 in) ceiling and taking into account reasonable aisle widths 1325 mm (52 in), cross-aisles and an allowance for a section of the service core, Henderson stated[12] that cubooks could be reduced to cubic feet by multiplying by 0.676 and to square feet by multiplying by 0.090. It is not convenient to translate his calculations into metric units, but the result can be obtained by multiplying the 'books per square foot', result by 10.76 to obtain the figure of 'books per square metre'.

These figures applied only in a 'typical reference library', but other formulae were provided for establishments which had higher or lower proportions of large books. The thesis is worth considering even now.

'For a rough estimate of the space in a normal stack to house a "typical reference library" stock:
ascertain the number of "standard" volumes to be housed [in a typical library no action, in an "untypical" one by using one of the formulae];
reduce to cubooks;
for stack volume in cubic feet, multiply by 0.676;
for deck [i.e. stack floor] area in square feet multiply by 0.09.'

Put at its crudest, this states that a reasonable closed stack in a typical reference library can house 119.4 books/m^2 or 51.9 books/m^3 (11.1 books/ft^2 or 1.5 books/ft^3). Although this refers to 'cubooks', it also applies to the actual books in a closely filled stack. This is lower than the figures from the diagrams here because it allows for oversize books and also service cores.

13:7. Closed stack: imperial sizes and metric sizes

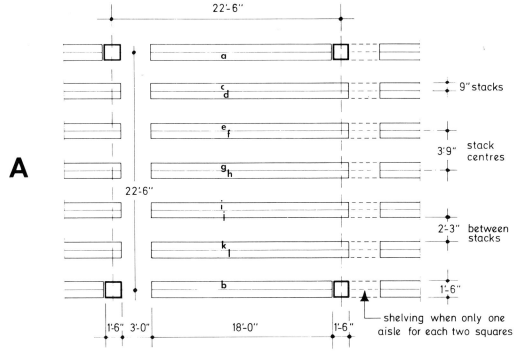

A

22'-6"

9" stacks

3'9" stack centres

2'-3" between stacks

1'-6"

22'-6"

1'-6" 3'-0" 18'-0" 1'-6"

↳ shelving when only one aisle for each two squares

A Example based on a grid of 6.9 m (22 ft 6 in)
One 3 ft cross-aisle per grid square
2 single-sided stacks (a and b) each
18 ft long = 36 ft
10 single-sided stacks (c to l) each
19 ft 6 in long = 195 ft
} = 231 ft

231 ft 7 shelves high = 1617 linear ft
1617 linear ft at 6 books per ft = 9702 books
= 19.16 books/ft².

One 3 ft cross-aisle every other grid square
Extra shelving = 12 × 3 ft = 36 ft

36 ft 7 shelves high = 252 linear ft
252 linear ft at 6 books per ft = 1512 books every other
square
= 756 books per square
9702 + 756 = 10 458 books
= 20.65 books/ft².

B Example based on a grid of 6.9 m (22 ft 6 in)
One 3 ft cross-aisle per grid square
2 single-sided stacks (a and b) each
18 ft long = 36 ft
8 single-sided stacks (c to j) each
19 ft 6 in long = 156 ft
} = 192 ft

192 ft 7 shelves high = 1344 linear ft
1344 linear ft at 6 books per ft = 8064 books
= 15.9 books/ft².

One 3 ft cross-aisle every other grid square
Extra shelving = 10 × 3 ft = 30 ft

30 ft 7 shelves high = 210 linear ft
210 linear ft at 6 books per ft = 1260 books every other
square
= 630 books per square
8064 + 630 = 8694 books
= 17.4 books/ft².

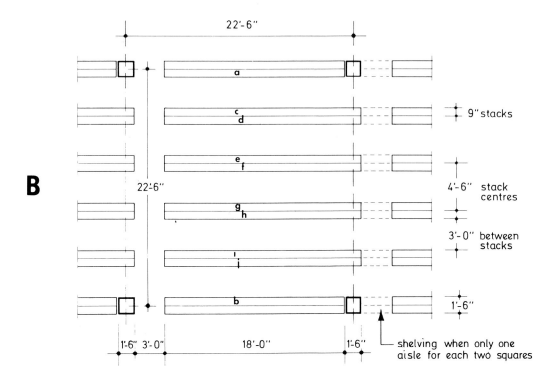

B

22'-6"

9" stacks

4'-6" stack centres

3'-0" between stacks

1'-6"

22'-6"

1'-6" 3'-0" 18'-0" 1'-6"

↳ shelving when only one aisle for each two squares

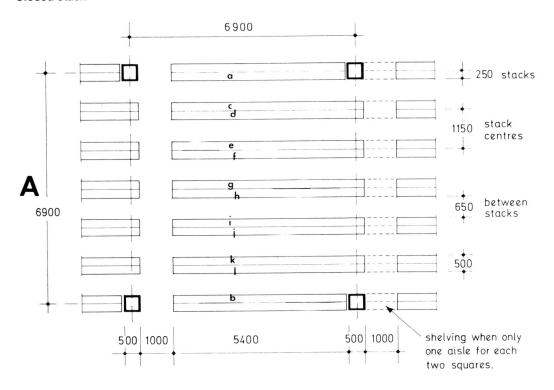

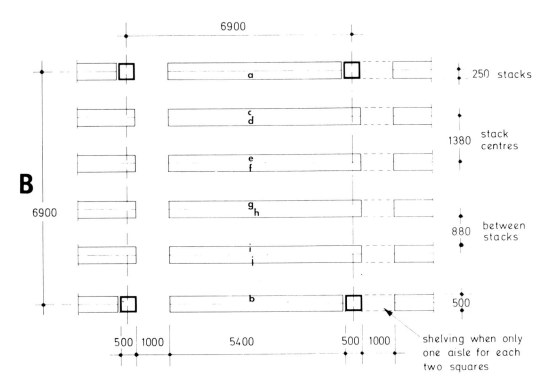

A Metric sizes based on a grid of 6.9 m (22 ft 6 in)
One 1 m cross-aisle per grid square
  2 single-sided stacks (a and b)
    each 5.4 m long   = 10.8 m }
10 single-sided stacks (c to l)   = 69.8 m
    each 5.9 m long   = 59 m }
69.8 m 7 shelves high = 488.6 linear m
488.6 linear m at 20 books per m = 9772 books
                            = 205 books/m^2.

One 1 m cross-aisle every other grid square
Extra shelving = 12 × 1 m = 12 m

12 m 7 shelves high = 84 linear m
84 linear m at 20 books per m = 1680 books every other
                               square
                           = 840 books per square
            9772 + 840 = 10 612 books
                           = 223 books/m^2.

B Metric sizes based on a grid of 6.9 m (22 ft 6 in)
One 1 m cross-aisle per grid square
  2 single-sided stacks (a and b)
    each 5.4 m long   = 10.8 m }
8 single-sided stacks (c to j)   = 58 m
    each 5.9m long   = 47.2 m }
58 m 7 shelves high = 406 linear m
406 linear m at 20 books per m = 8120 books
                               = 170.5 books/m^2.

One 1 m cross-aisle every other grid square
Extra shelving = 10 × 1 m = 10 m

10 m 7 shelves high = 70 linear m
70 linear m at 20 books per m = 1400 books every other
                               square
                           = 700 books per square
           8120 + 700 = 8820 books
                           = 185 books/m^2.

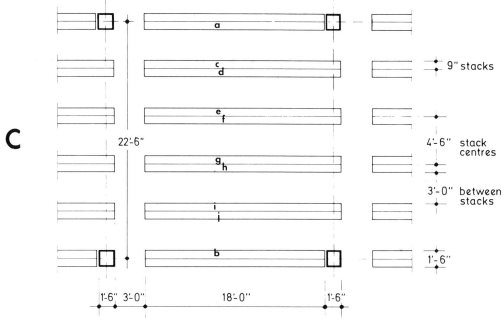

13:8. Open stack: imperial sizes and metric sizes

C Example based on a grid of 6.9 m (22 ft 6 in)

2 stacks (a and b) × 18 ft each = 36 ft ⎫
8 stacks (c to j) × 19 ft 6 in each = 156 ft ⎬ = 192 ft

192 ft 7 shelves high = 1344 linear feet
1344 linear feet at 6 books per ft = 8064 books
= 15.9 books/ft².

D Example based on a grid of 6.9 m (22 ft 6 in)

2 stacks (a and b) each 18 ft long = 36 ft ⎫
6 stacks (c to h) each 19 ft 6 in long = 117 ft ⎬ = 153 ft

153 ft 7 shelves high = 1071 linear feet
1071 linear feet at 6 books per ft = 6426 books
= 12.7 books/ft².

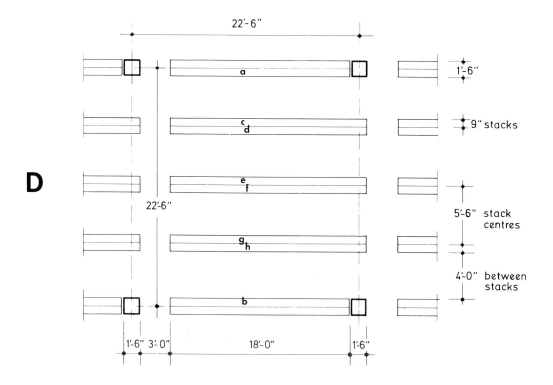

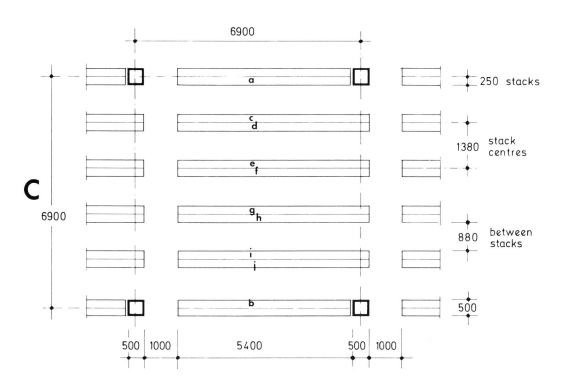

C Example based on a grid of 6.9 m (22 ft 6 in)

2 stacks (a and b) each 5.4 m long = 10.8 m ⎱
8 stacks (c to j)   each 5.9 m long = 47.2 m ⎰ = 58 m

58 m 7 shelves high = 406 linear m
406 linear m at 20 books per m = 8120 books
                              = 170.5 books/m².

D Example based on a grid of 6.9 m (22 ft 6 in)

2 stacks (a and b) each 5.4 m long = 10.8 m ⎱
6 stacks (c to h)   each 5.9 m long = 35.4 m ⎰ = 46.2 m

46.2 m 7 shelves high = 323.4 linear m
323.4 linear m at 20 books per m = 6468 books
                              = 135.85 books/m².

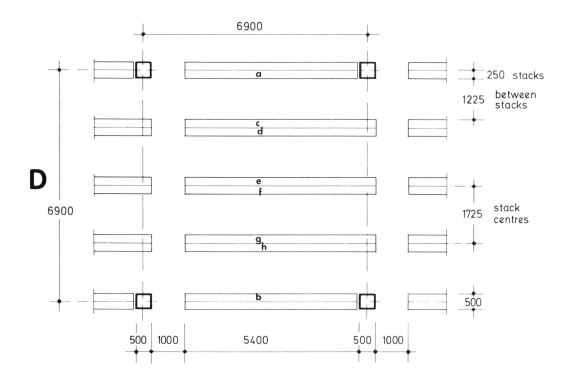

Table 13.4

Imperial sizes

Grid size (ft in)	Stack centres (ft in)	No. of double-sided stacks*	Books per grid square (one aisle per square)	Books per ft² (one aisle per square)
18	4 6	3	4914	15
20	5	3	5586	14
24	4 9	4	8694	15
25	5	4	9114	14½
25 6	5 1	4	9324	14
25 6	4 3†	5	11 214	17
27	5 5	4	9954	13½
27	4 6	5	11 970	16½

* Free-standing – includes the equivalent of the two single-sided stacks between columns which form part of the same square for calculations.
† If stacks are only 16 in deep the between-stack distance would be 2 ft 11 in.

Metric sizes

Grid size (m)	Stack centres (m)	No. of double-sided stacks*	Books per grid square (one aisle per square)	Books per m² (one aisle per square)
5.6	1.4	3	5012	160
6	1.5	3	5460	152
7.25	1.45	4	8610	164
7	1.55	4	9310	155
7.8	1.56	4	9380	154
	1.3	5	11 290	186
8.4	1.68	4	10 220	145
	1.4	5	12 292	174

Note These figures apply only when the following two qualifications are accepted:
They deal only with books which can be shelved seven shelves high and twenty to a metre and six to a foot, and a separate space allocation must be made for taller or deeper books.
Main aisles may be necessary if very heavy use is expected or if the stack area is large. Such aisles should be 1500 mm wide (5 ft).

Open stack

This is the most common form of shelving in university and college libraries. It takes up more space than closed stack, because more room must be left between stacks for readers to choose their books and for others to pass by. The minimum between-stack distance is 900 mm (3 ft) – i.e. 1375 mm (4 ft 6 in) centres – and where heavy use is to be expected, 1225 mm (4 ft) between stacks – 1680 mm (5 ft 6 in) stack centres – would be better. If wheelchair access is to be provided, 1060 mm (3 ft 6 in) should be the minimum between-stack distance, that is 1530 mm (5 ft) stack centres. The use of seating places within open stack complicates the issue and is not considered here.

Because the use is purposive rather than casual it is possible to shelve close to the floor, although one reader crouched low will block the passage-way; again the height of the top shelf must not exceed the comfortable reach of a short reader, and step-stools are certainly not advisable. Because most of the readers are young students, who will have little difficulty with high and low shelving, it is usual to have seven shelves to a tier to a top height of 2300 mm (7 ft 6 in), with a bottom shelf 150 mm (6 in) or less from the floor. Because of heavy use, it is preferable to have one cross-aisle for each grid square, the loss from the gross figure being, in a 5.5 m (18 ft) grid square, one-sixth, and in an 8.25 m square, one-ninth.

As with closed stack, all grid sizes are not equally hospitable: Table 13:4 gives possible alternatives and their capacities.

With free-standing stacks to a height of 2300 mm (7 ft 6 in) and with heavy use expected, the question of stack stability has to be taken seriously. If the easy answer of top bracing, stack-to-stack and stack-to-wall, is not acceptable on aesthetic grounds, then any other solution will affect either stack capacity (cases with wider bases, with the possible use of the wider bottom shelf for larger books) or flexibility (bolting the cases to the floor has an effect on carpets and layout). Manufacturers are not unaware of these problems, and in general these products can be relied upon for stability: where earthquakes are to be expected, the parameters are quite different, but so is the architect's approach to the whole building concept.

On the recommended grid of 6.86 m (22 ft 6 in) square, the two most appropriate layouts and resultant capacities are C and D in Figure 13:8.

In open stack conditions, calculations of book capacity for whole floors are complicated by the need for wider main aisles; how many will depend on the shape of the room. In the examples above, a cross-aisle of 1 m (3 ft 3 in) has been allowed for each grid square, but the addition of a main aisle every, say, four squares will make a small reduction in the overall capacity. The shelving of materials in large college and research library stacks is discussed in great detail by Metcalf,[13] and this is essential reading.

Table 13.4 *(Continued)*

Metric sizes with approximate equivalents in feet and inches*

Grid size (m)	(ft in)	No. of double-sided stacks	Stack centres (m)	(ft in)	Aisle widths (m)	(ft in)
5.5	18 1	4	1.1	3 7+	600	2 0−
5.6	18 4+	3	1.4	4 7+	900	3 0−
6	19 9	3	1.5	4 11+	1000	3 3+
		4	1.2	3 11+	700	2 4−
6.9	22 8−	3	1.725	5 8−	1225	4 0+
		4	1.38	4 6+	880	2 11−
		5	1.15	3 9+	650	2 2−
7.2	23 7½	5	1.2	3 11+	700	2 4−
7.25	23 9+	4	1.45	4 9+	950	3 1+
7.5	24 8	5	1.25	4 1+	750	2 5+
7.7	25 3	6	1.1	3 7	600	2 0−
7.75	25 5+	4	1.55	5 1+	1050	3 5+
7.8	25 7+	4	1.56	5 1+	1060	3 6−
		5	1.3	4 3+	800	2 8−
8.4	27 7−	4	1.68	5 6+	1130	3 8+
		5	1.4	4 7+	900	3 0−
		6	1.2	3 11+	700	2 4−

* Countries involved in changes between imperial and metric sizes may find this table helpful.

Periodical shelving within stack

Bound periodicals are treated as books. The various methods of shelving unbound periodicals are dealt with in Chapter 14, but if they are to be kept in piles, bundles or boxes on stack shelves, there should be a greater distance between stacks, because a shelf of periodicals is more frequently used than a shelf of books, and because readers take longer to find an issue than a book. A 1200 mm (4 ft) between-stack distance, which means 1675 mm (5 ft 6 in) stack centres, is the very least that should be allowed.

Open access

This method, in which books are spread out widely, attracting readers to browse round them, often in great numbers, is the most space-consuming of all, but it must form a large part of public lending, school and hospital libraries, and will be used to some extent in all libraries. The shelving here is not only a practical way of housing books but is itself one of the most important elements in the interior design of a room. The architect will therefore have strong feelings about the height, layout and material of the shelves; he will visualize them filled with brightly coloured books in plastic jackets. The shelving will be arranged informally and its relationship with the reading areas will be very much a matter of individual design. The shelving in British libraries is usually dispersed throughout the room, with browsing areas left between groups of bookcases, whereas in Scandinavia (and even more in the United States) some libraries have ranges of semi-formal shelving separate from larger reading and relaxing areas. The space left around bookcases will naturally vary widely according to the intensity of expected use. Figures 13:9 and 13:10 show the minimum that should be allowed.

Island bookcases cause less congestion than alcoves in busy libraries but they require more space around them. In less formal reading areas, space will have to be allowed for readers to consult books on nearby shelves, and also for trolleys to be pushed between tables. Figure 13:11 shows a typical layout in a combined study and browsing area.

The Danish State Library Inspectorate[14] recommends a 'browsing space' of about 900 mm (3 ft) in front of all shelving, and a 'passage space' of about 760 mm (2 ft 6 in) beyond that. This implies a minimum space between facing bookshelves of 2560 mm (8 ft 6 in); with 440 mm (1 ft 6 in) deep double-sided stacks it makes up the 3 m (10 ft) 'layout module' 13.13.

The inspectorate refers to a 'standard shelf unit', a bay with a total height of 1600 mm to 1850 mm (5 ft to 6 ft), with a shelf 20 mm (1¾ in) thick. The bottom shelf is 400 mm (16 in) from the floor. The adult shelving has five shelves to a height of 1850 mm (6 ft) and the children's shelving four shelves to a height of 1600 mm (5 ft 6 in): the between-shelf distance is given as 270 mm (10½ in). On such a tier 1 m wide, the capacity (allowing 20% of unoccupied space) is given as 165 volumes per five-shelf tier. If such a range of shelving is at 3 m (10 ft) centres, then a space 3 m (10 ft) × 1 m (3 ft 3 in) will include two such single-faced tiers, and the distance between will accommodate 330 volumes; this gives a capacity of 110 volumes/m² (10 volumes/ft²).

Later in the report[15] the inspectorate says:

'Sample surveys have shown that in libraries of the size under consideration (serving populations from about 5000 to about 25 000) the practical factors of daylight, traffic, and furniture other than shelving, account for about 40 per cent of the floor space in a well designed library area. A working measure of the capacity in the lending library can thus be reckoned as follows:
'110 volumes/m² less 40 per cent = about 65 volumes/m² [6 volumes/ft] of floor space.'

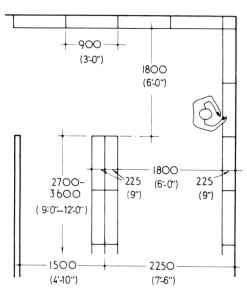

13:9. Recommended minimum plan dimensions in corner of open-access area

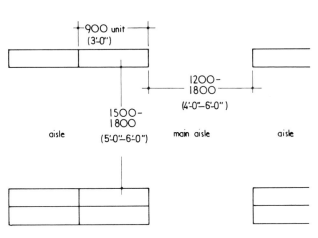

13:10. Recommended minimum plan dimensions in open-access area with shelving arranged in alcoves

13:11. Recommended minimum space between facing bookshelves in open-access area with high reader use

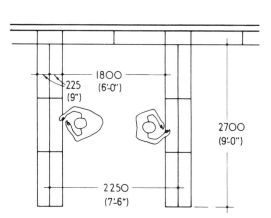

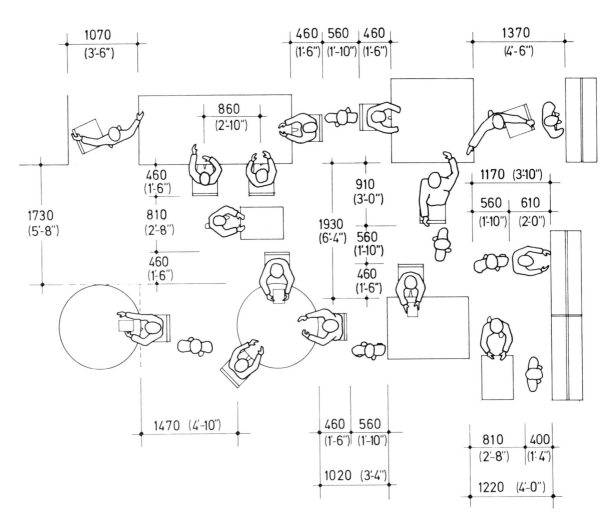

13:12. Minimum clearances in reading rooms

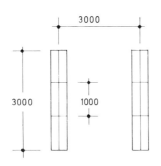

13:13 Danish State Library Inspectorate shelving module

14 Layouts and critical sizes: compact shelving and non-book materials

Desperate measures

The demand for more space to house books is always with us. Whether this will continue to eternity, whether the housing of ever more books in expensive space in expensive buildings is reasonable in the face of miniaturization and the new electronic technology, is discussed in Chapter 2. In the short term, however, the high cost of building, the shortage of space and the virtual certainty of the demand increasing year by year, force the librarian to take very seriously indeed any method which seems to offer space economies in shelving. He will therefore be most attracted by proprietary systems which offer space savings of the order of 100% to 150%. Even those which make more modest claims will still appeal, but he must first take a look at the overall situation.

Space savings in housing large quantities of books can be made in various ways but always at a price. The simplest and most quoted example is reducing aisle widths in closed stack from 900 mm (36 in) to 550 mm (22 in); this produces a saving of nearly 40% and leaves a 'practicable' aisle. The price to be paid for this is inconvenience to staff over the life of the library – no small matter. Many other examples of this kind were made familiar by the work of Rider,[1] and there is a copious literature on the subject; much of it is dated, but the principles have not changed.

Where the situation in an existing library really is desperate, the librarian has it within his power to rearrange his books so that they take up less space than they do when housed upright on shelves in the normal way. Before turning to the more elaborate methods, mention should be made of the simple ones:

1. *Shelving from floor to ceiling.* In an existing library where ceiling height allows, this means fitting extensions onto uprights so that more shelves can be arranged above existing shelves. Even simpler, in closed stack, is shelving on top of the canopy. Obvious gains are one-seventh added to stack capacity; equally obvious are the disadvantages in difficulty of access.
2. *Eliminating the space allowed* on each shelf for book movement: an easy gain where there is a fairly static book stock, at the expense of difficulty for the staff.
3. *Shelving a second row of books behind the first.* Very inconvenient and possibly calling for deeper shelving, but it can be done in a desperate situation where the shelves are deep enough, or the aisles wide enough for deeper shelves to be installed.
4. *Shelving books on the fore-edge* so that more shelves can be fitted into a tier. Again a certain minimum shelf and aisle depth are required and the inconvenience to users is obvious.
5. *Sizing* (see p. 35).

These are desperate measures and it is unlikely that a new library will be planned around any such methods.

In the past, ingenious ideas for space-saving shelving equipment have ranged from rotary cases suspended on overhead tracks to shelving books on endless bands. The compact-shelving methods described below are examples of proprietary products. Other, improved, ideas have replaced them, but they have in common the advantage of space saving in different degrees and the following disadvantages:

1. They cost much more than ordinary shelving.
2. They will almost certainly call for extra floor loading and bracing to accommodate the weight and movement.
3. They are less quick and easy to use than standard shelving units; unless special safeguards are incorporated, books may be damaged.

For these reasons such shelving is usually confined to specially designed stack areas accessible only to staff; in this capacity some improved types have been widely installed in libraries of all kinds.

Compact shelving

In a detailed (and perhaps over-elaborate) survey of compact shelving Gawrecki[2] distinguishes between:

1. Revolving shelves (better known in Britain as hinged shelf units).
2. Sliding drawers.
3. Sliding shelves (more usually known as rolling stacks).

The first two methods are chiefly seen in America: the third is universal.

Gawrecki's book contains sections by other authorities on compact shelving which show that such fittings have been devised and installed in libraries for very many years with varying success. Tracing the history of these experiments leads one to believe that human ingenuity and engineering skill will produce improved versions and that there is much to be gained by studying the problem. It is therefore not enough for the librarian to survey only what can be obtained today from equipment manufacturers; it may be that, in special circumstances, ingenuity can devise a specific design that will produce really worthwhile space savings. Each year that passes makes this matter more urgent: each rise in the cost of library space alters the economic balance of equipment cost and space saving.

Hinged shelf units

Many variants of these basic principles are possible, and an even greater variation of claims for space saving have been made for them. Without careful comparison of all factors involved it is impossible to dogmatize, but

14:1. Hinged shelf units: single-wing (left), single-faced and double-faced; double-wing (right), single-faced and double-faced

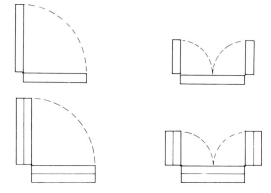

Gawrecki believes that of all these methods the greatest space saving is obtainable by the use of double-wing, double-faced methods. Considerable space has to be allowed between such cases, so normally this solution is helpful only in small libraries where the layout allows: it is of doubtful use to libraries with serried ranks of shelving units. A system by Snead and Company consisted of four rows of bookshelf units with the two outer rows hinged to swing out from the centre shelves, which were fixed. The hinging

14:2. Four rows of shelf units with outer two hinged to swing open

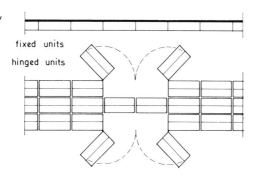

mechanism was so designed that when a hinged unit was fully open it projected only 400 mm (1 ft 4 in), and with a recommended between-stack dimension of 1 m (3 ft 3 in) there was space for people to pass while the bookshelves were being used. Compared with ordinary book stacks with 200 mm (8 in) shelves and 900 mm (3 ft) between-stack distances, capacity was increased by 66%.

Sliding drawers

The best-known examples of these were from American manufacturers and there were two basic types. The first, with 'single-headed' shelving, consisted of drawers which pulled outwards into aisles, each holding two rows of books, fore-edge to fore-edge, and a shorter front-facing shelf which was available from outside the stack when the drawer was recessed. This system was made by the

14:3. Drawer-type bookshelf units

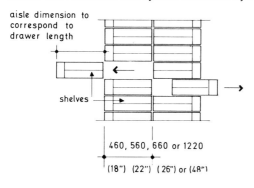

14:4. Drawer-type shelving withdrawable from either side

Hamilton Manufacturing Company. The second, 'double-headed' type was used in the Stor-mor system from W. R. Ames. Here the two fore-edge rows of books were shelved in a long drawer which could be withdrawn from either side of its stack. There was no shelf forming a front.

Even if such installations are still available, their use for large book stocks must cause considerable engineering problems. The mass of closely shelved books must be placed either at the lowest level of the building or directly above the load-bearing columns or girders; this in itself will limit planning freedom. In addition to the extra floor

loading, there will be special lighting requirements, because of the change of angle constantly presented by the movable stacks. This equipment is necessarily of very heavy construction and fairly complex, ball-bearing slides being essential. The systems are not common outside the United States, but their space-saving potential is not negligible. They have other advantages in that it may be possible for such space-saving fittings to be installed within existing bookcase frames if they are strong enough and of the right design.

At their best, sliding drawer methods have a less impressive space-saving ratio than hinged units. So many other considerations are involved, however, that this comparison should not be pressed.

Sliding and rolling cases

A sliding cabinet was used in the Iron Library of the British Museum many years ago, and that system is similar to one which is still offered today. The cases slid on overhead rails parallel to the range of fixed shelving in front of which they were placed. In a similar way the Conserv-a-file system developed by Supreme Equipment and Systems Corporation uses a set of shelves along the face of existing shelving, the front set being one unit shorter than the rear. The front set can slide from side to side, exposing a back shelf where needed; the back shelf itself can slide forward for ease of access. This method will give a large increase in shelving capacity while hardly increasing aisle widths, but at the expense of somewhat elaborate equipment. Naturally its use in large stack installations is limited.

Rolling stacks

The two most commonly used types of rolling stacks are those which move parallel to their length and those which roll at right angles to it.

Parallel rollers
These have been fitted in a large number of libraries for many years, the cases being either suspended from rails or running on tracks. In a simple example, single-sided shelf units slide on rails in the floor and may be free-standing up to 2200 mm (7 ft 3 in) high, after which a steadying guide rail is required at the top. The units are a standard 900 mm (3 ft) long and arranged up to three units deep. The back row is continuous and fixed, while the two sliding rows must omit one unit each to allow access. The units are propelled by hand. This principle is more effectively used in closely packed stacks where one of a row of cases can be pulled out for access from either side. Luxfer Ltd made steel cases of this kind: the cases were mounted on wide treads with ball-bearing rollers and when closed formed a solid block. One outstanding advantage of this system is that it may be used in any library area with a single floor level as it requires neither tracks nor overhead support.

Right-angle rollers
This is a system now in most common use for compact shelving. The stacks run at right angles to their length, leaving a gap in the solid rank of cases; the cases are rolled (by hand or by power) so that the 'adjustable' gap allows access to the required shelves, which are on metal frames mounted on bases. The various proprietary units move by means of wheels fixed to the chassis, running on rails either embedded in the floor screed or mounted upon the floor surface. To obtain appreciable space savings, the number of gangways in proportion to the number of stacks

must be low, and the stacks themselves must be long: this will usually mean that the stacks must be power-operated or at least power-assisted. This can be done either by pneumatic rams at the base of the units or by built-in electric motors linked to a drive. These power-operated stacks include safety devices with either mechanical or electronic detectors which halt the movement when any obstacle is encountered. These range from flaps which lock the movement when tripped by touching an obstruction, to electronic detectors and 'buttons of consent' which have to be operated before any stack movement can take place. Power-operated systems call for little human effort, although they are dearer and more subject to breakdown.

The space savings offered are very well illustrated by the example shown in advertisements issued by J. Glover and Sons: their Ingold-Compactus system (Figure 14:7) increases capacity by about 46%; 44 single-sided bays at 900 × 450 mm (36 × 18 in) replace 30 of the same size. The most-used systems are those with double-sided cases in a single line, the gangway for access being 'moved' along the stack run. In Figure 14:8 the double-sided cases move to give an increase of 140%. These diagrams can be used to work out potential space savings in an area of known size by trying out the different stack lengths and widths. Where the area was not designed to accommodate special compact storage devices, the gain is not usually as

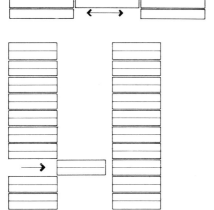

14:5. Single-sided sliding shelves

14:6. Parallel roller cases

14:7. Thirty single-sided units are replaced by 44: a gain of 46%

14:8. Twelve double-sided units are replaced by 29: a gain of 140%

The coming of cases with ratchets in their bases keying into floor tracks, operated by star-wheel handles on case ends and capable of moving many times the load of hand-pushed systems has altered the balance between hand and power operation. The drive is so low-geared that the cases can be moved with very little effort.

Normally the run of cases is beneath runs of fitted lighting (which must be at right angles to the cases), but an interesting variant from Bruynzeel is the bracket light fitted to the top of each case, the light coming on only when case movement exposes that particular shelving side to access. These rolling stacks are offered by a number of firms because they are used in storage situations throughout commerce and industry. The shelving mounted on the bases will be specifically designed for library use; it can be wood, but is usually metal and offers all the normal metal shelving alternatives, bracket and case, as well as the standard accessories. One firm at least offers a choice between hand-pushed, crank-driven, pneumatic-powered and electric power-driven systems, each bearing the same range of shelving alternatives but with very different movable loads and operating speeds. Because all the units running at right angles to their length will fit closely together, they can have rubber seals along the outer uprights to give a separation between shelf faces so that books which may protrude slightly from the shelves will not be damaged. Other advantages are exclusion of dust and greater than usual resistance to fire. A pair of adjacent cases or runs of cases can be lockable together to produce miniature 'strongrooms' with the shelving equivalent of a double-sided case.

There are so many proprietary examples that it is pointless to illustrate them here. They *appear* to be very similar, but whether they all work well is another matter. It is very difficult indeed to stipulate quality standards in such a field, where use and forces will be heavy, so it is the reputation of the manufacturer which is the best guide.

great, but Bruynzeel, who have supplied compact storage for well over a million volumes in the new Causewayside Building of the National Library of Scotland, as well as vast quantities for the new British Library building at St Pancras, have produced the 'Closing Aisle Storage Benefit Formula' to calculate gains. This states that the percentage saved =

$$\frac{100G\,(R-N)}{R\,(G+2S)}$$

where G = gangway width
R = number of runs per block
S = shelf depth
N = number of opening aisles required (normally one)

The greatest variant in normal use depends on how many cases need to be moved in order to produce a gangway. Bruynzeel claim that their equipment will fit 35 000 books into an area of 56 m² (600 sq ft), that is 624 volumes/m² (58 volumes/sq ft) – a considerable gain. It is perfectly possible for mobile shelving to be specifically designed to house oversize books, maps and other inconveniently sized items.

Obviously the simplest and easiest installations are those in single-floor buildings; to have the stacks in basements avoids loading problems, and many small and medium-sized public libraries find this the most economical way of housing their least-used stock. In multi-storey buildings, loading levels have to be higher than normal; a commonly proposed figure is 12 kN/m² (250 lb/sq ft). This is not enough in some circumstances; in the Causewayside Building in Edinburgh the extensive use of rolling stacks made 15 kN/m² (313 lb/sq ft) necessary. It must be understood that all floors will deflect under load and that normal design practice allows structural beams to deflect up to 1/360th of their length. This can result in floor gradients which could have an adverse effect upon closing aisle units, even causing them to move of their own accord. The deflection will not be only in a single direction, and the grid square will deflect proportionally and therefore with a cumulated deflection in the centre. This is a specialist matter, and very few architects or even structural engineers have experience in this field.

In the Causewayside Building the book storage areas were required to be the principal building element and to form the large core of the plan, the services and vertical means of access being on the perimeter. To permit densely packed mobile shelving to be installed throughout the building if required, a high loading was stipulated, and a shallow secondary floor system was specially developed to sit on top of the main structural floor. The steel rails supporting the mobile shelving were designed to accommodate suspended floor panels and to incorporate a levelling device to overcome deflection. A similar system is being used in the British Library building at St Pancras for its basement-suspended floor areas. In this way a large library can allow for a considerable increase in the compact shelving areas at some future date. Because of the weight problems and the matter of floor deflection it is certainly better if compact shelving can be planned for at the earliest stage rather than added as an extra after the structure has been built.

To assess possible overall cost savings is not easy; Gorman[3] Muller[4] and Hill[5] both discuss this question. Compact shelving equipment is always more expensive than normal shelving, and savings are apparent only in large buildings of regular shape with open floors. However, space in a library has a real value, and if double the quantity of books (or more) can be accommodated in a given area, then a real saving becomes apparent when it obviates (or postpones) the need for an extension to the building.

Although the major use of compact shelving is for the saving of space, the systems can be used for other purposes. For example, in multi-purpose libraries serving small communities it is possible for some of the bookcases to be movable to close up face-to-face together, freeing the area for meetings and other events. The price to be paid is the acceptance of tracks running beneath the shelving, but in a carpeted area this can be a very small drawback.

These systems are offered by many manufacturers, and there is no substitute for the inspection of systems in working conditions. However, the principles of moving cases on tracks are not secret and wooden cases can easily be mounted on rails by ingenious engineers in less-industrialized countries.

See also Chapter 5, which includes methods of mechanical retrieval of books; such systems can be used effectively only if the stack is designed specifically for the purpose. The question of the design of shelving is considered in Chapter 17.

Shelving other materials

In every library there will be materials other than printed books; in research libraries other forms may constitute a high proportion of the stock, and their shelving problems must be considered separately.

Very large books

Bound newspapers, atlases, 'elephant folios' and so on are best shelved flat because of the great strain on their bindings when they stand upright. A very few may be so large as to call for special accommodation, but generally shelves can be 900 mm (3 ft) long, and so conform to normal shelving modules. It is necessary for the shelves to be at least 150 mm (18 in) deep; it is better if each large volume can have a shelf to itself, the shelves being arranged at 70–100 mm (3–4½ in) centres, according to the depth of the book; here adjustable shelving is essential. Because of the wear on the covers of such heavy books when they are slid out of fixed shelves, it is preferable to have either pull-out trays (with stops to prevent them coming right out), or (much better) heavy rollers so that books can be moved out easily. Some sets of rollers can be adjustable for book thickness.

Because of the great weight of such books it is difficult for these shelves to be used above 1250 mm (4 ft) from the floor, and rather than waste stack shelving it is better for special low cases to be built. These can have sloping tops so that the books can be consulted in situ; the slopes should run 1 m to 1150 mm (3 ft 3 in to 3 ft 9 in) from the floor and should have upstands along the front edges to prevent the volumes sliding off. Such heavy volumes, if in constant use, will soon wear the surface of the case tops, so it is advisable to use steel or good plastic laminates for the top surfaces.

Very small books

Those less than 75 mm (3 in) square are best kept in boxes of normal book size, the boxes being shelved as books. In practice such books are kept in closed-access conditions.

Paperbacks

Some libraries, particularly college libraries which cater for students who are not 'bookish', may find it tactically valuable to keep stocks of paperback books in order to encourage reading among those for whom this is the only familiar book form. Paperbacks are also used in an ever-increasing proportion of popular libraries of all kinds. If they have been laminated into stiff covers or are within special stiffened containers, they present little problem, but if they are used in their limp form, special shelving arrangements may be needed. Display cases have been designed so that books may be shown face forwards and full advantage taken of the pictorial covers.

Current use of newspapers

Because newspapers are large and limp, the best method is to have each issue inside its own transparent-fronted stiff holder, but few libraries can afford the large amount of table space which consultation of several of these at a time would entail. There is still much to be said for the old-fashioned newspaper slope, each paper being spread out and held under a centre clip or clamping rod. Crude and space-consuming as this may seem, it has the advantage of confining users to a limited space and is

14:9. Flexible carrier for compact stacking at the Causewayside Building, National Library of Scotland, Edinburgh

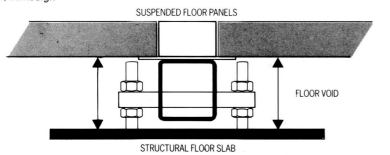

SUSPENDED FLOOR PANELS

FLOOR VOID

STRUCTURAL FLOOR SLAB

14:10. Newspaper slope: saves space and is useful when consultation of papers will be brief (City Business Library, London)

14:10. Newspaper slope: saves space and is useful when consultation of papers will be brief (City Business Library, London)

acceptable where papers are consulted briefly, as distinct from being studied or read for pleasure. Other methods include placing the folded paper in a special shelving rack or using the suspended filing system whereby a stick is placed in the centre of the paper, serving as a stop on the filing rack. All these methods have been in use for many years; none successfully combines convenience in use with efficiency in shelving. The field is open for an inventive designer.

14:11 and 14:12. Periodical storage system but without the appeal of the journal's cover (Schulz GMBH Speyer, GFR)

Current issues of periodicals

These form a large and very important part of the stock of many types of library; most libraries feature them prominently and the major problem is not of housing but of finding space for the eye-catching display of thousands of journals spread out for immediate use. The first step must

be selection according to frequency of use. Most-used titles will be displayed (preferably in individual transparent-fronted holders) in reading areas; this is of course extremely space-consuming. They can be housed on special display shelving, of which there are numerous designs, or on tilted shelves within system shelving units. An enterprising designer can create such a fitting as part of another piece of library furniture. More conventional cases can have the advantage of allowing storage space behind each issue for immediate back numbers, the 'home' space of each displayed issue of a journal being indicated by having the title lettered on the face of the slope, where it will be covered by the issue itself when the latter is not in use. Some methods simply hinge the front flap; more elaborate ones allow the lifted front flap to slide back horizontally into a recess, freeing the hands to get at the pile of back issues. Anyone who has attempted to find

back issues in these circumstances knows that the latter system is well worth its extra cost.

Designers have tackled the problem imaginatively: a solution which has the advantages of finding space for periodicals and spreading out their users is to place the current issues on single shelves running round otherwise unusable areas, under windows or along guard rails. To obtain the advantage of displaying the cover of the periodical without losing so much space there are systems which hold issues at an angle to the searcher. Less-used titles can be housed in individual holders, or without if they are sufficiently thick, shelved either vertically as if they were very narrow books or horizontally. They take up much less space, but the self-locating (and self-advertising) feature of the colourful cover is lost.

Back numbers of periodicals

Periodicals are difficult to house effectively because the same title can be in intense demand as it arrives hot from the press and then subject to intermittent recall over a number of years, by which time it has been joined by many thousands of its fellows. Because of the great and ever-growing practice of photocopying articles from periodicals, there is a tendency to leave them unbound. Bound volumes, the traditional way of keeping runs of periodicals, are very inconvenient for photocopying. This problem is being increasingly affected, first, by the issuing of long runs of back numbers of periodicals on microfilm, with its great advantages both in space saving and ease of reproduction, and, second, by the growing number of periodical runs which are available via the computer. It appears likely that runs of back numbers available on-line from compact disc will become normal long before electronic publishing replaces the current issues.

14:13. Lateral filing of pamphlets within the subject sequence

Unbound issues can be kept in open-sided boxes which are shelved like books; this is cheap, but, contrary to usual practice, it is advisable to stand the boxes on their backs (i.e. with the open sides at the top): it may call for deeper shelving but allows more shelves in the vertical space and can save a lot of trouble in the long run. Alternatively the issues can be tied up in bundles; again this is cheap, but it is very awkward indeed for access, and one can never rely on the user fastening them up after use. If loose issues are left unenclosed, piled flat on the shelves, they will inevitably stray.

Bound volumes

Because these are in book form they present little problem for shelving. The length of the run may lead the librarian to think of using fixed shelving for them, but note should be taken of the tendency of periodicals, even long-established ones, to change their format with disconcerting frequency. The main decision is whether bound volumes of a periodical shall be available close to the current issue in a reading area, or whether it is practicable to use the more economical plan of putting all bound volumes into stack. It can be assumed that in most libraries runs of bound volumes will seldom be required for browsing – except perhaps in art or history departments. Again, back numbers on CD/ROM (Compact disc, read only memory) may solve the problem.

Indexes and abstracts

Only experience of relative use and judgement of space priorities can decide whether indexes to periodicals should be kept on public shelving or with the run of journals, many

of which may be in stack. General periodical indexes and abstracts will certainly be housed in the main bibliographical areas; some specialist libraries also keep index volumes to individual periodicals there, the bound volumes being in stack. This enables the enquirer to identify the required article and to order a photocopy, which can be supplied by the photocopy service direct from the stack: for full efficiency these should duplicate the indexes bound in with the periodicals themselves. Again the growth of electronic publishing brings a totally new dimension to the problem.

Pamphlets and reports

These are particularly difficult to handle: any of individual importance may be fitted into a case with transparent covers and shelved in its subject sequence as a book. The chief difficulty with this method is that the spine is thin and it may be hard to find. If pamphlets form a finite series they can be bound and shelved as books. Perhaps the most usual method of shelving is in special pamphlet boxes, made to the appropriate size and shelved as books. (The power to obtain such special boxes to order is one of the advantages of the library's in-house bindery.) Vertical files, best arranged at right angles to the readers rather than facing them (lateral filing), are used to hold pamphlets but present a separate subject sequence for readers to search; such files, when freely used by readers, soon get out of order. Lateral filing close to the specific subject

sequence can be arranged as part of systems shelving units and has an advantage over separate units. In conventional vertical filing it is imperative to have the files suspended within the drawers to prevent them slithering down; moreover, except for holding separately numbers of short reports and keeping limp files without damage, these filing cases are extremely inefficient in their use of space. A normal vertical file case 450 × 700 × 1200 mm (1 ft 6 in × 2 ft 4 in × 4 ft) will occupy little over half of the possible 2300 mm (7 ft 6 in) of usable vertical space; lateral files with dimensions similar to those of a double-sided tier 900 × 450 × 2200 mm (3 ft × 1 ft 6 in × 7 ft) will hold up to three times the number of pamphlets or reports which vertical file cases would hold and are just as easily accessible. For pamphlets of immediate interest, various office-equipment firms have produced display fitments (rather like those for periodicals); when the immediate pressure of demand has lessened, the pamphlets can revert to storage by one of the less space-consuming methods.

Microforms

This is an important and still growing form of storing information; the coming of the computer, which may in the future make it obsolete, has at the moment added to its potential and its importance. In many circumstances microforms produced by computers give an information store which is more economical and requires less sophisticated access hardware than a computer. Presumably further developments of disc storage, laser-read, will change the equation. At present the existing holdings of long runs of unique books and journals on microform are so vast that it seems unlikely (if only for economic reasons) that they will be superseded in the near future; many different organizations are continuing to publish in this form. On the other hand it seems at the moment that microforms, as a method of storing runs of journals as well as archival materials, will be gradually replaced by CD/ROM (Compact disc, read only memory). This is because one CD/ROM can hold the equivalent of many reels of film and hundreds of fiche, can be searched more effectively than microforms, which normally use manual indexes, and is much more durable; and both reading and print-out are easier through the VDU. As CD/ROM is based on the large and growing audio compact disc industry, it is likely to become cheaper, even though laser-read discs are not yet standardized; it will remain a publishing medium, because the transfer of local records is very expensive.

There are many varieties of microforms, because special types have been developed especially for office, bank and other needs. Microfilm, which was the original medium, is now available as reel, cassette, cartridge, jacket and aperture card. Microfiche, also a transparency, is widely used as a replacement for the card catalogue. Microcard and microprint, both opaques, have been adopted for runs of specialized reports.

Transparencies

Reel microfilm in libraries is usually either 16 mm or 35 mm, the latter being much the more common. Both come in reels kept individually in an acid-free cardboard box. There are numerous proprietary filing systems on the market; the cheapest way is to shelve them as books, fitting the shelves 105 mm (4⅛ in) apart so that a normal stack shelving unit would hold sixteen such shelves and so about 300 boxes per tier. If boxes are shelved two deep, the capacity is doubled, but access will be less convenient, and a lip must be fitted at the back of each shelf to prevent the box from dropping off. Unless use is heavy it is better to put the microfilm boxes into larger boxes which can use shelf space more efficiently. A metal filing cabinet 660 × 760 mm (2 ft 2 in × 2 ft 6 in) of normal vertical file height is the next most common method, holding 675 rolls of 35 mm or 125 rolls of 16 mm film. Cabinets of much greater height are possible with corresponding gain in storage capacity, but they are heavy, and using the upper drawers can be hazardous. The great advantage of the cabinet is that it can be locked: a series of lockable vertical file cabinets is the most practical method for all but the largest collections. It must never be forgotten that microfilm is very easily damaged and particularly susceptible to changes in humidity. I have seen microfilm collections in tropical countries which have been so affected by the climate that they could never be used, even to make new copies from them. In these conditions the best answer undoubtedly is to keep a file of master negatives in a safe with strictly controlled atmospheric conditions, used only, with careful handling, for the production of positives for reader use. This is essential for microfilmed archive collections in humid climates; with commercially available films it might be cheaper to buy a new set. Short lengths of microfilm can be put in envelopes, particularly in transparent envelopes 125 × 205 mm (5 × 8 in), which offer both protection and speed of inspection; these will be filed upright in drawers.

Microfilm frames are also found as parts of aperture cards, whose sizes vary widely but which can be filed like catalogue cards.

Microfiche is in stiff rectangular form although transparent. The most usual sizes are 90 × 120 mm (3½ × 4¾ in), 75 × 125 mm (3 × 5 in), and 100 × 150 mm (4 × 6 in). This latter size is now that adopted by the British Standards Institution (BS 4187, *Specification for microfiche*, 1973). All can be filed as cards in drawers of the appropriate size but should be placed within individual protective envelopes. Another alternative is to file them in suitably sized boxes on standard shelves. As with microfilms, many proprietary holders are offered. Some libraries with large stocks store their 100 × 150 mm (4 × 6 in) fiche in an electro-mechanical unit which offers high-speed retrieval and will hold as many as 274 000 such fiche in a single piece of equipment. Microfiche in very heavy use (for example where they form the COM catalogue of the library) are housed in special containers with separate slots to hold thirty-two, sixty-four or a hundred fiche of 100 × 150 mm (4 in × 6 in) size. This holder can be a collection of viewing units on rotating bases, and it has obvious advantages for the quick identification of a fairly small collection of fiche.

The likelihood of misplacement of fiche is high and as they are small they are easily stolen (particularly as one fiche from a subject sequence makes a ready-made bibliography for a thesis). It is perhaps as well that a complete set of up-dated replacements is provided by the computer every few weeks.

Ultrafiche is microfiche with a much greater reduction ratio. These again are either 125 × 75 mm (5 × 3 in) or 150 × 100 mm (6 × 4 in) and can be filed as cards. The standard bibliography *Books in English* is on 150 × 100 mm (6 × 4 in) microfiche: each transparency contains 2380 frames of information below a title strip readable by the naked eye.

Opaques The term Microcard is often loosely, and wrongly, used to refer to all micro-opaques, but it is, in fact, covered by an American patent. Microcards are single-sided and their size is 125 × 75 mm (5 × 3 in). Other micro-opaques include Microprint, 225 × 150 mm (9 × 6 in), and Microlex (double-sided), 215 × 165 mm (8½ × 6½ in). Microprint tape presents no difficulty as it may be attached to cards of any size. As all these forms appear as rigid cards they will be filed in drawers of the appropriate dimensions.

The housing of microforms cannot be considered separately from the positioning of the machines on which they are to be read. The different forms require different machines, although there are combined film and fiche readers. All film can be damaged by misuse; but fiche is more durable, as are the opaques. It cannot be assumed that users will read the instructions with care, so the combination of a variety of machines and easily damaged materials makes this a difficult sphere of library management. If coin-operated reader-printers are also provided (and perhaps coin-change machines), the problems become greater. The safest, but most cumbersome and expensive, answer is to have staff supervision, but few libraries can afford this. A few universities contract out this work to firms who supervise and service the machines; where the use is really heavy this is a possibility if charging for use is acceptable; most libraries regard microform as just another way of making source materials available and would no more charge for their use than they would for the use of books.

Where microfilms are in heavy use (again the obvious example is the COM library catalogue) there will be a number of machines for use, each with a standard table and seat, and a desk-top holder of fiche within easy reach. If fiche catalogues are to be made available in several different parts of the library (one of the great advantages of the form for reader use) the problem of machine maintenance will loom large. Coin-operated reader-printers are popular, but they are soon put out of action (whatever the manufacturer may say). Perhaps this is too pessimistic; it may be that the durable and reliable reader-printer is on the horizon. We despaired of coin-operated photocopiers for many years but today they can be left open for use with confidence.

Slides

Slides (i.e. separate film transparencies) are usually 2 × 2 in frames holding a single 35 mm film. They can be mounted under glass for permanent storage or slipped into pockets within ready-made transparent sheets, which can themselves be suspended in vertical file drawers or in lateral filing. A sheet can be removed and placed in a viewer so that the required slide can be identified without being handled, and then removed for enlargement. The growing use of transparencies as part of the library's audio-visual service has led to the development of a number of new ways of handling them. Manufacturers of specialized library equipment offer illuminated frames on which transparencies are permanently displayed; the audio-cassette/slide package is popular in a form which is virtually that of a book. Filmstrips will be kept in their own cylindrical holders, preferably lined with paper to prevent scratching, and filed in drawers with close divisions. A recent innovation is to keep them in their holders, together with accompanying script, in transparent, labelled packets suspended from revolving frames.

Picture collections

These are a growing feature in libraries. Sometimes pictures are for loan; in other cases they may form part of the audio-visual stock for normal consultation. Paintings and prints are so cumbersome that their storage is a separate problem. If they are framed they can stand

14:14. Picture storage on sliding racks

upright between ad hoc vertical fittings; if unframed they can lie flat in solander boxes of a suitable size, with the usual handling risks when they are withdrawn for inspection. It seems reasonable that they should be displayed for pleasure as well as for consultation; in large libraries it is not unusual for them to be used simply as wall decoration in corridors and offices, but obviously there are risks. With larger collections, hinged or sliding double-sided fitments from specialist manufacturers offer great space economies as well as the easy opportunity for inspection. As in the case of planning art display areas, informed advice can often be obtained from colleagues on the staff of local art galleries.

Photographs, clippings and other illustrations

These are best attached to standard mounts and filed vertically in boxes either 325 × 260 × 75 mm (12¾ × 10¼ × 3 in) or 350 × 290 × 75 mm (13¾ × 11½ × 3 in), each holding between seventy and ninety mounts. The boxes can be stored on normal adjustable shelving sequences. Larger clippings, tipped to standard mounts, and other items, such as broadsides and prints, can be held flat in solander boxes 700 × 550 × 60 mm (27 × 21¼ × 2¼ in) or 1 m × 750 mm × 60 mm (38¾ × 29 × 2¼ in) and shelved horizontally in fixed shelving cases deep enough for the purpose. For such large items it is an advantage to have low cases with sloping tops for immediate consultation.

The easiest way of storing prints of a fairly consistent size is between clamps in the ubiquitous vertical file cabinet, but large collections mean many drawers, great weight and clumsy access. Once more it must be said that the future of all these forms seems to be with the computer. Collections of visual materials – prints, paintings, photographs and maps – can be held on video discs, whose storage capacity (more than 100 000 frames per disc) and power to reproduce in colour on a screen make them a solution to storage pressure, and they enable many users at any one time to retrieve the images (and images from other institutions). The possibility of obtaining on video disc vast specialist holdings from national libraries, and archives alters the whole relationship between student or researcher and the collections of his own library.

Maps

Bound volumes of maps must be treated as very large and very heavy books, shelved horizontally, preferably with rollers acting as shelves. Small collections of loose maps may be suspended in various types of vertical or lateral files; the architect will be very familiar with these methods because they are common in all planning offices. A typical metal vertical storage cabinet will take up to 750 sheet maps suspended from support bars; such a case could be from 1040 mm (41 in) to 1500 mm (59 in) high and 785 mm (31 in) to 916 mm (36 in) wide, with a depth of about 430 mm (17 in). Where there is a large collection this would take up a great deal of space. Sheet maps in libraries are usually laid horizontally, either in solander boxes or in proprietary metal map filing cabinets. Although sheet maps are thin they can be very heavy in quantity, especially if they are kept separate by folders. A 1 in (25 mm) deep drawer holds about a hundred maps with their folders; this may not seem many, but pulling more than a hundred maps about in order to get at one can soon damage them. It is much better to have many narrower drawers, but if there is a large collection there will be a weight problem. Two successful solutions I have seen are 2 m (6 ft 6 in) high cases of 25 mm (1 in) drawers housed in

14:15. Hinged system and pull-out fitment for maps in greatest demand (City Business Library, London)

a basement (steps are needed to reach the higher drawers) and a rather less tall run of cases placed along the lines of the beams in order to support the weight safely; the weight of such map cases is of course spread over the map size, not concentrated as much as is the weight of a heavily loaded tier of books. Individual maps (such as the Ordnance Survey series) may be mounted on linen, folded, reinforced and shelved as narrow books, even being in attractive transparent covers. Maps in constant use should be displayed permanently open, either in a pull-down fitment or on wall panels like wallpaper samples (see Figure 14:15). Rolled maps will be stored either in very deep pigeon holes (which uses a great deal of wall space) or horizontally on very narrow supporters along a wall. Once more it has to be said that video-disc storage is an ideal way of handling this form.

Music

Sheet music may be bound and shelved as books or stored unbound horizontally in drawers or in vertical file cabinets about 1200 mm (4 ft) high, 400 mm (15¾ in) wide and 300 mm (12 in) deep. Scores will normally be bound as books; the problem lies in making the correct shelf allocation for volumes of such varying depth, height and thickness. With adjustable shelving, miniature scores present no problems.

Audio discs (gramophone records)

These became common in libraries some forty years ago; at first they were 78 rpm, then 33 (and some 45). They were usually left in their folders (which were dull) and shelved upright, end-on, in lockable cupboards. When they were tightly packed (especially with expandable holders) little harm came to them. With the coming of the colourful cover it became usual to display them openly and to allow readers to handle and place them on turntables, either in listening carrels or in the open if headphones were used.

The librarian's judgement as to the reader's ability to do this with care determines the planning of the audio area: to have staff only playing the records from a central console and switching to headphones in one of a number of listening areas is safer but very expensive of staff time. To leave the user to help himself and use one of a number of turntables may be a risk. Such a decision affects not only the layout but the initial wiring provision, and once made may be expensive to change. The coming of the compact disc has altered the balance, as it is more durable, and it may be that we shall find the central console a thing of the past, except for the provision of a programme of music to headphones via sockets placed in many parts of the library.

Collections of 33 rpm discs can be stored on normal shelves; flat is theoretically best, but awkward for shelving. Upright, even if many vertical dividers are used, there is a risk of bending. For attractiveness and ease of use they are commonly shelved in open-topped troughs; a 'browser box', 350 mm (14 in) long, 75 mm (3 in) deep and 150 mm (6 in) high, mounted on short legs, is convenient and flexible. For large numbers of discs, a case 1500 mm (5 ft) high can have three rows of troughs vertically, each 350 mm (14 in) long and holding between 20 and 40 discs in each section. This case will accommodate between 60 and 120 discs in each running 350 mm (14 in); a double-sided case of this size, 2150 mm (7 ft) long, can hold between 700 and 1400 discs in conditions enabling the user to make his choice in comfort. Where pressure on space is less acute, lower troughs may be preferred. In theory it is said to be inadvisable to store discs leaning against each other in this way; in practice it seems to work perfectly well.

When planning such cases for discs it may be convenient to keep the disc storage at counter height and to incorporate shelving above for holding miniature scores, which are so often used in conjunction with them. A more recent method, of growing popularity in public libraries, consists of a lateral suspended file system in which the disc, within its coloured jacket, is placed in a transparent plastic holder suspended from a rail along which it slides; this can be part of a system shelving unit. A large number of discs can be held in a small space, and access is fairly easy.

Compact discs present fewer problems because they are smaller – 12 mm (4.72 in) in diameter – and have rigid, dust-protecting cases. They can be stored economically in drawers of appropriate size or in display cases (locked against pilfering), where their covers attract and are self-locating.

Audio tape, cassettes and cartridges

These (and video tape cassettes) are small and easy to house; they present a security rather than a shelving problem. Their sizes vary, and the answer until recently has been to file them on shelves, in drawers or pigeon-holes, and to make them available only on request to the staff. Because of the growing use of these forms, manufacturers now offer open display cases with shelves fixed at the appropriate intervals, and incorporating a security bar across the frame of each shelf, so that the cassettes can be on open display but are secured unless the bars are unlocked by staff: this is time-consuming. Another common method, imitating that used in music shops, is to have the attractive containers freely available in troughs or revolving display units, keeping the cassettes themselves under staff control. The reader brings the container to the staff counter, where the cassette is issued. The cassette is retained at the counter when returned, but the container is replaced on the display unit.

15 Reading and reader service areas

Although reading is a basic activity in libraries of all kinds, there is a fundamental difference between serious study and casual browsing. Entirely different space allowances have to be made for the two activities, the proportions depending on the aims of the library. Academic libraries will concentrate on serious study but they will not neglect to use the appeal of books in an informal setting to catch the students' interest and widen their horizons. Even in formal surroundings some eminent educationalists believe that serendipity is the library's great contribution to the acquisition of knowledge, more important than 'information' from the data bank.

Study areas

These will form the major part of university, college and public reference libraries. Overall space allowances will already have been determined from the product of the number of readers to be catered for (from the brief) and the space allocation per reader. The layout that gives the most economical use of space is rows of study tables in the centre of a room with shelving along the walls, and this was common in medium-sized reference libraries. The great drawback is the small and absolutely finite number of books which can be housed. This method is still used for special collection rooms, where the bookcases are usually glass-fronted and locked. The other layout is free-standing stacks down the centre of a room with seating by the windows. This, with refinements and changes of proportion, is the method in use in the majority of academic libraries.

The traditional relationship between reading accommodation and books in academic libraries is discussed by Thompson[1] and Brawne.[2] Until recently it was quite common for the stacks to be on one side of the room and rows of seating (like an examination hall) on the other side. This had some advantages in that there could be a good ceiling height over the reading area while stacking could be on two levels, the same ceiling height but with access by short stairs built into the stack. It also helped to solve the problem of direct sunlight, as the orientation could be arranged so that the reading half was on the shaded side, with windowless walls behind the stacks. Today most academic libraries have seating around the outside of the stacks on a number of subject floors. Seats are often to be found within the stacks also, but problems arise from the disturbance of readers by stack searchers, as well as economy of book housing.

Tables

Sizes per person of the surfaces of tables for serious study have been quoted by many experts, and once again the space needs seem to rise decade by decade. At present an acceptable figure seems to be 600 × 900 mm (2 × 3 ft); common sense and personal testing agree with this. The figure has sometimes grown to 1 m (3 ft 3 in) wide; it is claimed that the small increase gives the reader extra comfort, but judgement here is subjective and depends on local expectations. When planning to accommodate seating, space must be allowed for all readers to move about; a reasonable space allowance for a reader at a table might therefore be 1.35 m² (14½ sq ft). Where individual tables are placed against walls, or where multiple tables are used, this figure can be reduced to 1.25 m² (13½ sq ft) and 1.1 m² (12 sq ft) respectively.

This of course is not the whole picture; a share of the main access aisles and passage spaces within the room will be allocated to each reader, and these make up the normal allowance of 2.3 m² (25 sq ft) per reader. The difference here is between planning space allowances for readers in quantity and establishing layouts in actual reading areas.

These figures are based on the requirements of the 'average reader' or the undergraduate. There will be many cases where large numbers of readers need more table space (universities often allow research workers larger table space, while users of maps and prints need a great deal more room). In an extreme example special areas may be provided, for example for visiting professors (these will be referred to later when carrels are discussed).

There are different ways of providing tables, as follows.

Individual tables

These have psychological attractions but take up most space; and the stability of single tables needs to be carefully tested. They are particularly acceptable at right angles to a wall (and even more so to a window). Such a seat should be placed just ahead of the window so that

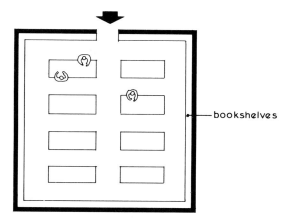

15:1. Reference library with shelving round walls and shelving in centre

bookshelves

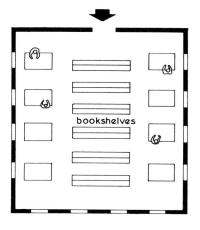

bookshelves

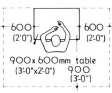

15:2. Minimum dimensions for one-person reading tables

600 (2'0") 600 (2'0")

900 × 600mm table (3'-0" × 2'-0") 900 (3'-0")

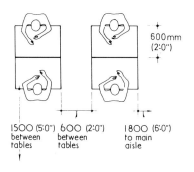

600mm
(2'-0")

1500 (5'-0") 600 (2'-0") 1800 (6'-0")
between   between   to main
tables   tables   aisle

15:3. Minimum dimensions for two-person reading tables

there is no distraction while working but with the opportunity to lean back, look out of the window and relax. Single tables in serried ranks in an open room produce a regimented feeling, and the arrival of new readers can disturb concentration. Readers' reactions to the arrangement of single tables seem to vary widely; some libraries use an informal, even an apparently haphazard, layout of tables, which might appear to embody all possible disadvantages, but they find it is popular with students. Experiment is easy. Complications can arise in such a situation if individual table lighting is to be provided and computer terminals are to be used. Floor sockets will be needed, and if flexibility is also required this will mean a network of electric supply conduits in the floor with sockets perhaps at intervals as frequent as 1400 mm (4 ft 6 in) – a very expensive provision. If the floor is carpeted, carpet plugs will be needed to block sockets that are not in use. This arrangement is used in the Birmingham Central Library on a very large scale, but the growing need for wiring for terminals complicates the matter further. If the tables are to be at right angles to a wall then the problem can be easily and neatly solved by running trunking both for power and other wires along the wall at table-top height.

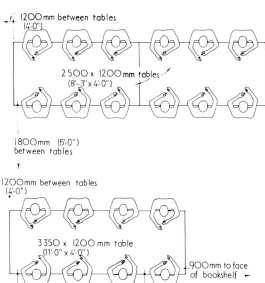

1200 mm between tables
(4'-0")

2500 x 1200 mm tables
(8'-3" x 4'-0")

1800 mm (6'-0")
between tables

1200 mm between tables
(4'-0")

3350 x 1200 mm table
(11'-0" x 4'-0")

900 mm to face
of bookshelf

1800 (6'-0")   1200 – 2100 (4'-0"-7'-10")
between tables   to face of bookshelf

1200 mm between tables
(4'-0")

3350 x 600mm table
(11'-0" x 2'-0")

1200 (4'-0")
between tables

15:4. Minimum dimensions for six-person and eight-person reading tables, and (below) for single-sided table for four persons

Dual tables

If without a centre division, dual tables with readers facing each other appear to have little to offer except the freedom of one reader to expand into the space not occupied by the other reader; this can lead to friction when the second reader arrives. A centre division prevents this overlap, for good or ill; it gives a feeling of privacy if the division is high enough to block the view ahead and prevent unwanted eye contact: if it does not do this it has little to commend it except that it can give a built-in bookrest. Although this latter idea has been out of fashion for some years, it has optical advantages in that a book on a flat surface is more tiring to read than one at an appropriate angle. Dunne[3] says, inter alia, 'For a reader sitting upright a range of bookrest angles from 50° to 61½° is needed, positioned so that the height of the bottom of the book can be varied from 260 mm to 400 mm (10¼ ins to 15¾ ins) below the level of the reader's eye.'

On a dual table with a centre division, local lighting can be installed; this allows a reader to control his own lighting (a very popular provision), but there is always the danger that light will shine into the eyes of the reader opposite. On the whole, dual tables are no more successful than other such compromises.

15:5. Minimum dimensions for a six-person reading table in an alcove

Long tables

These are certainly the most economical in use of space, but not outstandingly so because access aisles need to be wider. They have the advantage that, when the tables are not fully occupied, readers may spread their books into unused spaces. Long tables can be more solidly constructed and are consequently steadier. It is always a temptation to an architect to stipulate long regular tables, which look so much neater and more logical on a floor plan. These gains have to be balanced against readers' reluctance to sit in rows in what they may think of as school conditions; certainly it is noticeable that readers prefer separate seating when it is available. Long-table seating also has the disadvantage that the arrival and departure of readers seriously disturbs other readers' concentration.

Long tables can accommodate from four to twelve readers. Four is a reasonable number which avoids the feeling of regimentation but leads to a pleasant and flexible

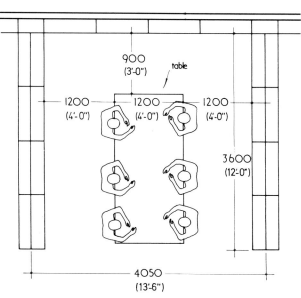

900
(3'-0")

table

1200   1200   1200
(4'-0")   (4'-0")   (4'-0")

3600
(12'-0")

4050
(13'-6")

15:6. Individual tables with their own lighting, overlooking the library floor. Always very popular with readers

layout. It also enables newcomers to go to an empty seat from either side. The width should not be less than 1200 mm (4 ft) and the lateral space allowance between readers never less than 900 mm (3 ft). Space between parallel tables should not be less than 1800 mm (6 ft), but it is possible to have 1500 mm (5 ft) spacing when shorter tables are used. Seating should never be allowed at the end of such tables.

Long tables can have centre divisions, but again it is difficult to see why unless the divisions are high enough to prevent readers catching the eye of the person opposite. The divisions can accommodate lighting fittings as well as providing jack points for audio-visual equipment. In such cases it would be better to have individual side divisions also in order to give some visual separation. When chairs are chosen they should be tested against the tables with which they are to be used. If the chairs have arms (and some readers have a strong preference for these) the chairs must fit easily under the table-tops.

Special tables

Almost inevitably some tables will have to be designed to meet special circumstances, for example the map-tracing table, which has a square of clouded glass let into the surface and lit from below. Archives (especially archive sorting) can require especially large tables with hard-wearing surfaces. A normal requirement today is for tables on which microform reading machines and VDUs will be used. To provide one or two of these, perhaps in carrels, was the practice of yesterday, but the stage has been reached when these are part of the normal equipment of a library and readers should be able to use them wherever they happen to be studying, not in some tucked-away corner. Users of these machines will need space for note-taking, and any table used in this way should be individual and longer than the usual ones, say 1250 × 750 mm (4 ft × 2 ft 6 in). This means an overall space allowance of 2.8 m^2 (30 sq. ft). Even so, the space left after the machine has been housed is small and it would be helpful to have pull-out panels or bracket-supported swivel tablets for note-taking. This will be an extra expense but the alternatives are carrels or much larger tables in quantity.

Such space allowances may be acceptable for the use of small viewing machines, but with the coming of

inter-active terminals accessing local or network bases, the larger keyboards of some personal computers, and above all printers, work-stations are needed. The choice of these is conditioned by what is on the market for a given system, but a possibility not to be ignored is the 1250 mm (4 ft) square table on wheels (lockable), which gives more flexibility in planning. Normally the overall space allowance for a workstation should be at least 4.5 m^2 (50 sq. ft).

It must not be forgotten also that if provision is to be made for more readers to use terminals, then either fewer readers than before can be seated or the total space available for readers will have to be increased. This can be an argument for increasing the size of the library.

In circumstances where it is necessary for general furniture to be constructed locally, design must be preceded by a study of what the highly organized computer technology industry has to offer. Tables for terminals must be specially chosen or planned; turntables giving tilt or swivel facilities are necessary where terminals are consulted by many different readers, for example as the main access to the library's on-line catalogue. It is pathetic to see readers having to bend to read screens when in search of quick information.

Because readers are individuals they have their own preferences for tables at which to study; perhaps they may have different preferences at different times and certainly when with different company. In an open-plan library particularly, it makes sense to meet their wishes. In one of the best-planned of British university libraries, Nottingham, there are four-seater open rectangular tables, circular ones, some free-standing semi-carrels and some more enclosed but still free-standing carrels, usually placed beside the vertical slit windows. The position of all these can be changed in a moment (preferably by the staff!). Cohen[4] tells us that readers tend to stake out their territory on four-seater tables; as they are unable to do this on circular tables they tend to be more gregarious and to converse.

Public libraries cater for all age groups, but it is reasonable to assume that the great bulk of users of academic libraries will be in their late teens and early twenties. The tendencies noted in undergraduates (those who like to be alone, those who are gregarious and those who vary between these trends from day to day) are not likely to apply in public libraries, where readers are of all kinds and are less predictable. The users of reference libraries in large central public libraries may have very different habits and desires from those in small suburban branch libraries: the local milieu has to be known and studied – one of the facets which makes public library work so fascinating. To take a simple example, students who have been working hard may like to relax in deep armchairs, and this can be a reasonable provision in academic libraries; but such chairs can be unpopular with elderly people, who may find it very difficult to get out of them. Design by age group may be a practical necessity. In public libraries there seems to be no limit to the different types which have to be catered for; and the proportion of the disabled will be higher and has to be taken into consideration.

Bright ideas are still possible. In the Central Library of Newcastle upon Tyne the tables are made up in threes, that is, two tables linked by a table-top. This reduces the number of table legs and also makes it possible to echelon (i.e. stagger) the table-tops, thus hindering the lateral spread of books and other material used by readers and achieving the effect of partitioning without the expense. This sounds complicated but seems to work well.

Large tables are often placed in bookcase alcoves, but

there is a serious disadvantage that readers wishing to use the books will disturb those working; it is particularly difficult to consult the bottom shelves when someone is seated at a table close behind. Circular tables should never be used for serious study. It has been my experience that the most popular of all reader seating is a single table with its own separately controllable table light, looking over the edge of a balcony on to a busy working floor beneath. In libraries in many countries I have observed that these are always the first to be occupied.

Carrels

These individual study rooms are necessary where serious workers need to be undisturbed and where they require the uninterrupted use of certain books for long periods. 'Long' is a relative term; such rooms may be reserved for readers for periods ranging from a day to a term. They may be equipped with typewriters, microform readers, television and video receivers and terminals, or users may bring their own machines, including personal computers. Power points for all such machines will certainly be needed, as well as wiring for audio-visual links and network connections. When planning carrels it is advantageous to have ducting, to take both power and low-current wiring, running along the walls at table-top height. The carrels will be lockable (although staff will have master keys) and will have a cupboard (possibly lockable) in which books can be kept in safety when they are not in use; but the library staff must have a record of the books and the right (and a key) to take them away if they are needed elsewhere. A coat-hanging fitment should be provided. If manuscript searches are to take place in the carrel, a washbasin might be needed, but then the provision begins to look like a small office. An inspection window (often a vertical slit) is desirable, if only because staff should be able to check that all is well. Carrels must be sound-proofed where possible, because the whole point is to provide study places away from the noise and bustle of other areas; it is helpful to have a group of carrels isolated from other reading areas and approached from a separate corridor. This, although space-consuming, has advantages. It is helpful if the carrels can be isolated from the library and have a separate approach for use after library hours. The size of carrels will vary, according to type of use, from 1500 × 1225 mm (5 × 4 ft) to 2450 × 3650 mm (8 × 12 ft) – the latter are virtually private offices. A good compromise is 1700 × 2100 mm (6 ft 10 in × 5 ft 7 in), which gives 3.6 m² (38.5 sq ft). 1500 × 2500 mm (5 × 8 ft) gives almost the 4 m² (40 sq ft) which is often recommended, but this seems generous unless a bookcase is to be installed; and it will certainly be needed if a full work-station is to be provided.

Closed carrels should be examined in other libraries; small enclosed spaces can be unpleasantly claustrophobic, and special attention must be given to the size of windows, the heating, lighting and particularly the air supply. Openable windows are not recommended: even if there is no air-conditioning to be affected, it is not reasonable to have the possibility of a fully open window in unsupervised conditions.

Because carrels are planned for people who are working seriously and need privacy (and as their use can be confined to such people) it hardly makes sense to provide a carrel unless the working surface is adequate for the tasks to be performed. The tables should be 1200 mm (4 ft) long and at least 600 mm (2 ft), preferably 750 mm (2½ ft) deep, clear of any bookcases, which may be fixed from table-level upwards and which will require another 225 mm (9 in). This is usually better than separate bookcases

15:7. Carrels off separate corridor

15:8. Possible carrel size, leaving room for bookcase use

15:9. Recommended minimum dimensions for four-person carrel room

15:10. Suggested arrangement for open carrels in bookshelf area

standing on the floor, which tend to enlarge the carrels unnecessarily. Again because carrels are for more serious study, double (or quadruple) person carrels seem to be a nonsense, popular as they are with couples or small groups. Closed carrels are spatially uneconomic; they serve few readers and they reduce the quantity (and often the quality) of nearby space available for the majority of seated readers. They are a form of privilege, and to provide them needs a serious policy decision.

Nevertheless the carrel has great psychological advantages for readers, and the demand is invariably greater than the supply. To meet this demand various compromises have been devised:

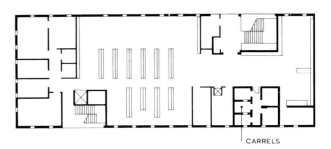

CARRELS

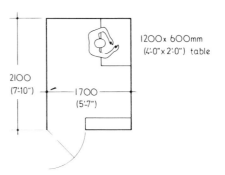

1200 × 600mm (4'-0" × 2'-0") table

2100 (7'-10")

1700 (5'-7")

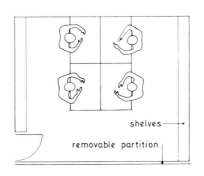

shelves

removable partition

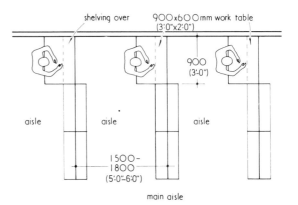

shelving over   900×600mm work table (3'-0"×2'-0")

900 (3'-0")

aisle   aisle   aisle

1500 – 1800 (5'-0"–6'-0")

main aisle

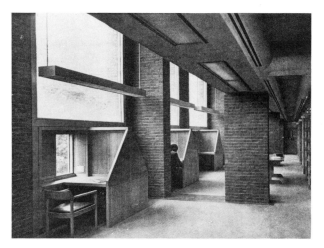

15:11. Leicester University Library

15:12. Free-standing semi-carrels, one to each slit window (Nottingham University Library)

1. Individual tables in book-lined alcoves: the reader is likely to be disturbed when other readers consult books housed there, and this is a serious disadvantage.
2. Individual tables, shielded or not, against window walls or attached to shelving rows: users of these tables will be disturbed less than those on bookcase alcoves, particularly if the tables are set at a slight angle to the window/wall.
3. Double or quadruple carrels, staggered so that the users are separated. Carrels such as these with shapes forming a cross to a swastika are also offered by manufacturers of library systems and because they can be dismantled and moved – some can even be stored flat when not in use – they are a valuable aid to flexibility. All commercial open carrels should be studied with care to help decide what degree of privacy is to be given; to face into a three-sided screen with one's back to human movement is far from perfect.

Naturally these compromises call for different allocations: Havard-Williams[5] suggests that a table of 1225 × 600 mm (4 × 2 ft) with a total cubicle area of 1525 × 1225 mm (5 × 4 ft) is acceptable.

Study table heights

A number of British Standards (particularly BS 3893 of 1965,[6] which is being revised) deal with anatomical, physiological and anthropometric considerations in the design of office furniture, including desks and chairs for machine operators. These generally recommend a table-top height of between 700 mm and 760 mm (28 in and 30 in). Van Buren[7] says 686 mm (27 in), Havard-Williams[8] 762 mm (30 in) with a kneehole height of not less than 635 mm (25 in). The standard height for a typing surface is 630 mm (25 in) to 650 mm (26 in). Experience in many countries leads me to recommend that 690 mm (27 in) is the most comfortable, but it is essential that local practice is studied. The needs of the disabled have to be given special consideration here (see p. 135). The minimum table-top height for wheelchair users is 660 mm (26 in), so the heights recommended above will be suitable. Table legs should always be about 150 mm (6 in) from ends of tables.

Chair heights

These need little comment, because they are a common factor in public buildings and the architect will have his own source of standards. Van Buren says they should be

430 mm (17 in) high, Havard-Williams says 460 mm (18 in); naturally there will be different requirements in school and children's libraries according to the age groups using them. Again architects and librarians must remember that people are of different average height in different parts of the world. International standards which emanate from Europe or the United States may be quite inappropriate in parts of Asia or Africa. Local architects will know.

Chairs which are normally used in lecture rooms may need tablets for note-taking and these can either be fitted permanently or be removable. Providing for left-handed users is a complication which the latter avoids, because they are not a permanent part of the chair. The tablets can be rigid or swivelling; the rigid ones are cheaper, but those which swivel are more convenient to use.

Browsing areas

Almost every type of library will need at least one area where readers can sit in relaxing and informal surroundings. In public, hospital and welfare libraries this will be a major requirement; the necessary amount of such provision in academic libraries will be indicated in the statement of aims. A college librarian may wish to attract students by having a lounge with reclining chairs where popular periodicals may be read. This should be spelled out clearly in the brief, because it is different from providing reclining chairs in the major current periodicals area (a growing practice which tends to limit the space for the serious study of periodicals). If the librarian really means to combine (or confuse) periodical reading with flopping in deep chairs, this can easily be planned. Other librarians feel that these activities are the province of the students' union building and waste valuable study space in libraries. They believe that the need is for formal study conditions and access to study materials. Perhaps the best way is to have only a few soft-seated chairs in a colourful area which can be used as a contrast to, and a break from, study in more spartan conditions.

In public lending and hospital patients' libraries the requirement will be for those users who have made a preliminary choice of books from the shelves and then wish to sit in comfort for a short time while they evaluate their selection. It could also be that the local community needs a place where people can spend an hour or two in comfort 'having a quiet read'. These are really two different needs; it is certainly possible for the architect to design one area for both purposes, but he should know that there are two purposes. It is only by analysing the problem that layout, decoration and furniture can be used to produce a good solution; too often a square of carpet and a few low soft chairs covered in a bright fabric, placed in a space that was otherwise unusable, have been regarded as the answer.

Questions to be asked are: how long is a reader expected to stay in the chairs? What is he to do there – read, write, relax, sleep? These questions will help the designer to know what and what not to provide if students are to be discouraged from working in this area, then tables can be designed at a height inconvenient for that purpose (e.g. 'coffee tables'). If readers must not sleep there, why provide deep upholstered lounge chairs which are so soporific? Is the intention really to reproduce a 'home' atmosphere? If not, then the need for body-support in comfort does not always have to be met by providing lounge chairs which may be difficult for an elderly person to use. If the intention is to have a somewhat less relaxed atmosphere then chairs can have tablet fittings so that note-taking can accompany reading.

The browsing area of a public library will be close to the books and preferably in an oasis of quiet. A school library may make a notational division by using low bookcases as a visual break between areas, and by change of decoration and floor covering. If small discussion groups have to be arranged, it is better to have a separate room for the purpose than to have part of the library acquire the air of a seminar room.

The layout of chairs in an academic library's informal reading area is more important than it may seem. Is conversation to be encouraged, tolerated or banned? If chairs are grouped in circles (or can be moved to form circles) talk sessions will inevitably result. If this is unwelcome, the chairs can be fixed into a less hospitable relationship, or be built into fitments. If total informality, including uninhibited conversation, is the aim there need be no chairs at all: children and students are very happy with carpeted or cushioned steps round an area of sunken floor – the average reader might even take to the idea.

Clearances

Figure 15:13 shows minimum clearances necessary between tables, furniture and bookcases in informal reading areas. Because readers will choose books from the shelves, and because trolley access will be needed, the layout of both study tables and casual seating needs careful consideration if congestion is to be avoided at peak times.

Subject or media departments

Large libraries will provide separate divisions for a number of special services which require more than the usual allowance of space for book stacks, reading tables and chairs. These include:

1. *Art departments* where facilities for working with graphic materials call for large tables and, if paints are used, impervious floors and nearby washing facilities.
2. *Music departments* with sound-proof performing and practice rooms, often supplied with pianos or other large instruments.
3. *Oral history rooms* with recording equipment and good acoustics.
4. *Local history departments* with lockable cases, reading slopes for the consultation of old newspapers, and full facilities for film and video viewing.
5. *Audio-visual departments* with a very wide range of media, and full wiring provided for a number of machines to be in use simultaneously: audio-video booths fitted with video, disc, cassette and CD play-back facilities are becoming common.
6. *Archive departments*, especially in university and public libraries; for the equipping of these departments recourse must be made to professional archivists.

Even the ubiquitous reference department may have to house its specialist materials in fast-service fitments (such

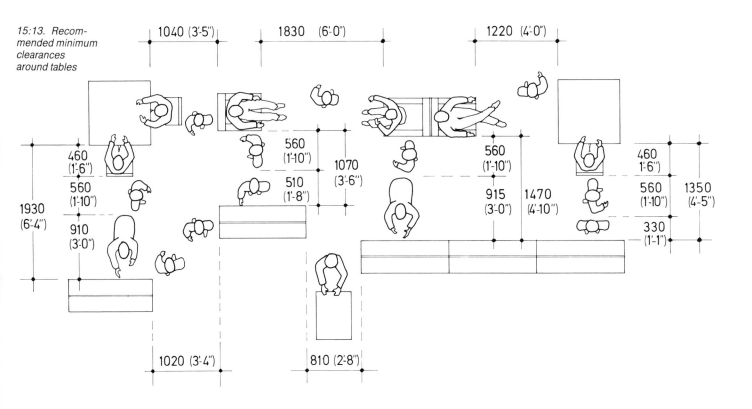

15:13. Recommended minimum clearances around tables

1040 (3'-5") 1830 (6'-0") 1220 (4'-0")

460 (1'-6") 560 (1'-10") 510 (1'-8") 1070 (3'-6") 560 (1'-10") 915 (3'-0") 1470 (4'-10") 460 1'-6" 560 (1'-10") 1350 (4'-5") 330 (1'-1")

1930 (6'-4") 910 (3'-0")

1020 (3'-4") 810 (2'-8")

as directories or dictionaries on revolving stands for easy access). It is impossible to generalize on the space layouts and allowances, for they will all differ widely. The important point is that the special furniture and equipment to be used has to be visualized, sketched to scale or plotted by placing cut-outs on a floor plan, estimating the space needed and the traffic routes which can be expected. If the facility is to be a new one the librarian must take full responsibility for planning ahead; solutions are not difficult to provide as long as real needs are recorded in the brief.

Other rooms

Colleges, universities and some schools will need group reading rooms, seminar rooms and even rooms for discussions. These can be furnished flexibly with groups of standard-sized 600 × 900 mm (2 × 3 ft) tables placed together to form larger units according to need. Walls of these rooms can also be shelved and the dimensions will be similar to those in a six-person reading alcove (see p. 162). Alternatively rooms can be created in open-stack libraries within systems stacking; such use of light partitions gives the advantage that they can be enlarged, reduced or placed in other parts of the stack as experience dictates. The use of demountable study kiosks for group use gives a very flexible use of space but, unless well thought out, can be visually hampering for the rest of the room.

Reader service areas

All libraries need prominently sited centres from which staff can give certain essential services. In multi-storey or sectionalized libraries such a centre may be needed for each major division.

The centres will have three main functions:

1. Control of the issue and return of books.
2. Supervision of user activities and security.
3. Bibliographical assistance to readers.

15:14. Simple bottleneck counter: one person can operate this at quiet periods, controlling both entrance and exit and having visual supervision of the library

15:15. Bottleneck counter separating returned books from open areas. At busy times three staff are needed (including an enquiries service). At quieter times two are enough (one for in-counter, one for out-counter). At very quiet times, one alone in the centre section can carry out all functions

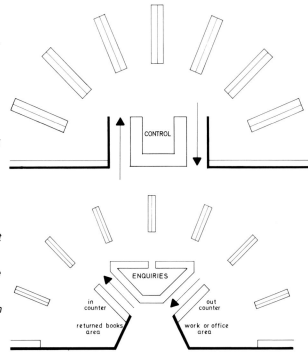

Issue and return of books

These will take place in a number of complicated patterns, but the place will be generally referred to as a 'counter'. The counter's size depends largely on the issue system in use; some academic libraries need elaborate issue methods to allow books and reader information to be searched in more than one way, so the space required at the counter can be large. This applies to a lesser degree to all busy libraries using card-and-ticket systems (such as Browne), but when planning for the future it is vital that the librarian bears in mind the requirements of more sophisticated systems. For this reason counters should wherever possible be sectional and free-standing, with provision of both electric power and low current wiring to allow for a future computer system.

The two functions of the counter, issue and return, require two separate traffic routes and it is obviously more efficient if the two routes can be kept apart. An island counter which stands between the two streams offers staffing economy and is the only possible answer in many small libraries, but it has psychological disadvantages for the staff; only severe discipline can keep it looking tidy.

In a busy library the receipt and issue of books will take place at separate desks. The issue desk need be no more than a simple top to hold the issue recording equipment. In the Browne system this will be only a date stamp and a tray to hold tickets but in computerized systems there will be either a hand-held scanner or one built flush into the table top, usually with a terminal to confirm that the operation has been completed. In some systems this can also validate the loan so that the reader is free to pass the security screen, but in others a separate activating device and a procedure for bypassing the screen have to be installed (see Chapter 12).

The return counter will be more elaborate: it needs

1. Space for staff to receive returned books, do the necessary recording and perhaps receive fines.
2. Space for loan records; in modern methods this can be small, just a hand-held scanner, or it can be built flush into the counter, with a terminal to handle the transaction. The Browne or other ticket-and-card method can require as much as 6 m (20 ft) of counter space.
3. Room for housing and movement of trolleys, if used to return books to the shelves.
4. Shelving for books to be retained at the counter: this is of several kinds. Sometimes reserved books are held here awaiting collection. In 'delayed discharge' systems, books have to be put aside for checking against a file of reservations; this calls for either a very large shelving allocation or, much better, a shelving room or behind-the-scenes sorting area (see 'Shelving rooms' below). In all systems, shelving is needed to hold books which may need physical attention before being returned to the shelves.
5. Cupboards and drawers for stationery; there may be space for these under the counter-top.
6. It is important to allow room for the maximum number of staff required at peak times; stools or chairs should be provided so that they can rest a little between rushes of business.

The comments and diagrams which follow will seem childishly simple for experienced librarians, but those who are not thoroughly familiar with the sequences of operations may find that a statement of basic principles can help in the planning of even the most complicated counter; considerable experience world-wide has taught me that every day 'beginners' are thrown into positions where they must make drastic decisions on new libraries. Moreover the design of counters is often very poorly thought out, especially by people who are not really sure what is to go on there. The architect can use his skills in producing interesting shapes and using unusual covering materials (so long as the top is hard-wearing), but it is the functional layout which is vital.

In small single-room libraries there will be only one counter, and as it will be the only staffed service point its position and shape will be of particular importance. In rather larger single-room libraries the all-purpose counter was traditionally placed to create a bottleneck for security reasons. For staffing economy it was an island placed to allow supervision of the whole room. This method dominated small public lending library design for many years. When pressure of readers increased and more staff had to be used, it gave way to a division of functions, with separate issue and return counters, the centre being usable for readers' enquiries. Both these layouts developed from 'safeguarded open access' and made possible lockable wicket gates across entrance and exit for greater security, but they produced a forbidding atmosphere and gave way to a freer layout of an unguarded entrance with counters placed deep within the room.

The relative emphasis on security on the one hand and an atmosphere of freedom on the other are for the librarian to assess. In some libraries, because of heavy book losses, it has become necessary to return to fully safeguarded exits, involving in many cases the installation of lockable wickets and/or theft-detection devices. This can mean layout decisions. If the basis of protection against theft is to be an electronic detection device, then it makes sense for it to be placed across the main exit. With this in operation the counter is freed of the security function and can be placed deeper in the room, where it can be associated with the short-loan book service or with the enquiries centre. (See Chapter 12.)

When planning layouts the basic considerations will be security, economy of staffing and expected reader traffic routes, but the interior design has still to be visualized at all times from the aesthetic viewpoint. What the reader sees as he enters the library matters enormously and this must be taken as seriously as the practical considerations. In the architect's preliminary sketches particular attention will be paid also to placing of enquiry desks, catalogues in whatever form they may be, and collections of bibliographies. The access routes to any area which may be under the supervision of the main control, for example children's libraries or reading rooms, will need special consideration. Libraries which serve separate classes of readers simultaneously need to be carefully planned, because to the usual priorities of security and economy of staffing is added separation between the two or more services. A good example is the library for a large hospital which serves medical staff, technicians and patients. Figure 15:17, reproduced here by kind permission of Mona Going from her standard book on hospital libraries,[9] shows how this is done in a combined library in Britain.

Examples of typical control layouts are to be seen in many books; Wheeler and Githens[10] in particular carried out an elaborate survey of American public library buildings, distinguishing a large number of various types and their relative advantages and disadvantages. Mevissen[11] gives examples of simple alternatives and also compares in detail four common counter placings.

Counter design

The detailed design of the counter is of great importance to the library because of the critical operations which take place there. The range of tasks is small but because they will be repeated hundreds of thousands (perhaps millions) of times annually a full method study of these operations must be made before counter design is begun. Such an operation should be carried out by a method study officer in close cooperation with the librarian, rather than by the librarian himself.

If all the different control operations for a small library are to be the work of a single member of the staff, the counter must be planned so that minimum movement is needed between operations. Figure 15:18 shows the maximum counter size which can be controlled by one person without unnecessary, and therefore tiring, movements.

Counters with special labour-saving fitments – sliding trays, circular revolving tray-holders, and so on – were common in the 1930s and are still offered by manufacturers specializing in library furniture. Most of these gadgets have long been abandoned because they were too inflexible to meet changing demands, but bright ideas are still needed.

When examining drawings, especially at the detail design stage, the librarian must give great attention to those of the counter because errors in planning counters (and desks) can affect the efficiency (and the comfort) of staff who will spend many thousands of working hours there. Seating heights, kneehole space, drawer clearances, positioning of handles and many other details must be checked. Operations should be simulated on existing equipment to make sure that the counter is efficient in human engineering terms. Time spent on this study will be repaid many times over.

Library equipment manufacturers offer complete counters. Some of these can be constructed from unit components similar to those used for the rest of the library equipment and will therefore fit well into the general appearance of the room. Terrapin Reska counters have a seated height of 700 mm or a standing height of 960 mm, both adjustable 20 mm by glides.

Librarians will have their own views about the need for special fitments such as rails or shelves along the front of the counter just below the working top to hold cases or shopping bags while readers are being served, but the absolute essentials are the right height to suit both readers and staff (best decided by measuring satisfactory furniture already in use) and a hard-wearing surface. The wear caused by books sliding across the top many thousands of times is greater than some architects can be induced to believe. Hard plastic laminates are certainly the best material here: to use vinyls and linos is not reasonable. Wood is the most attractive in traditional library environments, but the surface may have to be renewed at intervals and this can be inconvenient as well as expensive. No attributes other than durability and easy cleaning are required, and laminates are obtainable in attractive patterns and colours, including simulated wood surfaces. Similar attention should be paid to other parts of the counter which are liable to be handled constantly; light wood soon darkens in these conditions unless it really can be wiped clean.

Moving books

The greatest weakness in counter design has been the lack of attention to ways of handling expeditiously the very large number of books which come in at peak times. Books

15:16. Different counter positions in two single-room branch-libraries

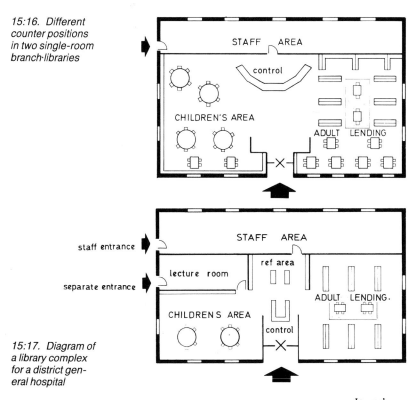

15:17. Diagram of a library complex for a district general hospital

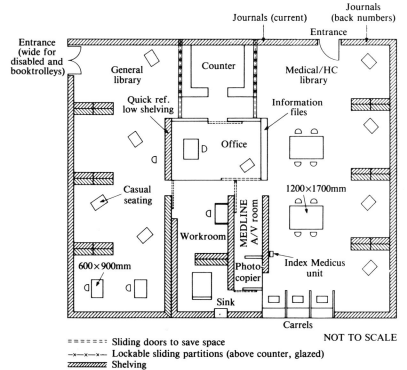

NOT TO SCALE

====== Sliding doors to save space
—x—x—x— Lockable sliding partitions (above counter, glazed)
////////// Shelving
Appropriate glazing of doors and walls for
supervision from counter, office and workroom

15:18. Maximum counter area usable conveniently by one person

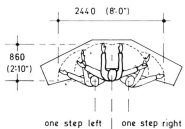

can be loaded at once onto shelving trolleys, which should fit into the counter itself and not stand in the way of working staff; but at peak times trolley loading and dispersing can be a disturbing and time-consuming operation. In very small libraries it is common for the trolleys when full to be placed outside the counter so that they can act as display shelves (and readers in fact do some of the book dispersal), but in a library of any size this is a step towards chaos.

For conveying books to a position from which they can be shelved by hand, the usual library trolley will be used. These are generally made with a slight slope on each side so that titles can easily be sorted into order: they serve a dual purpose in housing a ready-made display of books which have been newly returned to the library. While stationary, this trolley will have a foot-operated lock applied to the wheels. A more sophisticated version uses an arrangement of trolleys which form behind-counter shelving; books can be roughly sorted on to the four or six shelves of which the trolley is formed. When the trolley shelves are full they can be rolled out to the appropriate shelving bay, where the loaded shelves themselves are latched onto a special frame to form display shelving of returned books appropriate to that sequence. Many proprietary trolleys are available. Attention must be paid to their stability and the ease with which they can be pushed, particularly over carpets; the size and type of the castors are critical. As always, the exact function must be identified before a decision is made.

For books in boxes and, to a lesser extent, large books (such as bound periodicals) piled in heaps, the transport trolley is used. Here a flat and wide shelf is an obvious priority.

For hospital wards where bedridden patients need to be able to choose from a selection of titles, a special trolley is necessary. It must be light enough to be handled for long periods and over long distances, stand stable and be narrow enough to pass between beds. The angle at which the books stand on the trolley must be appropriate for choice by a patient who may be lying quite flat in bed.

Future developments include a motorized trolley for use in large libraries and hospitals where distances between wards can be considerable. The Hospitals and Handicapped Readers Group of the Library Association has done good work on this project, and *UNESCO Bulletin*[12] illustrated an electric trolley with two small revolving bookcases on a low carriage which enables bedridden patients to choose without having to stretch; but nothing more seems to have come of it. For those who have the energy and expertise, trolleys can be designed in-house for specific tasks. This has been done to great effect in the Alexandra Library Building, the State Library of Western Australia, but generally construction of such small quantities will make them expensive.

For the use of mothers accompanied by small children in a lending library there is a trolley which includes space for both books and a child, and this enables the mother to carry books around in comfort while keeping the child out of harm's way; another less elaborate one is designed for the disabled.

Whatever method is used, the operation of receiving books and placing them somewhere for disposal without disturbing the basic task of serving the next reader must be performed thousands of times a day. Two ideas which have been used are described below.

The book box A large box (say 750 mm (2 ft 6 in) square) stands close to the receiving position. Its top is a spring-loaded platform on which books are placed; under the growing load the platform sinks to make space for more. As the books are removed the platform rises so that the load is always at a height convenient for lifting. This method will be used only in small libraries where sudden peaks of use occur, for example when classes visit a school library and where lulls can be used to clear the accumulated books.

A conveyor belt can be used to take books to an adjoining sorting room. Early examples of this idea involved a travelling belt behind the assistant and parallel to the counter, so that the assistant had to turn round to place books on the belt. A later development placed the belt at right angles to the assistant; in Figure 15:20 it is between two assistants so that at busy times both positions can be manned, books dispatched without undue effort and the area kept uncluttered. Naturally this can only be arranged when the in-counter has no other function.

To place the sorting area in a basement and send the books down on a chute may be neat and labour-saving for the counter staff, but it will cause extra work in sending the books back from the basement to the eventual shelving area, even if lifts are used. If the counter is an island and a chute impossible, books can be sent on a belt to another area by using an underfloor conveyor. Unless such a system or a sorting area is used, there will inevitably be the problem of disposing of large numbers of books which, either on trolleys or carried by assistants, will continually cross the traffic flow of readers. This is a major and too little considered operational hazard which reduces the efficiency of some recent libraries with centrally placed return counters.

Some university and college libraries have to retain, close to the counter, short-loan collections, that is books which are in very great demand and which can be loaned for only very short periods, sometimes as little as two or three hours. To provide shelving for these books at the counter itself can be an embarrassment. One ingenious expedient has been to place two counters in tandem in a bottleneck area. Much more common in universities is for the issue-and-return counter to form a barrier to closed shelves, which often include short-loan stock. This can be efficient but it is very often unsightly because the proximity of the shelves tempts staff to dump 'queries' and 'awaitings' on the nearby shelves. The inevitable mess and debris of a busy library's operations ought to be kept out of sight as much as possible.

The problem can be made worse when terminals have been added to the existing equipment of an issue-and-return counter for answering reader enquiries; almost invariably the staff will find themselves explaining computer operations and limitations to readers. All these matters form a severe visual drawback to many university counters and can give an impression of muddle. My

15:19. Book box designed by Library Design and Engineering Ltd for the American School in London

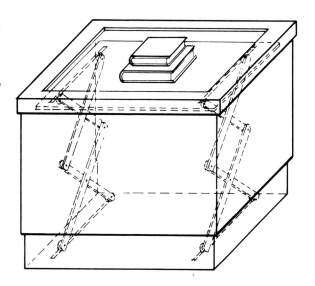

15:20. Plan of counter and sorting room

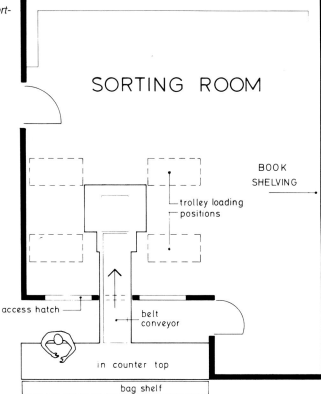

15:21. Handy position for small short-loan collection

15:22. Short-loan stock shelved in closed stack

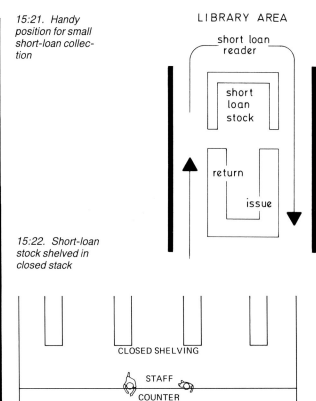

experience is that, once the architect has grasped the full range and frequency of operations, he is much better at designing a layout than the librarian is. It is a question of the trained eye against the long familiarity of working practice. The best answer is for a notional diagram and a written explanation of the counter's requirements to be produced by the librarian (or, much better, by the counter staff), followed by the preparation of sketches by the architect and the careful study of those sketches by the staff concerned.

Assistance to readers

Enquiry desk

In all except the smallest libraries there will be a separate desk manned by professional staff to give bibliographical assistance in response to readers' requests. The design of the desk may seem simple enough, but it will benefit from a method study of the operations which are to take place there. Certain essential books must be close at hand and the physical relationship with the reader is important: if readers usually stand, at what height should the adviser sit? If the reader is to be seated too (at any rate during lengthy enquiries), is it better for the adviser to face him across a desk, or would the relationship be easier if they sat side by side? If there is a desk-top VDU, is it to be seen by the reader or not? Too often one finds a student craning his neck and leaning over the counter to see what the assistant librarian is reading on the screen.

An obvious development of the growth of demand is that more readers' advisers will be needed, so the area should be planned to allow space for the maximum numbers of both staff and readers who will meet there.

The position of the desk will differ according to the type of library but it should always be close to the catalogue and to the main bibliographical tools; in a single-room library it will be in a position which allows a control view complementary to that of the counter.

In large libraries the placing of the desk will be a much more complex matter. Before deciding on the layout the librarian should try to put himself in the place of the potential user of the bibliographical services. This user must be led to the area by clear signs and must find before him visual guides to the catalogue and other tools. He will consult the bibliographies and catalogue and then go to the shelves. If he cannot find the book he wants he will go to the assistance centre, the readers' adviser's desk.

This desk may have to accommodate some of the following operations in addition to that of giving biblio-graphical advice:

1. Reserving books which are out on loan, and handing them over when they have arrived back; this necessitates space for books to be held (and possibly locked up) while awaiting collection by the reader.
2. Retrieving books from closed stacks and returning them to the stacks after use.
3. The photocopying service, which in research libraries can be a very large undertaking. Except where there are nearby photocopiers (operated by staff, contracting firms or self- (coin-)operated), this means taking the book the reader has selected to a photocopying point, receiving the book back with the copy and delivering the copy to the reader. Filling in forms may be necessary for copyright reasons, as well as the receipt of money in payment. If a photocopy has to be provided from a book in closed stack the procedure also involves having the book traced and transferred to the photo-copy centre. These activities alone show that the placing of such a point for efficient service can mean a

relationship with a document delivering system, a stack retrieval system and a book transfer system. Even if do-it-yourself photocopying machines are at hand, there will be many items which cannot be reproduced on these machines so that the book will have to go to a photographic section.

All these operations will take up space; again a method study and a well-thought-out traffic diagram are most valuable, not only for the layout and space allocation but also for the design of the often complex fitments.

The planning of such a central bibliographical service does not necessarily end the problem of assistance to readers. Subject departments, particularly on other floors, may need their own subject catalogues; with computer-produced catalogues there is likely to be at least one set on each floor, particularly if the library can afford service points in such departments. With a computer circulation system where the issue and return operations can take place in any or every department, this may be another duty of the readers' advisers' desks on each subject floor.

Catalogues

The catalogue is a most important piece of equipment. In small libraries it can be merely the record of the books in stock there, but if that library forms part of a system the catalogue may record the holdings of the whole system; in a research library dealing with information rather than books as such, it will be a major bibliographical tool which can be a valuable analysis of the contents of the literature on certain key subjects. In a library with a large closed stack the collection is completely inaccessible without the catalogue, which, if in card or sheaf form, will inevitably be very large. Sheaf catalogues are less used than card, chiefly because they take up more space and because revision is slower, but they have the great advantage that readers can remove the separate binders and use them at nearby tables, reducing congestion. The size of the slips in the binder can be 75 × 160 mm (3 × 6¼ in) or 125 × 200 mm (5 × 8 in). The smaller size is more often used in libraries, the binders being housed on shelves 100 mm (4 in) apart.

The traditional card catalogue is still used world-wide, despite the alternatives now available. It is either single or double-sided: cabinets with alternate rows of drawers facing in opposite directions can give a saving in depth of cabinet at the expensive of doubling the length. Because of the way in which readers consult the cards there are strict limits on the top and bottom height of thecabinet and thus on the number of drawers accommodated. Six drawers high is usually the maximum, and allowing 1000 cards per drawer and three cards per average book, one vertical row of drawers will represent only two thousand titles.

It is obviously an advantage if more drawers can be accommodated without inconveniencing readers. Figure 15:23 demonstrates that a seven-drawer unit is acceptable and even a ten-drawer unit, although in the latter case the reader will have to bend to consult the lower drawers.

Pull-out shelves, useful to aid note-taking, will increase the height, though only slightly. As bibliographies and the printed catalogues of major libraries are of great import-ance in searching, they will usually be kept together, and as they are always large volumes it can be convenient to house them below the runs of catalogue drawers. Some proprietary catalogue cabinets are offered in units where quite long runs of the vital bibliographies can be in a single long catalogue cabinet.

In a large library the catalogue will occupy a great deal of floor space – indeed some large libraries are being eaten up by their catalogues. A saving of open floor space can be achieved by having a single catalogue set against a wall, with the drawers designed to be removed and searched at special tables nearby. In such a case the drawers can start lower and continue higher, giving twelve vertical rows and, as readers do not have to stand immediately in front of the cabinets while using the catalogue, congestion is eased. The only disadvantages of such a scheme are that quick consultation for a single title is made more cumbersome and the great mass of the catalogue cabinet looks formidable.

When planning catalogue layout one should bear in mind that space will often be needed for staff to give introductory talks on the use of the catalogue to small groups of new readers.

Alternatively the drawers can be spread thinly along walls with books shelved above and below them, or as occasional tiers between tiers of books, but in a large library this is inflexible (except with some systems shelving methods) and will use up long wall runs; the method is better suited to small catalogues in separate subject rooms or to special libraries. On the European Continent separate catalogue rooms are often found, but these have not been generally adopted in Britain, partly because readers do not seem to like them and partly because they will be separated from the staff who offer bibliographical assistance. They will be found even less in future libraries.

Apart from these alternatives there is little choice in layout. The catalogues will be placed along walls or grouped in an area which they will entirely dominate. A large catalogue placed close to the bibliographies in research libraries (a collection of several hundred large volumes) produces a small library in itself. Because it must be used by readers of all subjects it is often associated with a collection of general reference books which are equally all-pervasive. The problem becomes one of planning a room that is conveniently placed *en route* to all departments and will hold perhaps 5000 books, most of them above normal size, with perhaps 18 m² (200 sq ft) of catalogues, with an effective reader's advisory service nearby and with space for very heavy use by readers. Little

seating is required, but shelves or narrow tables may have to be installed so that heavy bibliographies may be consulted. Because the great size of many card catalogue batteries themselves is limiting and because bibliographies are usually tall books, there can be little freedom in planning such a room.

For these reasons the practice has arisen in major libraries all over the world of planning a large 'catalogue hall', an open prime area leading off the entrance, entirely dominated by massive rows of card catalogue cabinets and with impressively large rows of bibliographies and reference books shelved around and between them. One of the greatest advantages the new technology brings is in freeing such an area for other functions. The massive card catalogue will no longer be a compulsory first step in the library for every reader. The problem of miniaturizing (almost certainly by computer techniques) the vast retrospective collections is only gradually being faced, but it would be irresponsible today to plan a large library without at least allowing for the use of the space which will be released in the future. The question is rather whether a library should opt for the technology at present easily available or go direct for the sophisticated on-line system, risking the hiccups which beset all developing systems. It is a serious decision to make: the long-term saving in space and freedom could revolutionize the operation of the library. Earlier efforts to end the space domination by these huge masses of card catalogues produced printed subject catalogues in book form, but most libraries have replaced them with computer-produced alternatives. The earlier ones, of which a widely used example was the computer print-out in large sheets bound like a book, took up less floor space but were most unattractive to use. The later computer-output-microfiche (COM) is very much smaller, but it is awkward to handle and individual fiche can be misplaced or stolen. This is not quite a disaster, because the COM (like the computer print-out) is expendable, in that a revised version replaces it every few weeks. Reading machines and display holders of COM are now to be found in libraries of all kinds – even small branch libraries. Their only space requirement is a table on which to stand the equipment, but in large libraries there must be a number of such machines and tables, because each machine serves

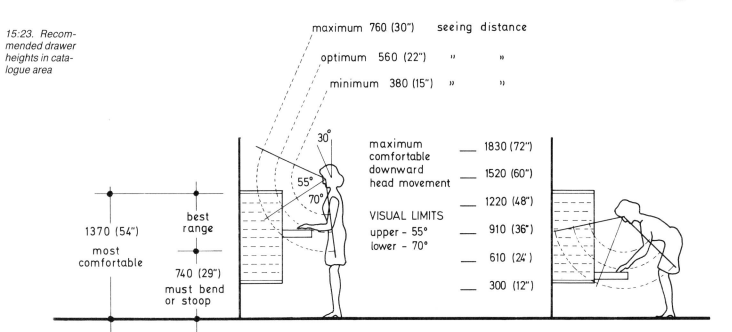

15:23. Recommended drawer heights in catalogue area

maximum 760 (30") seeing distance
optimum 560 (22") " "
minimum 380 (15") " "

30°
55°
70°

maximum comfortable downward head movement

VISUAL LIMITS
upper – 55°
lower – 70°

1830 (72")
1520 (60")
1220 (48")
910 (36")
610 (24')
300 (12")

1370 (54")
most comfortable

best range

740 (29")
must bend or stoop

15:24. Recommended minimum plan dimensions in card catalogue area

only one enquirer at a time. As the equipment is small (and not very expensive) it can be duplicated throughout the building, making the user of a subject department in a large library independent, almost for the first time, of a 'central catalogue hall'.

The change to on-line cataloguing which will be the trend in most libraries over the next few years will dramatically highlight the differences of operation. When information about the holdings of the entire library system (and whether the book is immediately available, reserved or even on order) is to be found easily from terminals placed all over the building, at branch libraries and even mobile libraries, then the role of the enquiry point has to be looked at in a different way. In universities with several floors it means, at the very least, a subject enquiry point with a terminal on each floor. In practice there will be limits: readers will be free to search the holdings of the library, probably a cooperative system and even a network, but it may be that access to outside databanks will be restricted, because of expense, to staff-controlled terminals. Much depends too on the development of security methods within the computer networks.

In large closed-access libraries (particularly national libraries) the fact that the catalogue is thus duplicated on several floors will increase the likelihood of requests for delivery of books from a central stack to any part of the reading areas: an expensive requirement. This is a matter which has been mentioned in the circulation section of the secondary brief and has also been considered under 'Outline planning' in Chapter 9.

The best answer is the directing (or, more politely, the encouragement) of readers to reading areas positioned near the stacks associated with the subject they require. This would reduce the delivery problem to a more manageable level.

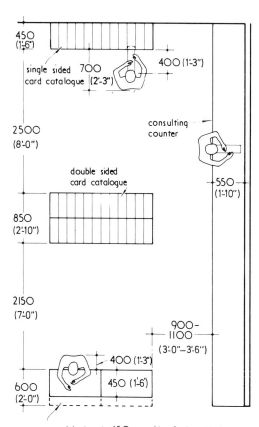

single sided card catalogue 700 (2'-3")
450 (1'-6")
400 (1'-3")
consulting counter
2500 (8'-0")
double sided card catalogue
850 (2'-10")
550 (1'-10")
2150 (7'-0")
900–1100 (3'-0"–3'-6")
600 (2'-0")
400 (1'-3")
450 (1'-6')

consulting bench: 450mm wide single sided
600mm wide double sided
(2'-0")

16 Other areas

Ancillary public amenities

Entrance hall

Smaller university and college libraries may lead from the main entrance directly into a reading area, particularly since circulation counters are commonly set deep inside the library. Larger university and large public libraries will have an entrance hall, often an area from which the different services radiate. As such it will need careful planning because of the entirely separate contributions which it has to make. The architect is sure to allow space and give a ceiling height which provides dignity and has an air both impressive and welcoming. As it has to admit people directly from the outside it will need a floor covering which is not easily soiled and which helps to protect the rest of the library from dirt. When the entrance is to a single open-room library, particularly if carpeted, this can be done by a large dirt-absorbing mat, but where the entrance is separate from the reading areas, the hall can have an impervious and easily cleaned floor – usually brick or tiles. Care must be taken that this is non-slip, as it will become wet in inclement weather.

The entrance doors must be acceptable to all, including the disabled, so the design of handles has to be studied. As most readers are carrying something (if only books) automatic doors can be a boon. Again in the case of an open room leading straight from the outside, a heat curtain is much to be desired. Care must always be taken when designing main entrance doors, as staff may be stationed in the area and draughts must be prevented: lobbies are very useful in this case.

The entrance space must be large enough for the visitor to orientate himself and to move around. The main guides to the library should be placed here, either a complete subject location guide (as in any department store) or a terminal where such information can be studied on-line. There will also be special notices and announcements: gadgets such as electronic signs catch the eye and put over the message. If the entrance hall is the place from which all public services radiate, then it is usually best to have a manned information point. Careful planning of this area is particularly important because of the impact which it makes on visitors.

Book display

As well as serried rows of bookcases, all librarians will wish to display special collections or selections. They can range from the permanent exhibition of an important collection of books or manuscripts to a changeable subject display and, most common of all, items newly added to stock. Neither the book form nor ways of displaying it are new: originality is hard to find in this field. In the past, book jackets were pinned onto boards. Now that these jackets are often sealed on to books, only the books themselves can be used. Display equipment has to be attractive and eye-catching and should possess some degree of originality. To produce it will be the sort of challenge for which an architect is well qualified, and he will certainly not want advice from a librarian in matters of design, although conditions of access, security and other practical matters will have to be spelled out. A measure of disagreement may, however, develop on this subject: the architect, seeing a blank space, wants to use it for an 'interesting feature' such as sculpture, mural or even flowers; the librarian wants to display books and yet more books. A very common compromise is for the librarian to give in gracefully on condition that the visual embellishment is free-standing and that the wall behind it could be shelved later if wished. It is easy, particularly if systems shelving is to be used, for exhibition panels and bookshelving to be quickly interchangeable. Apart from the use of shop windows and display cases, braced, like museum exhibit cases, from floor to ceiling, the only permanent provision needed is a supply of power points throughout the area.

Exhibition areas

Most libraries have the need for exhibition areas ranging from a group of free-standing cases to a room or open space in a prime position and with specially planned equipment. The architect may wish to combine (or at least associate) them with more permanent decorative features – murals, fixed sculpture, and so on. Within open areas it will be easy for him to provide demountable frameworks and the necessary spotlighting for changeable exhibitions, but in general the more permanent an exhibition, the more effective will be the design. It is for the librarian to say how much freedom for change he requires and to accept that 'changeable' is likely to mean less successful.

If the exhibition area is to be a part of a corridor or area leading off an entrance hall, agreement must be reached on size and likely maximum attendance so that clear passage can be guaranteed. In large libraries the librarian will be well advised to watch the planning of exhibition areas very carefully: it has been my experience that sooner or later the area will need to be taken over for a new subject library or reader service area; it is always important to allow for future change. In small libraries space can best be utilized by having open-backed or double-sided vertical display units which can serve as space dividers (like an island bookcase) without the need for a special display area. An idea which may have some originality (but will no doubt turn out to have been used in other places) is to be seen in the Hillingdon Central Library, where there are free-standing display 'boxes', 2 m (6 ft 6 in) high, covered with grooved cladding, movable on castors to form different layouts. The display appears to form part of the interior decor in a way that normal display screens would not do; also, because one side of each box is hinged, the interiors can be used for appropriate storage purposes.

Requirements for exhibitions or permanent displays must be indicated in the primary brief and elaborated in the secondary. Even the need for a board to hold statutory public notices (many libraries, alas, still suffer from these) should be recorded; to add a board to a wall which the architect had visualized as unblemished is to interfere with the overall design. Comments on exhibition cases are made in Chapter 17.

Lecture rooms

Libraries of all kinds need rooms for meetings, lectures, play-reading and similar community activities, often in the evenings when the main library service areas have closed for the day. For this reason they are usually placed in parts of the building which can easily be isolated; in a single-storey building this can be a wing, but in a multi-storey library the lecture room can be at the top (if there are sufficient lifts), or better still in the basement, which is easily reached and can usually be locked off from other areas.

In all cases lecture rooms are likely to need separate approaches from outside the building, and special arrangements such as external lighting must be made for security and public safety. Lavatories for the public may have to be associated with them, as well as simple kitchens and cloakrooms. To staff cloakrooms is always expensive, and the use of key-operated lockers should be explored. The County Libraries Section of the Library Association[1] says 'Lecture rooms [in public libraries] are not recommended for communities of under 25 000 population' and goes on to recommend flexibility in the

fittings of main rooms of small libraries, so that these can be adapted for lectures after library hours. This may be inevitable in very small libraries, but many librarians have found that dual-purpose rooms often satisfy neither purpose properly. It is true that lecture rooms are wasteful of space because they are in use for only limited periods, but if they are to be provided at all it is important that they be designed as such. Open and neutral rooms can be planned so that bringing in a simple lectern and some stacking chairs makes a lecture room (just as the erection of rows of screens makes it an exhibition hall, and a projector and screen make it a cinema); but the result is seldom satisfactory. Lighting, acoustics and good interior design are called for, particularly because it is important to give a good impression to visitors, who are potential readers.

If there is a need for a real lecture theatre, then its design must be taken seriously; special ventilation, public address system, raked seating – all these are specialist matters. In a permanent lecture theatre, seats will be fixed to the floor; if there is a possibility of change of use, chairs clamped to a bar unit are stable but still removable in rows at short notice. Stacking chairs are not acceptable. The advantages of tip-up seats should not be underestimated. Writing shelves or tablets, for note-taking, fixed or hinged, can be fastened on where needed but unscrewed and removed when not needed; the requirements of the left-handed should not be forgotten. If screens will be needed for showing films or video, the height, positioning, viewing distance and angles have to be considered.

These matters are within the architect's competence, but few librarians have experience of the practical considerations. The chapters on theatres and higher education facilities in the *New Metric Handbook*[2] give a good introduction.

For a smaller library the brief will say how many seats are needed and whether a stage, special lighting and changing rooms are to be provided. It is fair to say that there is more muddled, or at least inconclusive, thinking on this subject than on most other library questions, and that it is usually the librarian who is at fault. To provide a room with adequate seating, a simple stage, some spotlights, a basic proscenium and a public address system is easy enough, but even these provisions have to be thought out carefully in the anticipation of a possible full range of audio-visual equipment. If the librarian has in mind the escalation of activities at some future date, and perhaps the possibility of amateur stage performances in costume, then the matter is very different. To attempt to house these performances in a room not designed for the purpose and without specially planned fittings, acoustic treatment, changing rooms, washing and make-up facilities will mean failure or very expensive alterations. Public safety regulations (especially for gangways, entrances and exits) for 'theatres' are very different from those for meeting rooms. Lengthy plays need intervals, and intervals call for kitchens, refreshment rooms, lavatories, bars (and licences). Box office arrangements and ways of handling money are not to be taken lightly. To attempt such a transformation is always difficult and seldom satisfactory; clear identification of possible future needs before the brief is written is the only way to use the designer's talents.

Theatres

Because of the obvious connection between the written and the spoken word, libraries are becoming more closely linked with theatres. The association is simple enough in the large educational campus, where the theatre will be an

16:1. Lecture room seating and minimum dimensions (New Metric Handbook). Minimum dimensions: A Back-to-back distance between rows of seats: 760 mm (min) B Width of seats with arms: 510 mm (min) C Width of seat without arms: 460 mm (min) D Unobstructed vertical space between rows (seatway) 305 mm

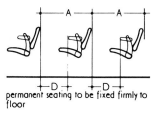

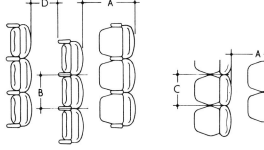

tip up seats to be actuated by weights

permanent seating to be fixed firmly to floor

16:2. Alternative forms of lecture room seating (New Metric Handbook)

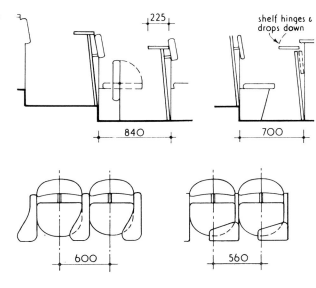

225

shelf hinges & drops down

840

700

600

560

independent partner to the library in its service to the community, but in the public library field it is common for the library and the theatre to be within the same building. The reasons given are that some facilities can be shared and that each will help to publicize the other; the true reason will be that prime sites are difficult to obtain. Because of the intense pressure of demand at perform-ance times, the great need for ease of entrance and egress (as well as for the publicity area required to lure in patrons), the theatre usually manages to get priority in the allocation of street-level space. The size of the auditorium and its immediate relationship with the stage and back-stage mean that a compact block around ground-floor level is requisitioned within the cubic space available for the combined building. My own experience in this field is that the theatre is an uncomfortable bedfellow for the public library. Nevertheless combined library and theatre build-ings have been erected recently in a number of London boroughs. A successful and even closer association began in the Manchester Public Libraries from a small theatre (with a professional company) in the basement of the central library; the system expanded and there are now two separate theatres in different parts of the city under the management of the city librarian, with lounge and refreshment areas serving both theatre and library patrons. The common use of these facilities has the great

advantage of publicizing each service to those familiar only with the other, as well as making them economically feasible.

The design of theatres is a matter so complicated and so technically involved that it cannot be dealt with here. In general, if the two services are to share a building, because of the problems of crowds and noise it is better if they are planned back-to-back, the only elements which might be shared being staff facilities. If large theatre companies are to be housed, even this arrangement is better avoided, because the working hours, rest times (and temperaments) of the two professions are so different. An excellent book for any librarian who may be even indirectly concerned with this subject is Roderick Ham's *Theatres*.[3]

Recreational facilities for readers

Many libraries will have no call for this fairly recent development, particularly those which are small or are part of an institution which already adequately serves the users. University libraries will certainly need restaurants, or at least cafeterias, for students who can be expected to spend many hours on the premises, but the campus may already have facilities near enough to serve the purpose. There is a growing tendency for libraries of all kinds to have coffee bars or food-and-drink vending machines in open areas as an encouragement to readers to regard the library as a hospitable centre. Opinions differ widely, some librarians holding that such noisy, smoky, splashy activities should be confined to a special area, perhaps off an entrance hall, where floors can be designed to stand the dirt and the spillage. The opposite view is well illustrated in Nottingham University Library, where the relaxing area with lounge chairs, refreshment facilities and a public tele-phone is housed on the wholly carpeted open-plan main floor (see p. 46); it is remarkably successful, mainly because of the superb acoustic treatment. In public libraries much will depend on the authority's policy; the coffee bar may be near the entrance as an attraction to passers-by or it may be deliberately placed deep inside the building so that it will serve only those using the long-term study facilities or the lecture theatre. The deliberate provision of large refreshment and relaxing areas in public libraries which are situated in a central position in a shopping area is a development of considerable interest. In Britain the best-known example is in the London Borough of Sutton, where the coffee and snack bar for shoppers is in a large area of changing exhibitions and leads directly to the lending library entrance without any barriers. In Holland the new public library in Middleburg uses a different technique: there is a pleasant café looking over the canal which is a feature of the centre of the little town, but to get to it the customers enter the library and go down an open and very attractive staircase. There is no doubt at all that these provisions are popular and are excellent for public relations; they ensure that the library is a natural meeting place and a centre of community life.

The question of providing special facilities for smokers has changed dramatically over the last few years. Earlier the feeling in Britain had been strongly against the practice of allowing smoking in general reading areas, but it was perhaps moving towards a United States' solution of special smoking rooms, despite troubles with insurance and fire regulations. Now feelings have swung strongly against any such provision, in line with the public attitude to the habit. If smoking is ever allowed in main reading areas, it is certainly necessary to provide at least one area for those who find the habit offensive.

16:3. Plan show-ing refreshment and exhibition area on ground floor, off shopping district and lead-ing to the library entrance counter: London Borough of Sutton. Note half-level changes in lending library with free-standing bookcases 'climb-ing the stairs'

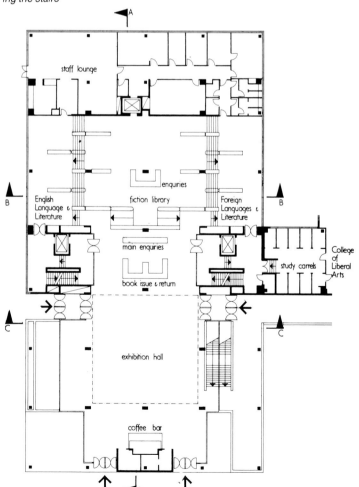

Toilet facilities for readers

It seems only civilized to provide adequate toilet facilities for readers who are to spend time on the premises, but like all other planning matters it is worth some thought. In long-stay institutions, especially colleges and universities, it will be normal to include lavatories for readers, but many public librarians oppose the provision of public lavatories (especially on the ground floor) because the library can become a convenient calling place for passers-by in that part of the town. If public lavatories are needed in these circumstances, they should be for longer-stay readers, and so the facilities could be placed deeper into the building rather than near the main entrance. In very small public libraries which double as community film and lecture rooms after library hours, such provision will certainly be necessary. Sometimes staff lavatories are made available to the public at these times, but this is a disagreeable expedient and the librarian should stand out strongly against it.

In a multi-storey building it is usual to provide toilets on every floor, but this is expensive unless the use of the library is likely to be heavy. Birmingham Central Library has placed toilets on every other floor and at corners, each (naturally) being associated with the corner service cores. In smaller libraries, even small university libraries, it is not unreasonable to have all toilet facilities on one floor; the basement is a place where space can often be spared. If lifts or escalators are provided this cannot be a hardship. I have met cases where toilets could only be sited outside the main security barriers, because a toilet close to a subject reading area is the ideal secluded place for unscrupulous readers to take books and tear sections out. In many countries this may seem laughable, but where the demand is enormous and the book supply limited, it is incumbent upon the librarian to protect his precious stock.

It is also reasonable to provide lockers in which readers can secure their smaller possessions such as briefcases, but care should be taken that these also are sited outside the security barrier so that library books cannot be locked within, to be smuggled out at a quiet moment. It also prevents readers 'reserving' for themselves books in great demand which cannot be issued to them. See Chapter 12.

Bookshops

Bookshops are a normal provision on academic campuses, but there seems little advantage in having them as part of the library building. There has been a move in Britain to find room for a bookshop when planning a new public library, chiefly to allow a bookseller an outlet on a key site at a reasonable cost. This is acceptable so long as the library gets all the space it needs. An alternative is for the library to use the new computer book-order methods allowing readers to utilize the library's terminal to send an order direct to a bookseller for books they have seen on the shelves of the library. This can be of real value to both readers and booksellers without the library having to lose valuable space.

Many public libraries now incorporate small shops (more likely to be called 'sales points') where the library's own publications can be purchased. These are normally reproductions of local prints, maps, postcards or even copies of historical documents of local interest. Apart from bringing in a small income (less in real terms than some librarians would have us think), the enterprise attracts people into the library and arouses interest in the library's holdings, particularly in the field of local history. The design of such a small shop is not a difficult matter, but

cash-handling, its security and space for the reserve stock need to be thought out.

Memorial rooms

Some university libraries, particularly in the United States, need to commemorate major donors by the creation of special rooms or even whole libraries of great dignity and attraction. This is not common elsewhere, but some newly independent countries may wish to celebrate national events or national leaders by the creation and dedication of a national or university library. Such a beginning may have a strong influence on the form of the building. A lesser memorial may take the form of a certain room, designed and fitted to a high standard of furnishing, where foreign visitors can be shown important documents and exhibitions on the country's history and development. I have been concerned with several of these rooms, and they can be very important to the people of the country. It is vital that such rooms should have as separate an approach as possible, preferably with a direct entrance from outside, certainly clear of normal library reader traffic routes. The furnishings are likely to include tables of specially selected local wood, glass-topped exhibition cases, bookcases and thick carpeting to produce an atmosphere of dignity.

It is strongly to be hoped that financial provision for this kind of room is provided separately and that the space does not come out of the overall allocation.

Staff areas

Staff work areas

Metcalf[4] said: 'If experience over the last fifty years applies today (and there is no reason to believe that it does not), it seems fair to say that in most library buildings accommodations for the staff tend to become inadequate before those for books or for readers.'

There is a fundamental difference between local work areas where immediate needs are met (the handling of reserves, new books, minor repairs etc.) and workrooms for the centralized operations common to the whole library or the whole system. In the smallest libraries all action will take place in the one workroom; in branch libraries the centralized operations may have already been carried out for the whole system in another building. The layout of work areas and the design of their furniture and equipment can usefully be discussed only with a knowledge of the requirements of the individual case. The following points are intended simply as a reminder of some of the actions for which allowance has to be made.

Arrival and dispatch of materials

The categories of materials arriving regularly are:

1. Cartons of new books from suppliers or, less often, on exchange (periodicals can be considered as part of the incoming mail).
2. Cartons of books back from rebinding.
3. Housekeeping supplies, from stationery to string and soap.

These will need a well-planned arrival area, under cover and with a ramp to facilitate loading and unloading without the need to lift heavy packages; if a ramp is not possible, then a pulley is necessary. The area should be planned against the known dimensions of the vans likely to be used and their approach routes, so that no difficulty will be met when backing in. Where deliveries could conveniently be made directly to more than one level (if, say, the accessions department is not on the same floor as the bindery), a double-level ramp is a great blessing. Plenty of space should be allowed for unpacking, and surfaces for packing and unpacking should be planned by staff who know how much bending and lifting will be needed if the right table heights are not chosen. There should be two levels of table: one on which to place the container and another, slightly higher, onto or from which the books are to be transferred. There should be an area (which can be shut off for fire reasons) where cartons can be stored for re-use within a short period. The amount of rubbish which will accumulate can be large, so wide-mouthed metal containers will be needed while periodic disposal is awaited.

The chief materials which are to be dispatched are cartons of books to branches or to rebinding firms and smaller parcels on exchange agreements. The essentials for work in the arrivals/dispatch area are strong, rough tables, and if any branches or other satellite libraries have to be supplied it will be necessary to have industrial racking to form pigeonholes so that books and other items can be accumulated until the time for the regular delivery. These should be lockable, as they are vulnerable to theft. Inter-library loan arrivals and departures do not normally involve items of great size, but a planned section with table, stores of packing materials, tape and string (and a file of reference books to check addresses) is worth thinking out.

Accessioning

Whatever the change in library procedures there is no reason to think that the arrival and accessioning of large quantities of books and periodicals will lessen for a very long time. Space for this work should not be under-estimated. Colleges and small universities should allow at least 50 m² (500 sq ft); large universities and central library headquarters will need several times as much. It is an ideal area for open-plan working, with free-standing tiers of shelving acting as screens between staff work desks. Because the operations are predictable it will be possible to arrange the layout as a production line. In practice there are always daily problems, and certain sections of shelving will be ear-marked for 'awaiting' or 'queries'. Movement of books is likely to be by trolley, except in the largest organizations, and working clusters should be planned so that trolleys are a part of the plan, not an encumbrance. Large libraries will need more sophisticated conveyors from the arrival area and to the cataloguing section: conveyor belt, hoist or other device. This is dealt with in Chapter 8.

The receipt of periodicals is a much larger and more complicated undertaking than an outsider would believe. The arrival of hundreds of current periodicals, the checking off, the identification of queries for investigation, and the delivery to different subject areas all call for careful planning. Methods of checking off have varied from the original card file to a number of patent control systems, but there is no doubt that this is a section ripe for the use of the general housekeeping computer. Apart from efficiency it gives the very great advantage of allowing reader service points (or readers using available terminals) to find instantly the position regarding the arrival of the latest issues. This in turn makes unnecessary the physical siting of the periodical control area close to where the periodicals are laid out for use; this proximity was useful for dealing with readers' questions but was a further constraint on the freedom of space planning.

Other necessary processes such as ordering, accounts and so on need ordinary offices; having them conveniently placed for the flow of activities must be a clear requirement in the notional space relationship diagrams, but they seldom need any facilities other than desks, files, telephones, telex, fax and terminals for order and accounts control.

Cataloguing and classifying

The layout of rooms for these activities will vary enormously, not only according to the size and type of library but according to the variations in the operations themselves. In major libraries the record produced by these skilled bibliographical processes will form the only guide to the holdings as well as the only way readers can trace the books. Because of the vast numbers of books in stock, full bibliographical cataloguing will be necessary so that the scholar can differentiate between one book, edition or variant and another. In medium-sized libraries of all kinds, the complexity of the bibliographical record will be less, but the procedures will be exactly the same. In a very small library the processes can be simplified to produce an entry which has only to help the reader to find a book among a small collection. In branch libraries the catalogue records may come already prepared along with each new book from the central organization or may be available through a terminal. Sometimes catalogue cards (or entries) are purchased pre-prepared (e.g. Library of Congress or British Library cards). A number of other activities, such as abstracting and indexing, though different in their procedures and purposes, may also be carried out in this open work area.

It has to be remembered that in work like this, consistency (that is, accordance with precedent) is all. In most cases the work has to be checked against current holdings and procedures, which means that the cataloguers must have access to a large card catalogue or terminal. In libraries on a single floor a considerable space saving can be made by placing the main public catalogue near enough to the cataloguing area for cataloguers to go to it for checking, rather than have a duplicate catalogue in the department. This is usually unpopular with cataloguers and is not reasonable if the library is on several floors. In either case a study should be undertaken of the traffic routes of cataloguers in the course of their work; in an open-plan room the layout can be changed as experience is obtained.

When the catalogue entry is provided by network or cooperative with a greater or lesser degree of local participation, the greater part of the work has been done at the centre of the organization and the record will be retrieved in the department onto a VDU. In a cooperative it may be the duty of the library to catalogue any book which is not already on the cooperative's data file, but with the commercial networks (with whom the future lies) it is only necessary for the library to amend the record transmitted by the network by bringing it into line with local practice.

The computer-based process should be very much faster but has very little effect on the layout of the department, apart from removing the need for a large catalogue cabinet once retrospective cataloguing is completed. Wiring for the terminals should be drawn from underfloor ducts, which can be planned in rows to serve the desks; despite the freedom which open-plan layouts give, in practice there will be a limited number of positions which each desk can occupy, and two lines of ducting should serve adequately. Modern desks are not only designed to accommodate terminals and the books which are being processed, but have channels built into them to receive the wires, which therefore do not have to trail as they would have done a few years ago.

The object will be a production line, which means that books will arrive from accessioning, be divided up as appropriate, according to the amount of attention they need, and after the processes have been completed, be transported to the next link in the chain. Again an open-plan area is to be desired in order to allow flexibility in the sequence of operations. Tiers of free-standing shelving can again form useful audial screens. Certain major reference tools will have to be shelved in a place convenient for all the staff of this department. Because of the large number of bibliographical tools needed to hand, 14 m² (150 sq ft) per cataloguer is a reasonable space allocation. A number of major multi-volume printed catalogues may need to be housed here, but as so many of these essential tools are now in microform the pressure on space in this department is tending to ease. Each cataloguer working in modern conditions will need space on, or adjacent to, the working desk for a live terminal (which includes a keyboard); when the catalogue entry appears on the screen it is amended according to local practice and then switched to become part of the library's record. In practice a form of this entry may be already on file from the ordering of the book by computer, but the space allocation is not affected.

In planning the layout and furniture for such working areas it is important to use the best possible source of information – those who work there. The cataloguers should be very much involved in the layout proposals, but the ideas which can come from asking each of them how he would like his own working area planned can be even more valuable. Unless the library is tied to contract furniture or is very short of funds, each desk and its book-holding fitments should be built as each cataloguer wishes, complete with bookcase fitments at the appropriate angle, swivel copy-holders, stationery containers and perhaps trolleys designed to fit in with the desk. The result will cost a little more, but this is seldom a vital matter in the cost of a new building. Cataloguers are replaced, but others will have similar needs, and the result can be a happier staff – and higher productivity.

Copy typing may have a place in the flow line, as may the reproduction of catalogue cards by machine duplicators or tape typewriters, although it may not be necessary for this to take place within the department. Certainly it will be quieter without it, but completed cards normally have to return to the professional staff for checking. In the case of computer-based cataloguing – and anyone planning a building must presume that this process will come sooner rather than later – it is vital to make arrangements for power and line connections by ducting, which must be installed while the building is being erected; if access points are added after the screed is laid, the result can be both unsightly and hazardous. In a smaller room (or in the case of an adaptation) the most satisfactory way is for desks to be placed near walls (preferably with windows) and for running ducting to be installed at table height.

Other offices

When books have been checked in the arrival or accessioning areas, invoices will be passed to clerical and accounts staff who will deal with the financial procedures. Although document conveyors can be used to pass invoices along the line, in practice it is preferable for the offices to be fairly close together for good communications. When readers have payments to make in this area it is obviously important for a well-signposted route to be used which avoids other non-public areas. These space-planning requirements may be difficult to arrange, but their successful solution can protect staff, already busy giving professional advice to readers, from being involved in the handling of cash.

Under the (British) Offices, Shops and Railway Premises Act 1963, persons habitually occupying a room are entitled to a minimum of 3.72 m² (40 sq ft) each, or 11.32 m³ (400 cu ft) if the ceiling is lower than 3 m (10 ft). The working space per head of staff in general work areas should be between 7 m² and 9.3 m² (75 sq ft and 100 sq ft); staff largely occupied at single desks (e.g. typists) will need only 7 m² to 8 m² (75 sq ft to 85 sq ft), but other specialists need 9.3 m² to 11.6 m² (100 sq ft to 125 sq ft), with more for senior staff, because they will be consulted by their colleagues. Individual offices will be from 9.3 m² to 28 m² (100 sq ft to 300 sq ft).

The sizes of desks and chairs for staff will be similar to those for readers, but because of the long hours they spend there it could be advantageous to have adjustable (even pneumatically adjustable) chairs; adjustable-height desks can also be purchased, and though expensive this could be worthwhile.

Even where large clerical offices are open-plan, furniture, and particularly bookcases, can be arranged to give each member of the staff some feeling of privacy and help to banish both visual and aural distraction.

Senior staff

Larger offices will be needed, often with adjoining secretarial support areas. In small libraries the chief librarian may also be the direct supervisor of public services and wish to be placed where he can exercise this function directly, but in large ones the supervisory duty will be delegated to departmental heads and the chief librarian can be accommodated on an upper floor where space is less precious. He may wish to be close to the clerical office or the accessions department: this will depend on the procedures and on his personal assessment of his role. He is also likely to require a reception/waiting area for visitors, with a minimum of 10 m² (100 sq ft), preferably audially separated from traffic routes. The relationships between the various areas will have been indicated in the primary brief. A size of 14 m² (150 sq ft) is often quoted for the office of the chief librarian of a medium to large library, but much will depend on the extent to which it is to be used for meetings of departmental heads or other small committees.

Processing

All library materials need some form of treatment before they are ready for use by readers. At the very least, books have to be labelled and lettered, and although in very small libraries this can be done in a general workroom, in most cases there will be a need for a special place in the flow-line for this work. Books received back after loan may need running repairs; older books may have to be taken off the shelves in a regular programme of repair or for leather dressing to be applied. Unless the library receives all its materials ready-prepared, new books will have to be jacketed, laminated or strengthened, and this may call for fairly heavy (and therefore static) machinery. It is helpful to get the sizes of the proposed machinery from the manufacturers' catalogues and plot the layout on a plan.

Bindery

In large libraries the above tasks will probably be carried out in a bindery, which, it should never be forgotten, is a factory laid out on production lines and operated by skilled technicians. The work to be carried out will depend on a number of factors: if an efficient commercial rebinding industry is to be found in the region it is normally more economical to send books there for treatment, but the in-house bindery is better where the librarian is unwilling to allow certain items off the premises. The speed of operation which is possible in the repetitive work of re-casing periodicals allows them to be consulted at almost any time while they are in the bindery, and the range of useful 'extras', such as the making of board, cloth, boxes and leather items which are not commercially available, should not be underestimated. The latter service can never be a reason for having a bindery, but it is of value when a bindery is otherwise justifiable. In libraries with valuable old books, especially those which are still acquiring items of this nature, a bindery will be essential (as will a conservation section: see below).

In Britain a bindery is likely to fall under the provisions of Factory Act legislation, and it will be the duty of the architect to familiarize himself with these regulations. Bookbinding work is dirty and noisy as well as highly skilled. The processes through which each volume passes should be organized as far as possible in a flow-line despite the difference in treatment which the various classes of books must receive. The most skilled work is still carried out by hand but has to fit in the flow-line for the economical use of machines such as presses and guillotines. The object is to have pre-prepared materials, made to the right size, fed into the flow-line at the right stage: a matter of skilled professional planning.

Hand operations will take place at tables, but there is a difference between the requirements of tables for work such as pulling-down (which is heavy and dirty), checking (which is cleaner and neater), glueing, forwarding and finishing (that is, lettering by hand), a particularly skilled operation needing a specially laid-out working space.

Some machinery will be on table-tops, but the larger machines, although theoretically free-standing, will be too heavy to be moved except in exceptional circumstances. A special power supply (3-phase) will be needed for these, but a running power supply needs to be ducted to most tables.

Because of the complexity of the operations and the size (and weight) of the machinery which will be used, it is not enough to make a flow-chart and leave it all to the architect. It is necessary to understand the operations which are to take place, and for this reason two typical bindery production lines are given here.

The first, largely handwork for binding books, may consist of the following sequence of actions:

1. Check in: prepare and insert instruction sheet.
2. Pull down (note: much rubbish to be collected for disposal).
3. Check sections.
4. *Apply endpapers.
5. Sew by hand (or by sewing machine on table-top or at hand).
6. Press by machine on table or free-standing press.
7. Trim by free-standing guillotine.
8. Round and back (by hand operations at table clamp or nearby press).
9. *Apply spine cloth.
10. *Fix boards; paste in endpapers.
11. *Cover with cloth or leather or both (in both covering operations a glue heater may be needed).
12. Press: as above, the books remaining in either a table-top or free-standing press.
13. Letter by hand with individual letter tools or pallet; in either case heated on table-top electric heater.
14. Inspect.

The processes marked with an asterisk call for the bringing in of materials which have previously been specifically prepared, usually in a sequence of normal sizes, with the use of table-top board cutter, shears and glueing machine.

When a programme of casing periodicals is the main work, the procedures are more repetitive and can be based much more on machine operations.

1. *Check in: insert instruction sheet and pre-prepared skiver panel which has been lettered by pallet and machine press in a series for that journal.
2. Remove staples.
3. Check sections.
4. Mill or trim spine (by free-standing machines).
5. *Add endpapers.
6. Sew (either all-along, cleat or oversewing) using different, usually free-standing, machines.
7. Press by free-standing presses.
8. Trim by free-standing guillotine.
9. Round and back (single operation by free-standing machine).
10. *Apply spine cloth by hand.
11. *Choose pre-cut boards.
12. *Make case, adding lettered skivers.
13. Paste and turn in endpapers.
14. Press by free-standing presses.
15. Inspect.

This is only a simple flow of operations; in a large library there will be other, more sophisticated machine operations, such as lettering by typesetter, sometimes computerized. A place will have to be planned for a foreman (supervisor) which will range from a desk to, in large establishments, a cubicle office.

These operations have been observed many times in many different countries, but because of variations of practice (and availability of special machines), it is certain that some bookbinders would disagree with the sequence in some respects. Nevertheless the list indicates that there are two basic requirements: a flow-line which involves a sequence of operations on heavy machines which have to be carefully sited; and a parallel series of operations which begin with the acquiring of material (cloth, leather, paper, gold for lettering, tapes etc.), which come in commercially produced packages and have to be stored, measured and prepared for use so that the flow is never held up for lack of the right material at the right time. Summarizing, it is necessary for there to be strong tables for pulling-down, work desks for individual craftsmen, machines (often special and heavy) in one or two rows, each with its own electrical power, and arrangements for the clearing away and disposal of masses of rubbish produced by the work.

Points to be noted are: the storing of cloths and leather rolls in racks along the walls, suitably sized pieces being cut off and stored under the appropriate working tables; at least two washbasins per flow-line; fitted toolracks convenient for each appropriate operation. For a suggested flow-line, see Chapter 5. It is obvious from this sketchy description that a bindery is a complex factory, and very great attention (with the assistance of a skilled and experienced bookbinder) is necessary before undertaking such a complicated venture.

Conservation

A library with many old and rare books and documents will need a section which can repair the ravages of time, wear and bad humidity. The section should be placed close to a fumigation room, which will itself have a direct connection with an arrival area. Suspect materials should always enter the library via a fumigation chamber (which will have its own extractor system to the exterior of the building), and it is common for them to be examined by the staff of the conservation section. Again, highly specialized work is involved; the conservation section may include its own small bindery, but if the library has a separate bindery the two departments will be located close to each other.

The layout of the department is based on slow and painstaking work on fragile material; a production-line layout would be quite inappropriate. The basis of the service is at least two large sinks, tables (some with ground-glass screens for delicate work and with fittings which allow them to be fixed at the angle suitable for the operator), standing presses, rotary trimmers, board choppers, and cupboards specially designed for the storage of the necessary chemicals. More advanced units will also contain leaf-casters and different kinds of mounters. A fume cupboard and suitable extractor system (independent of the general ventilation system) are vital. Flexibility of individual task lighting will be called for, as well as racks and cupboards for tools, acidity-test meters and other sophisticated items. Again a qualified and experienced conservationist will be essential to guide the planning of the section.

Artwork room

Most large libraries, particularly the headquarters of library systems, will need a centre for the production of display material, notices and so on; if lectures or theatrical performances are featured, the need will be much greater. Apart from specially adjustable work tables, cutting equipment and storage for both card and paints, the main question is whether actual printing work (that is, production in quantity rather than single items) is to take place. If it is, then all depends on the machines which are to be used, and the layout must be designed around them.

Photographic department

The range of work in this field can vary from the dry-copier, which requires little except the space on which it stands (plus an electric power point), to a full photographic laboratory complex employing many staff. Any library holding large and/or fragile material which may have to be photocopied will find that no single machine will economically do the whole range of work. Standing cameras need professional operators, and if one of these is to be employed, then his work must be scheduled so that his time is used most economically. Unless he is given non-professional assistance he will necessarily spend valuable time on tasks below his capability (and salary level). A large library therefore may need a full photographic department with both dark and light rooms; the tasks to be carried out have to be scheduled, and operation movements visualized. This information will be handed to the architect, who will plan the appropriate area.

Printing department

The work and equipment vary here more than in any other section, and it is impossible to generalize. A national library

may have the task of printing the national bibliography; but usually the range is from a small offset lithographic machine for display and public relations work to a workshop with filmsetter, colour camers, printing machines, collators and gatherers for the printing of brochures and journals. There may have to be stapling or stitching equipment, or (in extreme examples) the printed material will be passed to the in-house bindery. Computer (desk-top) publishing is an entirely different dimension; one can only list the requirements and get an expert to design the layout.

In all these workshops the theory is that the tasks, the equipment and the operations have to be visualized in some detail and recorded for the use of the architect. This is the theory; in practice I believe that there are four areas for which the architect is not the best person to produce a layout. These are conservation, bookbinding, photographic and printing departments. In each case it is better to have the layout designed by the professional concerned, preferably the one who is to run the department.

Maintenance section

In large libraries it is important that fully equipped workshops with associated storerooms be provided for those who have to maintain the elaborate service machinery. Even in a small library, if there is a caretaker-handyman who has to do the make-and-mend, he should be given the space and equipment to enable him to do the work properly. Benches, tool housing and storage for materials will be needed, as well as space for the inevitable furniture awaiting repair. In many libraries broken chairs can be found piled in odd corners where they are a hindrance and a potential fire hazard.

Cleaners will need space for storing materials as well as vacuum cleaners and brushes (which can be tall). There should be a central sink (in addition to one on each floor) where buckets can be filled and dirty water poured away; washbasins should never be used for either purpose. All these provisions should be made in all major areas; too often cleaners have to haul buckets and materials for long distances because these operations had not been considered seriously at the planning stage.

Where power supplies are suspect there must be stand-by generators; in very large libraries there will be sub-stations. Technicians may have to be housed: living quarters for technicians, security men, garages and workshops for vehicles (with oil and water points and perhaps inspection pits) – all these need to be spelled out very clearly in the brief. If a library also plans to provide accommodation for visiting scholars, then the architect has to bring some of the technique of hotel planning into his work.

Staff training section

In a large library a room will be needed for informal lectures given as part of an in-service training programme as well as for regular policy discussions. The headquarters of the system will need a large room for these and similar purposes. Such a room, if placed near the main staff rest areas, could also be made available to the staff for occasional social functions, but it should never, never be let to outside bodies. Blackboards, pinboards, projectors and screens can be free-standing; lighting dimmers are much to be desired. It is of course possible to use a public lecture room, but it is better management practice to have a special room which can be used as a centre where notices, and perhaps a collection of recent books and periodicals on librarianship, can be featured.

Committee rooms

A requirement often met is for a committee or board room for occasional use by representatives of the authority. This is likely to be accepted as an addition to the library's functional space requirements, but if the room is 'furnished' with lockable glass-fronted bookcases it can serve as a special collections room also. It may be used as an occasional office but it is always useful to have a room which has no specific function at the outset; a need will certainly arise, particularly when another office becomes temporarily out of action.

In national libraries as much as a whole floor may have to be devoted to the needs of the board and the directorate. This is because members may have to travel long distances to play their part; in these circumstances they will need, in addition to committee rooms and working offices, refreshment facilities and (in some examples I know) sleeping quarters.

Staff entrance

This is always necessary. It should be approachable by a well-paved path, with proper provision for disabled access. There should be facilities for staff car, motor-cycle and bicycle parking, separate from the public provision, secure, well lit and under cover.

Staff rest areas

The requirements for rest areas will differ widely among libraries, chiefly because of the working times of the staff. It shifts are worked, or if the library is in a place without easily accessible canteens or restaurants, fairly elaborate kitchen and dining facilities will be needed. Small libraries will have a combined kitchen and staffroom divided notionally between dining and lounge areas by furniture or by contrasting flooring materials. In others only an electric kettle, perhaps a microwave oven, small heater, storage cupboards and washing-up facilities may be needed, either within, or separate from, the staff lounge. This seems a simple stipulation but the design and the materials used can make a big difference to staff morale; it is worth forming a small, staff sub-committee to find out what is really needed. Too many uneasy compromises are to be found in this field.

Libraries which have many staff, are open long hours, but are not part of campuses must make more elaborate

plans. Dining facilities can be planned back-to-back with less elaborate ones for readers, thus allowing both to utilize the same kitchen services. An advantage of this is that when the library is closed both sets of refreshment areas can be used for major staff functions.

The positioning of the rest rooms is of some importance because of the potential waste of staff time in getting to those rooms from working areas. In a multi-storey building the architect will wish to group such areas vertically so as to simplify plumbing services within a service core, and this will largely determine the position; nevertheless the librarian should notionally 'time' the approach to each room by the staff who are to use it, taking into account lifts (which may be in use by others) and staircases. In many countries one finds washbasins in offices, seemingly a very civilized provision, but seldom seen in some countries (sadly including Britain). As they are easy to supply, it seems probable that it did not occur to the librarian to ask for them in the brief.

Libraries with a large staff should include a first-aid room; if there is a workshop or a bindery the provision will be compulsory. Whether such a room can be sited so as to serve readers in emergencies is a decision to be made by the librarian and intimated in the brief. A provision too seldom made, even in large libraries, is a small private rest area for women staff. This should be quite separate from the usual staff rest rooms. The first-aid room should not be used for this purpose: sooner or later both needs will arise at the same time.

In all these matters the librarian's task is to summarize the numbers of each sex to be catered for, give the times during which the facilities will be needed and indicate whether an average or a specially comfortable provision is to be made. When the sketch plans arrive he should arrange for members of the staff of different levels and sexes to examine them also. If there is a staff trades union its representatives should certainly be involved in accepting all proposed staff facilities. In all this planning it is obvious that expectations today are for something more spacious and elaborate than what would have been acceptable a generation ago.

It seems obvious too that there should be ample space for staff to get at their lockers, but the architect may forget that access to all lockers may be needed at the same time, for example at opening and closing times. The design of lockers often annoys staff because some proprietary types allow too little space for long coats to be hung without crushing them, and the result is that coats are hung on doors or across chairs throughout the staff areas. In addition to lockers, lockable drawers for women's handbags will be needed in all work areas, and this should be kept in mind when designing counters and desks.

17 Interiors: furniture, fittings and floors

To both librarian and reader the interior of the building is of more direct importance than the exterior. Both of them have to 'live with' the feeling produced by the layout, the choice of materials and the colours. Visual factors include the height and placing of the open-floor shelving, which determine the vista, the view across the room which is so important in giving a feeling of spaciousness. Colours have to be visualized carefully, for there are so many; colours of shelving, furniture and the greater blocks of colour formed by ceilings (even if white), curtains and floors. The effect of the colour of the books has to be borne in mind in the design, particularly in libraries where books are jacketed and protected by transparent covers, though to a lesser extent in libraries of all kinds. Indeed it is often said that a library interior designer should produce a neutral background as a foil to the mass of highly coloured books.

These factors are for the designer of the interior to balance. Some teams include a specialist interior designer, but in most cases the work is done by the architect or a member of his staff; certainly the librarian has no part to play as long as he has made clear in the primary brief what kind of feeling and atmosphere is to be created. He is concerned with the functional side of what is to be housed, and in particular with the furniture, the fittings and the floors. In the production of sketch designs and during estimating it is usual to draw a distinction between fixtures and fittings on the one hand and loose furniture on the other. The former, except for specialist library items, are usually chosen by the architect and shown on the outline plans. Loose furniture, because it has little practical influence on the building design (although it could affect bay sizes and will certainly influence the interior appearance) can be agreed between the architect and the librarian at a later stage. The quantity surveyor will have estimated the costs separately, furniture often being designated a 'prime cost' sum, which will be included in estimates but the spending of which is to be decided later. The distinction between the two categories is not entirely straightforward: formal book shelving in stacks is usually regarded as a 'fitting' even though it may be free-standing. The items discussed in this chapter therefore may fall into either category. Critical sizes and recommended layouts were considered in Chapters 13 and 14; it is now necessary to look at the materials, designs and relative costs of the more important items.

The librarian should always choose the shelving, catalogues and technical equipment. The architect should choose the chairs and tables, because they are elements with which he is concerned throughout his professional life; but with the choice of all furniture the librarian must be, at the very least, closely involved. He should look at a number of the coloured brochures issued by the many firms operating in this market, so as to have a good idea of what is available; visit libraries which use items which seem to be suitable; and have general discussions with the architect before meeting any salesmen: they are experts at selling. Close consultation is perhaps even more important than the decision who makes the choice: the architect chooses tables, but the librarian is vitally interested in their stability, the wearing quality of their top surfaces and so on. Similarly the librarian chooses the catalogue cabinets but the architect is very much concerned with the shape,

material and colour because of their effect on the interior design and on the cost. If, for reasons of economy or of design, the architect recommends the purchase of furnishings from a single proprietary range, the librarian must inspect every item in that range before agreeing. As furniture and equipment commonly account for between 10% and 15% of the total cost of a library project, this is not a matter to be treated lightly.

Shelving

Factors for the librarian to bear in mind are appearance, durability, suitability for purpose, and cost; in practice there are other factors, such as weight, stability, public safety and so on, which the architect will certainly take into account but which are likely to have already been given due attention by the highly efficient library furniture industry.

The relative importance of the qualities of bookshelving will vary, not only according to the type of library but also in different sections of each library. Almost every library will make a saving by having cheaper shelving in closed stack areas, where appearance is less important; an exception perhaps is the large library where the very size of the contract can produce economy by using the same proprietary shelving throughout. Except in the case of some special hardwood bookcases with glass fronts, the architect in industrial countries is less likely to have shelving constructed to his own designs; unless he has access to especially favourable labour conditions, he will find that manufacturers can offer library shelving more versatile and at a lower cost than any that can be specially made. There are many advantages in having shelving supplied by library equipment specialists; their wide experience over very many years and many countries, and the benefits of mass production, can outweigh the limitations which they place on the architect's freedom to design.

In some developing countries with large timber resources and active woodworking firms the position can be quite different. Here the saving of hard currency by using what is manufactured locally can be of prime importance. Because the shelving industry in developed countries is so expert and experienced, it may be inevitable that their products will be studied and perhaps copied. To start to design library shelving and specialist furniture without examining successful products is a hazardous operation.

A number of suppliers offer a consultancy service in planning and layout of shelving areas, which can add much to design teams' expertise. If the contract is eventually given to that firm, the costs of the consultancy will be 'free' (i.e. included in the total costs); if not, there may be a charge for the consultancy service, but this could be worthwhile for the ideas it might produce. It is like employing a specialist consultant on a specific task. The architect will retain overall design control, because the finished product must fit in with his concept.

This is very different from the turn-key operation offered by some firms and sometimes accepted by authorities who are without the guidance of either architect or librarian. Here the firm designs the interior layout and supplies the furniture. Not surprisingly, in these circumstances, the layout is planned to fit in with the furniture and equipment which that firm has to offer. This is a pernicious practice.

Valuable programmes of independent testing of what is available commercially exist under the Library Technology Program of the American Library Association and in Britain's *Library Equipment Reports*.[1] Otherwise the architect has to rely on the manufacturer's word and reputation as to the strength and durability of the products. As the furniture or equipment is to come from a commercial supplier, the first step is to obtain all the brochures and to compare them in detail. Here the value of visits to other libraries becomes apparent. Another very valuable exercise is to ask shelving suppliers to lend a unit of their production and to put this into use in the old library; after a few months' experience the librarian and architect will have more knowledge of the unit's suitability than could have been gained by reading hundreds of brochures.

The first consideration is the choice of materials – wood or metal; plastic shelving is not yet a feasible proposition (although plastic covering to metal shelves is on the market, and moulded glass fibre has been seen; plastic catalogue drawers are quite common).

Softwood

This can be the cheapest of all materials for shelves. Easily assembled softwood units, a by-product of the materials storage industry, were at one time thought suitable only for the roughest stack conditions, but they are now obtainable in designs and with finishes previously found only in hardwood at a much higher cost. In areas of high humidity, softwood shelving does tend to absorb moisture and become distorted when drying out unless it has been carefully prepared. Nevertheless, when cost is critical and atmospheric conditions are suitable, this material should not be discounted, especially in non-public areas. All examples must be carefully examined to see that they are not subject to splintering and surface roughness.

Softwood or pressed board shelves on metal racks are also offered by materials handling firms and give even greater freedom in dismantling and re-erection as well as a high cost saving. The librarian must consider carefully the load-bearing qualities of these shelves; experience has shown that rows of heavy books can easily cause softwood shelves to bow, even in only 900 mm (3 ft) lengths.

Some architects have used painted softwood shelving for public use, or it may have been forced on them by reason of economy. It is certainly cheap and has the advantage of complete freedom in choice of colour, both of which may be important considerations in small conversions; but it must not be forgotten that the constant movement of books soon disfigures painted shelves and that regular repainting is neither cheap nor convenient.

Hardwood

This was for centuries the only material in use in libraries and may still be preferred for its warm, mature appearance and its quietness. It can be cut to fit corners more easily than metal but is usually dearer. Poole,[2] writing in the 1960s, says that (in the United States) it 'may run to 20 per cent to 30 per cent more than steel'. In Britain the ratio may be higher. During the last thirty years a greater range of hardwoods has come on to the market, particularly from tropical countries. How the cost relationship will change in the future is still uncertain: hardwoods may be priced out of the library market completely within a few years. Most hardwoods today are in fact veneered plywood or high density board: in some circumstances these can be

stronger than real hardwood, which is becoming rare, but much depends on the method and quality of manufacture. Wooden shelving is made as a 'bookcase', backed or backless; in the latter case it must have cross-bracing to ensure rigidity, and this may cause damage to books which are pushed to the back of the shelf. I have seen unbraced shelving, held together by the ingenious fitting of fixed shelves, become trapezoid in a very short time. In wooden shelving, adjustability is supplied by the use of inlaid shelf supports such as the familiar Tonks fittings, or by pegs set into holes in the uprights.

Metal cases with brackets can be fitted with wooden shelves and decorative end panels: these are discussed under 'Systems metal shelving' below.

In some libraries hardwood shelving is essential because it gives a mellow atmosphere which may be appropriate in law or scholarly research libraries, or in memorial rooms. Case-made single-sided hardwood shelving with fitted glass-fronted doors gives an unrivalled appearance of dignity and luxury.

In theory, wooden shelving presents a greater fire hazard than metal, but in practice this has seldom to be taken seriously: fire detection equipment will have been alerted and fire control action taken long before the intensity of heat is high enough to ignite the shelving. Wood, even hardwood, does tend to absorb moisture. In countries of very high humidity (and in particularly where the humidity fluctuates violently) the period during which wooden shelving (and furniture) is travelling from air-conditioned surroundings (factory or ship) to the air-conditioned library can allow it to absorb moisture, which will cause it to twist, warp or bow when it dries out in the library.

Metal

Metal shelving is much the most common for tall stacks in large libraries where vast stocks of books have to be housed. The stacks are usually of steel, although some pillars and brackets are now made of lighter materials. The shelving is of considerable strength, and the shelves themselves, particularly with U-type construction, can now be fabricated up to 1400 mm (4 ft 6 in) long without intermediate support. On the other hand metal shelves of this kind are often thicker than wooden, so there could be a loss of vertical space, possibly a serious matter if it leads to a reduction of one shelf per tier.

Products of the materials handling industry can be used for shelving where cheapness is the only consideration, but there will usually be some reduction in adjustability. Some firms offer prefabricated strips which are cheap and can be bolted together and used with either metal or wood (or even pressed-board) shelves in storage areas.

Such methods can be acceptable provided that the shelf surfaces, and particularly the edges, do not damage the books; it is also important to see that no bolt heads or shanks protrude. The body of the bolt should be located within the shelf thickness, not below it. Where possible, clips are better than bolts for this purpose.

Metal shelving, constructed specially for library use, is always better but of course more expensive. This shelving will have enamelled or plastic-coated surfaces and it comes in a wide range of colours. The two main types are the 'case', in which the shelves slide (and possibly lock) into slots in the upright sides, and the 'brackets', in which shelf brackets fit into slots in the upright columns. The variations in style and methods of construction offered by different manufacturers are so large that it is perhaps better to say merely that the case type is enclosed and the bracket type open. Most other generalizations can be proved wrong by examples. Similarly the distinction between the bracket type and the systems shelving method (which will be referred to later) is becoming even more blurred.

Adjustability is usually based on lines of slots or holes at 25 mm (1 in) intervals, but another method is to have the brackets gripping the uprights by a fitment which can quickly be released, thus giving infinite adjustability. The latter costs more, and it must be seldom indeed that such a critical adjustment is necessary.

Rigidity can be obtained by cross-bracing, but in many examples today the top and bottom members alone are sufficiently strong to hold stacks rigid; such bracing is a drawback in that it can prevent books being shelved to their full depth in open-backed stacks.

17:1–3. Examples of system shelving units fitted with a reading shelf, a seat and transparency display racks (Library Design and Engineering)

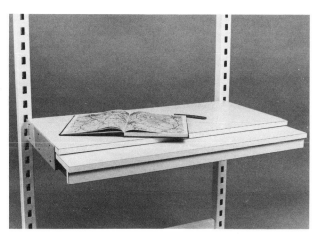

Stability is a matter of some importance because of possible 'card-castle' collapses, which can be very dangerous. The safest ways are certainly to anchor the stacks to the floor or to fasten the uprights to the ceiling by collars, but these obviously limit flexibility. In the past, stacks were often linked by rods fastened to the walls; these are seldom seen today, but they could be used as a safeguard in closed stacks. Case-type shelving is normally rigid enough in itself, but bracket-type often has wider feet for stability; the size and angle of these feet must be examined with care to see that they do not protrude into passageways. Many librarians consider that these feet give an unpleasing appearance in open-access rooms, but this is a subjective judgement. Because library floors are not always perfectly even, level adjusters under the feet can be a great asset.

Canopies can be supplied to bracket-type stacks to keep out dust, hold tier guiding or to serve as lighting holders; in stack conditions there seems little need for them, particularly in well-lit and air-conditioned buildings.

Systems metal shelving

Manufacturers now offer a very wide range of units which can be assembled to make both free-standing and wall-fixed shelving, and these are the most used type of shelving today. They are planned around a range of uprights, brackets and shelves, many different sizes and finishes being available. There are apertures in the uprights, and into these either shelf-supporting bracketrs or brackets with integral shelves are inserted. A less common variant is to have brackets integral with the shelves which fold away for neat storing when they are kept in reserve. Decorative end panels, of wood, laminated plastic or plastic-covered metal, can be supplied, and it is possible to change the appearance of a library merely by changing the colour, design and shape of these panels. Another great advantage is the very wide range of accessories made to fit into the unit systems: sloping shelves, display racks, catalogues, single study tables, seats – the range is constantly growing and offers the opportunity for internal flexbility at very low cost.

With the growing variety of media which libraries are having to house this flexibility can be a great asset. Perhaps the greatest facility is that of forming wall shelving without the need for uprights which stand out from the wall. Vertical wall strips, with the usual line of slots to take brackets, can be fastened to, or let into, the wall. Shelving can be bracketed in, or the wall left for display. In the latter case, only a vertical strip 8 mm (⁵⁄₁₆ in) wide will show, and panels, either as pure decoration or made of cloth-covered softboard for displays and notices, can be fitted to the walls between the strips. By using this system true flexibility of wall shelving can be obtained because a whole wall can be either used for shelving or left unshelved but decorated; if required, all walls of the building could be treated like this, with even greater flexibility, but the cost would be high.

Although shelves normally fit the distance between fixed uprights, it is possible with wall strips to have very long unbroken runs of shelving supported by brackets in hardly perceptible sunken wall strips. Special book supports will be necessary to keep the books upright. This kind of shelving is not needed in many libraries, but in some circumstances the architect might welcome the opportunity to provide a long straight run without vertical divisions. If brackets are to hold shelves running in both directions, a double strip will be needed, so the amount showing will be 13.6 mm (½ in) wide.

Summarizing, then, metal shelving is cheaper, stronger and can be more colourful than wood; but its great disadvantages are that it can feel 'cold and hard' and that it is noisy, books 'clanging' as they are placed on it.

Guides

Guides to the contents of the individual cases, tiers or even shelves will be needed, and an infinite variety of these is available. In closed-stack areas guides are less important because only the staff will have to locate books. Flat or tilted guides on ends of stacks, plus, possibly, slip-on shelf guides, are normally sufficient. When readers have to be guided to the required shelf, the matter is much more complicated.

General guides

In a prominent position near the reader entrance there should be a plan of the shelf layout of the entire library; another plan will be needed for each separate room. Ingenious systems have been devised, ranging from a layout map with coloured symbols (the colours being associated with the guides to individual shelving areas) to press-button systems which light up the required area on the map.

Many libraries today use terminals dedicated to giving detailed subject and location guiding on the VDU screen, but at present more people are likely to consult a large wall directory.

Guides to cases

Flat panels on the ends of bookcases are often built in by the manufacturers: they can be divided into two in order to show the contents of each side of the case. Where there are long runs of high bookcases in open-stack conditions, the guides have a limited use unless they give detailed information, shelf by shelf, but case guides are particularly useful on the ends of shorter runs of island cases. With these in place the tier guides can be minimal and so keep the overall height of the cases down, to provide a good vista.

Guides to tiers

Bookcases usually have a fascia guide strip at the top of each tier, but this is not possible when the top shelves have been left open either to accommodate large books or for a preferred 'bookshop' appearance. Because the position of the books on the shelves changes fairly rapidly in popular libraries, fascia tier guides must be easily changeable. Individual letters of cork or plastic can be fastened to fascias, by glue or pins. Cork lettering is available in a very wide range of founts for the purist, is comparatively cheap and can be coloured easily to particular requirements; plastic comes in a good range of colours and is stronger. These offer great advantages in flexibility, but cork particularly can be easily tampered with and removed. All these single-letter guiding systems tend to mark wooden fascias and this can limit theoretical flexibility. Lettered strips offer rather less flexibility but are interchangeable within tiers, and even reversible, and they can be slid and locked into grooves on the fascias. If desired, the lettering, either permanent or stuck on, can be on translucent material so that the guides can be back-lit. They can also be installed behind transparent material for protection.

Guides to shelves

In the forming of steel shelves narrow rails are often fitted so that lettered strips can be slid along the front edges of the shelves, either as complete words or, more rarely, letter-by-letter; in some systems a form of springing is incorporated to clip the guides into place. Where such provision is not made, sliding shelf clips can be used, but these have the disadvantage of protruding slightly onto the top of the shelf. Lettering can be fastened to the edges of wooden shelves, but this is a poor expedient. Individual shelf blocks can be made as guides to a shelf or to the whole tier. Where space can be spared on the shelves it is very helpful to the reader to have a block, perhaps 150 mm (6 in) cube, bearing on its face a guide to the contents of the shelf or tier. When neatly lettered such blocks can be attractive, and most readers seem to like them. They also serve as book supports.

Book supports

As shelves will seldom be completely full in open-access conditions, rows of books will tend to fall sideways, so some form of support is valuable, particularly for large books. On wooden shelves such supports can take the form of reversed U-shapes of rounded section rod, screwed onto the shelves (limiting book space), but on both wood and metal shelves movable supports are more usual. These can be of metal or plastic and can stand independently on the shelves, being moved along as books are inserted or removed; generations of librarians have grown to hate them. Systems shelving methods offer supports which can be clipped into the shelf above or slotted into the uprights. The latter is particularly useful where unbroken shelves beyond standard lengths are to be used. A more elaborate support can be spring-loaded and fixed to a rail mounted on the wall behind wall shelving. Whatever method is used, it is as well for the support to be at least 15 mm (½ in) thick, and rounded; wire or very narrow metal supports tend to get between pages of books when they are placed on the shelves in a hurry.

Tiers of oversized books, or awkwardly thin volumes, such as music scores or picture books, will need taller supports at closer intervals, since larger books exert considerable pressure when falling sideways. Because of the weight of these books the support should be permanently fastened to the shelves, top and bottom, or consist of sets of long rods which extend from top to bottom shelf of a whole tier, passing through holes in each shelf. These are offered by some manufacturers of systems shelving but presumably could be organized in any type of shelving, with some loss of flexibility. Spring-loaded rods have been offered for this purpose but are seldom very satisfactory. The best way is to have divisions running from front to back of each shelf to support the whole depth of the book.

A useful piece of shelf equipment is the narrow hollow block of wood or plastic, roughly the size of a book, which is substituted for a particular volume that has been removed from a reference shelf. Space is available on the 'spine' of the block for the book's title, while on the side can be a notice to the effect that the book is available elsewhere – usually on application to the staff. If the block has a built-in flange at the base it can serve as a book support. An old-fashioned notion, perhaps, but it can still serve a useful purpose. Lettered block guides to shelves, referred to earlier, also serve as book supports.

Manuscript storage

The librarian will have indicated the method of storage he wishes to use for manuscripts – usually deeper than for the shelving of books – and the size of document containers to be provided, but the architect should not choose them without the librarian's specific approval, because much damage can be done if containers made of material with a high acid content are allowed to come into contact with manuscripts (and other materials) for long periods. This is the specialist province of the archivist; the librarian who has no great experience in this field would be well advised to consult a professional archivist for advice.

Exhibition cases

This is another area where no home-produced items can compete successfully with the products of an industry which caters for museums and art galleries much more than for libraries. The librarian must think carefully and clearly identify his priorities before choosing from the large range of cases on the market. If security is all-important, then strong, thick glass is best for the viewing surface, preferably incorporating security alarms which go off even if the surface is merely tapped or scratched. Exhibition cases must keep out dust and should therefore be carefully sealed. To be entirely dust-free, the air must be prefiltered and forced into the case, preferably through the top, and vented out through the sides or bottom.

If clarity of display has a high priority, this calls for special lighting. If placed outside the case it may cause reflectance and glare, and so cases must be lit from the inside. Such lighting, or rather the heat and ultra-violet rays produced, can be a hazard to delicate objects on display; to avoid this, special and separate air-cooling equipment can be installed in the case – undoubtedly the best answer, but expensive. Fluorescent lights are cooler than incandescent but will need careful shielding to eliminate ultra-violet rays, and their colour rendering may not be acceptable; in general smaller low wattage incandescent lamps are best. This is another field where great improvements are to be expected from recent developments, and smaller and safer light fittings are already on the market. There is no substitute here for the advice of a museum or art gallery colleague.

Cases must be a suitable height for viewing, secure and yet easy to open without damaging the items on display. In most libraries, tall single-sided glass-fronted exhibition cases standing against a wall are most economical of space, but books displayed here can be damaged unless specially designed fitments are installed to hold them. Smaller, horizontal cases are safest for books; if the books are to be examined from two sides, the case will certainly take up a great deal of room, and again single-sided ones with their backs to a wall are less space-consuming.

Card catalogue cases

Although theoretically obsolescent, these large and impressive pieces of furniture will no doubt continue, in some countries, to dominate the appearance of open areas in libraries for many years. They still grow implacably with the size of the collection, and only the new technology can save many libraries from being overpowered.

The size of drawers is related to the size of the guide cards, which are naturally larger than the catalogue cards. The details of dimensions and fittings will not be discussed here because there is no substitute for the examination of examples of catalogues offered by specialized firms. Metal

catalogues are noisy if continuously in use. Softwood ones are usually unsatisfactory. The same used to be said of plastic ones, but they have improved greatly. Hardwood ones are expensive but almost inevitable. Proprietary catalogue cases, with label-holders, card-locking rods, safety catches and so on, are the result of years of experience. The production of catalogue cases, designed by the architect and made specially for the occasion by carpenters, is fraught with difficulty and expense, and from many year's experience I strongly urge that this temptation be resisted. Most library equipment firms offer standard carcasses for which special drawer fronts may be produced to meet the architect's design requirements. If more rows of drawers are decreed, despite the greater difficulty which the reader will find in consultation, these can be supplied (see Chapter 14).

Some catalogues incorporate consultation shelves below or between rows of drawers. Manufacturers of systems equipment offer small rows of catalogue drawers cantilevered off wall strips and thus completely interchangeable with wall shelving. This makes it possible for a subject catalogue to be dispersed, the cards for each subject being housed among the appropriate subject book tiers.

Chairs

There is little special about the chairs needed for libraries. The librarian's contribution is confined to providing information about the use to be expected, the categories of readers who will use them, and the atmosphere of the room: for example he may object to moulded plastic chairs for use in a very dignified ambience. Otherwise the material from which they are made concerns him little so long as the chairs are suitable for the predicted use, preferably un-tippable (leaning a chair backwards weakens the joints), durable[3] and easy to clean. Their covering materials must not make readers' clothes shine or deposit fluff on them. The chair legs must not damage the floor on which they will be used. Some readers much prefer chairs with arms, even when sitting at a table. If some of this type are to be provided they should be carefully tested at the tables where they are to be used. Deep, cloth-covered relaxing chairs become dirty in public use (even if it hardly shows), and for reasonf of hygiene should be carefully selected for ease of cleaning. Questions of fire safety and the dangers of materials like polyurethane are discussed in Chapter 12.

Tables

Tables, like chairs, are the common currency of the architect's world. The librarian will be concerned with rigidity and with the possible effect the feet may have on floor surfaces: in extreme cases castors or glides may be necessary. He should test a suggested table by piling books on one end of it: this test fails some very attractive tables, offered at low prices by makers of office furnishings, because they are not designed for library conditions. The position of the table legs in relation to readers' seating positions needs thought.

The material of the table-tops is certainly of concern to every librarian. Leather is particularly attractive to use but is easily marked; linoleum and rexine are harder; vinyl very much harder and available in a wide range of colours and patterns. When considering the relative resistance of these materials to the wear they will receive from books (particularly heavy manuscripts with metal clasps), it should be noted that if there is a strip of wood around resilient material on the table-top, it too will be vulnerable. If linoleum is chosen for the top because of its pleasant feel, accepting that it will have to be replaced at intervals, then the wood edging strip may need attention too, and this is a much more expensive matter. A compromise could be a linoleum top with plastic laminate edging, but many people dislike plastic laminates on table-tops.

A wooden table can be very attractive to the user; it feels right. It marks less easily than leather or linoleum but if marks do appear they are far more difficult to remove. To renew a complete surface is a major undertaking. New developments in polyester coatings may make wood more generally acceptable in the future; if veneered wood is to be used (as it usually is) it is important to see that the edges are protected against chipping, if necessary by edging them with a wooden strip or by having them bevelled.

The most durable materials are enamelled metal and plastic laminates, but they feel 'unfriendly', and writing on them in cool conditions can make the hand feel almost numb. Tables with spindly legs and hard plastic tops (usually white) are mass-produced and cheap; they are installed in far too many modern university libraries and are seldom popular. The librarian could well keep his eyes open in modern restaurants to see what new table materials are coming into use; their designers are usually ahead of the rest of the world.

Plastic-topped tables come in a wide range of colours and patterns (including imitation wood if prejudice can be overcome). It is important to test the surface in normal use conditions. If one tries to write with a ball-point pen on a single sheet of paper laid on various tops it will be found that some coverings are too soft (leather), some too uneven (oak or teak unless coated), some so hard that the ink will not flow in the pen (glass and some plastic laminates). But does a reader ever write like this on a single piece of paper? Questions of colour and reflectance are considered in Chapter 11.

Equipment

In the secondary brief the librarian will have indicated that he requires certain equipment – cameras, photocopiers, presses, guillotines, typewriters, duplicators and so on. The choice of this machinery is entirely his own; because so many different fields of activity are involved no attempt here is made to deal with the choice of models. Matters that concern the architect are the space needed, weight (for floor loading), electrical outlets and cost, if these items are to be included in the contract. The latter point is one for the authority to decide. If the cost is to be included, the librarian informs the architect how much money is to be allowed for each specific item, including installation and transport costs if relevant. In most cases these items will not be included in the general contract in order to save a possible contractor's percentage on all items in the contract.

Microform production and reading

This is a highly specialized field in which new equipment is constantly being marketed. At intervals the *Architects' Journal* publishes an information sheet on the subject, but much new equipment is produced between issues. The librarian must keep up to date with the latest articles on the subject and with makers' catalogues, although, as usual, it is necessary to treat manufacturers' claims with caution. It is always best to see the equipment in action (not as demonstrated by a salesman) and to speak to someone who has had experience of the machine in constant use. A

decision which must depend upon the particular situation is whether to have machines for each specific purpose or to use multi-purpose machines (film and fiche readers, for example); in general it is true that something designed for a single purpose tends to be more efficient than one with many uses.

In all cases a decision as to the number and positioning of the machines must be made at an early stage so that the architect can plan for space, weight, power supply and possibly variable lighting, but the model chosen does not affect him. The information given to the architect in the secondary brief will in any case be in general terms, if only because new models are likely to come on to the market during the planning process.

Audio-visual equipment

The great growth in the range of these media forces the librarian to study the market very carefully or his equipment will be out of date before the library is opened. There is a fundamental difference between machines which are only to be operated by staff and those which are suitable for use by readers. Many of the machines seem to be part of readers' home lives – television sets, video and audio recorders and players, for example – but this does not mean that they will be carefully used. Such machines should be chosen for their heavy-duty character and with as limited a range of controls as possible. There is an obvious difference between those built for individual use and those which are necessary to a 'performance' – large television sets, video and cine projectors, for example. To make one type serve both purposes is seldom satisfactory.

There is an infinite variety of ways to create (or to purchase ready-made) the viewing and/or listening booth. The most advanced will be the 'wet' carrel, which may have a computer terminal, an audio cassette and disc player and a television screen (or just the facility for using these machines when one or other is supplied on request from the library stock). An obvious alternative is to have different equipment fitted in different carrels, but this can be limiting in use. In popular libraries it is common to have semi-carrels (that is, small tables shielded audially and possibly visually from other users), but the difficulty here is to provide the necessary wide range of machine alternatives. This range is so wide that only a study of manufacturers' catalogues will give guidance.

Computer access equipment

Although it is not possible to comment on this in general terms (because all will depend on the computer hardware purchased) certain points have to be taken seriously. It is not good enough to presume that the reader will gaze at a screen rather than read a book and that therefore table space (with nearby power supply and ducting) is all that is required. Even if the local data is held in a staff-controlled area on CD/ROM, other optical disc or, soon perhaps, Digital Paper, the user may need print-out facilities; if he is to select from a stock of discs and use them himself, then extra equipment (disc-drive, mouse and and so on) will have to be provided. A major decision will be the number and complexity of the work-stations needed; because the number of users of these is certain to grow in the near future it will be a matter of deciding how many and of what kind – more a financial than a space problem. The factors involved in the choice of equipment are so complicated and so financially committing that this is fast becoming one of the greatest decisions the librarian has to make.

Table 17.1   Comparison of flooring materials in rising order of initial cost*

	Life in years	*Annual overall cost†*	*Wear resistance‡*	*Acoustic absorption‡*	*Water resistance‡*
Thermoplastic	10	3	5	1	2
Granolithic tile	20	1	1	5	3
Vinyl	15	3	3	3	2
Linoleum	15	4	3	3	3
Hardwood block	25–50	1–2	2	4	5
Thick rubber	25	4	2	1	1
Light carpet	20	7	3	1	3
Terrazzo	50	2	1	5	2
Heavy carpet	25	6	3	1	5
Slate	25	3	2	5	1
Marble	100	3	1	5	2

* Based on the *AJ Handbook of Building Enclosure*, Information Sheet, suspended floors (3), tables II and III.
† The higher number, the greater the cost.
‡ The higher number, the worse.

Floors

The wear to which floors in libraries are subjected is similar to that in other public buildings – theatres, shops, town halls and so on. With these and their problems the architect will be familiar. He will know all about the range of coverings available, their various properties and relative costs. The librarian's contribution will be to indicate the expected use, section by section, and his priorities with regard to such qualities as durability, quietness and ease of maintenance; later in the programme he will check the architect's recommendation against his own experience. In general, initial cost will dominate the choice of floor covering; it is unfortunate that because the cost of flooring is such a large element in the building, there is always a temptation to economize in order to reduce the overall price, with the result that appearance and readers' comfort suffer, and maintenance costs are increased (see Berkeley[4]) – a very serious matter, as floors are the biggest single item in library maintenance.

Standards in commercial buildings seem usually to be higher – a sad comment on the community's attitude to public buildings. Librarians could benefit from looking at the floor coverings used in supermarkets and the better-class department stores and considering why each was chosen. On the whole you get what you pay for. In each group of materials there is a cheap and an expensive grade and to expect one to give the same service as the other is unreasonable. In many cases the better, more expensive grade has a lower maintenance cost. To work out the balance of advantages, each library's peculiar problem must be studied. No library will use the same materials everywhere; in practice it is the choice or combination that matters. In areas exposed to the weather, subject to dirt and wet from shoes, or where noise is not an important consideration, terrazzo would give long-term savings, but it is too seldom seen in libraries; brick is often used with success. For each separate use the librarian must assess materials in terms of cost – initial and long-term – durability, ease of maintenance, quietness, comfort, safety (non-slip), thermal conductivity, reflectance (shine) and appearance. For each of these qualities there is a 'best choice'; but in order to make the correct overall decision it is necessary to know something of the properties of the different materials.

Factors to be considered

Cost
Costs can be compared only when materials are directly comparable; for example, poured concrete is cheaper than carpet, but they are unlikely to be alternatives for a particular floor area. For each type of material there will be wide differences in cost, according to thickness and quality, and this complicates comparison between types: some vinyl is dearer than some carpet, but generally carpet is much dearer than vinyl. Rolls are usually cheaper over a given area than square tiles of the same material, but not necessarily in a large contract: the question of whether tiles are to be stuck down is also a relevant cost factor. At the lower end of the price scale come concrete, asphalt, vinyl asbestos and linoleum; then rubber, cork, hardwood block and the better thermoplastics; towards the top come nylon carpet, polyesters and polyurethanes. Even higher are wool carpet and the best of the very hard surfaces – terrazzo and marble. These are initial costs; a truer comparison is the total cost, including maintenance, over the expected life of the flooring. Such comparisons are very difficult to obtain except from manufacturers, whose claims are seldom acceptable as evidence. As a very wide generalization it can be said that the initial extra cost of good-quality carpet will be between a quarter higher and double the price of the resilient materials which are its main competitors. It is widely stated that the higher initial cost will be offset by the much lower maintenance costs of carpeting; this seems likely, but after some experience the writer is a little uneasy about such a claim. Table 17:1 gives some comparative figures.

The *Architects' Journal*[5] quotes tests carried out in Louisville, Kentucky, reported by the American Carpet Institute, as showing that the labour costs of carpet cleaning were 65% to 73% less than for cleaning asphalt tile, vinyl asbestos, vinyl tile and terrazzo. Berkeley's figures on the matter are inconclusive.

Durability
The very hard materials are unchallengeable in this respect: marble, terrazzo, brick, wood block (in that order). Carpet, especially that with a proportion of man-made fibres, can be quite good, but the appearance suffers after a time. Rubber is much better than most vinyls and

linoleum. If the chief source of wear is grit carried on shoes off wet roads, cork can be a disaster. Stiletto heels ruin linoleum, vinyl and rubber. Different materials vary widely in their resistance to stains such as those made by cigarettes, tea, coffee and ink, but hard non-porous surfaces are obviously much the best.

Maintenance
Carpet is quickly cleaned by vacuum cleaner, but this is not the end of the story; in heavily used areas, particularly near entrances, a pattern of dirt will develop and the carpet will have to be shampooed – by no means a simple task. Carpets, if not kept clean, can cause respiratory problems. In a busy public library, routine vacuum cleaning is not enough. Carpet is also vulnerable to cigarette burns and stains of many kinds: it is not as hygienic as non-porous surfaces. Marble, tile and similar stone materials are very easily washed; hardwood blocks need more attention but the work is fairly simple. Other surfaces can be less easy to maintain. Linoleum needs both polishing and regular resealing, but requires less attention than cork. Vinyl is unsatisfactory both because of the regular cleaning it requires and because it is marked so easily, particularly by rubber heels. The way the material is laid – roll or tiles – affects the issue: see below.

Quietness
This is not so easy to assess as it might appear: carpet is so good a sound insulator that it is usually the most important piece of acoustic treatment for its area, but if other absorbent materials are present the result can be too 'dead' and inhuman (see Saunders[6] and Koderas[7]). Rubber, cork and linoleum are fairly good for quietness; vinyl is less good but better than wood. In general all the very hard floors are noisy, but even this generalization should not be accepted too easily: in the City Business Library, London, a marble floor, usually considered impossibly noisy, has proved very acceptable in an area where absolute quiet is not required.

Comfort
This is largely a matter of opinion. Carpet with a good backing gives a luxurious feel, but even sheet linoleum can be very soft to the feet if it has a rubber underlay. Is softness underfoot a desirable quality? Staff who have to be on their feet for long periods, in counter areas for example, may find that too soft a flooring can be tiring. On the other hand, staff should never be expected to spend long periods standing on very hard floors, which soon make ankles and feet painful. If a counter is set in the middle of a hard floor, the working area enclosed should be fitted with a resilient surface, because movement from hard to softer materials can cause accidents. In general, carpets are outstanding for comfort, rubber and linoleum good, cork and vinyl acceptable. For quick-reference areas, hard tiles (or marble) are possible; readers are familiar with them from their local supermarkets.

Safety
Highly polished marble and vinyl (and embossed vinyl) can be particularly dangerous, especially if wet, but for most materials correct maintenance according to the manufacturer's instructions will give safe conditions. Carpet (unless worn in patches) is excellent, as is cork. Some kinds of carpets, if fitted in dedicated computer rooms, may have to be earthed because of static build-up. This will not apply to terminals in usual library areas.

Thermal conductivity
The ability to conduct heat affects the decision as to choice of flooring materials in two opposite ways: where heat inside the building is to be conserved, low conductivity is desirable; conversely, when underfloor heating is installed, as much heat as possible has to pass upwards into the library, so high conductivity is desirable. Some of the harder materials have high conductivity (concrete, marble, and asphalt); vinyl and rubber have a higher conductivity than linoleum, cork very much less; carpet has least of all.
Generally, carpet is best for keeping a library warm and cosy, but it is worse for the efficient operation of underfloor heating.

Reflectance
Brock Arms[8] says: 'For study conditions where reading tasks require a long attention span, it is desirable to use only materials and colours within the field of vision which reflect percentages of light within the allowable contrast ratio of 1 to 10.' Vinyl in particular can offend here.

Appearance
Perhaps this should be left entirely to the architect, but the librarian is very much concerned with the results of his choice. It is legitimate to note that there are infinite varieties of colour and pattern available in vinyl. Where this material is laid in tiles rather than rolls, bright patterns are easily made; some librarians feel that the temptation to create jazzy patterns has been too much for some modern architects. Many librarians feel that wood block and cork offer the best 'mature' appearance in a library, but carpet is undoubtedly popular with readers.

Special areas
For entrance areas the librarian's priorities will be safety, durability and ease of maintenance, although he will naturally wish the architect to create a welcoming atmosphere. Durability is especially important in this area, where use is so heavy: not only is replacement expensive, it can bring the whole library to a standstill. The librarian may therefore place the highest priority on the need to have uninterrupted use of the area for many years, and might in this case favour marble, terrazzo, brick or a poured floor. Alternatively he may prefer thick rubber, which is quiet and can be replaced very easily.
For general public service areas the librarian will have to be sure that the architect fully understands the tremendous wear which certain traffic lanes in a library may undergo. The IN and OUT lanes beside lending library counters suffer very heavily, particularly if readers come to the IN counter direct from outside the building with grit on damp shoe soles. Here it is reasonable to have marble or terrazzo tiles or strips of thick rubber rather than replace sections of carpet, linoleum or vinyl as they wear out. Naturally this reduces flexibility, and the change of flooring is difficult to provide in open-plan libraries. The use of dirt-attracting mats at entrances, supplied on a contract basis, can be a great economy, but for safety they should be fitted in mat wells.
For corridors, closed stack rooms, and staff working areas the architect will use a suitable 'public building' material: cork, vinyl or linoleum. Perhaps surprisingly brick has been used effectively in many places. Even here, carpet, usually of a heavy-duty grade, is becoming common: when it is used throughout the building the large order can produce an advantageous price. It should not be forgotten that cheap plain carpet can stain easily (and permanently).

Materials and their qualities

Carpet

Carpets are unrivalled in their acoustic quality, their range of colours and their power to create a welcoming and luxurious atmosphere. The emphasis on luxury may seem impractical, but it can have real advantages, in that children are said to be more restrained in carpeted rooms: it may be that the effect wears off with familiarity. Until a few years ago carpet was specified only as a luxury for areas where hard use was not expected, but it is now found in most libraries which can afford it; it is reported that at least 90% of libraries in the United States are carpeted. It should not be forgotten, however, that carpeting does wear out and that at some future date it will have to be replaced, at considerable cost.

Carpet should have a pile density of 100 tufts per 645 mm^2 (1 sq in) and pile height of 15 mm to 18 mm. It can be composed of 100% wool or 100% man-made fibres; mixtures are common. Perhaps the most popular proportion at present is 80% wool–20% nylon. The differences between these types of carpets are important, advantages and disadvantages being present in each type in varying degrees.[9] It will be necessary to balance price, stain resistance, wearing qualities, anti-static qualities, and so on: this subject is worth studying by the librarian before he commits his library to heavy expenditure on this material. For example a newly completed library which I have visited reports considerable inconvenience from static even with a 80/20 wool/man-made fibre carpet.

A good-quality sponge rubber underlay will help to produce an even softer feel and a longer life. This underlay can either be laid as a roll, pre-fixed to a roll of carpet, or pre-fixed to each carpet tile. More common are backings of polypropylene, polyvinylchloride or bitumen, and these are normally stuck to the subfloor.

Many developments have recently taken place with the use of man-made fibre and animal bristles for non-woven carpets, such as Heugafloor and Heugafelt. These are often of very short pile, closely packed; the surface is resistant to dirt, but does not offer the same attractive appearance, or sense of luxury, as woven carpeting. Non-woven carpets have great advantages for areas such as stairs, where quietness, safety, hard wear and economy are needed. Manufacturers' ranges and claims must be studied carefully: this is the architect's business.

Vinyl

For some years this was the most used floor covering in British public libraries, replacing the linoleum which was ubiquitous before the Second World War. When bonded to its own soft backing, vinyl can be comfortable but without this it can feel hard. Many variations in plastics have been made, including vinyl asbestos, and cork covered with a transparent vinyl. On the whole such floor coverings are cheap, fairly durable and available in a wide range of patterns and colours, but they are not particularly quiet, they are easily scratched and marked and their shine may reflect overhead lights to the annoyance of users. Some consider that a large expanse of shining vinyl gives an institutional feeling: perhaps this is just a matter of taste.

Linoleum

This was once almost universal in libraries, usually of 'battleship' quality – 3.2 mm gauge: it is cheap and good to walk on, but the colours are less attractive than those of vinyl and it takes time and energy to maintain its apearance.

Rubber

This varies immensely, particularly in thickness. Thick rubber, now usually synthetic, has proved surprisingly long-lasting and comfortable in use. While it does not create an air of welcoming luxury, it is useful for quietness and durability in a very heavily used area. It tends to deteriorate in continuous direct sunlight.

Cork

When well maintained cork can look most attractive, but its maintenance is a serious problem in areas of heavy use. The grit carried in on readers' shoes can soon break down the surface seal, and resealing can be carried out only when the room is not in use. Cork is not particularly durable and after a time there will be a noticeable difference in colour between tiles which have received the heaviest wear, and have therefore been cleaned most often, and those close to furniture.

Wood

Hardwood blocks, parquet and softwoods of various kinds were widely used in the past but are seen less frequently today in reading and traffic areas. They are all noisy; wood block and parquet are expensive but look very attractive indeed. Certain newer composition floors contain finely ground wood among other elements; these are fairly cheap and are quieter than very hard floors, but as yet it is difficult to obtain reliable information about wearing qualities. Like all composition floors, these tend to look drab.

Tiles and bricks

These are obviously very durable and used mostly in entrance halls, where noise is not so damaging to the reader. Bricks can be very attractive, especially in regions where they are a familiar building material. Bricks are less liable to be slippery than tiles but are rather more expensive to maintain, as their surface is not usually exactly even.

It used to be the practice (for reasons of economy) to have raw concrete floors in basements, but if this is done it is most important for the surface to be well sealed (and kept sealed) to keep down the dust.

Roll or tiles

Some materials may be laid either in roll or in square tiles; each form has its advantages and disadvantages. As the question arises most often in the field of carpeting, comment will be restricted to that field, but it applies to flexible flooring in general.

Rolls of material are easier, and in some circumstances can be cheaper, to lay. Their appearance is even, there are no spaces in which dirt can accumulate and micro-organisms breed. When sections show signs of wear, patching can be difficult, although some rolls with bonded underlay can be cut easily and the edges do not fray.

In small quantities carpet tiles can turn out to be dearer than rolls of the same materials, partly because of the labour of sticking them down; but very large bulk purchase will reverse the differential. However well tiles are laid, the joints will show. Some designers see this as an advantage over plain carpet and point out that in roll carpet the seams will show as long lines and may be less acceptable visually. Other designers prefer to lay square carpet tiles with the pile running alternately in opposite directions to create a faint chequerboard pattern by use of the texture; with suitable colours this can be most attractive.

Tiles are less hygienic than roll, and if they do not fit closely they can be a safety hazard. Loaded trolleys can lift the edges of the tiles, and it may be necessary to have trolleys fitted with specially wide wheels. If the tiles are stuck down this should not apply: unstuck tiles give access to underfloor ducting, but this is seldom a vital factor. Perhaps an answer is for certain rows, running both ways, to be stuck down to act as anchor for the rest. The great advantage of tiles is said to be that worn ones can be interchanged with others from a less worn area, but the writer has not found this acceptable in practice, if only because wear is usually gradual over a number of tiles. Alternatively worn tiles may be replaced by new ones: if this is the intention it is advisable to buy a good many extra tiles when the floor is laid, as colours vary in different batches, and it is likely to be impossible later to make a good colour match. It is common (but pitiful) to see libraries which have had to transfer less-worn tiles from staff rooms to make a good replacement for worn ones in public areas, new tiles of a slightly different shade being acceptable in smaller rooms. Carpet tiles, in Britain, are usually 500 mm (20 in) square; when laid on a sound base they do knit together, but because they are affected by the moisture in the air and can expand between 2% and 6% an appropriate allowance may have to be made when they are first fitted. If they are to be stuck down – much the better policy in most situations – this allowance cannot be made.

18 Extensions and conversions

Extensions

It is not every architect (or librarian) who is fortunate enough to be able to create a library afresh on a clean and unencumbered site. There are many circumstances where it is necessary, or expedient, to use an existing building as the basis for a revived, modernized, extended service. The reasons are obvious; if the present library occupies an excellent site and there is land adjoining which can be used, it makes sense to extend. Not only will it usually be much cheaper but it allows a known service, with its built-in clientele, to be improved. Sometimes the task is not to extend but to modernise an existing library building and this is more difficult unless large under-used areas can be brought into service. More difficult still is the conversion of an alien building for library use; there have been so many of these, and the original buildings have varied so widely, that it is necessary to be quite sure what is needed before attempting to follow the example of others. In a survey of 'new' library buildings built in Britain between the years 1975 and 1983[1] it was found that, of the 581 buildings reported, 219 were either conversions or extensions. In the United States, of 256 academic libraries reported between 1976 and 1986,[2] 99 were additions and renovations. It is therefore a subject worth studying.

It is common today for libraries to be built in phases. There are a number of reasons for this; the most obvious is to allow the first part of a very large project to come into operation while plans for subsequent parts are being decided. A second is that a continuing need, but of unknown dimensions, has been identified. An extreme example of this is quoted by Metcalf[3]: 'The State of California planning authorities, because of the tremendous demand for additional space . . . have in certain circumstances ruled that new buildings should be large enough for five years only, after which a second stage of construction should be proposed.' More often, one suspects, a decision to build in phases is made because the cash for the first phase can be found but there is some doubt about the second. In such a case it is easier to call the building 'phase one' than to admit that it will be inadequate for its purpose. Leaving one wall with the option of being removed later should a second phase materialize can appear an enlightened decision; certainly if expansion is to come, even in the indefinite future, it is better to plan for it at the beginning. To do this properly, however, allowing access routes, mains services, and so on, can add appreciably to the cost of the first phase. This is discussed in a number of places under the heading 'expandability'.

Many expansions or extensions occur when a site becomes available alongside a library building which is famous as a piece of architecture, or one whose demolition for replacement would be unthinkable. Two very famous examples are the Boston Public Library and the Mitchell Library of Glasgow, both of which had large extensions in th 1970s. There are a number of similarities. Boston, by McKim, Mead and White, is one of the most famous public library buildings in the United States. A monumental building of 1897 with a vast reading hall, it was extended by Phillip Johnson on an adjoining rectangular site, the exterior of the buildings matching, although architectural licence allowed the architect to exaggerate the size of the arches which were a feature of the old building's face.

The Mitchell Library[4] is the main reference library of Glasgow, and its 1911 neoclassical facade is a feature of the city. Although there was an expansion in 1953 into adjoining space, this still did not meet the growing need. There was no opportunity for further expansion until a disastrous fire destroyed the St Andrews Hall, with which the library shared an island site; in fact it was only a fire-break which saved the library itself from destruction. The City Council agreed to the extension of the library but a number of constraints were evident:

1. The absolute necessity for any extension to fit in aesthetically with the existing Mitchell Library and the consequent decision to build within the still standing colonnaded walls of the old halls building.
2. The presence of a railway under part of the site.
3. The planning decision to align the floor levels to fit with the existing Mitchell Library, although the ground level was different.

The brief required the extension to provide space for public services arranged in large subject groupings, as well as display areas, a hall and a theatre.

On the site of one acre (0.4 hectares), three basements were possible. The lower two were devoted to book and newspaper stacks (the latter having much deeper shelves) and the upper basement to car parking. On the side adjoining the old library, seven book store levels were created, each associated with a subject department. The two buildings were linked chiefly at Floor 1 (the first above ground level) but there were doorway links on the ground floor and Floors 4–6. As part of the project the old library had to be altered, the old main reading hall and four other rooms being given subject commitments. At the same time the opportunity was taken to introduce on-line information services and a music lending library.

This example is given to show the great difficulties which can beset a major library when an extension is authorized. The project, which added 35 000 m^2 (375 000 sq ft) to a working library, imposed great strains on staff, who had to keep a public service going within the large building operation. To the importance of good relations between architect and librarian is added that of keeping everyone in the picture and making them feel that they are part of something exciting. Administratively this kind of project is more difficult to handle than the creation of a new building. The resultant building is certainly impressive, but it is not, and in these circumstances could never be, as good a functional solution as a new library would have been.

Another example of an interesting extension (if on a rather smaller scale) occurred when the Central Public Library of Amsterdam, which for many years had been inadequately housed, had the opportunity to take over a factory building behind the library building. The result was an extremely complicated exercise, mainly because of the separate elements of the two buildings and the height differences between street and ground levels. The facade, on the canal side, is particularly attractive because of the way the large frontage has been divided into four elements and, although completely modern, has retained sympathy with the spirit of the old warehouse buildings which face the Amsterdam canals.

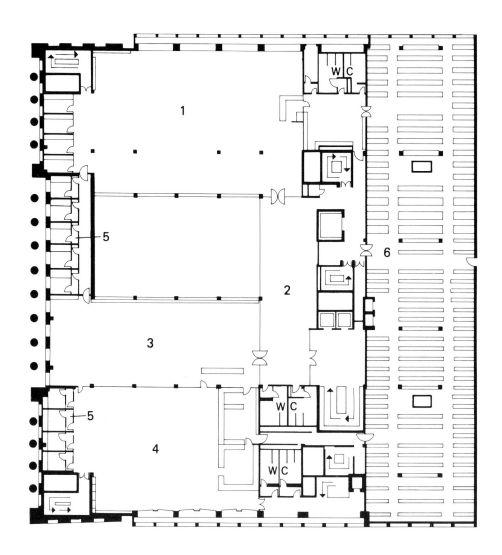

18:1. Mitchell Library, Glasgow: St Andrew's Halls (facade of old building conceals new building) Floor 4 (of twelve), showing position of stack between old and new buildings (Architects Sir Frank Mears and Partners)

Key: 1 Arts and recreation. 2: Display. 3: Music (lending). 4: Music (reference). 5: Carrels. 6: Book store

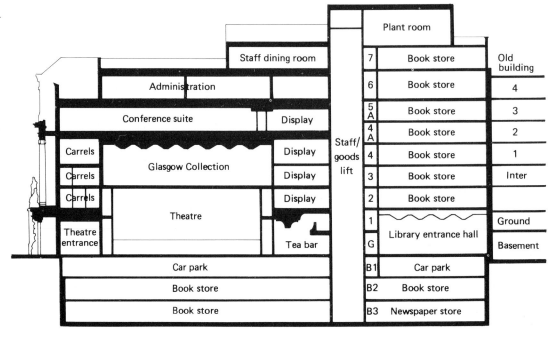

18:2. Mitchell Library: longitudinal section showing difficulty of linking with the old building

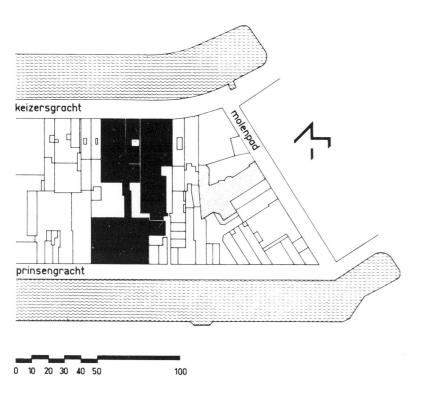

keizersgracht

molenpad

prinsengracht

0 10 20 30 40 50   100

18:3. Plan showing how Amsterdam Central Library was made from two separate buildings (Architect Architektenbureau G de Klerk of Amsterdam)

18:4. Amsterdam Central Library, showing frontage designed to accord with old warehouses, and also broken up to prevent mass dominating the area

Most extension projects are infinitely smaller than these. There is often some space to spare alongside or at the rear of an existing building, a legacy from the days when space in town centre positions was not as expensive as it is today. This area, be it loading bay, side access, or merely an awkward-shaped piece of land not worth including in the conventional outline of the old building, may prove invaluable to extend the building horizontally. Because such an extra piece of land will normally be at the side or rear it will not usually affect the main entrance, and there will be the problem of handling the greatly increased use of the future building through an entrance designed for a more modest purpose.

The operational decision is usually whether to erect book storage, thus freeing space in the old library which can be converted for public use, or to make an attractive new public service area to attract readers, leaving the old building, which is difficult to convert, to be book store and staff working areas. The creation of a lecture, exhibition or other hall on the vacant site, leaving the library untouched, is a wasted opportunity. To create a service within the shell of a building, that is, with only a facade standing, as in the case of the Mitchell Library Extension, can be done very successfully once it is accepted that the form has been predetermined and that no alteration of entrance or exit routes, and no further expansion, is possible. A good example illustrated in Figures 18:5 and 18:6 is in Stuttgart; the load-bearing pillars erected within the facade gave freedom for flexible service areas within.

The other obvious option – expansion vertically – is seldom possible with really old buildings unless the pillars and the lower beams are unusually strong. A structural survey will of course determine the matter, but even if it is technically possible one is faced in really old buildings with the problem of the great weight of the roof and the complications of its steep pitch. With buildings of the square type of the twenties and thirties the problems are

usually those of load-bearing (and of course planning consent to alter the building height). Perhaps a reason why expansion vertically is comparatively rarely used is the price to be paid in ground floor space in order to provide suitably wide stairs and/or lifts for access to the upper areas. A compromise of extra upper floors to be used only for storage and accessible only to staff means a waste of staff time when stock has to be fetched from the upper part of a building. The opposite, extension of the building downwards for storage purposes, is a very attractive one to a librarian, but may prove extremely expensive in operation unless there are rudimentary cellars.

Conversions

In very few parts of the world is the money available to put up sufficient new buildings to cater for increased library demand. With needs even sharper now that the private buying of books and other resources for learning have also come under pressure, the emphasis has shifted from the construction of imaginative new buildings to the alteration and use of old ones. Over the same period there has arisen a world-wide growth of interest in the conservation of old buildings. Architectural Heritage Year revealed the great need to find a way of bringing old buildings back into active use rather than to bulldoze away the heritage of the past. Because libraries, particularly public libraries, are largely self-contained social units, they can offer suitable uses for some old buildings, especially those which occupy key urban sites. Churches, warehouses, market halls and similar buildings of character can become effective libraries.

An extreme example is to be found in Italy, where some beautiful palazzi have lost their original purpose and where the municipalities have been very keen to find some practical use for buildings which are aesthetic assets to the area. Some have been made into libraries but, because the

18:5. Conversion of a ruined palace: Zentralbucherei im Wilhelmspalais, Stuttgart. The columns are being erected within the facade of the old palace

18:6. Here the columns (smaller at a higher level) support the new building

emphasis may be laid more on the preservation of the building than on the creation of a new service, there is a real danger that the functional needs of the library will be subordinated to an unacceptable degree to the appearance of the converted building. The librarian must be alive to this danger.

In the third world it is very seldom that old buildings are suitable for conversion as libraries. It is possible, however, in the more prosperous areas that some of the modest shop and office premises of the 1950s and 1960s, which are being superseded by much taller buildings, may be available for conversion, especially in oil-rich countries where capital and labour are available. Ironically in these countries the bulldozer usually clears the site.

The basic requirements of a library are comparatively simple. The housing of materials, chiefly books; the provision of space for readers to consult and to read them; reasonable lighting, heating and ventilating: these are not basically difficult to attain and a very wide range of buildings can be – and have been – used for the purpose. The number which have been effective as libraries is a very different matter. When the demand for libraries was particularly vocal and the supply of new building opportunities particularly low – immediately after each of the two world wars – a great number of conversions were made. Among the most common were unwanted churches or chapels, Nissen huts and semi-derelict shops. However workmanlike the conversions and well-planned the internal layouts, the results were seldom very satisfactory; they lacked not only aesthetic appeal but an indefinable rightness. The atmosphere created seldom offered that feeling of cheerful involvement which is the heart of a true library's appeal to the reader. It is a depressing thought that many people holding high office are so ready to assume that any old building will serve as a library – and the cheaper the better.

The need to preserve an old building is by no means the only reason why conversions are becoming frequent. There is the shortage of suitable sites for new buildings, but undoubtedly the greatest single reason is that it is cheaper to convert than to build anew. This is to over-simplify; other advantages include a shorter contract

period, less capital investment, the chance to build within a site where access will be easier. A reason which can be of great importance but which is difficult to assess is continuity in the character of an area which has been moulded over the years by this and other neighbouring buildings.

There is certainly logic in using an old building of character as the home of the public library, particularly as it will be the centre which holds and publishes the history of the locality. Many older buildings were solidly constructed with good-quality materials and offer advantages in energy conservation which would be expensive to obtain in a modern building. These reasons will appeal to the authorities concerned. An unfortunate consequence is that many libraries have been created which have proved quite unsuitable for their purpose. A conversion should not be considered as a cheap substitute but as an important creative project. Boards will often console themselves with the reflection that what is proposed is only a 'temporary' library but no professional will take this seriously, having known so many temporary library buildings which are still serving the same purpose fifty years later. Moreover the provision of a 'temporary' building may take the edge off vocal demand, making more difficult the task of obtaining a permanent one when funds are flowing again. The librarian must weigh all these factors.

If an existing building is to be converted to library use then the proposal requires, at all stages of the planning process, attention just as meticulous as that needed for a new library building. The process of planning should take exactly the same form, even though a number of the procedures can be taken as read. Too often the feasibility study for such a project consists of a few questions like 'Could we get planning consent?' and 'Is it big enough?'

Conversion has become a growth industry, and one advantage is that many architects have had experience of this kind of work; some have specialized in it. The points which follow in this chapter are meant for the guidance of librarians; they will be obvious, sometimes painfully obvious, to architects.

In Britain the most common conversions were the modernization of older libraries, particularly the many Carnegie Public Library buildings which had been erected between 1890 and 1914. To bring them into line with the requirements of the 1930s (or even the 1950s), the chief alterations were of internal allocations. The Carnegie libraries in the past had set great store by newspaper reading rooms (and sometimes by separate ladies' reading rooms), and this space was utilized to meet the

18:7. Conversion of a palazzo: Biblioteca Comunale di Como. Exterior with library windows (and window seats) added

18:8. Rear of the palazzo: use of the courtyard, with the new extension not visible from the street

greatly increased demand for lending services. At its simplest such a conversion might consist of exchanging the two areas, giving a large lending library and a small reading room, but the opportunity was usually taken to open out the rooms with more windows (and with clear rather than stained glass), to fit false ceilings under the great beams and to reduce the comparmentalism of the original buildings. Less often the front was altered; in many cases the piece of 'Railway Gothic' had become too much a part of the High Street to be altered.

Other internal conversions of an earlier day were arranged in order to substitute the Browne card-and-pocket charging system for the original closed-access Indicator system; ironically the large stretch of counter necessary for the Browne method is no longer needed with modern systems.

Changes in types of authority under local government reorganization can accentuate the need for change. On the one hand an old library may have to assume the duties of headquarters for a system, but it is more likely that a library which has been self-contained for many years becomes merely a branch library of a larger entity, the bulk of the book preparation work being taken over by a new regional headquarters. This can leave more space in the local library for service to readers. In such cases, and wherever the opportunity arises to add internally to the space for library service, the chief question to be asked is 'What are the present and future priorities for the use of this space?'

When we consider library buildings which were erected more than thirty years ago we can be sure that they were designed almost entirely to accommodate printed materials and that they were expected to serve a very much smaller readership than today. The basic problem is that of housing the new media attractively and finding space for readers to use them, and the book stock, in a way which was not conceived when the building was first built. The DES booklet *Designing a Medium-sized Public Library*[5] gives a good idea of the way in which a library can become very much a part of a local community, and shows how wide-ranging the needs of such a community can be. Moreover, the reader of today has higher expectations of both comfort and service than his predecessors; the interior of a library must offer a very different and more

welcoming atmosphere than libraries of the past. To arrange that audio and video discs and tapes shall be offered for loan is not in itself a space-consuming requirement, because the packages can be displayed and handled with little more trouble than books. Nevertheless the approach to this aspect of the service is quite different from that of a normal book-issuing service point, and if pictures and posters are also to be loaned, a new internal environment has to be created. The use of non-book media *within* a library, and particularly the library of an educational establishment, is a very different matter. In addition to housing the materials it is necessary to provide carrels or small study rooms for playing, listening, viewing or creating in all the media. This calls for a drastic rearrangement of space rather than positioning machines or facilities in odd corners. Even if the major use of the materials will take place outside the library there is still the problem of housing the reader or the small group wishing to use the media within the library, and this calls for a drastic re-thinking by both architect and librarian.

In addition to the pressures created by the growing requirements of both conventional and new media there are the problems of producing from an old shell an environment which will attract readers and make them feel comfortable. It is probable that the lack of real success of the public library movement in the eyes of the discerning public for many decades can be largely attributed to the dead atmosphere which the old 'free library' of an earlier generation produced. However important the conversion of an old building internally, to get the best out of the whole enterprise it is equally important that the image should be changed and that the users, both actual and potential, should be made fully aware that there has been a change which may offer them something of value.

Conversion by expansion

The easiest, cheapest and usually the most satisfactory conversion occurs when a library service is able to expand into another part of its own building which has become vacant. This was very common in older public library/ museum complexes when museums obtained their own buildings. It can also happen in any other area – school, college, hospital, for example – where the creation of a

18:9 and 18:10. Railway station before and after conversion: Lyminge Branch, Kent County Library

new building releases space in the old which in consequence can be made available either as a library extension or new library premises.

It is most important when expanding that the space available for the future library service should be considered as a whole. The two major problems will inevitably be the positioning of the main entrance and a rearrangement which avoids the need for extra supervisory staff. It is often expedient to move the administration sections of the library into the newly available space, thus releasing the old administration areas, already an integral part of the library building, for public service. A conversion of this kind can be comparatively cheap because there are seldom major structural difficulties in a building of unity. Little external work needs to be done (except for the creation of a satisfactory main entrance). To remove non-load-bearing walls and to reallocate furniture appears at first sight to constitute the major cost, but creating a continuity of feeling throughout the entire building can be quite expensive in finishes and floor coverings. Lighting will need careful thought, and some expenditure here will be necessary in order to create the right atmosphere throughout the library.

If the new area is to be used to extend the service itself, then obviously furniture must be purchased either to match the old (which may be difficult and expensive) or to provide a contrast with an area of different feeling. If, however, this new area is merely to be used to relieve pressure on the old, then the main cost may be chiefly the re-siting of existing furniture. The service fittings are another matter: in planning of this kind the opportunity will be taken to adopt changes in techniques, and a modern counter can be quite different in size and shape from the one it replaced. Computer services should also be carefully thought out; the idea of putting a terminal on any available table must be resisted. Allowance must be made in the estimates for 'making good', especially floors and their coverings, as

well as for lowering shelf case heights, re-positioning lighting and so on.

In cases where 'catwalk' galleries already exist it may be possible to widen them for public use or even to bridge the gap and create at least a partial mezzanine. Staircase access will already be adequate but there may be a need for an emergency fire exit.

To convert for library use levels which exist above the library can present many difficulties: floor loading, the need for book hoists or even lifts, ceiling heights, condition of roofs, disabled access, and the inevitable problems of fire safety. Consequent alterations to staircases may make the whole project too expensive. Thought must be given to the effect which changes in the upper part of a building will have on the lower: carrying out the alterations above will, at the very least, upset the plaster or rendering below, and allowance must be made for making good or even re-finishing. If the upper part has previously been used as a public building, then change of use may not be involved and the more stringent of the regulations could perhaps be avoided.

The easiest conversion of this type occurs where the original planning of the building allowed for temporary use by a non-library service of part of the building, usually the upper floors. Here, if adequate floor loading was allowed for in the original plans, the project is less a conversion than a simple move, requiring little more than new finishes.

Conversion of other buildings

The number of different building types which have been converted into libraries is quite astonishing. Apart from the well-known examples of houses, shops, offices, churches and warehouses which are mentioned below, I know of railway stations, market halls and even a fire station. Given a sound structure, an unencumbered floor area and a good site, these can become attractive and efficient service points. It all depends upon the imagination and skill of the architect.

Houses

Individual houses, if only because of their siting, are seldom appropriate for conversion as libraries of colleges, universities or schools, although in the shortages which followed the Second World War it was common in Britain for large houses to be made into education centres of which a room or two would be made into a library: not a satisfactory expedient, even at those times. Houses can be much more easily converted for use as public libraries, and many have been used for this purpose. Solid, middle-class houses of an earlier day, standing in the suburbs of many large industrial cities, have made very attractive branch libraries. With a position convenient for a residential community, a separate path leading often through a pleasant garden, such buildings can have a flying start. Because there will almost always be load-bearing walls within the house it may be difficult to open out the ground floor, and one would have to be content with widened door openings. Such conversions call for careful design or the pattern of rooms can feel like a rabbit warren. On the other hand a branch library within a fine old house has one outstanding advantage; it can feel comfortable and right to the people who use it. Many examples exist where readers are happier and more at ease than they would be in new and perhaps less familiar surroundings.

An inevitable problem is that of making use of the upper floors. If there is a wide staircase, then access will be simple without the use of a lift (although a book hoist may

18:11. First a railway station, then a market hall, then a corn exchange, and now Salisbury Divisional Library, Wiltshire County

18:12. Resource Centre, repeating the semicircular motif

18:13. Entrance hall, again repeating the semicircular motif of facade

floor readers? An obvious example is the staff rest and work areas, but in addition study rooms are a possibility. Personally I have always been against the placing of the children's library upstairs, for the obvious reasons of noise on the stairs and through the ceiling of the rooms below, but I have seen a number of examples where the arrangement works surprisingly well. Much depends on the habits of the local community, and here the local librarian's advice can be invaluable.

The change of use from a house used by a few people to a library used by large numbers will inevitably call for consents under the building regulations, particularly in respect of fire exits.

Shops

Perhaps the most common of all library conversions is that of a shop within a shoppintg district, chiefly because it offers a site where a popular library is best placed and partly because the basic elements of the two services are similar – attraction of customers, space for browsing, and service and facilities for storage of stock. The single most common feature of a shop is the large picture window for display and advertising, and it is surprising that for many years this feature was treated as a disadvantage, and indeed blotted out, when the shop was converted to a library. It is obviously one of the most valuable elements of the site, but it does have the disadvantage that it takes up useful shelvable wall space when lack of space is already the main drawback. Whereas a specialist shop can operate with a very small open display area, a library has a minimum size below which it cannot work as a reasonable public service.

The minimum open floor space which should ever be considered for use as a public library is 100 m^2 (1076 sq ft), and to this must be added 8 m^2 (86 sq ft) as an absolute minimum for staff facilities. Most librarians would strongly resist the argument (often put forward by ward councillors with a strong local patriotism) that some small space in a shopping area is better than nothing. The librarian knows that a shelf stock of 6000 books (which is all a space of 100 m^2 (1076 sq ft) would hold) could be quickly exhausted by even a small band of local users and that the very frequent change of stock necessary can be administratively very expensive.

It should be borne in mind also that if there is sufficient local demand for a new branch library, then at peak shopping hours it is likely that at least fifty people at a time will want to use the service; space for that number of people to circulate in comfort must be allowed.

Because a shop is designed for public use there is seldom any problem about safety regulations other than the provision of extra emergency exits; access for deliveries is also likely to be available. Planning consent for change of use will be needed but will almost certainly be given.

Offices

To take over a complete office block for conversion to a library has many advantages.' The site is likely to be good. There may be a wide main entrance and the whole building will have been designed with the needs of human beings in mind. In particular circulation routes will have been worked out and there will be physical conditions for people to read and write in comfort. The great disadvantage will be the compartmentalism; the building will probably be honeycombed with small rooms. If the structure permits the removal of internal walls, and in particular if it has been

be necessary). This means that disabled people cannot use the upper floor, and this can be illegal as well as anti-social. How to solve this problem, and indeed how to divide a small library between two floors, needs careful planning. What can be provided on the upper floor which cannot be available to disabled people, and which will not be used too intensively, causing disturbance to ground-

designed on the modern open-plan office principle, then a satisfactory conversion is possible.

Possible but not perfect: almost inevitably there will be a stiffness about the appearance and the result is not likely to be either aesthetically pleasing or particularly cosy, unless the architect can produce, with the aid of colour, design and ornament, a softening of the severe lines associated with office buildings.

A further disadvantage is that most office blocks have thin walls and it is highly likely that there will be acoustic problems. These can be solved by using sound-insulating layers, but it will add appreciably to the cost. When a smaller library is to be fitted out in an office block it must be on the ground floor. In a number of European countries, particularly France, it is common for public libraries to be found occupying upper floors, but this has disadvantages not only of access itself but of the psychological effect of indirect access. It has been my experience that only the librarian will ever take this point seriously: it *is* serious, and it is up to him to see that his views are forcefully presented.

Churches

Churches which have become redundant because of the movement of population away from town centres can be used to provide a public library service to workers, and in Britain a number of Victorian Gothic buildings have been used for this purpose. There are difficulties, and I have never seen a successful conversion. The main reason for this lack of success is the height of the nave; unless upper floors or false ceilings can be inserted (which is expensive to do properly and is often unacceptable because it would destroy the unity of the building), the result will be an over-imposing environment which is noisy and expensive to heat. If the windows extend down too low, the walls will not be usable for shelving unless the appearance of the interior is to be ruined. For a small and scholarly library for a college or other service where a 'Gothic' atmosphere is acceptable, it can be done satisfactorily. The conversion of All Saints Church, Oxford, into a library for Lincoln College is a particularly fine example.[6] Similar conversions of Victorian school buildings, redundant for the same reason as the churches, have made successful and quite attractive libraries because they have neither the high ceilings nor the large open spaces of a church.

Consents

In Britain planning consent is needed for every conversion, whether it involves alterations to the building or merely a change of use. In practice, because if every minor alteration were to be submitted to the planning authority for committee discussion an enormous bureaucracy would result, a simplified procedure allows automatic approval by the officers for various classes of minor work. On the other hand, if the building has been 'listed' by the Department of the Environment, either for the building's own quality or for its historical contribution to the area, or if the area itself is scheduled because of its general importance, then the limitation on alterations may be much more severe, and the project is likely to need 'listed building consent', which will inevitably mean delay.

Consents of this kind vary from country to country and it is part of the architect's job to be familiar with them. Undoubtedly the greatest legal hazard of conversion in Britain is the application of the Building Regulations. These regulations exist to ensure that building users are given a reasonable standard of protection in terms of health and personal safety. An existing structure may be defective, but it may be only when a new use is entertained that some aspect of the regulations will come into force. The regulations may apply even when physical alterations are not proposed; a change of use whereby a building serving a small number of people is to become a library and will therefore be used by a great number can need consent.

The regulations concerning fire can drastically affect ideas for the conversion. For example a warehouse may have attractive Victorian columns which appear to be sound, but by today's fire regulations much more fire-proof protection may be needed. The columns may have to be enclosed by fire-resistant materials before they can be accepted. Again, a vertical extension to a building may cause it to be within a different category of requirements for fire resistance. A structural survey will undoubtedly be needed not only to establish the soundness of the building for its new purpose but also to determine which walls are essentially load-bearing and which may be moved as part of the internal reorganization. Fenestration in particular may be a major problem. It may not be difficult to pierce the walls and put in extra windows, but if on a frontage, this will certainly require planning consent.

Services will present few problems to the architect, but lighting is quite another matter. All that has been said in Chapter 11 about the importance of lighting in libraries applies at least as much to converted buildings. If the interior is not entirely appropriate (if there are high ceilings, for example), then the lighting has an even greater task to perform. Good library lighting, free from reflectance and glare, of the correct intensity for reading in different human conditions, can be provided; but in an unusual building, with its own strengths and weaknesses, specially designed lighting can be the most important visual element.

As when planning a completely new building, the opportunity should be taken to carry out a survey of the library's proposed operating procedures and also those techniques and procedures which might, in the foreseeable future be introduced. To use an old building may be a calculated decision and many examples have shown how successful it can be, but to plan for yesterday is a recipe for disaster. It is just as important to prepare a full and carefully considered brief for a conversion as it is for a new building.

19 Published standards

Published standards are both a convenient yardstick when planning a service and an incentive to excellence. There are standards of objectives, of services, administration and funding, but here we are concerned with quantitative standards, particularly those which will guide us in making space allocations for a new library. The kind of space and equipment standards which any planning team would like to trace would be those exactly relating to their particular project and preferably emanating from the department of their own government which is concerned with libraries; failing that, another authoritative source which bears an obvious relevance to their problem. These sources are seldom to be found; if standards are laid down by the project's own top authority, usually a government department, they will in all probability be limiting and mandatory.

In the United States there are a number of official manuals, building project handbooks, and planning studies, which are issued to guide publicly supported educational establishments: a partial list is to be found in the bibliography of Metcalf. A very elaborate example, the series entitled *The Higher Education Facilities Planning and Management Manuals*, quoted in Edwards,[1] was produced by the Western Interstate Commission for Higher Education in Colorado; one of these manuals deals with the library, and though it is aimed at smaller educational establishments its figures can be a useful general guide.

More common are the recommendations of the various professional pressure groups, usually the specialist sections of the library associations of different countries. These are undoubtedly compiled with care by experts, but they are all too obviously an attempt to raise the level of service in their own fields. Because of this the recommendations will be pitched higher than existing levels, usually sufficiently higher to allow for bargaining with the authorities. Another difficulty is that conditions are seldom really comparable; it is the rich countries which produce most of the professional recommendations, and these may raise a wry smile in countries which could not possibly hope to obtain authority for such lavish levels. Nevertheless, with all their faults, specialist recommendations have a certain use, if only as a basis for compiling more suitable ones for a particular case. In the 1960s and 1970s numerous recommendations were published and were recorded in some detail in earlier editions of this book. Fewer of them are given here, partly because they are out of date and new ones have not appeared, but also because they take little cognizance of the changes which information technology has already brought to libraries. Another factor is that the great differences between conditions in various parts of the world tend to make universal recommendations of little value. Certainly IFLA's *Guidelines for Public Libraries*[2] is valuable, because it is specially designed to serve and to encourage the creation of public library services in many different countries, and also because the figures are so basic. Nevertheless after two editions had appeared under the title 'Standards . . .'[3] the new volume says: 'When needs and resources vary so widely there can be no common standards for services. For that reason we have called this volume not "Standards" but "Guidelines". We are offering not rules but advice, based on experience drawn from many countries and capable of general application.' In a different way the

recommendations of the Atkinson Report[4] are of great value everywhere, not for formulae and space standards but because of the clearly expressed reasoning behind the statements.

Before accepting the recommendations in any published standards we have to consider the circumstances under which the figures were compiled. For instance, when quoting allowances of space per reader we have to remember the differing expectations of readers across the world. Again, when we quote the number (or proportion) of readers in any community who are expected to use the library it is appropriate to take into account different patterns and frequencies of use which will arise because some readers have access to alternative sources, as well as the changes which are likely to come because of technological developments. Because these factors vary so much from place to place it is not reasonable to bludgeon the authority with bundles of statistics produced, perhaps, by pressure groups working in quite different situations. It is even worse if we try to mislead ourselves.

Public library standards

The most relevant document is of course IFLA *Standards for Public Libraries*,[3] the second edition appearing in 1977. The *Guidelines*[2] which replaced it in 1986 does not include revised quantitative statements, arguing (as quoted above) that in the present state of library development they are not likely to be universally relevant, but it does include a summary of the space recommendations of the 1977 *Standards*. The official British position is stated in the Working Party Reports[5] (one for England and Wales, one for Scotland), published in 1962, and in the government's Library Advisory Councils' recommendations[6] in 1971. Both of these sets of documents comment upon earlier editions of IFLA *Standards* and particularly on their relevance in British conditions.

Siting and accessibility

IFLA *Standards* says: 'In urban areas it will usually be found necessary to provide branch libraries within 1½ kilometres (1 mile) or so of most residents, and relatively large libraries within 3–4 kilometres (2–2½ miles) of most residents.' It adds: 'The relevant factor is the attractiveness of the focal centre as a whole, not that of the library alone, and this will usually point to the desirability of siting in shopping centres.'

On this point the Working Party said: 'it is . . . economical . . . if urban populations are served in units of not less than 15 000. . . . In urban areas no person should normally have to travel more than one mile to a library; the distance should be less in heavily built-up areas.'

The Library Advisory Councils Report comments on this:

'We do not consider it unreasonable that even in an urban area some readers should have to travel more than a mile in order to have the advantage of a full range of library services, including reference facilities, the assistance of professional staff and a level of stock which adequately reflects the tastes and interests of the community served. Good public transport, increased car ownership and adequate parking facilities are conditions that help to make a longer journey to the library acceptable.'

The Library Association[7] says:

'. . . maximum economy and efficiency are secured when a branch offers the maximum book stock to the maximum number of users. Thus the most economical unit is theoretically one with a shelf stock of between 15 000 and 20 000 serving a population of between 20 000 and 30 000. But for geographical and other reasons, it won't usually work out that way.'

In the long run the librarian has to depend on his professional judgement and knowledge of the peculiar requirements of a certain area in producing estimates of the size of service appropriate to a small community, and in persuading his authority to accept them. Reader-use surveys can offer general guidance but the pattern of use can vary enormously between apparently similar areas; the variation will be even greater between, on the one hand, sections of a vast conurbation and, on the other, sparsely populated rural areas. Research into the reasons behind these great variations is still needed. Three booklets have been produced which, although too long to be even summarized here, are worth studying. *Public Library Service Points*[8] interprets and adds to the Working Party Report. *Public Libraries and Their Use*[9] studies a number of existing public library situations and provides valuable statistics about current use, for example the effects of distance between service points, drawing some useful conclusions. The third, *Public Libraries and Cultural Activities*,[10] draws attention to the need to take seriously the contribution the public library should make in fields other than the provision of books.

Book stock

IFLA *Standards* considers a total book stock of two to three volumes per head of total population is a good basis for planning a service. The Working Party suggested that a library serving a population of 40 000 will normally be expected to add about 10 000 volumes a year if giving more than a basic service; libraries serving between 30 000 and 100 000 population should add (in addition to the basic figures quoted above) about 500 non-fiction titles for every 10 000 population served up to 100 000. In 1965 the DES[11] added: 'A book stock of not less than 1½ currently useful books per head of population may be considered reasonable for an authority of under 40 000 population.'

According to the Library Advisory Councils:

'The minimum shelf stock on display in a branch library open for thirty hours a week or more should be about 6000 volumes. If it is assumed that the number of volumes on loan at any one time is equivalent to about one per head for 50 per cent of the population, this implies a total branch stock of some 8000 volumes in a population of 4000.'

Withers,[12] summarizing the standards of fourteen different countries, says:

'In general it may be said that the recommended figures for bookstocks per inhabitant – which naturally are higher for small populations than large ones – range from about three volumes to one volume per inhabitant (sometimes less than one where populations exceeds one million).'

A report published in December 1986 by the Convention of Scottish Local Authorities[13] recommended (inter alia) that the annual addition to adult lending stocks of all materials should be 280 items per 1000 adult population.

Space standards

In their study of *The American Public Library Building*, Wheeler and Githens[14] produced a formula which can be used to determine the appropriate size of a public library from knowing the population eventually to be served. They called this the VSC formula, V being the total number of volumes (in both open shelf and stack), S the number of seats required for readers and C the circulation in volumes per year. In applying this formula the authors use certain conclusions of their own which the architect may not be willing to accept: that 1 m^2 is sufficient for housing 110 volumes (1 sq ft is sufficient for housing ten volumes), whether on stack or open shelf; that one reader seat require 3.72 m^2 (40 sq ft) and that 1 m^2 may be regarded as sufficient for a circulation of 430 volumes a year (1 sq ft of library space for a circulation of forty volumes a year).

With these figues in mind the VSC formula states that the required area in m^2 for a public library building is:

$$\frac{\text{No. of books}}{110} + (\text{seats} \times 3.7) + (\text{circulation} \div 430)$$

The imperial equivalent of this would be:

$$\frac{\text{No. of books}}{10} + (\text{seats} \times 40) + (\text{circulation} \div 40).$$

Note that the VSC formula had assumed an overall space per seated reader of 3.72 m^2 (40 sq ft) and this includes an allowance for circulation, service and architectural purposes.

In itself this formula cannot be very helpful for a future building, where the numbers of books, readers and circulation are all unknown quantities. If, however, the formula is used in conjunction with standards issued by an authoritative body, then helpful area figures for the new library can be deduced, and these will at least be a starting point for study and discussion. Anyone attempting to use this formula must certainly consult *The American Public Library Building*, as this summary represents only the outline of the method defined and amended more precisely in that book.

Mevissen[15] suggests space allocations for the main reader service areas for public libraries: 200 m^2 for those with stocks of 3000 volumes to 4808 m^2 for those with 200 000 volumes. In these allocations he estimates that most public libraries with fewer than 25 000 volumes will house 32.5 volumes/m^2, those with up to 200 000 volumes will house 70 volumes/m^2. He also suggests that libraries with over 200 000 volumes will have a further 100 000 volumes stored systematically at 150 volumes/m^2.

IFLA *Standards* recommends space allowances per population served as shown in Table 19:1. The Working Party commented:

'We do not think that [in Britain] the overall scale of provision can be reduced to the extent indicated [in the

Table 19.1 Space allowances per population	
Population served	*Allowance per 1000 of population*
10 000 to 20 000	42m^2 (450 sq ft)
20 000 to 35 000	39 m^2 (420 sq ft)
35 000 to 65 000	35 m^2 (375 sq ft)
65 000 to 100 000	31 m^2 (335 sq ft)
over 100 000	28 m^2 (300 sq ft)

table] as the population to be served increases. While the scale of provision in lending libraries may be reduced in relation to population, there is need for space to house larger reserve stocks, larger reference and local history collections and often also a commercial and technical library and other special departments and auxiliary services.

'We doubt whether any standards of general applicability can usefully be laid down, except perhaps strictly as minimum standards, for libraries serving populations over, say, 65 000.'

The standards for small public libraries issued in 1967 by the Danish State Library Inspectorate were specifically concerned only with public libraries serving populations between 5000 and 25 000, but in its space recommendations it is more categorical and helpful than other official bodies. The Inspectorate reports[16] that the space requirements for libraries serving populations of around 5000 (the lowest population figure for which full-time staff will be employed) will be somewhat under 600 m² (6400 sq ft) and that for libraries serving populations of 25 000 will be 1600 m² (17 075 sq ft). Within this range the requirements rise steadily with rise of population to be served. The Inspectorate's standards deal also with such matters as categories of rooms to be provided, readers' seats, numbers of staff and book stock provision.

In Finland a Building Committee[17] proposed that total space allocations should be decided on the basis of the number of inhabitants and the number of loans per head expected annually. It gave the example that an authority with a population of 20 000, aiming at 10 loans per head per year, would need 2070 m² (22 000 sq ft). This standard, it says, may be applied pro rata to library services with annual loans from 12 to 14 per inhabitant per year and serving populations from 3000 to 100 000.

Withers gives details of space allocations in the countries whose standards he surveys: although many of these figures are helpful, differences of local clientele, conditions and practice make it impossible to summarize them.

Adult lending areas

IFLA *Standards* says:

'Of the total bookstock of two or three volumes per head of total population, proposed [earlier], it will usually be found necessary to allocate not less than one volume per head of total population for the purpose of providing a lending service to adults. Of the total adult lending stock provided at each service point, it can be expected that approximately one third will be on loan at any one time, and this . . . suggests that as a general rule open access shelving should be provided in adult lending areas sufficient to accommodate 600 volumes per 1000 population. Libraries serving populations larger than 60 000 or so will usually be able to provide somewhat fewer books per 1000 population. The number of volumes displayed on open shelves in any adult lending library serving a population of 3000 or more should never be less than 4000. (See paragraph 25, which recommends a minimum total stock of 9000 volumes, of which one third might be for children. This leaves 6000 volumes for adults, most of which will be for loan, and about a third will be on loan at any one time.) In small branch libraries, however, there may be a considerable seasonal variation in the number of books on loan, and to allow for this the floor area in adult lending departments should never be less than 100 m² (1076 sq ft), with shelf capacity in proportion. In all larger libraries, allow

15 m² (161 sq ft) for every 1000 volumes on open shelves. Provision on this scale will allow for circulation of readers within the area, accommodation for staff counters and catalogues, informal seating without table space on the scale of one seat per 1000 population and a moderate amount of display equipment. If access to any part of the book stack is permitted, this should not result in any reduction in the number of volumes accommodated on freely accessible open shelves on the scale indicated above.'

These recommendations are summarized in Table 19:2.

Table 19.2　Adult lending facilities

Population served	Open-shelf accomodation		Floor area at 15 m² per 1000 volumes (minimum 100 m²)
	Volumes per 1000 population	Total capacity	
3000	1333	4000	100 m² (1076 sq ft)
5000	800	4000	100 m² (1076 sq ft)
10 000	600	6000	100 m² (1076 sq ft)
20 000	600	12 000	180 m² (1938 sq ft)
40 000	600	24 000	360 m² (3875 sq ft)
60 000	600	36 000	540 m² (5813 sq ft)
80 000	550	44 000	660 m² (7104 sq ft)
100 000	500	50 000	750 m² (8073 sq ft)

Children's libraries

IFLA *Standards* states that the area for children:

'must be sufficient to display the full variety of books needed to meet the demands of users, many volumes – particularly those for young children – being displayed face-forward for maximum effect. Allow 15 m² (161 sq ft) for every 1000 volumes on open shelves. This assumes that shelf units for children will be four shelves high. Provision on this scale will allow – as in the adult lending area – for circulation of readers, accommodation for staff counters and catalogues, informal seating without table space and a moderate amount of display equipment. In libraries serving a total population up to 10 000 the area needed for the above purposes will commonly be 75 to 100 m² (807 to 1076 sq ft). Between 10 000 and 20 000 population, an area of 100 to 150 m² (1076 to 1615 sq ft) will usually be needed. Libraries serving larger populations will need more accommodation than this, depending on local patterns of use. In all cases, there should be sufficient space to accommodate a class of schoolchildren without seriously disturbing other users.'

The *Standards* also reminds us that:

'Children's libraries are peculiarly prone to peaks of demand, especially during the hour or two after schools close. Space must be related to these periods of peak demand. Another important planning consideration is that children's libraries are commonly visited by school classes during the day, and must be able to accommodate such visits without disrupting the general service of the library.'

The Working Party considered this point:

'It is becoming increasingly necessary to provide space where children can do their homework and other forms of study with access to a good range of books. The suggested maximum size for a children's library 140

Table 19.3 IFLA Standards: adult reference facilities

Population served	Minimum total working stock of library		Adult reference facilities			
			Open-shelf accommodation		Seating area	
	Per head of population	Total number of volumes	Number of volumes (percentage of total stock in brackets)	Area required at 10 m² per 1000 volumes	No. of places at 1.5 per 1000 population*	Area required at 2.5 m² per place
3000	3	9000	100 (1)	1 m² (11 sq ft)	5	13 m² (140 sq ft)
5000	3	15 000	300 (2)	3 m² (32 sq ft)	8	20 m² (215 sq ft)
10 000	3	30 000	900 (3)	9 m² (97 sq ft)	15	38 m² (410 sq ft)
20 000	3	60 000	3000 (5)	30 m² (323 sq ft)	30	75 m² (807 sq ft)
40 000	2½	100 000	7000 (7)	70 m² (753 sq ft)	60	150 m² (1614 sq ft)
60 000	2	120 000	12 000 (10)	120 m² (1292 sq ft)	75	188 m² (2024 sq ft)
80 000	2	160 000	16 000 (10)	160 m² (1722 sq ft)	120	300 m² (3228 sq ft)
100 000	2	200 000	20 000 (10)	200 m² (2153 sq ft)	150	375 m² (4035 sq ft)

* This level of provision can sometimes be reduced in libraries serving populations larger than 100 000.

Table 19.4 Bassnett: summary of recommendations (areas)

Population group	Gross area ft² per capita*	Percentage of gross area						
		First floor	Readers' service	Stacks	Staff	Extension activities	Environmental features	Mechanical features
Group 1: 100 000 to 200 000	0.5 to 0.6	30	52	14	20	6	3	5
Group 2: 200 000 to 400 000	0.45 to 0.5	20	47	20	21	5	3	4
Group 3: 400 000 to 700 000	0.4 to 0.5	15	37† (38)	31	23	4† (3)	2	3
Group 4: 700 000 and above	0.25 to 0.4	15	34	35	23	3	2	3

* To stop unlimited increase of areas, subtract 10% of total for every 500 000 population over 2 000 000.
† P. J. Bassnett has pointed out in correspondence with the author that the figures in brackets are probably more correct statistically. He does say, however, that as large libraries of this kind tend to diversify their extension activities into branch libraries it may be that one city may need central extension activity areas greater than another city in a higher population bracket.

Table 19.5 Bassnett: summary of recommendations (seating)

Population group	No. of seats per 1000 population	Private carrel seats	Study seats	Lounge seats	Auditorium seats	Lecture and meeting room seats
		percentage				
Group 1: 100 000 to 200 000	3 to 4	5	75	20	200 to 300	50 to 100
Group 2: 200 000 to 400 000	2 to 3	5	80	15	250 to 500	100 to 200
Group 3: 400 000 to 700 000	2 to 2½	5	80	15	300 to 600	200 to 300
Group 4: 700 000 and above*	1½ to 2	5	80	15	400 to 600	200 to 600

* Subtract 10% of readers' seats for every 500 000 population over 2 000 000.

square metres (1500 sq ft) should be considerably increased to allow for this type of provision.'

Later it said:

'Since there is a limited number of worthwhile children's books available and since there is no reason to display large numbers of duplicate copies, we think that the optimum capacity for all children's libraries, except the smallest, might be between 4000 and 6000 volumes. If allowance is made fo the lower bookcases necessary this will give a children's department of 1000 to 1500 sq ft, with additional study space provided for the larger populations and to allow for class use. Extra space may be needed to allow for story hours, and when children up to fourteen years of age constitute 25–30 per cent of the population the children's books should comprise one third of the total stock.'

IFLA *Standards* again:

'There may still be a need, however, to set aside a specially designed room as an annex to the children's library, if justified by the extent, or by the nature, of children's activities. If it is to be used for activities in which children are essentially the audience, it will be sufficient to allow 1.5 m² (16 sq ft) per place. There might be more value however in developing a club-room atmosphere in which the children can participate in a range of creative activities, materials for which can be accumulated and used in the room without the need to tidy everything away after each session. For such purposes as this an area of up to 3 m² (32 sq ft) will be needed.'

Reference libraries

IFLA *Standards* considers the provision for study by readers as well as quick-reference facilities:

'A satisfactory level of provision in most circumstances would be 1.5 seats (each with a table space) per 1000 population, but it may sometimes be possible to reduce this level of provision in libraries serving populations larger than about 100 000. Allow about 2.5 m² (27 sq ft) per reader space, depending on the arrangement of seats and tables. No purpose-built library should provide fewer than 4 seats with table space suitable for study.'

On reference libraries in general, IFLA *Standards* again:

'Although reference books may require on average more shelf space per volume than books for loan, space for the circulation of readers in open-shelf areas does not need to be so generous as that prescribed for lending areas and it has been considered sufficient to allow 10 m² (108 ft²) per 1000 volumes on open shelves. [Table 19:3, p. 204 above] shows, for libraries serving populations of different sizes, the open-shelf reference stocks which are considered likely in most cases to be necessary and adequate as basic working collections, together with the space required for their accommodation, and the additional areas likely to be needed for seating. Together, these will allow sufficient space to accommodate any staff desks which are needed in the public area.'

The *Standards* emphasizes that space required for housing and consulting periodicals, and for storage and use of audio-visual materials, must be added to the areas recommended. On the question of periodicals it says: 'The number of seats needed for readers consulting periodicals will probably be at least one per 2000 population in libraries serving up to about 20 000 population but could well be reduced to one seat per 3000 population above

this figure. 3 m² (32 sq ft) of floor space should be provided per seat.' And on audio-visual materials: 'Any library serving a population of 20 000 or more will probably need to provide separate storage accommodation for audio-visual equipment. In libraries serving populations of 60 000 or more it will often be necessary to provide an additional area to accommodate a technician, laboratory and other photographic and recording equipment.'

The Library Association[18] issued standards for reference departments in public libraries, indicating that libraries need to provide one reference seat for each 500 population served (confirming the Working Party standard), and that the floor area for each seat should be 2.32 m² (25 sq ft). The amount of open-shelf reference stock should not be fewer than 200 volumes per 1000 population served, with a floor area of 8.36 m² (90 sq ft) per 1000 volumes. The remaining reference stock housed in stack requires a floor area of 4.18 m² (45 sq ft) per 1000 volumes. Periodicals should be at the rate of 0.09 m² (1 sq ft) of floor space per periodical for current periodicals on open access, 7 m² (75 sq ft) per 1000 volumes in stack when bound.

To store reserve stock, IFLA *Standards* tells us to allow (in closed stack)'5.5 m² (59 sq ft) per 1000 volumes (equivalent to 182 volumes per m², 17 per sq ft), but this capacity will be approximately doubled if compact shelving is employed. In stacks to which the public have access, provide 7 m² (75 sq ft) per 1000 volumes (equivalent to 143 volumes per m² (13.3 per sq ft).'

The IFLA *Standards* table showing recommended provision for adult reference libraries is given in Table 19:3, followed by the summaries of recommendations by population, one for area, one for seating, from studies of the provision of reference libraries in large cities produced by Bassnett[19] (Tables 19:4 and 19:5).

Staff work rooms, rest rooms, kitchens, toilets etc.

IFLA *Standards*: '20 per cent added to the total area of public departments will usually be found to provide adequately for work rooms and offices, and will be equivalent to about 10–12 m² (108–129 sq ft) of office or workroom space per staff member.' On rest rooms etc.: 'For each member of staff who may be expected to use the facilities (with generous allowance for probable increase in staff) allow 2–4 m² (22–43 sq ft) on a scale varying inversely with the size of the staff.' On circulation space or 'balance area' the *Standards* say: 'Allow 10–15 per cent of all public areas and 20–25 per cent of all staff areas.'

Table 19.6

Number of staff	Area per staff member	Total area
2	4.0 m² (43 sq ft)	8 m² (86 sq ft)
10	4.0 m² (43 sq ft)	40 m² (431 sq ft)
20	3.0 m² (32 sq ft)	60 m² (646 sq ft)
50	2.4 m² (26 sq ft)	120 m² (1292 sq ft)
100	2.2 m² (24 sq ft)	220 m² (2368 sq ft)
200	2.0 m² (22 sq ft)	400 m² (4306 sq ft)

University library standards

Withers says:

'[The university] covers a very wide range of libraries and this must be constantly borne in mind when considering the question of standards . . . the nature and extent of the collections and other facilities vary from the universities with a very high, and sometimes almost exclusive, load of postgraduate (particularly doctoral) work and other research work, to the universities whose role is mainly that of preparing students for first degrees. From the top to the bottom of the scale the differences in the collections of materials, staffing and other requirements are enormous.'

In his paper *Standards in university libraries*[20] Humphreys discusses this problem and quotes from standards from many different countries, clearly illustrating how figures vary, and says, '. . . almost all the standards I have quoted have little or no validity outside the environment for which they were invented.'

Two examples will make this clear: Humphreys quotes from the Association of College and Research Libraries Joint Committee on University Library Standards which based its finding on current practices of fifty leading university libraries in the US and Canada; this committee proposed that the total stock of a university library should be 2 000 000 volumes with an annual acquisition rate of 100 000 volumes; the average holding to be 100 volumes and one current periodical per student, the total number of periodicals currently received to be 15 000.

His second quotation is from the University Standards Committee of the Canadian Association of College and University Libraries, which suggests that 'a minimum collection of 100 000 volumes is desirable' and above that size '75 volumes per full-time student'. Both these examples emanate from North America and differ considerably from general European practice (or even recommendations); the distance between these figures and the hopes of most third world countries makes them of little help unless the financial authorities are prepared to accept the expenditure which the recommendations imply. As the financial allocation is so critical, and indeed is the main deciding factor, the basic element seems to be the percentage of total university funds which may be allocated to the library. In these circumstances, to attempt to provide detailed standards of building is an unprofitable exercise.

In planning a library for a new university there can be little conscious choice of a 'total book stock'; the range of subjects and the depth of research will affect selection, the money available will decide numbers to be purchased. In an institution of this kind the flow of new acquisitions is the life-blood, and, as there will be comparatively little discarding of older material, there is theoretically no limit to the optimum size. Withers quotes quantitative book stock standards of both the American and the Canadian Library Associations; both suggest a figure of around 300 000 volumes as a minimum for a university with 4000 students, but these are specifically stated to be minima. The ALA says: '. . . stronger institutions will demand considerably larger and richer collections'.

The Parry Report[21] referred to a medium-sized university with a stock of half a million volumes. Saunders[22] says:

'There should be no question of standardising or restricting the size of a library which is supposed to support research. . . . It is economic and educational common sense, and not empire building or wild extravagance, for any university library to aspire towards its first million volumes as rapidly as possible.'

Metcalf[23] referred to 'The average university library . . . at least 2 500 000 volumes. . . .', and in his introduction[24] says:

'Academic library collections tend to grow at the rate of four to five per cent a year until they become what may be called "mature". This growth which means doubling the collection size in perhaps sixteen or seventeen years has been true in the United States for at least two centuries. In due course libraries become increasingly "mature", and the growth rate slackens to the rate of two or three per cent a year – doubling in twenty-five to forty years instead of half that time. This slackening in the growth rate generally does not occur until the library is so large that even two per cent is a serious increment. For example at Harvard two per cent now amounts to some 200 000 or more volumes a year, requiring some 14 000 square feet (about 1300 square metres). . . .'

An entirely different approach to the problem came from Britain. Here the bulk of the funds to maintain universities (and so to regulate their libraries' growth) come from the University Grants Committee, a permanent body which assesses the claims of almost all British universities. For this reason the question of grants for increases in library space, and so the final book stock total, will lie between the university authority and the UGC, not with the librarian. The UGC set up a committee to consider the problem of continual growth in university library space needs:

'By the end of 1974 the University Grants Committee had come to the conclusion that they were clearly not going to have enough resources, either in the short term or the long term, to build new libraries at all universities on the scale needed to match an indefinitely growing number of books.'

This was the opening sentence of the foreword of the Atkinson Report.[25] The thinking behind this report was so fundamental, and its recommendations so well argued, that it should be studied with great care in all countries where unlimited funds are not likely to be found for the creation of new libraries and then for their maintenance. The conclusions of the report appear to be a series of mandatory formulae, but they differed very widely from those produced by most other bodies. The size of the library was to be assessed by the norm of 1.25 m² (13.455 sq ft) to planned full-time equivalent (FTE) student numbers, adding an assessed provision for special collections, then adding provision for further growth at a rate of 0.2 m² (2.15 sq ft) per FTE student applied to forecast numbers ten years ahead, with a final adjustment for special circumstances. Provision was to be made for a local reserve store where the existing buildings, together with any likely to be programmed in the near future, were insufficient to accommodate a university's holdings and no case could be made for a new building. Subject to local circumstances, the size of a reserve store was to be limited to the accommodation required for about five years' accessions at current rates. No library extension was to be considered 'unless it can be foreseen that the number of metres of shelving . . . per FTE student is likely to fall below 3.8 (12.35 feet)..'

Later discussions by the UGC added, to the norm per FTE student, '0.80 m² (8.6 sq ft) addition where necessary for each law student'. A figure for reserve stores was also added. However, the report stresses:

'This does not mean that a simple "norm" based on student numbers is applied indiscriminately by the UGC as a blunt instrument in assessing particular library projects . . . which a university may put forward for inclusion in a building programme. The application of the norm merely establishes the starting point for any such assessment and the Committee are always prepared to take careful account of the special factors and circumstances applying to individual cases and to make adjustments to meet them.'

This has been quoted at some length to emphasize a point which is of the greatest importance; although it is a mandatory ruling, it gives the librarian grounds on which to work out his basic needs, special factors being considered on their merits.

Emphasizing the limitation of national funding which forced these steps was the fact that 'present policy and practice, if continued, would demand the rebuilding, or the extension, of nearly five-sixths of all university libraries in Britain in the course of the next ten years.' The solution proposed was the 'self-renewing' library; that is, a library of a fixed size of book stock, so that the addition of books must be balanced by the withdrawal (in some way) of the equivalent of a similar number. It must be emphasized that while these proposals were based on the impossibility of accommodating the continual growth of libraries, they were made before the full effects of the electronic revolution were apparent. How much more worth studying are these recommendations today, when we can seen even more technological changes on the horizon.

Shelving requirements

The Atkinson Report said:

'. . . it is not unreasonable to assume that a library which provides 3.8 m (12½ ft) of shelving per FTE student should

Table 19.7 HGC norms for book storage

	Books: m^2 per 1000 vols	Bound journals: m^2 per 1000 vols
Open access	4.65	9.35
Closed access (fixed)	4.03	8.06
Closed access (rolling)	2.07	4.13

Table 19.8 UGC overall norms

	Unit per	Usable area m^2
Library		
Reader places (LUR)	each	2.39
Book storage (LUB)	1000	4.65
Bound journals (LUJ)	1000	9.35
Periodicals (LUP) assuming ¼ display ¾ storage	1000	25.13
Reader places (LUR+) including 18 per cent for administration	each	2.82
Book storage (LUB+) ditto	1000	5.49
Bound journals (LUJ+) ditto	1000	11.03
Periodicals (LUP+) assuming ¼ display ¾ storage and including 18 per cent for administration*	1000	29.65

The key to the 4 types of library units specified is:

Library Unit R (LUR) One reader place
Library Unit B (LUB) Storage for 1000 volumes of books
Library Unit J (LUJ) Storage for 1000 volumes of bound journals
Library Unit P (LUP) Storage for 1000 titles of periodicals

The plus sign (e.g. LUR+, LUB+) denotes an 18% addition for the requirements of administration.

* In the Atkinson Report the addition for administration was raised to 20%.

be adequate for normal working purposes, assuming:
1. The current degree of reliance by universities on the use of microform, inter-library borrowing and local inter-library co-operation; and
2. Storage facilities for additional little-used books and periodicals from which items can be fetched within twenty-four hours.'

The effect of computer access on the last point must not be underestimated. It is made clear that these shelving standards are based on a situation where 85% of the books are on open access and where shelves are considered full when 85% occupied. In these circumstances the 3.8 m (12½ ft) of occupied shelving translates into space allocation at 0.62 m² (96 sq in) per FTE.

Before this report, the UGC norms for book storage[26] were calculated to the scales shown in Table 19:7. With a typical mix, this suggests some 5.83 m² per 1000 volumes overall. These figures include provision for the margin needed for the reorganization of space or return of borrowed material, i.e. they assume that a shelf 85% occupied is effectively full (Table 19.7).

From these, and from the reader places formula of 1.5 for all arts students and 1.7 for all science students, the overall figures in Table 19:8 were given.

Housing of readers

The proportion of the future readers who can be expected to occupy seats at peak times will be affected by various factors. There may be departmental reading rooms, and in residential establishments study-bedrooms will cater for a fair number of readers. The study habits of postgraduate and research workers will almost certainly differ from those of undergraduates. Almost all educational libraries will have peak seating demands in the periods immediately preceding examination, but to base seating provision on these periodic explosions would mean half-empty rooms at other times; it may be preferable to open nearby class or tutorial rooms as overflow reading areas rather than cater for an artificial peak. A survey carried out at nine university and two polytechnic libraries in Britain by the Cambridge Library Management Research Unit[27] found that at least 93% of those responding to the questionnaire had visited the library within the previous two weeks and 85% within one week. The survey also recorded that 40% to 60% of the respondents, except academic staff and postgraduates, came to the library to use their own materials: those using the library's reference materials ranged from as low as 18% to 37%. Predictably more respondents at those universities with a larger number of halls of residence borrowed material. It would be unfair to draw too firm general conclusions from these findings, but the reports should certainly be studied.

According to the American Library Association, in *Standards for college libraries*,[28] 'Accommodation for at least one-third of the student body will be essential. The changing concept of the role of the library in the academic community may lead to an upward revision of this figure.' The Canadian Library Association[29] says: 'It is suggested that 25 per cent to 40 per cent of total student enrolment should be taken as the number of seats to be provided for students. . . . A new and small institution would normally use the higher figure.'

It seems to be generally accepted that the greatest use of the library is made by humanities (arts) readers, because science students spend much time in laboratories. On this point, however, the Atkinson Report says:

'We came to the initial conclusion that an appropriate norm

might be one seat for every four art students and one for every eleven science students. Over the country as a whole we decided that a broader norm of one place for every six students between arts and science would be more appropriate.'

As a contrast to this, the Association of American Law Schools is quoted by Metcalf[30] as recommending seating 'with generous table or desk spaces for 65 per cent of the student body'. Law students certainly sit and study books more than technology students, but the librarian has to decide whether such provision is reasonable in the light of his own situation.

Quoting the Atkinson Report again: 'We are also satisfied that 2.39 m² (25 sq ft) per place, which allows for a reasonably high proportion of single seat places, is adequate but not over-generous'. Later the report explains that the overall space normal of 1.25 m² (11 sq ft) per FTE student was arrived at by taking a notional 3.8 m (13 ft) of occupied shelving per FTE student, a figure based on an average of the present occupied shelving excluding special collections in the universities which the committee considered to be 'normal'. This figure was squared and 'adjusted' (for reasons which are given) to produce a 'book stack' space of 0.62 m² per FTE student. To this was added a seating space of 0.4 m² per student (derived from the figure of 2.39 m² per student and one seat for every six students) plus an overall allowance for administration of 20% (higher than the 18% in the existing norm because of the greater administrative load involved in operating a self-renewing library), rounding up the result to 1.25 m² per FTE student. This is an over-simplification of the committee's findings, which should be studied in the report itself.

Polytechnic library standards

In Britain, polytechnics are fairly small universities with an emphasis on science and technology and with much less research than universities. A recent survey established that each of them has up to ten staffed libraries on different sites, the mean being four. Their gross areas (mean) are 5573 m² (60 000 sq ft), that is 0.88 m² (9.5 sq ft) (mean) per student. Because polytechnics are a creation of the last thirty years, more attention has been given at official level to their space standards. Those issued by the Department of Education and Science[31] (the government body concerned) say:

'The appropriate usable area for polytechnic libraries is dependent on the pattern of studies and the physical location of departments in a particular establishment. This area may be up to 1.29 m² [14 sq ft] per FTE student, comprising a basic allowance of 0.8 m² [8½ sq ft] per FTE student, supplemented as necessary by an addition from the non-specialized teaching accommodation. The maximum area would permit the provision of readers' seats on a scale of one to every four FTE students, display and storage space for books and periodicals, audio-visual aids, counter and catalogue areas, a librarian's office, a workroom, seminar and tutorial rooms and carols [sic] for private study attached to the library suite and facilities for photocopying and a darkroom. The department approves the provision of a "calculated balance area", that is an allowance for corridors, stairs, foyers, toilets and so on, of 25 per cent of the library accommodation.'

The Council of Polytechnic Librarians Working Party[32] issued recommendations in 1980, but more detail is given in the older Library Association standards for polytechnic libraries,[33] which recommend a basic stock of 150 000 volumes and 3000 periodical titles; it also recommends that 80% of the stock should be on open access at 8.36 m² (90 sq ft) per 1000 volumes and 20% in limited access at 4.18 m² (45 sq ft) per 1000 volumes. For display of current periodicals it recommends a space allowance of 0.09 m² (1 sq ft) per periodical title. Space allowance for readers is to be calculated according to discipline, one place for every four students of scientific and technological disciplines, one place for every three students of other disciplines, and one place for every ten part-time students, irrespective of discipline. Seating space allowances recommended are: 2.3 m² (25 sq ft) for undergraduates generally and 3.2 m² (35 sq ft) for postgraduate students, and students of art, architecture and other similar disciplines.

Space allowances for library functions are given in some detail by the Library Association and are worth quoting:

'*Library staff* – cataloguing, 9.3 m² (100 sq ft) per person; stock selection, 7.43 m² (80 sq ft) per person; clerical staff, 3.72 m² (40 sq ft) per person. As some staff are on duty in public areas and others have split duties, only 70% of staff may need space allocation. Some members of staff require more space than others for interview and discussion. Thus librarian, deputy librarian and chief information officer, 13.94 m² (150 sq ft) minimum each. (Administrative offices should incorporate data processing equipment, which may need special environmental consideration.)

'*Committee room* – 18.58 m² (200 sq ft) minimum.

'*Staff room* – 0.93 m² (10 sq ft) per person (minimum 13.94 m² (150 sq ft)). (Kitchen facilities may be required, but these could be incorporated with a small self-service snack bar available to library users – an important feature of evening and weekend opening.)

'*Lecture, seminar and tutorial rooms* should be incorporated in the library suite. Lecture rooms should accommodate the maximum number of students likely to attend first-year degree courses (forty minimum), and there should be seminar rooms for a similar number – five seating eight students each. Tutorial rooms should be provided as generously as possible, particularly in those polytechnics with courses in social sciences, law and the humanities. All rooms should be equipped with visual and audio aids.

'*Audio and visual equipment* requires special facilities. Records and tapes may need a central control area, though listening booths or facilities for listening at study tables may be sited separately. Additionally, the technician may require a maintenance area – 37 m² (400 sq ft) minimum, excluding storage of records and tapes.

'*Repairs and preparation for binding* – 37 m² (400 sq ft) minimum.

'*Micro-storage* – a large collection needs to be housed under controlled humidity and temperature conditions. Some storage units which house large collections of a quarter of a million may need special floor loading.

'*Reprographic facilities* These have special space requirements – e.g. electrostatic copiers, 5.57 m² (60 sq ft); offset printing and plate making, 28 m² (300 sq ft) minimum; cameras, 9.29 m² (100 sq ft) each minimum; processors, 9.29 m² (100 sq ft) minimum.

'*Research and development* – depending on staff, but 14 m² (150 sq ft) minimum.

'*Issue, readers' and advisory points and catalogue space* (dependent on the possible requirements for branch libraries, computerised catalogues and other features), 93 m² (1000 sq ft) minimum.'

The Library Association recommendations end with the italicized comment '*Add the usual 40 per cent balance area*'. The two 'standards' quoted above clearly show the vast gap between what the interested parties claim and what the official body, which has to provide funding, is prepared to authorize.

College library standards

The differences between colleges are so great that comparison between them is a difficult (and probably uninformative) task. The (American) Association of College and Research Libraries produces standards for 'libraries supporting academic programs at the bachelor's and master's degree levels. They may be applied to libraries at universities which grant a small number of doctoral degrees, say fewer than ten per year'.[34] In Britain the term colleges is applied to comparatively small institutions, and the majority of them operate libraries on more than one site; they differ widely in size, as is shown by figures published in 1987.[35] The average total book stocks were quoted as ranging from 17 000 to 188 000 books and the number of periodical subscriptions ranging from 145 to well over 1000. There is an equally wide range in American colleges, although there are more at the top end of the range, perhaps because they include what in Britain would be polytechnics.

In Britain the Department of Education and Science has published *Area Guidelines*[36] covering further education and higher education colleges. The Library Association has produced guidelines for college libraries[37] (as well as others specifically for colleges of further education[38]), and NATFHE (the trade union for college staff) has also made brief recommendations on library areas.[39] Unless one is concerned with the specific type of college covered by these guidelines, it would be better to take most of the detailed space allocations from those quoted above for polytechnics. The salient point, as ever, is the space allowed for seating and for shelving per head of FTE students. The official British body, the DES,[40] said:

'The appropriate usable area for a college library is dependent not only on the number of students but also on the level of courses offered. It follows that more space is required for colleges with a high proportion of advanced work than for other colleges. For that reason there is a higher allowance for colleges where work at the advanced level is at least 30 per cent of the whole. The allowances are as follows:

'Colleges with at least 30 per cent advanced work: 390 m^2 (4200 sq ft) for the first 500 FTE students (0.78 m^2 (8.4 sq ft) each). 0.44 m^2 (4.75 sq ft) for each additional FTE student.

'Colleges with less than 30 per cent advanced work: 300 m^2 (3230 sq ft) for the first 500 FTE students (0.6 m^2 (6.5 sq ft) each). 0.38 m^2 (40.9 sq ft) for each additional student.

'The allowances are intended to permit the provision of readers' seats on a scale of one to every eight FTE students, display and storage space for books and periodicals, counter and catalogue areas, a librarian's office, a workroom, seminar and tutorial rooms and carols [*sic*] for private study attached to the library suite and possibly facilities for photocopying and a darkroom. Again a "calculated balance area" of 25 per cent of the above is recommended.'

Published figures for proportions of students to be provided with seats in university libraries will be helpful, but the availability of alternative study facilities will be different. Non-residential college libraries in towns may be used by students late into the night, while in country areas they may be unused at these times. Again the demand for seats at immediate pre-examination periods cannot be taken as an indication of reasonable needs.

The question of how many seats should be provided by the library for every hundred students is complicated by the possible provision of 'reading halls' in residential blocks. This is of course a very wide field of study, but there is much to be said for allowing the library to cater for all reading and study needs; if a large library with an expensive stock has to be provided it is more cost-efficient when it is heavily used; moreover it need be no more expensive to provide extra seats in libraries than in residential reading halls.

In the Library Association's guidelines for further education college libraries[38] it is stated that the basic stock for a college without degree work should not be fewer than 10 000 book titles and for a larger college with some degree work and specialized advanced courses not fewer than 25 000 titles. In a college with several degree courses this figure should be considerably exceeded. There are required also, in varying degrees, multiple copies of books as well as pamphlets, audio-visual and other non-book materials and special stocks for thesis and postgraduate work. The number of periodicals should range from around 100 for a small college to a minimum of 600 for a college with substantial advanced work.

College libraries[37] makes the following recommendations:

One reader place for every four FTE students in colleges doing advanced work, and one for fifteen in others
2.5 m^2 (27 sq ft) per reader place
Chief librarian's office 20 m^2 (215 sq ft). Other professional staff offices 15 m^2 (160 sq ft) each
Counter, catalogue, entrance area 30 m^2 (325 sq ft) minimum
Workroom 30 m^2 (325 sq ft) minimum
Book storage 9 m^2 (100 sq ft) per 1000 volumes
Journal storage 17 m^2 (180 sq ft) per 1000 volumes
Journal display 9 m^2 (100 sq ft) per 100 titles
Circulation space add 20%

Once again we see how the recommendations of the professionals concerned are much higher than the allowances from official sources.

The (British) Department of Education and Science's *New Colleges of Further Education*[41] lists the main areas to be included in the plans. For seating space it gives:

One place for every five students of technology and applied science
One place for every four students of pure science
One place for every three students of other disciplines
One place for every ten part-time students, irrespective of discipline
2.32 m^2 (25 sq ft) per undergraduate
3.25 m^2 (35 sq ft) for postgraduate students

Seats should be provided for not less than 10% of the total staff; there are advantages in having a staff study or, in higher-level colleges, a research room (both of which may contain lockers, individual desks or carrels for staff).

At least one classroom of 42 m^2 to 56 m^2 (450 sq ft to 600 sq ft) opening off the library should be divisible into smaller rooms for practical work or for seminars.

The space requirements are summarized as at 557 m^2 (6000 sq ft) for a small college and 1672 m^2 (18 000 sq ft) for a regional college, based on figures in DES Building Bulletin 5.

Table 19.9

Maximum student capacity*	Recommended area for library			
	Colleges with at least 30% advanced work		Colleges with less than 30% advanced work	
	(m²)	*(sq ft)*	*(m²)*	*(sq ft)*
500 or less	273.9	2975	237.8	2560
1000	438.5	4720	349.8	3765
1500	565.3	6085	461.7	4970
2000	695.8	7490	577.3	6215
2500	820.8	8835	685.6	7380
3000	957.8	10310	797.6	8585
3500	1085.6	11685	909.5	9790
4000	1222.6	13160	1023.8	11020
4500	1368.9	14735	1138.0	12250
5000	1505.9	16210	1252.3	13480

* 'Maximum student capacity' will usually be from 25% to 50% higher than the average day student population to permit some flexibility in the use of classrooms.

Table 19.10

Student numbers	Volumes
500 or less	30000
750	40500
1000	52500
1250	60300
1500	68820

Withers quotes the following from the *Notes on Procedure for the Approval of Further Education Project*, 1967 (the earlier and fuller version of item 40):

'The table [Table 19:9] shows the total library areas now recommended for different types of colleges. The areas shown are for actual library spaces: 25 per cent should be added for circulation, services etc.'

The recommended area is intended to provide readers' seats, display and storage space for books and periodicals, counter and catalogue areas and a micro-reader, librarian's office, workroom, seminar and tutorial rooms and carrels for private study attached to the library suite and possibly facilities for photocopying and a darkroom.

The DES[42] set the target shown in Table 19:10 for minimum book stocks for college of education libraries. The figures exclude provision for degree work and certain special facilities.

The New Zealand Library Association's *Standards for Teachers' College Libraries*[43] says:

'Reader accommodation is recommended at 20% of the combined staff and student rolls at 2.8 m² (30 sq ft) staff and 2.3 m² (25 sq ft) students. Space for books is estimated at 9.3 m² (100 sq ft) for each 1000 volumes. A net working area of 1280 m² (13800 sq ft) is suggested for a college of 1000 students.'

Again an addition of 25% would need to be made for circulation, services etc.

In the United States, *Standards for College Libraries*[44] were first prepared by a committee of the ACRL, approved

in 1959 and revised in 1975. The 1986 revision does not affect the quantitative standards which are given here. Book stock is to be provided according to Formula A:

1. Basic collection　　　　　　　　　　　85000 volumes
2. Allowance per FTE faculty member　　　100 volumes
3. Allowance per FTE student　　　　　　　15 volumes
4. Allowance per undergraduate major or minor field　　　　　　　　　　　　　350 volumes
5. Allowance per master's field, when no higher degree is offered in the field　6000 volumes
6. Allowance per master's field when a high degree is offered in the field　　3000 volumes
7. Allowance per 6th year specialist degree field　　　　　　　　　　　6000 volumes
8. Allowance per doctoral field　　　　25000 volumes

A 'volume' is defined as a printed work, and each reel of microfilm, or ten pieces of any other microform, is one volume-equivalent.

It is also stated that 'it is good practice for a library to own any [periodical] title that is needed more than six times per year'.

Formula B deals with staffing requirements and states that:

For each 500, or fraction thereof, FTE students up to 10000	1 librarian
For each 1000, or fraction thereof, FTE students, above 10000	1 librarian
For each 100000 volumes, or fraction thereof, in the collection	1 librarian
For each 5000 volumes, or fraction thereof, added per year	1 librarian

It adds that 'The support staff shall be no less than 65% of the total library staff, not including student assistants.'

The space standard, Formula C, states that:

'a. *Space for users* The seating requirements for the library of a college where less than 50% of the FTE enrollment resides on campus shall be one for each five students. That for the library of a typical residential college shall be one for each four FTE students. Each study station shall be assumed to require 25 to 35 square feet of floor space, depending upon its function.
b. *Space for books* The space allocated for books shall be adequate to accommodate a convenient and orderly distribution of the collection according to the classification system(s) in use, and should include space for growth. Gross space requirements may be estimated according to the following formula.

	Square feet/ volume	[m²/volume]
For the first 150000 volumes	0.10	[.0093 m]
For the next 150000 volumes	0.09	[.0084 m]
For the next 300000 volumes	0.08	[.0074 m]
For holdings above 600000 volumes	0.07	[.0065 m]

c. *Space for staff* Space required for staff offices, service and work areas, catalogs, files, and equipment, shall be approximately one-eighth of the sum of the space needed for books and users as calculated under a) and b) above.

'This formula indicates the net assignable area required by a library if it is to fulfill its mission with maximum effectiveness. . . .'.

It is obvious that these standards are produced by a professional body and not the authorities concerned, but it seems from a recent article that a high percentage of state universities in California meet the requirements for

Table 19.11   School library resource centres: calculated numerical levels of stock provision

Age group	No. of items which are assumed to be in simultaneous use by each pupil	No. of items additional which should be available in stock* per pupil	Total items in stock* per pupil†	Extent of stock* needed in school with roll as shown within each category				
				Up to 240‡	500	750	1000	1500
5–11	5	6	11	2640	5500	8250	11 000	
11–16	6	7	13	3120	6500	9750	13 000	19 500
Over 16	6	13	19	4560	9500	14 250		

* A unit of stock is any item packaged in one piece, e.g. a portfolio, a set of slides in a wallet and a cased collection of butterflies each count as one.

† 'The needs of an individual child are the same, whatever the size of the school he attends'. Bullock, *A language for life*.

‡ Schools of under 240 should be provided for as if they were that size.

Note Stock levels indicated in this table are inclusive of books and non-book materials but exclude textbooks and materials held in departments as working tools.

collections, although the figure is less high for library staff.

Also in the United States the question of quantitative library standards is given official attention at state level. Among many documents issued are those of the Western Interstate Commission for Higher Education in Colorado, which issued a series of manuals (quoted earlier[45]) dealing with the whole field of high education, of which one was appropriate to college libraries. This manual quotes the University of California space norms, which give a single-faced section of stack as having assignable space allowances ranging from 8.7 sq ft (0.8 m^2) for normal book and similar material shelving. In general they allow 8 to 10 books per square foot (86–110 m^2) in open-stack reading rooms, 10 to 12 per square foot (110–130 m^2) in open stack, 12 to 15 per square foot (130–160 m^2) in closed stack, and 40 to 60 per square foot (430–650 m^2) in compact storage. The basis of these calculations is a very complicated series of formulae based on the assignable square footage for each section of stack, for each user and member of staff, then multiplying these units by the proposed stock, number of reader seats, staff and service space needed. The categorizing of these spaces is done in some detail and may be useful in similar situations, but the differences in environment and reader expectations referred to so often here must be borne in mind.

School library standards

Withers quotes a wide range of standards from different countries and says:

'The three most comprehensive sets of school library standards come from three countries where an approach

Table 19.12

Age range	Size	Minimum teaching accommodation (m^2)	Amount of library accommodation 8% (m^2)
5–11	240	500	40
5–12	240	558	45
5–8	320	627	50
5–12	320	716	57
8–12	320	779	62
9–13	320	906	72
12–16	480	2140	171
11–16	600	2520	202
11–18	1500	6056	484
12–18	1500	6255	500

to education, defined recently as "a shift from teacher-orientated whole class instruction, where the textbook reigns supreme, to a pupil-oriented situation where the individual child learns actively from an environment rich in learning stimuli" is actively encouraged. These are Australia, Canada and the United States. . .'.

The standards which Withers quotes are certainly worthy of study, if only for purposes of comparison, but they are out of date now; there is no area where standards and recommendations are rising so rapidly. Even the Library Association, which in 1973 recommended 8 books per head in primary schools and 10 per head in others, was by 1977[46] recommending 11 to 19 per head.

Perhaps the greatest of changes is in the range of materials used, and this has led to the replacement of the term 'school library' by 'school library resource centres'. In looking for standards for stock provision today we must recognize that these will include not only books, pamphlets and periodicals, but maps, wallcharts, portfolios of cuttings, film strips and slides, transparencies of all kinds, discs, tapes, and packs of combined media. In the recommendations which follow, 'stock' is taken to include any or all of these items. The centre may be envisaged as a pool from which to draw when selecting materials for use for the entire school.

The Library Association's 1977 *Library Resource Provision in Schools*[46] gave guidelines and recommendations including those shown in Table 19:11.

To house the resource centre, the Library Association recommended that a formula of 8% of the minimum teaching area of the school should be applied. It gave the example shown in Table 19:12, based on DES standards for school premises regulations (1972).

The Library Association[46] also says that shelving should be provided for 75% of the school's ultimate book stock. Additional library spaces, such as quiet areas or book corners, would normally be considered as part of the classroom or home-base area. In addition secondary schools should have a workroom of not less than 14 m^2 (150 sq ft) and also an area for the preparation and organization of the different materials. For this a minimum area of 46 m^2 (500 sq ft) is recommended. For audio-visual work, particularly off-air recording, both for sound and vision, a separate work room should be provided, and this should be a minimum of 28 m^2 (300 sq ft); this does not include a dark room, which, if needed, should be provided in addition to the above. Finally the recommendations say that there should be at least one group room of not less than 46 m^2 (500 sq ft) with facilities for using all kinds of book and non-book materials. For middle and combined schools there should be a general work room of not less than 10 m^2 (100 sq ft), including as many as possible of the features listed above.

Hospital library standards

In 1969 IFLA published standards for libraries in hospitals.[47] The recommendations were helpful and are quoted below, but one feels they are a little half-hearted because of the vast gulf between services in different parts of the world. In countries where hospital provision is barely enough to meet health needs, libraries are likely to take a low priority. It is probable that there are no libraries in the majority of the world's hospitals; this does not absolve us from working to improve standards but it is necessary to realize that to very many nations these must represent long-term objectives. The variation of hospitals even in the developed countries is also large, because it includes hospital services provided from huge medical centres which may be part of universities, especially in North America. In Britain the coverage is more even, but there are still big differences between teaching hospitals, district general hospitals and the smaller ones – to say nothing of the many private hospitals. It is with these differences in mind that the recommendations below are given.

The basic necessities are a room solely for use as a library which patients can visit, and a ward trolley service. Two nations are recorded as having made recommendations for the size of the room:

Federal Republic of Germany: 30 m^2 minimum and

$$\frac{4 \times \text{book stock}}{1000} \times 25\,\text{m}^2$$

United Kingdom: 37 m^2 (400 sq ft) minimum for the general library with an additional 47 m^2 (500 sq ft) for the medical library, plus 20 m^2 (215 sq ft) for storage and work space.

Size of library room according to number of beds:

200 to 400 beds	56 m^2 (600 sq ft)
401 to 600 beds	65 m^2 (700 sq ft)
Over 600 beds	75 m^2 (800 sq ft)

Book stocks recommended in national standards are:

Czechoslovakia: Four books per bed in short-term institutions; eight books per bed in long-term institutions.

Federal Republic of Germany: Four books per bed; long-stay hospitals (six months) five books per bed; 7% to 10% of the books should be changed annually.

United Kingdom: Up to 50 beds, 1000 books; 51 to 100 beds, 1500 books; 101 to 150 beds, 2000 books; 151 to 200 beds, 2500 books; 201 to 300 beds, 3000 books; 300 to 600 beds, up to 5000 books.

United States: Up to 300 beds, eight books per bed; 301 to 500 beds, seven books per bed; 501 to 800 beds, six books per bed; 801 to 1100 beds, five books per bed; 1101 to 1500 beds, four books per bed. There is an increase of 25% for orthopaedic hospitals, children's hospitals, and 200–400-bed mental hospitals; 50% more for tuberculosis patients.

IFLA: 500 beds, eight books per bed; 500 to 1000 beds, six books per bed; over 1000 beds, five books per bed. There is an increase of 40% to 60% for long-stay hospitals.

The publication of the (British) Department of Health and Social Security *Library Service in Hospitals*[48] makes the following useful comment: 'Physical separation of staff and patients' libraries is desirable but they should be planned close together so that they can be administered as a single library and information service.'

Dealing with the staff library it says: 'The purpose of the staff library is to serve the needs of the hospital' – medical, dental, nursing and other professional and medical staff – and to provide a service for general practitioners, local authority doctors and other professional people who work in the National Health Service outside the hospital and who make use of hospital postgraduate training facilities. If the hospital has a nurses' training school a library will be required for that, and consideration should be given to the possibility of its being administered jointly with the main staff library.

The staff library will usually be sited in the postgraduate medical centre, if any; whether or not such a centre is provided, the library must be conveniently sited for those who use the staff library and should be accessible at all hours of the day. It should provide reading space which is available at all times, and not be used for lectures, discussion groups or other types of activity or as a medical staffroom.

Undergraduates and trainees	1 seat for 4
Student nurses	1 seat for 8
Other students and trainee technicians	1 seat for 8
Graduates, trained staff, consultants and medical staff	1 seat for 6
Trained technicians	1 seat for 10
General practitioners, dentists, nurses	1 seat for 20

Appendix

Metric equivalents of use to librarians –

1 in = 25.4 mm	1 mm = 1/24 in	1 sq ft = 0.093 m^2 (930 cm^2)	1 m^2 = 10.76 sq ft
1 ft = 0.305 m (305 mm)	1 cm = 13/32 in	1 cu ft = 0.028 m^3 (28 320 cc)	1 m^3 = 35.3 cu ft
3 ft = 0.914 m (914 mm)	1 m = 3 ft 3 in	1 lb = 0.45 kg	1 kg = 2.2 lb
1 mile = 1.61 km	1 km = 5/8 mile	1 lb/sq ft = 0.0479 kN/m^2	1 kN/m^2 = 20.88 lb/sq ft
£1/sq ft = £10.76 p/m^2			

References

Chapter 1

1. American Library Association. *Minimum Standards for Public Library Services.* ALA, Chicago, 1966.
2. Abdulaziz Mohamed Al-Nahari. *The Role of National Libraries in Developing Countries with special reference to Saudi Arabia.* Mansell, London and New York, 1984.
3. Metcalf, Keyes D. *Planning Academic and Research Library Buildings.* Second edition by Philip D. Leighton and David C. Weber. ALA, Chicago and London, 1986, p. 32.
4. University Grants Committee. *Report of the Committee on Libraries* (the Parry Report). HMSO, London, 1967, pp. 98–104.
5. ibid., Appendix 8, p. 267.
6. op. cit. p. 14.
7. *Library Journal*, Dec. 1986.
8. University Grants Committee. *Capital Provision for University Libraries: report of a working party* (the Atkinson Report). HMSO, London, 1976.
9. op. cit., pp. 44–49.
10. *Public Library Buildings 1975–1983.* Library Services Ltd, London, 1987.
11. *Library Journal*, Dec. 1986.
12. *Designing a Medium-sized Public Library.* Department of Education and Science, HMSO, London, 1980.
13. Department of Health and Social Security and Welsh Office. *Library Service in Hospitals.* HM(70)23, DHSS, London, 1970.
14. Library Association. *Hospital Libraries: recommended standards for libraries in hospitals.* LA, London, 1972.
15. Going, Mona (ed.). *Hospital Libraries and Work with the Disabled in the Community.* Third edition, Library Association, London, 1982.
16. Cohen, Elaine and Aaron. Trends in special library buildings. *Library Trends*, Fall 1987, p. 306.

Chapter 2

1. Rider, Freemont. *The Scholar and the Future of the Research Library: a problem and its solution.* Hadham Press, New York, 1944.
2. Williamson, R. *Knowledge Warehouse.* LIR Report 65, British Library, London, 1987.
3. *Information World Review*, March 1988, p. 1.
4. Adams, Roy J. *Information technology and libraries: a future for academic libraries.* Croom Helm, London, 1986.
5. Moran, Barbara B. and others. The electronic campus: impact of the scholar's workstation project on the libraries at Brown. *College and Research Libraries*, Jan. 1987, pp. 5–16.
6. Licklider, J. C. R. *Libraries of the Future.* MIT Press, Mass., 1965.
7. Licklider, J. C. R. A view from the halfway point on a journey to the future. In *Large Libraries and New Technological Development: proceedings of a symposium*, 29 Sept. to 1 Oct. 1982. K. G. Saur, Munich, New York, London, 1984.
8. Feigenbaum, E. A. The library of the future: a lecture. Aston University, Birmingham, 1986.
9. Educational Facilities Laboratories. *The Impact of Technology on the Library Building.* EFL, New York, 1967. *cf* Influence of computers on library buildings, *Liber Bulletin* (25), 1986.
10. op cit., pp. xiii and 15.
11. op cit. Rider was speaking and publishing on this subject from 1936.
12. University Grants Committee, op. cit.

Chapter 3

1. Library Association. *New Library Buildings.* LA, London. Irregular series under varying titles 1969–1983.
2. *Die neu Nationalbibliothek.* Buchhandler-Vereinigung Gmbh, Frankfurt-am-Main, 1983.
3. Royal Institute of British Architects. *Handbook of Architectural Practice and Management.* RIBA, London, updated; Part 3, 220.02.
4. RIBA. *Working with Your Architect.* RIBA, London, 1954.
5. University Grants Committee, op. cit.
6. RIBA *Handbook* (op. cit.). Appendix B, Part 3, 564 (05).
7. ibid. Appendix A, Part 3, 525.
8. Havard-Williams, Peter. In *Libri*, v 21, 1971, pp. 374–385.
9. International Federation of Library Associations and Institutions, Section of Public Libraries. *Guidelines for Public Libraries.* IFLA, Paris, 1986.
10. Withers, F. N. *Standards for Library Service.* UNESCO, Paris, 1970.

Chapter 4

1. Palmborg, Nils. New university library at Lund-UB2. *IATUL Proceedings*, Vol. 11, 1979, pp. 43–54.
2. Fussler, Herman H. and Julian L. Simon. *Patterns in the Use of Books in Large Research Libraries.* University of Chicago Press, Chicago, 1969.
3. Urquhart, J. A. and N. C. *Relegation and Stock Control in Libraries.* Oriel Press, London, 1976 (based on research on the specific subject of the title, it throws doubt on easy generalizations linking the age of the book with the frequency of use).
4. Cassata, Mary B. (ed.). Book storage. *Library Trends*, Vol. 19, No. 3, 1971 (contributions in this issue deal with possible solutions to book storage problems).
5. Cox, J. Grady. *Optimum Storage of Library Material.* Indiana Purdue University Libraries, Lafayette, 1964.
6. op. cit.
7. Metropolitan Toronto Library Board. *Metropolitan Toronto Central Library Programme and Site Selection Study.* The Board, Toronto, 1971.
8. *Bookseller*, 8 January 1988, p. 66.
9. Faulkner-Brown, Hendy, Watkinson, Stonor, architects. Nottingham University Library brochure. 1973.
10. Bristol University Library. Brochure. Bristol University, *c.* 1979.
11. Hoare, Peter A., Librarian, Nottingham University Library. Personal communication to the author.

Chapter 5

1. Konya, Allan. *Design Primer for Hot Climates.* Architectural Press, London, 1980.
2. op cit., p. 18.
3. University Grants Committee, op. cit., p. 92.
4. Illuminating Engineering Society. *Lighting of Libraries.* IES Technical Report No. 8, IES, London, 1966.
5. Osborn, E. The location of public libraries in urban areas. *Journal of Librarianship*, Vol. 3, No. 4, Oct. 1971, pp. 237–244.
6. op. cit.
7. *Open*, 19 (5), May 1987.
8. Brawne, Michael. *Libraries: architecture and equipment.* Pall Mall Press, London, 1970, pp. 141–143.
9. *Library Journal*, Dec. 1987.
10. *Architects' Journal*, 7 Jan. 1970, with subsequent discussion in the issues of 28 Jan., 11 and 28 Feb. and 4 March 1970.
11. op cit., Part 3, 270.

Chapter 6

1. RIBA, op cit., Part 3, 210: the process of design.
2. *AJ Handbook of Building Enclosures*, ed. A. J. Elder. Butterworth Architecture, London, 1974.
3. Mason, Ellsworth. *Mason on Library Buildings.* Scarecrow Press, Metuchen, New Jersey, 1979, p. 236.
4. op cit. p. 87
5. *Architects' Journal*, 16 April 1969.

6. op cit., pp. 32–34.
7. Faulkner-Brown, Harry. *Library Design; the impact of the '80s.* IFLA Pre-conference Seminar, Toronto, 1982.
8. op cit., p. 199.
9. *Architects' Journal*, editorial, 14 May 1975.
10. Wheeler, Joseph L. and Alfred Morton Githens. *The American Public Library Building.* Scribner, New York, 1941.
11. *Designing a Medium-sized Public Library* (op. cit.).
12. National Library of Scotland. *The Causewayside Building* (brochure). NLS, Edinburgh, 1986.
13. Plovgaard, Sven. *Public Library Buildings: standards and type plans for library premises in areas with populations of between 5,000 and 25,000.* 1967; trans. Oliver Stallybrass, Library Association, London, 1971.
14. Thompson, Anthony. *Library Buildings of Britain and Europe.* Butterworth, London, 1963, pp. 13–15.
15. op cit
16. BS Code CP3, Chapter V, Part 1, Table 1. London, 1967 (partially altered Nov. 1968).
17. Quoted in Faulkner-Brown, Harry. University library buildings. *Architects' Journal*, 21 Feb. 1968, pp. 457–460.
18. ibid.
19. Educational Facilities Laboratory. *Bricks and Mortarboards.* The Laboratory, New York, undated, p. 77.
20. Private communication to the author from E. Goodfellow, architect, of Perth, Western Australia.
21. Cohen, Aaron and Elaine. *Designing and Space Planning for Libraries: a behavioral guide.* Bowker, New York and London, 1979.
22. Tregenza, Peter. *The Design of Interior Circulation.* Crosby Lockwood Staples, London, 1976.
23. op. cit., p. 70.

Chapter 7

1. op. cit., pp. 13–15.
2. National Library of Scotland, op cit.
3. op. cit., pp. 32–33.
4. Quoted in *Architectural Record*, Nov. 1980, pp. 86–91.
5. op cit., pp. 176–177.
6. op. cit., p. 38.
7. *Library Journal*, 1 May 1971, p. 1582.
8. Quoted in Faulkner-Brown, Harry, *Library Design* (op. cit).
9. IES, *Lighting of Libraries* (op. cit).

Chapter 8

1. op. cit., Chapter 3 et seq.

Chapter 9

1. Wallace, A. In *Library World*, June 1971.
2. op. cit.

Chapter 10

1. op. cit.
2. Martin, P. L., and Oughton, D. R. *Faber and Kell's Heating and Air Conditioning of Buildings.* Seventh edition, Butterworth London, 1989.
3. Building revisited: New Zealand House. *Architects' Journal*, 10 March 1971.
4. Professor Dr G. Gattermann, in correspondence with the author.
5. Cunha, George Martin. Mass deacidification for libraries. *Library Technology Reports*, May/June 1987, ALA, Chicago.
6. University Grants Committee, op. cit., p. 92.
7. op. cit.
8. *Architects' Journal*, 21 May 1975, p. 1083.
9. op. cit.
10. *Library Journal*, 1 Dec. 1971, p. 3968.
11. op. cit.
12. *Architects' Journal*, 6 March 1968, p. 573.
13. op. cit. pp. 28–30.

Chapter 11

1. DSIR Technical Paper 17. HMSO, London, 1935.
2. *IES Lighting Handbook.* Fifth edition, IES of North America, New York, 1981, Chapter 7.
3. Thomson, Garry. *Conservation and Museum Lighting.* Museums Association Information Sheet, Museums Association, London, 1970, p. 2.
4. Hopkinson, R. G. and J. B. Collins. *The Ergonomics of Lighting.* Macdonald Technical and Scientific, London, 1970, p. 41.
5. Illuminating Engineering Society. *The IES Code.* London, 1973. *See also IES Lighting Handbook*, IES of North America (op. cit.).
6. Illuminating Engineering Society. *Lighting of Libraries* (op. cit.).
7. Holt, Raymond M. Trends in public library buildings. *Library Trends*, Fall 1987.
8. op. cit., p. 121. *See also* Metcalf, Keyes D., *Library Lighting*, Association of Research Libraries, Washington DC, 1970, for a general discussion of and recommendations for artificial lighting in libraries.
9. op. cit., p. 8.
10. Blackwell, H. Richard. Lighting the library: standards for illumination. In *The Library Environment: aspects of interior planning.* American Library Association, Chicago, 1965, pp. 26–27.
11. ibid., p. 26
12. Illuminating Engineering Society. *Lighting of Art Galleries and Museums.* IES Technical Report No. 14, IES, London, 1970.
13. ibid., Glossary, p. 29.
14. Arms, Brock. Principles of illumination for libraries. In *The Library Environment* (op. cit.), p. 32.
15. op. cit., pp. 29–30.
16. op. cit., p. 29.
17. *IES Code* (op. cit.), p. 5.
18. op. cit., p. 39.
19. op. cit., p. 30.

Chapter 12

1. *Protecting the Library and its Resources: a guide to physical protection and insurance.* Report on a study conducted by Gage-Babcock and Associates Inc., Library Technology Project, American Library Association, Chicago, 1963.
2. ibid.
3. Morris, John. *Managing the Library Fire Risk.* University of California, Berkeley, 1975.
4. Hillingdon Central Library, Uxbridge, brochure.
5. Fire Protection Association. *Fire Protection Design Guide.* FPA, London, 1970.
6. Leedham, John. *Live Safely with Fire.* Longmans for the FPA, London, 1969.
7. Poyner, Barry. *Design against crime: beyond defensible space.* Butterworths, London, 1983.
8. Cumming, Neil. *Security: the comprehensive guide to equipment,* Butterworth, London, 1987.
9. Underwood, Grahame. *The Security of Buildings,* Butterworth, London, 1984.

Chapter 13

1. Reed, J. B. *Handbook of Special Librarianship and Information Work.* Third edition, ASLIB, London, 1967, pp. 237–264.
2. Poole, Frazer G. The selection and evaluation of library bookstacks. *Library Trends*, April 1965, p. 419.
3. Plovgaard, op. cit., p. 39.
4. Library Association. *Library Resource Provision in Schools: guidelines and recommendations.* LA, London, 1977.
5. Anthony, L. J. Library planning. In *Handbook of Special Librarianship and Information Work.* Third edition, ASLIB, London, 1967, pp. 309–364.
6. op. cit., p. 420.
7. Library Association, County Libraries Section. *County Branch Libraries: report and recommended standards.* LA, London, 1958.

8. op. cit.

9. Plovgaard, op. cit., pp. 58–64.

10. op. cit., p. 419.

11. Henderson, Robert W. Tiers, books and stacks. *Library Journal*, Vol. 59, 1934, pp. 382–383.

12. Henderson, Robert W. Bookstack planning with the cubook. *Library Journal*, Vol. 61, 1936, pp. 52–54.

13. op. cit.

14. Plovgaard, op. cit., p. 41.

15. ibid., p. 43.

Chapter 14

1. Rider, Freemont. *Compact Book Storage*. Hadham Press, Middletown, Conn., 1949.

2. Gawrecki, Drahoslav. *Compact Library Shelving*. Library Technology Program, American Library Association, Chicago, 1968.

3. Gorman, Michael. Movable compact shelving: the current answer. *Library Hi-Tech,* 5(4), Winter 1987.

4. Muller, Robert H. Economics of compact book shelving. *Library Trends*, April 1965.

5. Hill, F. J. The compact storage of books. In Gawrecki, op. cit., p. 61.

Chapter 15

1. op. cit., pp. 13–15.

2. op. cit., pp. 12–20.

3. Dunne, Michael. The optimum values and range needed for the angle and height of book rests. *The Book Trolley*, Vol. 2, No. 10, June 1970.

4. *Designing and Space Planning for Libraries* (op. cit.), p. 23.

5. op. cit.

6. British Standards Institution. BS 3893: *Office desks, tables and seating.*

7. Van Buren, Martin. Design of library furniture. *Library Trends*, April 1965, pp. 392–393.

8. op. cit.

9. op. cit., p. 178.

10. op. cit., pp. 97–99.

11. Mevissen, Werner. *Public Library Building.* Ernst Heyer, Essen, 1958, pp. 45 and 58.

12. *UNESCO Bulletin,* March/April 1969, pp. 84–85.

Chapter 16

1. Library Association, County Libraries Section, op. cit.

2. *New Metric Handbook.* Architectural Press, London, 1979.

3. Ham, Roderick. *Theatres: planning guidance for design and adaptation.* Architectural Press, London, 1987.

4. op. cit., p. 129.

Chapter 17

1. *Library Equipment Reports.* Bi-monthly buyers' guide to equipment and services for librarians. Headland Press, London.

2. Poole, op. cit., p. 425.

3. Eckelman, Carl A. Evaluating the strength of library chairs and tables. *Library Technology Reports*, 13 (4), July 1977, pp. 341–343.

4. Berkeley, Bernard. *Floors: selection and maintenance.* Library Technology Program, American Library Association, Chicago, 1968 (useful citation of articles on different flooring materials in the bibliography).

5. *Architects' Journal Information Library*, 5 March 1969.

6. Saunders, D. J. Sound insulation and use of carpets. *Flooring and Carpet Specifier*, May 1970, pp. 2–7.

7. Koderas, M. J. Sound absorptive properties of carpeting. *Interiors*, June 1969, pp. 130–131.

8. op. cit., pp. 32–33.

9. Kreutzberg, H. The right answers on carpeting. *Architect*, October 1971, pp. 83–87, and November 1971, pp. 83–86.

Chapter 18

1. *Public Library Buildings 1975–1983* (op. cit.), pp. 1–12.

2. *Library Journal*, Dec. 1986.

3. op. cit., p. 313.

4. Alison, W. A. G. *The Mitchell Library Glasgow: the new extension.* City of Glasgow District Council, 1980.

5. op. cit.

6. *Country Life*, 6 July 1972, pp. 28–29.

Chapter 19

1. Edwards, H. M. University library planning: a comparative study. Witwatersrand University thesis, 1985

2. op. cit.

3. IFLA. *Standards for Public Libraries.* Verlag Dokumentation, Pullach, Munich, 1973 and 1977.

4. University Grants Committee, op. cit.

5. *Standards of Public Library Service in England and Wales: report of the working party appointed by the Minister of Education in March 1961.* HMSO, London, 1962.

6. Library Advisory Councils (England and Wales). *Public Library Service Points: a report with some notes on staffing.* Department of Education and Science, HMSO, London, 1971.

7. Library Association. *Public Library Buildings – the way ahead.* LA, London, 1960.

8. Library Advisory Councils, op. cit.

9. Taylor, John N. and Ian M. Johnson. *Public Libraries and their Use: a research report on the use of public library buildings with implications for their distribution, location and design.* HMSO, London, 1973.

10. Department of Education and Science. *Public Libraries and Cultural Activities.* Library Information Series No. 5, HMSO, London, 1975.

11. Department of Education and Science. Circular 4/65, March 1965, p. 13.

12. op. cit., p. 12.

13. Convention of Scottish Local Authorities. *Report on Standards for the Public Library Service in Scotland.* The Convention, Edinburgh, 1986.

14. op. cit.

15. op. cit.

16. Plovgaard, op. cit., p. 68.

17. *Scandinavian Public Library Quarterly,* 10 (2), 1977, pp. 34–43.

18. Library Association. Standards for reference services in public libraries. *Library Association Record*, Vol. 72, No. 2, Feb. 1970, pp. 53–57.

19. Bassnett, Peter J. Spatial and administrative relationships in large public libraries: an investigation into the planning of municipal libraries serving populations exceeding one hundred thousand. Library Association thesis, London, 1970.

20. Humphreys, K. W. Standards in university libraries. *Libri*, Vol. 20, 1970, pp. 144–155.

21. University Grants Committee, op. cit.

22. Saunders, W. L. *Journal of Librarianship*, Vol. 1, No. 4, Oct. 1969, p. 202.

23. op. cit., p. 14.

24. ibid., Introduction, p. XVIII.

25. University Grants Committee, op. cit.

26. Quoted ibid.

27. University of Cambridge Library Management Research Unit. Factors affecting the use of seats in academic libraries. *Journal of Librarianship*, Vol. 7, No. 4, Oct. 1975.

28. American Library Association. Standards for college libraries. *College and Research Libraries*, Vol. 20, No. 4, July 1959.

29. Canadian Library Association. *Report of University Library Standards Committee of Canadian Association of College and University Libraries: guide to Canadian university library standards 1961–1964*. Ottawa, 1967.

30. op. cit., p. 99.

31. Department of Education and Science. *Notes on Procedure for the Approval of Polytechnic Projects*. DES, London, 1971.

32. Council of Polytechnic Librarians Working Party on Polytechnic Library Buildings. *Polytechnic Library Planning*. COPOL, London, 1980.

33. Library Association. Libraries in the new polytechnics. *Library Association Record*, Vol. 70, No. 9, Sept. 1968, pp. 240–243.

34. Association of College and Research Libraries (ACRL). Standards for college libraries. *C&RL News*, Oct. 1975. Revised as 'Standards for college libraries, 1986', *C&RL News*, March 1986.

35. College libraries: annual survey. *Library Association Record*, 89 (3), March 1987.

36. Department of Education and Science. *Area Guidelines for Advanced Further Education Institutions*. DES Architects and Building Group, Design Note 44, 1981.

37. Library Association. *College Libraries: guidelines for professional services and resource provision*. Third edition, Library Association, London, 1982.

38. Library Association. *Recommended Standards of Library Provision in Colleges of Further Education*. Second edition, LA, London 1971.

39. National Association of Teachers in Further and Higher Education. *College Libraries: a policy statement*. NATFHE, London, 1982.

40. Department of Education and Science. *Notes on Procedure for the Approval of Further Education Projects (other than polytechnics)*. DES, London, 1972.

41. Department of Education and Science. *New Colleges of Further Education*. Building Bulletin 58, HMSO, London, 1959.

42. Department of Education and Science. College letter 2/68, ref. R34/65/01, March 1968.

43. New Zealand Library Association. *Standards for Teachers' College Libraries*. Wellington, 1967.

44. ACRL, op. cit.

45. Quoted in Edwards, op. cit.

46. Library Association, op. cit.

47. International Federation of Library Associations, Libraries in Hospitals Subsection. Standards for libraries in hospitals (general service). *UNESCO Bulletin for Libraries,* Vol. 23, No. 2, 1969.

48. op. cit.

Bibliography

The flow of books and articles on library planning, which rose to a flood between the late 1950s and the 1970s, has abated, although special issues of library journals worldwide continue to be devoted to the subject. Books from an earlier period which have been quoted over decades are now usually out of date: comments on space planning written before the coming of the new electronic technology are seldom relevant today, and it is for that reason that this bibliography is much reduced. There are many, many books on library automation but not on its effect on the planning of buildings. No doubt they will come when the effects of the new technology become less volatile, if they ever do.

Journal articles which covered new library buildings were listed in earlier editions of this book. It has been found that such articles are of little value outside the environment in which those libraries exist. It is certainly useful to study new buildings relevant to particular situations but coverage is best found in the professional press (library and architectural) of the country concerned. For an overall international survey there is no substitute for *Library and Information Science Abstracts* (LISA), which can now also be accessed on CD/ROM.

Planning and design – general

Brawne, Michael. *Libraries: architecture and equipment.* Pall Mall Press, London, 1970.
    A very general survey including historical examples.
Cohen, Aaron and Elaine. *Designing and Space Planning for Libraries: a behavioral guide.* Bowker, New York and London, 1979.
    An architect and a behavioral scientist deal with design, mainly internal design. Some new ideas; certainly a different approach.
Cohen, Aaron and Elaine. *Automation, Space Management and Productivity: a guide for libraries.* Bowker, New York, 1981.
    Concerned with the layouts of offices and libraries, chiefly the problems of accommodating new machinery.
Draper, James and James Brooks. *Interior Design for Libraries.* American Library Association, Chicago, 1979.
Fraley, Ruth A. and Carol Lee Anderson. *Library Space Planning: how to assess, allocate and reorganize collections, resources and physical facilities.* Neal-Schuman, New York and London, 1985.
Grey, S. M. and J. R. Wilson. *The Ergonomics of Library Issue desks: final report.* British Library R and D Report, London, 1983.
    A very detailed study carried out in an academic library but of general application: establishes sound principles.
Havard-Williams, Peter. Library design and planning in developing countries. *Libri,* 37 (2), June 1987, pp. 160–176.
Jones, Unity Robena Elizabeth. Analysis of the balance areas in selected large library buildings. Loughborough University thesis, 1975.
    Largely based on British practice but useful for a little-studied subject.
Konya, Allan. *Libraries: a design guide.* Architectural Press, London, 1986.
    The library volume in a useful series of design guides based on standard British procedures.
Library Buildings and *New Library Buildings.* Library Association, London.
    A survey of new British library buildings. From 1961 to 1964 this was published annually in the *Library Association Record,* but since 1966 it has been a separate, if irregular, publication. From 1961 to 1969 it was devoted to a survey of selected public library buildings erected in the previous year. For 1969–1970, 1971–1972, and 1973–1974, the volumes covered a selection of new library buildings of all types, giving information systematically, with tables, plans and photographs. The latest issue, entitled *Public Library Buildings,* uses the same technique but only covers public libraries built in Britain between 1975 and 1983.
Library Interior Layout and Design: proceedings of a seminar. IFLA Publication No. 24. Saur, London and New York, 1982.
    Twelve papers from a seminar held in Denmark: experts deal with different subjects.
Library Space Planning. Library Journal Special Report No. 1, LJ, 1976.
Lushington, Nolan and Willis N. Mills. *Libraries Designed for Users: a planning handbook.* Gaylord Professional Publications, Syracuse, New York, 1980.
Pierce, William S. *Furnishing the Library Interior.* M. Dekker, New York, 1980.
Pollet, Dorothy and Peter C. Haskell. *Sign Systems for Libraries.* Bowker, New York, 1979.
Pope, L. Gillian. Library signs and guiding. Loughborough University thesis, 1982.
Rawles, Beverly A. and Wessels, Michael B. *Working with Library Consultants.* Library Professional Publications, Hamden, Conn., 1984.
Robinson, Jeremy and Martin Filler. *Buildings for the Arts.* McGraw-Hill, New York, 1978.
    Wider in scope than most volumes quoted here but very useful when studying the planning of libraries as part of arts buildings.
Rohlf, Robert H. The consultant's role. In *Library Buildings: innovations for changing needs.* American Library Association, Chicago, 1972.
Schell, Hal B. (ed.). *Reader on the Library Building.* Microcard Edition Books, Englewood, Colo., 1975.
Seminar on *Library Buildings in India,* conducted by the National Information System for Science and Technology. Department of Science and Technology, New Delhi, 1982.
Shaw, Robert J. (ed.). *Libraries: building for the future.* American Library Association, Chicago, 1967.
Spencer, Herbert and Linda Reynolds. *Directional signing and labelling in libraries and museums: a review of current theory and practice.* Royal College of Art, London, 1977.
    This book and those of L. Gillian Pope and Pollet and Haskell exemplify very different approaches to the same problem.
Trezza, Alphonse (ed.). *Library Buildings: innovation for changing needs.* American Library Association, Chicago, 1972.
Withers, F. N. *Standards for Library Service.* UNESCO, Paris, 1970.
    An invaluable survey covering those countries which were willing to report. Particularly useful, despite its date, because it was compiled at a time when 'standards' were commonly used.
Zaman, Halimah Badioze. The design of library buildings in South-East Asia with special reference to national and university libraries. Loughborough University thesis, 1980.

National libraries

Abdulaziz Mohamed Al-Nahari. *The Role of National Libraries in Developing Countries with special reference to Saudi Arabia.* Mansell, London and New York, 1984.
    Tabulation and conclusions drawn from a questionnaire sent to directors of national libraries world-wide. The second half of the book is devoted to the need for a national library in Saudi Arabia.
Thompson, Anthony. *National Library Buildings: proceedings of a colloquium.* Verlag Dokumentation, Munich, 1975.
    Publication of an IFLA Seminar held in Rome (in English, French and Italian).
Zaman, Halimah Badioze. The role of national libraries and their consequent building requirements in developing countries. Loughborough University Ph.D. thesis, 1982.

Academic libraries

Braden, Irene A. *The Undergraduate Library.* American Library Association, Chicago, 1970.

Canadian Library Association. *Report of University Library Standards Committee of Canadian Association of College and University Libraries: guide to Canadian university library standards 1961–1964.* Ottawa, 1967.
> Although dated, this is still useful, because it shows how standards in one country developed over a number of years.

College Librarianship: the objective and the practice. Ed. A. Rennie McElroy, Library Association, London, 1984.

Council of Polytechnic Librarians Working Party on Polytechnic Library Buildings. *Polytechnic Library Planning.* COPOL, London, 1980.
> Short document with lists of recommended actions and equipment.

Council of Polytechnic Librarians. *Statistics of Polytechnic Libraries 1985–86.* COPOL, London, 1987.

Department of Education and Science. *Notes on Procedure for the Approval of Polytechnic Projects.* DES, London, 1971.
> British official statement about the then new educational entity: only a small part is concerned with libraries.

Department of Education and Science. *The Design of Libraries in Colleges of Education.* HMSO, London, 1969.

Department of Education and Science. *Notes on Procedure for the Approval of Further Education Projects (other than polytechnics).* DES, London, 1972.

Eatwell, R. F. A study of university library planning: with critical reference to three recent English university libraries. London. University thesis, 1973.
> Studies the universities of Salford, Surrey and East Anglia with photographs and some briefs.

Ellsworth, Ralph E. *Academic Library Buildings: a guide to architectural issues and solutions.* Colorado Associated University Press, Boulder, Colorado, 1973.
> Contains many photographs and floor plans of university libraries, not only in the USA.

Ellsworth, Ralph E. *Planning Manual for Academic Library Buildings.* Scarecrow Press, Metuchen, New Jersey, 1973.
> Systematic and useful.

Faulkner-Brown, Harry (ed.). *Planning the Academic Library: Metcalf and Ellsworth at York.* Oriel Press, Newcastle upon Tyne, 1971.
> Report of a conference, with some useful comments by two experts.

Gelfand, M. A. *University Libraries for Developing Countries.* UNESCO Manuals for Libraries 14, UNESCO, Paris, 1968.
> Cautious, because it has to cover so many situations, but still the official statement.

Kenny, Grace. *Polytechnics: the shared use of space and facilities.* DES Architects and Building Branch, London, 1977.
> Short, and only a few pages concern libraries.

Langmead, Stephen and Margaret Beckman. *New Library Design: guidelines to planning academic library buildings.* Wiley, Toronto, 1970.

Library Association. *Recommended Standards of Library Provision in Colleges of Further Education.* Second edition, LA, London, 1971.

Library Association. *College Libraries: guidelines for professional service and resource provision.* Third edition, LA, London, 1982.

Mason, Ellsworth. *Mason on Library Buildings.* Scarecrow Press, Metuchen, New Jersey, 1979.
> An expert's trenchant reviews of some modern university libraries. Strong words from someone who knows his subject.

Metcalf, Keyes D. *Planning Academic and Research Library Buildings.* Second edition by Philip D. Leighton and David C. Weber, American Library Association, Chicago and London, 1986.
> Revised after the author's death by two very expert editors. A huge book, packed with information and compulsory reading for anyone building a large university library in America. A little overpowering for the beginner.

National Association of Teachers in Further and Higher Education. *College Libraries: a policy statement.* NATFHE, London, 1982.
> The British trades union position; one chapter on libraries.

Rajwant Singh. *University Library Buildings in India.* Academic Publications, Delhi, 1984.
> Revision of the author's Ph.D. thesis, University of Rajasthan, 1983.

Smith, Lester K. A study of the architectural design of six university library buildings. University of Southern California Ph.D. thesis, 1973. Photocopy, University Microfilms, Ann Arbor, Michigan, 1982.

University Grants Committee. *Capital Provision for University Libraries: report of a working party* (the Atkinson Report). HMSO, London, 1976.
> Revolutionary proposals on the self-renewing library. The official British statement, but the argument should be studied by every university librarian.

University Grants Committee. *Report of the Committee on Libraries* (the Parry Report). HMSO, London, 1967.
> An official survey of the British position at that date, with some thoughtful comments. Although superseded in some ways by the Atkinson Report, it is still worth studying.

University Library Buildings in South East Asia: proceedings of a workshop. University of Singapore Library, 1977.
> Text with microfiche.

School libraries

Allan, Margaret. *The School Library Resource Centre.* Crosby, Lockwood, Staples, St Albans and London, 1974.

Department of Education and Science Architects and Building Group. *Area Guidelines for Secondary Schools.* Design Note 34, DES, London, 1984.

Department of Education and Science. *Area Guidelines for Sixth Form, Tertiary and NAFE Colleges.* DES, London, 1983.
> Both design notes give little attention to libraries, but they serve to show the official (British) attitude to the allocation of space (including library space) in schools.

Hannigan, Jane Anne and Glenn E. Estes (comps.). *Media Center Facilities Design.* American Library Association, Chicago, 1978.

Library Association. *Library Resource Provision in Schools: guidelines and recommendations.* LA, London, 1977.

Ray, Sheila. *Library Service to Schools.* Third edition, Library Association, London, 1982.
> Deals with both the running of the school library and the assistance which local public library services can give. A standard British text.

School Libraries: their planning and equipment. School Library Association, London, 1972.

School Media Centres. Prepared by School Planning and Building Research in conjunction with the Curriculum Committee on Learning Materials. Ontario Department of Education, Toronto, 1972.

Shifrin, Malcolm. *Information in the School Library: an introduction to the organisation of non-book materials.* C. Bingley, London, 1973.

Wild, Friedmann. *Libraries for Schools and Universities.* Van Nostrand Reinhold, New York, 1972.
> Translated from the German. Architectural plans with explanatory text.

Public libraries

Bassnett, Peter J. Spatial and administrative relationships in large public libraries: an investigation into the planning of municipal libraries serving populations exceeding one hundred thousand. Library Association thesis, London, 1970.

Designing a Medium-sized Public Library. Department of Education and Science, HMSO, London, 1980.
> A team appointed by the Department studied the need for a library in a British town and designed one which was eventually built. Not only the record of a job, but shows the way decisions were reached.

Hamilton, J. T. The planning of central library buildings in Scotland: a comparative study. University of Strathclyde thesis, Glasgow, 1974.

Hill, Ann B. *The Small Public Library.* University of Wisconsin School of Architecture and Urban Planning, Milwaukee, 1980.

International Federation of Library Associations and Institutions, Section of Public Libraries. *Guidelines for Public Libraries*. IFLA, Paris, 1986.

Replaces the earlier *Standards* but quotes figures from the 1977 edition.

Kronus, Carol and Linda Crowe (eds.). *Children's Services of Public Libraries*. University of Illinois Graduate School of Library Science, Urbana-Champaign, 1978.

Contains chapter on planning library facilities for children.

Library Architecture Pre-conference Institute. *An Architectural Strategy for Change: remodelling and expanding for contemporary public library needs*. American Library Association, Chicago, 1976.

One of the very few attempts to tackle this subject, which has been given too little attention.

Library Association, *Library Buildings* and *New Library Buildings*. See entry under 'Planning and design' above.

Library Association, County Libraries Section. *County Branch Libraries: report and recommended standards*. LA, London, 1958.

Very dated, but nothing else (except Plovgaard below) attempts to lay down standards for small branch libraries.

Mevissen, Werner. *Buchereibau: Public Library Building* (text in English and German). Ernst Heyer, Essen, 1958.

Again, very outdated, but worth looking at for some sound ideas from an experienced librarian.

Myller, Rolf. *The Design of the Small Public Library*. Bowker, New York, 1966.

Plovgaard, Sven. *Public Library Buildings: standards and type plans for library premises in areas with populations of between 5,000 and 25,000*. Originally issued by the Danish State Library Inspectorate's Committee for the Compilation of Standards for Library Buildings in 1967; trans. Oliver Stallybrass, Library Association, London, 1971.

As the title shows, this books deals with a very limited subject but the reasoning is simply explained and can be used in other situations. Excellent for absolute beginners.

Roberts, R. G. Rationalisation of the siting of public libraries. Sheffield Polytechnic thesis, 1970.

Taylor, John N. and Ian M. Johnson. *Public Libraries and Their Use: a research report on the use of public library buildings with implications for their distribution, location and design*. DES Library Information Series No. 4, HMSO, London, 1973.

An officially sponsored British study but quite simply written.

Veatch, Julian Lamar. Library architectural and environmental design: the application of selected environmental design factors to the planning of public library facilities. Florida State University Ph.D. thesis. Photocopy, University Microfilms, Ann Arbor, Michigan, 1980.

Hospital and welfare libraries

Association of Hospital and Institution Libraries Hospital Standards Committee and American Library Association. *Standards for Library Service in Health Care Institutions*. American Library Association, Chicago, 1970.

Brown, E. F. *Bibliotherapy and its Widening Applications*. Scarecrow Press, New Jersey, 1975.

Carmel, M. J. (ed.). *Medical Librarianship*. Library Association, London, 1981.

Cuthbert, M. J. (comp.). *Standards for Health Service Libraries: a select reading list*. Department of Health and Social Security, London, 1977.

Department of Health and Social Security and Welsh Office. *Library Service in Hospitals*. HM(70)23, DHSS, London, 1970.

The official British statement.

Foster, Eloise C. Library development and the joint commission on accreditation of hospital standards. Bulletin of the Medical Library Association, 67 (2) April 1979, pp. 226–231.

Going, Mona E. (ed.). *Hospital Libraries and Work with the Disabled in the Community*. Third edition, Library Association, London, 1982.

The most comprehensive and useful of all books on the subject.

Goldsmith, S. *Designing for the Disabled*. Third edition, RIBA, London, 1976.

Not specifically for libraries, but contains some very important points for the architect to consider.

International Federation of Library Associations, Libraries in Hospitals Subsection. Standards for libraries in hospitals (general service). *UNESCO Bulletin for Libraries*, Vol. 23, No. 2, 1969.

Just a few pages, but still the only international standard.

Kings Fund Centre. *A Library Service for the Mentally Handicapped*. Mental Handicap Paper 3, Kings Fund Centre, London, 1972.

Library Association. *Guidelines for Library Provision in the Health Service: a consultative document*. LA, London, 1980.

Library Association. *Hospital Libraries: recommended standards for libraries in hospitals*. LA, London, 1972.

Library Association. *Library Support for Health Care Services: a policy statement*. LA, London, 1980.

Library of Congress, National Library for the Blind and Physically Handicapped. *Planning Barrier-free Libraries*. LC, Washington DC, 1981.

Library Trends, 26 (1), Summer 1977.

Issue devoted to library services in correctional facilities.

Matthews, D. and F. Picken. *Medical Librarianship*. C. Bingley, London, 1969.

Phinney, E. (ed.). *The Librarian and the Patient: an introduction to library services for patients in health care institutions*. American Library Association, Chicago, 1977.

Ronnie, Mary. Standards for library service in health authorities. *New Zealand Libraries*, 41 (2), July 1978, pp. 55–56.

Standards approved by the Council of the New Zealand Library Association in 1978.

Yast, H. Standards for library service in institutions. B: In the health care setting. *Library Trends*, 21 (2), 1972.

All these books deal with the whole question of library service to hospitals and only incidentally with space planning and equipment.

Special libraries

Anthony, L. J. Library planning. In *Handbook of Special Librarianship and Information Work*. Third edition, ASLIB, London, 1967.

Association of Canadian Map Libraries. *University Map Libraries in Canada: a folio of selected plans*. ACML, Ontario, 1975.

Association of Canadian Map Libraries. *Federal, Provincial and Municipal Map Libraries in Canada, a folio of selected plans*. ACML, Ottawa, 1979.

Building Renovation in ARL Libraries. Systems and Procedures Exchange Centre, Association of Research Libraries, Washington DC, 1983.

Calderhead, Patricia (ed.). *Libraries for Professional Practice*. Architectural Press, London, 1972.

Planning libraries for architects' offices.

Kelly, R. Q. Planning update: commentary and bibliography. *Law Library Journal*, 66 (2), May 1973.

Lewis, Chester M. (ed.). *Special Libraries: how to plan and equip them*. Special Libraries Association Monograph No. 2, SLA, New York, 1963.

Lyles, Marjorie Appleman. Environmental design applications. *Special Libraries*, 63 (11), 1972

Overton, David. *Planning the Administrative Library* (IFLA Publication 26). Saur, Munich and London, 1983.

Planning the Special Library: a project of the New York Chapter, SLA. SLA Monograph No. 4, 1972.

Storage and use of books

Alley, Brian. A utility truck designed for moving library collections. *Library Acquisitions: practice and theory*, 3 (1), 1979, pp. 33–37.

Boll, John J. *To Grow or Not To Grow? A review of alternatives to new academic library buildings*. Library Journal Special Report No. 15, Bowker, New York, 1980.

Boll, John J. *Shelf Browsing, Open Access and Storage Capacity in Research Libraries*. University of Illinois Graduate School of Library and Information Science, Urbana–Champaign, 1985.

Cassata, Mary B. (ed.). Book storage. *Library Trends*, Vol. 19, No. 3, 1971.

Cox, J. Grady. *Optimum Storage of Library Material*. Indiana Purdue University Libraries, Lafayette, 1964.

Ellsworth, Ralph E. *The Economy of Book Storage in College and University Libraries*. ARL and Scarecrow Press, New Jersey, 1969.

Fussler, Herman H. and Julian L. Simon. *Patterns in the Use of Books in Large Research Libraries.* University of Chicago Press, Chicago, 1969.

Gawrecki, Drahoslav. *Compact Library Shelving.* Library Technology Program, American Library Association, Chicago, 1968.

Hill, Francis John. Compact storage of books: a study of methods and equipment. *Journal of Documentation*, December 1955.

Muller, Robert H. Economics of compact book shelving. *Library Trends*, April 1965.

> All the above titles, except Boll, are badly out of date but are the only standard sources on a subject which seems to receive little attention today – perhaps because electronic methods seem more relevant.

Remote Storage in ARL Libraries. Systems and Procedures Exchange Centre, Association of Research Libraries, Washington DC, 1977.

Running out of Space: what are the alternatives? Pre-conference proceedings, American Library Association, Chicago, 1978.

University of Cambridge Library Management Research Unit. Factors affecting the use of seats in academic libraries. *Journal of Librarianship*, 7 (4), October 1975.

Internal physical conditions

Berkeley, Bernard. *Floors: selection and maintenance.* Library Technology Program, American Library Association, Chicago, 1968.

Boud, John. *Lighting Design in Buildings.* Peter Peregrinus, Stevenage, 1973.

British Plastics Federation Building Group. *Floor Finishes.* The Federation, 1973.

Bullock, Cary G. and others. *Library Technology Reports*, 14 (4), July/August 1978, pp. 305–437.

> Devoted to energy conservation in libraries.

CIBS Lighting Guide, Libraries. Chartered Institute of Building Services, Lighting Division, London, 1982.

Durrant, ED. W. (ed.). *Interior Lighting Design.* Fourth edition, Lighting Industry Federation in association with the Electricity Council, London, 1973.

Henderson, S. T. and A. M. Marsden (eds.). *Lamps and Lighting.* Second edition, Edward Arnold, London, 1972.

Hopkinson, R. G. and J. B. Collins. *The Ergonomics of Lighting.* Macdonald Technical and Scientific, London, 1970.

Illuminating Engineering Society. *The IES Code: interior lighting.* IES, London, 1973.

Illuminating Engineering Society. *Lighting of Libraries.* IES Technical Report No. 8, IES, London, 1966.

Illuminating Engineering Society. *Lighting of Art Galleries and Museums.* IES Technical Report No. 14, IES, London, 1970.

Martin, P. L. and Oughton, D., Faber & Kell's *Heating and Air-conditioning of Buildings.* Seventh edition. Butterworth, London, 1989.

Metcalf, Keyes D. *Library Lighting.* Association of Research Libraries, Washington DC, 1970.

Salter, Walter L. *Floors and Floor Maintenance.* Applied Science Publishers, London, 1974.

Thomson, Garry. *Conservation and Museum Lighting.* Museums Association Information Sheet, Museums Association, London, 1970.

Torrance, J. S. A justification of air-conditioning in libraries. *Journal of Librarianship*, 7 (3), July 1975, pp. 199–206.

Security

Bahr, Alice H. *Book Thefts and Library Security Systems, 1981–2.* Knowledge Industry Publications, White Plains, NY, 1981.

Cumming, Neil. *Security: the comprehensive guide to equipment selection and installation.* Architectural Press, London, 1987.

> Not specifically for libraries but containing much useful information.

Fire Protection Association. *Fire Protection Design Guide.* FPA, London, 1970.

Leedham, John. *Live Safely with Fire.* Longmans for the FPA, London, 1969.

Lincoln, Alan J. *Crime in the Library: a study of patterns, impact, and security.* Bowker, New York, 1984.

Lynskey, Thomas A. Safety hazards in libraries. *Library Security Newsletter*, 2 (2), Summer 1978, pp. 7–8.

Morris, John. *Managing the Library Fire Risk.* University of California, Berkeley, 1975.

Powell, J. W. Architects, security consultants and security planning for new libraries. *Library Security. Newsletter*, 1 (Sept. 1975) 1.

Strassberg, Richard. *Conservation, Safety, Security and Disaster Considerations in Designing New or Renovated Library Facilities at Cornell University Libraries.* Cornell University Libraries, Ithaca, NY, 1984.

Theft Detection Systems for Libraries: a survey. Library Technology Reports, May 1974.

Underwood, Grahame. *The Security of Buildings.* Architectural Press, London, 1985.

> Concentrates on the security aspects of the building fabric.

Wright, K. G. *Cost-effective Security.* McGraw-Hill, London, 1972.

> Written by a security consultant with library experience.

Information technology

Adams, Roy J. *Information Technology and Libraries: a future for academic libraries.* Croom Helm, London, 1986.

> A good, up-to-date and succinct survey.

Anderla, G. *Information in 1985: a forecasting study of information needs and resources.* OECD, Paris, 1973.

> A chance to look at a forecast from an official source and see how much really did come true.

Collier, M. W. *Local Area Networks: the implication for library and information science.* LIR Report No. 19, British Library, London, 1984.

> A guide to the new LANs, which are chiefly used to link academic information resources within areas.

Forester, T. *The Information Technology Revolution.* Basil Blackwell, Oxford, 1985.

Koenig, Michael (ed.). *Managing the Electronic Library.* Special Libraries Association, Washington DC, 1984.

Lancaster, F. W. *Libraries and Librarians in an Age of Electronics.* Information Resources Press, Arlington, 1982.

Lancaster, F. W. *Library Automation as a Source of Management Information: clinic on library applications of data processing.* University of Illinois Graduate School of Library and Information Science, Urbana–Champaign, 1983.

> Writings of one of the best-known thinkers in this field.

Licklider, J. C. R. *Libraries of the Future.* MIT Press, Mass., 1965.

> Perhaps the first of the really visionary books; did it come true?

Licklider, J. C. R. A view fromt he halfway point on a journey to the future. In *Large Libraries and New Technological Development.* Saur, Munich and London, 1984.

Roberts, S. A. (ed.). *Costing and the Economics of Library and Information Services.* ASLIB, London, 1984.

Rohlf, Robert H. Building: planning implications of automation. In *Reader on the library building.* Microcard Edition Books, Englewood, Colo, 1975, pp. 261–265.

Rouse, Roscoe, Jr. *Whither the Book? Considerations for library planning in the age of electronics.* IFLA, Munich, 1983.

Simons, G. L. *Towards Fifth-generation Computers.* NCC Publications, Manchester, 1983.

Tedd, L. A. *An Introduction to Computer-based Library Systems.* Second edition, Wiley, New York, 1984.

Teskey, F. N. *Information Retrieval Systems for the Future.* LIR Report No. 26, British Library, London, 1984.

Weber, David C. The impact of computer technology on academic library buildings. In *Academic Libraries: myths and realities (Proc. of the Third National Conference of the Association of College and Research Libraries).* ARCL, Chicago, 1984.

Index